Koren Talmud Bavli

THE NOÉ EDITION

BAVA BATRA

Steinsaltz Center

KOREN

תלמוד בבלי

KOREN TALMUD BAVLI

THE NOÉ EDITION

בבא בתרא

BAVA BATRA

Daf 160a through Daf 176b

COMMENTARY BY

Rabbi Adin Even-Israel Steinsaltz

EDITOR-IN-CHIEF

Rabbi Dr Tzvi Hersh Weinreb

SENIOR CONTENT EDITOR

Rabbi Dr Shalom Z Berger

EXECUTIVE EDITOR

Rabbi Joshua Schreier

•

STEINSALTZ CENTER

KOREN PUBLISHERS JERUSALEM

Supported by the Matanel Foundation

Koren Talmud Bavli, The Noe Edition
Vol. 23h: Tractate Bava Batra, Daf 160a through Daf 176b
Paperback, ISBN, 978-965-7766-15-6

First Hebrew/English paperback edition, 2021

Koren Publishers Jerusalem Ltd.
PO Box 4044, Jerusalem 91040, ISRAEL
PO Box 8531, New Milford, CT 06776, USA
www.korenpub.com

Steinsaltz Center

Steinsaltz Center is the parent organization of institutions established by Rabbi Adin Even-Israel Steinsaltz

PO Box 45187, Jerusalem 91450 ISRAEL
Telephone: +972 2 646 0900, Fax +972 2 624 9454
www.steinsaltz-center.org

הִנֵּה יָמִים בָּאִים, נְאֻם אֲדֹנָי יֱהוִה, וְהִשְׁלַחְתִּי רָעָב בָּאָרֶץ,
לֹא־רָעָב לַלֶּחֶם וְלֹא־צָמָא לַמַּיִם, כִּי אִם־לִשְׁמֹעַ אֵת דִּבְרֵי יהוה.

Behold, days are coming – says the Lord God – I will send a hunger to the land, not a hunger for bread nor a thirst for water, but to hear the words of the Lord. (AMOS 8:11)

The Noé edition of the Koren Talmud Bavli
with the commentary of Rabbi Adin Even-Israel Steinsaltz
is dedicated to all those who open its covers
to quench their thirst for Jewish Knowledge,
in our generation of Torah renaissance.

This beautiful edition is for the young, the aged,
the novice and the savant alike,
as it unites the depth of Torah knowledge
with the best of academic scholarship.

Within its exquisite and vibrant pages,
words become worlds.

It will claim its place in the library of classics,
in the bookcases of the Beit Midrash,
the classrooms of our schools,
and in the offices of professionals and business people
who carve out precious time to grapple with its timeless wisdom.

For the Student and the Scholar

DEDICATED BY LEO AND SUE NOÉ

Steinsaltz Center

Executive Director, Steinsaltz Center

Rabbi Meni Even-Israel

Managing Editor

Rabbi Jason Rappoport

Senior Content Editor

Rabbi Dr. Shalom Z. Berger

Editors

Rabbi Dr. Joshua Amaru, *Coordinating Editor*
Rabbi Yehoshua Duker, *Final Editor*
Rabbi Avishai Magence, *Content Curator*
Yedidya Naveh, *Content Curator*
Tal Avrahami
Menucha Chwat
Rabbi Adin Krohn
Betzalel Philip Edwards
Rabbi Yonatan Shai Freedman
Raphael Friedman
Rabbi Ayal Geffon
Rabbi Uri Goldstein
Nechama Greenberg
Rabbi Tzvi Chaim Kaye
Rabbi Yonatan Kohn
Catriel Lev
Elisha Loewenstern
Adina Luber
Rabbi Simcha Mirvis
Rabbi Jonathan Mishkin
Rabbi David Sedley
Avi Steinhart
Rabbi David Strauss
Rabbi Yitzchak Twersky

Copy Editors

Aliza Israel, *Coordinator*
Ita Olesker
Debbie Ismailoff
Shira Finson
Ilana Sobel
Deena Nataf
Eliana Kurlantzick Yorav
Erica Hirsch Edvi
Nava Wieder
Sara Henna Dahan
Shalom Dinerstein

Language Consultants

Dr. Stephanie E. Binder, *Greek & Latin*
Rabbi Yaakov Hoffman, *Arabic*
Dr. Shai Secunda, *Persian*
Shira Shmidman, *Aramaic*

KOREN

Design & Typesetting

Dena Landowne Bailey, *Typesetting*
Tani Bayer, *Jacket Design*
Raphaël Freeman, *Design & Typography*

Images

Eliahu Misgav, *Illustration & Image Acquisition*
Daniel Gdalevich, *Illustration & Image Acquisition*

Introduction by the Publisher

The Talmud has sustained and inspired Jews for thousands of years. Throughout Jewish history, an elite cadre of scholars has absorbed its learning and passed it on to succeeding generations. The Talmud has been the fundamental text of our people.

Beginning in the 1960s, Rabbi Adin Even-Israel Steinsaltz שליט״א created a revolution in the history of Talmud study. His translation of the Talmud, first into modern Hebrew and then into other languages, as well the practical learning aids he added to the text, have enabled millions of people around the world to access and master the complexity and context of the world of Talmud.

It is thus a privilege to present the *Koren Talmud Bavli*, an English translation of the talmudic text with the brilliant elucidation of Rabbi Steinsaltz. The depth and breadth of his knowledge are unique in our time. His rootedness in the tradition and his reach into the world beyond it are inspirational.

Working with Rabbi Steinsaltz on this remarkable project has been not only an honor, but a great pleasure. Never shy to express an opinion, with wisdom and humor, Rabbi Steinsaltz sparkles in conversation, demonstrating his knowledge (both sacred and worldly), sharing his wide-ranging interests, and, above all, radiating his passion. I am grateful for the unique opportunity to work closely with him, and I wish him many more years of writing and teaching.

Our intentions in publishing this new edition of the Talmud are threefold. First, we seek to fully clarify the talmudic page to the reader – textually, intellectually, and graphically. Second, we seek to utilize today's most sophisticated technologies, both in print and electronic formats, to provide the reader with a comprehensive set of study tools. And third, we seek to help readers advance in their process of Talmud study.

To achieve these goals, the *Koren Talmud Bavli* is unique in a number of ways:

- The classic *tzurat hadaf* of Vilna, used by scholars since the 1800s, has been reset for great clarity, and opens from the Hebrew "front" of the book. Full *nikkud* has been added to both the talmudic text and Rashi's commentary, allowing for a more fluent reading with the correct pronunciation; the commentaries of *Tosafot* have been punctuated. Upon the advice of many English-speaking teachers of Talmud, we have separated these core pages from the translation, thereby enabling the advanced student to approach the text without the distraction of the translation. This also reduces the number of volumes in the set. At the bottom of each *daf*, there is a reference to the corresponding English pages. In addition, the Vilna edition was read against other manuscripts and older print editions, so that texts which had been removed by non-Jewish censors have been restored to their rightful place.

- The English translation, which starts on the English "front" of the book, reproduces the *menukad* Talmud text alongside the English translation (in bold) and commentary and explanation (in a lighter font). The Hebrew and Aramaic text is presented in logical paragraphs. This allows for a fluent reading of the text for the non-Hebrew or non-Aramaic reader. It also allows for the Hebrew reader to refer easily to the text alongside. Where the original text features dialogue or poetry, the English text is laid out in a manner appropriate to the genre. Each page refers to the relevant *daf*.

- Critical contextual tools surround the text and translation: personality notes, providing short biographies of the Sages; language notes, explaining foreign terms borrowed from Greek, Latin, Persian, or Arabic; and background notes, giving information essential to the understanding of the text, including history, geography, botany, archaeology, zoology, astronomy, and aspects of daily life in the talmudic era.
- Halakhic summaries provide references to the authoritative legal decisions made over the centuries by the rabbis. They explain the reasons behind each halakhic decision as well as the ruling's close connection to the Talmud and its various interpreters.
- Photographs, drawings, and other illustrations have been added throughout the text – in full color in the Standard and Electronic editions, and in black and white in the Daf Yomi edition – to visually elucidate the text.

This is not an exhaustive list of features of this edition, it merely presents an overview for the English-speaking reader who may not be familiar with the "total approach" to Talmud pioneered by Rabbi Steinsaltz.

Several professionals have helped bring this vast collaborative project to fruition. My many colleagues are noted on the Acknowledgments page, and the leadership of this project has been exceptional.

RABBI MENACHEM EVEN-ISRAEL, DIRECTOR OF THE STEINSALTZ CENTER, was the driving force behind this enterprise. With enthusiasm and energy, he formed the happy alliance with Koren and established close relationships among all involved in the work.

RABBI DR. TZVI HERSH WEINREB שליט״א, EDITOR-IN-CHIEF, brought to this project his profound knowledge of Torah, intellectual literacy of Talmud, and erudition of Western literature. It is to him that the text owes its very high standard, both in form and content, and the logical manner in which the beauty of the Talmud is presented.

RABBI JOSHUA SCHREIER, EXECUTIVE EDITOR, assembled an outstanding group of scholars, translators, editors, and proofreaders, whose standards and discipline enabled this project to proceed in a timely and highly professional manner.

RABBI MEIR HANEGBI, EDITOR OF THE HEBREW EDITION OF THE STEINSALTZ TALMUD, lent his invaluable assistance throughout the work process, supervising the reproduction of the Vilna pages.

RAPHAËL FREEMAN, EXECUTIVE EDITOR OF KOREN, created this Talmud's unique typographic design which, true to the Koren approach, is both elegant and user friendly.

It has been an enriching experience for all of us at Koren Publishers Jerusalem to work with the Steinsaltz Center to develop and produce the *Koren Talmud Bavli*. We pray that this publication will be a source of great learning and, ultimately, greater *avodat Hashem* for all Jews.

Matthew Miller, Publisher
Koren Publishers Jerusalem
Jerusalem 5772

Contents

For the vocalized Vilna Shas layout, please open as a Hebrew book.

Introduction to **Perek X**

And I bought the field that was in Anathoth from Hanamel, my uncle's son, and weighed him the money, seven shekels and ten pieces of silver. And I subscribed the deed, and sealed it, and called witnesses, and weighed the money in the balances. So I took the deed of the purchase, that which was sealed, the terms and the conditions, and that which was open.

(Jeremiah 32:9–11)

So said the Lord of hosts, the God of Israel: Take these deeds, this deed of the purchase, that which is sealed, and this deed that is open, and put them in an earthen vessel, that they may continue many days.

(Jeremiah 32:14)

In this chapter, the Gemara discusses the above verses and concludes that no practical halakhic deductions may be drawn from these verses in Jeremiah. Nevertheless, it is possible to learn from them that already in First Temple times there were distinct procedures involved in the formulation of deeds and intricate methods of acquisition associated with them. Since the Torah itself does not mention legal documents, with the exception of the bill of divorce mentioned in Deuteronomy 24:1, all the *halakhot* pertaining to such documents are rabbinic ordinances instituted through the ages, from the time of Moses down to the latter generations of talmudic Sages. This chapter, the final chapter of the tractate, discusses several fundamental issues concerning the legal documents relevant to the various kinds of business transactions dealt with throughout the tractate.

One issue is the correct method of writing the text and signing of witnesses on a document. In mishnaic times there were two types of documents: Ordinary documents and tied, or folded, documents. The proper procedure for preparing each of these documents is examined in this chapter: Where and how the witnesses should sign, under what circumstances a document may be written upon paper or parchment that had its original text written and erased, how to erase or correct errors in documents, and how to resolve apparent contradictions found in a document's text.

Other issues discussed are: May a document for a legal transaction be written with the consent of only one of the parties involved, or is it necessary to consult with and receive the consent of all the parties? Which party is required to pay the wages of the one who writes the document?

The Gemara also considers a somewhat related issue: If one has a document that has become erased or is fading and is bound to become illegible, is there a way to have the contents copied into a replacement document? The chapter addresses yet another question: If a promissory note is paid in part, should a new promissory note be written for the balance, or is the original promissory note to be retained, with a receipt issued to the debtor to protect him from subsequent collection of the full amount?

Toward the end of the chapter, the concept of a loan guarantee is raised. The basic idea of a guarantee is mentioned in the Torah, but its application to a loan guarantee is not clear. One question that arises is: What is the legal relationship between the creditor and the guarantor? Is the guarantor obligated to repay the loan only if the debtor defaults, or can the creditor approach the guarantor directly? Other issues discussed include the following: Is a guarantor legally bound by merely stating he will serve as a guarantor, or must his commitment be recorded in writing? What is the precise formulation that obligates a guarantor to honor his pledge? Can property that a guarantor has sold to others subsequent to undertaking the guarantee be seized as repayment?

Along with its analysis of these and similar topics, the Gemara addresses certain other subjects of a tangential nature, some of which are explored quite thoroughly.

מתני׳ גֵּט פָּשׁוּט – עֵדָיו מִתּוֹכוֹ, מְקוּשָּׁר – עֵדָיו מֵאֲחוֹרָיו.

MISHNA In an ordinary[N] document, its witnesses are to sign **inside it,** i.e., on the written side of the paper. In a folded and **tied document,**[N] **its witnesses are to sign on the back of it.**

פָּשׁוּט שֶׁכָּתְבוּ עֵדָיו מֵאֲחוֹרָיו, מְקוּשָּׁר שֶׁכָּתְבוּ עֵדָיו מִתּוֹכוֹ – שְׁנֵיהֶם פְּסוּלִין. רַבִּי חֲנִינָא בֶּן גַּמְלִיאֵל אוֹמֵר: מְקוּשָּׁר שֶׁכָּתְבוּ עֵדָיו מִתּוֹכוֹ – כָּשֵׁר, מִפְּנֵי שֶׁיָּכוֹל לַעֲשׂוֹתוֹ פָּשׁוּט. רַבָּן שִׁמְעוֹן בֶּן גַּמְלִיאֵל אוֹמֵר: הַכֹּל כְּמִנְהַג הַמְּדִינָה.

With regard to **an ordinary** document **whose witnesses wrote** their signatures **on the back of it,** and **a tied** document **whose witnesses wrote** their signatures **inside of it, both of these** are **not valid.**[N] **Rabbi Ḥanina ben Gamliel says: A tied** document **whose witnesses wrote** their signatures **inside of it is valid, because one can transform it into an ordinary** document by untying it. **Rabban Shimon ben Gamliel says: Everything is in accordance with regional custom.**[H]

גֵּט פָּשׁוּט – עֵדָיו בִּשְׁנַיִם, וּמְקוּשָּׁר – בִּשְׁלֹשָׁה. פָּשׁוּט שֶׁכָּתַב בּוֹ עֵד אֶחָד, וּמְקוּשָּׁר שֶׁכָּתַב בּוֹ שְׁנֵי עֵדִים – שְׁנֵיהֶם פְּסוּלִין.

An ordinary document is rendered valid **by** its having at least **two witnesses, and a tied** document is rendered valid **by** its having at least **three** witnesses. With regard to **an ordinary** document **in which a single witness wrote** his signature, **and a tied** document **in which** only **two witnesses wrote** their signatures, **they are both not valid.**

HALAKHA

Everything is in accordance with regional custom – הַכֹּל כְּמִנְהַג הַמְּדִינָה: Some say that any document that does not follow the procedures established by the Sages is not valid, even if there is nothing objectionable in its text. Therefore, if one writes a tied document today, when we have no firsthand knowledge of its proper preparation, it is not valid (*Nimmukei Yosef*). The Ramban notes that this opinion is not accepted as the authoritative *halakha* (*Shulḥan Arukh, Ḥoshen Mishpat* 42:1).

NOTES

Ordinary [*pashut*] – פָּשׁוּט: The word *pashut* has several meanings. In this context it appears that the most accurate interpretation would be flattened or spread out, in contrast to the other type of document, which is tied closed.

Folded and tied document – גֵּט...מְקוּשָּׁר: Tied documents in antiquity were used to ensure a more secure and tamper-resistant method of recording contracts and deeds. Preparing a tied document required a greater amount of time and expertise than preparing an ordinary document.

After the talmudic period and, it would appear from the Gemara, even at the close of the mishnaic period, the use of this type of document was severely limited and perhaps even discontinued altogether. In fact, the Rambam does not discuss it at all in the *Mishne Torah*. The commentaries who explain the details of its production and appearance are not speaking from firsthand knowledge, but are reconstructing these matters from information found in various discussions in the Gemara and traditions received from previous generations.

There are consequently several differing views as to how a tied document is written, which may be divided into two basic approaches. According to some, part of the document is folded back and forth several times, like a handheld fan or accordion. A line of text is written and the next line is left blank; the written line is then folded over the blank line and sewn closed. This procedure is repeated at least three times. Only the essential part of the document would be tied, with the rest of the document written below the folds in the ordinary manner (Rashi on *Gittin* 81a and *Kiddushin* 49b; Rabbeinu Gershom Meor HaGola; Rashbam; Rabbeinu Yehonatan of Lunel).

The second approach is that after the document is folded, it is tied with straps that emerge from its sides or ends (Ramah). In any event, the witnesses sign on the exposed side of the document, in the manner discussed in the Gemara. *Tosafot* subscribe in a large part to the former opinion, but maintain there is no system of alternating written and blank lines. Rather, the lines are written one after the other, and every other written line is folded over the written line that follows it.

In the 1960s, tied documents from the period of bar Kokheva were unearthed in a cave in Judea. On these, the entire text of the document was written twice on the same piece of parchment, with the first copy folded, tied, and sealed to ensure its integrity. The second copy was left open for easy reference. Witnesses signed on the back of the document, with one signature for every stitch tying the sealed copy. This model differs considerably from Rashi's explanation, more closely resembling the opinion of the Ramah.

Signed document, according to Rashi

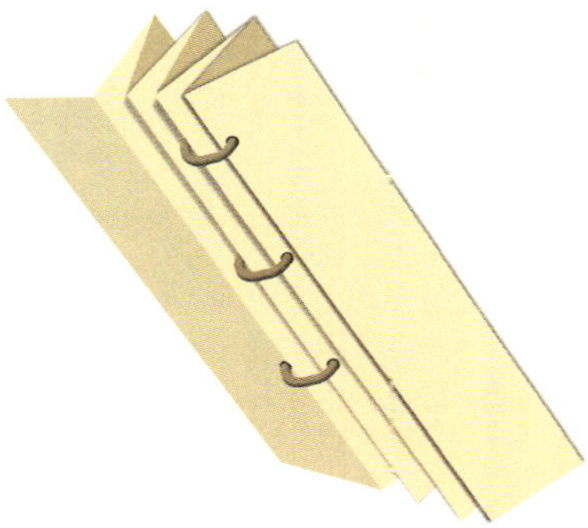

Manner of folding and stitching, according to Rashi

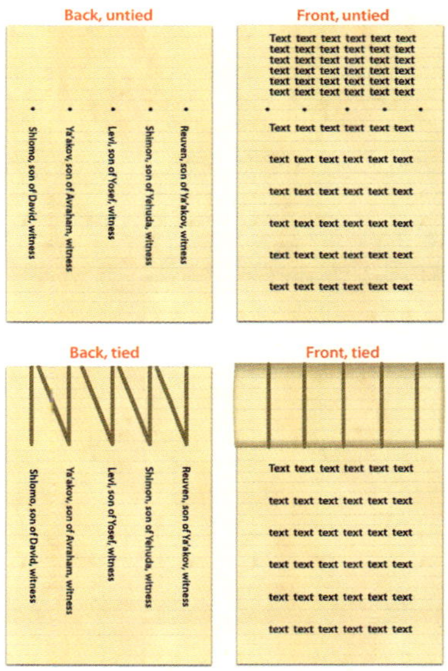

Illustrations of a tied document discovered in Nahal Hever. Pictured are the front of the document and its back, before and after being tied.

Both of these are not valid – שְׁנֵיהֶם פְּסוּלִין: These documents are invalidated because, as the Gemara explains (164b), different dating systems were used for ordinary and tied documents. It would therefore be possible to change the date of the transaction recorded in the document after it is signed by folding and sewing it, or by opening and unfolding it (*Tosafot*). According to the Ramban, the reason the document is disqualified is that a document is valid only if prepared by the scribe in accordance with the directions of the party who commissions it. This document, which meets the requirements of neither an ordinary document nor a tied one, is presumably not what the scribe was instructed to write. The Rashbam explains simply that any document that does not follow the procedures established for it by the Sages is *ipso facto* not valid.

גמ׳ מְנָהָנֵי מִילֵּי? אָמַר רַבִּי חֲנִינָא, דְּאָמַר קְרָא: ״שָׂדוֹת בַּכֶּסֶף יִקְנוּ וְכָתוֹב בַּסֵּפֶר וְחָתוֹם וְהָעֵד עֵדִים״; ״שָׂדוֹת בַּכֶּסֶף יִקְנוּ וְכָתוֹב בַּסֵּפֶר״ –

GEMARA The Gemara asks: **From where are these matters** derived? What biblical basis is there for the existence of these two types of documents? **Rabbi Ḥanina says: As the verse states: "They shall buy fields for money, and subscribe the deeds, and seal them, and call witnesses"** (Jeremiah 32:44). When the verse states: **"They shall buy fields for money, and subscribe the deeds,"**

Perek **X**
Daf **160** Amud **b**

זֶה פָּשׁוּט, ״וְחָתוֹם״ – זֶה מְקוּשָּׁר, ״וְהָעֵד״ – שְׁנַיִם, ״עֵדִים״ – שְׁלֹשָׁה, הָא כֵּיצַד? שְׁנַיִם לְפָשׁוּט, שְׁלֹשָׁה לִמְקוּשָּׁר.

this is referring to **an ordinary** document. When the verse states: **"And seal them," this** is referring to **a tied** document. The next phrase, "and call witnesses [*veha'ed edim*]," which more literally would be translated: And have witnesses bear witness, is interpreted as follows: **"And have bear witness [*veha'ed*],"** this indicates the need for **two** witnesses, as the term "witness [*ed*]" in the Torah generally refers to two witnesses. As to the word **"witnesses [*edim*],"** this additional term indicates the need for **three** witnesses. **How so?** How can the verse call for both two witnesses and three witnesses? Rabbi Ḥanina explains: **Two** witnesses are required **for an ordinary** document, and **three** are required **for a tied** document.

וְאֵיפוֹךְ אֲנָא! מִתּוֹךְ שֶׁנִּתְרַבָּה בִּקְשָׁרָיו נִתְרַבָּה בְּעֵדָיו.

The Gemara questions this explanation: **But I** can just as well **reverse** it, requiring two witnesses for a tied document and three for an ordinary one. The Gemara answers: **Since** the tied document requires **more** to be done **with regard to its ties,** it stands to reason that it requires **more** to be done **with regard to its witnesses,** requiring three rather than two.

רַפְרָם אָמַר, מֵהָכָא: ״וָאֶקַּח אֶת סֵפֶר הַמִּקְנָה אֶת הֶחָתוּם הַמִּצְוָה וְהַחֻקִּים וְאֶת הַגָּלוּי״; ״וָאֶקַּח אֶת סֵפֶר הַמִּקְנָה״ – זֶה פָּשׁוּט, ״אֶת הֶחָתוּם״ – זֶה מְקוּשָּׁר, ״וְאֶת הַגָּלוּי״ – זֶה פָּשׁוּט שֶׁבִּמְקוּשָּׁר,

Rafram says that there is a different source for two kinds of documents, **from here: "So I took the deed of the purchase, that which was sealed, the terms and conditions, and that which was open"** (Jeremiah 32:11). When the verse states: **"So I took the deed of the purchase," this** is referring to **an ordinary** document. When it states: **"That which was sealed," this** is referring to **a tied** document.[N] When it states: **"And that which was open," this** is referring to the **ordinary,** unfolded part **of a tied** document.

״הַמִּצְוָה וְהַחֻקִּים״ – אֵלּוּ דְּבָרִים שֶׁבֵּין פָּשׁוּט לִמְקוּשָּׁר, הָא כֵּיצַד? זֶה עֵדָיו שְׁנַיִם וְזֶה עֵדָיו שְׁלֹשָׁה, זֶה עֵדָיו מִתּוֹכוֹ וְזֶה עֵדָיו מֵאֲחוֹרָיו.

Rafram continues: With regard to the phrase: **"The terms and conditions," these are the matters that** distinguish **an ordinary** document **from a tied** one. **How so?** What are the details that differentiate the two types of documents? **This** one, the ordinary document, has **two witnesses, and that** one, the tied document, has **three witnesses.** And in **this** one, the ordinary document, **its witnesses** are signed **inside it,** on the front side, while in **that** one, the tied document, **its witnesses** are signed **on the back of it.**

וְאֵיפוֹךְ אֲנָא! מִתּוֹךְ שֶׁנִּתְרַבָּה בִּקְשָׁרָיו נִתְרַבָּה בְּעֵדָיו.

The Gemara questions this explanation: **But I** can just as well **reverse** it, requiring two witnesses for a tied document and three for an ordinary one. The Gemara answers: **Since** the tied document requires **more** to be done **with regard to its ties,** it stands to reason that it requires **more** to be done **with regard to its witnesses,** requiring three rather than two.

רָמִי בַּר יְחֶזְקֵאל אָמַר, מֵהָכָא: ״עַל פִּי שְׁנַיִם עֵדִים אוֹ עַל פִּי שְׁלֹשָׁה עֵדִים יָקוּם דָּבָר״, אִם תִּתְקַיֵּים עֵדוּתָן בִּשְׁנַיִם, לָמָּה פָּרַט לְךָ בִּשְׁלֹשָׁה? לוֹמַר לְךָ: שְׁנַיִם לְפָשׁוּט, שְׁלֹשָׁה לִמְקוּשָּׁר.

Rami bar Yeḥezkel said that there is a different source for two sets of *halakhot* for two types of documents **from here: "At the mouth of two witnesses or at the mouth of three witnesses shall a matter be established"** (Deuteronomy 19:15). **If** witnesses' **testimony is established with two** witnesses, **why** did the verse **specify for you** that it is also established **with three,** which is self-evident? Rather, this verse serves **to tell you** that there is a requirement for **two** witnesses **for an ordinary** document, and a requirement for **three** witnesses **for a tied** document.

NOTES

This is an ordinary document…this is a tied document – **זֶה פָּשׁוּט...זֶה מְקוּשָּׁר**: According to this interpretation, it emerges that Jeremiah wrote two documents for his purchase of this property from his cousin: An ordinary one and a tied one. The Ra'avad asks why Jeremiah would write two documents. The Ramah answers that both Jeremiah and his cousin were priests, living in a town of priests (see Jeremiah 1:1), and since the entire concept of tied documents was instituted for the benefit of priests, Jeremiah would naturally draw up a tied document. Since Jeremiah did not want the validity of the deed to be called into question at some time in the distant future, he wrote an ordinary document as well.

וְאֵיפוֹךְ אֲנָא! מִתּוֹךְ שֶׁנִּתְרַבָּה בִּקְשָׁרָיו נִתְרַבָּה בְּעֵדָיו.

The Gemara questions this explanation: **But I** can just as well **reverse** it, requiring two witnesses for a tied document and three for an ordinary one. The Gemara answers: **Since** the tied document requires **more** to be done **with regard to its ties,** it stands to reason that it requires **more** to be done **with regard to its witnesses,** requiring three rather than two.

וְהָנֵי לְהָכִי הוּא דְּאָתוּ? כָּל חַד וְחַד לְמִילְּתֵיהּ הוּא דַּאֲתָא, לִכְדִתְנַיָא: "שָׂדוֹת בַּכֶּסֶף יִקְנוּ וְכָתוֹב בַּסֵּפֶר וְחָתוֹם" – עֵצָה טוֹבָה קָא מַשְׁמַע לָן, "וָאֶקַּח אֶת סֵפֶר הַמִּקְנָה" – הָכִי הֲוָה מַעֲשֶׂה, "עַל פִּי שְׁנַיִם עֵדִים אוֹ עַל פִּי שְׁלֹשָׁה עֵדִים" – לְהַקִּישׁ שְׁלֹשָׁה לִשְׁנַיִם, בִּפְלוּגְתָּא דְּרַבִּי עֲקִיבָא וְרַבָּנַן!

The Gemara asks: **And** is it so that **these** verses **are coming for this** purpose, to teach that there are two types of documents? But **each and every one** of them **comes for its** own **purpose.** The first verse comes **for that which is taught** in a *baraita*: When the verse states: "**They shall buy fields for money, and subscribe the deeds, and seal them,** and call witnesses" (Jeremiah 32:44), it is merely to **teach us good advice,** that people should carefully document their purchases in order to provide permanent proof of purchase. When the verse states: "**So I took the deed of the purchase**" (Jeremiah 32:11), **this was** merely how that **incident** occurred, and the phrase is not intended to teach any *halakhot*. When the verse states: "**At the mouth of two witnesses or at the mouth of three witnesses** shall a matter be established" (Deuteronomy 19:15), this is stated in order **to juxtapose three** witnesses **with two** witnesses for several reasons, as delineated **in the dispute between Rabbi Akiva and the Rabbis** (*Makkot* 5b).

אֶלָּא, מְקוּשָּׁר מִדְּרַבָּנַן, וּקְרָאֵי אַסְמַכְתָּא בְּעָלְמָא.

The Gemara explains: **Rather,** the entire institution of the **tied** document is **rabbinic** in origin, **and** all these **verses** that were cited above by various *amora'im* were intended as **mere support**[B] for the concept of a tied document, as opposed to actual sources.

וְטַעְמָא מַאי תַּקִּינוּ רַבָּנַן מְקוּשָּׁר? אַתְרָא דְּכָהֲנֵי הֲווֹ, וַהֲווֹ קַפְדֵי טוּבָא וּמְגָרְשֵׁי נְשַׁיְיהוּ, וְעָבְדִי רַבָּנַן תַּקַּנְתָּא, אַדְּהָכִי וְהָכִי מִיתַּבָא דַּעְתַּיְיהוּ.

The Gemara asks: **And what is the reason** that **the Sages instituted** the **tied** document? The Gemara explains: There was a **place where there were** many **priests,**[N] **and they were very quick tempered, and they would** seek to **divorce their wives** impetuously. The *halakha* is that a priest may not marry a divorcée, even his own ex-wife. These priests, who acted impetuously, often regretted having divorced their wives. **And** therefore, **the Sages instituted an ordinance** that the bill of divorce for these people should be of the tied format, which is a long, drawn-out process, hoping that **meanwhile, their composure would be regained** and they would reconsider their decision to divorce.

הָתֵינַח גִּיטִּין, שְׁטָרוֹת מַאי אִיכָּא לְמֵימַר? כְּדֵי שֶׁלֹּא תַּחֲלֵק בֵּין גִּיטִּין לִשְׁטָרוֹת.

The Gemara asks: This **works out well** for **bills of divorce,** but **what can be said** with regard to other **documents?** Why is this procedure used for other documents as well? The Gemara answers: This was instituted **so that you should not differentiate between bills of divorce and** other **documents.**[N]

הֵיכָן עֵדִים חוֹתְמִין? רַב הוּנָא אָמַר: בֵּין קֶשֶׁר לְקֶשֶׁר, וְרַב יִרְמְיָה בַּר אַבָּא אָמַר: אֲחוֹרֵי הַכְּתָב וּכְנֶגֶד הַכְּתָב מִבַּחוּץ.

§ **Where do the witnesses sign** on a tied document? **Rav Huna says:** They sign **between each tied** fold. **And Rav Yirmeya bar Abba says:** They sign **on the back of the written** side, taking care that the signatures are exactly **opposite the writing, on the outside.**

אֲמַר לֵיהּ רָמֵי בַּר חָמָא לְרַב חִסְדָּא: לְרַב הוּנָא דְּאָמַר בֵּין קֶשֶׁר לְקֶשֶׁר, קָא סָלְקָא דַּעְתִּין בֵּין קֶשֶׁר לְקֶשֶׁר מִגַּוַּאי, וְהָא הַהוּא מְקוּשָּׁר דַּאֲתָא לְקַמֵּיהּ דְּרַבִּי, וַאֲמַר רַבִּי: אֵין זְמַן בָּזֶה? אֲמַר לֵיהּ רַבִּי שִׁמְעוֹן בְּרַבִּי לְרַבִּי: שֶׁמָּא בֵּין קְשָׁרָיו מוּבְלָע? פַּלְיֵיהּ וַחֲזַיֵיהּ; וְאִם אִיתָא, "אֵין זְמַן בָּזֶה וְאֵין עֵדִים בָּזֶה" מִיבְּעֵי לֵיהּ!

Rami bar Ḥama said to Rav Ḥisda: According to Rav Huna, who says that the witnesses sign **between each tied** fold, **it enters our mind** that he meant **between each tied** fold **on the inside** of the document. **But** this is difficult, as there was **a certain tied** document[N] **that came before Rabbi** Yehuda HaNasi,[P] **and** Rabbi Yehuda HaNasi, not realizing it was tied, **said: There is no date on this** document, so it is not valid. Then, **Rabbi Shimon,** son of **Rabbi** Yehuda HaNasi, **said to Rabbi** Yehuda HaNasi: **Perhaps** the date is **hidden between the tied** folds. Rabbi Yehuda HaNasi **opened it and saw** that the date was in fact between the tied folds. **And if it is so** that the witnesses sign between each tied fold on the inside of the document, Rabbi Yehuda HaNasi **should have** had two objections, and said: **There is no date on this** document, **and there are** also **no witnesses** signed **on this** document.

BACKGROUND

Mere support – אַסְמַכְתָּא בְּעָלְמָא: At times, the Gemara states that a verse cited as the basis for a *halakha* is merely an allusion to the *halakha* rather than its actual source. In such cases, the verse is called a support for the *halakha*. *Halakhot* of this kind are generally rabbinic enactments and not actually derived from the biblical text, which serves instead as a mnemonic device. This is indicated in the Talmud by the common phrase: The law is rabbinic, and the verse is a mere support.

NOTES

A place where there were many priests – אַתְרָא דְּכָהֲנֵי: *Tosafot* ask if this means that all priests, even today, are required to use a tied document when divorcing their wives. They conclude that today, when we do not have sufficient expertise to write a tied document, it is better to write an ordinary bill of divorce that fully complies with its *halakhot* than to write a tied document that might not fulfill its *halakhot*. Moreover, they suggest that the requirement to use tied documents was instituted only in one particular place and was not intended to be a general requirement for all priests. Finally, they maintain that it was never a requirement for any priests to use this format; rather, it was always presented to them as good advice.

So that you should not differentiate between bills of divorce and other documents – שֶׁלֹּא תַּחֲלֵק בֵּין גִּיטִּין לִשְׁטָרוֹת: *Tosafot* explain that if the procedures for writing documents were not uniform, people might refrain from using a tied document for bills of divorce as well. Rabbeinu Gershom Meor HaGola explains that if documents other than bills of divorce would be declared not valid in the tied format, people would be led to think that bills of divorce written in this format are also not valid, and this would lead to mistaken assumptions with regard to those women's marital status.

A certain tied document, etc. – הַהוּא מְקוּשָּׁר וכו׳: It is apparent from the Gemara later (164b) that Rabbi Yehuda HaNasi was not familiar with tied documents, as evidently they were already quite rare in his time. Therefore, he did not realize that it was a tied document, and he dismissed its validity because of the supposed lack of a date on it (see *Tosafot*).

PERSONALITIES

Rabbi Yehuda HaNasi – רַבִּי יְהוּדָה הַנָּשִׂיא: The period of *tanna'im* concluded with Rabbi Yehuda HaNasi's redaction of the Mishna. The son of Rabbi Shimon ben Gamliel II, Rabbi Yehuda HaNasi lived from 135 to 220 CE. When he was thirty years old he was appointed *Nasi*, or prince, but due to his great scholarship the Talmud refers to him simply as Rabbi. Rabbi Yehuda HaNasi spoke Greek, which was the language of the elite in Eretz Yisrael, and he was friendly with the Roman emperor Antoninus. His knowledge of Hebrew was legendary, to the extent that the Sages learned the meaning of difficult words from servants who worked in his house.

אָמַר לֵיהּ: מִי סָבְרַתְּ בֵּין קֶשֶׁר לְקֶשֶׁר מִגַּוַּאי? לָא, בֵּין קֶשֶׁר לְקֶשֶׁר מֵאַבְּרַאי.

Rav Ḥisda **said to him: Do you maintain** that Rav Huna meant that the witnesses sign **between the tied** folds **on the inside? No,** he meant **between the tied** folds **on the outside** of the document.

וְנֵיחוּשׁ דִּלְמָא זַיֵּיף וְכָתַב מַאי דְּבָעֵי, וַחֲתִימִי סָהֲדֵי!

The Gemara questions Rav Huna's opinion: **But let us be concerned** that **perhaps** the party holding the document **falsified** some information **and wrote whatever he wanted. And** this is a concern, as there are already **witnesses signed** on the document. In an ordinary document the witnesses sign immediately following the text, so there is no possibility of adding to the text. A tied document has part of its text written in the folds, but also has a part written on the face of the document on the unfolded paper, before or after the text in the folded part. If the witnesses sign between the folds there is the possibility of writing additional text in the unfolded section.

דִּכְתִיב בֵּיהּ "שָׁרִיר וְקַיָּים".

The Gemara explains: The case is one **where it is written in** the document: Everything is **confirmed and established.** That is, every folded document must contain this formula at the end of the text, to prevent forgery, as any writing after this formula would be disregarded.

וְנֵיחוּשׁ דִּלְמָא כָּתַב מַאי דְּבָעֵי, וַהֲדַר כָּתַב "שָׁרִיר וְקַיָּים" אַחֲרִינָא! חַד "שָׁרִיר וְקַיָּים" כָּתְבִינַן, תְּרֵי "שָׁרִיר וְקַיָּים" לָא כָּתְבִינַן.

The Gemara questions this explanation: **But let us be concerned** that **perhaps** the holder of the document **wrote whatever he wanted and afterward wrote another** time: Everything is **confirmed and established.** The Gemara explains: **We write** only **one** declaration of: Everything is **confirmed and established;**[H] **we do not write two** declarations of: Everything is **confirmed and established.** Therefore, anything written after the first declaration would be rejected, even if followed by a repetition of the declaration.

וְלֵיחוּשׁ דִּלְמָא מָחֵיק לֵיהּ לְ"שָׁרִיר וְקַיָּים", וְכָתַב מַאי דְּבָעֵי, וַהֲדַר כָּתַב "שָׁרִיר וְקַיָּים"! הָא אָמַר רַבִּי יוֹחָנָן: תְּלוּיָה מְקוּיֶּימֶת – כְּשֵׁרָה,

The Gemara questions further: **But let** there be **a concern** that **perhaps** the holder of the document **erased** the declaration: Everything is **confirmed and established, and** then **wrote whatever he wanted** over the erasure, **and afterward wrote** the declaration: Everything is **confirmed and established.** The Gemara responds: How could this happen? **Doesn't Rabbi Yoḥanan say:** A document that includes **a suspended** correction of text inserted between lines of the document, which is **verified**[H] at the end of the document, **is valid;**

HALAKHA

We write one declaration of: Everything is confirmed and established – חַד שָׁרִיר וְקַיָּים כָּתְבִינַן: Today, when it is the accepted practice to write at the end of all documents, even ordinary documents: Everything is confirmed and established, any document that is missing this formula is invalid. Therefore, witnesses may not sign any document where these words are not written. If this formula is written twice in a document, the document is valid, since the witnesses sign after the text, confirming the veracity of everything written before their signatures. The Rema, citing the Rosh, notes that nevertheless this formulation should not be written twice (*Shulḥan Arukh*, *Ḥoshen Mishpat* 44:9).

A suspended correction which is verified – תְּלוּיָה מְקוּיֶּימֶת: Letters or words that are suspended between the lines of a document or inserted between other letters or words are disregarded if not verified at the end of the document, but they do not invalidate the document in its entirety, in accordance with the statement of Rabbi Yoḥanan. If such corrections appear in the essential part of the document, where the names of the creditor and debtor and the amount of money involved are written, and the insertions were not verified at the end of the document, the entire document is invalid. If the unverified correction is to the date, the document is treated as a document that has no date (Rambam *Sefer Mishpatim*, *Hilkhot Malve VeLoveh* 27:8, and see *Sefer Nashim*, *Hilkhot Geirushin* 4:15; *Shulḥan Arukh*, *Ḥoshen Mishpat* 44:5, and see *Even HaEzer* 125:19).

Perek **X**
Daf **161** Amud **a**

מְחָק – פָּסוּל, וְאַף עַל פִּי שֶׁמְּקוּיָּים.

but a document with a reference to words written over an **erasure**[H] **is not valid, even if it is verified** at the end of the document. At the end of a document, before the formula: Everything is confirmed and established, is written, any corrections made in the document are verified by adding to the text: On line so-and-so, such and such a word has been added, or some similar formulation. This may be done only for inserted corrections, not for erasures.

HALAKHA

An erasure – מְחָק: In a case where a letter or word of a document is erased and others are written in its place, if the erasure is not verified the document is still valid, but the text written on the place of erasure is disregarded. Some say that if the erasure is not verified the entire document is invalid, unless it is clear from the context of the rest of the document that the text on the erasure is correct (Rema, citing *Tur* and *Nimmukei Yosef*). If the erasure was in the essential part of the document, i.e., where the names of the parties or the amount of money is written, the document is invalid (Rashba, citing *Tosefta*). If the erasure was in the place where the date is written, it is treated as an undated document (Rambam *Sefer Mishpatim*, *Hilkhot Malve VeLoveh* 27:8, and see *Sefer Nashim*, *Hilkhot Geirushin* 4:15; *Shulḥan Arukh*, *Ḥoshen Mishpat* 44:5, and see *Even HaEzer* 125:19).

וְלֹא אָמְרוּ מְחַק פָּסוּל אֶלָּא בִּמְקוֹם "שָׁרִיר וְקַיָּים", וּכְשִׁיעוּר "שָׁרִיר וְקַיָּים".

The Gemara clarifies this statement: **And they said that an erasure** on a document renders the document **not valid only** if it is **in a place** on the document where the declaration: Everything is **confirmed and established,**[H] should have been written, **and** only if the erasure **is the measure** of space in which the declaration: Everything is **confirmed and established,** can be written. The only concern with erasures is that the crucial formula: Everything is confirmed and established, might have been erased, as this would allow for unlimited forgery. If the erasure is such that this formula could not possibly have been erased, the document is valid.

וּלְרַב יִרְמְיָה בַּר אַבָּא דְּאָמַר: אֲחוֹרֵי הַכְּתָב וּכְנֶגֶד הַכְּתָב מִבַּחוּץ, לֵיחוּשׁ דִּלְמָא כָּתֵיב מִגַּוַּואי מַאי דְּבָעֵי וּמַחְתִּים סָהֲדֵי יְתֵירֵי מֵאַבְּרַאי, וְאָמַר: אֲנָא לְרַבּוֹת בְּעֵדִים הוּא דַּעֲבַדִי!

§ Rami bar Ḥama asked Rav Ḥisda: **And according to Rav Yirmeya bar Abba, who says** that the witnesses sign **on the back of the written** side, taking care that the signatures are exactly **opposite the writing, on the outside let** there be a **concern** that **perhaps** the party holding the document **will write whatever he wants on the inside,** i.e., the front of the document, adding to the text, **and** then **have extra witnesses sign on the outside, and** he will **say** to anyone questioning the number of witnesses being more than the minimum: **I did** this in order **to increase** the number of **witnesses,** the more to publicize the matters written in the document.

אֲמַר לֵיהּ: מִי סָבְרַתְּ עֵדִים כְּסִדְרָן חָתְמִי? עֵדִים מִמַּטָּה לְמַעְלָה חָתְמִי.

Rav Ḥisda **said to him: Do you maintain** that the **witnesses sign in order,** that is, one under the other, starting from the top of the page on the back? This is not correct; rather, the **witnesses sign from bottom to top.**[N] The witnesses sign in a perpendicular direction relative to the text of the document. The first signature begins at the reverse side of the last line of the document, and it continues upward toward the first line. There is therefore no possibility of adding to the text of the document, as, if the text extended beyond the beginning of the signatures, it would be recognized as a forgery.

וְלֵיחוּשׁ דִּלְמָא מִתְרַמְיָא רִיעוּתֵיהּ בְּשִׁיטָה אַחֲרוֹנָה, וְגָיֵיז לֵיהּ לְשִׁיטָה אַחֲרוֹנָה, וְגָיֵיז לֵיהּ לִרְאוּבֵן בַּהֲדֵיהּ, וּמִתְכַּשֵּׁר בְּ"בֶן יַעֲקֹב עֵד"; דִּתְנַן: "בֶּן אִישׁ פְּלוֹנִי עֵד" – כָּשֵׁר!

Rami bar Ḥama continues to question the method of signature prescribed by Rav Yirmeya bar Abba: **But let** there be **a concern** that **perhaps something detrimental** to the holder of the document **happens** to appear **in the final line** of the document, **and he excises the final line, and** in doing so **excises** the first name of the witness on the opposite side as well. For instance, if the witness's name is Reuven, son of Ya'akov, he will excise **Reuven along with** the final line of the document, **and** the document **will be rendered valid with** the remaining part of the signature: **"Son of Ya'akov, witness." As we learned** in a mishna (*Gittin* 87b): If one signs: **Son of so-and-so, witness,** without mentioning his own name, the document is **valid.**

NOTES

Sign from bottom to top – מִמַּטָּה לְמַעְלָה חָתְמִי: The Rashbam and others, citing the Jerusalem Talmud, explain this to mean that the signatures are written in a perpendicular direction relative to the document's text, the first signature beginning at the bottom line, heading up toward the top line, the second one following it on that same line, and so on, until the top of the document is reached (*Baḥ*). It would be difficult to add an additional signature after the original signatures, because that extra witness would have to begin his signature opposite the final line of text and finish it precisely before the first signature. To do so, he would have to squeeze or stretch his signature in order to finish in the desired place, and the forgery would be noticed (Rabbeinu Gershom Meor HaGola).

Tosafot ask why the Sages did not avoid these problems by simply requiring that the witnesses of a tied document sign on the face of the document immediately following the text, as is done in an ordinary document. They answer that the Sages wanted to make a clear distinction between the two types of documents and therefore instituted a different format for the signatures of each.

HALAKHA

In a place where the declaration, confirmed and established, etc. – בִּמְקוֹם שָׁרִיר וְקַיָּים וכו׳: If there was an erasure near the bottom of a document, covering enough space to have contained the words: Everything is confirmed and established, then the document is not valid, even if the erasure is verified, and even if nothing else was written on the place of the erasure (*Sma*). The reason for this is that there is a concern that this formulation may have been written there, designating the end of the document's text, and that it was subsequently erased so that additions could be inserted into the text, as the Gemara explains. This is the *halakha* only when there is no blank line between the end of the text and the beginning of the witnesses' signature. If there is one blank line there, the document is valid, and there is no concern that there might have originally been two blank lines and one of them was filled in after the signing of the document, since it is prohibited to leave two blank lines at the end of the text, as the Gemara explains later (162b). If it is suspected that the witnesses might be unfamiliar with the *halakha* that it is prohibited to leave two blank lines, the aforementioned concern is relevant and the document is not valid (Rambam *Sefer Mishpatim*, *Hilkhot Malve VeLoveh* 27:8, and see *Sefer Nashim*, *Hilkhot Geirushin* 4:15; *Shulḥan Arukh*, *Ḥoshen Mishpat* 44:5, and see *Even HaEzer* 125:19).

BACKGROUND

"Reuven, son of" on one line and "Ya'akov, witness" above it – רְאוּבֵן בֶּן בְּחַד דָּרָא, וְיַעֲקֹב עֵד עִלָּוֵויהּ:

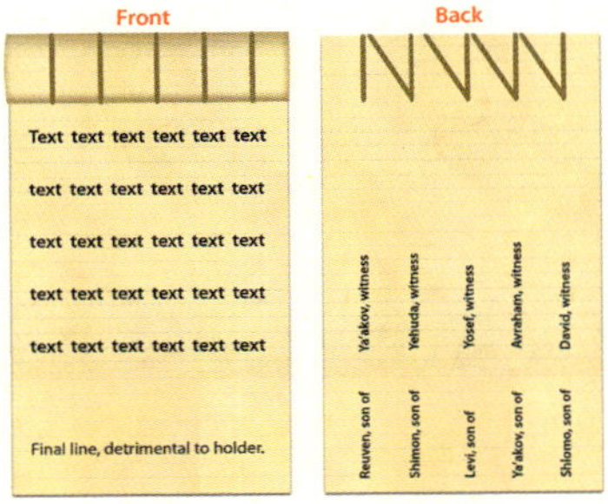

Document with signature according to the Gemara's response

דִּכְתִיב "רְאוּבֵן בֶּן" בְּחַד דָּרָא, וְ"יַעֲקֹב עֵד" עִלָּוֵויהּ.

The Gemara answers: It is a case **where it is written "Reuven, son of" on one line,** i.e., opposite the final line of the document, **and "Ya'akov, witness," above it,**[B] beginning from the penultimate line of the document and continuing upward in a perpendicular manner. That is, a tied document is valid only if the witnesses sign in this manner. In this case, if the final line of the document is excised, all that will remain of the signature will be: "Ya'akov, witness."

וְלֵיחוּשׁ דִּלְמָא גָּיֵיז לֵיהּ לִ"רְאוּבֵן בֶּן", וּמִתְכַּשַּׁר בְּ"יַעֲקֹב עֵד", דִּתְנַן: "אִישׁ פְּלוֹנִי עֵד" – כָּשֵׁר!

Rami bar Ḥama continues to ask: **But let** there be **a concern** that **perhaps he will excise** the final line of the document, along with the words **"Reuven, son of," and** the document **will be rendered valid with** the remaining part of the signature: **"Ya'akov, witness." As we learned** in a mishna (*Gittin* 87b): If someone signs just: **So-and-so, witness,** the document is **valid.**

דְּלָא כְּתִיב "עֵד".

The Gemara answers: It is a case **where** the word **witness is not written** after the witnesses' names. That is, a tied document is valid only if the word witness does not appear after the signatures. It is only in such a case that the document cannot be materially changed by excising the final line without rendering the witnesses' names disqualified.

וְאִיבָּעֵית אֵימָא: לְעוֹלָם דִּכְתַב "עֵד", דִּיָדְעִינַן בָּהּ דְּהָא חֲתִימוֹת יָדָא

And if you wish, say instead **that actually** the witness **did write "witness"** after his signature, and the case is one **where we know** for a fact **that this signature,** which consists of the words "Ya'akov, witness,"

Perek **X**
Daf **161** Amud **b**

NOTES

Fish – כְּוָורָא: The Rashbam writes that it is not known why the Sages listed here made their signatures with these signs, though he suggests that it is possible that each Sage had a particular association with the item in question, due to his eating habits or another connection.

LANGUAGE

Mast [*makhota*] – מַכּוֹתָא: This word is found in a number of languages, including the closely related Syriac Aramaic. It appears to ultimately derive from the Middle Persian makōg, meaning boat.

לָאו דְּיַעֲקֹב הוּא.

is not Yaakov's signature. That is, it is known for a fact that there is no one living in the city where the document was written who is named Ya'akov and whose signature matches the signature on this document. Therefore, the court will recognize that the signature must have originally stated: "So-and-so, son of Ya'akov, witness," and that the last line had been excised, and they will invalidate it.

וְדִלְמָא בִּשְׁמֵיהּ דַּאֲבוּהּ חָתַם! לָא שָׁבֵיק אִינִישׁ שְׁמֵיהּ דִּידֵיהּ וְחָתֵים בִּשְׁמֵיהּ דַּאֲבוּהּ.

Rami bar Ḥama challenges: **But perhaps** this witness **signed using the name of his father** instead of his own name, as a gesture of respect toward his father. The Gemara answers: This is not done; **a person does not discard his own name and sign using** only **the name of his father.**

וְדִלְמָא סִימָנָא בְּעָלְמָא הוּא דְּשָׁוְויֵהּ, דְּהָא רַב צָיֵיר כְּוָורָא, רַבִּי חֲנִינָא צָיֵיר חָרוּתָא, רַב חִסְדָּא – סמ"ך, רַב הוֹשַׁעְיָא – עי"ן, רָבָא בַּר רַב הוּנָא – מַכּוֹתָא! לָא חָצִיף אִינָשׁ לְשַׁוְּויֵהּ לִשְׁמֵיהּ דַּאֲבוּהּ סִימָנָא.

Rami bar Ḥama challenges further: **But perhaps** the witness **made** this name **into a mere distinguishing mark** that he uses as his signature, **as** it is known that **Rav** used to **draw a fish**[N] as his signature mark, rather than signing his name, and **Rabbi Ḥanina** used to **draw a palm branch** as his signature mark, and **Rav Ḥisda** used to sign just the letter ***samekh,*** and **Rav Hoshaya** used to sign just the letter ***ayin,*** and **Rava bar Rav Huna** used to sign his name by drawing a ship's **mast** [***makhota***].[L] The Gemara answers: **A person is not** so **insolent** as **to use his father's name as a distinguishing mark.**

מָר זוּטְרָא אָמַר: לָמָּה לָךְ כּוּלֵּי הַאי? כׇּל מְקוּשָּׁר שֶׁאֵין עֵדָיו כָּלִין בְּשִׁיטָה אַחַת – פָּסוּל.

Mar Zutra said: Why do you need all this? Why go to such lengths to answer the question posed above? There is a simpler answer: **Any tied** document **whose witnesses do not end on a single line** is **not valid.** The Gemara had previously assumed that the witnesses sign one after the other, beginning at the document's bottom line and going upward toward the first line; this arrangement leaves open the possibility that the signature of the first witness could be truncated by an unscrupulous party. Mar Zutra explains that this is not so; rather, the signatures are written with each one beginning opposite the bottom line and heading upward toward the beginning of the document. Therefore, if a line of text is excised from the bottom of the document, the names of all the witnesses on the reverse side will be truncated, and the forgery will become apparent.

אָמַר רַב יִצְחָק בַּר יוֹסֵף אָמַר רַבִּי יוֹחָנָן: כָּל הַמְּחָקִין כּוּלָּן – צָרִיךְ שֶׁיִּכְתּוֹב ״וְדִין קִיּוּמֵיהוֹן״. וְצָרִיךְ שֶׁיַּחֲזוֹר מֵעִנְיָנוֹ שֶׁל שְׁטָר בְּשִׁיטָה אַחֲרוֹנָה. מַאי טַעְמָא?

§ **Rav Yitzḥak bar Yosef says that Rabbi Yoḥanan says:** There are two *halakhot* with regard to documents: For **any erasures**[N] in a document, the scribe **must write** at the end of the document: **And this is their verification.**[H] That is, he must list the erasures, stating that on line so-and-so there is an erasure and a correction stating such and such, for each erasure. **And** the second *halakha* is that the scribe **must review** some **of the details of the document**[H] **in the final line** of the document. **What is the reason** for this second requirement?

NOTES

Any erasures – כָּל הַמְּחָקִין: Although Rabbi Yoḥanan himself said earlier that an erasure invalidates the document if it is of a size and position where the words: Confirmed and established, may have been erased, here he is speaking of erasures that do not fit that description. While such erasures do not invalidate the document, they must be verified. The early commentaries note that although the *halakhot* of erasures appear in the Gemara in the context of tied documents, they apply equally to ordinary documents.

HALAKHA

The scribe must write, and this is their verification – צָרִיךְ שֶׁיִּכְתּוֹב וְדִין קִיּוּמֵיהוֹן: If a document has erasures, or marginal or interlinear corrections, or words that have been crossed out, all such corrections must be verified at the end of the document, before the words: Everything is confirmed and established. The Rema, citing *Tosafot* and Mordekhai, rules that it is not necessary to write the specific words: And this is their verification (Rambam *Sefer Mishpatim, Hilkhot Malve VeLoveh* 27:8; *Shulḥan Arukh, Hoshen Mishpat* 44:5, 9).

And the scribe must review some of the details of the document, etc. – וְצָרִיךְ שֶׁיַּחֲזוֹר מֵעִנְיָנוֹ שֶׁל שְׁטָר וכו׳: It is required to review some of the details of a document in its final line. The reason for this is that no new information may be learned from the final line of a document, due to the possibility of its having been added later, after the witnesses have signed. If one did not review the content of the document in the final line, the document is not invalidated, but the content in the final line is disregarded. The Rema writes that this leniency is not in accordance with those authorities who maintain that any divergence from the *halakhot* of documents instituted by the Sages invalidates the document, even when the possibility of duplicity is eliminated. He also writes, citing the *Nimmukei Yosef*, that the last line is disregarded only if its content is to the benefit of the holder of the document; if it is to his detriment, there is no concern that it may have been added later, and its content is taken into account. Today, when it has become customary to write: Everything is confirmed and established, at the end of all documents, any text written prior to that formula is taken into account, even if it is on the last line, and it is no longer necessary to review in the last line (Rambam *Sefer Mishpatim, Hilkhot Malve VeLoveh* 27:3; *Shulḥan Arukh, Hoshen Mishpat* 44:1, 4, 9, and see 42:5).

אָמַר רַב עַמְרָם: לְפִי שֶׁאֵין לָמֵדִין מִשִּׁיטָה אַחֲרוֹנָה.

Rav Amram says: It is **because** one **may not learn** any new details **from the final line**[N] of a document. There is a concern that the holder of the document may have written in an extra line of text to his advantage, between the text and the witnesses' signatures. Therefore, any new information contained in the last line is disregarded. Since the final line is disregarded, it is necessary that the final line of a document contain only a review of what is already written in it.

אָמַר לֵיהּ רַב נַחְמָן לְרַב עַמְרָם: מְנָא לָךְ הָא? אֲמַר לֵיהּ, דְּתַנְיָא: הִרְחִיק אֶת הָעֵדִים שְׁנֵי שִׁיטִין מִן הַכְּתָב – פָּסוּל, שִׁיטָה אַחַת – כָּשֵׁר;

Rav Naḥman said to Rav Amram: From where do you know **this?** Rav Amram **said to him: As it is taught** in a *baraita* (*Tosefta* 11:1): If one writing a document **distanced the witnesses'** signatures[H] **two lines from the text** of the document, leaving two lines blank, the document is **not valid,** as it would be possible for the holder of the document to fill in false information in those lines. But if one distanced the signatures **one line** from the text, the document **is valid.**

מַאי שְׁנָא שְׁנֵי שִׁיטִין? דִּלְמָא מְזַיֵּיף וְכָתַב, שִׁיטָה אַחַת נַמִי מְזַיֵּיף וְכָתַב! אֶלָּא לָאו שְׁמַע מִינַּהּ: אֵין לָמֵדִין מִשִּׁיטָה אַחֲרוֹנָה, שְׁמַע מִינַּהּ.

Rav Amram analyzes the *baraita*: **What is different** in the case of **two** blank **lines** that that the document is not valid? If you say that **perhaps** the holder of the document will take advantage of those two blank lines, and **forge** unverified information **and write** it in those lines, then in the case of **one line** left blank **as well,** he can **forge** information **and write** it in that line. **Rather,** must one **not conclude from** the *baraita* that one **may not learn** any new details **from the final line** of a document? Therefore, only when two lines are left blank is there a concern that false information would be added to the penultimate line. The Gemara affirms: **Conclude from** this *baraita* that it is so.

NOTES

One may not learn from the final line – אֵין לָמֵדִין מִשִּׁיטָה אַחֲרוֹנָה: The early commentaries explain that perforce, there is often a blank line between the text and the witnesses' signatures, either because it is difficult for witnesses to sign exactly adjacent to the text (see Rashbam), or because a witness will at times leave a blank space before his signature, intending to allow a more senior or distinguished witness to sign in the first position (Ramah). This blank line can then be filled in unscrupulously by the holder of the document to his advantage. Since there is the possibility of tampering with the final line, nothing new may be learned from it.

HALAKHA

Distanced the witnesses' signatures, etc. – הִרְחִיק אֶת הָעֵדִים וכו׳: When signing a document, the witnesses should take care not to distance their signatures two lines from the end of the document's text. If they did leave a distance of two lines the document is invalid, even if the formulation of: Confirmed and established, is written at the end of the text, and even if it can be ascertained by testimony that nothing was added to the document after the witnesses signed it. This is because the document does not conform to the ordinances instituted by the Sages (*Sma*). Nevertheless, a loan recorded in such a document is still considered to be attested to the extent that the debtor cannot deny that it ever took place (Rambam *Sefer Mishpatim, Hilkhot Malve VeLoveh* 27:4, and see *Sefer Nashim, Hilkhot Geirushin* 1:18 and Ra'avad there; *Shulḥan Arukh, Hoshen Mishpat* 45:6–7, and see *Even HaEzer* 130:1).

איבעיא להו: שיטה ומחצה, מאי? תא שמע: הרחיק את העדים שני שיטין – פסול; הא שיטה ומחצה – כשר.

A dilemma was raised before the Sages: If the space of **a line and a half**[HN] is left blank, **what** is the *halakha*? The Gemara seeks a solution to the dilemma. **Come and hear** what was stated in the *baraita* cited earlier: If one writing a document **distanced the witnesses'** signatures **two lines** from the text of the document, leaving two lines blank, the document is **not valid.** One can infer: **But** if there is a gap of only **a line and a half,** the document is **valid.**

אימא סיפא: שיטה אחת – כשר; שיטה אחת הוא דכשר, הא שיטה ומחצה – פסול! אלא מהא ליכא למשמע מינה.

The Gemara deflects this proof: **Say the last clause** of the *baraita*: If one writing a document distanced the witnesses' signatures **one line** from the text of the document, the document is **valid.** One can infer: It is only when there is a gap of **one line that** the document **is valid, but** if there is a gap of **a line and a half** it is **not valid.** The Gemara states: **Rather, no** inference is **to be learned from this** *baraita*.

מאי הוי עלה? תא שמע, דתניא: הרחיק את העדים שני שיטין מן הכתב – פסול, פחות מכאן – כשר;

What halakhic conclusion **was reached about** this matter? **Come** and **hear** a proof from a different source, **as it is taught** in a *baraita* (*Tosefta* 11:10): If one writing a document **distanced the witnesses'** signatures **two lines from the text** of the document, the document is **not valid,** but if the gap is **less than that, it is valid.** It is clear from the *baraita* that any gap less than two full lines does not invalidate the document.

היו ארבעה וחמשה עדים חתומין על השטר, ונמצא אחד מהן קרוב או פסול – תתקיים עדות בשאר.

The *baraita* continues: If **there were four or five witnesses signed on the document, and one of them was found** to be **a relative** of one of the parties in the document, **or** one of them was found to be otherwise **disqualified**[H] from bearing witness, the **testimony** on the document may be **established via the other** witnesses.

מסייע ליה לחזקיה, דאמר חזקיה: מלאהו בקרובים – כשר;

The Gemara draws a further conclusion from this *baraita*: This **supports** the opinion of **Ḥizkiyya, as Ḥizkiyya says:** If one **filled in** the gap between the document and the signatures **with** signatures of **relatives,**[H] the document is **valid.**

ואל תתמה, שהרי אויר סוכה פוסל בשלשה, סכך פסול פוסל בארבעה.

Ḥizkiyya continued: **And do not be surprised** by this, as a similar situation is found with regard to the roofing of a *sukka*. Empty **space** in the roofing **of a *sukka***[N] **disqualifies** the *sukka* if the space extends for **three** handbreadths, whereas materials that are **unfit** to be used as **roofing disqualify** the *sukka* only if the unfit material extends for **four** handbreadths. If a *sukka* had a gap in its roofing of three handbreadths it is disqualified, but if the gap is filled in with unfit material the *sukka* is valid, since it is less than four handbreadths. This is comparable to the situation with a document: If there is a significant gap between the text and the signatures the document is not valid, but if the gap is filled in with signatures of those disqualified from bearing witness it is valid.

איבעיא להו: שני שיטין שאמרו

§ **A dilemma was raised before** the Sages: With regard to the gap of **two** blank **lines** between the text and the signatures, **which** the Sages **said** invalidates the document,

HALAKHA

A line and a half – שיטה ומחצה: If the witnesses distanced their signatures from the final line of a document by less than the thickness of two lines, the document is valid, in accordance with the conclusion of the Gemara, as explained by *Tosafot*. If the document's text ends in the middle of a line, and the rest of that line, plus another complete line, are left blank, the document is not valid, as it would be possible to add words to the text and then use the completely empty line to recapitulate some details of the document. Similarly, if the text ends at the end of a line and a completely empty line follows, with the witnesses' signatures in the second half of the line after that, this is also not valid, as it is possible to excise the last two lines and write a brief document preceding the witnesses' signatures, on the same line (Rambam *Sefer Mishpatim, Hilkhot Malve VeLoveh* 27:4; *Shulḥan Arukh, Even HaEzer* 45:6, 10, and see 44:3).

A relative or disqualified – קרוב או פסול: In a case where there are many witnesses signed on a document, and one of them was found to be a relative or someone who is otherwise not fit to bear witness, or if two of the witnesses are related to one another, and it cannot be ascertained why the unfit witnesses signed, if there is testimony that all of the signatories were present together at the time of the signing, the document is not valid. Some say that the document is invalid only if the valid witnesses were aware of the disqualified status of the unfit witnesses (see *Shakh*). If it is not known whether or not the witnesses were all present together at the time of signing, the document can be ratified based on the testimony of the fit witnesses. These *halakhot* apply whether the unfit witnesses were the first signatories or the later ones (see *Shakh*). Some maintain that the last two signatures on the document must be those of fit witnesses (Rema, citing *Tur*; see *Shakh*). The Rema adds that it is preferable not to have any relatives or unfit witnesses sign any document (Rambam *Sefer Shofetim, Hilkhot Edut* 5:6–7; *Shulḥan Arukh, Ḥoshen Mishpat* 45:12, and in the comment of Rema; *Ḥoshen Mishpat* 51:4).

Filled in the gap with signatures of relatives – מלאהו בקרובים: If witnesses on a document distanced their signatures from the text, leaving more than two blank lines, and the gap was then filled in with signatures of relatives or people otherwise unfit to bear witness, the document is valid, as it is no longer forgeable. These additional signatures may not be added after the document is presented for collection in court. While the Ra'avad and Rosh hold that the filling in of signatures may be done even without the knowledge of the obligated party, Rabbeinu Yona disagrees (Rambam *Sefer Mishpatim, Hilkhot Malve VeLoveh* 27:4; *Shulḥan Arukh, Ḥoshen Mishpat* 45:4).

NOTES

A line and a half – שיטה ומחצה: There are varying interpretations concerning the case of the Gemara's dilemma. Some say that the case is one where a complete blank line is left after the text, and then the witnesses sign in the middle of the following line (*Sefer HaIttur*; Ra'avad; see *Tosafot*). *Tosafot* claim that in this case the document would certainly be valid, as nothing new is learned from the final line of a document, i.e., the line of text preceding the signatures; such a document can consequently not be forged. Others disqualify such a document because it is possible to excise the single line containing the witnesses' signatures and write a one-line document on that same line, which would be a valid document; consequently, the possibility of forgery exists (Ramah; Rashba). According to *Tosafot*, the case in question is one where the thickness of the space between the text and the signatures is one and one-half lines.

Empty space of a *sukka* – אויר סוכה: A gap of three handbreadths disqualifies a *sukka* only if it breaks the continuity of roofing between the two opposite walls of a three-walled *sukka*, or if it is in a minimum-size *sukka*, in which case the lack of three handbreadths of roofing would reduce the roofing to less than the required minimum. Otherwise, a gap of three handbreadths does not disqualify the *sukka*. Nevertheless, one sitting in the area immediately below such a gap is not considered to be sitting in the *sukka* (*Tosafot*).

הֵן וַאֲוִירָן, אוֹ דִּלְמָא הֵן וְלֹא אֲוִירָן?

does this refer to the size of lines **with the space** between lines added? **Or** is it **perhaps** referring to lines of writing themselves, **without their spaces?**

אֲמַר רַב נַחְמָן בַּר יִצְחָק: מִסְתַּבְּרָא דְּהֵן וַאֲוִירָן, דְּאִי סָלְקָא דַּעְתָּךְ הֵן וְלֹא אֲוִירָן, שִׁיטָּה אַחַת בְּלָא אֲוִירָה לְמַאי חַזְיָא? אֶלָּא שְׁמַע מִינָּהּ הֵן וַאֲוִירָן, שְׁמַע מִינָּהּ.

Rav Naḥman bar Yitzḥak said: It stands to reason that it is referring to the lines **with their spaces.**[H] **As, if** it were to **enter your mind** that it is referring to the lines **without their spaces, for what is one line without its space fit?**[N] The *baraita* did not have to state that a document with a single blank line after the text, measured without counting spaces, is not forgeable; this is obvious. **Rather,** one may **conclude from** this claim that the reference is to two lines **with their spaces.** The Gemara affirms: **Conclude from** this claim that it is so.

רַבִּי שַׁבְּתַי אָמַר מִשְּׁמֵיהּ דְּחִזְקִיָּה: שְׁנֵי שִׁיטִּין שֶׁאָמְרוּ – בִּכְתַב יְדֵי עֵדִים וְלֹא כְּתַב יְדֵי סוֹפֵר; מַאי טַעְמָא? דְּכָל הַמְזַיֵּיף, לָאו לְגַבֵּי סַפְרָא אָזֵיל וּמְזַיֵּיף.

Rabbi Shabbtai says in the name of Ḥizkiyya: With regard to the gap of **two** blank **lines** between the text and the signatures, **which** the Sages **said** invalidates the document, the lines are measured **by the handwriting of witnesses,**[H] **and not** by **the handwriting of a scribe,** who is presumably skilled enough to write in a smaller script. **What is the reason** for this? **Anyone who forges** a document, adding additional lines to the document, **would not go to a scribe**[N] **and** ask him to **forge** it; he would execute the forgery himself, or have another unscrupulous person who is not a professional scribe forge it. Therefore, in order to present a concern for possible forgery, a document must have two blank lines that are measured by the handwriting of an ordinary person, such as one of the witnesses.

וְכַמָּה? אָמַר רַב יִצְחָק בֶּן אֶלְעָזָר: כְּגוֹן "לֵךְ לְךָ" זֶה עַל גַּבֵּי זֶה; אַלְמָא קָסָבַר: שְׁנֵי שִׁיטִּין וְאַרְבָּעָה אֲוִירִין.

The Gemara has established that the width of the gap required to invalidate the document is two lines with interlinear space. The Gemara clarifies: **And how much** interlinear space is necessary to invalidate the document? **Rav Yitzḥak ben Elazar says: For example,** enough to write the Hebrew word ***lekh*****, and** then the Hebrew word ***lekha*****, this** word **on top of that** one. These two words each consist of the two letters *lamed* and final *khaf*; the former has a projection that fully occupies the interlinear space above it, and the latter has a projection that fully occupies the interlinear space below it. Writing these words one under the other, then, would require an additional interlinear space above and below both lines. The Gemara concludes: **Apparently,** Rav Yitzḥak ben Elazar **maintains** that the empty space required to invalidate the document is the width of **two** written **lines with four** interlinear **spaces.**[N]

HALAKHA

The lines with their spaces – הֵן וַאֲוִירָן: The two blank lines of which the Sages spoke, stating that such a gap between the document's text and its signatures invalidates the document, is referring to two text-size lines with three interlinear spaces: One space between the two text-size lines, one above them, and one below them. This is sufficient to allow enough room for letters that extend above the text-line, e.g., *lamed*, and letters that extend below it, e.g., final *khaf*. The *halakha* is in accordance with the opinion of Rav Naḥman bar Yitzḥak, that the two lines include interlinear spaces, and in accordance with the opinion of Rav Ḥiyya bar Ami, that three such interlinear spaces are included. This opinion is adopted because it represents the intermediate position (Gra, explaining Rif), or because it is the most reasonable opinion (Rosh) and moreover because it does not conflict with Rav Naḥman bar Yitzḥak's statement (Rambam *Sefer Mishpatim, Hilkhot Malve VeLoveh* 27:4 and *Maggid Mishne* there; *Shulḥan Arukh, Ḥoshen Mishpat* 45:9).

By the handwriting of witnesses – בִּכְתַב יְדֵי עֵדִים: Two blank lines between the text of a document and its signatures invalidate a document; the size of these lines is measured in accordance with the handwriting of witnesses, which is usually larger than a scribe's handwriting. If the gap is only the size of two lines as measured by a scribe's handwriting, it is still valid. This is because one does not go to a scribe to commit forgery, as Rabbi Shabbtai said in the name of Ḥizkiyya (Rambam *Sefer Mishpatim, Hilkhot Malve VeLoveh* 27:4; *Shulḥan Arukh, Ḥoshen Mishpat* 45:8).

NOTES

For what is one line without its space fit – שִׁיטָּה אַחַת בְּלָא אֲוִירָה לְמַאי חַזְיָא: The Rashbam prefers a different version of the text: If it were to enter your mind that it is referring to the lines without their spaces, for what are they fit? That is, the question relates to the case of a document with two blank lines between the text and the signatures, which is not valid because it is susceptible to forgery. Accordingly, Rav Naḥman bar Yitzḥak's statement is: If the blank space is just large enough to write two lines without any space between lines, in order to add two lines of text the forger would have to compress the writing by using smaller-size letters than the rest of the document, and the forgery would be immediately noticeable.

Would not go to a scribe – לָאו לְגַבֵּי סַפְרָא אָזֵיל: One need not be concerned with the possibility that another person would participate in the duplicitous act of the one holding the document. Moreover, a professional scribe would not risk his reputation by engaging in forgery (see Rashbam).

Two lines with four interlinear spaces – שְׁנֵי שִׁיטִּין וְאַרְבָּעָה אֲוִירִין: Although the text of a document normally has only a single blank line between written lines, the assumption is that a person would not engage in a forgery unless he had enough room to write any word that could be required in any scenario, including the possibility of having the word *lekh* appear over the word *lekha* (see *Tosafot*).

רַב חִיָּיא בַּר אַמִי מִשְּׁמֵיהּ דְּעוּלָּא אָמַר: כְּגוֹן לְמ״ד מִלְמַעְלָה וְכ״ף מִלְּמַטָּה; אַלְמָא קָסָבַר: שְׁנֵי שִׁיטִין וּשְׁלֹשָׁה אֲוִירִין.

Rav Ḥiyya bar Ami states a different opinion in the name of Ulla: For example, enough to write a *lamed* on the upper line and a final *khaf* on the lower line. The Gemara concludes: Apparently, Ulla maintains that the empty space required to invalidate the document is the width of two written lines with three interlinear spaces, one above the first line, one between the two lines, and one beneath the second line.

רַבִּי אַבָּהוּ אָמַר: כְּגוֹן ״בָּרוּךְ בֶּן לֵוִי״ בְּשִׁיטָה אַחַת; קָא סָבַר: שִׁיטָה אַחַת וּשְׁנֵי אֲוִירִין.

Rabbi Abbahu states a different opinion: **For example,** enough to write the name **Barukh ben Levi on one line.** Barukh contains a final *khaf*, and Levi contains a *lamed*. The Gemara concludes: **Apparently,** Rabbi Abbahu **maintains** that the empty space required to invalidate the document is the width of **one** written **line with two** interlinear **spaces,** one above the line and one beneath the line.

אָמַר רַב: לֹא שָׁנוּ אֶלָּא בֵּין עֵדִים לַכְּתָב, אֲבָל בֵּין עֵדִים לְאַשַּׁרְתָּא – אֲפִילּוּ טוּבָא נַמִי כָּשֵׁר.

§ Rav says: **They taught** in the *baraita* that a gap of two lines invalidates the document **only** if that space is **between the witnesses'** signatures **and the text** of the document. **But** if there is a gap **between the witnesses'** signatures **and** a court's **ratification**[N] of the document, which follows the witnesses' signatures, then **even** if there is **more** space than this, the document is **valid.**

מַאי שְׁנָא בֵּין עֵדִים לַכְּתָב – דִּלְמָא מְזַיֵּיף וְכָתַב מַאי דְּבָעֵי וַחֲתִימִי סָהֲדֵי; בֵּין עֵדִים לְאַשַּׁרְתָּא נַמִי מְזַיֵּיף וְכָתַב מַאי דְּבָעֵי וַחֲתִימִי סָהֲדֵי!

The Gemara asks: **What is different** about the case where the gap is **between the witnesses and the text,** that it invalidates the document? There is a concern that **perhaps** the holder of the document **may forge** additional lines **and write whatever he wants, and the witnesses** have already **signed** at the bottom, giving the appearance that they attest to the added lines as well. But the same concern can be raised concerning a gap **between the witnesses'** signatures **and** the court's **ratification as well:** There, too, he can **forge** additional lines **and write whatever he wants,** and have **witnesses sign it,**[N] with the court's ratification giving the appearance that it attests to the added lines and signatures as well. Why is this document valid?

דִּמְטַיֵּיט לֵיהּ. אִי הָכִי, בֵּין עֵדִים לַשְּׁטָר נַמִי מְטַיֵּיט לֵיהּ!

The Gemara explains: When is a gap between the witnesses' signatures and the court's ratification not problematic, according to Rav? Only **when** someone **inks in**[N] the blank space[H] with lines or dots, to prevent information from being added there. The Gemara asks: **If so,** the gap **between the witnesses'** signatures **and** the text of **the document** should **also** be made irrelevant in this manner: **Let** the scribe **ink in** [*metayyet*][L] the blank space. Why, then, was it taught categorically that the witnesses must sign within two lines of the text?

אָמְרִי: סָהֲדֵי אַטִּיּוּטָא הוּא דַּחֲתִימִי. בֵּין עֵדִים לְאַשַּׁרְתָּא נַמִי, אָמְרִי: בֵּי דִינָא אַטִּיּוּטָא הוּא דַּחֲתִימִי! בֵּי דִינָא אַטִּיּוּטָא לָא חָתְמִי.

The Gemara answers: Inking in the gap between the text and the signatures of the witnesses will not help, as people might **say,** i.e., the concern might be raised: **The witnesses are signed** only **on the inking in.**[H] It is possible that the witnesses' signatures were affixed only to attest that the inking was done in their presence and that the inking in is not a sign of duplicity, and their signatures do not relate to the actual text of the document. The Gemara asks: If so, raise the same concern when the gap **between the witnesses'** signatures **and the court's ratification** is inked in; there too, people might **say: The court's** ratification **is signed** only **for the inking in,** and not for the actual text of the document. The Gemara answers: **A court does not sign on** mere **inking in;** their ratification is always in reference to the entire document.

NOTES

Court's ratification [*asharta*] – אַשַּׁרְתָּא: An *asharta*, also known as a *henpek*, is a written declaration signed by three judges of a court, usually affixed at the bottom of a document, which states that the judges have determined that the signatures of the witnesses were found to be authentic. This determination can be made on the basis of the judges' personal recognition of the signatures, by comparison to another ratified document with the same signatures, through the testimony of witnesses who personally recognize these signatures, or through the oral testimony of the signatories themselves, affirming that the signatures are in fact theirs. The standard formulation of this declaration, as it appears in the Talmud (*Ketubot* 21a) is the following: In light of the fact that so-and-so came and testified with regard to so-and-so's signature…we have ratified and established it as is fit.

And write whatever he wants and witnesses sign it – וְכָתַב מַאי דְּבָעֵי וַחֲתִימִי סָהֲדֵי: This question is difficult to understand, as the added text would be beneath the signatures of the witnesses, and as a result not attested to by their signatures. *Penei Shlomo* suggests that when a document has a court's ratification, all of the information detailed in that document is presumed to be accurate, even what is written beneath the signatures of the witnesses. The Ramah explains that the concern is that he may forge witnesses' signatures beneath the added text and suggests an emendation of the text of the Gemara to reflect this explanation.

When someone inks in – דִּמְטַיֵּיט: *Tosafot* explain that this does not mean that the entire gap is inked in with a solid black block; as if so, a person could blacken an entire document along with its witnesses, and then write another document, with forged signatures in the margin, which would then be thought to be ratified by the court's declaration of ratification appearing on the document. Rather, Rabbeinu Tam explains that it means that the gap is filled in with a number of dots or other symbols that prevent filling the space with text and at the same time indicate that there was no previous text written in the inked-in space. By contrast, the Rashbam appears to understand that the area is totally blacked out with a solid block of ink (see *Shakh*).

LANGUAGE

Ink in [*metayyet*] – מְטַיֵּיט: The *Arukh* cites a variant reading, *medayyet*. It would appear that the source of the word *metayyet* is *tit*, meaning dirt or mud; i.e., the space is dirtied, as it were, with ink. The word *medayyet* is related to the word *deyo*, meaning ink.

HALAKHA

When someone inks in the blank space – דִּמְטַיֵּיט לֵיהּ: If a document bears a court's ratification, and there are two or more blank lines left between the signatures and the ratification, the blank space must be filled with inked lines, as then the document will not be forgeable. There is no concern that the ratifying judges intended to ratify only the inked-in marking rather than the document itself. This is in accordance with Rav's opinion, as Rabbi Yoḥanan does not disagree with him (*Maggid Mishne*). According to others, it is only Rav who maintains that this concern is not raised, and the *halakha* is not in accordance with his opinion (*Maggid Mishne*, explaining Rif). The *Sma* writes that the inking in of the gap must be done with lines or the like, but if the entire space is blackened with a block of ink the document is not valid. According to the *Shakh*, even such a document is valid (Rambam *Sefer Mishpatim*, *Hilkhot Malve VeLoveh* 27:4; *Shulḥan Arukh*, *Ḥoshen Mishpat* 46:32).

The witnesses are signed only on the inking in, etc. – סָהֲדֵי אַטִּיּוּטָא וכו׳: If the witnesses distanced their signatures from the end of the document's text by two or more lines, then even if the gap is inked in, the document is not valid, as one could argue that the signatures attest only to the inking in and not to the document itself. The *Shakh* maintains that if the inking in was done by drawing lines, as opposed to a solid block of ink, the document is valid (Rambam *Sefer Mishpatim*, *Hilkhot Malve VeLoveh* 27:4; *Shulḥan Arukh*, *Ḥoshen Mishpat* 45:6, 11).

וְלֵיחוּשׁ דִּלְמָא גָּיֵיז לֵיהּ לְעֵילָּא, וּמָחֵיק לֵיהּ לַטִּיוּטָא וְכָתַב מַאי דְּבָעֵי וּמַחְתִּים סָהֲדֵי, וְאָמַר רַב: שְׁטָר הַבָּא הוּא וְעֵדָיו עַל הַמְּחָק – כָּשֵׁר!

The Gemara raises another issue: **And let** there be **a concern** that **perhaps** the holder of the document will **excise** the entire text that appears **above** the signatures, **and** then **erase the inked-in** part **and write**[N] **whatever he wants** in that erased area, **and** have unscrupulous **witnesses sign** it. **And** this would be a valid document, as **Rav says: A document that comes** before the court for ratification in which **its** content **and** the signatures of **its witnesses are** both written **over an erasure is valid.** The court ratification would then be assumed to be referring to this new, forged document.

NOTES

And erase the inked-in part and write, etc. – וּמָחֵיק לֵיהּ לַטִּיוּטָא וְכָתַב וכו׳: The early commentaries note that this concern could be raised with regard to any document with a court's ratification: The holder of the document could erase the entire text of the document, along with the signatures of its witnesses, and forge a new text over the erasure with false witnesses, and the ratification would be assumed to be relating to the forged document. The Rashbam in fact states (163b) that the Gemara's question is meant to apply to all documents. By contrast, *Tosafot* explain there that it is assumed to be too difficult to smoothly erase a text with words and signatures without arousing suspicion, whereas it is easier to erase dots and forge a new document on top of the erasure.

הָנִיחָא לְרַב כָּהֲנָא דְּמַתְנֵי לָהּ מִשְּׁמֵיהּ דִּשְׁמוּאֵל – שַׁפִּיר, אֶלָּא לְרַב טַבְיוּמֵי דְּמַתְנֵי לָהּ מִשְּׁמֵיהּ דְּרַב – מַאי אִיכָּא לְמֵימַר?

This works out well, i.e., this concern does not apply, **according to Rav Kahana, who teaches in the name of Shmuel** that a document in which its content and its witnesses' signatures are both written over an erasure is valid; according to him, all **is well.** It is Rav who says that an inked-in gap between the witnesses' signatures and the court's ratification is acceptable, and it is Shmuel who says that a document that is written and signed over an erasure is acceptable. **But according to Rav Tavyumei, who teaches** this latter statement **in the name of Rav, what can be said?** According to him, Rav said both statements, and taken together they pose a difficulty: The inked-in gap between the witnesses' signatures and the ratification can easily be erased and a new document with signatures can be written over the erasure.

קָסָבַר: כָּל כִּי הַאי גַּוְונָא, אֵין מְקַיְּימִין אוֹתוֹ מִן הָאַשְׁרָתָא שֶׁבּוֹ, אֶלָּא מִן הָעֵדִים שֶׁבּוֹ.

The Gemara answers: Rav **maintains** that in **all cases like this,** where a document and its witnesses' signatures are written over an erasure and there is a court ratification on a non-erased part of the paper, the later court **ratifies** the document **not on the basis of the** previous court's **ratification that is on it,**[H] **but** only **on the basis of the** signatures of the **witnesses that are on it.** Therefore, the forging of a document in this manner is impossible, as the prior ratification of the court is disregarded, and the witnesses will attest to what they signed upon.

וְרַבִּי יוֹחָנָן אָמַר: לֹא שָׁנוּ אֶלָּא בֵּין הָעֵדִים לַכְּתָב, אֲבָל בֵּין עֵדִים לְאַשְׁרְתָא – אֲפִילּוּ שִׁיטָה אַחַת פָּסוּל.

The Gemara cites another opinion: **And Rabbi Yoḥanan says: They taught** in the *baraita* that a gap of one line does not invalidate the document **only** in the case where that space is **between the witnesses'** signatures **and the text** of the document. **But** if the gap is **between the witnesses'** signatures **and** a court's **ratification**[H] of the document, then a space of **even one line**[N] renders the document **not valid.**

מַאי שְׁנָא בֵּין עֵדִים לְאַשְׁרְתָא? דִּלְמָא גָּיֵיז לְעֵילָּאֵי וְכָתַב הוּא וְעֵדָיו בְּשִׁיטָה אַחַת, וְקָסָבַר: שְׁטָר הַבָּא הוּא וְעֵדָיו בְּשִׁיטָה אַחַת – כָּשֵׁר;

The Gemara asks: **What is different** about the case where there is a one-line gap **between the witnesses'** signatures **and** the court's **ratification** that you say it is not valid? The Gemara answers: There is a concern that **perhaps** the holder of the document will **excise** the entire text of the document at **the top** of the paper **and** then **write** a new, brief document, with **its** text **and** the signatures of **its witnesses on one line.** The court's ratification will appear to verify the new, forged document. **And** Rabbi Yoḥanan **holds** that **a document that comes** before the court with **its** text **and** the signatures of **its witnesses** appearing **on one line**[H] **is valid.**

HALAKHA

Ratifies the document not on the basis of the court's ratification that is on it – אֵין מְקַיְּימִין אוֹתוֹ מִן הָאַשְׁרָתָא שֶׁבּוֹ: A document whose text and signatures are both written over an erasure, with the court's ratification on a non-erased part of the paper, may not be ratified on the basis of a previous court's written ratification. Rather, the witnesses' signatures must be verified. This is due to the concern that there may have been another text to which the court's ratification was affixed, with a gap of several lines between the document and the ratification, and that gap is inked in with dots. Therefore, it would be possible to excise the entire original document, erase the dots filling in the empty space, and then write a new, false document over the erasure.

Some disagree and maintain that such a document may be ratified on the basis of a previous court's written ratification, since according to the opinion of Rabbi Yoḥanan, in accordance with whom the *halakha* is ruled, it is forbidden to leave a gap between the witnesses' signatures and the court's ratification, even if the space is inked in, and it is therefore unlikely that such a gap was present in contravention of the *halakha* (*Beit Yosef*, explaining Rif and Rosh). The *Shakh* rules in accordance with the former opinion (Rambam *Sefer Mishpatim*, *Hilkhot Malve VeLoveh* 27:10; *Shulḥan Arukh*, *Ḥoshen Mishpat* 46:33, and see *Sma* there).

Between the witnesses' signatures and a court's ratification – בֵּין עֵדִים לְאַשְׁרְתָא: The court's ratification of a document must be written immediately following the witnesses' signatures, or in the document's side margin, or, if there is no room in the side margin (Rema, citing Rambam and *Maggid Mishne*), on the back of the document, opposite the writing. If there is a gap the size of a line of text and two interlinear spaces between the witnesses' signatures and the court's ratification, the ratification is not valid, as this leaves open the possibility of forgery; it would be possible to excise the entire document and write a new one, along with witnesses' signatures, in the gap. This is in accordance with the opinion of Rabbi Yoḥanan, as the *halakha* generally follows his opinion in his disputes with Rav (Rambam *Sefer Mishpatim*, *Hilkhot Malve VeLoveh* 27:6; *Shulḥan Arukh*, *Ḥoshen Mishpat* 46:31).

Its text and its witnesses on one line – הוּא וְעֵדָיו בְּשִׁיטָה אַחַת: If the entire document, including witnesses' signatures, is written on a single line, the document is valid, as there is no possibility of duplicity in such a case (Rambam *Sefer Mishpatim*, *Hilkhot Malve VeLoveh* 27:4; *Shulḥan Arukh*, *Ḥoshen Mishpat* 45:19).

NOTES

Even one line – אֲפִילּוּ שִׁיטָה אַחַת: The Ramban explains that the Sages allowed the witnesses to leave a gap between their signatures and the text because witnesses are not necessarily used to writing, and as a result are not always able to affix their signatures in immediate proximity to the text. Consequently, in order to prevent the possibility of falsification, the Sages instituted that no new details may be learned from the final line of a document. By contrast, the judges in a court are experienced and can easily write their ratification in immediate proximity to the witnesses' signature; therefore the Sages did not provide them with the leniency of leaving a gap.

According to the Rashbam, Rabbi Yoḥanan disagrees with Rav and rules that a document in which there is a gap between the witnesses' signatures and the court's ratification, even if the gap is inked in, is not valid.

אִי הָכִי, בֵּין עֵדִים לִכְתָב נַמִּי, דִּלְמָא גָּיֵיז לֵיהּ לְעֵילָּאֵי וְכָתַב מַאי דְּבָעֵי וַחֲתִימִי סָהֲדֵי! קָא סָבַר: שְׁטָר הַבָּא הוּא בְּשִׁיטָּה אַחַת וְעֵדָיו בְּשִׁיטָּה אַחֶרֶת – פָּסוּל.

The Gemara suggests: **If so,** the same problem **also** exists when there is a one-line gap **between the witnesses'** signatures **and the text:** There should be a concern that **perhaps** he will **excise** the entire text of the document at **the top** of the paper **and** then **write whatever he wants** in a brief, one-line document. **And the witnesses'** signatures on the next line, which are there from the old document, will still be **signed** there, appearing to attest to the veracity of the new one-line document. The Gemara answers: Rabbi Yoḥanan **holds** that **a document that comes** before the court with **its** text **on one line and** the signatures of **its witnesses** appearing **on another line,**[H] i.e., on the following line, is **not valid.**[N]

וְלֵיחוּשׁ דִּלְמָא כָּתַב הוּא וְעֵדָיו בְּשִׁיטָּה אַחַת, וְאָמַר: אֲנָא לְרַבּוֹת בְּעֵדִים הוּא דַּעֲבַדִי!

The Gemara suggests: **And let** there be **a concern** that **perhaps** the holder of the document will excise the entire document, leaving only the blank line and the signatures that follow it, and he will **write** a brief document in which **its** text **and** the signatures of **its witnesses** are **on one line,** followed by the original signatures that remained from the original document, **and** he will **say: I did this** in order **to increase** the number of **witnesses,** the more to publicize the matter written in the document. The document is therefore still forgeable.

קָסָבַר: כָּל כִּי הַאי גַּוְונָא, אֵין מְקַיְּימִין אוֹתוֹ מִן הָעֵדִים שֶׁלְּמַטָּה אֶלָּא מִן הָעֵדִים שֶׁלְּמַעְלָה.

The Gemara answers: Rabbi Yoḥanan **maintains** that in **all cases like this,** where a document and its witnesses' signatures are written on one line, followed by other signatures on subsequent lines, the court **ratifies** the document **not on the basis of the** signatures of the **witnesses that** are **on the bottom, but on the basis of the** signatures of the **witnesses that** are **on top,** on the same line as the text. Therefore, the forging of a document in this manner is impossible. The false signatures of the witnesses will be discovered when those witnesses attest to what they signed upon.

גּוּפָא, אָמַר רַב: שְׁטָר הַבָּא הוּא וְעֵדָיו עַל הַמְּחָק – כָּשֵׁר.

§ Having cited Rav's statement, the Gemara discusses **the** matter **itself. Rav says: A document that comes** before the court in which **its** content **and** the signatures of **its witnesses are** both written **over an erasure is valid.**

Perek **X**
Daf **164** Amud **a**

וְאִם תֹּאמַר: מוֹחֵק וְחוֹזֵר וּמוֹחֵק – אֵינוֹ דּוֹמֶה נִמְחַק פַּעַם אַחַת לְנִמְחַק שְׁתֵּי פְּעָמִים.

And if you say: There is a possibility of forgery with such a document, as the holder of the document can **erase** the original writing on the paper, then write the text of the document and have witnesses sign on the part that had been erased, **then erase** the document text **once again,** substituting for it a text that is more to his advantage, leaving the original signatures in place, this is not a valid argument. Paper that has been **erased once is not similar** in appearance **to** paper that has been **erased twice.** It will be seen that the signatures are on a place that had been erased once and that the text is written on a place that had been erased twice, and the forgery will be noticed.

וְלֵיחוּשׁ דִּלְמָא שָׁדֵי דְּיוֹתָא אַמְּקוֹם עֵדִים מֵעִיקָּרָא וּמָחֵיק לֵיהּ, דְּכִי הֲדַר מָחֵיק לֵיהּ לְהַאי, הֲוָה לֵיהּ אִידִי וְאִידִי נִמְחַק שְׁתֵּי פְּעָמִים!

The Gemara suggests: **But let** there be **a concern** that **perhaps** the holder of the document will **initially,** after the entire original document, including the signatures, has been erased, but before the second one is written, **throw** some **ink on the place** where the **witnesses** are to sign under the text of the second document, **and** then **erase** that ink. He will do this **so that when,** after the witnesses have signed, **he then erases** the document text and writes a false text, it will emerge that both **this,** the new document's text, **and that,** the signatures, will be on paper that had been **erased twice.**

HALAKHA

Its text on one line and its witnesses on another line – הוּא בְּשִׁיטָּה אַחַת וְעֵדָיו בְּשִׁיטָּה אַחֶרֶת: A document whose text consists of a single line, followed by witnesses' signatures in the following line, is not valid. This is because of the possibility that there was originally another document with a one-line gap between its text and its signatures, and that original text was excised, the remaining paper being used to write this new document, using the signatures from the original document (Rambam *Sefer Mishpatim, Hilkhot Malve VeLoveh* 27:5; *Shulḥan Arukh, Ḥoshen Mishpat* 45:18).

NOTES

And the signatures of its witnesses on another line is not valid – וְעֵדָיו בְּשִׁיטָּה אַחֶרֶת פָּסוּל: The Rashbam explains that this is for the same reason as the requirement to review the content of a document in the last line of a document: No new details may be learned from the final line of a document due to the possibility of falsification by excising the original text and writing a one-line text in the gap.

אֲמַר אַבַּיֵי, קָסָבַר רַב: אֵין הָעֵדִים חוֹתְמִין עַל הַמְּחָק אֶלָּא אִם כֵּן נִמְחַק בִּפְנֵיהֶם.

Abaye said in response: **Rav holds** that **witnesses may not sign** a document written over **an erasure unless** the paper **was erased in their presence,** i.e., unless they saw the paper after its old text had been erased, before the new text was written. They will then see that the place where they are to sign has been erased twice, while the place where the document is to be written has been erased only once. They will realize that this leaves open an opportunity of subsequent erasing and falsification, and they will refrain from signing.

מֵיתִיבֵי: הוּא עַל הַנְּיָיר וְעֵדָיו עַל הַמְּחָק – כָּשֵׁר; וְנֵיחוּשׁ דִּלְמָא מָחֵיק לֵיהּ וְכָתֵיב מַאי דְּבָעֵי, וְהָוֵי לֵיהּ הוּא וְעֵדָיו עַל הַמְּחָק!

The Gemara **raises an objection** to the opinion of Rav from a *baraita*: A document in which **its** text **is on** a part of the **paper** that has never had writing erased **and** the signatures of **its witnesses are on an erasure**[H] **is valid.** The Gemara suggests: **But let us be concerned** that **perhaps** the holder of the document will **erase** the text **and write** in its place **whatever he wants, and it will** then **be** a document where both **its** text **and** the signatures of **its witnesses** are **on an erasure.** Since Rav maintains that such a document is valid, it is easily forgeable in this manner.

דְּכָתְבִי הָכִי: ״אֲנַחְנָא סָהֲדֵי חָתַמְנָא עַל מְחָקָא וּשְׁטָרָא כְּתַב עַל נְיָירָא״.

The Gemara answers: Such a document is valid only in a case **where** the witnesses **write this: We, the witnesses,**[N] **signed on an erasure, but the document** text **was written on** a part of the **paper** that never had writing erased. If the holder of the document then tries to erase the original text and write new text in its place, the forgery will be noticed.

דְּכָתְבִי הֵיכָא? אִי מִלְּתַחַת – גָּיֵיז לֵיהּ, אִי עִילָּאֵי – מָחֵיק לֵיהּ! דְּכָתְבֵי בֵּין סָהֲדָא לְסָהֲדָא.

The Gemara asks: **Where** do the witnesses **write** this declaration? **If** they write it **underneath** their signatures, the holder of the document can simply **excise it.** And **if** they write it **above** their signatures, the holder of the document can **erase it** along with the text of the document. The Gemara answers: **They write** the declaration **between** the signature of one **witness and** the signature of the other **witness.**

אִי הָכִי, אֵימָא סֵיפָא: הוּא עַל הַמְּחָק וְעֵדָיו עַל הַנְּיָיר – פָּסוּל; אַמַּאי פָּסוּל? הָכָא נַמִי נִכְתְּבוּ הָכִי: ״אֲנַחְנָא סָהֲדֵי חָתַמְנָא עַל נְיָירָא וּשְׁטָרָא עַל מְחָקָא״!

The Gemara asks: **If that is so,** that the *baraita* is discussing a case in which the witnesses write a declaration about the circumstances of the document's condition, **say the latter clause** of the *baraita*: A document in which **its text is on an erasure and** the signatures of **its witnesses are on** a part of **the paper**[H] that never had writing erased is **not valid.** The Gemara presents its question: **Why is** such a document **not valid? Here, too, let** the witnesses **write this: We,** the **witnesses, signed on paper** that never had writing erased, **but the document** text was written **on an erasure.**[N]

[הָשְׁתָּא נַמִי] מַאי אָמְרַתְּ? מוֹחֵק חוֹזֵר וּמוֹחֵק – הָא אָמְרַתְּ: אֵינוֹ דּוֹמֶה נִמְחַק פַּעַם אַחַת לְנִמְחַק שְׁתֵּי פְּעָמִים! הָנֵי מִילֵּי הֵיכָא דַּחֲתִימִי סָהֲדֵי אַמְּחָקָא, הֵיכָא דְּלָא חֲתִימִי סָהֲדֵי אַמְּחָקָא אֶלָּא אַנְּיָירָא – לָא יְדִיעַ.

Now in this case **as well** it should be valid, as **what** can **you say** to argue that it is a forgeable document? If you say that the holder of the document, having **erased** the original document, can **erase** the writing **once again** and write a new, false document, this is not a concern, as **didn't you say** that paper that has been **erased once is not similar** in appearance **to** paper that has been **erased twice?** It would therefore be noticeable that the document had been erased a second time, and the forgery would be noticeable. The Gemara answers: **That statement** applies only **when the witnesses are signed on an erasure,** and the appearance of that erasure can be compared with the appearance of a double erasure. But in a case **where the witnesses are signed not on an erasure but on paper** that has not had its writing erased, so that there is no contrast between a single erasure and a double erasure, the forgery would **not** be **known.**

וְלֵיתֵי מְגִילְּתָא אַחֲרִיתִי וְלִמְחוֹק וְלִידַמֵּי! לָא דָּמֵי מְחָקָא דְּהָא מְגִילְּתָא לִמְחָקָא דְּהָא מְגִילְּתָא.

The Gemara suggests: **But** let the court **bring another parchment,** write something on it **and erase it, and** then **compare** this single erasure with the erasure on the document in question. If the document were erased twice, a contrast would be seen between a single erasure and a double erasure. The Gemara answers: **The erasure of this parchment is not** necessarily **similar to the erasure of that parchment.** A single erasure on one parchment might resemble a double erasure on a different parchment.

HALAKHA

Its text is on paper and its witnesses are on an erasure – הוּא עַל הַנְּיָיר וְעֵדָיו עַל הַמְּחָק: A document is not valid if its text is written on paper that never had writing erased but the witnesses are signed over an erasure. This is because there is a concern that the holder of the document may then erase the original text of the document and substitute text more to his advantage; this new document would then be accepted due to Rav's ruling that a document that has both its text and its signatures over an erasure is valid. The former document is valid if the witnesses write the following declaration between their signatures: We, the witnesses, signed on an erasure, but the document text was written on paper that never had writing erased. If they wrote this declaration before both signatures or after both signatures it is not valid, as the Gemara teaches (Rambam *Sefer Mishpatim, Hilkhot Malve VeLoveh* 27:11; *Shulḥan Arukh, Ḥoshen Mishpat* 45:21, and see *Sma* and *Taz* there).

Its text is on an erasure and its witnesses are on the paper – הוּא עַל הַמְּחָק וְעֵדָיו עַל הַנְּיָיר: A document whose text is written over an erasure and whose witnesses' signatures are on paper that never had writing erased is invalid, even if the witnesses explicitly write between their signatures: We, the witnesses, signed on paper that never had writing erased but the document text was written on an erasure. The reason for this is that there is a concern that the holder of the document might erase the second document and write a falsified text, which would then be accepted since the difference between a double erasure and a single erasure is not noticeable unless there is a contrast between the two on the same paper. This is in accordance with the *baraita* and the Gemara's explanation of it (Rambam *Sefer Mishpatim, Hilkhot Malve VeLoveh* 27:12; *Shulḥan Arukh, Ḥoshen Mishpat* 45:22).

NOTES

We the witnesses, etc. – אֲנַחְנָא סָהֲדֵי וכו׳: Some early commentaries note that the document is still forgeable, as the holder of the document can simply erase this written declaration of the witnesses, which is, after all, written over an erasure. It will therefore not be noticeable that it had been erased again. Then the entire document can be erased and rewritten with false information. They answer that if this declaration would be erased it would be noticed, as that line would then be written on a double erasure, whereas the rest of the document would be written on a single erasure (Rabbeinu Gershom Meor HaGola; Rabbi Yitzḥak ben Meir in *Tosafot*).

But the document text was written on an erasure – וּשְׁטָרָא עַל מְחָקָא: The Rashba and several other early commentaries discuss the following issue: If this written declaration appears between the two signatures, meaning that it was written after the first witness signed, this indicates only that it is attested to by the second witness; the first witness may not have been aware at all that the declaration was written. It therefore emerges that in validating the document on the basis of this declaration, the court is relying on the testimony of only one witness, whereas two witnesses are required.

The Rashba (see responsa attributed to Ramban, 94), explains that one can assume that the second witness was not lying when he wrote, in the plural: We, the witnesses, signed on an erasure, but the document text was written on paper that never had writing erased. There are certain matters for which a single witness is deemed credible by Torah law, and one can assume that the declaration was made on behalf of both witnesses. The Rashba concludes from this that the verification of an erasure may be written between the two witnesses' signatures. The Ritva concurs with the Rashba's explanation. The Ra'ah disagrees, claiming that while the Gemara could have raised this objection, it did not need to, since the present argument of the Gemara is rejected for other reasons. The Meiri understands the Gemara to be saying that each of the witnesses must write out this declaration following his signature, so that there is in fact the testimony of two witnesses that the signatures, or, in other cases, the text, was written on an erasure (see *Shulḥan Arukh, Ḥoshen Mishpat* 44:10 and *Shakh* there).

וְלִקַבְּלָה לַחֲתִימוֹת יָדָא דְּסָהֲדֵי בְּבֵי דִינָא, וְלִמְחוֹק וְלִידַמֵּי! אָמַר רַב הוֹשַׁעְיָא: אֵינוֹ דּוֹמֶה נִמְחַק בֶּן יוֹמוֹ לְנִמְחַק בֶּן שְׁנֵי יָמִים.

The Gemara continues to suggest: **But let us accept,** i.e., verify, **the signatures of the witnesses** on the document **in court,** after which they may safely be erased; **and** then **erase** the signatures **and compare** that erasure to the erasure of the document text, to see if it was erased once or twice. In response to this question **Rav Hoshaya says:** That which is **erased on the same day** that it was written **is not** necessarily **similar to** that which was **erased two days** ago, i.e., more than a day after it was written. An older erasure looks different from a new one, so the comparison might not show that there was a double erasure in the document.

וְלִישַׁהְיֵיהּ! אָמַר רַבִּי יִרְמְיָה: חָיְישִׁינַן לְבֵית דִּין טוֹעִין.

The Gemara suggests: **But let us retain** the document for an extra day, at which point both erasures will be old and can be compared. **Rabbi Yirmeya said** in response: **We are concerned for** the possibility of **an erring court.** If such complicated procedures were used in order to declare a document valid, there would be a chance that a particular court would not apply them properly, and that court would end up ratifying a document that was not valid.

״רַבִּי חֲנִינָא בֶּן גַּמְלִיאֵל אוֹמֵר: מְקוּשָּׁר״ וכו׳. הֵשִׁיב רַבִּי לְדִבְרֵי רַבִּי חֲנִינָא בֶּן גַּמְלִיאֵל:

§ The mishna teaches that **Rabbi Ḥanina ben Gamliel says: A tied** document whose witnesses wrote their signatures inside of it is valid, because one can transform it into an ordinary document by untying it. **Rabbi** Yehuda HaNasi **raised an objection to the statement of Rabbi Ḥanina ben Gamliel:**

Perek **X**
Daf **164** Amud **b**

NOTES

Reigned for one year, etc. – מָלַךְ שָׁנָה וכו׳: The practice was to date documents according to the number of years of the ruling king's reign. Often the government was insistent upon this, as a sign of loyalty. There were places where it was customary to add a year to the length of the reign recorded in the document. This was done to give honor to the king by indicating that he had ruled even longer than he actually did. The Sages instituted that this extra year should be written specifically in a tied document, in order to further distinguish between a tied document and an ordinary document.

וַהֲלֹא אֵינוֹ דּוֹמֶה זְמַנּוֹ שֶׁל זֶה לִזְמַנּוֹ שֶׁל זֶה; פָּשׁוּט, מָלַךְ שָׁנָה – מוֹנִין לוֹ שָׁנָה, שְׁתַּיִם – מוֹנִין לוֹ שְׁתַּיִם; מְקוּשָּׁר, מָלַךְ שָׁנָה – מוֹנִין לוֹ שְׁתַּיִם, שְׁתַּיִם – מוֹנִין לוֹ שָׁלֹשׁ.

But the date of this one, a tied document, **is not the same as the date of that one,** an ordinary document. In **an ordinary** document, when the king has **reigned** for one **year,**[N] one **year is counted for him,** and when he has reigned for **two** years, **two** years **are counted for him.** By contrast, in **a tied** document, when the king has **reigned** for one **year, two** years **are counted for him,** and when he has reigned for **two** years, **three** years **are counted for him.** If a tied document is simply opened up and used as an ordinary document, then it will emerge that it is postdated by a year.

וְזִימְנִין דְּיָזֵיף מִינֵּיהּ זוּזֵי בִּמְקוּשָּׁר וּמִיתְרַמֵי לֵיהּ זוּזֵי בֵּינֵי בֵּינֵי וּפָרַע לֵיהּ, וְאָמַר לֵיהּ: הַב לִי שְׁטָרַאי, וְאָמַר לֵיהּ: אִירְכַּס לִי, וְכָתַב לֵיהּ תַּבְרָא,

Rabbi Yehuda HaNasi continues: **And** there are **times** this can be problematic, as in a case **where** the debtor **borrows money from** the creditor, and the details of the loan are written **in a tied** document. **And** the debtor **chances upon** some **money in the interim,** i.e., during the first year after the document was written, **and** he **repays** the creditor, **and says to him: Give me** back **my** promissory **note,** as I have just repaid you. **And** the creditor **says to** the debtor: **I lost** the document and cannot give it to you. **And** in lieu of returning the promissory note, the creditor **writes a receipt** for the debtor, as protection against a second collection.

וְכִי מָטֵי זִמְנֵיהּ מְשַׁוֵּי לֵיהּ פָּשׁוּט, וְאָמַר לֵיהּ: הָנֵי הָשְׁתָּא דְּיָזְפַתְּ מִינַּאי!

Rabbi Yehuda HaNasi continues: **And** then, **when the time for** repayment written in the promissory note **arrives,** the creditor will **make it** into **an ordinary** document by undoing its stitches and opening it up, **and** he can then **say to** the debtor: **It is now that you borrowed this** money **from me,** as attested in this promissory note, and the receipt you have in your possession is for a previous debt, as its date precedes the date on my document.

קָא סָבַר: אֵין כּוֹתְבִין שׁוֹבֵר.

The Gemara answers: Rabbi Ḥanina ben Gamliel **holds** that **one does not write a receipt** in such cases. If a creditor loses his promissory note, the debtor need not pay him at all, out of concern that the debt may one day be collected again when the promissory note is found. He is not required to pay the debt and accept only a receipt, which he will then have to guard permanently to protect himself against a second collection.

וּמִי בָּקִי רַבִּי בִּמְקוּשָּׁר? וְהָא הַהוּא מְקוּשָּׁר דַּאֲתָא לְקַמֵּיהּ דְּרַבִּי, וְאָמַר רַבִּי: שְׁטָר מְאוּחָר זֶה! וְאָמַר לוֹ זוּנִין לְרַבִּי: כָּךְ מִנְהָגָהּ שֶׁל אוּמָּה זוֹ, מָלַךְ שָׁנָה – מוֹנִין לוֹ שְׁתַּיִם, שְׁתַּיִם – מוֹנִין לוֹ שָׁלֹשׁ!

The Gemara asks with regard to the previous discussion: **And was Rabbi** Yehuda HaNasi **expert in the** *halakhot* of **tied** documents? **But** wasn't there **a certain tied** document **that came before Rabbi** Yehuda HaNasi, **and** when **Rabbi** Yehuda HaNasi saw the date he **said: This is a postdated document. And** a Sage named **Zunin**[P] **said to Rabbi** Yehuda HaNasi: **Such is the custom of this nation;** when the king has **reigned** for one **year, two** years **are counted for him,** and when he has reigned for **two** years, **three** years **are counted for him.** The document is therefore not postdated. From this anecdote it is clear that Rabbi Yehuda HaNasi himself had not been familiar with this practice.

בָּתַר דִּשְׁמָעָהּ מִזּוּנִין סְבָרָהּ.

The Gemara answers: **After** Rabbi Yehuda HaNasi **heard it from Zunin** he accepted the explanation **and held this** way himself, and that is what prompted him to raise his objection.

הַהוּא שְׁטָרָא דַּהֲוָה כָּתַב בֵּיהּ ״בִּשְׁנַת פְּלוֹנִי אַרְכָן״, אָמַר רַבִּי חֲנִינָא: יִבָּדֵק אֵימָתַי עָמַד אַרְכָן בְּאַרְכָנוּתֵיהּ.

§ There was **a certain document on which was written,** as its date: **In the year of so-and-so, Archon** [*Arkhan*],[NL] a title for a ruler, without stating any particular year of his reign. **Rabbi Ḥanina said: Let it be investigated when** it was that this **Archon rose to his** position of **archon,** i.e., find out the year he came to power, and the validity of the document is established from that year.

וְדִלְמָא דַּאֲרִיךְ מַלְכוּתֵיהּ! אָמַר רַב הוֹשַׁעְיָא: כָּךְ מִנְהָגָהּ שֶׁל אוּמָּה זוֹ, שָׁנָה רִאשׁוֹנָה קוֹרִין לוֹ ״אַרְכָן״, שְׁנִיָּה – קוֹרִין לוֹ ״דִּיגוֹן״.

The Gemara suggests: **But perhaps** the writer of the document was using an Aramaic or Hebrew term, and intended to say **that the reign of** so-and-so had already **extended** [*arikh*] for several years. **Rav Hoshaya says: Such** is **the custom of this nation** where the document was written: In the **first year** of the king's reign **they refer to him** with the title **Archon;** in his **second** year **they refer to him** with the title ***Digon.***

וְדִלְמָא עֲבוּרֵי עַבְרוּהוּ וַהֲדַר אוֹקְמוּהוּ! אָמַר רַבִּי יִרְמְיָה: הַהוּא – ״אַרְכָן דִּיגוֹן״ קָרְאוּ לֵיהּ.

The Gemara suggests: **But perhaps** the people **deposed** the ruler **and then reinstated him,** and the document was written in the first year of his second reign. **Rabbi Yirmeya**[P] **said:** In **that** case, **they** would **refer to him** with the title **Archon *Digon.***

תָּנוּ רַבָּנַן: ״הֲרֵינִי נָזִיר הֵינָא״, סוּמְכוֹס אוֹמֵר: ״הֵינָא״ – אַחַת, ״דִּיגוֹן״ – שְׁתַּיִם, ״טְרִיגוֹן״ – שָׁלֹשׁ, ״טֶטְרִיגוֹן״ – אַרְבַּע, ״פֶּנְטִיגוֹן״ – חָמֵשׁ.

§ Apropos these Greek terms, the Gemara cites two *baraitot* that mention them. **The Sages taught** (*Tosefta, Nazir* 1:2) that if one said: **I am hereby a nazirite**[B] ***heina,***[L] or stated a similar expression with other comparable Greek terms, **Sumakhos said** that his status depends on which term he used. If he used the word ***heina,*** he is a nazirite for **one** term of naziriteship, i.e., thirty days; if he said ***digon,***[L] he is a nazirite for **two** terms of thirty days each; if he said ***terigon,*** he is a nazirite for **three** terms; ***tetrigon,*** for **four** terms; ***pentigon,*** for **five** terms.

תָּנוּ רַבָּנַן: בַּיִת עָגוֹל, דִּיגוֹן, טְרִיגוֹן, פֶּנְטִיגוֹן – אֵינוֹ מִטַּמֵּא בִּנְגָעִים, טֶטְרִיגוֹן – מִטַּמֵּא בִּנְגָעִים.

The Sages taught in another *baraita* (*Tosefta, Nega'im* 6:3): **A round house,**[H] or one that is shaped like **a *digon,*** i.e., it has two walls, one straight and one curved, or one that is shaped like **a *terigon,*** i.e., a triangle, or one that is shaped like **a pentagon, does not become susceptible to the ritual impurity of leprous spots.** If it is shaped like **a *tetrigon,*** i.e., a quadrilateral, it **becomes susceptible to the ritual impurity of leprous spots.**

מְנָא הָנֵי מִילֵּי? דְּתָנוּ רַבָּנַן: לְמַעְלָה אוֹמֵר ״קִיר״ ״קִירוֹת״ – שְׁתַּיִם, לְמַטָּה אוֹמֵר ״קִיר״ ״קִירוֹת״ שְׁתַּיִם – הֲרֵי כָּאן אַרְבַּע.

The Gemara asks: **From where are these matters** derived? The Gemara answers: It is **as the Sages taught** in a *baraita*: The Torah **states above:** "If the plague be in the walls of the house" (Leviticus 14:37). The verse did not state: **A wall,** but **"walls,"** indicating that the house in question has at least **two** walls. And where it **states below:** "If the plague has spread in the walls of the house" (Leviticus 14:39), instead of stating: **A wall,** the verse states **"walls,"** indicating another **two** walls. There **are** a total of **four** walls mentioned **here** in order to indicate that a house can become impure through leprous spots only if it has four sides.

PERSONALITIES

Zunin – זוּנִין: Zunin, a man with the Greek name Ζήνων, Zeno, was apparently in charge of the finances and business dealings of the household of the *Nasi*. Baitos ben Zunin (see *Pesaḥim* 37a) was probably his son, and he too was close to the household of the *Nasi*. Zunin was known for his great wealth and dedication to the punctilious fulfillment of mitzvot, as may be seen from the many stories related about him in the Talmud.

Rabbi Yirmeya – רַבִּי יִרְמְיָה: Born in Babylonia, Rabbi Yirmeya was one of the leading *amora'im* of the third and fourth generations. He studied in Babylonia in his youth, but soon emigrated to Eretz Yisrael, where he became a disciple of the most prominent Sages of the generation, Rabbi Zeira and Rabbi Abbahu, who were the preeminent students of Rabbi Yoḥanan. Rabbi Yirmeya possessed great acuity and had a unique method of understanding the law. He was known for posing provocative questions to his teachers and colleagues. Since these questions gave the impression that Rabbi Yirmeya was seeking to undermine the accepted conventions of halakhic dialectic, he was criticized, and even expelled from the study hall for a brief period (see 23b). Rabbi Yirmeya's statements are quoted extensively in both the Babylonian Talmud and the Jerusalem Talmud, so much so that when the Babylonian Talmud simply says: They say in the West, i.e., in Eretz Yisrael, it generally refers to the opinion of Rabbi Yirmeya.

NOTES

In the year of so-and-so Archon [*Arkhan*] – בִּשְׁנַת פְּלוֹנִי אַרְכָן: The Rashbam asserts that the title *Arkhan* is used to refer to a king, and is used specifically in the first year of his reign. The Rashbam relates the term to the word *arikh*, found in the Bible (Ezra 4:14), meaning: Set in place. *Tosafot* explain that the term refers to a local ruler or governor, a functionary whom the monarch replaces after a year or two in office. According to this interpretation it is easier to understand the Gemara's discussion later of the archon being deposed and reinstated, a situation that is not usually applicable to a monarch. Although the Gemara uses the term *malakh*, meaning reign, this is not difficult, as this word is often employed by the Gemara in the sense of holding high office.

LANGUAGE

Archon [*Arkhan*] – אַרְכָן: Adopted from Greek ἄρχων, *arkhon*, meaning an appointed person or the leader of a city or organization. In many places an archon, or a consul, would be appointed for a single year, and documents would be dated citing his name.

Heina – הֵינָא: The Gemara is referring to the Greek word ἕν, *hen*, meaning one.

Digon, etc. – דִּיגוֹן וכו׳: *Digon* is from the Greek word δίγωνον, *digonon*, meaning a shape with two corners. The related word δίγονον, *digonos*, means double or twins, and the Greek suffix *gonos* refers to birth or generation. Similarly, τρίγωνον, *trigonon*, means something with three corners, a triangle, whereas τρίγονος, *trigonos*, means three times or third. The word τετράγωνον, *tetragonon*, means a shape with four corners, a quadrilateral, and τετράγονος, *tetragonos*, means four times. The word πεντάγωνος, *pentagonon*, refers to a five-cornered shape.

HALAKHA

Round house – בַּיִת עָגוֹל: A house becomes susceptible to the ritual impurity of leprous spots only if it has four walls. If it is round, or has more or fewer than four walls, it does not become susceptible to the ritual impurity of leprous spots (Rambam *Sefer Tahara*, *Hilkhot Tumat Tzara'at* 14:6).

BACKGROUND

Naziriteship – נְזִירוּת: As detailed in the Torah (Numbers 6:1–21), one who takes a vow of naziriteship must refrain from eating or drinking any product of a grapevine, must avoid contracting ritual impurity imparted by a corpse, and may not cut his hair. A nazirite who violates any of these prohibitions is liable to be flogged. One can vow to be a nazirite for any length of time, but the minimum term of naziriteship is thirty days, which is also the length of the term for one who does not specify how long he wishes to be a nazirite. The *halakhot* of a nazirite are discussed in tractate *Nazir*.

הַהוּא מְקוּשָּׁר דַּאֲתָא לְקַמֵּיהּ דְּרַבִּי, וַאֲמַר רַבִּי: אֵין זְמַן בָּזֶה? אֲמַר לֵיהּ רַבִּי שִׁמְעוֹן בַּר רַבִּי לְרַבִּי: שֶׁמָּא בֵּין קְשָׁרָיו מוּבְלָע? פַּלְיֵיהּ וְחַזְיֵיהּ. הֲדַר חֲזָא בֵּיהּ רַבִּי בְּבִישׁוּת, אֲמַר לֵיהּ: לָאו אֲנָא כְּתַבְתֵּיהּ, רַבִּי יְהוּדָה חַיָּיטָא כְּתָבֵיהּ. אֲמַר לֵיהּ: כְּלָךְ מִלָּשׁוֹן הָרַע הַזֶּה.

§ The Gemara relates: There was **a certain tied** document **that came before Rabbi** Yehuda HaNasi, **and Rabbi** Yehuda HaNasi, not realizing it was a folded document, **said: There is no date on this** document, so it is not valid. **Rabbi Shimon, son of Rabbi** Yehuda HaNasi, **said to Rabbi** Yehuda HaNasi: **Perhaps** the date is **hidden between its tied** folds. Rabbi Yehuda HaNasi **opened it and saw** that the date was in fact between the tied folds. **Afterward, Rabbi** Yehuda HaNasi **looked at** his son **disapprovingly,** as he held that one should not write a tied document. His son **said to him: I did not write it; Rabbi Yehuda Ḥayyata wrote it.** Rabbi Yehuda HaNasi **said to** his son: **Turn away from** uttering **this** kind of **malicious speech.**[H]

זִימְנִין הֲוָה יָתֵיב קַמֵּיהּ וְקָא פָּסֵיק סִידְרָא בְּסֵפֶר תְּהִלִּים, אֲמַר רַבִּי: כַּמָּה מְיוּשָּׁר כְּתָב זֶה, אֲמַר לֵיהּ: לָאו אֲנָא כְּתַבְתֵּיהּ, יְהוּדָה חַיָּיטָא כְּתָבֵיהּ. אֲמַר לֵיהּ: כְּלָךְ מִלָּשׁוֹן הָרַע הַזֶּה.

Another **time,** Rabbi Shimon **was sitting before** his father **and reciting a section of the book of Psalms. Rabbi** Yehuda HaNasi **said** to him: **How straight** and neat is **this writing** in this book from which you are reading. Rabbi Shimon **said to him: I did not write it; Yehuda Ḥayyata wrote it.** Rabbi Yehuda HaNasi **told** his son: **Turn away from** uttering **this** kind **of malicious speech.**

בִּשְׁלָמָא הָתָם אִיכָּא לָשׁוֹן הָרַע, אֶלָּא הָכָא מַאי לָשׁוֹן הָרַע אִיכָּא? מִשּׁוּם דְּרַב דִּימִי. דְּתָנֵי רַב דִּימִי אֲחוּהּ דְּרַב סָפְרָא: לְעוֹלָם אַל יְסַפֵּר אָדָם בְּטוֹבָתוֹ שֶׁל חֲבֵירוֹ, שֶׁמִּתּוֹךְ טוֹבָתוֹ בָּא לִידֵי רָעָתוֹ.

The Gemara asks: **Granted, there,** in the first episode, **there is malicious speech** involved, since Rabbi Yehuda HaNasi was displeased with the writer of the document, **but here,** in the second episode, **what malicious speech is there?** Rabbi Yehuda HaNasi was complimenting the writer of the book of Psalms, not criticizing him. The Gemara answers: It is **because of** what **Rav Dimi** teaches. **As Rav Dimi, the brother of Rav Safra, teaches: A person should never speak the praises of another,**[HN] **as out of the praise** spoken about **him** someone may **come to** speak to **his detriment.**

אֲמַר רַב עַמְרָם אָמַר רַב, שָׁלֹשׁ עֲבֵירוֹת אֵין אָדָם נִיצּוֹל מֵהֶן בְּכָל יוֹם: הִרְהוּר עֲבֵירָה, וְעִיּוּן תְּפִלָּה, וְלָשׁוֹן הָרַע. לְשׁוֹן הָרַע סָלְקָא דַּעְתָּךְ?!

Rav Amram says that **Rav says:** There are **three sins from which a person is not spared each day.** They are: Having **sinful thoughts,**[N] **and** committing sins concerning **deliberation in prayer,**[N] **and** uttering **malicious speech.** The Gemara asks: Can it **enter your mind** that a person cannot go through the day without uttering **malicious speech?**

HALAKHA

Turn away from this malicious speech – כְּלָךְ מִלָּשׁוֹן הָרַע הַזֶּה: One who speaks negatively about another, even if his words are true, is considered as one who slanders another. With regard to him, the verse (Psalms 12:4) states: "May the Lord cut off all flattering lips, the tongue that speaks proud things" (Rambam *Sefer HaMadda*, *Hilkhot Deot* 7:2).

A person should never speak the praises of another – לְעוֹלָם אַל יְסַפֵּר אָדָם בְּטוֹבָתוֹ שֶׁל חֲבֵירוֹ: If one praises another person in the presence of that person's enemies, this is considered a hint of malicious speech, as he thereby indirectly prompts the enemies to speak disparagingly of that person. It is concerning this matter that Solomon said: "He who blesses his friend with a loud voice, rising early in the morning, it shall be counted a curse to him" (Proverbs 27:14), because as a result of this praise the friend experiences negative effects (Rambam *Sefer HaMadda*, *Hilkhot Deot* 7:4).

NOTES

A person should never speak the praises of another – אַל יְסַפֵּר אָדָם בְּטוֹבָתוֹ שֶׁל חֲבֵירוֹ: Many commentaries ask: Can it be that it is forbidden to praise any person? Moreover, the Sages often praised their students and colleagues. Some explain that the Gemara means that one should not praise another excessively, because this may lead a listener to feel that he has to balance the embellished claims with statements to the contrary (Rashi on *Arakhin* 16a; Meiri). Others explain that the intent is that one should not praise another person in the presence of that person's enemy, as that will provoke him to refute the praise (Rambam). In a similar vein, the Ramah explains that one may not speak someone's praises in public, lest someone present be an enemy of his, who will then contest the claims. Another explanation given is that one should not speak the praises of a person who has many negative aspects to his character as well, since this may lead to a discussion of those negative traits (*Shita Mekubbetzet*). The *Ḥatam Sofer* adds that the prohibition applies to the praises of one's physical or material gains, and not to one's accomplishments in the spiritual or ethical realm.

Sinful thoughts, etc. – הִרְהוּר עֲבֵירָה וכו׳: The Maharal writes that the uniqueness of these three sins is that they are transgressed with great ease. The first two are sins of mere thought, and the third is a sin of mere speech, not requiring physical exertion. It is therefore common for people to transgress in these areas without noticing. He also writes that these three sins represent three types of mitzvot: Those between a person and himself, those between a person and God, and those between one person and another. The Gemara's point is that one can easily transgress each of these categories of mitzvot.

Deliberation in prayer – עִיּוּן תְּפִלָּה: The commentaries note that as the term deliberation in prayer is employed elsewhere in a positive sense, in each case it must be understood in context. Most commentaries explain that here the Gemara is referring to the lack of deliberation in prayer, meaning that one does not pray with proper intent. They cite anecdotes related in the Jerusalem Talmud in which even great Torah scholars were unable at times to concentrate properly throughout the prayers or were unable to avoid thinking about other matters while praying (*Tosafot*).

Some explain that the term deliberation in prayer is referring here to one who believes that since he has prayed so fervently, God must answer his prayers to his satisfaction (Rashbam). A similar interpretation is that one prays fervently on the condition that God answer his prayers, in effect testing God (Rabbeinu Gershom Meor HaGola).

אֶלָּא, אֲבַק לָשׁוֹן הָרָע.

The Gemara answers: **Rather,** Rav was referring to uttering **a hint,** i.e., words with a bare trace, **of malicious speech.**[N]

אָמַר רַב יְהוּדָה אָמַר רַב: רוֹב בְּגָזֵל, וּמִיעוּט בַּעֲרָיוֹת, וְהַכֹּל בְּלָשׁוֹן הָרָע. בְּלָשׁוֹן הָרָע סָלְקָא דַּעְתָּךְ? אֶלָּא, אֲבַק לָשׁוֹן הָרָע.

Rav Yehuda says that **Rav says:** The **majority** of people succumb to sin **with regard to robbery,**[N] **and** a **minority** of people succumb to sin **with regard to sexual matters, and everyone** succumbs to sin **with regard to malicious speech.** The Gemara asks: Can it **enter your mind** that all people sin **with regard to malicious speech?** The Gemara answers: **Rather,** Rav was referring to uttering **a hint of malicious speech.**

״רַבָּן שִׁמְעוֹן בֶּן גַּמְלִיאֵל אוֹמֵר: הַכֹּל כְּמִנְהַג הַמְּדִינָה״. וְתַנָּא קַמָּא לֵית לֵיהּ מִנְהַג מְדִינָה?!

§ The mishna teaches, with regard to documents, that **Rabban Shimon ben Gamliel says: Everything** is **in accordance with regional custom.** The Gemara wonders: **And does the first** *tanna* **not accept** that one should follow the **regional custom?** It is not reasonable that he would take issue with such a basic concept.

אָמַר רַב אַשִׁי: בְּאַתְרָא דְּנָהִיגִי פָּשׁוּט, וַאֲמַר לֵיהּ: ״עֲבֵיד לִי פָּשׁוּט״, וַאֲזַל עֲבַד לֵיהּ מְקוּשָּׁר – קְפֵידָא; נָהִיגִי מְקוּשָּׁר, וַאֲמַר לֵיהּ: ״עֲבֵיד לִי מְקוּשָּׁר״, וַאֲזַל עֲבַד לֵיהּ פָּשׁוּט – קְפֵידָא;

Rav Ashi said in explanation: **In a place where the custom** is to write **an ordinary** document, **and** one **said to** a scribe: **Make an ordinary** document **for me, and** the scribe **went** and **made a tied** document **for him,** it is assumed that he was **particular** about wanting an ordinary document. Similarly, in a place where **the custom** is to write **a tied** document, **and** one **said to** a scribe: **Make a tied** document **for me, and** the scribe **went** and **made an ordinary** document **for him,** it is assumed that he was **particular** about wanting a tied document. In both of these cases, the document is considered to have been written without the consent of the one who requested it. If it is a bill of divorce it may not be used, as a bill of divorce must be written with the knowledge and consent of the husband.

כִּי פְּלִיגִי – בְּאַתְרָא דְּנָהִיגִי בְּפָשׁוּט וּמְקוּשָּׁר, וַאֲמַר לֵיהּ: ״עֲבֵיד לִי פָּשׁוּט״, וַאֲזַל עֲבַד לֵיהּ מְקוּשָּׁר – מָר סָבַר: קְפֵידָא, וּמָר סָבַר: מַרְאֶה מָקוֹם הוּא לוֹ.

When the *tanna'im* of the mishna **disagree** is **in a place where the custom** is to write **both an ordinary** document **and a tied** document, **and** one **said to** a scribe: **Make an ordinary** document **for me, and** the scribe **went and made a tied** document **for him.** In such a case, one **Sage,** the first *tanna*, **holds** that the one requesting the document was **particular** about wanting an ordinary document, and since the scribe wrote a tied document, it is considered to have been written without his consent. **And** one **Sage,** Rabban Shimon ben Gamliel, **holds** that the one requesting the document was merely **indicating** his **position to** the scribe, stating that if the scribe wanted to save himself the trouble of writing a tied document there would no objection.

אָמַר אַבָּיֵי: רַבָּן שִׁמְעוֹן בֶּן גַּמְלִיאֵל וְרַבִּי שִׁמְעוֹן וְרַבִּי אֶלְעָזָר, כּוּלְּהוּ סְבִירָא לְהוּ: מַרְאֶה מָקוֹם הוּא לוֹ.

Abaye said: Concerning **Rabban Shimon ben Gamliel, and Rabbi Shimon, and Rabbi Elazar, they all hold** that when one gives instructions to an agent, he is merely **indicating** his **position to him,** as opposed to expressing an insistence on certain details.

רַבָּן שִׁמְעוֹן בֶּן גַּמְלִיאֵל – הָא דַּאֲמָרַן. רַבִּי שִׁמְעוֹן – דִּתְנַן,

Rabban Shimon ben Gamliel holds this is the case, **as we have** just **said. Rabbi Shimon** holds this as well, **as we learned** in a mishna (*Kiddushin* 48a), as explained by the Gemara there, that the first *tanna* rules that if a woman appoints an agent to accept her betrothal money and tells him that the man will be giving a golden dinar, or that he will be giving a silver dinar, and he in fact gives the other type of dinar, the betrothal is not valid, as in accepting the wrong dinar the agent did not follow the woman's instructions exactly.

רַבִּי שִׁמְעוֹן אוֹמֵר: אִם הִטְעָהּ לְשֶׁבַח – הֲרֵי זוֹ מְקוּדֶּשֶׁת.

But **Rabbi Shimon says: If he misled her to her advantage,**[H] i.e., he told her he was going to give a silver dinar and gave her a golden dinar, **she is betrothed.** When the woman told the agent to receive the silver dinar she did not mean to insist that the dinar be silver as opposed to gold, but was only indicating her position, which is that she would have no objection to receiving only a silver dinar.

NOTES

A hint of malicious speech – **אֲבַק לָשׁוֹן הָרָע:** Malicious speech is speech that disparages another, even if the statement is true. A hint of malicious speech is a statement that is not inherently disparaging but can be interpreted in a negative light or may lead to disparaging comments. The Rashbam cites an example from tractate *Arakhin* (15b), where someone declares: There is always a fire in so-and-so's house, which can be taken to indicate that the people in that house are constantly cooking and eating. Another example is the anecdote here about Rabbi Shimon, son of Rabbi Yehuda HaNasi, who spoke in praise of Yehuda Ḥayyata; there was a concern that disparaging words may be spoken as a result of those praises. Rav notes that statements such as these, which are not themselves malicious speech, and often are not spoken with any ill intent, are very difficult to avoid.

The majority succumb with regard to robbery – **רוֹב בְּגָזֵל:** The intent here is not to outright robbery but to various types of deceitful behavior that people engage in while doing business, through which they take or withhold money of others in a manner that is not completely just (Rashbam; Rabbeinu Gershom Meor HaGola).

HALAKHA

If he misled her to her advantage, etc. – **הִטְעָהּ לְשֶׁבַח וכו׳:** If someone betroths a woman on the condition that he is a rich man, and it is found out that he is actually poor, or vice versa, the betrothal does not take effect, in accordance with the unattributed opinion in the mishna in tractate *Kiddushin* (Rambam *Sefer Nashim*, *Hilkhot Ishut* 8:1; *Shulḥan Arukh*, *Even HaEzer* 38:24).

רַבִּי אֶלְעָזָר – דִּתְנַן: הָאִשָּׁה שֶׁאָמְרָה ״הִתְקַבֵּל לִי גִּיטִּי מִמָּקוֹם פְּלוֹנִי״, וְקִיבְּלוֹ לָהּ מִמָּקוֹם אַחֵר – פָּסוּל, וְרַבִּי אֶלְעָזָר מַכְשִׁיר; מָר סָבַר: קְפֵידָא, וּמָר סָבַר: מַרְאֶה מָקוֹם הוּא לוֹ.

Abaye continues: **Rabbi Elazar** also holds this, **as we learned** in a mishna (*Gittin* 65a): With regard to **the woman who,** when designating her agent for receipt of her bill of divorce, **said** to her agent: **Receive my bill of divorce for me**[H] **in such and such a place, and he received it for her in another place,** the divorce is **invalid; and Rabbi Elazar deems** it **valid.** One **Sage,** the first *tanna*, **holds** that the woman is **particular** that her instructions be followed, **and** one **Sage,** Rabbi Elazar, **holds** that she was merely **indicating** her **position to** the agent, informing him of where she thought her husband would be.

[״פָּשׁוּט שֶׁכָּתוּב בּוֹ עֵד אֶחָד״ כו׳.] בִּשְׁלָמָא מְקוּשָּׁר שֶׁכָּתוּב בּוֹ שְׁנֵי עֵדִים פָּסוּל – אִיצְטְרִיךְ, סָלְקָא דַּעְתָּךְ אָמִינָא: הוֹאִיל וּבְעָלְמָא כָּשֵׁר הָכָא נַמִי כָּשֵׁר, קָא מַשְׁמַע לָן דְּפָסוּל. אֶלָּא פָּשׁוּט שֶׁכָּתוּב בּוֹ עֵד אֶחָד – פְּשִׁיטָא!

§ The mishna teaches: With regard to **an ordinary** document **in which** the signature of **a single witness is written,** and a tied document in which the signatures of only two witnesses are written, they are both not valid. The Gemara asks: **Granted,** it **was necessary** for the mishna to teach that **a tied** document **in which** the signatures of only **two witnesses are written** is **not valid,** as it might **enter your mind to say** that **since generally** a document is **valid** with two signatures, **here too** it is valid; therefore, the mishna **teaches us that** it is in fact **not valid. But** why was it necessary to state that **an ordinary** document **in which** the signature of **a single witness is written** is not valid; isn't this **obvious?**

אֲמַר אַבַּיֵי: לָא נִצְרְכָא, דַּאֲפִילּוּ עֵד אֶחָד בִּכְתָב וְעֵד אֶחָד בַּפֶּה.

Abaye said: It **is necessary** to state this *halakha* **only** to teach **that even** if there is **one witness** signed on the document **in writing and,** in addition, **one witness** testifies **orally**[H] to the contents of the document, the document is not valid.

אַמֵימָר אַכְשַׁר בְּעֵד אֶחָד בִּכְתָב וְעֵד אֶחָד עַל פֶּה. אֲמַר לֵיהּ רַב אַשִׁי לְאַמֵימָר: וְהָא דְּאַבַּיֵי מַאי? אֲמַר לֵיהּ: לָא שְׁמִיעַ לִי, כְּלוֹמַר לָא סְבִירָא לִי.

The Gemara relates: **Ameimar deemed** a document **valid**[N] **in the** case of **one witness** signed on the document **in writing and one witness** testifying **orally** to the contents of the document. **Rav Ashi said to Ameimar: And what of that** statement **of Abaye,** which deemed such a document invalid? Ameimar **said to him: I did not hear** of it, as though **to say: I do not hold** like it; I disagree with Abaye.

אֶלָּא קַשְׁיָא

Rav Ashi asks: **But** if you disagree, the **difficulty**

HALAKHA

The woman who said: Receive my bill of divorce for me, etc. – **הָאִשָּׁה שֶׁאָמְרָה הִתְקַבֵּל לִי גִּיטִּי וכו׳**: If a woman said to an agent: Receive my bill of divorce in such and such a place, and the agent received it in a different place, the divorce is invalid, in accordance with the opinion of the Rabbis (Rambam *Sefer Nashim, Hilkhot Geirushin* 9:34; *Shulḥan Arukh, Even HaEzer* 141:49).

One witness in writing and one witness orally – **עֵד אֶחָד בִּכְתָב וְעֵד אֶחָד בַּפֶּה**: If one witness is signed on a promissory note and a second witness corroborates this promissory note with oral testimony, their testimonies may be combined into a single unit, preventing the possibility of the debtor altogether denying the debt. The *Sma* notes that the debtor would not be deemed credible if he issued such a denial, even if he took an oath to contradict the testimony of each of the two witnesses (Rambam *Sefer Shofetim, Hilkhot Edut* 4:5; *Shulḥan Arukh, Ḥoshen Mishpat* 30:10, 51:1).

NOTES

Ameimar deemed valid – **אַמֵימָר אַכְשַׁר**: The Rashbam maintains that according to the opinion of Ameimar, the document is as valid as any other document, and collection may even be made based on such a document from liened property that has been sold by the debtor. Rabbeinu Gershom Meor HaGola and *Sefer HaIttur* agree. By contrast, the majority of the early commentaries hold that only a document with two signed witnesses can be used to collect liened property that had been sold by the debtor, and that Ameimar deemed such a document valid only insofar as it may be used to collect unsold property from the debtor (Ri Migash; Ramban; Rid).

Perek **X**
Daf **165** Amud **b**

מַתְנִיתִין!

with **the mishna** remains: Why does the mishna state that which is obvious, that a document with a single witness's signature is not valid?

הָא קָא מַשְׁמַע לָן, דִּשְׁנַיִם בִּמְקוּשָּׁר כְּעֵד אֶחָד בְּפָשׁוּט, מָה הָתָם פְּסוּלָא דְּאוֹרַיְיתָא, אַף הָכָא נַמִי פְּסוּלָא דְּאוֹרַיְיתָא.

The Gemara answers that the mishna **teaches us this: That** the case of **two** witnesses signed **on a tied** document is **similar to** the case of **one witness** signed **on an ordinary** document: **Just as there,** in the case of a single witness signed on an ordinary document, **the disqualification** is **by Torah law,**[N] **so too here,** in the case of two witnesses signed on a tied document, **the disqualification** is **by Torah law.**

תֵּדַע, דִּשְׁלַחוּ מִתָּם חֶבְרַיָּיא לְרַבִּי יִרְמְיָה.

Ameimar added: **Know** that the signature of one witness on a document and the oral testimony of one person about it can be combined into a single testimony, **as the colleagues** of the academy **sent** a question **from there,** i.e., Eretz Yisrael, **to Rabbi Yirmeya**[N] seeking clarification of a *baraita*. The *baraita* states that the first *tanna* holds that the testimony of two witnesses to an event can be combined into a single testimony only if both of them witnessed the event together, while Rabbi Yehoshua ben Korḥa holds that the testimony can be combined even if they saw the event one after the other. Furthermore, the first *tanna* holds that their testimony is accepted only if they both testify together. By contrast, Rabbi Natan holds that the testimony of one witness may be accepted today, and when the other witness comes the next day his testimony may be accepted, and the two testimonies may thereby be combined.

NOTES

Just as there, the disqualification is by Torah law – **מָה הָתָם פְּסוּלָא דְּאוֹרַיְיתָא**: As it is stated in the Torah: "One witness shall not rise up against a man" (Deuteronomy 19:15), meaning that the testimony of a single witness cannot serve as the basis to collect money from another party or to establish any other fact that requires witness testimony. Not only is a document with one signatory witness considered insufficient testimony to collect money from another party, but if money was collected on the basis of such a document, it must be returned (*She'iltot deRav Aḥai Gaon*). If the document was a bill of divorce, a divorce executed through it is not valid, and if the woman remarries on the basis of such a bill of divorce, the offspring of this marriage is a *mamzer* (see *Tosafot*).

As the colleagues sent from there to Rabbi Yirmeya – **דִּשְׁלַחוּ מִתָּם חֶבְרַיָּיא לְרַבִּי יִרְמְיָה**: The Rashash suggests an emendation of the text of the Gemara, deleting the term: From there, as Rabbi Yirmeya himself lived in Eretz Yisrael. Ya'avetz suggests that after Rabbi Yirmeya was expelled from the academy in Eretz Yisrael (see 23b) he traveled to Babylonia.

עֵד אֶחָד בִּכְתָב וְעֵד אֶחָד עַל פֶּה, מַהוּ שֶׁיִּצְטָרְפוּ?

The dilemma they posed to Rabbi Yirmeya was this: In the case of a loan for which there is **one witness in writing,** signed on a promissory note, **and one** other **witness** who testifies to the loan **orally, what is** the *halakha* with regard to the possibility **that** the two of them **will combine** to testify as two witnesses?

אַלִּיבָּא דְּתַנָּא קַמָּא דְּרַבִּי יְהוֹשֻׁעַ בֶּן קָרְחָה לָא תִּיבְּעֵי לָךְ, דַּאֲפִילּוּ שְׁנַיִם בִּכְתָב וּשְׁנַיִם עַל פֶּה לָא מִצְטָרְפִי, אֶלָּא כִּי תִּיבְּעֵי לָךְ – אַלִּיבָּא דְּרַבִּי יְהוֹשֻׁעַ בֶּן קָרְחָה: שְׁנַיִם בִּכְתָב וּשְׁנַיִם עַל פֶּה הוּא דְּמִצְטָרְפִי, אֲבָל עֵד אֶחָד בִּכְתָב וְאֶחָד עַל פֶּה לָא מְצָרְפִינַן, אוֹ דִּלְמָא לָא שְׁנָא?

The dilemma is clarified: **According to** the opinion **of the first** ***tanna*** of the *baraita,* who engages in a dispute **with Rabbi Yehoshua ben Korḥa, you should not raise the dilemma, as** according to his opinion there are situations where **even two** testimonies **in writing or two oral** testimonies **are not combined** into a single testimony. All the more so they are not combined when one is written and one is oral. **Rather, when should you raise the dilemma?** Raise it **according to** the opinion **of Rabbi Yehoshua ben Korḥa.** The dilemma is: Is it only testimonies of **two** witnesses **in writing** or **two oral** witnesses **that are combined** into a single testimony, **but we do not combine** testimony of **one witness in writing and one** orally? **Or perhaps** there **is no difference** between these cases.

שְׁלַח לְהוּ: אֲנִי אֵינִי כְּדַאי שֶׁשְּׁלַחְתֶּם לִי, אֶלָּא כָּךְ דַּעַת תַּלְמִידְכֶם נוֹטָה – שֶׁיִּצְטָרְפוּ.

Rabbi Yirmeya humbly **sent** back his response **to** the colleagues of the academy: **I am not worthy** of being the recipient of the query **that you sent to me. But this** is how **the opinion of your student,** i.e., himself, **leans: That** the testimonies **should be combined.**[N] This exchange between Rabbi Yirmeya and his questioners indicates that Ameimar's opinion is accepted.

אֲמַר לֵיהּ: אֲנַן הָכִי מַתְנִינַן לָהּ, דִּשְׁלַחוּ לֵיהּ חֲבֵרַיָּא לְרַבִּי יִרְמְיָה: שְׁנַיִם שֶׁהֵעִידוּ אֶחָד בְּבֵית דִּין זֶה וְאֶחָד בְּבֵית דִּין זֶה, מַהוּ שֶׁיָּבוֹאוּ בֵּית דִּין אֵצֶל בֵּית דִּין וְיִצְטָרְפוּ?

Rav Ashi **said to** Ameimar: **We teach** this entire incident with Rabbi Yirmeya differently, **as follows: That the colleagues** of the academy **sent** this question **to Rabbi Yirmeya:** If there **are two** witnesses **who testified, one in this court and one in that court,**[H] **what is** the *halakha* with regard to the possibility **that** the judges of one **court could come** to the other **court and** in this manner the two testimonies **will be combined** to become a valid testimony of two witnesses?

אַלִּיבָּא דְּתַנָּא קַמָּא דְּרַבִּי נָתָן לָא תִּיבְּעֵי לָךְ, דַּאֲפִילּוּ בְּחַד בֵּית דִּינָא נַמִי לָא מִצְטָרְפִי, אֶלָּא כִּי תִּיבְּעֵי לָךְ – אַלִּיבָּא דְּרַבִּי נָתָן: בְּחַד בֵּי דִינָא הוּא דְּמִצְטָרְפִי, אֲבָל בִּתְרֵי בֵּי דִינָא לָא מִצְטָרְפִי, אוֹ דִּלְמָא לָא שְׁנָא?

The dilemma is clarified: **According to** the opinion **of the first** ***tanna*** of the *baraita,* who also engages in a dispute **with Rabbi Natan, you should not raise the dilemma, as** according to his opinion, testimonies that are not given concurrently **are not combined even in one court;** all the more so when they are given in two different courts. **Rather, when should you raise the dilemma?** Raise it **according to** the opinion **of Rabbi Natan.** The dilemma is: Is it **in one court that** the two separate testimonies **are combined, but** when they are given **in two** separate **courts they are not combined? Or perhaps** there is **no difference.**

וּשְׁלַח לְהוּ: אֲנִי אֵינִי כְּדַאי שֶׁאַתֶּם שְׁלַחְתֶּם לִי, אֶלָּא כָּךְ דַּעַת תַּלְמִידְכֶם נוֹטָה – שֶׁיִּצְטָרְפוּ.

And Rabbi Yirmeya **sent** back his response **to them: I am not worthy** of being the recipient of the query **that you sent to me. But this** is how **the opinion of your student leans: That they should be combined.** According to this version of the exchange between Rabbi Yirmeya and his questioners there is no relevance to Ameimar's statement.

מָר בַּר חִיָּיא אֲמַר, הָכִי שְׁלַחוּ לֵיהּ: שְׁנַיִם שֶׁהֵעִידוּ בְּבֵית דִּין זֶה וְחָזְרוּ וְהֵעִידוּ בְּבֵית דִּין זֶה, מַהוּ שֶׁיָּבוֹא אֶחָד מִכׇּל בֵּית דִּין וְיִצְטָרְפוּ?

Mar bar Ḥiyya said yet a third version, that the dilemma the colleagues of the academy **sent to** Rabbi Yirmeya is **as follows:** If there are **two** witnesses **who testified in this court and then testified in that court,**[H] **what is** the *halakha* with regard to the possibility **that one** judge would **come from each court** to one location and relate the testimony he had heard to the other, **and** in this manner the two testimonies **will be combined?**

אַלִּיבָּא דְּרַבִּי נָתָן לָא תִּיבְּעֵי לָךְ, הָשְׁתָּא עֵדִים מְצָרְפִינַן, דַּיָּינֵי מִיבַּעְיָא? אֶלָּא כִּי תִּיבְּעֵי לָךְ – אַלִּיבָּא דְּתַנָּא קַמָּא דְּרַבִּי נָתָן: עֵדִים הוּא דְּלָא מְצָרְפִינַן, אֲבָל דַּיָּינֵי מְצָרְפִינַן, אוֹ דִּלְמָא לָא שְׁנָא?

The dilemma is clarified: **According to** the opinion **of Rabbi Natan you should not raise the dilemma. Now** that he maintains that **we combine** two individual **witnesses, is** it **necessary** to ask if **judges** may be combined in this manner? They certainly can be combined. **Rather, when should you raise the dilemma?** Raise it **according to** the opinion **of the first** ***tanna*** of the *baraita,* who engages in a dispute **with Rabbi Natan.** The dilemma is: **Is** it only testimony of **witnesses that we do not combine** into a single testimony, **but we do combine judges** from two different courts? **Or perhaps** there **is no difference.**

NOTES

The opinion of your student leans that the testimonies should be combined – **דַּעַת תַּלְמִידְכֶם נוֹטָה שֶׁיִּצְטָרְפוּ:** In the discussion of this question in the Jerusalem Talmud, the opinion is expressed that a document with one witness signed on it is not valid even if it is supported by oral testimony of one witness. It states there that if there is any dilemma at all, it is in a case in which there actually are two witnesses signed on the document but one signature cannot be verified, so that the remaining signature stands alone in the sense that it is the sole verified signature. Some interpret the Gemara's discussion here in this manner as well, while others write that the Babylonian Talmud and the Jerusalem Talmud disagree concerning this issue. The Ramban and others cite *Halakhot Gedolot,* which rules that a document with a single signed witness is valid to the extent that it would require an oath on the part of the debtor who seeks to contradict it, as is the case in general with a single oral witness in monetary cases (*Sefer Hashlama*; see Ran).

HALAKHA

Two who testified, one in this court and one in that court – **שְׁנַיִם שֶׁהֵעִידוּ אֶחָד בְּבֵית דִּין זֶה וְאֶחָד בְּבֵית דִּין זֶה:** If one witness testifies in one court, and another witness testifies in another court, the judges of the two courts can form one large court, and in this manner the two testimonies can be combined (Rambam *Sefer Shofetim, Hilkhot Edut* 4:6; *Shulḥan Arukh, Ḥoshen Mishpat* 30:11).

Two who testified in this court and then testified in that court, etc. – **שְׁנַיִם שֶׁהֵעִידוּ בְּבֵית דִּין זֶה וְחָזְרוּ וְהֵעִידוּ בְּבֵית דִּין זֶה וכו׳:** If two witnesses testify in one court and then testify in another court, and testify again in a third court, three judges, one from each court, can form a new court, in which they may pronounce judgment based on the testimony they had all heard (Rambam *Sefer Shofetim, Hilkhot Edut* 4:6; *Shulḥan Arukh, Ḥoshen Mishpat* 30:12).

שְׁלַח לְהוּ: אֲנִי אֵינִי כְּדַיי שֶׁאַתֶּם שְׁלַחְתֶּם לִי, אֶלָּא כָּךְ דַּעַת תַּלְמִידְכֶם נוֹטָה – שֶׁיִּצְטָרְפוּ.

Rabbi Yirmeya **sent** back his response **to them: I am not worthy** of being the recipient of the query **that you sent to me. But this** is how **the opinion of your student leans: That they should be combined.**

רָבִינָא אֲמַר, הָכִי שְׁלַחוּ לֵיהּ: שְׁלֹשָׁה שֶׁיָּשְׁבוּ לְקַיֵּים אֶת הַשְּׁטָר, וּמֵת אֶחָד מֵהֶן, צְרִיכִי לְמִכְתַּב: ״בְּמוֹתַב תְּלָתָא הֲוֵינָא וְחַד לֵיתוֹהִי״, אוֹ לָא?

Ravina said a fourth version, that the dilemma the colleagues of the academy **sent to** Rabbi Yirmeya is **as follows:** If there were **three** judges **who sat** as a court **to ratify a document, and,** after verifying the signatures of the witnesses, **one of** the judges **died, must they** mention this in their statement of ratification, to account for why the declaration is signed by only two judges, and **write: We were sitting in** a group of **three** judges, **and one of** the judges **is no** longer alive? **Or** perhaps they are **not** required to write this.

שְׁלַח לְהוּ: אֲנִי אֵינִי כְּדַיי שֶׁאַתֶּם שְׁלַחְתֶּם לִי, אֶלָּא כָּךְ דַּעַת תַּלְמִידְכֶם נוֹטָה – שֶׁצְּרִיכִין לְמִכְתַּב ״בְּמוֹתַב תְּלָתָא הֲוֵינָא וְחַד לֵיתוֹהִי״.

Rabbi Yirmeya **sent** back his response **to them: I am not worthy** of being the recipient of the query **that you sent to me. But this is** how **the opinion of your student leans: That they are required to write: We were sitting in** a group of **three** judges, **and one of** the judges **is no** longer alive.

וְעַל דָּא עַיְּילוּהוּ לְרַבִּי יִרְמְיָה בְּבֵי מִדְרְשָׁא.

The Gemara relates: **And** it was **because of this** fitting answer, to whichever version of the dilemma that is adopted, that the Sages **brought Rabbi Yirmeya into the study hall** after he had been expelled, as related earlier in this tractate (23b).

מתני׳ כָּתוּב בּוֹ ״זוּזִין מְאָה דְּאִינּוּן סְלָעִין עֶשְׂרִין״ – אֵין לוֹ אֶלָּא עֶשְׂרִין; ״זוּזִין מְאָה דְּאִינּוּן תְּלָתִין סְלָעִין״ – אֵין לוֹ אֶלָּא מָנֶה.

MISHNA If **it is written in** a document that someone owes: **One hundred dinars, which are**[N] **twenty** ***sela***,[H] which is internally inconsistent since there are twenty-five *sela* in a hundred dinars, the holder of the document **has** the right to claim **only twenty** ***sela***, the lower of the two amounts. If it is written that he owes: **One hundred dinars, which are thirty** ***sela***, the holder of the document **has** the right to claim **only one hundred dinars,** again the lower of the two amounts.

״כֶּסֶף זוּזִין דְּאִינּוּן״ וְנִמְחַק – אֵין פָּחוֹת מִשְּׁתַּיִם. ״כֶּסֶף סְלָעִין דְּאִינּוּן״ וְנִמְחַק – אֵין פָּחוֹת מִשְּׁתַּיִם. ״דַּרְכּוֹנוֹת דְּאִינּוּן״ וְנִמְחַק – אֵין פָּחוֹת מִשְּׁתַּיִם.

If it is written that someone owes: **Silver dinars that are, and** the remainder of the text, where the number of dinars should be specified, **was erased,**[NH] the amount must be **no less than two** dinars, the lowest amount to which the plural word dinars can be referring. That is what the creditor can claim. Similarly, if it is written: **Silver** ***sela*** **that are, and** the remainder of the text **was erased,** the amount must be **no less than two** *sela*. And if it is written: **Darics that are, and** the remainder of the text **was erased,** the amount must be **no less than two** darics.

כָּתוּב בּוֹ מִלְמַעְלָה מָנֶה וּמִלְּמַטָּה מָאתַיִם, מִלְמַעְלָה מָאתַיִם וּמִלְּמַטָּה מָנֶה – הַכֹּל הוֹלֵךְ אַחַר הַתַּחְתּוֹן. אִם כֵּן, לָמָּה כּוֹתְבִין אֶת הָעֶלְיוֹן? שֶׁאִם תִּמָּחֵק אוֹת אַחַת מִן הַתַּחְתּוֹן – יִלָּמֵד מִן הָעֶלְיוֹן.

If it is **written in** the document **above,** in an earlier place in the document, that someone owes **one hundred dinars, and below,** toward the end of the document, it is written that the amount owed is **two hundred**[H] dinars, or if **above** it is written **two hundred** dinars **and below one hundred dinars, everything follows the bottom** amount. **If so, why** does one **write** the information in **the upper** part of the document at all? It is a safety measure, **so that if one letter is erased from the lower** part of the document, thereby rendering it illegible, the information **can be learned from the upper** part of the document.

NOTES

One hundred dinars which are, etc. – **זוּזִין מְאָה דְּאִינּוּן וכו׳**: The principle in these cases is that whenever there is a contradiction, one can claim only the lowest possible amount. This is in accordance with the principle that the burden of proof always rests upon the claimant; the corollary of this principle is that the holder of a document is at a disadvantage. The Rid writes that if the document lists several smaller amounts and then presents a total sum of those amounts, and that total does not match the sum of the individual amounts, it is the individual amounts that are followed, as the assumption is that there was probably a mistake in the addition of the smaller amounts.

Silver dinars that are, and the remainder was erased – **כֶּסֶף זוּזִין דְּאִינּוּן וְנִמְחַק**: The early commentaries conclude from this statement that if part of a document is erased, the document is not thereby invalidated. The erased part should be inferred, if possible, from the context (see Ramah and Ritva).

HALAKHA

One hundred dinars which are twenty ***sela*** – **זוּזִין מְאָה דְּאִינּוּן סְלָעִין עֶשְׂרִין**: If one presents a promissory note containing two contradictory statements with regard to the amount, with both expressions related to one another by wording such as: One hundred, which is two hundred, or: Two hundred, which are one hundred, the holder of the document is at a disadvantage and can collect only one hundred, the lower of the two stated contradictory values (Rambam *Sefer Mishpatim, Hilkhot Malve VeLoveh* 27:14, 17; *Shulḥan Arukh*, *Ḥoshen Mishpat* 42:5).

Silver dinars that are, and the remainder was erased – **כֶּסֶף זוּזִין דְּאִינּוּן וְנִמְחַק**: If one presents a promissory note in which it is written that another owes him a number of coins of a certain denomination, and the actual amount is erased beyond recognition, the holder of the document can collect only two of those coins (*Shulḥan Arukh*, *Ḥoshen Mishpat* 42:11).

It is written in the document above one hundred dinars, and below two hundred – **כָּתוּב בּוֹ מִלְמַעְלָה מָנֶה וּמִלְּמַטָּה מָאתַיִם**: If one presents a promissory note in which two different amounts are written as the amount owed, e.g., one hundred earlier in the document and two hundred later in the document, or vice versa, and it is impossible to reconcile the two figures, the bottom amount is followed, provided it does not appear on the final line of the document, as explained earlier in the chapter (162b). The Rema writes that if the amount that appears later in the document is the lesser of the two amounts, it is taken as the authoritative amount even if it is on the final line.

If a series of individual amounts are recorded in the document, followed by a total, and that total does not correspond to the sum of the individual amounts, there is an opinion that it should be assumed that there was an error of calculation and the individual amounts should be taken as authoritative, even though the total sum is written later (Rid). The *Shulḥan Arukh* writes that this opinion appears to be correct (Rambam *Sefer Mishpatim, Hilkhot Malve VeLoveh* 27:14; *Shulḥan Arukh*, *Ḥoshen Mishpat* 42:5).

גמ׳ תָּנוּ רַבָּנַן: אָמַר ״כֶּסֶף״ – אֵין פָּחוֹת מִדִּינָר כֶּסֶף; ״כֶּסֶף דִּינָרִין״ וְ״דִינָרִין כֶּסֶף״ – אֵין פָּחוֹת מִשְּׁנֵי דִּינָרִין כֶּסֶף; ״כֶּסֶף בְּדִינָרִין״ – אֵין פָּחוֹת מִבִּשְׁנֵי דִּינָרִין דְּהַב, כֶּסֶף.

GEMARA **The Sages taught** (*Tosefta* 11:2): If a document **states** that someone owes **silver,**[H] without specifying which silver coin, the amount must be **no less than a silver dinar.** If it states: **Silver dinars, or: Dinars silver,** the amount must be **no less than two silver dinars,** the lowest amount to which that phrase can refer. If it states: **Silver, in dinars,** the amount must be **no less than two golden dinars'** worth **of silver.**

אָמַר מָר: ״כֶּסֶף״ – אֵין פָּחוֹת מִדִּינָר כֶּסֶף. וְאֵימָא: נַסְכָא! אָמַר רַבִּי אֶלְעָזָר: דִּכְתוּב בֵּיהּ ״מַטְבֵּעַ״. וְאֵימָא: פְּרִיטֵי! אָמַר רַב פַּפָּא: בְּאַתְרָא דְּלָא סָגֵי פְּרִיטֵי דְּכַסְפָּא.

The Gemara analyzes the beginning of the *baraita*. **The Master says:** If a document states that someone owes **silver,** without specifying which silver coin, the amount must be **no less than a silver dinar.** The Gemara asks: **But** why not **say** that the intention of the word silver is not to a coin at all, but to a small **piece** of silver? **Rabbi Elazar said:** The case of the *baraita* is **where** the word **coin is written in** the document. The Gemara asks further: **But** why not **say** that the intent is not a dinar, but smaller coins, such as *perutot*? **Rav Pappa said:** The *halakha* of the *baraita* is stated **with regard to a place where silver *perutot* do not circulate.**

תָּנוּ רַבָּנַן: ״דְּהַב״ – אֵין פָּחוֹת מִדִּינָר דְּהַב; ״דְּהַב דִּינָרִין״ וְ״דִינָרִין דְּהַב״ – אֵין פָּחוֹת מִשְּׁנֵי דִּינָרִין דְּהַב; ״דְּהַב בְּדִינָרִין״ – אֵין פָּחוֹת מִבִּשְׁנֵי דִּינָרִין כֶּסֶף, דְּהַב.

The Sages taught in the continuation of the *baraita*: If it is written in a document that someone owes **gold,** the amount must be **no less than a golden dinar.** If it is written: **Golden dinars, or: Dinars golden,** the amount must be **no less than two golden dinars.** If it is written: **Gold, in dinars,** the amount must be **no less than two silver dinars'** worth **of gold.**

אָמַר מָר: ״דְּהַב״ – אֵין פָּחוֹת מִדִּינָר דְּהַב. אֵימָא: נַסְכָא! אָמַר רַבִּי אֶלְעָזָר: דִּכְתַב ״מַטְבֵּעַ״.

The Gemara analyzes the beginning of this section of the *baraita*. **The Master says:** If it is written in a document that someone owes **gold,** the amount must be **no less than a golden dinar.** The Gemara asks: But why not **say** that the intention of the word gold is not to a coin at all, but to a small **piece** of gold? **Rabbi Elazar said:** The case of the *baraita* is **where** the word **coin is written** in the document.

Perek **X**
Daf **166** Amud **a**

וְאֵימָא: פְּרִיטֵי! פְּרִיטֵי דְּדַהֲבָא לָא עָבְדִי אֱינָשֵׁי.

The Gemara asks further: **But** why not **say** that the intent is not a dinar, but smaller coins, such as *perutot*? The Gemara answers: **People do not make *perutot* of gold.**

״זָהָב בְּדִינָרִין״ – אֵין פָּחוֹת מִבִּשְׁנֵי דִּינָרִין כֶּסֶף, זָהָב. וְאֵימָא: דַּהֲבָא פְּרִיכָא בִּתְרֵי דִּינָרֵי דַּהֲבָא קָאָמַר! אָמַר אַבָּיֵי: יַד בַּעַל הַשְּׁטָר עַל הַתַּחְתּוֹנָה.

The Gemara continues its analysis of the *baraita*, which states: If it is written: **Gold, in dinars,** the amount must be **no less than two silver dinars'** worth **of gold.** The Gemara asks: **But** why not **say** that the document **is speaking of two golden dinars'** worth of **pieces of gold? Abaye says:** This interpretation is also possible, but the guiding principle in all interpretations of ambiguities is that **the holder of the document** is **at a disadvantage.**

רֵישָׁא דְּקָתָנֵי: ״כֶּסֶף בְּדִינָרִין״ – אֵין פָּחוֹת מִשְּׁנֵי דִּינָרִין זָהָב, כֶּסֶף; אַמַּאי? אֵימָא: כַּסְפָּא, נַסְכָא בִּתְרֵי דִּינָרֵי כַּסְפָּא קָאָמַר!

The Gemara asks a question from **the first clause** of the *baraita*, **which teaches** that if the document states: **Silver in dinars,** the amount must be **no less than two golden dinars'** worth **of silver. Why** is he entitled to so much? **Say** that the document **is speaking of silver** only, and means: **Two silver dinars'** worth of silver **pieces.** This interpretation would be a lower value than the interpretation assigned to it by the *baraita*, and would be in keeping with the principle that the holder of the document is at a disadvantage.

אָמַר רַב אַשִׁי: רֵישָׁא – דִּכְתַב ״דִּינָרֵי״, סֵיפָא – דִּכְתַב ״דִּינָרִין״.

Rav Ashi said in reply that the text of the *baraita* should be emended: In **the first clause** the case is **that** the scribe **wrote:** Silver in dinars, using the plural form ***dinarei***, which refers specifically to golden dinars. In **the latter clause,** the case is **that** the scribe **wrote:** Gold in dinars, using the plural form ***dinarin***,[H] which denotes silver dinars specifically.

HALAKHA

States that someone owes silver – אָמַר כֶּסֶף: If a document states: So-and-so borrowed silver from so-and-so, the debtor needs to pay only one small piece of silver, of the smallest unit of weight. In the case of a document that states that someone owes a silver coin, if there are *perutot* of silver in that place the debtor pays one silver *peruta*. If there are no *perutot* of silver in that place, he pays the silver coin of lowest value that circulates in that place (*Shulḥan Arukh, Ḥoshen Mishpat* 42:13).

HALAKHA

***Dinarei, dinarin* – דִּינָרֵי, דִּינָרִין:** If a promissory note states that someone owes: *Dinarei* silver, or: Silver *dinarei*, the creditor collects two silver dinars. All the more so, this is the *halakha* if the word *dinarin* is used instead of *dinarei* (see *Sma* and *Shakh*). If it states: Silver, in *dinarei*, he collects silver coins equal in value to two golden dinars. If it states: Gold, in *dinarei*, he collects gold pieces equal in value to two golden dinars. If it states: Silver, in *dinarin*, he collects pieces of silver equal in value to two silver dinars. If it states: Gold, in *dinarin*, or: *Dinarei* of gold, he collects two golden dinars. If it states: Gold, in *dinarin*, he collects gold with the value of two silver dinars, reflecting Rav Ashi's conclusion, that there is a distinction between the terms *dinarei* and *dinarin*. The Rema, citing the *Maggid Mishne*, writes that in contemporary parlance there is no difference between these two terms, and in any case the creditor collects the lowest of any possible interpretation of the terms of the note (Rambam *Sefer Mishpatim, Hilkhot Malve VeLoveh* 27:17; *Shulḥan Arukh, Ḥoshen Mishpat* 42:13, and in the comment of Rema).

וּמְנָא תֵּימְרָא דְּשָׁאנֵי בֵּין ״דִּינָרֵי״ לְ״דִינָרִין״?

The Gemara supports its assertion that there is a difference between these two plural forms: **And from where do you say that there is a difference between the words *dinarei* and *dinarin*?**

דְּתַנְיָא: הָאִשָּׁה שֶׁהָיוּ עָלֶיהָ סְפֵק חָמֵשׁ לֵידוֹת, סְפֵק חָמֵשׁ זִיבוֹת – מְבִיאָה קׇרְבָּן אֶחָד וְאוֹכֶלֶת בִּזְבָחִים, וְאֵין הַשְּׁאָר עָלֶיהָ חוֹבָה. הָיוּ עָלֶיהָ חָמֵשׁ לֵידוֹת וַדָּאוֹת, חָמֵשׁ זִיבוֹת וַדָּאוֹת – מְבִיאָה קׇרְבָּן אֶחָד וְאוֹכֶלֶת בִּזְבָחִים, וְהַשְּׁאָר עָלֶיהָ חוֹבָה;

This is **as it is taught** in a mishna (*Karetot* 8a): In the case of a **woman for whom there was uncertainty** with regard to **five births,**[HN] and likewise a woman for whom there was **uncertainty** with regard to **five** irregular **discharges** of blood from the uterus [*ziva*],[N] **she brings one offering, and** then **she may partake of** the meat of **offerings. And the remaining** offerings **are not an obligation for her.**[N] If she **has** in her case **five definite births** or **five definite discharges of a *zava*, she brings one offering, and** then **she may partake of** the meat of **offerings. And the remaining** offerings **are an obligation for her.**

מַעֲשֶׂה וְעָמְדוּ קִינִּים בִּירוּשָׁלַיִם בְּדִינְרֵי זָהָב, אָמַר רַבָּן שִׁמְעוֹן בֶּן גַּמְלִיאֵל: הַמָּעוֹן הַזֶּה! אִם אָלִין הַלַּיְלָה עַד שֶׁיְּהוּ בְּדִינָרִין; נִכְנַס לְבֵית דִּין וְלִימֵּד: הָאִשָּׁה שֶׁהָיוּ עָלֶיהָ חָמֵשׁ לֵידוֹת וַדָּאוֹת, חָמֵשׁ זִיבוֹת וַדָּאוֹת – מְבִיאָה קׇרְבָּן אֶחָד וְאוֹכֶלֶת בִּזְבָחִים, וְאֵין הַשְּׁאָר עָלֶיהָ חוֹבָה.

That mishna continues: There was **an incident where** the price **of nests,**[B] i.e., pairs of birds, **stood in Jerusalem at golden *dinarei*,** as the great demand for birds for the offerings of a woman after childbirth and a *zava* led to an increase in the price. **Rabban Shimon ben Gamliel said:** I take an oath by **this abode** of the Divine Presence that **I will not lie down tonight until** the price of nests **will be in *dinarin*.** Ultimately, **he entered the court and taught: A woman for whom there were five definite births** or **five definite discharges of a *zava* brings one offering, and** then **she may partake of** the meat of **offerings. And the remaining** offerings **are not an obligation for her.**

BACKGROUND

Nests – קִינִּים: There are various circumstances in which one is required to sacrifice a nest, consisting of two birds, either turtledoves or pigeons. One bird is sacrificed as a burnt-offering and the other as a sin-offering. A poor person who is required to bring a sliding-scale offering brings a bird pair (Leviticus 5:7–10), as does a poor woman after giving birth (Leviticus 12:8), a poor leper (Leviticus 14:22), and a *zav* or *zava* following their purification (Leviticus 15:29–30).

HALAKHA

In the case of a woman for whom there was uncertainty with regard to five births, etc. – הָאִשָּׁה שֶׁהָיוּ עָלֶיהָ סְפֵק חָמֵשׁ לֵידוֹת וכו׳: A woman who has had five incidents of uncertain birth or five incidents of uncertain discharges of a *zava* brings one purification offering, and thereafter she may partake of sacrificial meat; the remaining offerings are not obligatory for her. If she had five definite births or five definite discharges of a *zava*, she may partake of sacrificial meat after bringing just one offering, but in that case the remaining four offerings are obligatory for her. The Ra'avad disagrees, maintaining that even in the latter case the remaining offerings are not obligatory, in accordance with Rabban Shimon ben Gamliel's statement (Rambam *Sefer Korbanot*, *Hilkhot Meḥusrei Kappara* 1:10, and see *Kesef Mishne*, *Leḥem Mishne*, and *Mishne LaMelekh* there).

NOTES

Uncertainty with regard to five births – סְפֵק חָמֵשׁ לֵידוֹת: A woman after childbirth is required to bring a lamb or bird for a burnt-offering and a bird for a sin-offering (see Leviticus 12:6–8). Before bringing this offering, the woman would not be permitted to partake of sacrificial meat or enter the Temple grounds. A separate offering is required for each birth. This requirement applies to both a live birth and a miscarriage, provided the fetus reached a certain stage of development. The case described here is where a woman had five miscarriages, and in each case she was unsure if the miscarried fetus had reached the minimum stage of development. Since her obligation to bring the offerings is in question, one offering suffices for all five.

Uncertainty with regard to five irregular discharges of blood from the uterus [*ziva*] – סְפֵק חָמֵשׁ זִיבוֹת: Once a woman's menstrual period begins, any bleeding that occurs during the first seven days is considered menstrual blood; bleeding that takes place thereafter is considered a flow of *ziva*. If such *ziva* bleeding occurs on three consecutive days, then in order to achieve ritual purity the woman waits seven days after the bleeding ceases and brings an offering of one bird for a burnt-offering and another for a sin-offering (see Leviticus 15:29–30). Before bringing these offerings, the woman is not be permitted to partake of sacrificial meat or enter the Temple grounds. A separate set of offerings is required for each series of *ziva* bleeding. The case described here is where the woman experienced three days of bleeding five times, but was not sure if these incidents were within the first seven days of her menstrual period or after them. Since her obligation to bring the offerings is in question, one set of offerings suffices for all five.

And the remaining offerings are not an obligation for her – וְאֵין הַשְּׁאָר עָלֶיהָ חוֹבָה: It is forbidden to slaughter a non-sacrificial animal in the Temple courtyard; therefore, there is a principle that if there is uncertainty with regard to whether one is obligated to bring an offering, he should refrain from doing so, unless it is a type of offering that can be brought voluntarily. The exception to this *halakha* is a bird sin-offering. While a sin-offering may not be brought voluntarily, a bird sin-offering may be brought even in cases where there is uncertainty as to whether or not one is obligated to bring the offering. Nevertheless, the employment of this allowance is kept to a minimum, and for this reason only one set of offerings is brought for all five cases of uncertain childbirth or of uncertain *ziva*.

וְעָמְדוּ קִינִּין בּוֹ בַּיּוֹם בִּרְבָעְתַּיִם.

The mishna concludes: **And** as a result, the price of the **nests stood that day at one-quarter** of a silver dinar, as the demand for nests decreased. It is clear in the mishna that the term *dinarei* indicates a higher value than the term *dinarin*.

״כָּתוּב מִלְמַעְלָה״ וכו׳. תָּנוּ רַבָּנַן: יִלָּמֵד הַתַּחְתּוֹן מִן הָעֶלְיוֹן בְּאוֹת אַחַת, אֲבָל לֹא בִּשְׁתֵּי אוֹתִיּוֹת,

§ The mishna teaches: If it is **written** in the document **above** that someone owes one hundred dinars, and below it is written two hundred dinars, or if above it is written two hundred and below one hundred, everything follows the bottom amount. If so, why does one write the information in the upper part of the document at all? It is a safety measure, so that if one letter is erased from the lower part of the document, thereby rendering it illegible, the information can be learned from the upper part of the document. **The Sages taught** in a *baraita* (*Tosefta* 11:4): Information concerning what is written **below may be learned from** what is written **above** if the lower text is missing **one letter, but not** if it is missing **two letters.** In that case, in the event of a discrepancy between information written above and information written below, the document is not valid.

כְּגוֹן: ״חָנָן״ מֵ״חֲנָנִי״ וְ״עָנָן״ מֵ״עֲנָנִי״.

For example, if the name of one party is written as **Ḥanan** below and Ḥanani above, it may be derived **from** the word **Ḥanani** written above that the party is named Ḥanani. **And** similarly, if a name is written **Anan** below, it may be learned **from** the name **Anani** written above that the party is named Anani.

מַאי שְׁנָא שְׁתֵּי אוֹתִיּוֹת דְּלָא? דִּלְמָא מִיתַּרְמֵי שֵׁם בֶּן אַרְבַּע אוֹתִיּוֹת, וַהֲוָה לֵיהּ פַּלְגֵיהּ דִּשְׁמָא; אִי הָכִי, אוֹת אַחַת נַמִי – דִּלְמָא מִיתַּרְמֵי שֵׁם בֶּן שְׁתֵּי אוֹתִיּוֹת, וַהֲוָה לֵיהּ פַּלְגֵיהּ דִּשְׁמָא!

The Gemara asks: **What is different** about **two letters** missing, that the *baraita* teaches **that** the name written below **cannot** be corrected from the name written above? The Gemara suggests: It is out of concern that **perhaps** it will **occur** by chance that there is a **four-letter name, and** the omission of two letters **would be half of the name,** and for this reason the Sages extended this concern to all cases where two letters are missing. The Gemara challenges: **If so,** the same could be said when **one letter** is missing **as well,** as **perhaps** it will **occur** by chance that there is **a two-letter name, and** the omission of one letter **would be half of the name.**

אֶלָּא, שְׁתֵּי אוֹתִיּוֹת הַיְינוּ טַעְמָא – דִּלְמָא מִיתַּרְמֵי שֵׁם בֶּן שָׁלֹשׁ אוֹתִיּוֹת, וַהֲוָה לֵיהּ רוּבָּא דִּשְׁמָא.

The Gemara explains: **Rather, this is the reason** that when **two letters** are missing the name written below cannot be corrected from the name written above: The concern is that **perhaps** it will **occur** by chance that there is **a three-letter name, and** the omission of two letters **would be a majority of the name.** The Sages applied this concern to all cases where two letters are missing.

אָמַר רַב פַּפָּא: פְּשִׁיטָא לִי, ״סֵפֶל״ מִלְמַעְלָה וְ״קֶפֶל״ מִלְּמַטָּה – הַכֹּל הוֹלֵךְ אַחַר הַתַּחְתּוֹן.

The Gemara continues to discuss discrepancies between the information written above and below in a document. **Rav Pappa said:** It is **obvious to me** that if a document states **above** that one owes **a** ***sefel*****,**[N] a type of cup, **and below** it states ***kefel*****,**[NH] a type of garment, **everything is determined by the** information written **below.** In this case there is not a missing letter at the bottom but an altered letter. Therefore, the information written below is not corrected from the information written above.

בָּעֵי רַב פַּפָּא: ״קֶפֶל״ מִלְמַעְלָה וְ״סֵפֶל״ מִלְּמַטָּה, מַאי? מִי חָיְישִׁינַן לִזְבוּב, אוֹ לָא? תֵּיקוּ.

Rav Pappa raises a dilemma: What if it is stated ***kefel*** **above and** ***sefel*** **below?**[B] The difference between the two words is that the former begins with *kuf*, whereas the latter begins with *samekh*. The orthographical difference between these two letters is a single stroke that extends downward, as the omission of the extension of this stroke would change *kuf* into *samekh*. Rav Pappa's dilemma is: **Are we concerned for** the possibility that **a fly** landed on the stroke of the *kuf*, removing the ink and changing it into *samekh*? **Or** are we **not** concerned with this possibility? The Gemara comments: The dilemma **shall stand** unresolved.

NOTES

Sefel – סֵפֶל: The Rashbam understands the word *sefel* to mean cup, as it does in the Bible (see Judges 6:38). Rabbeinu Tam, cited in *Tosafot*, explains that the word is an abbreviation, composed of the letter *samekh*, meaning sixty, followed by an abbreviation of the word *palgei*, meaning halves. In a similar vein, Rabbeinu Ḥananel sees it as an abbreviation meaning a *se'a* and a half [*se'a ufalga*], and many other early commentaries follow this interpretation. Rabbi Yitzḥak Karkusha notes that in some Gemara manuscripts the words *sefel* and *kefel* have punctuation marks, indicating that they are abbreviations.

Kefel – קֶפֶל: The explanations given for this term parallel those for *sefel*. The Rashbam explains that it is a kind of garment, which can be folded [*mekupal*]. Others understand it to be referring to a kind of key or lock (Ra'avad). Rabbeinu Tam writes that the term is an abbreviation of the letter *kuf*, meaning one hundred, followed by an abbreviation of the word *palgei*, meaning halves, while Rabbeinu Ḥananel understands it to be an abbreviation for a *kav* and a half [*kav ufalga*].

HALAKHA

Sefel…kefel – סֵפֶל...קֶפֶל: If a document contains contradictory amounts owed, for example, when it is written above *sefel*, an abbreviation for one and one-half *se'a* (see *Sma*), and below *kefel*, an abbreviation for one and one-half *kav*, the correct amount is determined by the latter description; the holder of the document would collect only one and one-half *kav*. If *kefel* is written above and *sefel* below, the possibility is taken into account that a fly might have removed the extra stroke of ink that distinguishes between the two words (see *Sma*), and only one and one-half *kav* is collected. This follows the principle that the burden of proof rests upon the claimant, in this case the holder of the document. Therefore, since the Gemara states about this latter case that it shall stand unresolved, it is a case of uncertainty concerning liability, and no collection of the money in question is allowed (Rambam *Sefer Mishpatim, Hilkhot Malve VeLoveh* 27:15; *Shulḥan Arukh, Ḥoshen Mishpat* 42:7).

BACKGROUND

Kefel…sefel – קֶפֶל...סֵפֶל:

ק ס

Orthographical similarity between a *kuf* and a *samekh*

הַהוּא דַּהֲוָה כְּתַב בֵּיהּ ״שִׁית מְאָה וְזוּזָא״, שַׁלְחָהּ רַב שֵׁרֵבְיָא קַמֵּיהּ דְּאַבָּיֵי: שִׁית מְאָה אִיסְתֵּירֵי וְזוּזָא, אוֹ דִּלְמָא: שִׁית מְאָה פְּרִיטֵי וְזוּזָא? אֲמַר לֵיהּ: דַּל פְּרִיטֵי, דְּלָא כָּתְבִי בִּשְׁטָרָא, דְּאַסּוֹכֵי מַסְכָן לְהוּ

§ The Gemara relates: There was **a certain** document **in which it was written** that the amount due was **six hundred**[H] **and a dinar** without specifying to which denomination the six hundred amount referred. **Rav Sherevya sent** this question **before Abaye:** Does the holder of the document collect **six hundred *istira* and a dinar?** *Istira* is another name for a *sela*, which equals four dinars. **Or** is he **perhaps** entitled to collect only **six hundred *perutot* and a dinar,** a *peruta* being a small fraction of a dinar? Abaye **said to him: Remove** the possibility of six hundred ***perutot*, since** people **do not write** large numbers of *perutot* **in a document, as they** instead **combine them** into larger denominations

HALAKHA

A certain document in which it was written six hundred, etc. – הַהוּא דַּהֲוָה כְּתַב בֵּיהּ שִׁית מְאָה וכו׳: If a document lists an amount of money described with a number without citing a denomination, the local custom determines the meaning of the document. For example, in the case cited in the Gemara, where a document stated six hundred and a dinar, the possibility that the denomination is *perutot* can be ruled out, as it is not customary to record a large sum of *perutot* but rather to express such sums in terms of larger denominations. The highest and lowest remaining possibilities are six hundred *istira* or six hundred dinars and the lower of the two values is followed. Similarly, in any locality where certain expressions are used, even if these expressions are colloquial and not based on determinations made by the Sages, it is the local custom that determines the meaning of these expressions in a document (Rambam *Sefer Mishpatim, Hilkhot Malve VeLoveh* 27:15; *Shulḥan Arukh, Ḥoshen Mishpat* 42:15).

Perek **X**
Daf **167** Amud **a**

וּמְשַׁוֵּי לְהוּ זוּזֵי, מַאי אָמְרַתְּ? שִׁית מְאָה אִיסְתֵּירֵי וְזוּזָא, שִׁית מְאָה זוּזֵי וְחַד זוּזָא – יַד בַּעַל הַשְּׁטָר עַל הַתַּחְתּוֹנָה.

and change them into a smaller number of **dinars.** Therefore, **what can you say?** The highest and lowest remaining possibilities are: **Six hundred *istira* and a dinar,** and **six hundred dinars and one** more **dinar.** The guiding principle is that **the holder of the document** is **at a disadvantage,** and the lesser of these two values is assumed.

אֲמַר אַבָּיֵי: הַאי מַאן דְּבָעֵי לְמַחְוֵי חֲתִימוֹת יְדֵיהּ בְּבֵי דִינָא, לָא לַחְוֵי בְּסוֹף מְגִילְּתָא, דִּלְמָא מַשְׁכַּח לָהּ אַחֵר וְכָתֵיב דְּמַסִּיק בֵּיהּ זוּזֵי, וּתְנַן: הוֹצִיא עָלָיו כְּתַב יָדוֹ שֶׁהוּא חַיָּיב לוֹ – גּוֹבֶה מִנְּכָסִים בְּנֵי חוֹרִין.

§ **Abaye said:** With regard to **this one who needs to show his signature**[H] **in court** for the purpose of corroborating his signature on a document, he **should not show** it by writing it **at the end of the parchment, lest another,** unscrupulous, person **find** the parchment **and write** above the signature **that** the signatory **owes him money. And** such a document would be valid, as **we learned** in a mishna (175b): If one **presents to** a debtor a document in the **handwriting of** the debtor stating **that he owes** money **to him,** but without witnesses signed on the document, the creditor **can collect** only **from unsold property,**[B] i.e., property that is currently in the possession of the debtor.

HALAKHA

This one who needs to show his signature, etc. – הַאי מַאן דְּבָעֵי לְמַחְוֵי חֲתִימוֹת יְדֵיהּ וכו׳: If a claimant presents a handwritten note in which the one who wrote the note admits to owing the claimant money, the claimant can collect the debt from the writer of the note, albeit only from unsold property (see 175b). This *halakha* also applies if the note itself was written by a third party and the debtor signed it as well. If one's signature is at the top of a paper, and the text where the debt is recorded is written by a third party underneath the signature, the document is not valid, as it is possible that he signed his name when the paper was blank and another subsequently took advantage of the signature to write a false document (Rambam *Sefer Mishpatim, Hilkhot Malve VeLoveh* 11:3; *Shulḥan Arukh, Ḥoshen Mishpat* 69:1).

BACKGROUND

Unsold property – נְכָסִים בְּנֵי חוֹרִין: Unsold property stands in contrast to liened property. If a debtor sells his liened property, his creditor can repossess that property from the purchaser. The creditor cannot repossess this property from the purchaser if the debtor has property of his own, even if it is inferior in quality to the sold property.

הַהוּא בַּזְבִּינָא דַּאֲתָא לְקַמֵּיהּ דְּאַבָּיֵי, אֲמַר לֵיהּ: נֶיחֱזֵי לִי מָר חֲתִימוֹת יְדֵיהּ, דְּכִי אָתוּ רַבָּנַן מַחְווּ לִי – מַעֲבַרְנָא לְהוּ בְּלָא מִכְסָא. אַחֲוֵי לֵיהּ בְּרֵישׁ מְגִילְּתָא, הֲוָה קָא נָגֵיד בֵּיהּ, אֲמַר לֵיהּ: כְּבָר קְדָמוּךָ רַבָּנַן.

The Gemara relates: There was **a certain** Jewish **tax collector who came before Abaye** and **said to him: Let the Master show me his signature** on a piece of paper to keep in my records, **as when rabbis come** to me and **show me** a note with your signature on it, attesting to the fact that they are Torah scholars, **I let them pass without** paying the **tax. Abaye showed him** his signature **at the top of the parchment,** though the unscrupulous tax collector kept **pulling** the parchment away from Abaye so that the signature would be at the bottom. Abaye noticed this and **said to him: The Sages** have **already anticipated** people such as **you** and advised that one should never write his signature at the bottom of a paper.

אֲמַר אַבָּיֵי: מִתְּלָת וְעַד עֶשֶׂר לָא לִכְתּוֹב בְּסוֹף שִׁיטָה, דִּלְמָא מְזַיֵּיף וְכָתַב. וְאִי אִיתְרְמֵי לֵיהּ – נִיהַדְרֵיהּ לְדִבּוּרֵיהּ תְּרֵין תְּלָתָא זִימְנֵי, אִי אֶפְשָׁר דְּלָא מִיתְרְמֵי לֵיהּ בְּאֶמְצַע שִׁיטָה.

§ **Abaye said:** When writing a promissory note, one **should not write** any number **from three until ten at the end of a line, lest** someone **commit forgery and write** an extension to the number, since it is at the end of the line. In Hebrew and Aramaic, the words for the numbers three through nine can be changed to thirty through ninety, respectively, by appending to them the suffix *in*, written with the letters *yod* and *nun*. Ten can be changed to twenty in a similar manner. **And if** by chance **it occurs for him** that these numbers fall out at the end of a line, **he should repeat his words two** or **three times,** stating and restating the agreement in question, as **it is impossible that** the number will **not** eventually **occur for him in the middle of a line.** When there is a contradiction, it is the final mention of the amount that is authoritative, as the mishna teaches.

ההוא דהוה כתיב ביה "תילתא בפרדיסא", אזל מחקיה לגגיה דבי"ת וכרעיה, ושויה "ופרדיסא"; אתא לקמיה דאביי, אמר ליה: מאי טעמא רויח ליה עלמא להאי וי"ו? כפתיה ואודי.

The Gemara relates: There was **a certain** bill of sale **in which it was written** that the item sold was: In my garden, **one-third of the orchard.** The purchaser **went** and **erased the roof and the foot of the** ***beit***[B] of the term: Of the orchard [*befardeisa*], **and** thereby **changed** the prefix *beit* into a *vav*, yielding: In my garden one-third, **and the orchard [*ufardeisa*],** indicating that the sale included one-third of the garden in addition to all of the orchard. The document **came before Abaye,** who **said to** the purchaser: **What is the reason** that there is **so much space around this** ***vav*****?** Since the letter *vav* is narrower than the letter *beit*, a larger space between letters emerged as compared to the spacing of letters in the rest of the document. Abaye **bound** the purchaser,[N] i.e., he subjected him to physical coercion, **and he admitted**[H] to the forgery.

ההוא דהוה כתב ביה "מנת ראובן ושמעון אחי", הוה להו אחא דשמיה "אחי", אזל כתב ביה וי"ו, ושויה "ואחי"; אתא לקמיה דאביי, אמר ליה: מאי טעמא דחיק ליה עלמא להאי וי"ו כולי האי? כפתיה ואודי.

The Gemara relates: There was **a certain** bill of sale **in which it was written** that the item being sold was: **The portions of Reuven and Shimon, brothers [*aḥei*].** Reuven and Shimon happened to **have a brother whose name** was **Aḥai,** which, when writing without vowels, is spelled identically to *aḥei*. The purchaser **went** and **wrote** a conjunctive ***vav*** **in** the document before the word *aḥei*, **and changed** the wording into: The portions of Reuven and Shimon **and Aḥai.** The document **came before Abaye,** who **said to the** purchaser: **What is the reason** that it is **so crowded around this** ***vav*****?** By inserting the extra *vav*, a smaller space between letters emerged as compared to the spacing of letters in the rest of the document. Abaye **bound** the purchaser, i.e., he subjected him to physical coercion, **and he admitted** the forgery

ההוא שטרא דהוה חתים עליה רבא ורב אחא בר אדא, אתא לקמיה דרבא, אמר ליה: דין חתימות ידא דידי היא, מיהו קמיה דרב אחא בר אדא לא חתימי לי מעולם! כפתיה ואודי. אמר ליה: בשלמא דידי זייפת, אלא דרב אחא בר אדא דרתית ידיה, היכי עבדת? אמר: אנחי ידאי אמצרא, ואמרי לה: קם אזרנוקא וכתב.

The Gemara relates: There was **a certain document upon which** the signatures of **Rava and Rav Aḥa bar Adda**[P] **were signed.** The one holding the document **came before Rava,** who **said to him: This is my signature, but I never signed** any document **before Rav Aḥa bar Adda.**[N] Rava **bound** the holder of the document, i.e., he subjected him to physical coercion, **and he admitted** the forgery. Rava **said to him: Granted, you** were able to **forge my** signature, **but how did you perform** a forgery **of Rav Aḥa bar Adda's** signature, **since his hands shake** and as a result his signature is distinctive? The man **said: I placed my hands on** the rope **of a narrow footbridge [*amitzra*],**[L] and was thereby able to duplicate Rav Aḥa's signature. **And some say** that the forgery was accomplished when the forger **stood upon a wobbly water skin [*azarnuka*]**[L] **and wrote** the signature.

NOTES

Bound the purchaser – כפתיה: The Ramah understands from here that when a court suspects forgery in a document, a judge is permitted to subject the suspect to physical coercion to induce him to confess. Others explain that Abaye did not actually physically harm the suspect, as there was no proof of wrongdoing to justify physical punishment, but only threatened to do so, and it was the psychological pressure that induced him to admit the forgery (see Meiri).

But…before Rav Aḥa bar Adda, etc. – מיהו קמיה דרב אחא וכו׳: Some explain that Rava meant to say that he regarded Rav Aḥa bar Adda as his superior and would never have placed his signature on a document before that of Rav Aḥa bar Adda (Ramah; Meiri).

HALAKHA

Bound him, and he admitted – כפתיה ואודי: One of the precautions taken when writing or examining a document is that the narrow letters *vav* and *zayin* should not appear as if they are squeezed in, as in such a case there is a suspicion that they were added after the document was signed. Likewise, they should also not be spaced too broadly, as in that case there is a suspicion that a wider letter, such as *ḥet* or *heh*, was partially erased and reduced to the *vav* or *zayin*. In general, a scribe should be careful to write the entire document in a uniform style and with uniform spacing, so as to avoid the possibility of subsequent forgery. Consequently, witnesses should not sign a document in which these precautions were not taken, and a judge should not allow the use of such a document without careful clarification. It is permitted to exert pressure, even physical force, on one who produces a document that appears to have been forged. Some say that if the defendant does not claim that the document is forged, the document is not subjected to the aforementioned scrutiny. The Ramah comments that if the defendant is not present, e.g., in the case of a debt being collected from an heir or a third party, all possible suspicions of forgery are raised in favor of the party from whom collection is sought (Rambam *Sefer Mishpatim, Hilkhot Malve VeLoveh* 27:12; *Shulḥan Arukh, Ḥoshen Mishpat* 42:3).

BACKGROUND

Erased the roof and the foot of the *beit* – מחקיה לגגיה דבי"ת וכרעיה:

The letter *beit* made to look like *vav* through partial erasure

PERSONALITIES

Rav Aḥa bar Adda – רב אחא בר אדא: Rav Aḥa bar Adda, a second- and third-generation Babylonian *amora*, apparently lived early enough to study under the great *amora* Rav, as he transmits statements in the latter's name, although it appears that he was mainly a student of Rav's disciples, Rav Hamnuna and Rav Yehuda. It seems that he lived for a time in Eretz Yisrael, and upon his return to Babylonia he transmitted several statements he had heard from the Sages of Eretz Yisrael. Rav Aḥa bar Adda lived a very long life, and was still active in the time of the great fourth-generation *amora*, Rava. His son, Rav Pappa, is also mentioned in the Talmud.

LANGUAGE

Narrow footbridge [*mitzra*] – מצרא: The literal meaning of this term is narrow passage, but was used in practice to denote a particular type of bridge, as follows: Sometimes, to enable passage over a stream, instead of a proper bridge, two ropes would be fastened on either side of the waterway and suspended over it. A person would walk on one of the ropes while grasping the other as a sort of railing. This rope would naturally shake and sway when people were on it.

Water skin [*zarnuka*] – זרנוקא: Possibly related to the Arabic زرنوق, *zurnūq*, meaning a water channel or stream. In the Sages' parlance it refers to a water skin, which functioned as a canteen for transporting water.

MISHNA

מתני׳ כּוֹתְבִין גֵּט לָאִישׁ אַף עַל פִּי שֶׁאֵין אִשְׁתּוֹ עִמּוֹ, וְהַשּׁוֹבֵר לָאִשָּׁה – אַף עַל פִּי שֶׁאֵין בַּעְלָהּ עִמָּהּ, וּבִלְבַד שֶׁיְּהֵא מַכִּירָן. וְהַבַּעַל נוֹתֵן שָׂכָר.

MISHNA A scribe may **write a bill of divorce for a man**[H] who requests one, **even if his wife is not with him** to give her consent when he presents his request, as there is no possibility that he will misuse the document. **And** a scribe may write **a receipt for a woman**[NH] upon her request, attesting to the payment of her marriage contract, **even if her husband is not with her** to give his consent. This is true **provided that** the scribe **recognizes** the parties requesting the document, to prevent misrepresentation. **And** for both documents, **the husband gives** the scribe his **wages.**[H]

NOTES

And a receipt for a woman, etc. – וְהַשּׁוֹבֵר לָאִשָּׁה וכו׳: The receipt is for the benefit of the husband, as it exempts him from further payment of the marriage contract, and the guiding principle is that one can act in a person's interest in his absence. By contrast, having the receipt written before the husband is ready to pay the woman the value of her marriage contract is detrimental for the wife for the same reason, and for this reason her request or consent is required in order for it to be written. Thereafter she will have to be careful not to lose the receipt so that it not fall into the possession of the husband, who would then be able to use it to claim that he had already paid the marriage contract.

HALAKHA

A scribe may write a bill of divorce for a man, etc. – כּוֹתְבִין גֵּט לָאִישׁ וכו׳: If a man requests a bill of divorce, one may be written for him even if his wife is not present, provided that the witnesses who sign the bill of divorce know that the names therein are the correct names of the one requesting the bill of divorce and his wife. The Rema adds, citing the *Tur*, that there are some who require that the scribe also know that the names in the bill of divorce are correct (Rambam *Sefer Mishpatim*, *Hilkhot Malve VeLoveh* 24:1 and *Sefer Nashim*, *Hilkhot Geirushin* 2:3; *Shulḥan Arukh*, *Even HaEzer* 120:3).

And a receipt for a woman, etc. – וְהַשּׁוֹבֵר לָאִשָּׁה וכו׳: A receipt may be written on a woman's behalf stating that she has received the payment of her marriage contract, even if her husband is not present with her, as such a document benefits the husband, and one can act in another's interest in his absence. It is noted in *Ḥelkat Meḥokek* that this is the *halakha* provided that the scribe knows both the woman and her husband (Rambam *Sefer Mishpatim*, *Hilkhot Malve VeLoveh* 24:1–2; *Shulḥan Arukh*, *Even HaEzer* 110:1).

The husband gives his wages – הַבַּעַל נוֹתֵן שָׂכָר: When a receipt of payment of a marriage contract is written for a woman, the husband pays the scribe for his work. If the reason she requests the receipt is that she lost her marriage contract, it is she who must pay his wages (see *Beit Shmuel*). With regard to a bill of divorce, it is the woman who pays the scribe's wages, in accordance with the conclusion in the Gemara (Rambam *Sefer Mishpatim*, *Hilkhot Malve VeLoveh* 24:1 and *Sefer Nashim*, *Hilkhot Geirushin* 2:3; *Shulḥan Arukh*, *Even HaEzer* 110:1, 120:3).

Perek **X**
Daf **167** Amud **b**

כּוֹתְבִין שְׁטָר לַלֹּוֶה אַף עַל פִּי שֶׁאֵין מַלְוֶה עִמּוֹ, וְאֵין כּוֹתְבִין לַמַּלְוֶה עַד שֶׁיְּהֵא לֹוֶה עִמּוֹ וְהַלֹּוֶה נוֹתֵן שָׂכָר.

A scribe may **write** a promissory **note for a debtor**[NH] who requests one, **even if** the **creditor is not with him** when he requests the document, **but** a scribe may **not write** a promissory note **for a creditor** who requests it **unless** the **debtor is with him** and consents. **And** it is **the debtor** who **gives** the scribe his **wages.**

כּוֹתְבִין שְׁטָר לַמּוֹכֵר אַף עַל פִּי שֶׁאֵין לוֹקֵחַ עִמּוֹ, וְאֵין כּוֹתְבִין לַלּוֹקֵחַ עַד שֶׁיְּהֵא מוֹכֵר עִמּוֹ; וְהַלּוֹקֵחַ נוֹתֵן שָׂכָר.

A scribe may **write a bill** of sale **for a seller**[H] of a field who requests one **even if the purchaser is not with him** when he presents his request, **but** a scribe may **not write** a bill of sale **for a purchaser** who requests it **unless the seller is with him** and consents. **And** it is **the purchaser** who **gives** the scribe his **wages.**[H]

NOTES

A scribe may write a promissory note for a debtor – כּוֹתְבִין שְׁטָר לַלֹּוֶה: At times, a prospective debtor might desire to have a promissory note prepared in advance, so that he will be able to borrow money from the prospective creditor as soon as he meets him, without delay. The early commentaries note that in tractate *Bava Metzia* (13a) the Gemara clarifies that the writing of promissory notes in advance is permitted only when the note contains a clause indicating an immediate lien on the debtor's property, regardless of the actual date of the loan.

HALAKHA

A scribe may write a promissory note for a debtor, etc. – כּוֹתְבִין שְׁטָר לַלֹּוֶה וכו׳: A scribe may write a promissory note for a debtor who requests one, even if the creditor recorded in the document is not present, provided that the identity of the debtor making the request is established. The identity of the creditor need not be established (*Sma*). This applies only when the document contains a clause indicating that the debtor's real estate is liened to the creditor immediately, irrespective of the date when the loan actually takes place (Rema; see *Shakh*). If the document does not contain such a clause, the document may not be written at the debtor's request, even if the creditor is present, and even if the transfer of the loaned money is witnessed, unless the document is immediately handed over to the creditor or to someone else acting on his behalf (*Sma*, citing *Nimmukei Yosef*). This is because a promissory note whose specification of the date on which the loan is given predates that of the actual loan is not valid, and it is prohibited for a creditor to possess the document before the loan is granted. If the creditor explicitly protests, the document may not be written (Rema, citing Rashba).

A scribe may not write a promissory note at the request of a creditor without the consent of the debtor. Even if a creditor requests that a document be written and then entrusted to the court or witnesses for safekeeping until the debtor authorizes its transfer to the creditor, the request may not be honored. All this reflects the conclusion of the Gemara in *Bava Metzia* 13a (Rambam *Sefer Mishpatim*, *Hilkhot Malve VeLoveh* 23:5; *Shulḥan Arukh*, *Ḥoshen Mishpat* 39:13, and see 49:2).

A scribe may write a bill of sale for a seller, etc. – כּוֹתְבִין שְׁטָר לַמּוֹכֵר וכו׳: A scribe may write a bill of sale for one who is selling a field even if the purchaser is not present. Some say that this is the *halakha* only if the seller states that he has already received the money for the sale (Ri Migash). The scribe may write the bill of sale only if the sale takes place through an act of acquisition immediately by means of a third party, in the presence of the court, or if the seller states that such acquisition has already taken place. The reason is that if the sale will take place at a later date, the purchaser, holding an antedated document, would have an unfair advantage over others who lay claim to the property. The scribe may write the bill only if the witnesses who sign it know that the recorded names of the seller and purchaser correspond to their true names (see *Sma*). A scribe may not write a bill of sale at the request of the purchaser without the consent of the seller. The Ramban rules that even if witnesses testify that a sale has taken place, a scribe may not write a bill of sale at the purchaser's request, because it is not automatically assumed that the seller desires that the sale be recorded in writing (Rambam *Sefer Mishpatim*, *Hilkhot Malve VeLoveh* 23:1; *Shulḥan Arukh*, *Ḥoshen Mishpat* 238:1, 3).

And it is the purchaser who gives the wages – וְהַלּוֹקֵחַ נוֹתֵן שָׂכָר: The expenses involved in writing a bill of sale are borne by the purchaser, even if the seller is anxious to sell the property, in accordance with the conclusion of the Gemara (Rambam *Sefer Mishpatim*, *Hilkhot Malve VeLoveh* 23:2 and *Sefer Kinyan*, *Hilkhot Mekhira* 30:1; *Shulḥan Arukh*, *Ḥoshen Mishpat* 238:2).

אֵין כּוֹתְבִין שִׁטְרֵי אֵירוּסִין וְנִשּׂוּאִין אֶלָּא מִדַּעַת שְׁנֵיהֶם, וְהֶחָתָן נוֹתֵן שָׂכָר.

A scribe may **not write documents of betrothal and** documents of **marriage**[HB] **except with the consent of both** parties, the groom and the bride. **And** it is **the groom** who **gives** the scribe his **wages.**[H]

אֵין כּוֹתְבִין שְׁטַר אֲרִיסוּת וְקַבְּלָנוּת אֶלָּא מִדַּעַת שְׁנֵיהֶם, וְהַמְקַבֵּל נוֹתֵן שָׂכָר.

A scribe may **not write contracts for sharecroppers and contractors**[HN] **except with the consent of both** parties, i.e., the sharecropper or contractor and the one who hires him. **And** it is **the** sharecropper or **contractor** who **gives** the scribe his **wages.**

אֵין כּוֹתְבִין שִׁטְרֵי בֵירוּרִין וְכָל מַעֲשֵׂה בֵית דִּין אֶלָּא מִדַּעַת שְׁנֵיהֶם, וּשְׁנֵיהֶם נוֹתְנִין שָׂכָר; רַבָּן שִׁמְעוֹן בֶּן גַּמְלִיאֵל אוֹמֵר: לִשְׁנֵיהֶם כּוֹתְבִין שְׁנַיִם, לָזֶה לְעַצְמוֹ וְלָזֶה לְעַצְמוֹ.

A scribe may **not write documents** testifying to **arbitration** agreements **or any** other **court enactment**[N] **except with the consent of both** parties to the litigation. **And both** parties **give** the scribe his **wages. Rabban Shimon ben Gamliel says:** The scribe **writes two** documents **for the two** parties, one **for this** one **by himself, and** one **for that** one **by himself.**

גמ׳ מַאי ״וּבִלְבַד שֶׁיְּהֵא מַכִּירָן״? אָמַר רַב יְהוּדָה אָמַר רַב: וּבִלְבַד שֶׁיְּהֵא מַכִּיר שֵׁם הָאִישׁ בַּגֵּט וְשֵׁם הָאִשָּׁה בַּשּׁוֹבֵר.

GEMARA What is meant by: **Provided that** the scribe **recognizes** the parties requesting the document? **Rav Yehuda says** that **Rav says:** It means **provided that he recognizes the man's name in the** case of **the bill of divorce and the woman's name in** the case of **the receipt.**

יָתֵיב רַב סָפְרָא וְרַב אַחָא בַּר הוּנָא וְרַב הוּנָא בַּר חִינָּנָא, וְיָתֵיב אַבָּיֵי גַּבַּיְיהוּ, וְיָתְבִי וְקָמִיבַּעְיָא לְהוּ: שֵׁם הָאִישׁ בַּגֵּט – אִין, שֵׁם הָאִשָּׁה לָא? שֵׁם הָאִשָּׁה בַּשּׁוֹבֵר – אִין, שֵׁם הָאִישׁ לָא?

The Gemara relates: **Rav Safra**[P] **and Rav Aḥa bar Huna and Rav Huna bar Ḥinnana were sitting, and Abaye**[P] was **sitting near them. And** as **they were sitting, they raised a dilemma:** Did Rav mean that with regard to **the man's name in the** case of bill of divorce **bill, yes,** it must be known to the scribe, but **the woman's name** need **not** be known to the scribe? And did he mean that with regard to **the woman's name in** the case of **the receipt, yes,** it must be known to the scribe, but **the man's name** need **not** be known to the scribe?

וְלֵיחוּשׁ דִּלְמָא כָּתַב גִּיטָּא וְאָזֵיל וּמַמְטֵי לֵיהּ לְאִיתְּתֵיהּ דְּהַיאךְ,

But if so, **let** there be **a concern** that **perhaps** the man who made the request **writes the bill of divorce and** intends **to go and give it to the wife of another** man with the same name.

NOTES

Sharecroppers and contractors – אֲרִיסוּת וְקַבְּלָנוּת: A sharecropping arrangement is an agreement between a landowner and an individual who undertakes to work his field in exchange for a percentage of the crops. A contractor is one who pays a set amount to the landowner for the right to work the field and keep all of the crops for himself. Since the contract between these workers and the landowner obligates both of them, both parties must give their consent in order for the document to be written (Ri Migash).

Or any other court enactment – וְכָל מַעֲשֵׂה בֵית דִּין: The commentaries explain, based on the Gemara elsewhere (*Bava Metzia* 16b), that this is referring to documents with which the court allows a creditor to seize the property of a defaulting debtor [*adrakhta*], or documents with which the court vouches for the creditor's right to occupy the property he collected for the debt [*haltata*], or other documents of a similar nature. The reason consent of both parties is required is that there is a concern that the debtor might have paid off his debt after the court instructed that the document be written, and the *adrakhta* would thereby enable the creditor to seize his property unjustly (Ramah).

PERSONALITIES

Rav Safra – רַב סָפְרָא: Rav Safra was a third- and fourth-generation *amora* in Babylonia. The Talmud records that Rav Safra discussed halakhic matters as a student and colleague with the greatest Sages of the third generation of *amora'im*, such as Rabba and Rav Yosef, and he continued to teach in the time of their students, Abaye and Rava. Apparently Rav Safra was a merchant and visited Eretz Yisrael, where he interacted with Sages such as Rabbi Abba and Rabbi Abbahu. His primarily expertise was in the area of *halakha*, and he did not devote himself to the study of *aggada* or Bible. Rav Safra was also renowned for his exemplary character, particularly his desire to entirely avoid falsehood. Because he was an itinerant merchant, he never established his own yeshiva and was not a constant presence in the study hall. Therefore some Sages maintained that he did not have the status of one whom the *halakha* requires that all must mourn his passing.

Abaye – אַבָּיֵי: One of the outstanding Sages of the Talmud, Abaye was a fourth-generation Babylonian *amora*. Abaye was orphaned at the time of his birth and raised by his paternal uncle, Rabba. Some say that his real name was Naḥmani or Kelil, and that Abaye was a nickname.

Abaye was the primary student of Rabba and of Rav Yosef. After Rav Yosef's death, Abaye succeeded him as the head of the yeshiva in Pumbedita. In addition to Abaye's prominence as a Torah scholar, he was known for his righteousness and his acts of kindness.

Abaye's exchanges and halakhic arguments with his uncle and, even more so, with Rav Yosef, can be found throughout the Talmud. His disputes with his colleague Rava are especially significant. These disputes, known as the discussions of Abaye and Rava, are examples of profound and edifying disputes and are among the foundations of the Babylonian Talmud. In these disputes, with six exceptions, the *halakha* is ruled in accordance with the opinion of Rava.

HALAKHA

Documents of betrothal and marriage – שִׁטְרֵי אֵירוּסִין וְנִשּׂוּאִין: A scribe may not write a document of betrothal without the bride's consent. If a scribe did so, and it is used to effect the betrothal, it is uncertain if the woman is betrothed (Rambam *Sefer Mishpatim, Hilkhot Malve VeLoveh* 23:2 and *Sefer Nashim, Hilkhot Ishut* 3:4; *Shulḥan Arukh, Even HaEzer* 32:1, and see *Ḥelkat Meḥokek* and *Beit Shmuel* there, and see 51:1, and in the comment of Rema).

And it is the groom who gives the wages – וְהֶחָתָן נוֹתֵן שָׂכָר: The expenses involved in writing a document that records the amounts the groom and bride or their parents undertake to bring to the marriage are borne by the groom, even if he is a Torah scholar (*Beit Shmuel*), in accordance with the conclusion of the Gemara. If a copy of the document is written up for each of the two parties, each party pays the scribe for his copy (*Shulḥan Arukh, Even HaEzer* 51:1, and in the comment of Rema).

Contracts for sharecroppers and contractors – שְׁטַר אֲרִיסוּת וְקַבְּלָנוּת: A scribe may not write a contract for a sharecropping agreement without the consent of both the landowner and the sharecropper, since a written document binds both sides and prevents them from reneging on their agreements. The expenses involved in writing the contract are borne by the sharecropper, even if he will receive no payment in the current year, in accordance with the conclusion of the Gemara (Rambam *Sefer Mishpatim, Hilkhot Malve VeLoveh* 23:1; *Shulḥan Arukh, Ḥoshen Mishpat* 320:2, and in the comment of Rema, and see *Sma* there).

BACKGROUND

Betrothal and marriage – אֵירוּסִין וְנִשּׂוּאִין: There is a two-stage process through which a man and a woman become husband and wife. Betrothal is the first stage of the marriage process. The bond created by betrothal is so strong that a betrothed woman must be divorced before she can marry another man. Similarly, intercourse with other men is considered adulterous and is punishable by death. Nevertheless, a betrothed couple may not yet live together as husband and wife, and most of the couple's mutual obligations do not yet apply.

Marriage is effected by the bride and groom coming under the bridal canopy together, symbolizing their union. This immediately confers the privileges and the responsibilities associated with marriage upon the newlywed couple, including all of the monetary rights and obligations applying to married couples. After marriage, if one spouse dies, all the *halakhot* of mourning for a close blood relative apply to the surviving spouse. If the wife of a priest dies, it is permitted for him to become ritually impure to bury her. Today, betrothal and marriage are performed in a single ceremony, but in the talmudic period there was usually a yearlong gap between the two stages.

וְזִמְנִין אָזְלָא כָּתְבָה אִשָּׁה שׁוֹבֵר וְיָהֲבָה לְגַבְרָא דְּלָאו דִּילַהּ!

And similarly, in the case of the receipt let there be a concern that there will be **times** when **the woman writes** the **receipt and** intends to **give** it **to a man who is not her** husband, whose wife shares her name.

אֲמַר לְהוּ אַבָּיֵי, הָכִי אָמַר רַב: שֵׁם הָאִישׁ בַּגֵּט, וְהוּא הַדִּין לְשֵׁם הָאִשָּׁה; שֵׁם הָאִשָּׁה בַּשּׁוֹבֵר, וְהוּא הַדִּין לְשֵׁם הָאִישׁ.

Abaye said to them: You are not understanding Rav's statement correctly. **This** is what **Rav says: The man's name in** the case of **the bill of divorce** must be known to the scribe, **and the same is true of the woman's name,** which must also be known to the scribe. And **the woman's name in** the case of **the receipt** must be known to the scribe, **and the same is true of the man's name,** which must also be known to the scribe.

וְלֵיחוּשׁ לִשְׁנֵי יוֹסֵף בֶּן שִׁמְעוֹן הַדָּרִים בְּעִיר אַחַת, דִּלְמָא כָּתֵיב גִּיטָּא וְאָזֵיל וּמַמְטֵי לֵיהּ לְאִיתְּתֵיהּ דְּהֵיאָךְ! אֲמַר לְהוּ רַב אַחָא בַּר הוּנָא, הָכִי אָמַר רַב: שְׁנֵי יוֹסֵף בֶּן שִׁמְעוֹן הַדָּרִים בְּעִיר אַחַת, אֵין מְגָרְשִׁין נְשׁוֹתֵיהֶן אֶלָּא זֶה בִּפְנֵי זֶה.

They continued their line of questioning: **And** even if both names are known to the scribe, **let** there be **a concern for** the possibility of **two** men with the same name, such as two men named **Yosef ben Shimon, who live in one city**[H] and whose wives share the same name as well, and **perhaps** the man who made the request will **write the bill of divorce and** intend to **go and give it to the wife of the other** man who bears the same name as him. **Rav Aḥa bar Huna said to them** in reply that **this** is what **Rav says:** If there are **two** men named **Yosef ben Shimon who live in one city** and are married to women who share the same name, **they may divorce their wives only in the presence of one another.**

וְלֵיחוּשׁ דִּלְמָא אָזֵיל לְמָתָא אַחֲרִיתָא וּמַחְזֵיק לֵיהּ לִשְׁמֵיהּ בְּיוֹסֵף בֶּן שִׁמְעוֹן, וְכָתֵיב גִּיטָּא וּמַמְטֵי לֵיהּ לְאִיתְּתֵיהּ דְּהֵיאָךְ!

They continued to ask: **But** even if the scribe knows the man's name and the name of the man's wife, **let** there be **a concern** that **perhaps** someone will **go to another city and establish** a false **name for himself as Yosef ben Shimon, and** he **will write the bill of divorce and give it to the wife of the other** man, whose name really is Yosef ben Shimon.

אֲמַר לְהוּ רַב הוּנָא בַּר חִינָּנָא, הָכִי אָמַר רַב: כׇּל שֶׁהוּחְזַק שְׁמוֹ בָּעִיר שְׁלֹשִׁים יוֹם – אֵין חוֹשְׁשִׁין לוֹ.

Rav Huna bar Ḥinnana said to them that **this** is what **Rav says:** With regard to **anyone whose name has been established in a city** for **thirty days,**[H] there is **no concern** harbored **about him** that his name is false. It is assumed that this is his true name.

לָא אִיתְחֲזַק, מַאי? אָמַר אַבָּיֵי: דְּקָרוּ לֵיהּ וְעָנֵי. רַב זְבִיד אָמַר: רַמָּאָה בְּרַמָּאוּתֵיהּ זָהִיר.

They continued to ask: **What** if his name has **not** been **established** for thirty days? How can a newcomer in a town have a bill of divorce drawn up for him? **Abaye said:** It is sufficient **that** people **call him** by the name he claims for himself **and he responds**[H] to that call. **Rav Zevid said: A liar is careful about** upholding **his lies,** and just because he responds to being called by a particular name does not prove he is telling the truth. A newcomer would therefore have to wait thirty days before requesting that a scribe write him a bill of divorce.

HALAKHA

Two people with the same name, such as Yosef ben Shimon, who live in one city – שְׁנֵי יוֹסֵף בֶּן שִׁמְעוֹן הַדָּרִים בְּעִיר אַחַת: If two men with identical names live in the same city, and they are married to women with identical names, neither couple may divorce unless the other couple is present. The concern is that one of the husbands may fraudulently write a divorce document for the other man's wife. Even if one of the two wives has a bill of divorce in her possession, it is not considered proof of divorce unless she proves that her husband divorced her in the presence of the other couple of the same name or produces witnesses who saw her receive the document from her own husband (Rema). The Rema adds that there are some who say that even if the names of the wives are not identical, if the names of the husbands are identical, the scribe should include a unique identifying feature of the divorcing man, such as if he is a priest, or a nickname. The custom of giving a bill of divorce in public developed out of a concern that there might be another couple in town with the same names as the divorcing couple (Rambam *Sefer Nashim, Hilkhot Geirushin* 2:3; *Shulḥan Arukh, Even HaEzer* 120:3 and 136:1, and in the comment of Rema).

Anyone whose name has been established in a city for thirty days – כׇּל שֶׁהוּחְזַק שְׁמוֹ בָּעִיר שְׁלֹשִׁים יוֹם: If one's name has been established in a city for thirty days, that name may be used in writing a bill of divorce or any other document for him. At that point there is longer any concern that he has assumed a false name in order to engage in fraudulent behavior (Rambam *Sefer Mishpatim, Hilkhot Malve VeLoveh* 24:4; *Shulḥan Arukh, Ḥoshen Mishpat* 49:3 and *Even HaEzer* 136:1, and in the comment of Rema).

That people call him and he responds – דְּקָרוּ לֵיהּ וְעָנֵי: In the case of one who arrives in a location and calls himself by a particular name, and a document is written in that name that obligates him financially, and he later claims that it is, in fact, not his real name and the document should not obligate him financially, if he answers to this name when he is called it is assumed that it is his real name, even if he has not been settled in the town for thirty days (*Shulḥan Arukh, Ḥoshen Mishpat* 49:4).

ההוא תַּבְרָא דַּהֲוָה חָתִים עֲלַהּ רַב יִרְמְיָה בַּר אַבָּא, אֲתָא לְקַמֵּיהּ הַהִיא אִיתְּתָא, אֲמַרָה לֵיהּ: לָאו אֲנָא הֲוַאי, אֲמַר: אֲנָא נַמִי אֲמַרִי לְהוּ לָאו אִיהִי הִיא, וַאֲמַרוּ לִי: מֵיקַשׁ הוּא דְּקַשְׁאָ לַהּ וּבְגַר לַהּ קָלָא;

§ There was **a certain receipt** of payment of a marriage contract **upon which Rav Yirmeya bar Abba was signed** as a witness. **That woman,** whose name matched the name on the receipt, **came before** Rav Yirmeya, seeking to collect payment of her marriage contract. Rav Yirmeya recognized her name, but not her appearance. The woman **said to him: It was not I** whose name was on the receipt that you signed, but another woman with the same name; I have not collected payment of my marriage contract. Rav Yirmeya **said: I, too, said to** the other witnesses signed on the document: The woman for whom we signed the receipt **is not she. But they said to me:** It is in fact the same woman, but **she has aged and her voice has matured** and changed, and that is why you do not recognize her.

אֲמַר אַבַּיֵי, אַף עַל גַּב דַּאֲמוּר רַבָּנַן:

Abaye said that **although the Sages said:**

Perek **X**
Daf **168** Amud **a**

כֵּיוָן שֶׁהִגִּיד שׁוּב אֵינוֹ חוֹזֵר וּמַגִּיד – צוּרְבָא מֵרַבָּנַן לָאו אוֹרְחֵיהּ לְמֵידַק.

Once one **has stated** his testimony **he may not then state a revision,** this case of Rav Yirmeya is an exception, and he can retract his initial statement in which he supported the woman's claim. The reason is that **it is not the manner of a Torah scholar to be careful**[NH] about identifying women, for reasons of modesty.

ההוא תַּבְרָא דַּהֲוָה חָתִים עֲלֵיהּ רַב יִרְמְיָה בַּר אַבָּא, אֲמַרָה לֵיהּ: לָאו אֲנָא הֲוַאי, אֲמַר לַהּ: אִיבְרָא אַנְתְּ הֲוַת. אֲמַר אַבַּיֵי: אַף עַל גַּב דְּצוּרְבָא מֵרַבָּנַן לָאו אוֹרְחֵיהּ לְמֵידַק, כֵּיוָן דְּדָדֵיק – דָּק.

The Gemara relates: There was **a certain receipt** of payment for a marriage contract **upon which Rav Yirmeya bar Abba was signed.** A woman whose name appeared on the receipt, who was seeking to collect payment of her marriage contract, **said to him: It was not I,** but another woman with the same name, who had this receipt written. **He said to her: But it was you,** and you are lying now. **Abaye said: Although** I said that **it is not the manner of a Torah scholar to** be **careful** about identifying women, **once he is careful** about such an identification and states positively that he recognizes a particular woman, **he is careful.**[N]

אֲמַר אַבַּיֵי: הַאי צוּרְבָא מֵרַבָּנַן דְּאָזֵיל לְקַדּוּשֵׁי אִיתְּתָא, נִידְבַּר עַם הָאָרֶץ בַּהֲדֵיהּ, דִּלְמָא מְחַלְּפוּ לַהּ מִינֵּיהּ.

Abaye said: A Torah scholar who goes to betroth a woman should take an ignoramus with him to establish a positive identity of the woman, **lest** people **exchange** another woman for **her** when given to **him** for marriage, taking advantage of his innocence.

"וְהַבַּעַל נוֹתֵן שָׂכָר" וכו׳. מַאי טַעְמָא? דְּאָמַר קְרָא: "וְכָתַב...וְנָתַן". וְהָאִידָּנָא דְּלָא עָבְדִינַן הָכִי, שַׁדְיוּהוּ רַבָּנַן אַאִשָּׁה כִּי הֵיכִי דְּלָא לְשַׁהְיֵיהּ.

§ The mishna teaches that **the husband gives** the scribe's **wages** for writing a bill of divorce. The Gemara asks: **What is the reason** for this? The Gemara answers: **As the verse states:** "When a man takes a wife and marries her, and it comes to pass, if she finds no favor in his eyes, because he has found some unseemly matter in her, **he shall write** her a scroll of severance **and give** it in her hand" (Deuteronomy 24:1). It is therefore the husband's responsibility to have the bill of divorce written. The Gemara adds: **But today,** the reason **that we do not do so,** but instead have the woman pay the scribe, is that **the Sages placed** the burden **upon the woman,**[H] **so that** the husband **should not delay** the divorce by refusing to pay the scribe.

"כּוֹתְבִין שְׁטָר לַלֹּוֶה אַף עַל פִּי שֶׁאֵין מַלְוֶה עִמּוֹ" וכו׳. פְּשִׁיטָא! לָא צְרִיכָא, בְּעִיסְקָא.

The mishna teaches: A scribe may **write** a promissory **note for a debtor** who requests one, **even if** the **creditor is not with him,** and it is the debtor who gives the scribe his wages. The Gemara asks: Isn't it **obvious** that the debtor pays the wages? After all, he is the beneficiary of the loan. The Gemara answers: **No,** it is **necessary** for the mishna to state this, as there are times when the loan is beneficial to the creditor as well, as **in** a case of **a joint venture,** where the creditor receives a share of the profits engendered by the money provided to the borrower (see *Bava Metzia* 104a).

NOTES

It is not the manner of a Torah scholar to be careful – צוּרְבָא מֵרַבָּנַן לָאו אוֹרְחֵיהּ לְמֵידַק: The commentaries discuss the limits of this statement, but the most likely explanation is that of the Rashbam. He understands the Gemara to be referring specifically to the identification of women, as for reasons of modesty it is not usual for Torah scholars to gaze at women to familiarize themselves with their appearance. Therefore, if a Torah scholar changes his mind with regard to the identification of a woman, it is not considered to be a retraction of testimony. The Ba'al HaMaor in tractate *Rosh HaShana* generalizes this principle, and states that whenever a situation arises in which a witness's testimony was based on a readily understandable mistake, it may be retracted.

Once he is careful, he is careful – כֵּיוָן דְּדָדֵיק דָּק: Just as a Torah scholar is deemed credible to say that he was not careful in identifying a woman, so too, he is he deemed credible on other occasions to say that he in fact does recognize a specific woman (Rashbam). *Tosafot* find the Rashbam's interpretation difficult, and explain this line otherwise: If the Torah scholar claimed initially that he positively recognizes a specific woman, he is not allowed to retract this identification subsequently on the grounds that he is not careful in identifying women. The *Piskei HaRid* interprets the Gemara this way as well.

HALAKHA

It is not the manner of a Torah scholar to be careful – צוּרְבָא מֵרַבָּנַן לָאו אוֹרְחֵיהּ לְמֵידַק: If a Torah scholar wrote a receipt for a woman for payment of her marriage contract, he may later claim that he had mistaken her identity and that his intention was to write it for another woman, as it is not the manner for a Torah scholar to be careful about identifying women (see *Ḥelkat Meḥokek*), in accordance with the Gemara's description of the incident with Rav Yirmeya bar Abba. No other person can make a similar claim, as it is assumed that he was careful in establishing the identity of the woman before writing the document. Similarly, in any case where witnesses claim that they had made an understandable mistake in their testimony, they may retract it (*Shulḥan Arukh, Even HaEzer* 110:1, and in the comment of Rema, and *Ḥoshen Mishpat* 29:1, 49:1, and in the comment of Rema).

The Sages placed the burden upon the woman – שַׁדְיוּהוּ רַבָּנַן אַאִשָּׁה: Although the Torah places the obligation of writing a bill of divorce on the husband, the Sages shifted the financial responsibility to the woman in order to avoid situations where wives wait for their bills of divorce for long periods of time (Rambam *Sefer Mishpatim, Hilkhot Malve VeLoveh* 24:2 and *Sefer Nashim, Hilkhot Geirushin* 2:4; *Shulḥan Arukh, Even HaEzer* 120:1).

"כּוֹתְבִין שְׁטָר לַמּוֹכֵר אַף עַל פִּי שֶׁאֵין לוֹקֵחַ" וכו׳. פְּשִׁיטָא! לָא צְרִיכָא, בְּמוֹכֵר שָׂדֵהוּ מִפְּנֵי רָעָתָהּ.

The mishna teaches: A scribe may **write a bill** of sale **for a seller** of property who requests one, **even if the purchaser is not with him** when he presents his request, and it is the purchaser who provides the scribe's wages. The Gemara asks: Isn't it **obvious** that the purchaser pays the wages? After all, he is the beneficiary of the sale. The Gemara answers: **No,** it is **necessary** for the mishna to state this, as sometimes the sale is beneficial to the seller as well, as **in** a case of **one who sells a field because of its poor** quality, as he is anxious to be rid of it.

"אֵין כּוֹתְבִין שִׁטְרֵי אֵירוּסִין" וכו׳. פְּשִׁיטָא! לָא צְרִיכָא, דַּאֲפִילּוּ צוּרְבָא מֵרַבָּנַן, דְּנִיחָא לֵיהּ לַחֲמוּהּ לְקָרוּבֵיהּ.

The mishna teaches: A scribe may **not write documents of betrothal** and documents of marriage except with the consent of both the groom and the bride, and it is the groom who provides the scribe's wages. The Gemara asks: Isn't it **obvious** that the groom pays the wages? After all, he is the one acquiring his betrothed. The Gemara answers: **No,** it is **necessary** for the mishna to state this, to teach us **that** it applies **even** when the groom is **a Torah scholar,** in **which** case **it gives his father-in-law satisfaction to bring him into his family** by having him marry his daughter. Even in such a case, where the bride's family is a beneficiary, it is the groom who pays the wages.

"אֵין כּוֹתְבִין שְׁטַר אֲרִיסוּת וְקַבְּלָנוּת" וכו׳. פְּשִׁיטָא! לָא צְרִיכָא, בְּבוּרָה.

The mishna teaches: A scribe may **not write contracts for sharecroppers and contractors** except with the consent of both parties, i.e., the sharecropper or contractor and the one who hires him, and it is the sharecropper or contractor who provides the scribe's wages. The Gemara asks: Isn't it **obvious** that the contractor pays the wages? After all, the contract details his rights to the field. The Gemara answers: **No,** it is **necessary** for the mishna to state this, as sometimes the deal is detrimental to the contractor, as **in** the case of **a fallow** field. It might have been thought that in this case the cost of the document is borne by the landowner.

"אֵין כּוֹתְבִין שִׁטְרֵי בֵּירוּרִין אֶלָּא מִדַּעַת שְׁנֵיהֶם" וכו׳. מַאי שִׁטְרֵי בֵּירוּרִין? הָכָא תַּרְגִּימוּ: שִׁטְרֵי טַעֲנָתָא. רַב יִרְמְיָה בַּר אַבָּא אָמַר: זֶה בּוֹרֵר לוֹ אֶחָד וְזֶה בּוֹרֵר לוֹ אֶחָד.

The mishna teaches: A scribe may **not write documents** testifying to **arbitration** or any other court enactment **except with the consent of both** parties to the litigation. The Gemara asks: **What** is meant by **documents** testifying to **arbitration? Here** in Babylonia the Sages **interpreted** it to mean **documents recording the claims**[H] of the two parties to the litigation. **Rav Yirmeya bar Abba says:** A document testifying to arbitration is one that records the procedure in which the composition of the court is chosen, as described in tractate *Sanhedrin* (23a), whereby **this** litigant **chooses one** judge **and that** litigant **chooses one** judge,[H] and these two judges choose the third one.

"רַבָּן שִׁמְעוֹן בֶּן גַּמְלִיאֵל אוֹמֵר: לִשְׁנֵיהֶם כּוֹתְבִין שְׁנַיִם, לָזֶה בְּעַצְמוֹ וְלָזֶה בְּעַצְמוֹ". לֵימָא, בְּכוֹפִין עַל מִדַּת סְדוֹם קָא מִיפַּלְגִי,

§ The mishna teaches that **Rabban Shimon ben Gamliel says:** The scribe **writes two** documents **for the two** parties, one **for this** one **by himself and** one **for that** one **by himself.** The Gemara analyzes the disagreement between Rabban Shimon ben Gamliel and the first *tanna*, who did not call for two separate documents: **Shall we say** that they **disagree with regard to** the principle that the court **coerces** people to prevent **conduct** characteristic **of Sodom,** i.e., selfish behavior? That is, the case is where one of the litigants does not want to contribute to the writing of a joint document, and insists that each litigant pay to have his own document written, which would entail an additional expenditure on the part of the other party.

דְּמָר סָבַר: כּוֹפִין, וּמָר סָבַר: אֵין כּוֹפִין?

The dispute is then as follows: **As one Sage,** the first *tanna*, **holds** that the court **coerces** people to prevent this conduct, so the obstinate litigant is forced to pay his share of a joint document, **and one Sage,** Rabban Shimon ben Gamliel, **holds** that the court does **not coerce** people to prevent this conduct, and a litigant can insist upon paying only for a document of his own.

לָא, דְּכוּלֵּי עָלְמָא – כּוֹפִין, וְהָכָא הַיְינוּ טַעֲמָא דְּרַבָּן שִׁמְעוֹן בֶּן גַּמְלִיאֵל, דְּאָמַר לֵיהּ: לָא נִיחָא לִי דְּתֶהֱוֵי זְכוּתָךְ גַּבֵּי זְכוּתִי, דְּדָמֵית עֲלַאי כִּי אַרְיָא אַרְבָּא.

The Gemara rejects this analysis: **No, everyone** in the mishna holds that the court **coerces** people to prevent conduct characteristic of Sodom, **and here this is the reason** for the ruling **of Rabban Shimon ben Gamliel:** It is because the litigant demanding separate documents is not making a pointless, selfish request at all, **as he says to** the other litigant: **It is not amenable for me that your defense,** i.e., the record of your claims, **should be together with my defense,**[N] **as you are to me like an ambushing lion,** i.e., our interests are in conflict.

HALAKHA

Documents recording the claims – שִׁטְרֵי טַעֲנָתָא: A litigant is not required to present his claims in writing. In fact, a judge may not accept a claim submitted in writing but must instead hear the claims presented by the parties to the dispute themselves. These claims, presented orally, are then recorded. This record of the claims should not be made without the prior consent of both parties, and both of them contribute to the payment made to the scribe. The Rema writes that if both parties consent to allow the submission of claims in writing instead of in person, it is allowed, but they may not subsequently alter these claims with various excuses and explanations. This is all in accordance with the mishna and with the Gemara's explanation that the term: Documents of arbitration, is referring to documents recording the claims of the litigants (*Shulḥan Arukh, Ḥoshen Mishpat* 13:3; 14:2, and in the comment of Rema).

This litigant chooses one judge and that litigant chooses one judge – זֶה בּוֹרֵר לוֹ אֶחָד וְזֶה בּוֹרֵר לוֹ אֶחָד: If the two litigants in a case cannot agree on a court before which to bring their case, each litigant chooses a judge of his liking, and the two judges together choose a third judge; this system helps ensure a fair trial. The court must draw up a document of arbitration stating: So-and-so chose so-and-so to be a judge, and so-and-so chose so-and-so to be a judge. As long as the choice is not recorded in the document, either party may change his mind. Once the document is written they may no longer retract their choices, and for this reason the document may be written only with the consent of both parties. The expense of writing the document is shared by both parties. This is all in accordance with the mishna and the interpretation of Rav Yirmeya bar Abba that the term: Document of arbitration, is referring to this kind of document (Rambam *Sefer Mishpatim, Hilkhot Malve VeLoveh* 24:1–2; *Shulḥan Arukh, Ḥoshen Mishpat* 13:1–2).

NOTES

It is not amenable for me that your defense should be together with my defense – לָא נִיחָא לִי דְּתֶהֱוֵי זְכוּתָךְ גַּבֵּי זְכוּתִי: The early commentaries offer differing explanations of this claim. The Rashbam explains that the litigant wants each of the two parties to have a document listing only his own rights. Writing the documents in this manner will lead to a decrease in ill will between the parties, as each will not be constantly exposed to the record of the rights of the other. The Ramban explains that both documents would be identical, and the claim is that he does not want to be subject to the whims of the other in terms of having access to the document, or alternatively, of having to present the document to the other whenever he demands it.

מתני׳ מִי שֶׁפָּרַע מִקְצָת חוֹבוֹ, וְהִשְׁלִישׁ אֶת שְׁטָרוֹ וְאָמַר לוֹ: "אִם לֹא נָתַתִּי לְךָ מִכָּאן וְעַד יוֹם פְּלוֹנִי – תֵּן לוֹ שְׁטָרוֹ"; הִגִּיעַ זְמַן וְלֹא נָתַן – רַבִּי יוֹסֵי אוֹמֵר: יִתֵּן, רַבִּי יְהוּדָה אוֹמֵר: לֹא יִתֵּן.

MISHNA In the case of a debtor who **repaid part of his debt**[H] **and** with the agreement of the creditor **deposited** the promissory **note with a third party** serving as a trustee to ensure that the creditor would not collect the full amount, **and** the debtor **said to** the trustee: **If I have not given you** the balance **from now until such and such a day, give** the creditor **his** promissory **note,** thereby enabling him to collect the full amount stated on the note, if the stipulated **time arrived and** the debtor **did not give** the balance to the trustee, **Rabbi Yosei says:** The trustee **should give** the promissory note to the creditor, in accordance with the debtor's stipulation. **Rabbi Yehuda says:** The trustee **should not give** it, as the stipulation is void.

גמ׳ בְּמַאי קָמִיפַּלְגִי? רַבִּי יוֹסֵי סָבַר: אַסְמַכְתָּא קָנְיָא, וְרַבִּי יְהוּדָה סָבַר: אַסְמַכְתָּא לָא קָנְיָא.

GEMARA **With regard to what** principle **do** Rabbi Yosei and Rabbi Yehuda **disagree? Rabbi Yosei holds** that **a transaction with inconclusive consent** [*asmakhta*][N] **effects acquisition.** In this case, the debtor willingly undertook a penalty if he would not repay the remainder of the debt on time. Yet, he did not think that he would miss the deadline and be held accountable to pay that penalty. Rabbi Yosei holds that he is nevertheless bound by his word. **And Rabbi Yehuda holds** that **an *asmakhta* does not effect acquisition,** i.e., it is not binding.

אָמַר רַב נַחְמָן אָמַר רַבָּה בַּר אֲבוּהּ אָמַר רַב: הֲלָכָה כְּרַבִּי יוֹסֵי. כִּי אֲתוֹ לְקַמֵּיהּ דְּרַבִּי אַמִי, אֲמַר לְהוּ: וְכִי מֵאַחַר שֶׁרַבִּי יוֹחָנָן מְלַמְּדֵנוּ פַּעַם רִאשׁוֹנָה וּשְׁנִיָּה הֲלָכָה כְּרַבִּי יוֹסֵי, אֲנִי מָה אֶעֱשֶׂה?

Rav Naḥman says that **Rabba bar Avuh says** that **Rav says:** The ***halakha*** **is in accordance with** the opinion of **Rabbi Yosei. When** questioners **came before Rabbi Ami,** inquiring of him what the *halakha* is in this matter, **he said to them: But since** it is the case **that Rabbi Yoḥanan taught us a first time and a second** time, i.e., repeatedly, that the ***halakha*** is **in accordance with** the opinion of **Rabbi Yosei, what can I do** to contradict his words?

וְאֵין הֲלָכָה כְּרַבִּי יוֹסֵי.

The Gemara concludes: **But in fact the *halakha*** **is not in accordance with** the opinion of **Rabbi Yosei,** i.e., an *asmakhta* is not binding.

HALAKHA

A debtor who repaid part of his debt, etc. – מִי שֶׁפָּרַע מִקְצָת חוֹבוֹ וכו׳: In the case of a debtor who repaid part of his debt and then deposited the promissory note with a third party serving as a trustee, saying to the trustee: If I do not give you the balance by a certain day give the note to the creditor, then even if the payment is not made by the stipulated date, the trustee should not give the document to the creditor, as this agreement is considered a transaction with inconclusive consent [*asmakhta*], which is null and void. If at the time of stating the agreement the parties performed an act of acquisition in the presence of a distinguished court formalizing this arrangement, such a stipulation is binding if the debtor transfers the relevant documents to the court. All this does not apply if the stipulated condition was not met because of some event beyond the control of the obligated party, such as unexpected illness or travel irregularities. This is in accordance with the conclusion of the Gemara in *Nedarim* 27b (Rambam *Sefer Kinyan, Hilkhot Mekhira* 11:5; *Shulḥan Arukh*, *Ḥoshen Mishpat* 55:1, 207:12).

NOTES

A transaction with inconclusive consent [*asmakhta*] – אַסְמַכְתָּא: An *asmakhta* is an obligation that one undertakes that is dependent upon some future development. Usually it is referring to a situation in which the one undertaking the obligation does so under the assumption that the conditions that will cause the obligation to take effect will never materialize. The clarification of the *halakhot* of *asmakhta*, as well as the difference between an *asmakhta* and any other condition stipulated in the course of a transaction, is the subject of much discussion among the commentaries.

Rav Se'adya Gaon maintains that in order to qualify as an *asmakhta*, the obligation undertaken must be disproportionate to whatever inconvenience or loss might be caused by the specified condition. He also maintains that a condition is considered an *asmakhta* if the specified condition is completely beyond the control of the one obligating himself. These positions are also adopted by Rabbeinu Tam in *Sefer HaYashar*.

The Rif, Rabbeinu Ḥananel, and others hold that any obligation voluntarily undertaken by a party to an agreement is an *asmakhta* unless it is initiated by the beneficiary of that obligation; however, there are certain exceptions. The Ramah distinguishes between different formulations of a statement accepting an obligation. When the self-obligating party states: If such and such occurs, I obligate myself it is an *asmakhta*, but if he states: I obligate myself on the condition that such and such occurs, or: The obligation is binding as of this moment, it is not an *asmakhta*.

The Ritva, citing his teachers Ra'ah and Rashba, concludes as follows: For an *asmakhta* to be not binding, the proposed penalty must be exaggerated, the self-obligating party must not want the event to occur that will cause the obligation to take effect, and the event that will cause the obligation to take effect is one that is partially under the control of the self-obligating party. If the event is completely under the control of the self-obligating party or is not at all under his control, it is not considered an *asmakhta* (see Rabbeinu Yona and Ran).

מתני׳ מִי שֶׁנִּמְחַק שְׁטַר חוֹבוֹ – מַעֲמִיד עָלָיו עֵדִים, וּבָא לִפְנֵי בֵּית דִּין וְעוֹשִׂין לוֹ קִיּוּם: ״אִישׁ פְּלוֹנִי בֶּן פְּלוֹנִי נִמְחַק שְׁטָרוֹ בְּיוֹם פְּלוֹנִי,

MISHNA In the case of a creditor **whose promissory note has become erased,** he should **produce witnesses** who remember the details of the document to testify **about it. And** they **come before the court, and they ratify** his promissory note **for him,** stating: The promissory **note of so-and-so was erased,** and it stated that a loan for such and such an amount took place **on such and such a date,**

Perek **X**
Daf **168** Amud **b**

וּפְלוֹנִי וּפְלוֹנִי עֵדָיו״.

and so-and-so and so-and-so were its witnesses. The ratification document is signed, and it may be used as a replacement for the erased document.

גמ׳ תָּנוּ רַבָּנַן: אֵיזֶהוּ קִיּוּמוֹ: ״בְּמוֹתַב תְּלָתָא הֲוֵינָא אֲנוּ פְּלוֹנִי וּפְלוֹנִי וּפְלוֹנִי, הוֹצִיא פְּלוֹנִי בֶּן פְּלוֹנִי שְׁטָר מָחוּק לְפָנֵינוּ בְּיוֹם פְּלוֹנִי, וּפְלוֹנִי וּפְלוֹנִי עֵדָיו״; וְאִם כָּתוּב בּוֹ ״הוּזְקַקְנוּ לְעֵדוּתָן שֶׁל עֵדִים וְנִמְצֵאת עֵדוּתָן מְכוּוֶּנֶת״ – גּוֹבֶה וְאֵינוֹ צָרִיךְ לְהָבִיא רְאָיָה, וְאִם לָאו – צָרִיךְ לְהָבִיא רְאָיָה;

GEMARA **The Sages taught** (*Tosefta, Bava Metzia* 1:16): **What is** the text of **the ratification** document **of** an erased document? The court writes as follows: **We, so-and-so and so-and-so and so-and-so, were sitting as three** judges, and **so-and-so, son of so-and-so, produced an erased document before us,** which was written **on such and such a date, and so-and-so and so-and-so** were **its witnesses. And if it is written in** this ratification document also: **We engaged in** the investigation of **the testimony of the witnesses and their testimony has been found** to be **congruent,** the creditor can **collect** his debt on the basis of this ratification document, **and he does not need to bring** further **proof. But if** this formula is **not** written, the creditor **needs to bring** further **proof** of the loan in order to collect it.

נִקְרַע – פָּסוּל, נִתְקָרַע – כָּשֵׁר; נִמְחַק אוֹ נִטְשְׁטֵשׁ, אִם רִישּׁוּמוֹ נִיכָּר – כָּשֵׁר.

The *baraita* continues with its discussion of damaged documents: If a promissory note was **torn** intentionally it is **not valid,** but if it **became torn** accidentally it is **valid.** In a case where it **was erased**[H] **or smudged, if its imprint is recognizable,** i.e., if the words are still legible, though barely, it is **valid.**

הֵיכִי דָּמֵי ״נִקְרַע״ הֵיכִי דָּמֵי ״נִתְקָרַע״? אָמַר רַב יְהוּדָה: ״נִקְרַע״ – קֶרַע שֶׁל בֵּית דִּין, ״נִתְקָרַע״ – קֶרַע שֶׁאֵינוֹ שֶׁל בֵּית דִּין.

The Gemara seeks to clarify the terms in the second part of the *baraita*: **What are the circumstances,** i.e., what are the defining characteristics, of a document that was **torn,** and **what are the circumstances** of a document that **became torn? Rav Yehuda says:** A document that was **torn** means that it had **a tear** created **by the court,** because they wished to render it not valid due to payment of the loan or some other circumstance. A document that **became torn** means it had **a tear that** was **not** created **by the court.**

הֵיכִי דָּמֵי קֶרַע שֶׁל בֵּית דִּין? אָמַר רַב יְהוּדָה: מְקוֹם עֵדִים וּמְקוֹם הַזְּמַן וּמְקוֹם הַתּוֹרֶף. אַבָּיֵי אָמַר: שְׁתִי וָעֵרֶב.

The Gemara seeks further clarification: **What are the circumstances,** i.e., what are the signs, of a document that had **a tear** created **by the court? Rav Yehuda says:** The document has a tear that ruins **the place of the witnesses'** signatures **and the place of the date and the place of the essential part** of a document. **Abaye says:** It has a **tear** that goes both **lengthwise and widthwise.**

HALAKHA

Torn, erased – נִקְרַע, נִמְחַק: If a document comes before the court and it is torn in the manner that a document is usually torn by a court, namely, it is torn in the place of the witnesses' signatures, the date, and the essential part of the document, or if it is torn lengthwise and widthwise, the document is not valid. If it is clear that it was cut by means of a knife, which indicates that it was most likely torn deliberately (*Sma*), even if it is not torn in the manner described above, it is also not valid. If it is torn into two pieces is all the more so not valid. If there are witnesses that the document was torn inadvertently, it is treated like a document that has become erased (Rema). If the document is torn along its fold, it is valid, as the tear is attributed to normal wear and tear (*Sma*; see *Shakh*). If the writing on the document is erased or smudged, than provided its imprint is recognizable it is still valid. If the document is partially disintegrated or is punctured with many holes it is valid. The Rema, citing the Rosh and *Teshuvot Maimoniyyot*, rules that if a document has been partially devoured by moths or mice at the top, then as long as the names of the debtor and creditor and the main details of the document at the end can still be read it is valid (Rambam *Sefer Mishpatim*, *Hilkhot Malve VeLoveh* 23:14, and see *Sefer Nashim*, *Hilkhot Geirushin* 4:15–17; *Shulḥan Arukh*, *Ḥoshen Mishpat* 52:1, and see *Even HaEzer* 125:20–21).

הנהו ערבאי דאתו לפומבדיתא, דהוו קא אנסי ארעתא דאינשי; אתו מרוותיהו לקמיה דאביי, אמרו ליה: ליחזי מר שטרין ולכתוב לן מר שטרא אחרינא עליה, דאי מיתנים חד – נקיטינן חד בידן.

§ The Gemara relates: There was once **a certain** group of **Arabs who came to Pumbedita** and **who would rob people's land** and force the victims to surrender the deeds to their property to prevent subsequent legal action. **The owners of** land who had not yet had fallen victim to these Arabs **came before Abaye** and **said to him: Let the Master look at our deeds** to our property **and let the Master write us another deed for it,** so **that if one** of the deeds **is robbed we will have** the other **one in our possession.**

אמר להו: מאי אעביד לכו? דאמר רב ספרא: אין כותבין שני שטרות על שדה אחת, דלמא טריף והדר טריף.

Abaye **said to them: What can I do for you?** I cannot comply with your request, as **Rav Safra says:** One may **not write two deeds** of ownership **for one field, lest** the owner of that land **repossess property** once **and** then **go back and repossess** it once again. Generally, whenever real estate is sold there is a guarantee given to the purchaser in the event that the land is repossessed by the seller's creditor or by someone else who proves that the land rightfully belongs to him. If the seller of the repossessed land has no money to honor the guarantee, the purchaser can repossess property from others who had purchased property from the same seller subsequent to the sale of the repossessed land. In order to do so, he would have to produce the bill of sale proving that he had purchased the repossessed property. If he has two such deeds, he would be able to collect payment twice. To eliminate this possibility, duplicate property deeds are not written.

הוו קא טרדי ליה, אמר ליה לספריה: זיל כתוב להו הוא על המחק ועדיו על הנייר, דפסול.

The landowners **kept badgering** Abaye to write the duplicate documents, until, in order to be rid of them, **he said to his scribe: Go write** the document **for them,** but first write on paper and then erase it, and then write the desired document over the erased text, so that the text of the document will be written **over an erasure,**[N] **and the** signatures of **its witnesses** will be **on** a part of **the paper** where the writing had not been erased, a situation in **which** the document is **not valid.**

אמר ליה רב אחא בר מניומי לאביי: ודלמא רישומו ניכר, ותניא: נמחק או נטשטש, אם רישומו ניכר – כשר! אמר ליה: מי קאמינא שטרא מעליא? אל"ף בי"ת בעלמא קאמינא.

Rav Aḥa bar Minyumi said to Abaye: But perhaps the first writing on the paper was not erased thoroughly, so **its imprint is recognizable,**[N] **and it is taught** in the *baraita* that in a case where the writing on a document **was erased or smudged, if its imprint is recognizable,** the document is **valid. Abaye said to him: Did I say** that he should write **a proper document** and then erase it? **I said,** i.e., I intended, that he should **merely** write letters of the **alphabet** [*alef beit*], not actual words.

תנו רבנן: הרי שבא ואמר "אבד שטר חובי", אף על פי שאמרו עדים "אנו כתבנו וחתמנו ונתננו לו" – אין כותבין לו את השטר; במה דברים אמורים – בשטרי הלואה, אבל שטרי מקח וממכר – כותבין, חוץ מן האחריות שבו;

§ **The Sages taught** in a *baraita*: In a case where one **came** to court **and said: My promissory note was lost,**[HN] **even if witnesses said: We wrote and signed** such a promissory note **and gave** it **to** this man, the court may **not write** a new **document for him.** The Gemara asks: **In what** case **is this statement said? In** the case of **documents** detailing **loans. But** in a case of **deeds of buying and selling** land,[H] the court may **write** a replacement document, **excluding the** standard **guarantee that** was **in** the first document, which states that if the field is repossessed the seller will compensate the purchaser for his loss.

HALAKHA

My promissory note was lost – אבד שטר חובי: If a creditor lost his promissory note and appears before a court to request a replacement document, the court may not write one for him, even if he produces the witnesses signed on the lost document to testify that they had signed it and transferred it to him, and even if the date for repayment of the loan has not yet arrived. Even if witnesses testify that they saw the document get lost, the court may not write a replacement document for him, lest the original be found one day and be used for collection. Only if witnesses testify that they saw the document destroyed may the court write a replacement. If the document had been entrusted to a third party and that third party lost it, the court may write a replacement, as there is no concern that it may be found one day by the creditor. The Rema, citing the Maharik, rules that if one left his documents in a city that was conquered in war, the court may write a replacement, as it is assumed that the original document is not retrievable (Rambam *Sefer Nashim*, *Hilkhot Geirushin* 4:11; *Shulḥan Arukh*, *Even HaEzer* 41:3–4).

Deeds of buying and selling land – שטרי מקח וממכר: If one appears before a court and claims to have lost a bill of sale for land, and he produces the witnesses of the original document to support his claim, the court may write a replacement document for him, but the following clause must be added: This document may not be used for collection, neither from sold property nor from unsold property, and we have written it only to prove that such and such a field belongs to so-and-so to prevent the seller or his heirs from denying the sale and repossessing the field from him. This is in accordance with the *baraita* and Rav Naḥman's interpretation (169b). Some say that the date in the replacement document should be the date of the original sale, as if the later date is written there is a concern that perhaps the purchaser had resold the field to the seller in the interim, and the later date would enable him to unjustly get it back (Rabbeinu Yitzḥak of Dampierre, in *Tosafot*). All these *halakhot* apply to a deed of gift of land as well (Rambam *Sefer Mishpatim*, *Hilkhot Malve VeLoveh* 23:10; *Shulḥan Arukh*, *Ḥoshen Mishpat* 239:1, 41:3, and in the comment of Rema).

NOTES

Over an erasure, etc. – על המחק וכו׳: This document would not be valid, but the landowners would not realize this, so they would cease harassing Abaye (Rashbam). Rabbeinu Gershom Meor HaGola writes that Abaye did not intend to deceive the landowners, and that the document he gave them was sufficient to prove their ownership of the land. Nevertheless, it would be insufficient proof of ownership for the purpose of repossessing other people's property in the event the land was repossessed as payment for a debt.

Perhaps its imprint is recognizable – ודלמא רישומו ניכר: Rav Aḥa bar Minyumi thought that Abaye had instructed his scribe to write out a bill of sale, then erase it, and then rewrite it over the erasure. Rav Aḥa bar Minyumi was concerned that the imprint of the first document would not be erased thoroughly and would still be recognizable if the holder of the document would erase the upper layer of writing (Rashbam).

My promissory note was lost – אבד שטר חובי: The case is one where the creditor does not have witnesses that saw the document destroyed (Rashbam). The reason a replacement document may not be written is that there is a concern that the document is not actually lost, or that it is lost now and will be found later; in such cases a replacement document would enable double collection of a loan. The case differs from the case in the mishna, in which the erased document is shown in court, or there are witnesses who saw it being erased, so that the possibility of the creditor possessing two documents is eliminated.

HALAKHA

Because the court may not write two deeds for one field – שֶׁאֵין כּוֹתְבִין שְׁנֵי שְׁטָרוֹת עַל שָׂדֶה אַחַת: With regard to a bill of sale of property containing a guarantee of reimbursement in the event of repossession, or a similar deed of gift, if it becomes worn out or erased, the court can write a replacement as long as it destroys the first document or writes in the replacement document: This document is not intended to be used for collection based on the guarantee of reimbursement, but only to prove ownership of the land on behalf of the purchaser so that the seller or giver will not be able to take it back from him unjustly. This procedure is necessary to prevent double collection (see *Sma* and *Shakh*). The Rema, citing the Rashba, adds that two or more deeds of sale may be written in this manner at the time of sale, even *ab initio* (Rambam *Sefer Mishpatim*, *Hilkhot Malve VeLoveh* 23:10; *Shulḥan Arukh*, *Ḥoshen Mishpat* 41:1, 239:1, and in the comment of Rema).

Authorization to repossess liened property…document of authorization to seize a debtor's property…appraisal in which it is not written, etc. – ...טִירְפָּא...אַדְרַכְתָּא...שׁוּמָא דְּלָא כְּתִיב וכו׳: Any document of authorization [*adrakhta*] in which it is not written that the court has torn the creditor's promissory note is not a valid document. Any document of authorization to repossess liened property [*tirfa*] in which it is not written that the court has torn the document of authorization is not a valid document. Any document of appraisal [*shuma*] in which it is not written that the court has torn the document of authorization to repossess liened property is not a valid document. This is in accordance with the Rambam's version of the text of the Gemara, which varies from the standard printed version (Rambam *Sefer Mishpatim*, *Hilkhot Malve VeLoveh* 22:13, and see 22:1–12; *Shulḥan Arukh*, *Ḥoshen Mishpat* 98:10, and see 98:1–9).

NOTES

Come based on his claim of his ancestors – דְּקָאָתֵי מִכֹּחַ אֲבָהָתֵיהּ: In this case, the claimant would collect his land without the need to produce any documentation that could be torn to prevent a repeat claim.

רַבָּן שִׁמְעוֹן בֶּן גַּמְלִיאֵל אוֹמֵר: אַף שִׁטְרֵי מִקָּח וּמִמְכָּר אֵין כּוֹתְבִין; וְכֵן הָיָה רַבָּן שִׁמְעוֹן בֶּן גַּמְלִיאֵל אוֹמֵר: הַנּוֹתֵן מַתָּנָה לַחֲבֵרוֹ וְהֶחֱזִיר לוֹ אֶת הַשְּׁטָר – חָזְרָה מַתְּנָתוֹ, וַחֲכָמִים אוֹמְרִים: מַתְּנָתוֹ קַיֶּימֶת.

The *baraita* continues: **Rabban Shimon ben Gamliel says:** The court may **not write** a replacement document **even** for **deeds of buying and selling** land. **And Rabban Shimon ben Gamliel says as well:** With regard to **one who gives a gift** of land **to another, and the** recipient **returned the deed to him, his gift** of land **returns** to him as well. **But the Rabbis say: His gift** of land **remains** in the possession of the recipient.

אָמַר מָר: חוּץ מֵאַחֲרָיוּת שֶׁבּוֹ. מַאי טַעְמָא?

The Gemara analyzes the *baraita*: **The Master says** in the *baraita*: With regard to deeds of buying and selling land, the court may write a replacement document, **excluding the guarantee that** was **in** the first document. **What is the reason** that the guarantee may not be written?

אָמַר רַב סַפְרָא: לְפִי שֶׁאֵין כּוֹתְבִין שְׁנֵי שְׁטָרוֹת עַל שָׂדֶה אַחַת, דִּלְמָא אָזֵיל בַּעַל חוֹב טָרֵיף לֵיהּ לְהַאי, וְאָזֵיל הַאי וּמַפֵּיק חַד וְטָרֵיף לָקוֹחוֹת, וְאָמַר לֵיהּ לְבַעַל חוֹב: שׁוּף לִי דְּאֵיקוּם בַּהּ וַהֲדַר תָּא טִירְפַן. וּמַפֵּיק אַחֲרִינָא וַהֲדַר אָזֵיל טָרֵיף לָקוֹחוֹת אַחֲרִינֵי.

Rav Safra says: It is **because** the court may **not write two deeds** of sale **for** the same sale of **one field,**[H] **lest a creditor** of the seller **go** and **repossess** the field sold **to this** purchaser, **and that** purchaser **go and take out one** deed, **and** in accordance with the guarantee clause of the sale, **repossess** land from other **purchasers** who purchased land from the same seller at a later date, **and say to the creditor: Remain quiet** [*shof*][L] about this matter for a few years, **while I become established in** the property I repossessed. **And then, come** and claim your loan again, and then you will **repossess** this property **from me. And** then, after it is taken from him a second time, the purchaser will then **take out the other** document of sale, the replacement that the court had written for him, **and then go** and **repossess** land from **other purchasers** who purchased land from the same seller. In short, a replacement document with a guarantee will enable double collection on that guarantee.

וְכֵיוָן דְּקָרְעִנֵיהּ לִשְׁטָרָא דְּמִלְוֶה, בְּמַאי הָדַר טָרֵיף לַהּ?

The Gemara asks with regard to Rav Safra's scenario: How would it be possible for this to occur? **But once** the creditor repossessed the land the first time as payment of the debt, **we,** the court, **tore the** promissory **note of** the seller's **creditor; with what** document could the creditor **repossess** the purchaser's land **again?**

וְכִי תֵּימָא דְּלָא קָרְעִנֵיהּ – וְהָא אָמַר רַב נַחְמָן: כׇּל טִירְפָּא דְּלָא כְּתִיב בֵּיהּ ״קָרְעִנֵיהּ לִשְׁטָרָא דְּמִלְוֶה״ – לָאו טִירְפָּא הוּא; וְכׇל אַדְרַכְתָּא דְּלָא כְּתִיב בַּהּ ״קָרְעִנֵיהּ לְטִירְפָּא״ – לָאו אַדְרַכְתָּא הוּא; וְכׇל שׁוּמָא דְּלָא כְּתִיב בֵּיהּ ״קָרְעִנֵיהּ לְאַדְרַכְתָּא״ – לָאו שׁוּמָא הִיא!

And if you would say that we did not tear the creditor's promissory note in the course of the first collection, that cannot be. **But doesn't Rav Naḥman say** that **any** document of **authorization to repossess** liened property from its purchaser **in which it is not written: We have torn the creditor's** promissory **note, is not** a valid document of **authorization to repossess** liened property; **and any document of authorization** used **to** seize a debtor's property **in which it is not written: We have torn the** creditor's document of **authorization to repossess** liened property, **is not** a valid **document of authorization; and any document of appraisal** of an article's value **in which it is not written:**[H] **We have torn** the creditor's **document of authorization, is not** a valid **document of appraisal.**

לָא צְרִיכָא, דְּקָאָתֵי מִכֹּחַ אֲבָהָתֵיהּ.

The Gemara answers: **No,** it is **necessary** to explain Rav Safra's case as follows: The concern is not that a creditor will repossess the field, but **that** someone will **come** to repossess it **based on** his claim to the land as the property of **his ancestors.**[N] That is, he proved that the field had belonged to his ancestors, and by extension belongs to himself as their heir, and the one who sold the field was in fact a thief. It was for this reason that he repossessed the field from the purchaser, and the concern is that the purchaser will seek reimbursement, as stipulated in the guarantee, from other property sold subsequently by the seller. If the purchaser has two deeds of sale with guarantees, he can collect payment twice.

LANGUAGE

Remain quiet [*shof*] – שׁוּף: In this context the meaning of *shof* is to remain quiet, to hold one's peace and not attract attention. Some assert that the primary meaning of the term is to smooth a rough surface and that here it is extended to be referring to a situation that is smooth in the sense that there is no disturbance or commotion.

אֲמַר לֵיהּ רַב אַחָא מִדִּפְתִּי לְרָבִינָא וְלָמָּה לֵיהּ לְמֵימַר לֵיהּ לְבַעַל חוֹב ״שׁוֹף לִי בְּהַאי אַרְעָא וְאֵיקוּם בָּהּ״? תֵּיפוֹק לֵיהּ, דְּכֵיוָן דְּנָקֵיט תְּרֵי שְׁטָרֵי – טָרֵיף וַהֲדַר טָרֵיף!

The Gemara presents another question pertaining to Rav Safra's case. **Rav Aḥa of Difti said to Ravina: And why did** Rav Safra have **to** include in his case that the purchaser will **say to the creditor:**[N] **Remain quiet** about this matter for a few years **while I become established in this land** I repossessed, and then come and claim your loan again? Why did he devise a case in which the seller's creditor collects payment twice? Let the problem **derive** from the fact **that since** the purchaser **holds two deeds** he will be able to **repossess** land based on his guarantee once **and** then **repossess** land **again,** even if the creditor does not collect his debt twice.

אִם כֵּן, נְפִישִׁי עֲלֵיהּ בַּעֲלֵי דִינִין.

Ravina answered: **If so,** if the purchaser attempts to repossess land twice based on a single repossession of the creditor, **he will have** too **many litigants** to deal with at once, and his dishonest dealings will be discovered.

וְלִכְתּוֹב לְהַאי שְׁטָרָא מְעַלְּיָא, וְלִכְתּוֹב תַּבְרָא לַמּוֹכֵר: ״כָּל שְׁטָרֵי דְּיִפְּקוּן עַל אַרְעָא דָּא פְּסוּלִין, לְבַר מִן דְּיִפּוֹק בְּזִמְנָא דָּא״!

The Gemara asks further: **But let** the court **write** a **proper bill** of sale, one that includes a guarantee, **for this** purchaser, **and** then **let** the court **write a receipt for the seller,** stating: **All documents that are issued with regard to** the purchase of **this field are not valid, except for** the one **issued on this date,** referring to the replacement document written by the court. This will prevent double collection, as if the purchaser attempts to collect on his guarantee with a second document, the seller will foil this attempt by showing this receipt.

אֲמַרוּהָ רַבָּנַן קַמֵּיהּ דְּרַב פַּפָּא, וְאָמְרִי לָהּ קַמֵּיהּ דְּרַב אַשִׁי: זֹאת אוֹמֶרֶת, אֵין כּוֹתְבִין שׁוֹבֵר?

The Rabbis said before Rav Pappa in response to this question, **and some say** it was said **before Rav Ashi: Is that to say** that the *tanna* of the *baraita* holds that in general the court does **not write a receipt**[N] in such cases?

NOTES

To the creditor – לְבַעַל חוֹב: Although the Gemara has already modified Rav Safra's case to be one that does not involve an actual creditor, but one who claims the field as his ancestral property, the Gemara here and throughout its discussion continues to refer to the one repossessing the sold field as a creditor, since this is the way the case was described initially.

Does not write a receipt – אֵין כּוֹתְבִין שׁוֹבֵר: There is a dispute between *tanna'im* (see 170b) involving cases where there is a danger of double collection, such as when a creditor has lost his promissory note and seeks to collect the debt anyway. According to some *tanna'im*, he is able to collect the debt, and a receipt is given to the debtor to protect him from suffering a second collection in the event that the lost document is found. According to others, a receipt is not written. These latter *tanna'im* consider it unfair to transfer the burden of preserving and producing documentation from the creditor, who generally must produce documentation to receive payment, to the debtor, who must now produce the documentation to avoid paying. In the case of the *baraita* there is a danger of double collection that could be neutralized by giving a receipt to the seller of the field. Since this option is not pursued, the Gemara infers that the *tanna* of this *baraita* is in agreement with those who maintain that a receipt is not written in such cases.

Perek **X**
Daf **169** Amud **b**

אֲמַר לְהוּ: בְּעָלְמָא כּוֹתְבִין שׁוֹבֵר, וְהָכָא הַיְינוּ טַעֲמָא, דְּדִלְמָא אָזֵיל בַּעַל חוֹב וְטָרֵיף מִינֵּיהּ דְּלוֹקֵחַ, וְאָזֵיל אִיהוּ וְטָרֵיף לָקוֹחוֹת, וְשׁוֹבֵר גַּבֵּי לָקוֹחוֹת לֵיכָּא.

Rav Pappa or Rav Ashi **said to** them: Do not draw this conclusion. It is possible that the *tanna* of the *baraita* holds that **generally** the court **writes a receipt** when a creditor has lost his promissory note. **And here, this is the reason** that it does not write a receipt: **As, perhaps the creditor,** i.e., the one from whom the property was stolen, will **go and repossess** property **from the purchaser** who bought the stolen land, **and** the purchaser, seeking reimbursement in accordance with the guarantee, will **go and repossess** property from other **purchasers** who had later bought property from the same seller. **And the receipt** will not help, because it **is not with the purchasers** who bought property from the seller, but is in the possession of the seller himself. The purchasers, who are the ones who will suffer from the double collection, have no protection; they will in fact not even be aware that they are the victims of a double collection.

סוֹף סוֹף, לָקוֹחוֹת לָאו אַמָּרֵי דְּאַרְעָא הָדְרִי?

The Gemara asks: **Ultimately, don't** these **purchasers go back to the owner,** i.e., the seller, **of the land** to demand reimbursement? At that point the seller will produce the receipt, exposing the double collection, and the entire process will be reversed, so that ultimately the purchaser who suffered from the unjust collection will obtain possession of his property.

אַדְּהָכִי וְהָכִי שָׁמֵיט וְאָכֵיל פֵּירֵי;

The Gemara answers: While it is true that ultimately the deception will be discovered, **in the interim,** between the time the land was unjustly repossessed from the purchaser and the time when the injustice is reversed, the one who repossessed the land **seizes** the land **and consumes** its **produce,**[N] i.e., he enjoys the profits produced by the land, and it will be difficult to receive full reimbursement for this stolen produce.

NOTES

Seizes the land and consumes its produce – שָׁמֵיט וְאָכֵיל פֵּירֵי: As the Sages teach elsewhere (*Ḥullin* 89a), stolen property that has been consumed is difficult to repay. It is difficult to accurately evaluate that which is no longer extant and to ensure that proper reimbursement for it is made. Therefore, the produce of the field that has been consumed by the party who has unjustly seized land, between the time of the seizure and the time that the injustice is discovered, will constitute a loss for the party who suffered the unjust seizure of his land (Rashbam; Rabbeinu Gershom Meor HaGola).

אִי נַמִי, לְלוֹקֵחַ שֶׁלֹּא בְּאַחֲרָיוּת.

Alternatively, the reason the option of writing a receipt for the seller of the land is not pursued here is that there is a concern **about one who purchases** land **without a guarantee.** As such a purchaser knows that he has no recourse to be reimbursed from the seller if the land he bought is repossessed, he will never contact the seller and discover that the seller has a receipt and that he has been the victim of an unjust double collection.

אִי הָכִי, שִׁטְרֵי הַלְוָאָה נַמִי!

The Gemara asks: **If so,** the same concern should be taken into consideration in the case of **promissory notes as well.** And yet Rav Pappa or Rav Ashi, said that the *tanna* of the *baraita* concedes that a receipt may be written for the debtor to enable the collection of a debt in the event of the loss of the promissory note. Why are the aforementioned concerns not applicable to the case of debt collection?

הָתָם דְּזוּזֵי מַסֵּיק, אָמְרִי: פַּיְּיסֵיהּ בַּעַל חוֹב בְּזוּזֵי, הָכָא דְּאַרְעָא מַסֵּיק, מֵידַע יָדְעִי דְּמַאן דְּמַסִּיק אַרְעָא – בְּזוּזֵי לָא מִפַּיֵּיס.

The Gemara answers: **There, where** the debtor **owes money,** when the creditor seeks to repossess sold land, the purchaser of that land **will say** to himself: There is a possibility that the debtor **appeased the creditor by** paying him **money,** since debts are usually settled with money. I will therefore investigate the matter with the debtor before allowing the creditor to repossess my land. At that point the receipt, held by the debtor, will be discovered, and double collection will be prevented. **Here, where he owes land,** as the issue is that the claim is based on reimbursement for having bought stolen land, the purchaser **knows that** it is **not** common for one **who is owed land** to be **appeased with money** in such cases. The purchaser will therefore allow his land to be repossessed and will seek reimbursement at a later time.

אָמַר מָר: חוּץ מִן הָאַחֲרָיוּת שֶׁבּוֹ. הֵיכִי כָּתְבִינַן? אֲמַר רַב נַחְמָן, דְּכָתְבִי הָכִי: "שְׁטָרָא דְּנַן דְּלָא לְמִיגְבֵּי בֵּיהּ לָא מִמְּשַׁעְבְּדֵי וְלָא מִבְּנֵי חָרֵי, אֶלָּא כִּי הֵיכִי דְּתֵיקוּם אַרְעָא בִּידֵיהּ דְּלוֹקֵחַ".

§ The Gemara returns to the *baraita* and analyzes one of its statements. **The Master says** in the *baraita*: With regard to deeds of buying and selling land, the court may write a replacement document, **excluding the guarantee**[H] **that** was **in** the first document that if the field is repossessed the seller will compensate the purchaser for his loss. **How do we write** a bill of sale in such a way that it does not include this guarantee? **Rav Naḥman said** that the case is one in **which** the court **writes as follows: Our deed is not** intended **to enable** the **collection** of reimbursement in event of repossession, **neither** collection **from liened** property that has been sold **nor** collection **from unsold** property; **rather,** it is intended merely to ensure **that the land is established in the possession of the purchaser.**

אָמַר רַפְרָם, זֹאת אוֹמֶרֶת: אַחֲרָיוּת – טָעוּת סוֹפֵר הוּא; טַעְמָא דְּכָתַב לֵיהּ הָכִי, הָא לָא כָּתַב לֵיהּ הָכִי – גָּבֵי.

Rafram says: This statement of Rav Naḥman serves **to say** that the omission of the **guarantee** of the sale from a document **is a scribal error.**[H] That is, it is assumed that when one purchases land he expects to have his purchase guaranteed, and that if such a clause is not stated in the document it is presumed to be a mere scribal oversight, and a guarantee is in effect. Rav Naḥman said, in explaining the *baraita*, that **the** only **reason** a land purchase would not have a guarantee **is that** the scribe **wrote this for him,** i.e., he wrote that there is no guarantee, explicitly in the deed; **this** indicates that if the scribe **did not write this** explicitly **for** the purchaser, but left out the subject of the guarantee altogether, the purchaser **would** nevertheless have the guarantee and would be able to **collect** reimbursement from the seller in the event of repossession.

רַב אַשִׁי אָמַר: אַחֲרָיוּת – לָאו טָעוּת סוֹפֵר הוּא, וּמַאי "חוּץ מֵאַחֲרָיוּת שֶׁבּוֹ"? דְּלָא כְּתִיב בֵּיהּ אַחֲרָיוּת.

Rav Ashi disagrees and **says:** The omission of the **guarantee** of the sale from a document **is not a scribal error.** Accordingly, if mention of a guarantee is omitted from a bill of sale, there is in fact no guarantee. **And what** does the *baraita* mean when it says: **Excluding the guarantee that** was **in** the first document? It means simply **that** in this case there was **no** clause about a **guarantee written in it** at all.

הַהִיא אִיתְּתָא דִּיהַבָה לֵיהּ זוּזֵי לְהַהוּא גַּבְרָא לְמִיזְבַּן לָהּ אַרְעָא, אֲזַל זְבַן לָהּ שֶׁלֹּא בְּאַחֲרָיוּת; אָתְיָא לְקַמֵּיהּ דְּרַב נַחְמָן,

The Gemara relates: There was **a certain woman who gave money to a certain man to** act as her agent and **purchase land for her.** The agent **went** and **purchased** land **for her,** but he conducted the purchase in such a way that it was **without a guarantee.**[H] The woman wanted to take action against the agent and **came before Rav Naḥman** to ask what recourse she had.

HALAKHA

Excluding the guarantee – חוּץ מִן הָאַחֲרָיוּת: If one appears before the court and states that he has lost a bill of sale for land he has purchased from another, the court may write a replacement deed for him. The replacement deed must state: This document is not intended for the collection of a guarantee, neither from sold property nor from unsold property; we have written this document only to provide proof that the land belongs to this person, so that the seller or his heirs should not be able to take it from him. This is in accordance with the *baraita*, as interpreted by Rav Naḥman. A similar *halakha* applies to a deed of gift, although, as noted by the *Sma*, in that case it is not necessary to explicitly state that the replacement document is not intended to be used for the collection of a guarantee (Rambam *Sefer Mishpatim, Hilkhot Malve VeLoveh* 22:10; *Shulḥan Arukh, Ḥoshen Mishpat* 239:1, 41:3, and in the comment of Rema).

Omission of the guarantee is a scribal error – אַחֲרָיוּת טָעוּת סוֹפֵר: With regard to any document testifying to a loan or to a sale of land, even if no guarantee clause is written in it, it is considered as if one were written, as it is assumed to be an inadvertent omission on the part of the scribe, and a guarantee is applied in these transactions. This is in accordance with the ruling of Rava in tractate *Bava Metzia* (15b). The only way for a transaction not to be subject to a guarantee is if it is written explicitly in the document that there is no guarantee, as Rafram states here (Rambam *Sefer Nezikin, Hilkhot Gezeila VaAveda* 18:1; *Sefer Kinyan, Hilkhot Mekhira* 19:1; and *Hilkhot Zekhiya UMattana* 5:8; *Shulḥan Arukh, Ḥoshen Mishpat* 39:1, 49:2, and in the comment of Rema).

He went and purchased land for her without a guarantee – אֲזַל זְבַן לָהּ שֶׁלֹּא בְּאַחֲרָיוּת: If one gives money to an agent to purchase land for him, and the agent purchases the land without a guarantee, he is considered to have mishandled his mission and the agency is rendered void, as the one who appointed him can claim: I sent you to act for my benefit, not to my detriment. The agent must purchase the property for himself without a guarantee and then resell it with a guarantee to the one who appointed him, so that the burden of reimbursement falls upon the agent. The Rema adds that this is the procedure only if the one who appointed the agent is satisfied with the guarantee of the agent; otherwise, he has the option of canceling the sale altogether. Some say that if the agent has the money to return to the one who appointed him, he can do so and does not have to purchase the property without a guarantee (Rambam *Sefer Kinyan, Hilkhot Sheluḥin VeShutafin* 1:3, and see 2:4; *Shulḥan Arukh, Ḥoshen Mishpat* 182:6).

אֲמַר לֵיהּ: ״לְתַקּוֹנֵי שַׁדַּרְתִּיךְ וְלָא לְעַוּוֹתֵי״, זִיל זְבְנָה מִינֵּיהּ שֶׁלֹּא בְּאַחֲרָיוּת, וַהֲדַר זַבְנָהּ נִיהֲלָהּ בְּאַחֲרָיוּת.

Rav Naḥman **said to** the agent: The principle with regard to an agent is that if he acts to the detriment of the one who appointed him, the one who appointed him can say: **I sent you to act for my benefit**[N] **and not to my detriment.** Therefore, the entire agency is null and void, thereby negating the purchase. Nevertheless, you agreed to purchase the land without a guarantee. Therefore, **go** yourself and **purchase** the land **from him without a guarantee, and then sell it to** this woman **with a guarantee** that you will reimburse her in the event the land is repossessed.

״רַבָּן שִׁמְעוֹן בֶּן גַּמְלִיאֵל אוֹמֵר: הַנּוֹתֵן מַתָּנָה לַחֲבֵירוֹ וְהֶחְזִיר לוֹ אֶת הַשְּׁטָר – חָזְרָה מַתְּנָתוֹ, וַחֲכָמִים אוֹמְרִים: מַתְּנָתוֹ קַיֶּימֶת״. מַאי טַעְמָא דְּרַבָּן שִׁמְעוֹן בֶּן גַּמְלִיאֵל? אֲמַר רַב אַסִי, נַעֲשָׂה כְּאוֹמֵר לוֹ: שָׂדֶה זוֹ נְתוּנָה לְךָ כׇּל זְמַן שֶׁהַשְּׁטָר בְּיָדְךָ.

§ The *baraita* teaches that **Rabban Shimon ben Gamliel says:** In the case of **one who gives a gift** of land **to another, and** the recipient **returned the deed to him, his gift** of land **returns** to him as well. **But the Rabbis say: His gift** of land **remains** in the possession of the recipient. The Gemara asks: **What is the reason** for the opinion **of Rabban Shimon ben Gamliel? Rav Asi says: It becomes as if** the giver **said to** the recipient: **This field is given to you** only **as long as the deed** remains **in your possession.** Therefore, by returning the deed to the giver, the recipient is canceling the gift.

מַתְקִיף לַהּ רַבָּה: אִי הָכִי, נִגְנַב אוֹ אָבַד נָמֵי!

Rabba objects to this: If that is so that these are the conditions of the gift, then when the deed is **stolen** from **or lost** by the recipient, the gift should **also** be canceled.

אֶלָּא אָמַר רַבָּה: בְּאוֹתִיּוֹת נִקְנוֹת בִּמְסִירָה קָמִיפַּלְגִי, רַבָּן שִׁמְעוֹן בֶּן גַּמְלִיאֵל סָבַר: אוֹתִיּוֹת נִקְנוֹת בִּמְסִירָה, וְרַבָּנַן סָבְרִי: אֵין אוֹתִיּוֹת נִקְנוֹת בִּמְסִירָה.

Rather, Rabba said a different explanation: Rabban Shimon ben Gamliel and the Rabbis **disagree about** whether or not the **letters,** i.e., the contents of a promissory note, **are acquired by** merely **transferring** the document from one holder of the document to another. **Rabban Shimon ben Gamliel holds** that the **letters are acquired by transferring**[N] the document. Therefore, if the recipient returns the bill of sale to the giver, the land returns to the giver as well. **And the Rabbis hold** that the **letters are not acquired by transferring**[H] the document.

תָּנוּ רַבָּנַן: הַבָּא לָדוּן בִּשְׁטָר וּבַחֲזָקָה – נִידּוֹן בִּשְׁטָר, דִּבְרֵי רַבִּי; רַבָּן שִׁמְעוֹן בֶּן גַּמְלִיאֵל אוֹמֵר: בַּחֲזָקָה.

The Sages taught in a *baraita*: With regard to **one who comes** to court **to be judged** over a claim that land that is in his possession belongs to another, if he claims ownership **based on a deed,** i.e., a bill of sale, **and** claims further that he is the owner **based on presumptive ownership** of the land, as it was in his uncontested possession for three years, and he therefore does not need the deed as proof, his claim is **judged based on the deed.** This is **the statement of Rabbi** Yehuda HaNasi. **Rabban Shimon ben Gamliel says:** His claim is judged **based on** his **presumptive ownership.**

בְּמַאי קָמִיפַּלְגִי? כִּי אֲתָא רַב דִּימִי אָמַר: בְּאוֹתִיּוֹת נִקְנוֹת בִּמְסִירָה קָא מִיפַּלְגִי,

The Gemara analyzes the *baraita*: **With regard to what do** Rabbi Yehuda HaNasi and Rabban Shimon ben Gamliel **disagree? When Rav Dimi came** from Eretz Yisrael to Babylonia **he said: They disagree** about whether or not **letters are acquired by transferring** the document from one holder of the document to another.

HALAKHA

Letters are not acquired by transferring – אֵין אוֹתִיּוֹת נִקְנוֹת בִּמְסִירָה: How does one transfer ownership of a promissory note or a bill of sale to another party? The seller writes a separate document, or may even add the following statement into the original document being sold (*Sma*; *Shakh*): You, so-and-so; acquire from me, so-and-so, this document, along with all the rights embodied therein. The document is then transferred to the new owner. It thereby emerges that the document has been acquired through writing and transferring. If this statement is not written, the document cannot be transferred to another party, as the letters of a document are not acquired through merely transferring the document, in accordance with the conclusion of the Gemara earlier in this tractate (77a), and in accordance with the opinion of the Rabbis (Rambam *Sefer Kinyan*, *Hilkhot Sheluḥin VeShutafin* 6:10; *Shulḥan Arukh*, *Ḥoshen Mishpat* 66:1).

NOTES

I sent you to act for my benefit, etc. – לְתַקּוֹנֵי שַׁדַּרְתִּיךְ: The early commentaries understand this case in different ways. According to some, the agent did not inform the seller that he was purchasing the land on behalf of the woman; rather, he purchased it without specifying the identity of the purchaser. Therefore, although the man's agency was rendered void by virtue of the fact that he acted to the woman's detriment, the sale remained in effect. Had the agent informed the seller that he was acting as an agent for the woman, the entire transaction would have been rendered void and no further action would be necessary (Ran on Rif in *Kiddushin* 17a; see Rambam). Others say that the agent did inform the seller that the purchase was on behalf of the woman, and the sale is completely void. By right, the agent should simply return the money to the woman, but in the case here the agent does not have enough money to do so. Therefore, Rav Naḥman told him to return to the seller and repurchase the land in his own name, even without a guarantee if the seller insists on this.

Letters are acquired by transferring – אוֹתִיּוֹת נִקְנוֹת בִּמְסִירָה: Rabban Shimon ben Gamliel holds that the legal rights listed in a document are transferred from one party to another merely by handing over the document. In the case of a bill of sale, this means that the ownership of the land is transferred by handing over its deed, and stating: Acquire this document and all the rights therein. It is for this reason that Rabban Shimon ben Gamliel said in the first clause of the *baraita* that a replacement bill of sale may not be written for a purchaser who lost the original. The concern is that the purchaser may have resold the land to the original owner in the interim by merely transferring the deed to him. A replacement bill of sale would enable him to unjustly reclaim the land. The Rabbis, by contrast, maintain that ownership cannot be transferred merely by transferring possession of the deed; a new document would have to be written, and the date on that new document would prevent the purchaser from using his replacement document, with its prior date, to reclaim the land from the seller (Ramah; Rid).

רַבָּן שִׁמְעוֹן בֶּן גַּמְלִיאֵל סָבַר: אֵין אוֹתִיּוֹת נִקְנוֹת בִּמְסִירָה, וְרַבִּי סָבַר: אוֹתִיּוֹת נִקְנוֹת בִּמְסִירָה.

The Gemara explains: This is a case where one party sold land to another, who then sold it to a third party by transferring the bill of sale to him. **Rabban Shimon ben Gamliel holds** that the **letters are not acquired by transferring** possession of the document. Handing the bill to the third party is therefore not a valid act of acquisition. In in order to establish that the land is his, one must prove presumptive ownership by demonstrating that he has lived in the land uncontested for three years. **And Rabbi** Yehuda HaNasi **holds** that the **letters are acquired by transferring** possession of the document. Therefore, if the third party produces the bill of sale that had been transferred to him, this is sufficient proof that the land is his.

אֲמַר לֵיהּ אַבַּיֵי: אִם כֵּן, פְּלוּגְתָּא לְדְמָר! אֲמַר לֵיהּ: וְתִפְלוֹג.

Abaye objected and **said to** Rav Dimi: **If that is so,** that Rabban Shimon ben Gamliel holds that letters are not acquired by transferring possession of the bill of sale, this would be in **disagreement with** what **the Master,** Rabba, said earlier, that Rabban Shimon ben Gamliel maintains that letters are acquired by transferring possession of the bill of sale. Rav Dimi **said** back **to him: And let it be in disagreement.** I am not obligated to be in agreement with Rabba.

אֲמַר לֵיהּ, הָכִי קָאָמִינָא לָךְ: מַתְנִיתָא לָא מִיתַּרְצָא אֶלָּא כְּדִמְתָרְצָא מָר, וְאִם כֵּן קַשְׁיָא דְּרַבָּן שִׁמְעוֹן בֶּן גַּמְלִיאֵל אַדְּרַבָּן שִׁמְעוֹן בֶּן גַּמְלִיאֵל!

Abaye clarified his objection and **said to him: This is what I** meant to **say to you. The** ***baraita*** (168b), which Rabba was explaining, **can be explained only** the way the **Master,** Rabba, **explained** it. **And if so,** i.e., if you do not agree with Rabba's understanding of the opinion of Rabban Shimon ben Gamliel, there is **a difficulty,** as there is a contradiction **between** one statement **of Rabban Shimon ben Gamliel and** the other statement **of Rabban Shimon ben Gamliel.**

אֶלָּא אֲמַר אַבַּיֵי: הָכָא בְּמַאי עָסְקִינַן – כְּגוֹן שֶׁנִּמְצָא אֶחָד מֵהֶן קָרוֹב אוֹ פָּסוּל;

Rather, Abaye said that the explanation of the *baraita* concerning one who appears before a court to be judged is as follows: **With what are we dealing here?** We are dealing with a case **where one of** the witnesses signed on the bill **was found to be a relative** to one of the parties, **or** he was found to be **disqualified** from bearing witness for another reason, and therefore the document is rendered invalid.

וּבִפְלוּגְתָּא דְּרַבִּי מֵאִיר וְרַבִּי אֶלְעָזָר קָא מִיפַּלְגִי, רַבִּי סָבַר לָהּ כְּרַבִּי אֶלְעָזָר, דְּאָמַר: עֵדֵי מְסִירָה כָּרְתֵי;

Abaye continues: **And** the two opinions in the *baraita* disagree **with regard to** the issue that is the subject of **the dispute between Rabbi Meir and Rabbi Elazar. Rabbi** Yehuda HaNasi **holds in accordance with** the opinion of **Rabbi Elazar, who says: The witnesses of the transmission** of the document **effect** the transaction,[H] meaning that witnesses are not required to be signed on a document at all, provided that there are witnesses who saw the transfer of the document to the relevant party. It is therefore inconsequential that one of the witnesses that signed the document is disqualified. This is why Rabbi Yehuda HaNasi says that the claim is judged based on the deed, i.e., the deed is valid.

וְרַבָּן שִׁמְעוֹן בֶּן גַּמְלִיאֵל סָבַר לָהּ כְּרַבִּי מֵאִיר, דְּאָמַר: עֵדֵי חֲתִימָה כָּרְתֵי.

And Rabban Shimon ben Gamliel holds in accordance with the opinion of **Rabbi Meir, who says: The signatory witnesses** on the document **effect** the transaction, meaning that it is necessary for a document to have witnesses sign it. If there are no witnesses or if one or both of them are disqualified, the document is not valid even if its transmission is witnessed by qualified witnesses. This is why Rabban Shimon ben Gamliel says that the claim is judged based on the claimant's presumptive ownership; this is his only valid proof since the deed he possesses is not valid.

וְהָא אָמַר רַבִּי אַבָּא: מוֹדֶה הָיָה רַבִּי אֶלְעָזָר בִּמְזוּיָּיף מִתּוֹכוֹ שֶׁהוּא פָּסוּל!

The Gemara objects to Abaye's explanation: **But doesn't Rabbi Abba say** that **Rabbi Elazar concedes** that **in** the case of a document whose **falsification is inherent in it**[H] **that it is not valid?** Rabbi Elazar said only that a document that has no witnesses signed on it at all is valid if its transmission was witnessed. If the document has disqualified witnesses, he agrees it is not valid.

HALAKHA

The witnesses of the transmission effect the transaction – עֵדֵי מְסִירָה כָּרְתֵי: There must be two valid witnesses present when a bill of divorce is handed from a husband to a wife, as the *halakha* is in accordance with the opinion of Rabbi Elazar, that witnesses of the transmission of the bill of divorce effect the divorce. The Sages instituted for the betterment of the world that witnesses should also sign the bill of divorce, lest the witnesses who saw the transmission not be available later to attest to the divorce. If a bill of divorce signed by witnesses is transmitted not in the presence of witnesses, some say it is a valid divorce after the fact (Rif; Rambam), while others say that it is not valid (*Ge'onim*; *Tur*, citing Rabbeinu Tam and Rosh). In the opposite case, when there are witnesses to the transmission of the bill of divorce but no witnesses signed the bill of divorce, all agree that the divorce is valid.

The same is true with regard to documents other than bills of divorce. If witnesses see the transmission of the document, even if no witnesses signed the document, the transaction is valid and the document can be used to collect even liened property that has been sold. This is in accordance with the statement of Shmuel (*Gittin* 86b), that the *halakha* is in accordance with the opinion of Rabbi Elazar with regard to all kinds of documents. By contrast, the *Shakh* notes that some authorities disagree with this and maintain that the *halakha* is in accordance with the opinion of Rabbi Elazar only with regard to bills of divorce (Rambam *Sefer Nashim, Hilkhot Geirushin* 1:15, 18 and *Sefer Mishpatim, Hilkhot Malve VeLoveh* 11:2; *Shulḥan Arukh, Even HaEzer* 133:1 and *Ḥoshen Mishpat* 51:7).

In the case of a document whose falsification is inherent in it – בִּמְזוּיָּיף מִתּוֹכוֹ: If a document has just two witnesses signed on it (see *Sma*), and one of them is discovered to be related to one of the parties or disqualified from bearing witness for another reason, then even if there were witnesses who saw the transmission of the document, in the case of a bill of divorce the document cannot be used to effect a divorce, and if it is a financial document it cannot be used to collect a debt from liened property that has been sold. Some say that the document has the status of a document with the signature of one witness (Rambam *Sefer Nashim, Hilkhot Geirushin* 1:17; *Shulḥan Arukh, Even HaEzer* 130:17 and *Ḥoshen Mishpat* 51:3, 7).

אֶלָּא אָמַר רַבִּי אָבִינָא: הַכֹּל מוֹדִים, שֶׁאִם כָּתוּב בּוֹ: "הוּזְקַקְנוּ לְעֵדוּתָן שֶׁל עֵדִים, וְנִמְצֵאת עֵדוּתָן מְזוּיֶּיפֶת" – שֶׁהוּא פָּסוּל, כִּדְרַבִּי אַבָּא. לֹא נֶחְלְקוּ אֶלָּא בִּשְׁטָר שֶׁאֵין עָלָיו עֵדִים כְּלָל, דְּרַבִּי סָבַר לַהּ כְּרַבִּי אֶלְעָזָר, דְּאָמַר: עֵדֵי מְסִירָה כָּרְתֵי, וְרַבָּן שִׁמְעוֹן בֶּן גַּמְלִיאֵל סָבַר לַהּ כְּרַבִּי מֵאִיר, דְּאָמַר: עֵדֵי חֲתִימָה כָּרְתֵי.

Rather, Rabbi Avina said a modification of Abaye's explanation. **All concede that if it is written in** the document: We, the court, **engaged in** an investigation of **the testimony of the witnesses** and have determined that they signed the document, **and their testimony was found** to be **false,** the document **is not valid, in accordance with** the statement **of Rabbi Abba. They disagree only with regard to a document upon which there are no witnesses** signed **at all. As Rabbi** Yehuda HaNasi **holds in accordance with** the opinion of **Rabbi Elazar, who says: The witnesses of the transmission** of the document **effect** the transaction. Signatory witnesses are not necessary, and the deed can therefore be used as proof. **And Rabban Shimon ben Gamliel holds in accordance with** the opinion of **Rabbi Meir, who says: The signatory witnesses** on the document **effect** the transaction, so the deed cannot be used. Therefore, the only valid proof would be based on his presumptive ownership.

וְאִיבָּעֵית אֵימָא: בְּמוֹדֶה בִּשְׁטָר שֶׁכְּתָבוֹ צָרִיךְ לְקַיְּימוֹ קָא מִיפַּלְגִי,

The Gemara suggests: **And if you wish, say** instead: The case in the *baraita* is one where the alleged purchaser has a bill of sale for the land, but the alleged seller, although he admits that the document was written with his consent, claims that the sale did not ultimately occur, and that the alleged purchaser took the document from him. And the *tanna'im* in the *baraita* **disagree, with regard to** the *halakha* in the case of a debtor **who admits that he wrote** a promissory **note,**[N] whether the creditor **is required to ratify it** in court in order to collect, and, by extension, in a case where a seller admits that he wrote a bill of sale, whether the purchaser must ratify it in court in order to establish its validity.

דְּרַבִּי סָבַר: מוֹדֶה בִּשְׁטָר שֶׁכְּתָבוֹ – אֵין צָרִיךְ לְקַיְּימוֹ, וְרַבָּן שִׁמְעוֹן בֶּן גַּמְלִיאֵל סָבַר: צָרִיךְ לְקַיְּימוֹ.

As, Rabbi Yehuda HaNasi **holds** that in the case of a debtor **who admits that he wrote** a promissory **note,** the creditor **is not required to ratify it** in court in order to collect what is owed to him. In this case as well, the purchaser can use the bill of sale as proof that he is the rightful owner of the property. **And Rabban Shimon ben Gamliel holds** that in the case of a debtor who admits that he wrote a promissory note, the creditor **is required to ratify it** in court in order to use it to collect the debt. In this case as well, since the purchaser is unable to ratify it, his only recourse to prove his ownership is showing that he lived in the land uncontested for three years.

וְהָא אִיפְּכָא שָׁמְעִינַן לְהוּ! דְּתַנְיָא: שְׁנַיִם אֲדוּקִין בִּשְׁטָר, מַלְוֶה אוֹמֵר: "שֶׁלִּי הוּא, וְנָפַל מִמֶּנִּי וּמְצָאתוֹ", וְלֹוֶה אוֹמֵר: "שֶׁלְּךָ הוּא, וּפְרַעְתִּיו לְךָ" – יִתְקַיֵּים הַשְּׁטָר בְּחוֹתְמָיו, דִּבְרֵי רַבִּי. רַבָּן שִׁמְעוֹן בֶּן גַּמְלִיאֵל אוֹמֵר: יַחֲלוֹקוּ;

The Gemara asks: **But didn't we hear the opposite concerning** Rabbi Yehuda HaNasi and Rabban Shimon ben Gamliel? **As it is taught** in a *baraita* (*Tosefta, Bava Metzia* 1:8) that if **two** people, the debtor and the creditor, **are grasping** a promissory **note,**[H] and the **creditor says: It is mine,** i.e., the debt has not yet been paid, **and it fell from me, and you,** the debtor, **found it, and** the **debtor says: It is** in fact **yours,** i.e., I did borrow the money from you, **but I paid you** and was given the promissory note, and it fell from me, and you found it, **the** promissory **note must be ratified through its signatories,** even though the debtor admits it is a valid document. **This is the statement of Rabbi** Yehuda HaNasi. **Rabban Shimon ben Gamliel says: They should divide** the amount written in the promissory note, i.e., the debtor must pay half of the recorded sum to the creditor.

וְהָוֵינַן בָּהּ, וְלֵית לֵיהּ לְרַבִּי הָא דִּתְנַן: שְׁנַיִם אוֹחֲזִין בְּטַלִּית, זֶה אוֹמֵר "אֲנִי מְצָאתִיהָ" וְזֶה אוֹמֵר "אֲנִי מְצָאתִיהָ" – זֶה יִשָּׁבַע שֶׁאֵין לוֹ בָּהּ פָּחוֹת מֶחֶצְיָהּ, וְזֶה יִשָּׁבַע שֶׁאֵין לוֹ בָּהּ פָּחוֹת מֶחֶצְיָהּ, וְיַחֲלוֹקוּ?

The Gemara explains: **And we discussed it** once before and asked the following question about it: **But doesn't Rabbi** Yehuda HaNasi agree to **that which we learned** in a mishna (*Bava Metzia* 2a), with regard to **two** people who came to court **holding a garment,** where **this one is saying: I found it, and that** one is **saying: I found it;** that **this one takes an oath that he does not have** claim to **less than half of it, and that** one **takes an oath that he does not have** claim to **less than half of it, and they divide** it? Why does Rabbi Yehuda HaNasi not maintain that in a case where the debtor and creditor are grasping a promissory note, there too they should divide the money?

NOTES

Who admits that he wrote a promissory note – מוֹדֶה בִּשְׁטָר שֶׁכְּתָבוֹ: The case is one where the alleged purchaser, who presently occupies the land, is confronted by the alleged seller, who claims that the land still belongs to him and was never sold to the present occupant. The alleged purchaser presents a bill of sale, and the seller admits that the document was prepared with his consent and that the witnesses' signatures are genuine. Despite this, he claims that the document had been in his possession, having been prepared in advance of a sale that never occurred, and it was lost or stolen from him and ultimately came to be in the possession of the alleged purchaser, or it had been given to the alleged purchaser in trust that he would not use it until the sale was finalized. All these claims are generally too weak to be accepted if the document is ratified by the court through external evidence. In this case, it is the alleged seller himself who vouches for the authenticity of the document. The question therefore is whether or not the seller's claims can be accepted if the document is not ratified through the usual process using external evidence.

HALAKHA

Two people are grasping a promissory note, etc. – שְׁנַיִם אֲדוּקִין בִּשְׁטָר וכו׳: If the debtor and the creditor are grasping a promissory note, each one claiming that it was in his possession and fell from him with the other person then grasping it, if it is possible to ratify the note, each party takes an oath that he does not have claim to less than half of the amount of money recorded in the promissory note, and the debtor pays half the sum stated in the document. If it is not possible to ratify the note, the debtor takes an oath that he owes nothing, and he is exempt from paying. The *halakha* is in accordance with the opinion of Rabbi Yehuda HaNasi, that in the case of a debtor who admits that he wrote a promissory note, the creditor is required to ratify it in court in order to collect the debt (Rambam *Sefer Nashim, Hilkhot Geirushin* 1:14; *Shulḥan Arukh, Ḥoshen Mishpat* 65:15).

HALAKHA

With regard to verifying – **בִּלְבָרֵר**: If one has possession of a parcel of land and a previous owner of the land contests his claim, saying that he, the previous owner, had never sold it, and the occupier counters that he purchased it or received it as a gift from the previous owner and that he has a bill of sale or deed of gift, as well as three years of uncontested possession to prove his claim, the court instructs him to ratify his deed. As long as the witnesses signed on the deed are available, he must bring them to court to ratify their signatures. If the witnesses are not available to ratify it, his three years of uncontested possession are sufficient to establish his ownership of the land. This is in accordance with the conclusion of the Gemara, that the dispute between Rabbi Yehuda HaNasi and Rabban Shimon ben Gamliel concerns the issue of verification of claims, and that the *halakha* is in accordance with the opinion of Rabbi Yehuda HaNasi (Rambam *Sefer Mishpatim*, *Hilkhot To'en VeNitan* 15:1; *Shulḥan Arukh*, *Ḥoshen Mishpat* 140:4).

וַאֲמַר רָבָא אָמַר רַב נַחְמָן: בִּמְקוּיָּים – דְּכוּלֵּי עָלְמָא לָא פְּלִיגִי דְּיַחְלוֹקוּ; כִּי פְּלִיגִי – בְּשֶׁאֵינוֹ מְקוּיָּים, רַבִּי סָבַר: מוֹדֶה בִּשְׁטָר שֶׁכְּתָבוֹ צָרִיךְ לְקַיְּימוֹ, וְאִי מְקַיֵּים לֵיהּ – גָּבֵי פַּלְגָּא, וְאִי לָא – חַסְפָּא בְּעָלְמָא הוּא;

And in response to this question **Rava said** that **Rav Naḥman said: In** the case of **a ratified** promissory note, **everyone agrees that they should divide it. Where they disagree** is in the case of a note **that is not ratified. Rabbi** Yehuda HaNasi **holds** that in the case of a debtor **who admits that he wrote** a promissory **note,** the creditor **is required to ratify it** in court in order to collect the debt from him. **And if he** successfully **ratifies it,** the creditor **collects half** of the recorded sum, since the two parties are contesting ownership of the document. **And if** he is **not** successful in ratifying the note, it **is merely a shard,** i.e., a worthless piece of paper.

וְרַבָּן שִׁמְעוֹן בֶּן גַּמְלִיאֵל סָבַר: מוֹדֶה בִּשְׁטָר שֶׁכְּתָבוֹ אֵין צָרִיךְ לְקַיְּימוֹ, וְיַחְלוֹקוּ!

And Rabban Shimon ben Gamliel holds that in the case of a debtor **who admits that he wrote** a promissory **note,** the creditor **is not required to ratify it** in court in order to collect payment. Since the note is valid and fit for collection, **they should divide** it, i.e., the creditor collects half the sum, as the ownership of the document is contested. The positions of Rabbi Yehuda HaNasi and Rabban Shimon ben Gamliel are therefore the reverse of what the Gemara proposed in its explanation of the first *baraita*.

אֵיפוּךְ.

The Gemara answers: **Reverse** the way the opinions of Rabbi Yehuda HaNasi and Rabban Shimon ben Gamliel are recorded in one of the two *baraitot* so that they are consistent in both *baraitot*.

וְאִיבָּעֵית אֵימָא: לְעוֹלָם לָא תֵּיפוּךְ, אֶלָּא הָכָא בִּלְבָרֵר קָמִיפַּלְגִי;

And if you wish, say instead: **Actually, do not reverse** their opinions. There is no contradiction between them, because the issue in the first *baraita* is not whether or not a bill of sale must be ratified when the seller admits that he wrote it. **Rather, here** the *tanna'im* **disagree with regard to verifying,**[H] i.e., they disagree about whether a litigant is required to verify all his claims in circumstances where his case is strong enough to have the court rule in his favor even if they were to disregard some of his claims. Generally, if one has evidence of presumptive ownership of a field he does not have to produce a bill of sale for it. Here, Rabbi Yehuda HaNasi holds that since the one occupying the land claims that he has a bill of sale, he must verify this claim by producing it. Rabban Shimon ben Gamliel holds that he is not required to produce it, as the claim of presumptive ownership suffices.

כִּי הָא דְּרַב יִצְחָק בַּר יוֹסֵף הֲוָה מַסֵּיק בֵּיהּ זוּזֵי בְּרַבִּי אַבָּא, אֲתָא לְקַמֵּיהּ דְּרַבִּי יִצְחָק נַפָּחָא, אֲמַר: פְּרַעְתִּיךְ בִּפְנֵי פְּלוֹנִי וּפְלוֹנִי. אֲמַר לֵיהּ רַבִּי יִצְחָק: יָבוֹאוּ פְּלוֹנִי וּפְלוֹנִי וְיָעִידוּ. אֲמַר לֵיהּ: אִי לָא אָתוּ לָא מְהֵימְנִינָא? וְהָא קַיְימָא לַן: הַמַּלְוֶה אֶת חֲבֵירוֹ בְּעֵדִים – אֵינוֹ צָרִיךְ לְפָרְעוֹ בְּעֵדִים!

The Gemara explains: It is **like this** case **where Rav Yitzḥak bar Yosef was owed money by Rabbi Abba.** The case **came before Rabbi Yitzḥak Nappaḥa.** Rabbi Abba **said:** I already **repaid you** the debt **in the presence of so-and-so and so-and-so. Rabbi Yitzḥak** Nappaḥa **said to** Rabbi Abba: The witnesses you have named, **so-and-so and so-and-so, must come and testify** that they saw you repay the loan. Rabbi Abba **said to** Rabbi Yitzḥak Nappaḥa: **If they do not come, am I not deemed credible** to say that I repaid the loan? **But don't we maintain** that with regard to **one who lends** money **to another in** the presence of **witnesses,**[H] the debtor **need not repay him in** the presence of **witnesses,** as he is deemed credible to say he repaid the debt even with no supporting testimony?

אֲמַר לֵיהּ: אֲנָא בְּהַהִיא כִּשְׁמַעְתָּא דְּמָר סְבִירָא לִי, דְּאָמַר רַבִּי אַבָּא אָמַר רַב אַדָּא בַּר אַהֲבָה אָמַר רַב: הָאוֹמֵר לַחֲבֵירוֹ ״פְּרַעְתִּיךְ בִּפְנֵי פְלוֹנִי וּפְלוֹנִי״ – צָרִיךְ שֶׁיָּבוֹאוּ פְּלוֹנִי וּפְלוֹנִי וְיָעִידוּ. [אֲמַר לֵיהּ:] וְהָא אָמַר רַב גִּידֵּל אָמַר רַב: הֲלָכָה כְּדִבְרֵי רַבָּן שִׁמְעוֹן בֶּן גַּמְלִיאֵל. וְאַף רַבִּי לָא

Rabbi Yitzḥak Nappaḥa **said to** Rabbi Abba: **With regard to this** issue, **I hold like the *halakha*** said **by the Master,** i.e., you yourself. **As Rabbi Abba says** that **Rav Adda bar Ahava said** that **Rav says:** If **one says to another,** i.e., if a debtor says to his creditor: **I repaid you in the presence of so-and-so and so-and-so,** it is **required that so-and-so and so-and-so come** to court **and testify** that they witnessed the repayment. Rabbi Abba **said to** Rabbi Yitzḥak Nappaḥa: **But doesn't Rav Giddel say** that **Rav says** that the ***halakha*** is **in accordance with the statement of Rabban Shimon ben Gamliel,** that it is not required that a litigant verify all his stated claims if his case is sufficiently strong without those claims? **And** moreover, **even Rabbi** Yehuda HaNasi **did not**

HALAKHA

One who lends money to another in the presence of witnesses – **הַמַּלְוֶה אֶת חֲבֵירוֹ בְּעֵדִים**: If one lends money to another in the presence of witnesses, without written documentation and without performing an act of acquisition, the debtor's repayment of the loan need not be in the presence of witnesses. Whenever he claims that he has repaid the loan he is deemed credible (Rambam *Sefer Mishpatim*, *Hilkhot Malve VeLoveh* 11:1; *Shulḥan Arukh*, *Ḥoshen Mishpat* 70:1).

אָמַר אֶלָּא לְבָרֵר! אֲמַר לֵיהּ: אֲנָא נַמִּי לְבָרֵר קָאָמִינָא.

say that the litigant loses the case if he cannot produce verification of his extraneous claims, but **only** that he is told **to verify** those claims if he can. Rabbi Yitzḥak Nappaḥa **said to** Rabbi Abba: **I, too, am saying** only that you are required **to verify** your claim if you can; if you cannot, you will not be required to pay.

מתני׳ מִי שֶׁפָּרַע מִקְצָת חוֹבוֹ – רַבִּי יְהוּדָה אוֹמֵר: יַחֲלִיף; רַבִּי יוֹסֵי אוֹמֵר: יִכְתּוֹב שׁוֹבֵר. אָמַר רַבִּי יְהוּדָה: נִמְצָא זֶה צָרִיךְ לִהְיוֹת שׁוֹמֵר שׁוֹבְרוֹ מִן הָעַכְבָּרִים! אָמַר לוֹ רַבִּי יוֹסֵי: כָּךְ יָפֶה לוֹ, וְלֹא יֵרַע כֹּחוֹ שֶׁל זֶה.

MISHNA In the case of a debtor **who repaid part of his debt,**[H] **Rabbi Yehuda says:** The creditor **should exchange** the promissory note for a new one stating the current balance and tear up the first promissory note. **Rabbi Yosei says:** The creditor may keep the original promissory note, and he **should write a receipt** for the payment he has received and give it to the debtor as proof of his partial payment of the sum recorded in the old note. **Rabbi Yehuda said** with regard to this arrangement: It is **found** that **this** debtor **must** now **guard his receipt against** being destroyed by **mice,**[B] as if he no longer has the receipt, he will have to pay the entire sum recorded in the promissory note. **Rabbi Yosei said to him: This** situation **is fitting for him;**[N] it is better that this procedure be followed, **and the strength of** the claim of **this** creditor **not be weakened.**

גמ׳ אָמַר רַב הוּנָא אָמַר רַב: אֵין הֲלָכָה לֹא כְּרַבִּי יְהוּדָה וְלֹא כְּרַבִּי יוֹסֵי, אֶלָּא בֵּית דִּין מְקָרְעִין הַשְּׁטָר וְכוֹתְבִין לוֹ שְׁטָר אַחֵר מִזְּמַן רִאשׁוֹן.

GEMARA Rav Huna says that Rav says: The *halakha* is not in accordance with the opinion of Rabbi Yehuda, nor** is it **in accordance with** the opinion of **Rabbi Yosei. Rather,** the *halakha* is that **the court tears up the** original promissory **note and writes a different** promissory **note for** the creditor, listing the new sum owed, dated **from the time** of the **first** document.

אֲמַר לֵיהּ רַב נַחְמָן לְרַב הוּנָא, וְאָמְרִי לַהּ רַב יִרְמְיָה בַּר אַבָּא לְרַב הוּנָא: אִי שְׁמִיעַ לֵיהּ לְרַב הָא [בָּרַיְיתָא,] דְּתַנְיָא: עֵדִים מְקָרְעִין אֶת הַשְּׁטָר וְכוֹתְבִין לוֹ שְׁטָר אַחֵר מִזְּמַן רִאשׁוֹן – הֲוָה הָדַר בֵּיהּ.

Rav Naḥman said to Rav Huna, and some say it was **Rav Yirmeya bar Abba** who said this **to Rav Huna: If Rav would have heard this** following ***baraita*, as it is taught** in a *baraita* that according to Rabbi Yehuda the proper procedure is that the **witnesses tear the** original promissory **note and write another** promissory **note for** the creditor listing the new sum owed, dated **from the time** of the **first** document, **he would have retracted**[N] his statement that the court tears the promissory note and writes a new one.

אֲמַר לֵיהּ: שְׁמִיעַ לֵיהּ וְלָא הֲדַר בֵּיהּ,

Rav Huna **said to him:** Rav **heard** the *baraita*, **and** nevertheless **he did not retract** his statement. While Rabbi Yehuda says in the *baraita* that the witnesses write a new promissory note, Rav maintains that this must be done specifically by a court. Why is this?

BACKGROUND

Against mice – מִן הָעַכְבָּרִים: Although mice do not eat parchment and paper, they often nibble at inedible items to obtain bits and pieces with which to line their burrows.

HALAKHA

A debtor who repaid part of his debt, etc. – מִי שֶׁפָּרַע מִקְצָת חוֹבוֹ וכו׳: If a debtor repays part of a debt recorded in a promissory note, the creditor has a choice: If he desires, the court can write a new promissory note for the remaining amount of the debt, using the date of the original loan. Alternatively, he may write a receipt for the sum received and give it to the debtor (see *Baḥ*, *Sma*, and *Shakh*), as the *halakha* is in accordance with the opinion of Rabbi Yosei. The Rema, citing *Haggahot Asheri*, rules that a new promissory note may be written by the witnesses, dated from the time of the partial repayment, provided that they obtain permission from the debtor (Rambam *Sefer Mishpatim*, *Hilkhot Malve VeLoveh* 23:16; *Shulḥan Arukh*, *Ḥoshen Mishpat* 54:1).

NOTES

This situation is fitting for him – כָּךְ יָפֶה לוֹ: The Rashbam explains that this situation is fitting, i.e., advantageous, to the creditor, because the fact that he holds a promissory note stating a sum that is more than the debtor truly owes will pressure the debtor to repay the remainder of his debt as soon as possible, out of concern that he might lose his receipt. If one must choose between serving the interests of the creditor or the debtor, the creditor's interests take precedence, as he is the one who benefited the debtor by loaning him money.

He would have retracted – הֲוָה הָדַר בֵּיהּ: According to *Tosafot*, Rav Naḥman at first misunderstood Rav's intent in his disagreement with Rabbi Yehuda. He thought that Rav understood Rabbi Yehuda to mean that the new promissory note should contain the current date rather than the date of the original loan, and that Rav disagreed and maintained that the original date should be written in the new document. Since the presentation of the *baraita* of Rabbi Yehuda's opinion states explicitly that the original date is used, Rav Naḥman asserted that had Rav been aware of this *baraita* he would not have disagreed with Rabbi Yehuda.

NOTES

Witnesses may write even ten, etc. – עֵדִים כּוֹתְבִין אֲפִילּוּ עֲשָׂרָה וכו׳: The Rashbam and *Tosafot* explain that the case here is one where the original deed has been lost or destroyed. Others explain that these ten replacement documents can be written all at once if the purchaser desires to have several copies (Ramah).

HALAKHA

Witnesses may write even ten deeds for one field – כּוֹתְבִין אֲפִילּוּ עֲשָׂרָה שְׁטָרוֹת עַל שָׂדֶה אַחַת: When a field is sold, the witnesses may write several deeds attesting to the sale as long as the additional deeds do not contain a guarantee of compensation in the event of the repossessing of the field, which would lead to the possibility of multiple collections. The *Shakh*, citing the Rosh, comments that it is best to avoid the writing of multiple documents for no reason (*Shulḥan Arukh*, *Ḥoshen Mishpat* 239:1, and in the comment of Rema).

בִּשְׁלָמָא בֵּי דִינָא – אַלִּימֵי לְאַפְקוּעֵי מָמוֹנָא, אֶלָּא עֵדִים שֶׁעָשׂוּ שְׁלִיחוּתָן – חוֹזְרִין וְעוֹשִׂין שְׁלִיחוּתָן?!

Granted, **a court** can write a new document, because the court **has the power to confiscate money.** A creditor has the right to seize any property that the debtor had owned on the day the promissory note was written, even if that property was subsequently sold to others; the earlier the date on the note, the more properties it applies to. By dating the new document on the date of the original document the creditor is once again given the right to seize properties from those who had purchased land from the debtor in between the date of the original loan and the date the new promissory note is actually written. The court has such confiscatory power. **But** with regard to **witnesses, who** already **performed their agency,** i.e., fulfilled their assigned role, the first time they wrote the promissory note, can **they return and perform their agency** again by writing a second promissory note?

וְלָא? וְהָא אָמַר רַב יְהוּדָה אָמַר רַב: עֵדִים כּוֹתְבִין אֲפִילּוּ עֲשָׂרָה שְׁטָרוֹת עַל שָׂדֶה אַחַת!

The Gemara asks: **And** is it so that witnesses are **not** empowered to do so? **But doesn't Rav Yehuda say** that **Rav says: Witnesses** who were commissioned to write a deed for the transfer of property **may write even ten**[N] **deeds for one field?**[H] If the original deed is lost or destroyed, the witnesses may write a replacement deed for the purchaser, even if the deed is lost many times.

רַב יוֹסֵף אָמַר: בִּשְׁטַר מַתָּנָה,

Rav Yosef says an answer to this question: Rav Yehuda's statement was concerning **a deed of gift,** not a bill of sale. A gift of land has no guarantee; if it is repossessed from the recipient by the giver's creditor to repay the giver's debt, the recipient has no recourse and cannot collect any money from anyone. Therefore, in this case no one is jeopardized by the writing of many replacement deeds, which are intended only to serve as a proof that the recipient is actually entitled to the land.

וְרַבָּה אָמַר: בִּשְׁטָר שֶׁאֵין בּוֹ אַחֲרָיוּת.

And Rabba says: It is possible to say that Rav Yehuda's statement applied even **with regard to a bill** of sale **that does not have a guarantee in it.** In that case as well, there is no potential loss to any purchasers of land. By contrast, in the case of a promissory note, which can be used to repossess property from those who have purchased land from the debtor, witnesses do not have the authority to predate a document and thereby subject more purchasers to possible land seizures due to the predating of the document.

מַאי בָּרַיְיתָא? דְּתַנְיָא: הֲרֵי שֶׁהָיוּ נוֹשִׁין בּוֹ אֶלֶף זוּז, וּפָרַע מֵהֶן חֲמֵשׁ מֵאוֹת זוּז – עֵדִים מְקָרְעִין אֶת הַשְּׁטָר וְכוֹתְבִין לוֹ שְׁטָר אַחֵר מִזְּמַן רִאשׁוֹן, דִּבְרֵי רַבִּי יְהוּדָה; רַבִּי יוֹסֵי אוֹמֵר: שְׁטָר זֶה יְהֵא מוּנָּח בִּמְקוֹמוֹ וְיִכְתְּבוּ שׁוֹבֵר;

The Gemara cited an excerpt from a *baraita* earlier. It now cites it in full: **What** is the full text of the ***baraita*****? As it is taught: If one thousand dinars are owed by** a debtor, and the debt is recorded in a promissory note, **and** the debtor **repaid five hundred dinars out of** the total, the **witnesses tear the** original promissory **note and write another** promissory **note for him,** dated **from** the **time of** the **first** note. This is **the statement of Rabbi Yehuda. Rabbi Yosei says: This** original promissory **note shall remain in its place,** in the custody of the creditor, **and** witnesses **write a receipt** for the five hundred dinars that were repaid. This receipt is given to the debtor to protect himself against a possible attempt by the creditor to use the promissory note to collect the entire one thousand dinars.

וּמִפְּנֵי שְׁנֵי דְבָרִים אָמְרוּ כּוֹתְבִין שׁוֹבֵר: אַחַת – כְּדֵי שֶׁיָּכוֹף לְפוֹרְעוֹ, וְאַחַת – כְּדֵי שֶׁיִּגְבֶּה מִזְּמַן רִאשׁוֹן.

Rabbi Yosei continues: **And** there are **two reasons why** the Sages **said** that **they write a receipt,** as opposed to writing a new promissory note: **One** reason is **so that** the creditor **can coerce** the debtor **to repay him,** i.e., the psychological pressure for the debtor of knowing that the creditor has a promissory note with a larger amount listed than what he owes him will induce the debtor to repay the remainder promptly. **And** the other **one** is **so that he,** the creditor, **should** be able to **collect** liened property **from** the **first date,** that of the original document.

וְהָא רַבִּי יְהוּדָה נַמִּי מִזְּמַן רִאשׁוֹן קָאָמַר! הָכִי קָאָמַר לֵיהּ רַבִּי יוֹסֵי לְרַבִּי יְהוּדָה: אִי מִזְּמַן רִאשׁוֹן קָאָמְרַתְּ – פְּלֵיגְנָא עֲלָךְ בַּחֲדָא, אִי מִזְּמַן שֵׁנִי קָאָמְרַתְּ – פְּלֵיגְנָא עֲלָךְ בְּתַרְתֵּי.

The Gemara asks with regard to Rabbi Yosei's second reason: **But doesn't Rabbi Yehuda also say** that the new document must be dated **from the time of** the **first** document? The Gemara answers: Rabbi Yosei did not hear a full explanation of Rabbi Yehuda's opinion; he heard only that Rabbi Yehuda prescribed writing a new promissory note recording the new balance. And **this** is what **Rabbi Yosei is saying to Rabbi Yehuda: If you** mean to **say** that the new promissory note is dated **from** the **time of** the **first** document, **I disagree with you on one** count, as I hold a receipt should be written to pressure the debtor. **If** you mean to say that the second promissory note is dated **from** the **second date,** i.e., from when the second promissory note was written, **I disagree with you on two** counts.

תָּנוּ רַבָּנַן: שְׁטָר שֶׁזְּמַנּוֹ כָּתוּב בְּשַׁבָּת אוֹ בַּעֲשָׂרָה בְּתִשְׁרֵי – שְׁטָר מְאוּחָר הוּא וְכָשֵׁר, דִּבְרֵי רַבִּי יְהוּדָה; רַבִּי יוֹסֵי פּוֹסֵל. אָמַר לוֹ רַבִּי יְהוּדָה: וַהֲלֹא מַעֲשֶׂה בָּא לְפָנֶיךָ בְּצִפּוֹרִי וְהִכְשַׁרְתָּ! אָמַר לוֹ: כְּשֶׁהִכְשַׁרְתִּי – בָּזֶה הִכְשַׁרְתִּי.

§ The Gemara discusses a related *halakha*. **The Sages taught** in a *baraita* (*Tosefta, Makkot* 1:3): If there is a promissory **note whose date is written as a Shabbat or as the tenth of Tishrei,**[H] i.e., Yom Kippur, it **is** assumed to be **a postdated** promissory **note,**[N] as writing is forbidden on Shabbat and Yom Kippur, **and it is** therefore **valid.** This is **the statement of Rabbi Yehuda. Rabbi Yosei deems** the promissory note **invalid. Rabbi Yehuda said to** Rabbi Yosei: **But didn't** such **an incident come before you in Tzippori, and you** yourself **deemed** the promissory note **valid?** Rabbi Yosei **said to him: When I deemed** the promissory note **valid,** it was **in** a case like **this,** where the date was a Shabbat or Yom Kippur, that **I deemed** it **valid.**

וְהָא רַבִּי יְהוּדָה נַמִּי בָּזֶה קָאָמַר!

The Gemara is puzzled by Rabbi Yosei's response at the end of the *baraita*: **But Rabbi Yehuda was also speaking in** a case like **this,** where the date was a Shabbat or Yom Kippur, and yet Rabbi Yosei's opinion was that the promissory note is invalid.

אָמַר רַבִּי פְּדָת: הַכֹּל מוֹדִים, שֶׁאִם הוּזְקַקְנוּ לְעוֹנָתוֹ שֶׁל שְׁטָר, וְנִמְצֵאת עוֹנָתוֹ מְכוּוֶּנֶת בְּשַׁבָּת אוֹ בַּעֲשָׂרָה בְּתִשְׁרֵי – שֶׁשְּׁטָר מְאוּחָר הוּא וְכָשֵׁר,

Rabbi Pedat says: All parties to this dispute **agree that if we engaged in** an investigation of **the date of the document, and its date was found to be exactly on Shabbat or on the tenth of Tishrei,** that it is self-evident **that it is a postdated** promissory **note and is valid.**

Perek **X**
Daf **171** Amud **b**

לֹא נֶחְלְקוּ אֶלָּא בִּשְׁטָר מְאוּחָר בְּעָלְמָא,

The two Sages **disagree only with regard to** a case of **a postdated** promissory **note in general,** i.e., one in which the fact that it is postdated is not readily discernible from the dating of the document, as opposed to one dated on Shabbat or Yom Kippur.

דְּרַבִּי יְהוּדָה לְטַעֲמֵיהּ, דְּאָמַר: אֵין כּוֹתְבִין שׁוֹבֵר, וְלָא נָפֵיק מִינֵּיהּ חוּרְבָּא;

As Rabbi Yehuda conforms **to his** line of **reasoning, as he says:** One does **not write a receipt** for a debtor when he pays his debt; rather, the original document is torn, and in the case of partial repayment a new document is written, attesting to the balance due. **And** consequently, **no harm can emerge from** a postdated document. There is no concern that the date on the postdated document may have been recorded after the writing of a receipt.

וְרַבִּי יוֹסֵי לְטַעֲמֵיהּ, דְּאָמַר: כּוֹתְבִין שׁוֹבֵר, וְנָפֵיק מִינֵּיהּ חוּרְבָּא.

And Rabbi Yosei conforms **to his** line of **reasoning, as he says:** One **writes a receipt** for a debtor when he pays his debt, in lieu of tearing the promissory note. **And** consequently, **harm can emerge from** a postdated promissory note. Harm can occur in a case such as the following: The loan was given on the first of Nisan. The debt was paid on the following day and, rather than tearing the promissory note, a receipt was written and dated on the second of Nisan. If the original note had been postdated to the third of Nisan or thereafter, the creditor could use it to collect his debt a second time, arguing that the debtor's receipt is irrelevant, as its date is prior to the date in the promissory note.

HALAKHA

A promissory note whose date is written as a Shabbat or as the tenth of Tishrei – **שְׁטָר שֶׁזְּמַנּוֹ כָּתוּב בְּשַׁבָּת אוֹ בַּעֲשָׂרָה בְּתִשְׁרֵי**: A promissory note that is dated with the date of a Shabbat or Yom Kippur is assumed to be a postdated document and is therefore valid. Although it is also possible that the document is antedated and therefore not valid, the validity of the document is upheld in the absence of evidence to the contrary. Some say that if the debtor demands of the creditor that he take an oath that the document is not antedated, this demand is honored (*Baḥ*; *Sma*; see *Shakh*). All this applies only if the document had been ratified by the court; if it had not been ratified the creditor would have to prove that the document is not antedated in order to collect the debt (Rambam *Sefer Mishpatim*, *Hilkhot Malve VeLoveh* 23:4; *Shulḥan Arukh*, *Ḥoshen Mishpat* 43:14, and see *Netivot HaMishpat* there).

NOTES

It is assumed to be a postdated promissory note – **שְׁטָר מְאוּחָר הוּא**: A postdated promissory note is valid, and an antedated one is invalid (*Shevi'it* 10:4). The early commentaries raise the question that in the case being discussed here, all that is known is that the document was not written on the day that is recorded as its date. Why, then, is it assumed that it is postdated, and therefore valid, as opposed to being antedated and therefore invalid? The answer given is that it is assumed that the witnesses would not have signed an antedated document, as they would not sign a document that they know is invalid. Moreover, a document is not disqualified unless there is proof that it is not valid. A document is never invalidated because of a mere possibility that it is so (Rabbeinu Ḥananel; Ri Migash; Rashbam).

אָמַר רַב הוּנָא בְּרֵיהּ דְּרַב יְהוֹשֻׁעַ: אֲפִילּוּ לְמַאן דְּאָמַר כּוֹתְבִין שׁוֹבֵר, הָנֵי מִילֵּי אַפַּלְגָא, אֲבָל אַכּוּלֵּיהּ לָא.

§ **Rav Huna, son of Rav Yehoshua, says: Even according to the one who says** that one **writes a receipt** for the debtor when he pays, in lieu of tearing the promissory note, **this statement** applies only **with regard to** a case where the debtor pays **half,** i.e., a portion, of the debt. **But with regard to** a case where the debtor comes to repay **all of** the debt and the creditor has lost the promissory note and cannot tear it, all agree that one does **not** write a receipt.[N] Rather, the debtor will not be required to repay the loan unless the creditor can produce the promissory note.

וְלָא הִיא, אֲפִילּוּ אַכּוּלֵּיהּ כָּתְבִינַן;

The Gemara rejects this opinion: **But it is not so; we write** a receipt **even in** a case where the debtor pays **all of** the debt.[H]

כִּי הָא דְּרַב יִצְחָק בַּר יוֹסֵף הֲוָה מַסֵּיק בֵּיהּ זוּזֵי בְּרַבִּי אַבָּא, אֲתָא לְקַמֵּיהּ דְּרַבִּי חֲנִינָא בַּר פַּפִּי, אֲמַר לֵיהּ: הַב לִי זוּזַי. אֲמַר לֵיהּ: הַב לִי שְׁטָרַאי וּשְׁקוֹל זוּזָךְ. אֲמַר לֵיהּ: שְׁטָרָךְ אִירְכַּס לִי, אֶכְתּוֹב לָךְ תַּבְרָא. אֲמַר לֵיהּ, הָא רַב וּשְׁמוּאֵל דְּאָמְרִי תַּרְוַיְיהוּ: אֵין כּוֹתְבִין שׁוֹבֵר!

The Gemara proves its assertion: This is **like that** case **where Rav Yitzḥak bar Yosef was owed money by Rabbi Abba.** Rav Yitzḥak bar Yosef **came before Rabbi Ḥanina bar Pappi,** and **said to** Rabbi Abba: **Give me my money.** Rabbi Abba **said to him:** First **give me my** promissory **note, and** then **take your money.** Rav Yitzḥak bar Yosef **said to him: I lost your** promissory **note;** instead, **I will write a receipt for you.** Rabbi Abba **said to him: Isn't** there the opinion of **Rav and Shmuel, who both say** that the *halakha* is that one does **not write a receipt?**

אֲמַר: מַאן יָהֵיב לָן מֵעַפְרֵיהּ דְּרַב וּשְׁמוּאֵל רָמֵינַן בְּעַיְינִין, הָא רַבִּי יוֹחָנָן וְהָא רֵישׁ לָקִישׁ דְּאָמְרִי תַּרְוַיְיהוּ: כּוֹתְבִין שׁוֹבֵר.

Rabbi Ḥanina bar Pappi, the judge, thereupon **said: Who will give us** some **of the dust of Rav and Shmuel,** and **I will place it on my eyes,** so highly do I regard them. Nevertheless, **isn't** there the opinion of **Rabbi Yoḥanan and Reish Lakish, who both say** that one **writes a receipt?**

וְכֵן כִּי אֲתָא רָבִין אָמַר רַבִּי אֶילְעָא: כּוֹתְבִין שׁוֹבֵר.

And similarly, when Ravin came from Eretz Yisrael to Babylonia, he said that **Rabbi Ilai says:** The *halakha* is that one **writes a receipt.**

וּמִסְתַּבְּרָא דְּכוֹתְבִין שׁוֹבֵר, דְּאִי סָלְקָא דַּעְתָּא אֵין כּוֹתְבִין שׁוֹבֵר, אָבַד שְׁטָרוֹ שֶׁל זֶה – יֹאכַל הַלָּה וְחָדֵי?

The Gemara concludes: **And it stands to reason that** one **writes a receipt. As, if** it would **enter your mind that** one does **not write a receipt,** then **if the** promissory **note of this** creditor **is lost, should this** debtor **eat and rejoice?** Is it fair that he should keep money that he knows he owes the creditor?

מַתְקִיף לָהּ אַבַּיֵי: וְאֶלָּא מַאי, כּוֹתְבִין שׁוֹבֵר? אָבַד שׁוֹבְרוֹ שֶׁל זֶה – יֹאכַל הַלָּה וְחָדֵי? אֲמַר לֵיהּ רָבָא: אִין, "עֶבֶד לֹוֶה לְאִישׁ מַלְוֶה".

Abaye objects to this line of reasoning: **Rather, what** should the *halakha* be, that one **writes a receipt** when the creditor cannot find the promissory note? If **the receipt of** the debtor **is lost, should this** creditor **eat and rejoice?**[N] Once the debtor has lost his receipt, there is nothing to prevent the creditor from collecting the debt a second time. This, too, is unfair. In either case, whether a receipt is written or not, an injustice could result. Why should it be preferred that the potential of suffering an injustice should be borne by the debtor rather than the creditor? **Rava said to** Abaye: **Yes,** it is preferable, because, as it is written: **"The borrower is a servant to the lender"** (Proverbs 22:7). The debtor's interests are subordinated to those of the creditor.

HALAKHA

We write a receipt even in a case where the debtor pays all of the debt – אֲפִילּוּ אַכּוּלֵּיהּ כָּתְבִינַן: If a debtor seeks to repay his debt and the creditor informs him that the promissory note attesting to the loan has been lost, the debtor is obligated to pay the debt, and the debtor is issued a receipt to protect himself against double collection. If the debtor asserts that the creditor is purposely hiding the promissory note, the creditor must counter this claim by taking an oath that the document is in fact lost, and then he can proceed to collect the debt and write the receipt. This is all in accordance with the opinion of Rabbi Yosei, whose opinions are generally accepted in his disputes with Rabbi Yehuda, and in accordance with the opinion of Rabbi Yoḥanan and Reish Lakish and Rava, whose opinions are generally accepted over those of Abaye (Rambam *Sefer Mishpatim, Hilkhot Malve VeLoveh* 23:16; *Shulḥan Arukh, Ḥoshen Mishpat* 54:2).

NOTES

With regard to all of the debt, one does not write a receipt – אַכּוּלֵּיהּ לָא: The reason for this distinction is that in a case where the debtor has paid part of the debt, the most equitable way to ensure the protection of both parties going forward is to write a receipt. In a case where the debtor is willing to repay the entire debt, it is his interests that need to be considered, and since it is through the creditor's negligence that the promissory note was lost, the creditor bears responsibility for his inattention.

If the receipt…is lost, should this creditor eat and rejoice – אָבַד שׁוֹבְרוֹ...יֹאכַל הַלָּה וְחָדֵי: Abaye is pointing out that according to either opinion there is a possibility that injustice will occur. Ya'avetz notes that in fact the two injustices are quite different. In the case where the debtor is excused from paying when the promissory note is lost, it is in accordance with the *halakha* that he withholds payment, as he cannot be forced to repay the debt before proof of the debt is produced. By contrast, in the case where the debtor loses his receipt, it is only through deception and fraud that the debt would be collected a second time, and there is no reason to assume that the creditor would do this. Nevertheless, Abaye apparently was concerned about the possibility that this could happen.

תְּנַן הָתָם: שְׁטָרֵי חוֹב הַמּוּקְדָּמִין – פְּסוּלִין, וְהַמְאוּחָרִין – כְּשֵׁרִין.

§ **We learned** in a mishna **elsewhere** (*Shevi'it* 10:5): **Promissory notes that are antedated**[H] **are not valid, but those that are postdated**[H] **are valid.**

אָמַר רַב הַמְנוּנָא: לֹא שָׁנוּ אֶלָּא שִׁטְרֵי הַלְוָאָה, אֲבָל שִׁטְרֵי מִקָּח וּמִמְכָּר – אֲפִילּוּ מְאוּחָרִין נַמִי פְּסוּלִין; מַאי טַעֲמָא? זִימְנִין דְּמַזְבֵּין לֵיהּ אַרְעָא בְּנִיסָן וְכָתֵיב לֵיהּ בְּתִשְׁרֵי, וּמִתְרַמֵּי לֵיהּ זוּזֵי בֵּינֵי בֵּינֵי וְזָבֵין לֵיהּ מִינֵּיהּ. וְכִי מָטֵי תִּשְׁרֵי מַפֵּיק לֵיהּ וְאָמַר לֵיהּ: הֲדַר זְבַנְתָּהּ מִינָּךְ.

Rav Hamnuna says: They taught this *halakha* **only** with regard to **promissory notes, but** with regard to **deeds of buying and selling** property, **even postdated**[H] documents **are not valid. What is the reason** for this stringency in the case of bills of sale? If postdated documents were allowed, there could be **times that** the seller **sells land to** the purchaser **in** the month of **Nisan** of a particular year **and writes** a postdated deed **for him** stating that the sale took place **in** the following **Tishrei, and some money happens to** reach the seller **between** Nisan and Tishrei **and he purchases** the land back **from** the purchaser. **And** then, **when Tishrei arrives**, the purchaser **takes out** the original bill of sale **and says to** the seller: It is true that you purchased the field from me, but **I then purchased it from you** again now, in Tishrei, as stated in this document.

אִי הָכִי, שִׁטְרֵי הַלְוָאָה נַמִי, זִימְנִין דְּיָזֵיף בְּנִיסָן וְכָתֵיב לֵיהּ שְׁטָרָא בְּתִשְׁרֵי, וּמִתְרַמֵּי לֵיהּ זוּזֵי בֵּינֵי בֵּינֵי וּפָרַע לֵיהּ, וְאָמַר לֵיהּ: הַב לִי שְׁטָרַאי, וְאָמַר לֵיהּ: אִירְכַּס לִי, וְכָתֵיב לֵיהּ תַּבְרָא. וְכִי מָטֵי זִמְנֵיהּ מַפֵּיק לֵיהּ וְאָמַר לֵיהּ: הָנֵי הָשְׁתָּא הוּא דִּיזַפְתְּ מִינַּאי!

The Gemara asks: **If so,** a similar scenario could occur with **promissory notes as well:** There could be **times that one borrows** money **in Nisan and writes** a promissory **note for** the creditor stating that the loan took place **in** the following **Tishrei, and** some **money happens to** reach the debtor **between** Nisan and Tishrei **and he repays** his debt **to** the creditor early **and says to him: Give me my** promissory **note. And** the creditor **says to him: I lost** it, **and he writes him a receipt** instead. **And** then, **when the time** written in the note **arrives,** the creditor **takes out** the supposedly lost promissory note **and says to** the debtor: It is true that you repaid me previously, but **it is now,** after you repaid that loan, **that you borrowed from me these** dinars recorded in this document, which is dated in Tishrei.

קָסָבַר: אֵין כּוֹתְבִין שׁוֹבֵר.

The Gemara answers: Rav Hamnuna **holds that** one does **not write a receipt,** so that scenario cannot occur. Like Rabbi Yehuda, Rav Hamnuna maintains that if a creditor loses his promissory note the debtor does not have to repay the loan. Rabbi Yosei, who does allow the creditor to collect his debt in such a case and write a receipt for the debtor, is concerned about that scenario, and consequently he holds that postdated promissory notes are not valid.

אֲמַר לֵיהּ רַב יֵימָר לְרַב כָּהֲנָא, וְאָמְרִי לָהּ רַב יִרְמְיָה מִדִּיפְתִּי לְרַב כָּהֲנָא: וְהָאִידָּנָא דְּכָתְבִינַן שְׁטָרֵי מְאוּחָרֵי וְכָתְבִינַן תַּבְרָא, אַמַּאי קָעָבְדִינַן הָכִי? אֲמַר לֵיהּ: בָּתַר דַּאֲמַר לְהוּ רַבִּי אַבָּא לְסָפְרֵיהּ: כִּי כָּתְבִיתוּ שְׁטָר מְאוּחָר, כִּתְבוּ הָכִי: "שְׁטָרָא דְּנַן לָא בִּזְמְנֵיהּ כְּתַבְנֵיהּ, אֶלָּא אַחֲרְנוּהוּ וּכְתַבְנוּהוּ".

Rav Yeimar said to Rav Kahana, and some say it was **Rav Yirmeya of Difti** who said this **to Rav Kahana: And today, when we write postdated** promissory **notes, and we** also **write a receipt** in cases where the creditor loses his promissory note, **why do we do this?** The combination of allowing postdated promissory notes and allowing the writing of a receipt instead of producing the promissory note would enable double collection of the loan to take place. Rav Kahana **said to him:** The problem was rectified **after Rabbi Abba told his** court **scribe: When you write postdated** promissory **notes, write as follows: We did not write this document on its date,** i.e., on the date written within the document; **rather, we postdated it and wrote it.** Since it is clear from the text of the document that it was postdated, double collection of the loan is avoided.

אֲמַר לֵיהּ רַב אַשִׁי לְרַב כָּהֲנָא: וְהָאִידָּנָא דְּלָא קָא עָבְדִינַן הָכִי! בָּתַר דַּאֲמַר לֵיהּ רַב סַפְרָא לְסָפְרֵיהּ: כִּי כָּתְבִיתוּ הָנֵי תַּבְרֵי, אִי יָדְעִיתוּ זִימְנָא דִּשְׁטָרָא – כִּתְבוּ, אִי לָא – כִּתְבוּ סְתָמָא, דְּכָל אֵימַת דְּנָפֵיק לִרְעֵיהּ.

Rav Ashi said to Rav Kahana: But what about **today, when we do not do this,** i.e., we do not follow Rabbi Abba's instructions? How do we avoid double collection of the loan? Rav Kahana replied: The problem was rectified **after Rav Safra said to his** court **scribe: When you write these receipts** for debtors who pay debts without the original promissory note being torn, **if you know the date** written **in the** missing promissory **note, write** it into the receipt. But **if** you do **not** know the date written in the promissory note, **write** the receipt **without specification,**[N] i.e., do not write any date at all in the receipt, so **that whenever** the creditor **produces**[H] the promissory note, the undated receipt **can weaken it,** i.e., exempt the debtor from payment.

אֲמַר לֵיהּ רָבִינָא לְרַב אַשִׁי, וְאָמְרִי לָהּ רַב אַשִׁי לְרַב כָּהֲנָא:

Ravina said to Rav Ashi, and some say it was **Rav Ashi** who said **to Rav Kahana:**

HALAKHA

Promissory notes that are antedated – שְׁטָרֵי חוֹב הַמּוּקְדָּמִין: Antedated promissory notes are not valid. This is because they enable the creditor to repossess assets that were owned by the debtor on the recorded date, even though the loan did not take place until later. This could cause a loss to anyone who purchased assets from the debtor between the date written on the promissory note and the date the loan was made. Since such a document can be misused, the Sages decreed that it should not be used at all to repossess liened property that has been sold to others. Nevertheless, the document is valid insofar as the debtor cannot claim, when the creditor produces the note, that he has already paid the debt. Similarly, the debtor is not deemed credible if he denies that the loan ever took place. The Rema writes that there are those who maintain that the document is completely invalid (*Tur*; Rabbeinu Yitzhak of Dampierre; Rosh; Rivash). This means that the debtor can claim that he has already paid the debt, but he cannot deny that the loan took place altogether (*Sma*). The *Shakh*, holds that he can even deny that the loan took place (Rambam *Sefer Mishpatim*, *Hilkhot Malve VeLoveh* 23:1; *Shulḥan Arukh*, *Ḥoshen Mishpat* 43:7, and see *Netivot HaMishpat* there).

Promissory notes…that are postdated – שְׁטָרֵי חוֹב...הַמְאוּחָרִין: A postdated promissory note is valid, as the later date merely limits the collection possibilities of the creditor. Even if the postdated note does not state explicitly that it is postdated, it is valid. The Rema, citing Rabbeinu Yona, writes that although a postdated promissory note is valid, a document should not be postdated *ab initio*, as it gives the appearance of a falsehood (Rambam *Sefer Mishpatim*, *Hilkhot Malve VeLoveh* 23:2; *Shulḥan Arukh*, *Ḥoshen Mishpat* 43:12).

Deeds of buying and selling property, even postdated – שִׁטְרֵי מִקָּח וּמִמְכָּר אֲפִילּוּ מְאוּחָרִין: A bill of sale of property with an incorrect date is not valid, whether the incorrect date is earlier or later than the date of the sale, unless the document states explicitly that it is dated incorrectly. A postdated bill of sale is not valid because there is a concern that the seller might repurchase the property before the arrival of the date written in the bill of sale, and then the postdated bill of sale might be used by the purchaser to claim that he purchased the field once again on the specified date. This is in accordance with the opinion of Rav Hamnuna (Rambam *Sefer Mishpatim*, *Hilkhot Malve VeLoveh* 23:7; *Shulḥan Arukh*, *Ḥoshen Mishpat* 43:13).

So that whenever the creditor produces, etc. – דְּכָל אֵימַת דְּנָפֵיק וכו׳: When a postdated promissory note is written, if it is subsequently lost and there is consequently a need to write a receipt for the debtor when he repays the debt, the receipt should be written without a date, so that if the postdated promissory note is found and presented in court in the future, the undated receipt will be used to counter it. If the debtor accepted a receipt with a date in it, he bears the consequences if the promissory note is found and presented in the future. This is in accordance with what Rav Safra told his scribe and the conclusion of the Gemara (Rambam *Sefer Mishpatim*, *Hilkhot Malve VeLoveh* 23:7; *Shulḥan Arukh*, *Ḥoshen Mishpat* 43:24).

NOTES

Write without specification – כִּתְבוּ סְתָמָא: The date should not be specified in the receipt so it can be used at any time. The sum of money recorded in the promissory note, which is now being repaid, would certainly be written in the receipt. The Rashbam notes that the creditor would have to take care to refrain from lending the debtor this precise sum of money in the future, since the receipt, which has no date, could be used to counter any future promissory note for the specified sum.

וְהָא הָאִידָּנָא דְּלָא קָעָבְדִינַן הָכִי! אֲמַר לֵיהּ: רַבָּנַן תַּקּוּנֵי תַּקִּינֵי, מַאן דְּעָבֵיד – עָבֵיד, מַאן דְּלָא עָבֵיד – אִיהוּ הוּא דְּאַפְסֵיד אַנַּפְשֵׁיהּ.

But today, when we do not do this either when writing receipts, how can we avoid double collection of a loan? Rav Kahana **said to him: The Sages instituted** taking this precaution. **One who does** what the Sages instituted **does** it and protects himself from loss; and as for **one who does not do** so, **he has brought the loss upon himself,** and will suffer the consequences if the promissory note is found and presented in the future.

אֲמַר לְהוּ רָבָא בַּר רַב שֵׁילָא לְהָנְהוּ כָּתְבֵי שְׁטָרָא אַקְנָיָאתָא: כִּי כָּתְבִיתוּ שְׁטָרֵי אַקְנָיָאתָא, אִי יָדְעִיתוּ יוֹמָא דִּקְנִיתוּ בֵּיהּ – כִּתְבוּ, וְאִי לָא – כִּתְבוּ יוֹמָא דְּקָיְימִיתוּ בֵּיהּ, כִּי הֵיכִי דְּלָא מִתְחֲזֵי כְּשִׁקְרָא.

Rava bar Rav Sheila said to those who wrote deeds of acquisition, i.e., deeds of sale or deeds of gifts for property they acquired: **When you write deeds of acquisition** after the acquisition was performed, **if you know the day on which you effected the acquisition,**[NH] **write** that date on the document. **But if** you do **not** know the day on which you effected the acquisition, **write the date on which you are currently** writing the document. You should follow this procedure, and not write an approximate or estimated date, **so that** the document shall **not appear as a falsehood.**

אֲמַר לְהוּ רַב לְסָפְרֵיהּ, וְכֵן אֲמַר לְהוּ רַב הוּנָא לְסָפְרֵיהּ: כִּי קָיְימִיתוּ בְּשִׁילֵי – כִּתְבוּ בְּשִׁילֵי, וְאַף עַל גַּב דִּמְסִירָן לְכוּ מִילֵּי בְּהִינִי; כִּי קָיְימִיתוּ בְּהִינִי – כִּתְבוּ בְּהִינִי, וְאַף עַל גַּב דִּמְסִירָן לְכוּ מִילֵּי בְּשִׁילֵי.

Rav said to his scribe, and Rav Huna said similarly to his scribe: When you are writing a document and you **are situated in Shili, write** that the document was written **in Shili, and** you should do so **even if the matters were given over to you,** i.e., the transaction attested to in the document took place, **in Hini.**[B] **When you are situated in Hini, write** that the document was written **in Hini, even if the matters were given over to you in Shili.**

אֲמַר רָבָא: הַאי מַאן דְּנָקֵיט שְׁטָרָא בַּר מְאָה זוּזֵי, וְאָמַר: שַׁוְּיֵהּ נִיהֲלִי תְּרֵי בְּנֵי חַמְשִׁין חַמְשִׁין – לָא מְשַׁוֵּינַן לְהוּ.

§ **Rava said:** With regard to **this one who is holding** a promissory **note of one hundred dinars,**[H] **and he says** to the court: **Prepare** this note **for me,** i.e., exchange it, **for two** notes **of fifty** dinars **each,** so that if the debtor pays half the debt I will be able to give him one document and keep the other, **we do not prepare** the new notes for him.

מַאי טַעְמָא? עֲבַדוּ רַבָּנַן מִילְּתָא דְּנִיחָא לֵיהּ לַמַּלְוֶה וְנִיחָא לֵיהּ לַלֹּוֶה; נִיחָא לֵיהּ לַמַּלְוֶה – כְּדֵי שֶׁיָּכוֹף לְפוֹרְעוֹ, וְנִיחָא לַלֹּוֶה – כִּי הֵיכִי דְּנִיפַּגַם שְׁטָרֵיהּ.

What is the reason? The Sages have performed a matter here **that** is **beneficial to the creditor and** is **beneficial to the debtor** as well. It is **beneficial to the creditor** to keep the promissory note with the larger sum **so that** he can **coerce** the debtor **to repay him,** as there is a greater incentive to pay off a larger promissory note than a smaller one. **And** it is **beneficial to the debtor, so that** when he pays half the debt **his** promissory **note becomes vitiated,** and the remainder of the sum written in the vitiated promissory note can be collected only if the creditor takes an oath that he has not received the entire sum.

NOTES

If you know the day on which you effected the acquisition – אִי יָדְעִיתוּ יוֹמָא דִּקְנִיתוּ בֵּיהּ: This would not be considered an antedated note and consequently not valid, because the date on the document does in fact reflect the date of the transaction, and it is on the date of the transaction that the liens on the seller's property are activated.

BACKGROUND

Shili, Hini – שִׁילֵי, הִינִי: These two towns, which were less than a kilometer apart from each other, were primarily market towns, centers for the sale of produce. It appears that they were close to the Euphrates River and within the jurisdiction of the larger city of Sura. Some maintain that these two towns eventually merged into a single small city called Shilahin, which is located south of the city of Kufa, in Iraq.

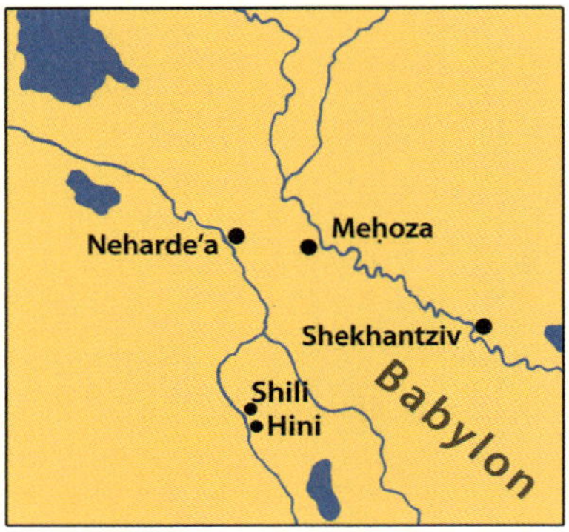

Location of Shili and Hini

HALAKHA

If you know the day on which you effected the acquisition, etc. – אִי יָדְעִיתוּ יוֹמָא דִּקְנִיתוּ וכו׳: A document may be written to attest to an acquisition even long after the acquisition occurred. Therefore, if there are two people who witnessed such an acquisition and delayed writing the document attesting to it until a later date, they should write the date on which the acquisition occurred; if they do not recall the precise date, they should record the date of the writing of the document, in accordance with the statement of Rava bar Rav Sheila. The witnesses may not say, for example: We are certain that the acquisition took place in Tishrei, so we will date the document in Marḥeshvan, the month following Tishrei; such a document has a semblance of falsehood. Rav Yaakov Beirav writes that they may write a date range, such as: The first third of month so-and-so, or the middle of month so-and-so (Rambam *Sefer Mishpatim, Hilkhot Malve VeLoveh* 23:6; *Shulḥan Arukh, Ḥoshen Mishpat* 43:16, 18–19).

This one who is holding a promissory note of one hundred dinars – הַאי מַאן דְּנָקֵיט שְׁטָרָא בַּר מְאָה זוּזֵי: If one holds a promissory note that says another owes him one hundred dinars, and he requests of the court that they exchange this note for two notes of fifty dinars each; or conversely, if he has two notes of fifty dinars each and he requests that the court exchange them for a single note of one hundred dinars, the court does not honor these requests, even if it is definitively known that no repayment had been received, unless both parties consent to the exchange. This is in accordance with the statements of Rava (Rambam *Sefer Mishpatim, Hilkhot Malve VeLoveh* 23:17; *Shulḥan Arukh, Ḥoshen Mishpat* 53:1, and in the comment of Rema).

וְאָמַר רָבָא: הַאי מַאן דְּנָקֵיט תְּרֵי שְׁטָרֵי בְּנֵי חַמְשִׁין חַמְשִׁין, וְאָמַר: שַׁוִּינְהוּ נִיהֲלִי חַד בַּר מְאָה – לָא מְשַׁוֵּינַן לֵיהּ,

And Rava said further: With regard to **this one who is holding two** promissory **notes, each of fifty dinars,** owed by the same person, **and he says** to the court: **Prepare** this note **for me** into a **single** note **of one hundred** dinars, **we do not prepare** the new note for him.

עֲבוּד רַבָּנַן מִילְּתָא דְּנִיחָא לֵיהּ לְמַלְוֶה וְנִיחָא לֵיהּ לְלֹוֶה; נִיחָא לֵיהּ לְמַלְוֶה – כִּי הֵיכִי דְּלָא נִיפְגּוֹם שְׁטָרֵיהּ, וְנִיחָא לֵיהּ לְלֹוֶה – כְּדֵי שֶׁלֹּא יָכוֹף לְפוֹרְעוֹ.

What is the reason? **The Sages have performed a matter** here **that** is **beneficial to the creditor and** is **beneficial to the debtor** as well. It is **beneficial to the creditor** to keep the smaller notes, **so that** if the debtor pays fifty dinars, **his** promissory **note will not become vitiated,** which would require the creditor to take an oath before collecting the remainder. **And** it is **beneficial to the debtor, so that** the creditor **will not** be able to **coerce him to repay** the debt quickly, as there is a greater incentive to repay a larger sum than a smaller one.

אָמַר רַב אַשִׁי: הַאי מַאן דְּנָקֵיט שְׁטָרָא בַּר מְאָה זוּזֵי, וַאֲמַר: שַׁוּוּנְהִי נִיהֲלִי חַד בַּר חַמְשִׁין – לָא מְשַׁוֵּינָא לֵיהּ.

Rav Ashi says: With regard to **this one who is holding** a promissory **note of one hundred dinars, and he said** to the court: **Prepare** this note **for me** into **one** note **of fifty** dinars,[H] as the debtor has paid me half, **we do not prepare** the new note for him.

מַאי טַעֲמָא? אָמְרִינַן: הַאי מִיפְרַע פַּרְעֵיהּ, וַאֲמַר לֵיהּ: הַב לִי שְׁטָרַאי, וַאֲמַר לֵיהּ: אִירְכַּס לִי, וְכָתֵיב לֵיהּ תַּבְרָא, וּמַפֵּיק לֵיהּ הַאי וְאָמַר לֵיהּ: הַאי אַחֲרִינָא הוּא.

What is the reason? We say, i.e., we are concerned, that the following may have happened: **This** debtor actually **repaid** all one hundred dinars, **and** when he did so he **said to the** creditor: **Give me** back **my** promissory **note. And** the creditor **said to him: I lost it. And** the creditor **wrote a receipt for him** in lieu of handing over the promissory note. **And** now, if we write a new promissory note of fifty dinars for the creditor, **he will present this** note **and say to** the debtor, who presents his receipt for a hundred dinars: **That** receipt **is** for **a different** loan that you repaid.

מתני׳ שְׁנֵי אַחִין, אֶחָד עָנִי וְאֶחָד עָשִׁיר, וְהִנִּיחַ לָהֶן אֲבִיהֶן מֶרְחָץ וּבֵית הַבַּד; עֲשָׂאָן לְשָׂכָר – הַשָּׂכָר לָאֶמְצַע. עֲשָׂאָן לְעַצְמוֹ – הֲרֵי הֶעָשִׁיר אוֹמֵר לֶעָנִי: קַח לְךָ עֲבָדִים וְיִרְחֲצוּ בַּמֶּרְחָץ, קַח לְךָ זֵיתִים וּבֹא וַעֲשֵׂה בְּבֵית הַבַּד.

MISHNA In a case where there are **two brothers, one poor and one rich, and their father left them a bathhouse**[H] **or an olive press** as an inheritance, if the father had **built** these facilities **for profit,**[N] i.e., to charge others for using them, **the profit** that accrues after the father's death **is shared equally**[N] by the two brothers. If the father had **built them for himself** and for the members of his household to use, the poor brother, who has little use for these amenities, cannot force the rich brother to convert the facilities to commercial use; rather, **the rich** brother can **say to the poor** brother: Go **take servants for yourself, and they will bathe in the bathhouse.** Or he can say: Go **take olives for yourself, and come and make** them into oil **in the olive press.**

שְׁנַיִם שֶׁהָיוּ בְּעִיר אַחַת, שֵׁם אֶחָד יוֹסֵף בֶּן שִׁמְעוֹן וְשֵׁם אַחֵר יוֹסֵף בֶּן שִׁמְעוֹן – אֵין יְכוֹלִין לְהוֹצִיא שְׁטַר חוֹב זֶה עַל זֶה, וְלֹא אַחֵר יָכוֹל לְהוֹצִיא עֲלֵיהֶן שְׁטַר חוֹב.

If there are **two** people **who were** living **in one city,**[H] **one named Yosef ben Shimon and the other** also **named Yosef ben Shimon, one cannot present a promissory note against the other,** as the purported debtor can claim: On the contrary, it is you who owed me money; you repaid me and I returned this note to you upon payment. **Nor can another,** third person, **present a promissory note against** either of **them,** as each one can claim: It is not I but the other Yosef ben Shimon who owes you money.

נִמְצָא לְאֶחָד בֵּין שְׁטָרוֹתָיו: ״שְׁטָרוֹ שֶׁל יוֹסֵף בֶּן שִׁמְעוֹן פָּרוּעַ״ – שְׁטָרוֹת שְׁנֵיהֶן פְּרוּעִין.

If a document **is found among one's documents** stating: **The promissory note against Yosef ben Shimon is repaid,** and both men named Yosef ben Shimon owed this man money, **the promissory notes of both of them** are considered **repaid,** as it cannot be determined which debt was repaid and which is outstanding.

HALAKHA

Prepare this note for me into one note of fifty dinars – שׁוּוּנְהִי נִיהֲלִי חַד בַּר חַמְשִׁין: If a creditor appears before the court holding a promissory note for one hundred dinars and requests that it be exchanged for another note for fifty dinars, as the debtor has paid half the debt, the court may not honor this request. This is because of the concern that the debtor might have in fact repaid the entire debt of one hundred dinars and been issued a receipt to that effect, a receipt that would be now be ineffective against a promissory note of fifty dinars (Rambam *Sefer Mishpatim*, *Hilkhot Malve VeLoveh* 23:18; *Shulḥan Arukh*, *Ḥoshen Mishpat* 53:1).

Two brothers…and their father left them a bathhouse, etc. – שְׁנֵי אַחִין...וְהִנִּיחַ לָהֶן אֲבִיהֶן מֶרְחָץ וכו׳: In a situation in which two brothers, one rich and one poor, inherited a bathhouse or olive press that cannot be divided between them, the *halakha* is as follows: If the father built these facilities for profit, they should continue to operate them under that arrangement, the profits being divided among the brothers. If the father built them for personal use and the poor brother would have no benefit from such amenities, he cannot force his brother to convert them into commercial facilities; rather, both brothers should continue using them as the father had intended them, as personal amenities, the rich brother saying to the poor one: Go purchase servants and attendants to use the bathhouse, or: Go purchase olives to press.

If the poor brother proposes: Either purchase my half from me or I will purchase your half from you, the rich brother must accept the offer. According to some opinions, this option, which is standard in cases of joint property in which one partner wants to terminate the partnership, is not applicable to this case (Rambam *Sefer Kinyan*, *Hilkhot Shekhenim* 1:2; *Shulḥan Arukh*, *Ḥoshen Mishpat* 171:6, and in the comment of Rema; and see *Sma* there).

Two people who were living in one city, etc. – שְׁנַיִם שֶׁהָיוּ בְּעִיר אַחַת וכו׳: If two people in a city share the same name and father's name, neither of them can present a promissory note against the another, as the purported debtor can claim: This note in fact attests to the fact that you owed me money. You repaid the loan, whereupon I returned the document to you. Similarly, no third party can collect the debt from either of them with a promissory note bearing their shared name, as each can claim that the note applies to the other. If the witnesses who signed the document appear before the court and testify that the loan was given to one or the other of these men, the loan is collectible from the party so identified, but only as a loan by oral contract, which would allow for the possibility of the debtor to successfully claim that the debt has been paid (*Maggid Mishne*, citing Ritva).

What solution is available in such a case to allow these two to conduct their business? They should identify themselves in a unique manner in their documents, such as by writing the names of their grandfathers or an identifying physical or familial trait. This is all in accordance with the mishna.

The Rema, citing the *Tur*, writes that if two people with identical names live in different cities, these limitations do not apply to them, as the names of their respective hometowns would be recorded in the note. See *Netivot HaMishpat*, where it is noted that others maintain it is not necessary to record the hometown of the parties in a promissory note, and nonetheless the limitations do not apply to them. He writes that this is the accepted practice (Rambam *Sefer Mishpatim*, *Hilkhot Malve VeLoveh* 24:8; *Shulḥan Arukh*, *Ḥoshen Mishpat* 49:7).

NOTES

If the father had built these facilities for profit – עֲשָׂאָן לְשָׂכָר: According to *Tosafot* (cited in Rosh), the deciding factor is not whether or not the father actually built these facilities for profit, but whether or not they are currently capable of being put to commercial use (see Ritva, *Bava Batra* 13a).

The profit is shared equally – הַשָּׂכָר לָאֶמְצַע: This is to say that the poor brother cannot claim that he would prefer to sell the facility and divide the proceeds, and the rich brother cannot claim that he would prefer to divide the days rather than the profits so that he may have half the days available for his own use (Ba'al HaMaor).

כֵּיצַד יַעֲשׂוּ? יְשַׁלְּשׁוּ, וְאִם הָיוּ מְשׁוּלָּשִׁין – יִכְתְּבוּ סִימָן, וְאִם הָיוּ מְסוּמָּנִין – יִכְתְּבוּ כֹּהֵן.

What should two people with the same name in a single city **do** in order to conduct their business? **They should triple** their names by writing three generations: Yosef ben Shimon ben so-and-so. **And if they have** identical **triple** names, i.e., not only their fathers but their grandfathers had identical names, **they should write an indication** as to which one is referred to, such as: The short Yosef ben Shimon or the dark Yosef ben Shimon. **And if they have** identical **indications, they should write:** Yosef ben Shimon **the priest,** if one of them is a priest.

גמ׳ הַהוּא שְׁטָרָא דִּנְפַק לְבֵי דִינָא דְּרַב הוּנָא, דַּהֲוָה כְּתִיב בֵּיהּ ״אֲנִי פְּלוֹנִי בַּר פְּלוֹנִי לָוִיתִי מָנֶה מִמְּךָ״,

GEMARA

There was **a certain** promissory **note that was presented at the court of Rav Huna, in which it was written: I, so-and-so son of so-and-so, borrowed one hundred dinars from you.** No name was given as the creditor, but the one presenting the document claimed that the money was owed to him.

Perek **X**
Daf **172** Amud **b**

אֲמַר רַב הוּנָא: ״מִמְּךָ״ – אֲפִילּוּ מֵרֵישׁ גָּלוּתָא, וַאֲפִילּוּ מִשָּׁבוֹר מַלְכָּא.

Rav Huna said: The term: **From you,**[H] in the document does not identify anyone in particular, and can mean **even: From the Exilarch,**[B] **or even: From King Shapur.**[P]

אֲמַר לֵיהּ רַב חִסְדָּא לְרַבָּה: פּוֹק עַיֵּין בָּהּ, דִּלְאוּרְתָּא בָּעֵי לָהּ רַב הוּנָא מִינָּךְ.

Rav Ḥisda said to Rabba: Go out and **investigate** this matter, **as tonight Rav Huna will ask this** question **of you.**

נְפַק דַּק וְאַשְׁכַּח, דְּתַנְיָא: גֵּט שֶׁיֵּשׁ עָלָיו עֵדִים וְאֵין בּוֹ זְמַן, אַבָּא שָׁאוּל אוֹמֵר: אִם כָּתוּב בּוֹ ״גֵּרַשְׁתִּיהָ הַיּוֹם״ – כָּשֵׁר.

Rabba **went out, examined** the matter, **and discovered** a relevant source. **As it is taught** in a *baraita*: Concerning **a bill of divorce in which there are** the signatures of **witnesses on** the document **but there is no date** written **on it, Abba Shaul says** that **if it is written in it: I divorced her today,**[H] **it is valid.**

אַלְמָא: ״הַיּוֹם״ – הַהוּא יוֹמָא דְּנָפֵיק בֵּיהּ מַשְׁמַע, הָכָא נַמִי ״מִמְּךָ״ – מֵהַהוּא גַּבְרָא דְּנָפֵיק מִתּוּתֵי יְדֵיהּ מַשְׁמַע.

Rabba concludes: **Apparently,** the term: **Today, indicates that day on which** the bill of divorce **emerges** in the presence of the court. **Here too,** the term: **From you,** in a promissory note **indicates that man from whose possession it emerges.**

אֲמַר לֵיהּ אַבַּיֵי: וְדִלְמָא אַבָּא שָׁאוּל כְּרַבִּי אֱלִיעֶזֶר סְבִירָא לֵיהּ, דְּאָמַר: עֵדֵי מְסִירָה כָּרְתֵי, אֲבָל הָכָא לֵיחוּשׁ לִנְפִילָה!

Abaye said to him: But this is not a valid proof, as **perhaps Abba Shaul holds in accordance with** the opinion of **Rabbi Eliezer,** who **says** that **witnesses of the transmission** of the bill of divorce **effect** the divorce.[N] **But here, let** there be **a concern for** the possibility of the promissory note **falling** from its rightful owner and being found by the present holder of the document.

אֲמַר לֵיהּ: לִנְפִילָה לָא חָיְישִׁינַן. וּמְנָא תֵּימְרָא דְּלָא חָיְישִׁינַן לִנְפִילָה?

Rabba **said to** Abaye: **We are not concerned for** the possibility of a promissory note **falling** from its rightful owner and being found by another. **And from where do you say,** i.e., from where can it be proven, **that we are not concerned for** the possibility of a promissory note **falling** and being found by another?

HALAKHA

From you – מִמְּךָ: Concerning a promissory note in which it is written: I, so-and-so, borrowed one hundred dinars from you, anyone who claims to be the creditor and is in possession of such a document can collect the stated debt with it. This is the *halakha* provided that the holder of the promissory note claims to be the creditor; otherwise it is unreasonable to assume that a debtor would obligate himself to anyone who might happen to be holding the document (*Shakh*; *Netivot HaMishpat*). The concern that perhaps the true creditor lost the note and the current holder found it is not taken into consideration, in accordance with Rabba's statement. This applies only if the note is signed by witnesses. If it was written or signed by the debtor himself, since he has the right to claim that the debt has been repaid, he also is deemed credible if he claims: I borrowed the money from someone else, who apparently lost the note, and you found it. He would then be exempt from repaying the debt (Rambam *Sefer Mishpatim*, *Hilkhot Malve VeLoveh* 24:9; *Shulḥan Arukh*, *Ḥoshen Mishpat* 50:1, and in the comment of Rema; 61:10).

If it is written in it: I divorced her today – אִם כָּתוּב בּוֹ גֵּרַשְׁתִּיהָ הַיּוֹם: A bill of divorce in which there is no date recorded, and instead it is written: I divorced her today, is valid, as the word today is taken to be referring to the specific day on which the bill of divorce is brought to the court, in accordance with the statement of Rabba. See *Shiltei Gibborim*, who maintains that it is valid only if it can be established, via the witnesses who saw the transmission of the bill of divorce to the woman, what the date of the divorce was (Rambam *Sefer Nashim*, *Hilkhot Geirushin* 1:26; *Shulḥan Arukh*, *Even HaEzer* 127:7 and *Beit Shmuel* and *Ḥokhmat Shlomo* there).

BACKGROUND

Exilarch – רֵישׁ גָּלוּתָא: The person who filled the position of Exilarch, who was descended from the kings of the house of David, was recognized by the Jews as the heir to the scepter of Judah (see Genesis 49:10) and entrusted with broad official powers. He was the leader of the Jews of the Persian Empire and their representative to the authorities, who regarded him as a member of a royal dynasty. Consequently, the Exilarch enjoyed a lofty position within the Persian court.

PERSONALITIES

King Shapur – שָׁבוֹר מַלְכָּא: This refers to the Persian king Shapur I, 241–272 CE, the second ruler of the Sassanid dynasty. He was one of the great Persian kings who expanded the borders of the kingdom. He waged several wars against the Romans and conquered extensive territory from them, reaching as far as Syria. He even managed to take the Roman Emperor Valerianus captive. Despite this, he did not always win his wars, and was defeated by the Romans in several battles.

Unlike most of the kings of that dynasty, King Shapur I was tolerant of other religions. The Gemara relates at length his close relationship with the Jews, and how he valued and appreciated Jewish customs. On several occasions the Talmud recounts his friendship with the *amora* Shmuel.

NOTES

Witnesses of the transmission effect the divorce – עֵדֵי מְסִירָה כָּרְתֵי: The Rashbam explains: According to the opinion of Rabbi Eliezer, there is no need for signatures on a bill of divorce at all except by a rabbinic enactment; the only absolute requirement is the presence of witnesses at the time of the transmission of the bill of divorce. Moreover, he maintains that there is no need for a bill of divorce to have a date written on it, as the witnesses to the transmission of the document can themselves testify to the date of the divorce. It is for this reason that Abba Shaul allows the bill of divorce to state simply: Today. It is not because this term is considered a valid date, but because he does not require a date altogether. Therefore, nothing can be inferred from this case to the case of the promissory note.

דְּתְנַן: שְׁנַיִם שֶׁהָיוּ בְּעִיר אַחַת, שֵׁם אֶחָד יוֹסֵף בֶּן שִׁמְעוֹן וְשֵׁם אַחֵר יוֹסֵף בֶּן שִׁמְעוֹן – אֵינָן יְכוֹלִין לְהוֹצִיא שְׁטַר חוֹב זֶה עַל זֶה, וְלֹא אַחֵר יָכוֹל לְהוֹצִיא עֲלֵיהֶן שְׁטַר חוֹב; הָא הֵם עַל אֲחֵרִים – יְכוֹלִין, וְאַמַּאי? לֵיחוּשׁ לִנְפִילָה! אֶלָּא לָאו שְׁמַע מִינָּהּ: לִנְפִילָה לָא חָיְישִׁינַן.

As we learned in the mishna: If there are **two** people **who were** living **in one city, one named Yosef ben Shimon and the other** also **named Yosef ben Shimon, one cannot present a promissory note against the other,** as the purported debtor can claim: On the contrary, it is you who owed me money; you repaid me and I returned this note to you upon payment. **Nor can another,** third person, **present a promissory note against** either of **them. This** indicates that one of **them can** present a promissory note **against others.**[H] **But why** can they do so? **Let** there be **a concern for** the possibility of the promissory note **falling** from one Yosef ben Shimon and being found by the other. **Rather,** must one **not conclude from this** mishna that **we are not concerned for** the possibility of the promissory note **falling** from one Yosef ben Shimon and being found by the other?

וְאַבַּיֵי? לִנְפִילָה דְּחַד לָא חָיְישִׁינַן, לִנְפִילָה דְּרַבִּים חָיְישִׁינַן.

The Gemara asks: **And** why did **Abaye,** who is concerned for this possibility, not see a proof to the contrary from the mishna? He would counter: **We are not concerned for** the possibility of a promissory note **falling from one** particular person and being found by the other person with the same name, which is the case in the mishna, as that is extremely unlikely. **We are concerned for** the possibility of a promissory note **falling from** one of the general **public** and being found by someone else.

HALAKHA

One of them…against others – הֵם עַל אֲחֵרִים: If there are two people in the same city with identical names and fathers' names, although they cannot collect debts from one another based on promissory notes, they can collect such debts from others. The debtor cannot claim: I did not borrow from you but from the other man with the same name, and he must have lost the note, which you now found. This is because it is assumed that the holder of the note is the true creditor; the concern that it may have fallen and been found by another man with the same name is not taken into consideration, in accordance with the Gemara here (Rambam *Sefer Mishpatim, Hilkhot Malve VeLoveh* 24:9; *Shulḥan Arukh, Ḥoshen Mishpat* 49:7).

Perek **X**
Daf **173** Amud **a**

וְאֶלָּא הָא דְּתַנְיָא: כְּשֵׁם שֶׁאֵין מוֹצִיאִין שְׁטַר חוֹב זֶה עַל זֶה – כָּךְ אֵין מוֹצִיאִין עַל אֲחֵרִים, בְּמַאי קָמִיפַּלְגִי?

The Gemara asks: **And** what of **that which is taught** in another *baraita*:[N] **Just as** the two men named Yosef ben Shimon **cannot produce a promissory note, this** one **against that** one, **so they cannot produce** promissory notes **against others,** as those others can claim: I did not borrow from you but from the other Yosef ben Shimon, and somehow the note he was holding is in your possession? This *baraita* contradicts the mishna, from which it was inferred that one of the two men named Yosef ben Shimon can produce promissory notes to collect the debt from others. **With regard to what** principle **do** the mishna and *baraita* **disagree?**

בְּאוֹתִיּוֹת נִקְנוֹת בִּמְסִירָה קָמִיפַּלְגִי,

They disagree with regard to whether **letters,** i.e., the content of a promissory note, **are acquired by** merely **transferring**[N] the document to a new owner. In other words, they disagree about whether or not a creditor can transfer his right to collect a debt to another by merely transferring the document to him.

תַּנָּא דִּידַן סָבַר: אוֹתִיּוֹת נִקְנוֹת בִּמְסִירָה, וְתַנָּא בָּרָא סָבַר: אֵין אוֹתִיּוֹת נִקְנוֹת בִּמְסִירָה.

The *tanna* **of our** mishna **maintains** that **letters are acquired by transferring** the document. There is no concern that the promissory note was inadvertently transferred from one Yosef ben Shimon to the other by being lost and then found, as explained earlier. Nevertheless, there is still the possibility that one Yosef ben Shimon deliberately transferred the promissory note to the other, transferring the right of collection to him. According to this *tanna*, the second Yosef ben Shimon is fully entitled to collect the debt by producing the promissory note. **And the** *tanna* **of the** *baraita* **holds** that **letters are not acquired by transferring**[H] the document, so that even if one Yosef ben Shimon transferred his promissory note to the other, the new holder of the document is not entitled to collect the debt.

NOTES

And what of that which is taught in another *baraita* – וְאֶלָּא הָא דְּתַנְיָא: This *baraita* disagrees with the mishna, and maintains that it is possible for a promissory note written for one Yosef ben Shimon to find its way into the possession of the other Yosef ben Shimon. Despite this, the *baraita* assumes that this did not take place by its being dropped by one Yosef ben Shimon and then found by the other, as both Abaye and Rabba earlier agreed that this is extremely unlikely. Therefore, the Gemara seeks to explain the ruling of the *baraita* in another manner.

They disagree with regard to whether letters are acquired by transferring – בְּאוֹתִיּוֹת נִקְנוֹת בִּמְסִירָה קָמִיפַּלְגִי: This is a dispute recorded earlier in this chapter (169b–170a). Some hold that the ownership of a promissory note and the rights associated with it can be transferred by merely transferring the document to its new owner. Others maintain this is not sufficient. Rather, a separate document of transfer must be written, or the document can be acquired in conjunction with the acquisition of land.

HALAKHA

Letters are not acquired by transferring – אֵין אוֹתִיּוֹת נִקְנוֹת בִּמְסִירָה: How can the holder of a promissory note or a bill of sale transfer ownership of the document to another? The seller of the document writes a separate document of sale, or it is written into the note itself being sold, stating: You, so-and-so, acquire from me, so-and-so, this document along with all the financial rights associated with it. Both the document being transferred and the new document attesting to the transferal are then given to the acquirer. The document is thereby transferred through a process of writing and transmission. If this procedure was not followed, the document has not been legally transferred, and is not acquired even as a piece of paper. This is in accordance with the Gemara in a previous chapter (*Bava Batra* 77a), which concludes that letters cannot be acquired by transferring (Rambam *Sefer Kinyan, Hilkhot Mekhira* 6:10; *Shulḥan Arukh, Ḥoshen Mishpat* 66:1).

HALAKHA

One of several brothers who has a promissory note in his possession – אֶחָד מִן הָאַחִין שֶׁהַשְּׁטָר חוֹב יוֹצֵא מִתַּחַת יָדוֹ: If several brothers have inherited their father's estate and have yet to divide the estate among them, and one of the brothers produces a promissory note of their father that he claims belongs to him exclusively, he must bring proof that the father transferred the note to him, or that the father bequeathed it to him on his death bed. If he cannot prove his claim, the promissory note is assumed to be joint property of all the brothers. This is in accordance with the *baraita* cited in the Gemara. This is the *halakha* even according to the opinion that ordinarily the holder of a promissory note with another's name as creditor is not required to prove he acquired it legally; as it is common for brothers who are co-heirs to seize property belonging to the estate from one another (Rambam *Sefer Mishpatim*, *Hilkhot Naḥalot* 9:9–10; *Tur* and *Shulḥan Arukh*, *Ḥoshen Mishpat* 62:1, and in the comment of Rema).

וְאִי בָּעֵית אֵימָא: דְּכוּלֵּי עָלְמָא – אוֹתִיּוֹת נִקְנוֹת בִּמְסִירָה, וְהָכָא בְּצָרִיךְ לְהָבִיא רְאָיָה קָא מִיפַּלְגִי; תַּנָּא דִּידַן סָבַר: אֵין צָרִיךְ לְהָבִיא רְאָיָה, וְתַנָּא בְּרָא סָבַר: צָרִיךְ לְהָבִיא רְאָיָה.

And if you wish, say that everyone, i.e., both the *tanna* of the mishna and the *tanna* of the *baraita*, holds that **letters are acquired by transferring** the document, **and here they disagree with regard to** whether or not the new holder of the promissory note is **required to bring proof** that the original creditor transferred it to him for collection, as opposed to his having received it for safekeeping or having found it by chance. **The *tanna* of our** mishna **holds** that the present holder of the document is **not required to bring proof** that the debt was transferred to him and therefore he can collect the debt through the promissory note in his possession. **And the *tanna* of the *baraita* holds** that he is **required to bring** such **proof,** and in its absence he cannot collect the debt with the document he holds.

דְּאִיתְּמַר: אוֹתִיּוֹת נִקְנוֹת בִּמְסִירָה – אַבַּיֵי אָמַר: צָרִיךְ לְהָבִיא רְאָיָה, וְרָבָא אָמַר: אֵינוֹ צָרִיךְ לְהָבִיא רְאָיָה.

This is **as it was stated: Letters are acquired by transferring** the document. **Abaye says:** The new holder of the document is **required to bring proof** that he has in fact acquired the right to collect the debt. **And Rava says: He is not required to bring** such **proof;** it is assumed that if he is holding the document it was transferred to him knowingly by the original creditor.

אֲמַר אַבַּיֵי: מְנָא אָמֵינָא לַהּ? דְּתַנְיָא: אֶחָד מִן הָאַחִין שֶׁהַשְּׁטָר חוֹב יוֹצֵא מִתַּחַת יָדוֹ – עָלָיו לְהָבִיא רְאָיָה; מַאי לָאו הוּא הַדִּין לַאֲחֵרִינֵי?

Abaye said: From where do I say that he is required to bring proof? This is **as it is taught** in a *baraita*: In the case of **one of** several **brothers,** heirs of an estate, **who has a promissory note in his possession**[H] listing a debt owed to the deceased father, and he seeks to collect the debt for himself, it is **upon him to bring proof** that the document was transferred to him legally by his father in his lifetime, or that it was bequeathed to him specifically and he did not appropriate it from the other brothers. Abaye concludes from this: **What, is the same not true for** all **others** in a similar situation? In other words, whenever someone holds a promissory note that did not initially belong to him he is required to prove that he acquired it legally.

וְרָבָא אָמַר: שָׁאנֵי אַחִין, דְּשָׁמְטוּ מֵהֲדָדֵי.

And Rava said in response: Proof is not generally required in such a case. But the case of **brothers** who are heirs **is different, as** it is common for brothers who are co-heirs to **seize** property belonging to the estate **from one another.**

אִיכָּא דְּאָמְרִי, אָמַר רָבָא: מְנָא אָמֵינָא לַהּ? דְּתַנְיָא: אֶחָד מִן הָאַחִין שֶׁהַשְּׁטָר חוֹב יוֹצֵא מִתַּחַת יָדוֹ – עָלָיו לְהָבִיא רְאָיָה; אַחִין הוּא דְּשָׁמְטוּ מֵהֲדָדֵי, אֲבָל אַחֲרִינֵי לָא.

There are those **who say** there is a different version of this exchange between Abaye and Rava. According to this version, **Rava said: From where do I say** that no proof is required? **As it is taught** in a *baraita*: In the case of **one of** several **brothers,** heirs of an estate, **who has a promissory note in his possession** listing a debt owed to the deceased father, and he seeks to collect the debt for himself, it is **upon him to bring proof** that the document was transferred to him legally by his father in his lifetime, or that it was bequeathed to him specifically and that he did not appropriate it from the other brothers. The implication is that **it is** only **brothers** who must bring such proof, as it is common for brothers who are co-heirs to **seize** property belonging to the estate **from one another. But others** in a similar situation do **not** have to bring proof that they acquired the promissory note legally.

וְאַבַּיֵי? אַחִין אִיצְטְרִיכָא לֵיהּ, סָלְקָא דַּעְתָּךְ אָמֵינָא: כֵּיוָן דְּשָׁמְטוּ מֵהֲדָדֵי – אֵימָא מִיזְדַּהַר זְהִירִי, וְלָא צְרִיכִי לְהָבִיא רְאָיָה, קָמַשְׁמַע לַן.

And how would **Abaye** counter this proof? He would say: There is no difference between **brothers** and anyone else; they all have to bring proof. The *baraita* specifies brothers because it **was necessary for it** to mention that case, as it might **enter your mind to say** that **since** it is common for brothers who are co-heirs to **seize** property belonging to the estate **from one another,** one might **say** that **they are careful** to prevent such attempts. **And** therefore, when brothers produce a promissory note, **they are not required to bring proof** that they obtained it legally, as it is assumed that the other brothers would not have allowed the note to escape their possession otherwise. To counter this, the *baraita* **teaches us** that brothers, too, must bring proof when they produce promissory notes.

וְאֶלָּא הָא דְּתַנְיָא: כְּשֵׁם שֶׁמּוֹצִיאִין הֵן שְׁטַר חוֹב עַל אֲחֵרִים – כָּךְ מוֹצִיאִין זֶה עַל זֶה, בְּמַאי קָמִיפַּלְגִי?

§ The Gemara returns to discuss the case of two men with the same name. **But** what about **that which is taught** in another *baraita*: **Just as** the two men named Yosef ben Shimon **can produce a promissory note against others, so can they produce** promissory notes **against one another.** This represents a third opinion, standing in opposition to both the mishna and the previous *baraita*. The Gemara asks: **With regard to what do** the mishna and first *baraita* on the one hand, and this *baraita* on the other, **disagree?**

בְּכוֹתְבִין שְׁטָר לַלֹּוֶה וְאַף עַל פִּי שֶׁאֵין מַלְוֶה עִמּוֹ, קָמִיפַּלְגִי;

The Gemara answers: **They disagree about** whether or not a scribe **may write** a promissory **note for a debtor even if** the **creditor is not with him.**

תַּנָּא דִּידַן סָבַר: כּוֹתְבִין שְׁטָר לַלֹּוֶה וְאַף עַל פִּי שֶׁאֵין מַלְוֶה עִמּוֹ. זִימְנִין דְּאָזֵיל לְגַבֵּי סָפְרָא וְסָהֲדֵי, וְאָמַר לְהוּ: "כִּתְבוּ לִי שְׁטָרָא, דְּבָעֵינַן לְמֵיזַף מִיּוֹסֵף בֶּן שִׁמְעוֹן חֲבֵרִי", וּבָתַר דְּכָתְבִי וְחָתְמִי לֵיהּ, נָקֵיט לֵיהּ וְאָמַר לֵיהּ: "הַב לִי מְאָה דְּיזַפְתְּ מִינַּאי";

The *tanna* of our mishna **holds** that a scribe **may write** a promissory **note for a debtor even if the creditor is not with him.** The Gemara explains: At **times,** it could happen **that** one of the men named Yosef ben Shimon **goes to a scribe and** to **witnesses and says to them: Write** a promissory **note for me, as I wish to borrow** money **from another Yosef ben Shimon. And** then, **after they write** the document **and sign it for him,** he will **take it and say to** the other Yosef ben Shimon: **Give me the hundred** dinars **that you borrowed from me,** as attested to in this document. That is the reason why the mishna rules that two people of the same name cannot collect a debt through a promissory note from one another, thereby preventing this occurrence.

תַּנָּא בָּרָא סָבַר: אֵין כּוֹתְבִין שְׁטָר לַלֹּוֶה עַד שֶׁיְּהֵא מַלְוֶה עִמּוֹ.

By contrast, **the *tanna* of the** other ***baraita*** **holds** that a scribe **may not write** a promissory **note for a debtor unless** the **creditor is with him** and consents to the writing of the document. If one Yosef ben Shimon consents to the writing of the document before the other, they apparently trust one another, and there is no concern that the one holding the promissory note will defraud the other.

"נִמְצָא לְאֶחָד בֵּין שְׁטָרוֹתָיו: "שְׁטָרוֹ שֶׁל יוֹסֵף בֶּן שִׁמְעוֹן פָּרוּעַ" – שְׁטָרוֹת שְׁנֵיהֶם פְּרוּעִין" וכו׳. טַעֲמָא דְּנִמְצָא, הָא לֹא נִמְצָא – מָצֵי מַפֵּיק; וְהָאֲנַן "וְלֹא אַחֵר יָכוֹל לְהוֹצִיא עֲלֵיהֶן שְׁטַר חוֹב" תְּנַן!

§ The mishna teaches: If a document is **found among one's documents** stating: The promissory **note against Yosef ben Shimon is repaid,** and both men named Yosef ben Shimon owed this man money, **the** promissory **notes of both of them are** considered **repaid,** as it cannot be determined which debt was repaid and which is outstanding. The Gemara comments: The implication of the mishna is that **the reason** this man cannot collect his debt is **that** this note **was found** among his papers; **but if it** was **not** suddenly found, rather he was always aware of its existence, **he could present** a promissory note against one of the men named Yosef ben Shimon and collect the debt from him. The Gemara asks: **But didn't we learn** earlier in the mishna: **Nor can another present a promissory note against** either of **them?**

אָמַר רַבִּי יִרְמְיָה: בִּמְשׁוּלָּשִׁין.

Rabbi Yirmeya said: This later line in the mishna is stated **with regard to** a promissory note in which the debtors Yosef ben Shimon are identified by having their names **tripled,** i.e., through mentioning the name of their respective grandfathers, as is explained at the end of the mishna.

וְנֶחֱזֵי תַּבְרָא בִּשְׁמָא דְּמַאן דִּכְתִיב! אָמַר רַב הוֹשַׁעְיָא: בִּמְשׁוּלָּשִׁין בַּשְּׁטָר וְאֵין מְשׁוּלָּשִׁין בַּשּׁוֹבֵר.

The Gemara questions this explanation: **But let us see in whose name the receipt,** i.e., the note stating that Yosef ben Shimon's debt has been repaid, **is written.** Why is there uncertainty as to which Yosef ben Shimon is referred to in the document? **Rav Hoshaya said:** The case is **where** the debtors are identified by having their names **tripled in the** promissory **note, but** the names are **not tripled in the receipt.**[H]

אַבַּיֵּי אֲמַר, הָכִי קָאָמַר: נִמְצָא לַלֹּוֶה בֵּין שְׁטָרוֹתָיו "שְׁטָרוֹ שֶׁל יוֹסֵף בֶּן שִׁמְעוֹן עָלַי פָּרוּעַ" – שְׁטָרוֹת שְׁנֵיהֶם פְּרוּעִין.

Abaye stated a different answer to this question, that the mishna is speaking about the debtor, not the creditor, and **this** is what **it is saying:** If a receipt is **found among the debtor's documents**[H] stating: **The** promissory **note of Yosef ben Shimon against** me has been **repaid,** and this debtor had borrowed money from both men named Yosef ben Shimon, **the** promissory **notes of both of them are** considered **repaid,**[N] i.e., they are not valid for collection, as it cannot be determined which debt was paid and which one is outstanding.

HALAKHA

Where the names are tripled in the promissory note, but not tripled in the receipt – **בִּמְשׁוּלָּשִׁין בַּשְּׁטָר וְאֵין מְשׁוּלָּשִׁין בַּשּׁוֹבֵר:** If one lent money to two people named Yosef ben Shimon, and each of the two promissory notes indicated the debtors' grandfathers' names so that they could be distinguished from each other, and the creditor finds a receipt stating that the debt of Yosef ben Shimon has been repaid, without mentioning the grandfather's name, and both promissory notes are stored among the creditor's torn promissory notes, i.e., notes that have already been repaid, although these promissory notes themselves were not torn, the presumptive status of both notes is undermined and neither one can be collected. This is in accordance with the mishna, as it is explained by Rabbi Yirmeya and Rav Hoshaya (*Shulḥan Arukh, Ḥoshen Mishpat* 49:9).

Found among the debtor's documents – **נִמְצָא לַלֹּוֶה בֵּין שְׁטָרוֹתָיו:** If two people named Yosef ben Shimon lent money to a single debtor, who has a receipt stating that he has repaid a loan to Yosef ben Shimon, neither creditor can collect his debt with his promissory note, as the debtor can say to whichever of them attempts to collect: This receipt pertains to your loan. This is in accordance with Abaye's interpretation of the mishna. If one Yosef ben Shimon then authorizes the other to collect his loan for him, so that the second Yosef ben Shimon is empowered to collect both debts, he can collect with the lesser of the promissory notes, since the debtor concedes that one of the debts is not repaid (*Sefer Mishpatim, Hilkhot Malve VeLoveh* 24:8; *Shulḥan Arukh, Ḥoshen Mishpat* 49:7).

NOTES

The promissory note of Yosef ben Shimon has been repaid, the promissory notes of both of them are considered repaid – שְׁטָרוֹ שֶׁל יוֹסֵף בֶּן שִׁמְעוֹן עָלַי פָּרוּעַ, שְׁטָרוֹת שְׁנֵיהֶם פְּרוּעִין: If either Yosef ben Shimon attempts to collect with his promissory note, the debtor can claim: It is not known for certain that my debt to you has not been repaid, and therefore he can avoid payment to both of them. If one of the men named Yosef ben Shimon authorizes the other to collect his debt for him, the authorized one can approach the debtor acting on behalf of both himself and the other man, and collect the lesser of the two debts (Rashbam; see Rashba and Ritva). The *Sefer HaShlama* and the Meiri note that when the Gemara here states that the debtor need not repay either debt, this is referring only to the inability of the court to force repayment; on a moral level the debtor is in fact obligated to pay both debts, as explained elsewhere (see *Bava Kamma* 118a).

"כֵּיצַד יַעֲשׂוּ? יְשַׁלְּשׁוּ" כו׳. תָּנָא: אִם הָיוּ שְׁנֵיהֶם כֹּהֲנִים – יִכְתְּבוּ דּוֹרוֹת.

The mishna teaches: **What should** two people with the same name in a single city **do** in order to conduct their business? **They should triple** their names by writing three generations: Yosef ben Shimon ben so-and-so. If their grandfather's names are identical and they have no prominent physical difference to indicate who is the one listed in the document, they write that the one referred to in the document is a priest, if that is the case. The Sages **taught** the following continuation of the mishna in a *baraita*: And **if both of them were priests, they should write** several **generations** of ancestors, until a divergence in names is found that can serve as a means of identification.

מתני׳ הָאוֹמֵר לִבְנוֹ "שְׁטָר בֵּין שְׁטָרוֹתַי פָּרוּעַ וְאֵינִי יוֹדֵעַ אֵי זֶהוּ" – שְׁטָרוֹת כּוּלָּן פְּרוּעִין; נִמְצָא לְאֶחָד שָׁם שְׁנַיִם – הַגָּדוֹל פָּרוּעַ, וְהַקָּטָן אֵינוֹ פָּרוּעַ.

MISHNA In the case of **one who says to his son** before dying: One promissory **note among the** promissory **notes in my** possession **is repaid, but I do not know which one,**[H] **the** promissory **notes of all of** those who owe him money **are** considered **repaid,** i.e., they are not valid for collection, as it cannot be determined which debt was repaid and which are outstanding. If there were **found** among his papers **two** promissory notes owed **by one** person, the one for **the greater** amount **is** considered **repaid, and** the one for **the smaller** amount **is not** considered **repaid** and can be collected; the debtor is favored in the case of an uncertainty.

גמ׳ אָמַר רָבָא: "שְׁטָר לְךָ בְּיָדִי פָּרוּעַ" – הַגָּדוֹל פָּרוּעַ, וְהַקָּטָן אֵינוֹ פָּרוּעַ; "חוֹב לְךָ בְּיָדִי פָּרוּעַ" – שְׁטָרוֹת כּוּלָּן פְּרוּעִין.

GEMARA **Rava says** that if a creditor says to a debtor who borrowed money twice from him: One promissory **note** of the two that I have **of yours in my possession is repaid,**[H] without specifying which one, the one for **the greater** amount **is** considered **repaid, and** the one for **the smaller** amount **is not** considered **repaid,** and can be collected. If the creditor said instead: **The debt of yours** that I have **in my possession is repaid, all** the promissory **notes** this creditor has from this debtor **are** considered **repaid,** as the term debt covers all the loans at once.

אֲמַר לֵיהּ רָבִינָא לְרָבָא: אֶלָּא מֵעַתָּה, "שָׂדִי מְכוּרָה לְךָ" – שָׂדֶה גְּדוֹלָה מְכוּרָה לוֹ, "שָׂדֶה שֶׁיֵּשׁ לִי מְכוּרָה לְךָ" – כׇּל שְׂדוֹתָיו מְכוּרִין לוֹ?

Ravina said to Rava: If that is so that when one makes an ambiguous statement it is interpreted to his detriment, does the same *halakha* apply to sales? If a seller of land writes a document for a purchaser stating: **My field is** hereby **sold to you,**[H] without specifying which of his two fields he is referring to, is it the **larger field** that is **sold to him?** And if he writes a document for the purchaser stating: The **field that I have is sold to you,** is it so that **all of his fields are sold to him,** as the Hebrew word for field can refer to several fields as well as a single field?

הָתָם יַד בַּעַל הַשְּׁטָר עַל הַתַּחְתּוֹנָה.

Rava explains: **There, the holder of the document** of sale **is at a disadvantage,**[N] as it is he who seeks to take more property from the seller, and must accept the minimal meaning. Here too, in the case of the promissory notes, it is the holder of the document, the creditor, who seeks to collect more money from the debtor. Therefore, the creditor is at a disadvantage.

מתני׳ הַמַּלְוֶה אֶת חֲבֵירוֹ עַל יְדֵי עָרֵב – לֹא יִפָּרַע מִן הֶעָרֵב,

MISHNA **One who lends** money **to another with** the assurance of **a guarantor cannot collect** the debt **from the guarantor.**

Perek **X**
Daf **173** Amud **b**

וְאִם אָמַר לוֹ "עַל מְנָת שֶׁאֶפָּרַע מִמִּי שֶׁאֶרְצֶה" – יִפָּרַע מִן הֶעָרֵב; רַבָּן שִׁמְעוֹן בֶּן גַּמְלִיאֵל אוֹמֵר: אִם יֵשׁ נְכָסִים לַלֹּוֶה – בֵּין כָּךְ וּבֵין כָּךְ לֹא יִפָּרַע מִן הֶעָרֵב.

But if the creditor **said to** the debtor: I am lending the money **on the condition that I will collect** the debt **from whomever I wish,** i.e., either the debtor or the guarantor, he **can collect** the debt **from the guarantor. Rabban Shimon ben Gamliel says: If the debtor has property** of his own, then **whether** in **this** case, where the creditor stipulated this condition, **or that** case, where he did not, he **cannot collect** the debt **from the guarantor.**

HALAKHA

One promissory note among the promissory notes in my possession is repaid, but I do not know which one, etc. – שְׁטָר בֵּין שְׁטָרוֹתַי פָּרוּעַ וְאֵינִי יוֹדֵעַ אֵי זֶהוּ וכו׳: If one says to his children: One of the promissory notes in my possession is repaid, but I do not know which one it is, all of his promissory notes are considered repaid, in accordance with the mishna. There is no difference whether the man who said this is still alive, or has since died. If he is still alive, and he subsequently claims to have examined the matter and determined which document it is that was repaid, he is deemed credible, and he can then collect all his other debts (*Shakh*). If there are among the man's promissory notes two notes relating to the same debtor, he can collect the lesser of the two debts, in accordance with the mishna. The Rema, citing *Nimmukei Yosef*, writes that if the debtor has a receipt for the lesser debt, the greater debt can then be collected (Rambam *Sefer Mishpatim, Hilkhot Malve VeLoveh* 16:12; *Shulḥan Arukh, Ḥoshen Mishpat* 65:23).

One promissory note of yours in my possession is repaid – שְׁטָר לְךָ בְּיָדִי פָּרוּעַ: If a creditor says to a debtor: One of the promissory notes I have of yours is repaid, and the creditor has two notes of this debtor, the larger of the two loans is considered repaid, and he can collect the smaller loan. If the creditor said to him instead: The debt of yours that I have in my possession is repaid, all the promissory notes in his possession are considered repaid. Since he did not mention any particular amount, it is assumed that when he used the term debt he was including all the amounts loaned to this debtor over time, in accordance with Rava's statement (*Shulḥan Arukh, Ḥoshen Mishpat* 65:24, and see *Sma* there).

My field is hereby sold to you, etc. – שָׂדִי מְכוּרָה לְךָ וכו׳: If one says to another: I am hereby selling you one of my houses, or: I am hereby selling you one of my oxen, without specification, he gives him the smallest house or ox in his possession. If one of the seller's oxen dies before he has given any to the purchaser, or if one of his houses collapses, he can tell the purchaser that it was that ox or house that was sold, and the purchaser is not refunded his money, because the holder of the document of sale is always at a disadvantage (Rambam *Sefer Kinyan, Hilkhot Mekhira* 21:19; *Shulḥan Arukh, Ḥoshen Mishpat* 214:12).

NOTES

There, the holder of the document is at a disadvantage, etc. – הָתָם יַד בַּעַל הַשְּׁטָר וכו׳: The underlying principle in these cases is: The burden of proof rests upon the claimant. Therefore, in both the case of the promissory note and the case of the sale, whoever attempts to receive more than the minimum must prove his case.

וְכֵן הָיָה רַבָּן שִׁמְעוֹן בֶּן גַּמְלִיאֵל אוֹמֵר: הֶעָרֵב לְאִשָּׁה בִּכְתוּבָּתָהּ, וְהָיָה בַּעְלָהּ מְגָרְשָׁהּ – יַדִּירֶנָּה הֲנָאָה, שֶׁמָּא יַעֲשׂוּ קְנוּנְיָא עַל נְכָסִים שֶׁל זֶה וְיַחֲזִיר אֶת אִשְׁתּוֹ.

And so Rabban Shimon ben Gamliel would say:[N] If there is **a guarantor for a woman for her marriage contract,**[H] from whom the woman can collect payment of her marriage contract instead of collecting it from the husband, **and her husband was divorcing her,** the husband **must take a vow** prohibiting himself from deriving any **benefit from her,** so that he can never remarry her. This precaution is taken **lest** the couple **collude** [*kenunya*][L] to divorce in order to collect payment of the marriage contract **from this** guarantor's **property, and** then the husband **will remarry** his wife.

גמ׳ מַאי טַעְמָא? רַבָּה וְרַב יוֹסֵף דְּאָמְרִי תַּרְוַויְהוּ: גַּבְרָא אַשְׁלִימַתְ לִי, גַּבְרָא אַשְׁלִימִי לָךְ.

GEMARA

The mishna teaches: One who lends money to another with a guarantor cannot collect the debt from the guarantor. The Gemara at first understands that the mishna is ruling that a guarantor's commitment is limited to when the debtor dies or flees. **What is the reason** the guarantor's commitment is limited? **Rabba and Rav Yosef both say** that the guarantor can tell the creditor: **You gave a man over to me,** to take responsibility for him if he dies or flees; **I have given a man back to you.** The debtor is here before you; take your money from him, and if he has nothing, suffer the loss yourself.

מַתְקִיף לָהּ רַב נַחְמָן: הַאי דִּינָא דְפַרְסָאֵי!

Rav Naḥman objects to this: This is Persian law.

אַדְּרַבָּה, בָּתַר עָרְבָא אָזְלִי!

The Gemara interjects: **On the contrary,** the Persian courts **go after the guarantor** directly, without even attempting to collect the debt from the debtor himself. Why, then, did Rav Naḥman say that excusing the guarantor from payment is Persian law?

אֶלָּא, בֵּי דִינָא דְפַרְסָאֵי, דְּלָא יָהֲבִי טַעְמָא לְמִילְּתַיְיהוּ.

The Gemara clarifies Rav Naḥman's intent: **Rather,** Rav Naḥman meant to say that this kind of ruling would be appropriate for the members of **a Persian court, who do not give a reason for their statements,** but issue rulings by whim. Rav Naḥman was saying that it is not fair or logical to excuse the guarantor and cause a loss to the creditor who was depending on him.

אֶלָּא אָמַר רַב נַחְמָן: מַאי לֹא יִפָּרַע מִן הֶעָרֵב – לֹא יִתְבַּע עָרֵב תְּחִלָּה.

Rather, Rav Naḥman said: What does the mishna mean when it says that the creditor **cannot collect** the debt **from the guarantor?** It means that he **cannot claim** payment from the **guarantor at the outset,** until after it is established that the debtor has no means to repay the debt. After the borrower defaults, the creditor can collect the debt from the guarantor.

תַּנְיָא נַמִּי הָכִי: הַמַּלְוֶה אֶת חֲבֵירוֹ עַל יְדֵי עָרֵב – לֹא יִתְבַּע עָרֵב תְּחִלָּה, וְאִם אָמַר ״עַל מְנָת שֶׁאֶפָּרַע מִמִּי שֶׁאֶרְצֶה״ – יִתְבַּע עָרֵב תְּחִלָּה.

This *halakha* **is also taught** in a *baraita*: One **who lends** money **to another with** the assurance of **a guarantor cannot claim** payment of the debt **from the guarantor at the outset,** rather, he must first attempt to collect the debt from the debtor. **But if** the creditor **said to** the debtor: I am lending the money **on the condition that I will collect** the debt **from whomever I wish,** he can **claim** payment of the debt **from the guarantor at the outset,** bypassing the debtor.

אָמַר רַב הוּנָא: מִנַּיִן לְעָרֵב דְּמִשְׁתַּעְבֵּד? דִּכְתִיב: ״אָנֹכִי אֶעֶרְבֶנּוּ מִיָּדִי תְּבַקְשֶׁנּוּ״.

§ **Rav Huna said: From where** is it derived that **a guarantor becomes obligated** to repay a loan he has guaranteed? **As it is written** that Judah reassured his father concerning the young Benjamin: **"I will be his guarantor;**[N] **of my hand shall you request him"** (Genesis 43:9). This teaches that it is possible for one to act as a guarantor that an item will be returned to the giver.

מַתְקִיף לָהּ רַב חִסְדָּא: הָא קַבְּלָנוּת הִיא, דִּכְתִיב: ״תְּנָה אֹתוֹ עַל יָדִי וַאֲנִי אֲשִׁיבֶנּוּ״!

Rav Ḥisda objects to this: This incident involving Benjamin is not a case of a standard guarantor, but a case of **an unconditional guarantee, as it is written,** also in the context of Benjamin, that Reuben said: **"Deliver him into my hand, and I will bring him back to you"** (Genesis 42:37). One who undertakes unconditional responsibility for a loan has a different status than a standard guarantor, as will soon be elaborated. Therefore, a biblical source has yet to be adduced to teach that one can become a standard guarantor.

אֶלָּא אָמַר רַבִּי יִצְחָק, מֵהָכָא: ״לְקַח בִּגְדוֹ כִּי עָרַב זָר וּבְעַד נָכְרִיָּה חַבְלֵהוּ״;

Rather, Rabbi Yitzḥak said that the source is **from here: "Take his garment that is surety for a stranger; and hold him in pledge that is surety for an alien woman"** (Proverbs 20:16). The verse advises a creditor to take the garment of the debtor's guarantor as payment for the loan.

NOTES

And so Rabban Shimon ben Gamliel would say – וְכֵן הָיָה רַבָּן שִׁמְעוֹן אוֹמֵר: The term: And so, indicates that there is a connection to Rabban Shimon's previous statement in the mishna. The Ramah explains that in both *halakhot*, Rabban Shimon ben Gamliel expresses concern for the guarantor's welfare, that he not be exploited.

I will be his guarantor – אָנֹכִי אֶעֶרְבֶנּוּ: Although there was no monetary obligation involved in this incident, the Gemara nevertheless derives from this verse that there is a concept of serving as a guarantor (*Levush*).

HALAKHA

A guarantor for a woman for her marriage contract, etc. – עָרֵב לְאִשָּׁה בִּכְתוּבָּתָהּ וכו׳: If there is a guarantor for a woman to pay her marriage contract, and her husband divorces her and has no property from which to pay the marriage contract, collection from the guarantor is permitted only after the husband takes a vow prohibiting himself from deriving any benefit from his divorcée. This vow is taken in order to eliminate the possibility that a couple would collude to divorce only in order to collect the money, planning all along to remarry thereafter (Rambam *Sefer Mishpatim, Hilkhot Malve VeLoveh* 25:6 and *Sefer Nashim, Hilkhot Ishut* 17:9; *Shulḥan Arukh, Even HaEzer* 102:7).

LANGUAGE

Collusion [*kenunya*] – קְנוּנְיָא: From the Greek κοινωνία, *koinonia*, meaning partnership or joint ownership.

וְאוֹמֵר: "בְּנִי אִם עָרַבְתָּ לְרֵעֶךָ תָּקַעְתָּ לַזָּר כַּפֶּיךָ, נוֹקַשְׁתָּ בְאִמְרֵי פִיךָ נִלְכַּדְתָּ בְּאִמְרֵי פִיךָ, עֲשֵׂה זֹאת אֵפוֹא בְּנִי וְהִנָּצֵל כִּי בָאתָ בְכַף רֵעֶךָ לֵךְ הִתְרַפֵּס וּרְהַב רֵעֶיךָ", אִם מָמוֹן יֵשׁ לוֹ בְּיָדְךָ – הַתֵּר לוֹ פִּיסַת יָד, וְאִם לָאו – הַרְבֵּה עָלָיו רֵיעִים.

And it is stated: "My son, if you have become surety for your neighbor, if you have shaken your hands for a stranger, you have become ensnared by the words of your mouth, you have been caught by the words of your mouth. Do this now, my son, and save yourself, seeing that you have come into the hand of your neighbor: Go, humble yourself [*hitrappes*], and assemble your neighbors" (Proverbs 6:1–3). This last part of the passage means: **If** your neighbor's **money is in your possession,** as you owe it as a guarantor, **open up [*hatter*] the palm [*pissat*] of your hand** and repay him. **And if** it is **not** money that you owe him, but rather "you have become ensnared by the words of your mouth" and owe him an apology for a personal slight, **gather together many neighbors** through which to seek his forgiveness.

אֲמַר אַמֵּימָר: עָרֵב דְּמִשְׁתַּעְבֵּד – מַחְלוֹקֶת רַבִּי יְהוּדָה וְרַבִּי יוֹסֵי; לְרַבִּי יוֹסֵי דְּאָמַר: אַסְמַכְתָּא קָנְיָא – עָרֵב מִשְׁתַּעְבֵּד, לְרַבִּי יְהוּדָה דְּאָמַר: אַסְמַכְתָּא לָא קָנְיָא – עָרֵב לָא מִשְׁתַּעְבֵּד.

§ **Ameimar said:** The issue of **whether** or not **a guarantor** in fact **becomes obligated** to repay the loan he has guaranteed is **a dispute**[N] between **Rabbi Yehuda and Rabbi Yosei. According to Rabbi Yosei, who says** that **a transaction with inconclusive consent [*asmakhta*] effects acquisition, a guarantor becomes obligated** to repay the loan, whereas **according to Rabbi Yehuda, who says** that an ***asmakhta* does not effect acquisition, a guarantor** does **not become obligated** to repay the loan. Any obligation one undertakes that is dependent on the fulfillment of certain conditions that he does not expect will be fulfilled, in this case the debtor's default on the loan, is considered an *asmakhta*.

אֲמַר לֵיהּ רַב אַשִׁי לְאַמֵּימָר: הָא מַעֲשִׂים בְּכׇל יוֹם, דְּאַסְמַכְתָּא לָא קָנְיָא, וְעָרֵב מִשְׁתַּעְבֵּד!

Rav Ashi said to Ameimar that he was conflating these two issues: **But** it is **a daily occurrence,** i.e., it is taken for granted, **that an *asmakhta* does not effect acquisition, and** it is also taken for granted that **a guarantor becomes obligated** to repay the loan he has guaranteed.

אֶלָּא אֲמַר רַב אַשִׁי: בְּהַהוּא הֲנָאָה דְּקָא מְהֵימַן לֵיהּ – גָּמַר וּמְשַׁעְבֵּד נַפְשֵׁיהּ.

Rather, Rav Ashi said: Through that satisfaction that the guarantor feels when the creditor **trusts him** and loans the money based on his guarantee, the guarantor **resolves** to **obligate himself**[N] to repay the loan. Guaranteeing a loan is unlike a usual case of an obligation undertaken that is dependent on the fulfillment of certain conditions that he does not expect will be fulfilled, in which the commitment is not considered a real one. Here, the one obligating himself experiences a sense of satisfaction when the money is loaned to the debtor, and due to that, fully commits to fulfill his obligation.

NOTES

Whether a guarantor becomes obligated is a dispute, etc. – עָרֵב דְּמִשְׁתַּעְבֵּד מַחְלוֹקֶת וכו׳: Undertaking the guarantee of a loan is considered a transaction with inconclusive consent [*asmakhta*] because the guarantor assumes that the debtor will repay the loan himself so that the guarantor will never be obligated to do so. The Ritva, in his discussion of *asmakhta* earlier in the chapter (168a), states that an agreement is considered an *asmakhta* only if the party undertaking the obligation makes it conditional upon his own actions; if the condition involves the actions of another party it is not considered an *asmakhta*. He explains that nevertheless, in the case of a loan guarantee, although the obligation is dependent upon the actions of another person, i.e., the default of the debtor, it is still considered an *asmakhta*, since the guarantor is performing a kindness for the debtor and therefore does not expect him to default, thereby causing him a loss.

Resolves to obligate himself – גָּמַר וּמְשַׁעְבֵּד נַפְשֵׁיהּ: In this situation, unlike cases of *asmakhta*, the guarantor undertaking the obligation is so pleased that the loan was given on his guarantee that it is considered as if he himself is a beneficiary of the loan. The underlying principle is that an act of acquisition is a demonstration of conclusive intent; in certain instances, such as here, the context of a given situation can demonstrate such intent even without an act of acquisition.

"וְאִם אָמַר עַל מְנָת שֶׁאֶפָּרַע מִמִּי שֶׁאֶרְצֶה" כו׳. אָמַר רַבָּה בַּר בַּר חָנָה אָמַר רַבִּי יוֹחָנָן: לֹא שָׁנוּ אֶלָּא שֶׁאֵין נְכָסִים לַלֹּוֶה, אֲבָל יֵשׁ נְכָסִים לַלֹּוֶה – לֹא יִפָּרַע מִן הֶעָרֵב.

§ The mishna teaches: **But if** the creditor **said** to the debtor: I am lending the money **on the condition that I will collect** the debt **from whomever I wish,** he can collect the debt from the guarantor. **Rabba bar bar Ḥana says** that **Rabbi Yoḥanan says: They taught** this **only when the debtor has no property** of his own from which to repay the loan, **but if the debtor has property** the creditor **cannot collect** the debt **from the guarantor.**

וְהָא מִדְּקָתָנֵי סֵיפָא, רַבָּן שִׁמְעוֹן בֶּן גַּמְלִיאֵל אוֹמֵר: אִם יֵשׁ נְכָסִים לַלֹּוֶה – לֹא יִפָּרַע מִן הֶעָרֵב, מִכְּלָל דְּתַנָּא קַמָּא סָבַר: לָא שְׁנָא הָכִי וְלָא שְׁנָא הָכִי!

The Gemara questions this assertion: **But from** the fact **that the latter clause** of the mishna **teaches** that **Rabban Shimon ben Gamliel says: If the debtor has property** of his own, then whether in this case, where the creditor stipulated this condition, or that case, where he did not, he **cannot collect** the debt **from the guarantor, by inference** one can understand **that the first *tanna* maintains** that there **is no difference** if it is **like this and** there **is no difference** if it is **like that.** Whether or not the debtor has property from which to repay the loan, the creditor can collect the debt from the guarantor.

חַסּוֹרֵי מִחַסְּרָא וְהָכִי קָתָנֵי: הַמַּלְוֶה אֶת חֲבֵירוֹ עַל יְדֵי עָרֵב – לֹא יִפָּרַע מִן הֶעָרֵב, וְאִם אָמַר "עַל מְנָת שֶׁאֶפָּרַע מִמִּי שֶׁאֶרְצֶה" – יִפָּרַע מִן הֶעָרֵב; בַּמֶּה דְּבָרִים אֲמוּרִים – בְּשֶׁאֵין נְכָסִים לַלֹּוֶה, אֲבָל יֵשׁ נְכָסִים לַלֹּוֶה – לֹא יִפָּרַע מִן הֶעָרֵב; וְקַבְּלָן, אַף עַל פִּי שֶׁיֵּשׁ נְכָסִים לַלֹּוֶה – יִפָּרַע מִן הַקַּבְּלָן;

The Gemara clarifies: The mishna **is incomplete and this** is what **it is teaching: One who lends** money **to another with** the assurance of **a guarantor**[H] **cannot collect** the debt **from the guarantor** before first claiming the debt from the debtor. **But if** the creditor **said** to the debtor: I am lending the money **on the condition that I will collect** the debt **from whomever I wish,**[H] he **can collect** the debt **from the guarantor. In what case is this statement said? When the debtor has no property** of his own from which to repay the debt; **but if the debtor has property,** the creditor **cannot collect** the debt **from the guarantor.** This is the *halakha* with regard to a standard guarantor, **but** in the case of **an unconditional guarantor, even if the debtor has property** of his own, the creditor **can collect** the debt **from the unconditional guarantor.**

HALAKHA

One who lends money to another with a guarantor – הַמַּלְוֶה אֶת חֲבֵירוֹ עַל יְדֵי עָרֵב: If one lends money to another with the assurance of a guarantor, the guarantor is bound to honor his commitment, but the creditor cannot collect from the guarantor before attempting to collect from the debtor. Even if the debtor's property, from which the loan will be collected, is of inferior quality, the creditor must settle for this, rather than turn to the guarantor for collection. Even if the debtor has no land, the creditor must first attempt to collect the debt from movable property owned by the debtor rather than collect the debt from the guarantor. The *Sma*, citing Rabbeinu Yeruḥam, rules that if a court mistakenly allowed the creditor to collect the debt from the guarantor first, the property seized from the guarantor must be returned to him (Rambam *Sefer Mishpatim*, *Hilkhot Malve VeLoveh* 25:3; *Shulḥan Arukh*, *Ḥoshen Mishpat* 129:8).

But if the creditor said: On the condition that I will collect the debt from whomever I wish – וְאִם אָמַר עַל מְנָת שֶׁאֶפָּרַע מִמִּי שֶׁאֶרְצֶה: If the creditor stipulated that he reserves the right to collect the debt from whomever he wishes, i.e., either the debtor or the guarantor, he may bypass the debtor and collect the debt from the guarantor, even if the debtor has property from which to pay (Ri Migash). Some authorities disagree with this (Rabbeinu Tam). All agree that if the wording of the creditor's stipulation was: I am lending on the condition that I can collect first from whomever I wish, he can then collect the debt from the guarantor directly, even if it is known that the debtor has property (Rambam *Sefer Mishpatim*, *Hilkhot Malve VeLoveh* 25:4; *Shulḥan Arukh*, *Ḥoshen Mishpat* 214:14).

Perek **X**
Daf **174** Amud **a**

רַבָּן שִׁמְעוֹן בֶּן גַּמְלִיאֵל אוֹמֵר אִם יֵשׁ נְכָסִים לַלֹּוֶה – אֶחָד זֶה וְאֶחָד זֶה לֹא יִפָּרַע מֵהֶן.

Rabban Shimon ben Gamliel says: If the debtor has property, in **both this** case and in **that** case, i.e., whether the guarantor is a standard guarantor or an unconditional guarantor, the creditor **cannot collect** the debt **from** either type of guarantor.

אָמַר רַבָּה בַּר חָנָה אָמַר רַבִּי יוֹחָנָן: כׇּל מָקוֹם שֶׁשָּׁנָה רַבָּן שִׁמְעוֹן בֶּן גַּמְלִיאֵל בְּמִשְׁנָתֵנוּ – הֲלָכָה כְּמוֹתוֹ, חוּץ מֵעָרֵב, וְצַיְדָּן, וּרְאָיָה אַחֲרוֹנָה.

Rabba bar Ḥana says that **Rabbi Yoḥanan says: Wherever Rabban Shimon ben Gamliel taught** a *halakha* **in** the corpus of **our Mishna,** the ***halakha*** is **in accordance with his** opinion, **except for** the following three cases: The responsibility of the **guarantor, and** the incident that occurred in the city of **Tzaidan** (see *Gittin* 74a), **and** the dispute with regard to **evidence** in the **final** disagreement (see *Sanhedrin* 31a).

אָמַר רַב הוּנָא: "הַלְוֵהוּ וַאֲנִי עָרֵב", "הַלְוֵהוּ וַאֲנִי פּוֹרֵעַ", "הַלְוֵהוּ וַאֲנִי חַיָּיב", "הַלְוֵהוּ וַאֲנִי נוֹתֵן" – כּוּלָּן לְשׁוֹן עַרְבוּת הֵן;

§ The Gemara discusses which expressions confer upon a person the status of a standard guarantor, and which confer the status of an unconditional guarantor. **Rav Huna says** that if one says to a potential creditor: **Lend** money **to him and I am a guarantor,**[H] or: **Lend** money **to him and I will repay** the debt, or: **Lend** money **to him and I** am **obligated** to repay the debt, or: **Lend** money **to him and I will give** the money back to you, **all these are expressions** that confer the status of a standard **guarantee.**

"תֵּן לוֹ וַאֲנִי קַבְּלָן", "תֵּן לוֹ וַאֲנִי פּוֹרֵעַ", "תֵּן לוֹ וַאֲנִי חַיָּיב", "תֵּן לוֹ וַאֲנִי נוֹתֵן" – כּוּלָּן לְשׁוֹן קַבְּלָנוּת הֵן.

If one says: **Give** money **to him and I am an unconditional guarantor,** or: **Give** money **to him and I will repay** the debt, or: **Give** money **to him and I** am **obligated** to repay the debt, or: **Give** money **to him and I will give** the money back to you, **all these are expressions** that confer the status of **an unconditional guarantee.** The usage of the word give, as opposed to lend, confers the status of an unconditional guarantor.

HALAKHA

Lend to him and I am a guarantor, etc. – הַלְוֵהוּ וַאֲנִי עָרֵב וכו׳: When does one become a standard guarantor and when does he become an unconditional guarantor? If one says to the creditor: Lend money to him and I am a guarantor, or: Lend money to him and I will repay, or: Lend money to him and I am obligated to repay, or: Lend money to him and I will give the money back to you, or: Lend money to him and I am an unconditional guarantor, or: Give money to him and I am a guarantor, or: Give money to him and I will repay, or: Give money to him and I am obligated to give it back to you, or even: Give money to him and I am an unconditional guarantor, these expressions all result in the status of a standard guarantor. Only if one said to the creditor: Give money to him and I will give it back to you, is he an unconditional guarantor. This is in accordance with the opinion of Rava, the latest of all the Sages involved in this discussion. In a case where one said to a creditor after a loan had already been granted: I will give back to you the money that you have given to that person, if the declaration is accompanied by an act of acquisition, he becomes an unconditional guarantor as well. The Rema writes that there are those who disagree with regard to the statement: Give money to him and I am an unconditional guarantor, and maintain that this confers the status of an unconditional guarantor (see Rosh; Rashba), and he adds that this is the opinion that should be followed (Rambam *Sefer Mishpatim*, *Hilkhot Malve VeLoveh* 25:5; *Shulḥan Arukh*, *Ḥoshen Mishpat* 129:17–18).

אִיבַּעְיָא לְהוּ: ״הַלְוֵהוּ וַאֲנִי קַבְּלָן״, ״תֵּן לוֹ וַאֲנִי עָרֵב״, מַאי?

A dilemma was raised before the Sages: **What** is the *halakha* if one says: **Lend** money to **him and I** am **an unconditional guarantor?** On the one hand, the word lend is used, as opposed to give, but on the other hand, he explicitly states that he will be an unconditional guarantor. What is the *halakha* if one says: **Give** money **to him and I** am **a guarantor?** On the one hand, the word give is used, as opposed to lend, but on the other hand, he states that he will be a guarantor.

אָמַר רַבִּי יִצְחָק: לְשׁוֹן עַרְבוּת – עַרְבוּת, לְשׁוֹן קַבְּלָנוּת – קַבְּלָנוּת.

Rabbi Yitzḥak says in resolving this dilemma: When one employs **the language of** a standard **guarantee,** it is a standard **guarantee,** even if he also used the word give. And when one employs **the language of an unconditional guarantee,** it is **an unconditional guarantee,** even if he also used the word lend.

רַב חִסְדָּא אָמַר: כּוּלָּן לְשׁוֹן קַבְּלָנוּת הֵן, בַּר מֵ״הַלְוֵהוּ וַאֲנִי עָרֵב״.

Rav Ḥisda says: All of the expressions mentioned in this discussion **are expressions of an unconditional guarantee, except for: Lend** money **to him and I am a guarantor.**

רָבָא אָמַר: כּוּלָּן לְשׁוֹן עַרְבוּת הֵן, בַּר מִ״תֵּן לוֹ וַאֲנִי נוֹתֵן״.

Rava says: All of the expressions mentioned in this discussion **are expressions of** a standard **guarantee, except for: Give** money **to him and I** will **give** the money back to you.

אֲמַר לֵיהּ מָר בַּר אַמֵּימָר לְרַב אַשִׁי, הָכִי אֲמַר אַבָּא: ״תֵּן לוֹ וַאֲנִי נוֹתֵן״ – אֵין לַמַּלְוֶה עַל הַלֹּוֶה כְּלוּם.

Mar bar Ameimar said to Rav Ashi: My father said the following: If one says: **Give** money **to him and I** will **give** the money back to you, this expression binds the guarantor to such an extent that **the lender has no** claim **against the debtor at all;** his only option is to collect the debt from the guarantor.

וְלָא הִיא, לָא מִיפַּטַר לֹוֶה מִינֵּיהּ דְּמַלְוֶה עַד שֶׁיִּשָּׂא וְיִתֵּן בַּיָּד.

The Gemara rejects this last statement: **But that is not so.** Rather, **the debtor is not exempted from** dealing with the **creditor unless** the guarantor **takes** the money from the creditor **and gives** it to the debtor **with** his own **hand.**[H]

הַהוּא דַּיָּינָא דְּאַחְתֵּיהּ לַמַּלְוֶה לְנִכְסֵי [דְּלֹוֶה] מִקַּמֵּי דְּלִתְבְּעֵיהּ לַלֹּוֶה, סַלְּקֵיהּ רַב חָנִין בְּרֵיהּ דְּרַב יֵיבָא.

§ The Gemara relates: There was once **a certain judge who permitted a creditor to enter the debtor's property** and collect it for his debt **before lodging a claim against the debtor** himself. **Rav Ḥanin, son of Rav Yeiva,** overruled that judge and **expelled** the creditor from the seized property.

אֲמַר רָבָא: מַאן חַכִּים לְמֶעְבַּד כִּי הָא מִילְּתָא, אִי לָאו רַב חָנִין בְּרֵיהּ דְּרַב יֵיבָא! קָסָבַר: נִכְסֵיהּ דְּבַר אִינִישׁ אִינּוּן מְעָרְבִין יָתֵיהּ; וּתְנַן: הַמַּלְוֶה אֶת חֲבֵירוֹ עַל יְדֵי עָרֵב – לֹא יִפָּרַע מִן הֶעָרֵב; וְקַיְימָא לָן: לֹא יִתְבַּע עָרֵב תְּחִלָּה.

When **Rava** heard about this he **said: Who is wise** enough **to perform**[N] **such a matter,** i.e., to issue this ruling, **if not Rav Ḥanin, son of Rav Yeiva? He holds that a person's property is a guarantee for him,** i.e., it acts as a guarantor for the loan if the debtor does not repay it; **and we learned** in the mishna: **One who lends** money **to another with** the assurance of **a guarantor cannot collect** the debt **from the guarantor. And we established** that the mishna means that he **cannot collect** the debt **from the guarantor at the outset,** before seeking payment from the debtor himself. So too, he cannot collect the debt by taking the debtor's property without first seeking payment from the debtor himself.

HALAKHA

The guarantor takes the money from the creditor and gives it with his own hand – שֶׁיִּשָּׂא וְיִתֵּן בַּיָּד: If the unconditional guarantor takes the money being loaned directly from the creditor and gives it to the debtor, the creditor has no legal recourse to seek payment from the debtor. His dealings are limited to the guarantor only, in accordance with the Gemara's conclusion. Some say that the same applies when it is a standard guarantor who personally transfers the money to the debtor (Rosh; *Tur*). If the guarantor has no assets from which to pay, the creditor can then approach the debtor for collection, based on Rabbi Natan's principle that a creditor can collect the debt from the debtor of his debtor. If the guarantor forgives the debtor's debt to him, the creditor can no longer claim payment from the debtor, although the *Shakh* maintains that one cannot forgive a loan if this causes a loss to others (Rambam *Sefer Mishpatim, Hilkhot Malve VeLoveh* 25:3; *Shulḥan Arukh, Ḥoshen Mishpat* 129:19).

NOTES

Who is wise enough to perform, etc. – מַאן חַכִּים לְמֶעְבַּד וכו׳: Rav Ḥanin followed the procedure for what is done in the case of a judge who errs by overlooking an explicitly recorded ruling: The judge's decision is overturned (Ritva). Rava expressed his amazement because the *halakha* involved in this case is not recorded explicitly, but follows from the logically sound contention that liened property plays an equivalent role in a loan to that of a guarantor.

הַהוּא עָרְבָא דְּיַתְמֵי דְּפָרְעֵיהּ לְמַלְוֶה מִקַּמֵּי דְּלוֹדְעִינְהוּ לְיַתְמֵי,

§ The Gemara relates: There was once **a certain guarantor for orphans** whose father borrowed money and died, and the orphans were minors, and this guarantor **repaid** the debt **to the creditor before informing the orphans** that he was repaying the debt for them. The guarantor now sought reimbursement from the orphans.

אֲמַר רַב פַּפָּא: פְּרִיעַת בַּעַל חוֹב מִצְוָה, וְיַתְמֵי לָאו בְּנֵי מֵיעֲבַד מִצְוָה נִינְהוּ;

Rav Pappa said: Repaying a creditor is **a mitzva,**[NH] **and orphans** who are minors **are not obligated in performing a mitzva.**[N] They therefore do not have to repay any debts owed by their deceased father until they reach the age of majority.

וְרַב הוּנָא בְּרֵיהּ דְּרַב יְהוֹשֻׁעַ אֲמַר: אֵימַר צְרָרֵי אַתְפְּסֵיהּ.

And Rav Huna, son of Rav Yehoshua, also **said** that the orphans do not have to repay the guarantor until reaching majority, but for a different reason: **Say** that perhaps the deceased **gave bundles** of money **to** his creditor before his death, and therefore some or all of the debt has been paid. As long as they are minors, the heirs would not be aware of this payment, but upon reaching majority there is a chance that they may examine their father's papers and discover that their father had done this. Therefore, payment is deferred until they reach majority.

HALAKHA

Repaying a creditor is a mitzva – פְּרִיעַת בַּעַל חוֹב מִצְוָה: Just as it is a mitzva for a debtor to repay his debt, so is it a mitzva for his heirs to repay it, and they can be forced to do so. This is relevant in a case where the heirs inherited real estate from the debtor. If they inherited only movable property they are not forced to pay, although it is still a mitzva for them to do so. In post-talmudic times, the *ge'onim* instituted that debts can be collected from inherited movable property as well. If the heirs inherit no property at all from the debtor, they are not obligated to repay his debts out of their own property, and it is not even a mitzva for them to do so (Rambam *Sefer Mishpatim, Hilkhot Malve VeLoveh* 11:8; *Shulḥan Arukh, Ḥoshen Mishpat* 107:1).

NOTES

Repaying a creditor is a mitzva – פְּרִיעַת בַּעַל חוֹב מִצְוָה: Many commentaries maintain that repaying a debt is a mitzva by Torah law (Radbaz, citing Rambam; Mabit). By contrast, Rashi (*Ketubot* 91b) writes that there is no explicit mitzva by Torah law to repay a debt. Rather, the Gemara means that it is a mitzva by rabbinic law. Others are of the opinion that while repaying a debt that one has personally incurred is a mitzva by Torah law, repaying debts incurred by one's parents is a mitzva by rabbinic law. At any rate, whether it is a mitzva by Torah law or Rabbinic law, this requirement is subject to the same measures as any positive mitzva: If one refuses to fulfill it the court may coerce him to do so. If the person is not obligated to fulfill the Torah's mitzvot, e.g., a minor or someone who is halakhically not competent, coercion is, perforce, not relevant.

And orphans are not obligated in performing a mitzva – וְיַתְמֵי לָאו בְּנֵי מֵיעֲבַד מִצְוָה נִינְהוּ: The Rashbam explains that this statement applies only to a loan by oral contract. If the loan is attested to in a promissory note, the debtor's property is liened to the creditor and he is entitled to seize it even if the debtor is a minor. In the case recounted by the Gemara, even if the loan was recorded in a promissory note, a debtor's obligation to reimburse a guarantor who has repaid his debt is not written in a document, and is considered an obligation by oral contract. Since the people who owe the money to the guarantor are minors, they are exempted from performing the mitzva of paying him until they reach majority. The Ramban explains the Gemara differently. According to his understanding, since the repayment of the debt is a mitzva, the guarantor, by repaying the loan himself without informing the orphans, has shown that he desires to fulfill this mitzva himself, and the orphans are exempt from reimbursing him even when they reach adulthood.

Perek **X**
Daf **174** Amud **b**

מַאי בֵּינַיְיהוּ?

The Gemara asks: **What is** the difference **between** the opinion of Rav Pappa and that of Rav Huna, son of Yehoshua, as both agree that the orphans are exempt from repaying the debt until they reach majority?

אִיכָּא בֵּינַיְיהוּ כְּשֶׁחַיָּיב מוֹדֶה. אִי נַמִי, דְּשַׁמְּתוּהוּ וּמֵת בְּשַׁמְתֵּיהּ.

The Gemara answers: The difference **between them** is in a case **where the one who owed** the money, i.e., the deceased, **admits** explicitly just before his death that he did not yet repay any of his loan. **Alternatively,** there is a difference between them in a case **where** the court **excommunicated** the deceased[B] for not cooperating with the court in repaying his debt, **and he died** while still **in** a state of **excommunication,** which demonstrates that the debt had not been repaid prior to his death. In both of these cases Rav Pappa would exempt the minor orphans from payment, as minors are not obligated to perform mitzvot, while Rav Huna, son of Yehoshua, would require them to repay the debt immediately, as there is no possibility that their father had repaid the debt.

BACKGROUND

Excommunicated the deceased – שַׁמְּתוּהוּ: One who violates certain *halakhot* may be subjected to excommunication, either as a punishment or in order to compel him to alter his conduct. The Talmud specifies twenty-four transgressions that are punishable by excommunication, and any Jew is authorized to excommunicate one guilty of these offenses. A scholar may also excommunicate someone who offended him and thereby denigrated his honor. One who has been excommunicated may not wear leather shoes or cut his hair, and other people must maintain a distance of at least four cubits from him. Nevertheless, it is permitted to conduct business with him, to study with him, or to teach him. If one was excommunicated and did not mend his ways, he may be subjected to an even more severe ban. The duration of the excommunication and the manner of its dissolution vary, depending on the cause of the excommunication and the status of the one who imposed it (see Meiri).

שלחו מתם: שמתוהו ומת בשמתיה – הלכתא כרב הונא בריה דרב יהושע.

The Sages of Eretz Yisrael **sent** a ruling **from there** to Babylonia: In a case where the court had **excommunicated** a debtor for not cooperating in repaying his debt, **and** the debtor **died** while still **in** a state of **excommunication, the** ***halakha*** **is in accordance with** the opinion of **Rav Huna, son of Rav Yehoshua,** and the orphans must repay the debt immediately.

מיתיבי: ערב שהיה שטר חוב יוצא מתחת ידו – אינו גובה, ואם כתוב בו "התקבלתי ממך" – גובה;

The Gemara **raises an objection** from a *baraita* (*Tosefta* 11:15): **A guarantor** for a debt **who has the promissory note** for that debt **in his possession,**[H] indicating that he has repaid the debt, and now seeks reimbursement from the debtor, **cannot collect** if the debtor has died and the obligation for the debt has fallen to his minor heirs. **But if it is written** by the creditor **in** the promissory note: **I received** repayment **from you,** the guarantor, then the guarantor **can collect** the debt from the minor heirs.

בשלמא לרב הונא בריה דרב יהושע משכחת לה – כשחייב מודה, אלא לרב פפא קשיא!

The Gemara explains the objection: **Granted, according to** the opinion of **Rav Huna, son of Rav Yehoshua, you find** a case where the minor heirs would be required to repay the debt, such as **when the one who owed** the money, i.e., the deceased, **admits** explicitly just before his death that he did not yet repay the loan. **But according to** the opinion of **Rav Pappa,** who maintains that minor heirs never have to repay their father's debts, it is **difficult.** What is the case discussed in the *baraita*?

שאני התם, להכי טרח וכתב ליה "התקבלתי".

The Gemara answers: It is **different there,** as it is **for this** reason that the creditor **troubled himself and wrote for** the guarantor: **I received** repayment from you. Once the creditor writes this in the promissory note, it attains the status of a promissory note of the guarantor held directly against the debtor, and even Rav Pappa agrees that a debt that is recorded in a promissory note can be collected from the deceased's property immediately, even from the minor heirs.

ההוא ערבא דגוי דפרעיה לגוי מקמי דלתבעינהו ליתמי. אמר ליה רב מרדכי לרב אשי, הכי אמר אבימי מהגרוניא משמיה דרבא: אפילו למאן דאמר חיישינן לצררי – הני מילי ישראל, אבל גוי, כיון דבתר ערבא אזיל – לא חיישינן לצררי.

The Gemara relates: There was **a certain guarantor** who had guaranteed a loan given **by a gentile, who repaid the gentile** creditor **before** the gentile creditor **claimed** repayment **from the orphans** who survived the debtor. The guarantor now sought reimbursement from the orphans. **Rav Mordekhai said to Rav Ashi: This is** what **Avimi of Hagronya said in the name of Rava: Even according to the one who says** that **we are concerned for** the possibility that the deceased may have given **bundles** of money to the creditor before his death, **this statement** applies only in the case of **a Jewish** creditor. **But** in the case of **a gentile** creditor, **since** according to gentile law he is entitled to **go** directly **to a guarantor, we are not concerned for** the possibility that the deceased may have given **bundles** of money. The debtor would not repay the gentile before the loan is due, as the latter has the right to collect directly from the guarantor, and would thereby receive double payment.

אמר ליה: אדרבה: אפילו למאן דאמר לא חיישינן לצררי – הני מילי ישראל, אבל גוים, כיון דדינייהו בתר ערבא אזלי, אי לאו דאתפסיה צררי מעיקרא – לא הוה מקבל ליה.

Rav Ashi **said to** Rav Mordekhai: **On the contrary, even according to the one who says** that **we are not concerned for** the possibility that the deceased may have given **bundles** of money, **this statement** applies only in the case of **a Jewish** creditor. **But** in the case of **a gentile** creditor,[H] **since** according to gentile **law they** are entitled to **go** directly **to a guarantor, no** guarantor **would accept** upon himself to guarantee such a loan **if the debtor had not given bundles** of money as collateral to the gentile creditor **from the outset.**

HALAKHA

A guarantor who has the promissory note in his possession – ערב שהיה שטר חוב יוצא מתחת ידו: A guarantor who claims that he has paid a loan for a debtor cannot collect restitution from the debtor unless he produces witnesses to verify his claim that he has repaid the debt. Without such proof he cannot collect payment, even if he has the promissory note in his possession. Nevertheless, if the creditor wrote a statement to the effect that he had received payment from the guarantor, the guarantor can collect the sum he repaid to the creditor from the debtor. For the guarantor to collect payment from the debtor, it is also necessary that he be identified in the document, or alternatively, that the debtor admit that this person is a guarantor for his loan (Rambam *Sefer Mishpatim, Hilkhot Malve VeLoveh* 26:6; *Shulḥan Arukh, Ḥoshen Mishpat* 130:4, and see 130:5).

This statement applies in the case of a Jewish creditor, but in the case of a gentile creditor, etc. – הני מילי ישראל אבל גוים וכו׳: In a case of a gentile creditor, if the debtor died and the guarantor repaid the debt without first informing the heirs, the heirs are not obligated to repay the guarantor. This is because there is a concern that perhaps the deceased had already paid the debt before his death. Since it is the custom among gentiles to seek payment from the guarantor before confronting the debtor or his heirs, this is a reasonable possibility. If the guarantor did inform the heirs before repaying the debt, they must repay him. The Rema, citing *Beit Yosef*, rules that if the guarantor was forced to pay by the court, it is considered equivalent to his having informed the heirs before paying (Rambam *Sefer Mishpatim, Hilkhot Malve VeLoveh* 26:6; *Shulḥan Arukh, Ḥoshen Mishpat* 130:7).

"וְכֵן הָיָה רַבָּן שִׁמְעוֹן בֶּן גַּמְלִיאֵל אוֹמֵר הֶעָרֵב לְאִשָּׁה בִּכְתוּבָּתָהּ" [וכו']. מֹשֶׁה בַּר עַצְרִי עַרְבָא דִּכְתוּבָּתָהּ דְּכַלָּתֵיהּ הֲוָה, רַב הוּנָא בְּרֵיהּ צוּרְבָא מִדְּרַבָּנַן הֲוָה וּדְחִיקָא לֵיהּ מִילְּתָא, אֲמַר אַבַּיֵי: לֵיכָּא דְּנֵיזִיל דְּנַסְבֵּיהּ עֵצָה לְרַב הוּנָא, דְּנִגָרְשָׁהּ לִדְבֵיתְהוּ, וְתֵיזִיל וְתִגְבֵּי כְּתוּבָּה מֵאֲבוּהּ, וַהֲדַר נַהְדְּרָהּ?

§ The mishna teaches: **And so Rabban Shimon ben Gamliel would say:** If there is **a guarantor for a woman for her marriage contract,** and her husband is divorcing her, the husband must take a vow prohibiting himself from deriving any benefit from her so that he can never remarry her. The Gemara relates an incident pertaining to this ruling: Someone named **Moshe bar Atzari was a guarantor for the marriage contract of his daughter-in-law,** guaranteeing the money promised by his son in the event of death or divorce. **His son,** named **Rav Huna, was a young Torah scholar, and was in financial straits. Abaye said: Is there no one who will go advise Rav Huna that he should divorce his wife, and she will go and collect her marriage contract from** Rav Huna's **father, and then** Rav Huna should **remarry her?**

אֲמַר לֵיהּ רָבָא: וְהָא יַדִּירֶנָּה הֲנָאָה תְּנַן! אֲמַר לֵיהּ אַבַּיֵי: אַטּוּ כׇּל דִּמְגָרֵשׁ – בְּבֵי דִינָא מְגָרֵשׁ?

Rava said to Abaye: **But didn't we learn** in the mishna that when a husband divorces his wife in such circumstances he **must take a vow** prohibiting himself from deriving any **benefit** from **her,** thereby precluding the possibility of remarriage? **Abaye said to him: Is that to say** that **everyone who divorces** his wife **divorces** her **in a court?** Rav Huna could be advised to divorce his wife outside the court, in which case he could do so without being forced to take the prescribed vow.

לְסוֹף אִיגַּלַּאי מִילְּתָא דְּכֹהֵן הוּא. אֲמַר אַבַּיֵי, הַיְינוּ דְּאָמְרִי אֱינָשֵׁי: בָּתַר עַנְיָא אָזְלָא עֲנִיּוּתָא.

Ultimately, it was revealed that this Rav Huna **was a priest,** who may not marry a divorcée, even his own ex-wife. Abaye's suggestion was therefore not an option for him. Upon hearing this, **Abaye said: This** is in accordance with the adage **that people say: Poverty follows the poor.**

וּמִי אֲמַר אַבַּיֵי הָכִי? וְהָא אָמַר אַבַּיֵי: אֵיזֶהוּ רָשָׁע עָרוּם? זֶה הַמַּשִּׂיא עֵצָה לִמְכּוֹר בִּנְכָסִים כְּרַבָּן שִׁמְעוֹן בֶּן גַּמְלִיאֵל!

The Gemara asks: **But did Abaye** really **say this?** Would he really encourage giving such advice? **But doesn't Abaye** himself **say: Who is a cunning, wicked person?**[NH] **This is one who provides advice to sell property in accordance with** the ruling of **Rabban Shimon ben Gamliel.** As taught elsewhere (*Ketubot* 95b), if one says: My property is hereby bequeathed to you, and after you die it will pass to so-and-so, Rabban Shimon ben Gamliel rules that the first recipient can sell the property, which would thereby deprive the second recipient from receiving it. Abaye said that giving advice to someone to pursue such action, though it is legally sound, is considered wicked. Here as well, why would he give advice to Rav Huna to divorce his wife only in order to force his father to pay the marriage contract?

בְּנוֹ שָׁאנֵי, וְצוּרְבָא מֵרַבָּנַן שָׁאנֵי.

The Gemara answers: When dealing with one's **son it is different.**[N] It is not considered wickedness to force a father to give money to his own son. Moreover, when dealing with a **Torah scholar it is different.** It is not considered wickedness to procure money for a Torah scholar, because the money enables him to pursue his studies.

וְהָא עָרֵב הוּא, [וְקַיְימָא לַן:] עָרֵב דִּכְתוּבָּה לָא מִשְׁתַּעְבֵּד! קַבְּלָן הֲוָה.

The Gemara asks another question with regard to this incident: **But wasn't** Moshe bar Atzari **a guarantor? And we maintain,** as the Gemara will soon note, that **a guarantor for a marriage contract does not become obligated** to pay. The Gemara answers: **He was an unconditional guarantor.**

הָנִיחָא לְמַאן דְּאָמַר: קַבְּלָן דִּכְתוּבָּה אַף עַל גַּב דְּלֵית לֵיהּ נִכְסֵי לְבַעַל מִשְׁתַּעְבֵּד – שַׁפִּיר, אֶלָּא לְמַאן דְּאָמַר: אִי אִית לֵיהּ מִשְׁתַּעְבֵּד, אִי לֵית לֵיהּ לָא מִשְׁתַּעְבֵּד – מַאי אִיכָּא לְמֵימַר?

The Gemara objects: **This works out well according to the one who says** that **an unconditional guarantor for a marriage contract becomes obligated** to pay it **even if the husband has no property** of his own at the time of the marriage. According to this opinion all is **well. But according to the one who says: If** the husband **has** his own property the unconditional guarantor **becomes obligated** to pay, but **if** the husband **does not have** his own property **he does not become obligated, what is there to say?** Rav Huna obviously did not have any property of his own. Why, then, was his father held responsible for paying his marriage contract according to this latter opinion?

NOTES

Who is a cunning wicked person – אֵיזֶהוּ רָשָׁע עָרוּם: The early commentaries explain that this negative description is directed at one who gives such advice, not at one who actually pursues this course of action himself. The one giving the advice is criticized because he is involving himself in a situation that does not affect him personally and promotes the interest of one party over another. He is referred to as cunning because his advised action is legally sound, and he is called wicked because his advice violates the spirit and intent of the agreement, whereby the property was supposed to revert to a second recipient upon the death of the first recipient. In the case in the Gemara as well, the advice violates the spirit and intent of the guarantor's taking of responsibility, which was in order to pay the marriage contract in the event that a divorce would become necessary, not to pay the marriage contract in the event of a staged divorce.

One's son is different, etc. – בְּנוֹ שָׁאנֵי וכו׳: That is, in this case there is a combination of two factors that enables the guarantee to be binding: It is a case of a father guaranteeing the debt of his son, so it is a sound assumption that he does so willingly and sincerely, and moreover it is a case involving a poor Torah scholar, whose financial welfare should be an important concern. The early commentaries write that where only one or the other of these two factors is present, one may not offer such advice.

HALAKHA

Who is a cunning wicked person, etc. – אֵיזֶהוּ רָשָׁע עָרוּם וכו׳: It is forbidden to advise a married man to divorce his wife only in order to collect her marriage contract from its guarantor, and then subsequently remarry. The exception to this is where the guarantor is the man's father and the man is a poor Torah scholar and is not receiving any financial assistance from his father. In this case, it is permitted to advise him to do so, as occurred in the incident with Moshe bar Atzari (*Shulḥan Arukh*, *Even HaEzer* 102:7 and *Ḥelkat Meḥokek* there).

אִיבָּעֵית אֵימָא: מֶיהֱוֵי הֲוָה לֵיהּ וְאִישְׁתַּדּוּף. וְאִיבָּעֵית אֵימָא: אַבָּא לְגַבֵּי בְּרֵיהּ שַׁעְבּוּדֵי מְשַׁעְבֵּד נַפְשֵׁיהּ.

The Gemara answers: **If you wish, say** that Rav Huna **had** property when he got married, so that his father's guarantee took effect, **but it became blighted,** i.e., it was ruined or lost in the interim. **And if you wish, say** instead: **A father, vis-à-vis his son,** sincerely **obligates himself** to guarantee his marriage contract, even when the son has no property of his own.

דְּאִיתְּמַר: עָרֵב דִּכְתוּבָּה – דִּבְרֵי הַכֹּל לָא מִשְׁתַּעְבֵּד, קַבְּלָן דְּבַעַל חוֹב – דִּבְרֵי הַכֹּל מִשְׁתַּעְבֵּד, קַבְּלָן דִּכְתוּבָּה וְעָרֵב דְּבַעַל חוֹב – פְּלִיגִי, מָר סָבַר: אִי אִית לֵיהּ נִכְסֵי לַלֹּוֶה – מִשְׁתַּעְבֵּד, אִי לֵית לֵיהּ – לָא מִשְׁתַּעְבֵּד; וּמָר סָבַר: בֵּין אִית לֵיהּ וּבֵין לֵית לֵיהּ – מִשְׁתַּעְבֵּד.

The Gemara elaborates on the issue under discussion. This is **as it was stated: Everyone agrees** that a standard **guarantor for a marriage contract does not become obligated** to pay the marriage contract, and **everyone agrees** that **an unconditional guarantor for a creditor,** i.e., for a loan, **becomes obligated** to repay the loan. With regard to **an unconditional guarantor for a marriage contract and** a standard **guarantor for a creditor,** the Sages **disagree.** One **Sage holds** that **if the debtor** or husband **has** his own **property,** these guarantors **become obligated** for the guarantees they have undertaken, but **if he does not have** his own property the guarantor **does not become obligated. And** one **Sage holds** that **whether** the debtor or husband **has** property **or does not have** property, the guarantor **becomes obligated** to pay it.

וְהִלְכְתָא: עָרֵב, בֵּין אִית לֵיהּ וּבֵין לֵית לֵיהּ – מִשְׁתַּעְבֵּד, בַּר מֵעָרֵב דִּכְתוּבָּה, דְּאַף עַל גַּב דְּאִית לֵיהּ לַבַּעַל – לָא מִשְׁתַּעְבֵּד; מַאי טַעֲמָא? מִצְוָה הוּא דַּעֲבַד וְלָאו מִידֵּי חַסְּרָהּ.

And the ***halakha*** is that **a guarantor becomes obligated** to pay, **whether** the debtor **has** his own property **or does not have** property. This is **to the exclusion of a guarantor for a marriage contract,** in which case **even if the husband has** his own property **he does not become obligated** to pay. **What is the reason** for this? The intention of the guarantor **is to perform** the **mitzva** of facilitating a marriage by encouraging the woman to consent to the marriage as a result of his involvement, but he does not truly intend to obligate himself. **And** furthermore, in contrast to a guarantor for a loan, where the creditor stands to suffer a loss if he is not repaid, the woman **does not** suffer any concrete **loss,** as the husband does not borrow money from the woman. Therefore, the level of commitment of the guarantor in this case is lower. Accordingly, the Sages instituted that the guarantor does not become responsible for payment of the marriage contract from his own property.

אָמַר רַב הוּנָא: שְׁכִיב מְרַע שֶׁהִקְדִּישׁ כׇּל נְכָסָיו, וְאָמַר "מָנֶה לִפְלוֹנִי בְּיָדִי" – נֶאֱמָן, חֲזָקָה אֵין אָדָם עוֹשֶׂה קְנוּנְיָא עַל הֶקְדֵּשׁ.

§ **Rav Huna says** that **a person on his deathbed who consecrated all his property**[H] to the Temple treasury, **and** then **says: So-and-so has one hundred dinars in my possession,** i.e., I owe one hundred dinars to so-and-so, is **deemed credible,** and the money is to be repaid to that person. The reason for this is that there is **a presumption** that **a person does not collude against** the **Temple** treasury. He would not lie about owing money to someone, thereby causing a loss to the Temple treasury.

מַתְקִיף לַהּ רַב נַחְמָן: וְכִי אָדָם עוֹשֶׂה קְנוּנְיָא עַל בָּנָיו? דְּרַב וּשְׁמוּאֵל דְּאָמְרִי תַּרְוַיְיהוּ: שְׁכִיב מְרַע שֶׁאָמַר "מָנֶה לִפְלוֹנִי בְּיָדִי", אָמַר "תְּנוּ" – נוֹתְנִין, לֹא אָמַר "תְּנוּ" – אֵין נוֹתְנִין; אַלְמָא אָדָם עָשׂוּי שֶׁלֹּא לְהַשְׂבִּיעַ אֶת בָּנָיו,

Rav Naḥman objects to this ruling: **And does a person collude against his children?** Of course not. Yet, as **Rav and Shmuel both say** that in the case of **a person on his deathbed who says: So-and-so has one hundred dinars in my possession,**[H] only if **he says** explicitly: **Give** him the money, the children **give** it, but if **he did not say** explicitly: **Give** him the money, the children do **not give** it. The person on his deathbed is not assumed to be telling the truth about owing the money unless he explicitly instructs that the money be given. **Apparently,** then, it is assumed that **a person is prone** to make false statements so as **not to make his sons** appear **sated,** i.e., wealthy. A person on his deathbed may falsely claim that he is in debt in order to dispel the notion that his children are wealthy heirs.

HALAKHA

A person on his deathbed who consecrated all his property, etc. – **שְׁכִיב מְרַע שֶׁהִקְדִּישׁ כׇּל נְכָסָיו וכו׳:** If a person on his deathbed consecrated all his property to the Temple treasury, and immediately thereafter added: I owe so-and-so one hundred dinars, he is deemed credible, as there is a presumption that a person on his deathbed would not cause a loss to the Temple treasury in order to benefit another party. Therefore, if he said: Give the money to him, the person to whom the money is owed can collect it, even without taking an oath that it is owed to him. But if the person on his deathbed did not say: Give the money to him, the person to whom the money is supposedly owed cannot collect the debt, unless he has a ratified promissory note, in which case he can collect the debt without taking an oath (*Sma*). If the person on his deathbed said: Give the money to him, but he said this sometime after having consecrated all his property, the person to whom the money is supposedly owed can collect the debt if he has a ratified promissory note, but only if he takes an oath. Even then he can collect the debt only from one who has redeemed the property from the Temple treasury, but not if it is still in the possession of the Temple treasury (Rambam *Sefer Hafla'a, Hilkhot Arakhin VaHaramim* 7:19; *Shulḥan Arukh, Ḥoshen Mishpat* 255:3).

HALAKHA

A person on his deathbed who says, so-and-so has one hundred dinars in my possession, etc. – **שְׁכִיב מְרַע שֶׁאָמַר מָנֶה לִפְלוֹנִי בְּיָדִי וכו׳:** In the case of a person on his deathbed who said: I owe one hundred dinars to so-and-so, if he added: Give the money to him, the money is given to him, but if he did not give instructions to give him the money, it is not given, as it is possible that he said he owed this money only in order to avoid the impression that he or his heirs are wealthy. This is in accordance with the statements of Rav and Shmuel in the Gemara here. Therefore, if it is clear from his words that his admission of owing money is sincere, the money is given even if he did not explicitly say: Give the money to him, in accordance with Rava's explanation given later in the Gemara. Similarly, if a person on his deathbed admitted in writing that all of his property is owed to so-and-so, it is considered a sincere admission (Rambam *Sefer Kinyan, Hilkhot Zekhiya UMattana* 10:3–4; *Shulḥan Arukh, Ḥoshen Mishpat* 255:2).

הָכָא נַמִי, אָדָם עָשׂוּי שֶׁלֹּא לְהַשְׂבִּיעַ אֶת עַצְמוֹ!

Here, too, with regard to the Temple treasury, apply the same principle and say: **A person is prone** to make false statements so as **not to make himself** appear **sated.** It is therefore possible that the money was not owed, and payment should not be made from the consecrated property.

כִּי קָאָמַר רַב הוּנָא הָתָם – דְּנָקֵיט שְׁטָרָא.

The Gemara answers: **When does Rav Huna say** that payment should be made **there,** in the case of a person on his deathbed who consecrated all his property? In a case **where** the creditor, to whom the deceased admitted owing money, **holds** a promissory **note** corroborating the deceased's admission.

מִכְּלָל דְּרַב וּשְׁמוּאֵל – דְּלָא נָקֵיט שְׁטָרָא; אָמַר ״תְּנוּ״ – נוֹתְנִין?! מִלְוֶה עַל פֶּה הָוֵה, וְרַב וּשְׁמוּאֵל דְּאָמְרִי תַּרְוַיְיהוּ: מִלְוֶה עַל פֶּה – אֵינוֹ גּוֹבֶה לֹא מִן הַיּוֹרְשִׁין וְלֹא מִן הַלָּקוֹחוֹת!

The Gemara comments: **By inference,** the statement **of Rav and Shmuel,** where the money is not given to the creditor unless the person on his deathbed explicitly requests that it be given, is applicable in a case **where** the creditor **does not hold** a promissory **note** corroborating the admission. The Gemara asks: If so, how can it be that if the deceased **says: Give** him the money, the children **give** it to him, i.e., it is collected from the estate left to the heirs, as **it is a loan by oral** contract,[N] **and as Rav and Shmuel both say: One does not collect a loan by oral** contract **from heirs nor from purchasers** who bought land from the debtor after the loan was granted?

אֶלָּא אָמַר רַב נַחְמָן: אִידֵּי וְאִידֵּי דְּנָקֵיט שְׁטָרָא, וְלָא קַשְׁיָא: הָא דִּמְקוּיָּים, הָא דְּלָא מְקוּיָּים; אָמַר ״תְּנוּ״ – קַיְּימֵיהּ לִשְׁטָרֵיהּ, לָא אָמַר ״תְּנוּ״ – לָא קַיְּימֵיהּ לִשְׁטָרֵיהּ.

The Gemara gives a different answer to this question. **Rather, Rav Naḥman said:** Both **this** case **and that** case are discussing **where** the creditor **holds** a promissory **note** corroborating the deceased's admission. **And** yet it is **not difficult.** In **this** ruling of Rav Huna, the case is **where** the creditor's promissory note has been **ratified** by the court, and in **that** ruling of Rav and Shmuel, the case is **where** the creditor's promissory note has **not** been **ratified** by the court. Therefore, in the latter case, if the person on his deathbed **says: Give** him the money, he **has** in effect **ratified** the creditor's promissory **note,** and if he did **not say: Give** him the money, he has **not ratified** the creditor's promissory **note.**

אָמַר רַבָּה: שְׁכִיב מְרַע שֶׁאָמַר ״מָנֶה לִפְלוֹנִי בְּיָדִי״, וְאָמְרוּ יְתוֹמִין ״פְּרַעְנוּ״ – נֶאֱמָנִין; ״תְּנוּ מָנֶה לִפְלוֹנִי״, וְאָמְרוּ יְתוֹמִין ״פְּרַעְנוּ״ – אֵין נֶאֱמָנִין.

§ **Rabba says** that in the case of **a person on his deathbed who says: So-and-so has one hundred dinars in my possession, and the orphans** who inherited his property subsequently **said:**[H] **We repaid** the debt, **they are deemed credible.** But if the father said: **Give one hundred dinars to so-and-so,** as I owe it to him, **and** subsequently **the orphans said: We repaid** him the money, **they are not deemed credible.**

כְּלַפֵּי לַיָּיא? אִיפְּכָא מִסְתַּבְּרָא! אָמַר ״תְּנוּ מָנֶה״, כֵּיוָן דִּפְסַקָה אֲבוּהוֹן לְמִילְּתָא – אִיכָּא לְמֵימַר דִּפְרַעֵיהּ. ״מָנֶה לִפְלוֹנִי בְּיָדִי״ – כֵּיוָן דְּלָא פְּסַק אֲבוּהוֹן לְמִילְּתָא – אִיכָּא לְמֵימַר דְּלָא פְּרַעֵיהּ!

The Gemara objects: **Isn't it the opposite** [*kelappei layya*]?[L] **The opposite is** more **reasonable.** If the father **says: Give one hundred dinars** to so-and-so, **since their father stated the matter assertively,** as he gave an explicit directive, **it could be said that** the heirs **repaid** the money. But if he said: **So-and-so has one hundred dinars in my possession, since** the orphans' **father did not state the matter assertively, it could be said that** the heirs **did not repay** the creditor.

אֶלָּא אִי אִיתְּמַר הָכִי אִיתְּמַר: שְׁכִיב מְרַע שֶׁאָמַר ״מָנֶה לִפְלוֹנִי בְּיָדִי״, וְאָמְרוּ יְתוֹמִין: חָזַר וְאָמַר לָנוּ אַבָּא ״פָּרַעְתִּי״ – נֶאֱמָנִין, מַאי טַעְמָא? אִדְּכוּרֵי מִידְּכַר; ״תְּנוּ מָנֶה לִפְלוֹנִי״, וְאָמְרוּ יְתוֹמִין: חָזַר וְאָמַר אַבָּא ״פָּרַעְתִּי״ – אֵין נֶאֱמָנִין, דְּאִם אִיתָא דִּפְרַעֵיהּ, לָא הֲוָה אָמַר ״תְּנוּ״.

The Gemara reformulates Rabba's statement: **Rather, if** Rabba's statement **was stated, it was stated as follows:** In a case of **a person on his deathbed who says: So-and-so has one hundred dinars in my possession, and the orphans** subsequently **said:** After his admission, **Father retracted** his words **and said to us: I repaid** the debt,[H] **they are deemed credible. What is the reason** for this? At first the father had forgotten, but subsequently **he remembered** repaying the debt. But if the father says assertively: **Give one hundred dinars to so-and-so, and the orphans** subsequently **said:** Afterward **Father retracted** his words **and said: I repaid** the debt, **they are not deemed credible.** The reason is **that if it is so that** the father **repaid** the debt or was uncertain about the matter, **he would not say** with such assertiveness: **Give** the money to him.

NOTES

It is a loan by oral contract – מִלְוֶה עַל פֶּה הָוֵה: The Rashbam raises a difficulty: Although heirs need not repay debts incurred by the deceased through loans by oral contract, there is a principle that states: It is a mitzva to fulfill the statement of the dead (*Ketubot* 70a). For this reason alone the heirs should be required to give the money to the party mentioned by the deceased. He answers that there is a mitzva to give the money after the death of the deceased, but not before that. The Ramah suggests that Rav and Shmuel, whose opinion the Gemara is discussing, disagree with the principle that it is a mitzva to fulfill the statement of the dead. There are others who say that the principle applies only when the money in question has already been transferred to a third party or to a court (Ra'avad; Rashba; see Ritva).

HALAKHA

A person on his deathbed who says, so-and-so has one hundred dinars in my possession, and the orphans said, etc. – שְׁכִיב מְרַע שֶׁאָמַר מָנֶה לִפְלוֹנִי בְּיָדִי וְאָמְרוּ יְתוֹמִין וכו׳: If a person on his deathbed said: I owe one hundred dinars to so-and-so, and the orphans subsequently said: We repaid the debt, they are not deemed credible. Since the father did not say assertively: Give the hundred dinars to him, it would be expected that they would not repay the debt. If the father did say: Give the money to him, and subsequently the orphans said: We repaid the debt, they are deemed credible, although they would be subject to the requirement by rabbinic law to take an oath of inducement to substantiate their claim. There are others who maintain that in both cases the orphans are deemed credible to say that they have subsequently repaid the debt (Rema, citing Ra'avad and Rid), and the *Shakh* concurs (Rambam *Sefer Kinyan, Hilkhot Zekhiya UMattana* 10:10–11; *Shulḥan Arukh, Ḥoshen Mishpat* 255:4).

Father retracted and said to us, I repaid the debt, etc. – חָזַר וְאָמַר אַבָּא פָּרַעְתִּי וכו׳: If a person on his deathbed said that he owes another money, and after his death the heirs said: After his admission, Father retracted his words and told us that he had in fact repaid the debt, they are deemed credible (see *Sma* and *Shakh*), but they would be subject to the requirement by rabbinic law to take an oath of inducement to substantiate their claim (see *Shakh*). If the father had said: Give the money to him, and then the heirs claimed that the father had subsequently retracted his directive, they are not deemed credible. This is all in accordance with the Gemara's conclusion (Rambam *Sefer Kinyan, Hilkhot Zekhiya UMattana* 10:8–9; *Shulḥan Arukh, Ḥoshen Mishpat* 255:5).

LANGUAGE

Isn't it the opposite [*kelappei layya*] – כְּלַפֵּי לַיָּיא: This exclamation is used when a statement appears to be the exact opposite of what logic would dictate. Some translate the words to mean: Toward where? or: Where are you going? Others explain that the words mean: Toward the tail. It refers to one riding on a horse while he is facing its tail rather than facing frontward, and became an expression denoting any statement that seems to be the opposite of what is reasonable.

בָּעֵי רָבָא: שְׁכִיב מְרַע שֶׁהוֹדָה, מַהוּ? צָרִיךְ לוֹמַר "אַתֶּם עֵדַי", אוֹ אֵין צָרִיךְ לוֹמַר "אַתֶּם עֵדַי"? צָרִיךְ שֶׁיֹּאמַר "כְּתוֹבוּ", אוֹ אֵין צָרִיךְ לוֹמַר "כְּתוֹבוּ"? אָדָם מְשַׁטֶּה בִּשְׁעַת מִיתָה, אוֹ אֵין אָדָם מְשַׁטֶּה בִּשְׁעַת מִיתָה?

§ **Rava raises a dilemma:** With regard to **a person on his deathbed who,** upon hearing someone's monetary claim against him, **admitted**[NH] owing the money to him, **what is the** *halakha*? Is it **required** for him **to say** to two people: **You are my witnesses,** as is usually necessary in order to prove that an admission is stated in earnest and not in jest? **Or** is it perhaps **not required** for him **to say: You are my witnesses,** since he is a person on his deathbed, whose instructions are generally binding? Is it **required that he say** to two people: **Write** my admission in a document, as is usually required, **or** is it **not required** for him **to say: Write** my admission in a document? The issue in question here is: Does **a person** sometimes **jest at the time of death,** i.e., while on his deathbed, **or** can it be assumed that **a person** does **not jest at the time of death?**

בָּתַר דִּבְעָיָא הֲדַר פַּשְׁטַהּ: אֵין אָדָם מְשַׁטֶּה בִּשְׁעַת מִיתָה, וְדִבְרֵי שְׁכִיב מְרַע כִּכְתוּבִין וְכִמְסוּרִין דָּמוּ.

After Rava **raised the dilemma, he then resolved it,** and ruled: **A person** does **not jest at the time of death, and** therefore **the statements of a person on his deathbed are considered as** if they were **written** in a document **and transmitted**[NH] to the relevant party.

מתני׳ הַמַּלְוֶה אֶת חֲבֵירוֹ בִּשְׁטָר – גּוֹבֶה מִנְּכָסִים מְשׁוּעְבָּדִים, עַל יְדֵי עֵדִים – גּוֹבֶה מִנְּכָסִים בְּנֵי חוֹרִין.

MISHNA **One who lends** money **to another by means of** a promissory **note can collect** the debt **from liened property** that had been sold to others by the debtor after the loan was granted. One who lends money **by means of witnesses,**[H] without recording the loan in a promissory note, **can collect** the debt only **from unsold property.**

NOTES

A person on his deathbed who admitted – שְׁכִיב מְרַע שֶׁהוֹדָה: There seems to be a contradiction between the Gemara here, which rules that the money must be given based on the deceased's admission, and the Gemara earlier on this *amud*, where the heirs need not give the money mentioned by the deceased to the supposed creditor, as it is possible that the deceased's statement was not sincere, but made only to avoid the impression that his heirs are wealthy. Some early commentaries answer that the situation here is one where it is clear from context that the deceased's admission is made in earnest (Rif; see also Ramban). Others explain that the case here is one in which the creditor himself made a claim against the person on his deathbed, and the latter admitted the veracity of the claim (Rashbam; Ra'avad).

And the statements of a person on his deathbed are considered as if written and transmitted – וְדִבְרֵי שְׁכִיב מְרַע כִּכְתוּבִין וְכִמְסוּרִין דָּמוּ: This principle is mentioned many times in the Talmud. Usually it is employed in a different sense, i.e., that it is not necessary for a person on his deathbed, as opposed to a healthy person, to perform an act of acquisition to confirm the transfer of money or property to the stated beneficiary. Here, the intent is that an admission of debt by a person on his deathbed is sufficient to have the admission recorded in writing, even without his explicit consent (*Tosafot*; see Rashba).

HALAKHA

A person on his deathbed who admitted – שְׁכִיב מְרַע שֶׁהוֹדָה: If a person on his deathbed, upon hearing someone's monetary claim against him, admitted owing the money to him, or if another person admits owing money to the person on his deathbed (Rema, citing Mordekhai), the one who admitted owing the money cannot subsequently claim that he was not serious, even if he did not tell two men: You are my witnesses to this admission, as a person does not jest at the time of death, as Rava concludes here. See the *Shakh*, who writes that there are those who say that while the concern of jesting is not raised without basis, if the person on his deathbed states explicitly that he was not being serious, he is deemed credible (Rambam *Sefer Kinyan, Hilkhot Zekhiya UMattana* 8:4; *Shulḥan Arukh, Ḥoshen Mishpat* 81:2, 27, and see 255:1).

And the statements of a person on his deathbed are considered as if written and transmitted – וְדִבְרֵי שְׁכִיב מְרַע כִּכְתוּבִין וְכִמְסוּרִין דָּמוּ: A person on his deathbed, when apportioning all of his property (*Sma*), who bequeaths a gift is not obligated to perform any act of acquisition to finalize the transferal of the gift, as the statement of a person on his deathbed is considered as if it were written in a document and transmitted (Rambam *Sefer Kinyan, Hilkhot Zekhiya UMattana* 8:2; *Shulḥan Arukh, Ḥoshen Mishpat* 250:1).

By means of witnesses – עַל יְדֵי עֵדִים: If one lends money in the presence of witnesses, or if a debtor admits to owing money to a creditor in the presence of witnesses, but the debt is not recorded in a promissory note, this is a loan by oral contract, and it cannot be collected from property sold by the debtor to others subsequent to the loan or admission (Rambam *Sefer Mishpatim, Hilkhot Malve VeLoveh* 11:4; *Shulḥan Arukh, Ḥoshen Mishpat* 39:1).

הוֹצִיא עָלָיו כְּתַב יָדוֹ שֶׁהוּא חַיָּיב לוֹ – גּוֹבֶה מִנְּכָסִים בְּנֵי חוֹרִין.

If one **presents to** a debtor a document in the **handwriting of** the debtor stating **that he owes** money **to him**, but without witnesses signed on the document, the creditor **can collect** only **from unsold property.**

עָרֵב הַיּוֹצֵא לְאַחַר חִיתּוּם שְׁטָרוֹת – גּוֹבֶה מִנְּכָסִים בְּנֵי חוֹרִין.

In the case of a **guarantor whose** commitment **emerged after the signing of** the promissory **note,**[H] the creditor **can collect** the sum only **from unsold property** of the guarantor.

מַעֲשֶׂה וּבָא לִפְנֵי רַבִּי יִשְׁמָעֵאל, וְאָמַר: גּוֹבֶה מִנְּכָסִים בְּנֵי חוֹרִין. אָמַר לוֹ בֶּן נַנָּס: אֵינוֹ גּוֹבֶה לֹא מִנְּכָסִים מְשׁוּעְבָּדִים וְלֹא מִנְּכָסִים בְּנֵי חוֹרִין.

The mishna relates: **An incident** occurred where such a case **came before Rabbi Yishmael,**[P] **and he said:** The creditor can **collect** the sum **from unsold property** of the guarantor, but not from liened property that he has sold to others. **Ben Nannas**[LP] **said to** Rabbi Yishmael: The creditor **cannot collect** the sum from the guarantor at all, **not from liened property** that has been sold, **nor from unsold property.**

אָמַר לוֹ: לָמָּה? אָמַר לוֹ: הֲרֵי הַחוֹנֵק אֶת אֶחָד בַּשּׁוּק, וּמְצָאוֹ חֲבֵירוֹ וְאָמַר לוֹ ״הַנַּח לוֹ [וַאֲנִי אֶתֵּן לָךְ]״ – פָּטוּר, שֶׁלֹּא עַל אֱמוּנָתוֹ הִלְוָהוּ; אֶלָּא אֵיזֶה הוּא עָרֵב שֶׁהוּא חַיָּיב? ״הַלְוֵהוּ וַאֲנִי נוֹתֵן לָךְ״ – חַיָּיב, שֶׁכֵּן עַל אֱמוּנָתוֹ הִלְוָהוּ.

Rabbi Yishmael **said to him: Why** not? Ben Nannas **said to him: If one was strangling someone in the marketplace,**[H] demanding repayment of a loan, **and another** person **found him** doing so and **said** to the attacker: **Leave him alone and I will give you** the money he owes, the person who intervened is **exempt** from paying, as the creditor **did not loan** the money in the first place **based on his trust** of the one who intervened. **Rather, who is a guarantor who is obligated** to repay the loan he has guaranteed? One who tells the creditor before the loan takes place: **Lend** money to **him, and I will give you** the repayment, as in that case the creditor **did loan** the money **based on his trust** of the guarantor.

וְאָמַר רַבִּי יִשְׁמָעֵאל: הָרוֹצֶה שֶׁיַּחְכִּים – יַעֲסוֹק בְּדִינֵי מָמוֹנוֹת, שֶׁאֵין לָךְ מִקְצוֹעַ בַּתּוֹרָה יוֹתֵר מֵהֶן, וְהֵן כְּמַעְיָין הַנּוֹבֵעַ, וְהָרוֹצֶה שֶׁיַּעֲסוֹק בְּדִינֵי מָמוֹנוֹת – יְשַׁמֵּשׁ אֶת שִׁמְעוֹן בֶּן נַנָּס.

And Rabbi Yishmael thereupon **said: One who wants to become wise should engage in** the study of **monetary law,**[N] **as there is no greater discipline in the Torah, and it is like a flowing spring. And,** he added, **one who wants to engage in** the study of **monetary law should attend to,** i.e., become a disciple of, **Shimon ben Nannas.**

HALAKHA

A guarantor whose commitment emerged after the signing of the note – עָרֵב הַיּוֹצֵא לְאַחַר חִיתּוּם שְׁטָרוֹת: If a guarantor writes beneath the signatures on a promissory note: And I am the guarantor, and his handwriting can be verified, he is obligated to honor his guarantee, and the debt can be collected from his unsold property, in accordance with the mishna here. There is a dispute between halakhic authorities as to whether the guarantee must be accompanied by a formal act of acquisition (Ramah) or not (Ra'avad; Ramban). According to the Rambam, even if the guarantor writes his guarantee above the signatures on the promissory note, if his guarantee was not given until after the loan was transferred he is obligated only if his guarantee was accompanied by a formal act of acquisition (Rambam *Sefer Mishpatim, Hilkhot Malve VeLoveh* 26:1; *Shulḥan Arukh, Ḥoshen Mishpat* 129:4).

If one was strangling someone in the marketplace, etc. – הַחוֹנֵק אֶת אֶחָד בַּשּׁוּק וכו׳: If a creditor was strangling a debtor in the marketplace, seeking to coerce him to repay his debt, and one who saw this assault stepped forward and said: Leave him alone, and I will guarantee payment for him if he does not repay you by a certain time (see *Sma*), the guarantor is not obligated to honor his commitment to repay the debt. If the guarantor said: Leave him alone and I will assume complete responsibility for the debt in his stead, he is considered like a guarantor at the time of the loan, and is obligated to pay (Rambam *Sefer Mishpatim, Hilkhot Malve VeLoveh* 25:1; *Shulḥan Arukh, Ḥoshen Mishpat* 129:1, and *Sma* and *Shakh* there).

PERSONALITIES

Rabbi Yishmael – רַבִּי יִשְׁמָעֵאל: Rabbi Yishmael ben Elisha II is the Rabbi Yishmael widely quoted in the Mishna and the Talmud. As related in the Gemara, he was taken into captivity, and was redeemed by Rabbi Yehoshua for a significant ransom. He then became a student of Rabbi Yehoshua and one of the prominent speakers in Yavne. Rabbi Yishmael was a friend of Rabbi Akiva, with whom he engaged in many disputes. Each established significant halakhic-exegetical schools of thought. The thirteen hermeneutic principles of the Torah, as articulated by Rabbi Yishmael, are the foundations of midrash and *halakha*. Many statements are attributed to him in the Mishna, and a large number of his opinions appear in the Gemara introduced with the formulation: The school of Rabbi Yishmael taught. The Sages of the following generation studied from him, and Rabbi Yoshiya and Rabbi Yonatan were his primary students.

Apparently, Rabbi Yishmael died before the bar Kokheva revolt. His sons and daughters are mentioned in the Gemara, and it is possible that the *tanna* Rabbi Eliezer, son of Rabbi Yishmael, was his son.

Ben Nannas – בֶּן נַנָּס: The reference is to Rabbi Shimon ben Nannas, a *tanna* of the third generation of *tanna'im*. He was one of the Sages of Yavne, and a contemporary of Rabbi Akiva and Rabbi Yishmael, with whom he is frequently cited as discussing halakhic issues. Nothing is known of his life's events or his family.

LANGUAGE

Nannas – נַנָּס: This name appears to be adopted from the Greek νάννας, *nannas*, meaning uncle, specifically a mother's brother.

NOTES

Should engage in the study of monetary law – יַעֲסוֹק בְּדִינֵי מָמוֹנוֹת: Monetary law differs from other areas of Torah law in that it relies largely on the application of logic and deduction, as opposed to the interpretation of biblical verses. Although monetary law is based on the Torah's command: "In righteousness shall you judge your neighbor" (Leviticus 19:15), there are few explicit instructions with regard to how this is to be implemented, and judgment is dependent upon deep investigation and analysis of the facts. Moreover, in ritual matters it is always possible to lean toward stringency when an uncertainty arises concerning Torah law, whereas in cases of monetary law, which involve two opposing parties, any decision will perforce benefit one at the expense of the other. It is therefore necessary to carefully deliberate the claims of the two parties and reach an equitable and accurate decision (*Tiferet Yisrael*).

גמ׳ אָמַר עוּלָּא: דְּבַר תּוֹרָה, אֶחָד מַלְוֶה בִּשְׁטָר וְאֶחָד מַלְוֶה עַל פֶּה – גּוֹבֶה מִנְּכָסִים מְשׁוּעְבָּדִים, מַאי טַעֲמָא? שִׁעְבּוּדָא דְּאוֹרַיְיתָא, וְאֶלָּא מַה טַּעַם אָמְרוּ: מַלְוֶה עַל פֶּה אֵינוֹ גּוֹבֶה אֶלָּא מִנְּכָסִין בְּנֵי חוֹרִין? מִשּׁוּם פְּסֵידָא דְּלָקוֹחוֹת.

GEMARA **Ulla says: By Torah law,** a creditor, **whether** in the case of **a loan with a** promissory **note or** the case of **a loan by oral** contract, can **collect** the debt **from liened property** that has been sold by the debtor subsequent to his receiving the loan. **What is the reason** for this? The property of a debtor at the time of the loan, even an oral loan, is **liened by Torah law.**[NH] **And what is the reason** the Sages **said** that one who gives **a loan by oral** contract can **collect** the debt **only from unsold** property? **Because of the loss** that would be incurred **by purchasers** of land if the seller's creditors could seize the land they have purchased.

אִי הָכִי, מַלְוֶה בִּשְׁטָר נַמִי! הָתָם אִינְהוּ נִינְהוּ דְּאַפְסִידוּ אַנַּפְשַׁיְיהוּ.

The Gemara asks: **If so, a loan with** a promissory **note** should **also** not be collected from purchasers of property, as this would cause them a loss. The Gemara answers: **There,** in the case of a loan recorded in a promissory note, the purchasers, who neglected to investigate the financial status of the seller before purchasing land from him, **brought the loss upon themselves.** By contrast, loans by oral contract are often impossible to discover, even with a thorough investigation.

וְרַבָּה אָמַר: דְּבַר תּוֹרָה, אֶחָד מַלְוֶה בִּשְׁטָר וְאֶחָד מַלְוֶה עַל פֶּה – אֵינוֹ גּוֹבֶה אֶלָּא מִנְּכָסִים בְּנֵי חוֹרִין, מַאי טַעֲמָא? שִׁעְבּוּדָא לָאו דְּאוֹרַיְיתָא, וּמַה טַּעַם אָמְרוּ: מַלְוֶה בִּשְׁטָר גּוֹבֶה מִנְּכָסִים מְשׁוּעְבָּדִים? כְּדֵי שֶׁלֹּא תִּנְעוֹל דֶּלֶת בִּפְנֵי לוֹוִין.

And Rabba says: By Torah law, a creditor, **whether** in the case of **a loan with** a promissory **note or** the case of **a loan by oral** contract, can **collect** the debt **only from** the debtor's **unsold property. What is the reason** for this? The property of a debtor is **not liened by Torah law. And what is the reason** the Sages **said** that one who gives **a loan with** a promissory **note can collect** the debt **from liened property** that has been sold? **So as not to lock the door in the face of** potential **borrowers.** If one could not collect a debt by taking liened property that has been sold, people would be hesitant to put their money at risk by lending it.

אִי הָכִי, מַלְוֶה עַל פֶּה נַמִי! הָתָם לֵית לֵיהּ קָלָא.

The Gemara asks: **If that is so,** that there is a desire to encourage people to lend money by granting greater power of collection to creditors, **a loan by oral** contract should **also** be collectible from liened property that has been sold. The Gemara answers: **There,** in the case of a loan by oral contract, **it has no publicity** associated with it, so that purchasers often cannot find out about it, even after a thorough investigation, and it would be an unfair burden on them to have the property purchased by them seized in such cases.

וּמִי אֲמַר רַבָּה הָכִי? וְהָא אָמַר רַבָּה: גָּבוּ קַרְקַע – יֵשׁ לוֹ, גָּבוּ מָעוֹת – אֵין לוֹ!

The Gemara asks: **And did Rabba** really **say this? But doesn't Rabba say,** in the case of a firstborn son, that if he and his brothers **collected** a debt from **land, he has** the right to receive a double portion of that payment, but if **they collected** a debt from **money, he does not have** the right to a double portion? A firstborn son is entitled to a double share of inheritance of any property that was owned by his father at the time of his death, but not to profits or income that accrue to the estate after his death. If a debt owed to the father is collected from land after his death, Rabba said that the firstborn is entitled to a double portion, indicating that the land was considered in the father's possession even before he died, which indicates that Rabba holds that the property of a debtor is liened to a creditor by Torah law.

וְכִי תֵּימָא: אֵיפוּךְ דְּרַבָּה לְעוּלָּא וּדְעוּלָּא לְרַבָּה, וְהָא אָמַר עוּלָּא: דְּבַר תּוֹרָה, בַּעַל חוֹב דִּינֵיהּ בְּזִבּוּרִית!

And if you would say: The opinions as they were cited earlier are attributed incorrectly, and it is necessary to **reverse** the two opinions, and exchange the opinion **of Rabba for** that of **Ulla, and** that **of Ulla for** that **of Rabba,** there is a difficulty: **But doesn't Ulla say** elsewhere: **By Torah law** the ***halakha* of a creditor** is to collect his debt only **from inferior-quality land?**[HB]

אֶלָּא רַבָּה טַעֲמָא דִּבְנֵי מַעֲרָבָא קָאָמַר, וְלֵיהּ לָא סְבִירָא לֵיהּ.

The Gemara resolves the contradiction between Rabba's two statements: **Rather, Rabba was stating an explanation for** the opinion of the **people of the West,** Eretz Yisrael, cited earlier (125a), **but he himself does not hold accordingly,** as he holds that a firstborn son is not entitled to a double portion of a debt collected from land.

NOTES

Liened by Torah law – שִׁעְבּוּדָא דְּאוֹרַיְיתָא: It is clear that a debtor is personally obligated by Torah law to repay his loan. The issue in this discussion is the basis for the creation of a lien on the debtor's property, which remains in effect even if the property is subsequently sold or given to another. Ulla, who maintains here that the lien is in effect by Torah law, does not cite a biblical verse as a proof text. Some early commentaries write that it is based on the verse: "The man to whom you have lent shall bring forth the pledge to you" (Deuteronomy 24:11). The commentaries maintain that it is from this verse that Ulla himself derives that when a creditor seizes land for his debt he can take only from the debtor's inferior-quality land (see *Bava Kamma* 8a), as the verse assigns to the debtor, who would certainly prefer to repay his debt with his inferior-quality land, the decision as to which property is given as payment. This same verse could also be seen as a proof text for the debtor's property, even his real estate, being subject to collection by, or by extension liened to, the creditor (Rashbam; Rabbi Avraham *Av Beit Din*; Ramah). Such a line of reasoning is found in the Jerusalem Talmud (*Gittin* 5:1).

HALAKHA

Liened by Torah law – שִׁעְבּוּדָא דְּאוֹרַיְיתָא: A debtor's property is liened to his debt by Torah law. Some hold that the lien is not by Torah law but is a rabbinic enactment (*Tosafot*). According to the *Shakh*, this matter is an unsettled question in *halakha* (Rambam *Sefer Mishpatim, Hilkhot Malve VeLoveh* 11:4, and see *Sefer Korbanot, Hilkhot Meḥusrei Kappara* 1:13; *Shulḥan Arukh, Ḥoshen Mishpat* 39:1).

The *halakha* of a creditor is to collect from inferior-quality land – בַּעַל חוֹב דִּינֵיהּ בְּזִבּוּרִית: By Torah law, a creditor collects his debt from the inferior-quality land of the debtor. The Sages instituted that he can collect the debt from intermediate-quality land, so as not to lock the door in the face of potential borrowers, in accordance with the statement of Ulla (Rambam *Sefer Mishpatim, Hilkhot Malve VeLoveh* 19:1).

BACKGROUND

Inferior-quality land – זִיבּוּרִית: When one repays a debt with land rather than with money, differences among gradations of land quality must be taken into consideration. Even though the monetary value of the land one receives will be the same whether the debt is repaid with a larger parcel of inferior-quality land or a smaller parcel of intermediate- or superior-quality land, the court assesses that people prefer to receive a smaller parcel of superior-quality land, as this requires less maintenance. Generally speaking, the following guidelines apply: Compensation for damage must be paid from the superior-quality land, debts must be repaid from land that is at least of intermediate quality, and one's obligations to one's wife resulting from her marriage contract can be paid from inferior-quality land. The Torah states explicitly that injured parties receive payment for damage caused to them from superior-quality land, in the verse: "Of the best of his own field, and of the best of his own vineyard, shall he pay" (Exodus 22:4). By Torah law, creditors receive their payment from inferior-quality land, but the Sages instituted that a creditor collects the debt from intermediate-quality land, so as to maintain the incentive to lend money.

רַב וּשְׁמוּאֵל דְּאָמְרִי תַּרְוַיְיהוּ: מִלְוָה עַל פֶּה – אֵינוֹ גּוֹבֶה לֹא מִן הַיּוֹרְשִׁין וְלֹא מִן הַלָּקוֹחוֹת, מַאי טַעְמָא? שִׁעְבּוּדָא לָאו דְּאוֹרַיְיתָא.

The Gemara continues to discuss the issue of the extent of liens on a debtor's property. **Rav and Shmuel both say:** In the case of **a loan by oral** contract, the creditor **can collect** the debt only from the one who took the loan, but **not from the heirs** of the debtor after his death, **and not from purchasers** of his property. **What is the reason** for this? They maintain that the property of a debtor is **not liened by Torah law.**

רַבִּי יוֹחָנָן וְרַבִּי שִׁמְעוֹן בֶּן לָקִישׁ דְּאָמְרִי תַּרְוַיְיהוּ: מִלְוָה עַל פֶּה – גּוֹבֶה בֵּין מִן הַיּוֹרְשִׁין וּבֵין מִן הַלָּקוֹחוֹת, מַאי טַעְמָא? שִׁעְבּוּדָא דְּאוֹרַיְיתָא.

Rabbi Yoḥanan and Rabbi Shimon ben Lakish both say: In the case of **a loan by oral** contract, the creditor **can collect** the debt **both from the heirs** of the debtor after his death **and from the purchasers**[N] of his property. **What is the reason** for this? They maintain that the property of a debtor is **liened by Torah law.**

מֵיתִיבֵי: הַחוֹפֵר בּוֹר בִּרְשׁוּת הָרַבִּים, וְנָפַל עָלָיו שׁוֹר וַהֲרָגוֹ – פָּטוּר; וְלֹא עוֹד, אֶלָּא שֶׁאִם מֵת הַשּׁוֹר – יוֹרְשֵׁי בַּעַל הַבּוֹר חַיָּיבִים לְשַׁלֵּם דְּמֵי שׁוֹר לִבְעָלָיו!

The Gemara **raises an objection** to the opinion of Rav and Shmuel from a *baraita* (*Tosefta, Bava Kamma* 6:2): **If one was digging a pit in the public domain,**[H] **and an ox fell on him and killed him** as he was in the pit, the owner of the ox is **exempt** from paying for the damage caused, as it is the one who dug the pit who is at fault. **Moreover, if** it occurred **that the ox died** as a result of the fall, **the heirs of the owner of the pit are liable to pay the value of the ox to its owner.** Compensation for damages is comparable to a loan by oral contract, and yet the *baraita* states that the heirs of the culpable party must pay it.

אָמַר רַבִּי אֶלְעָא אָמַר רַב: בְּשֶׁעָמַד בַּדִּין.

Rabbi Ela says that **Rav says:** The *baraita* is discussing a case **in which** the one who dug the pit **stood trial** for the damage before he died, and once judgment is rendered by a court, the resulting financial liability is comparable to a loan with a promissory note.

וְהָא הֲרָגוֹ קָתָנֵי! אָמַר רַב אַדָּא בַּר אַהֲבָה: שֶׁעֲשָׂאוֹ טְרֵפָה.

The Gemara objects: **But it is taught** in the *baraita* that the ox **killed him** by falling on him. How then can one say that he stood trial? **Rav Adda bar Ahava says:** The *baraita* does not mean that the ox killed him instantly, but **that it rendered him one who has a wound that will cause him to die within twelve months** [*tereifa*], and there was enough time before his death to try him and deem him liable to pay for damages.

וְהָא אָמַר רַב נַחְמָן, תָּנֵי תַּנָּא: מֵת וּקְבָרוֹ! הָתָם, דְּיָתְבִי דַּיָּינֵי אַפּוּמָּא דְּבֵירָא וְחַיְּיבוּהוּ.

The Gemara objects that there is a different version of the *baraita* according to which this interpretation is not possible: **But doesn't Rav Naḥman say** that a certain ***tanna* taught** the *baraita* with a different formulation, stating that the one who dug the pit **died** from the impact of the ox **and** the ox in effect **buried him** in the ground at the bottom of the pit? In this scenario it would be impossible to take the one who dug the pit to court to stand trial. The Gemara answers: **There,** according to that second version, it is discussing a case **where judges sat at the opening of the pit and deemed liable** the one who dug the pit to pay for the damage before he died.

NOTES

And from the purchasers – וּבֵין מִן הַלָּקוֹחוֹת: Rabbi Yoḥanan and Rabbi Shimon ben Lakish mean that in the case of a loan by oral agreement, the creditor can collect the debt from purchasers by Torah law, although of course it cannot be collected from purchasers in practice, as the mishna states explicitly, due to the rabbinic enactment (Ramah).

HALAKHA

If one was digging a pit in the public domain, etc. – הַחוֹפֵר בּוֹר בִּרְשׁוּת הָרַבִּים וכו׳: If one was digging a pit in a public domain and an ox fell into the pit, crushing the former to death, the owner of the ox is exempt from paying for the damage caused. If the ox died as a result of the fall, the ox's owner can collect the value of his ox from the heirs of the one who dug the pit. This is in accordance with the straightforward reading of the *baraita*, as the limitations set by the Gemara for this case were necessitated only according to the opinion that one cannot collect a loan by oral contract from heirs, whereas the *halakha* is in accordance with the opposing opinion, that one can collect a loan by oral contract from heirs (*Maggid Mishne*). The *Sma* notes that the heirs are not deemed credible if they claim that their father had paid for the damage while he was alive, even if he survived after the animal fell on him (Rambam *Sefer Nezikin, Hilkhot Nizkei Mamon* 12:22; *Shulḥan Arukh, Ḥoshen Mishpat* 410:38).

Perek **X**
Daf **176** Amud **a**

אָמַר רַב פַּפָּא, הִלְכְתָא: מִלְוָה עַל פֶּה – גּוֹבֶה מִן הַיּוֹרְשִׁין וְאֵינוֹ גּוֹבֶה מִן הַלָּקוֹחוֹת; גּוֹבֶה מִן הַיּוֹרְשִׁין – כְּדֵי שֶׁלֹּא תִּנְעוֹל דֶּלֶת בִּפְנֵי לֹוִין, וְאֵינוֹ גּוֹבֶה מִן הַלָּקוֹחוֹת – דְּלֵית לֵיהּ קָלָא.

Rav Pappa said: The *halakha* is that when a creditor gives **a loan by oral** contract, he can **collect** the debt **from the heirs**[H] of the debtor after his death, **but he cannot collect** the debt **from the purchasers**[H] of the debtor's property. He can **collect** the debt **from the heirs so as not to lock the door in the face of** potential **borrowers. But he cannot collect** the debt **from the purchasers, as a** loan by oral contract **has no publicity** associated with it.

HALAKHA

A loan by oral contract, he can collect from the heirs – מִלְוָה עַל פֶּה גּוֹבֶה מִן הַיּוֹרְשִׁין: Any loan, even if it is by oral contract, can be collected from heirs, in accordance with Rav Pappa's opinion. By talmudic law, one can collect only from land that the heirs inherited from the debtor. The *ge'onim* later instituted that one can collect even from the inherited movable property (Rambam *Sefer Mishpatim, Hilkhot Malve VeLoveh* 11:4; *Shulḥan Arukh, Ḥoshen Mishpat* 107:1).

HALAKHA

But he cannot collect from the purchasers – וְאֵינוֹ גּוֹבֶה מִן הַלָּקוֹחוֹת: One who loans money by oral contract can collect the debt only from property that is presently in the possession of the debtor or his heirs. He cannot seize property that the debtor had sold or given as a gift to others subsequent to the loan, in accordance with Rav Pappa's statement here (Rambam *Sefer Mishpatim, Hilkhot Malve VeLoveh* 11:4; *Shulḥan Arukh, Ḥoshen Mishpat* 39:1, 111:1).

"הוֹצִיא עָלָיו כְּתַב יָדוֹ שֶׁהוּא חַיָּיב לוֹ – גּוֹבֶה מִנְּכָסִים בְּנֵי חוֹרִין" וכו׳. בְּעָא מִינֵּיהּ רַבָּה בַּר נָתָן מֵרַבִּי יוֹחָנָן: הוּחְזַק כְּתַב יָדוֹ בְּבֵית דִּין, מַאי? אֲמַר לֵיהּ: אַף עַל פִּי שֶׁהוּחְזַק כְּתַב יָדוֹ בְּבֵית דִּין – אֵינוֹ גּוֹבֶה אֶלָּא מִנְּכָסִים בְּנֵי חוֹרִין.

§ The mishna teaches: If one **presents to** a debtor a document in the **handwriting of** the debtor stating **that he owes** money **to him,** but without witnesses signed on the document, the creditor **can collect** only **from unsold property. Rabba bar Natan asked Rabbi Yoḥanan:** If the document in the **handwriting of** the debtor **was ratified in court** at a later time, **what** is the *halakha*? Would it then be possible to collect the debt from liened property that has been sold? Rabbi Yoḥanan **said to him** in reply: **Even if** the document in the **handwriting of** the debtor **was ratified in court,** the creditor **can collect** the debt **only from unsold property.**

מֵתִיב רָמִי בַּר חָמָא: שְׁלֹשָׁה גִּיטִּין פְּסוּלִין, וְאִם נִישֵּׂאת – הַוָּלָד כָּשֵׁר, וְאֵלּוּ הֵן: כָּתַב בִּכְתַב יָדוֹ וְאֵין עָלָיו עֵדִים, יֵשׁ עָלָיו עֵדִים וְאֵין בּוֹ זְמַן, יֵשׁ בּוֹ זְמַן וְאֵין בּוֹ אֶלָּא עֵד אֶחָד – הֲרֵי אֵלּוּ שְׁלֹשָׁה גִּיטִּין פְּסוּלִין, וְאִם נִישֵּׂאת – הַוָּלָד כָּשֵׁר;

Rami bar Ḥama raises an objection from a mishna (*Gittin* 86a), which states: There are **three** types of **bills of divorce** that **are not valid** *ab initio*, **but if** the woman **marries** another man on the basis of one of these bills of divorce the lineage of **the offspring** from this marriage **is unflawed.** In other words, she is not considered to be a married woman who engaged in sexual intercourse with another man, which would impair the lineage of their child. **And they are these:** A bill of divorce that the husband **wrote in his handwriting**[H] **but there are no** signatures of **witnesses in** the document at all; a bill of divorce where **there are** the signatures of **witnesses in** the document **but there is no date** written **in it;**[H] and a bill of divorce where **there is a date** written **in it, but it contains only one witness. These are the three bills of divorce** that are **not valid** with regard to which the Sages said: **And if she marries,** the lineage of **the offspring is unflawed.**

רַבִּי אֶלְעָזָר אוֹמֵר: אַף עַל פִּי שֶׁאֵין עָלָיו עֵדִים, אֶלָּא שֶׁנְּתָנוֹ לָהּ בִּפְנֵי עֵדִים – כָּשֵׁר, וְגוֹבָה מִנְּכָסִים מְשׁוּעְבָּדִים!

Rabbi Elazar says: Even though there are no signatures of **witnesses in** the document,[H] **but he handed it to her in the presence** of two **witnesses,**[N] it is **a valid** bill of divorce. **And** on the basis of this bill of divorce the woman can **collect** the amount written to her in her marriage contract even **from liened property**[N] that has been sold. This indicates that even when no witnesses signed the document, the debt listed therein can be collected from liened property that has been sold, as long as witnesses saw the document being transferred to the creditor. All the more so a debt listed in a document in the handwriting of the debtor that has been ratified by a court should be eligible for collection from liened property that has been sold.

HALAKHA

Wrote in his handwriting – **כָּתַב בִּכְתַב יָדוֹ**: If the husband writes a bill of divorce in his own handwriting, and had one witness sign the document, it is not valid. Nevertheless, if it was used in an attempt to effect a divorce, it would be prohibited for the wife, as a divorcée, to marry a priest after the death of her husband (Rambam *Sefer Nashim, Hilkhot Geirushin* 1:14; *Shulḥan Arukh, Even HaEzer* 130:20).

But there is no date written in it – **וְאֵין בּוֹ זְמַן**: One is required to record the date in a bill of divorce. If a woman is given a bill of divorce without a date she may not remarry on the basis of that document. Despite this, if she did remarry, she need not leave her second husband, even if she has no children with him (Rambam *Sefer Nashim, Hilkhot Geirushin* 1:25; *Shulḥan Arukh, Even HaEzer* 127:1).

There are no witnesses in the document – **אֵין עָלָיו עֵדִים**: There is a requirement that two fit witnesses see a bill of divorce transmitted to the wife, in accordance with the opinion of Rabbi Elazar. Preferably, there should be two witnesses signed on the document as well, but after the fact the divorce is valid if there are no signatory witnesses, as long as the document was transmitted in the presence of witnesses. There are those who say that if it is known for certain that a bill of divorce was transmitted to the wife without the transmission being witnessed, the divorce is not valid even if there are signatory witnesses. Nevertheless, as long as witnesses are signed in the document it may be assumed that it was transmitted in the presence of witnesses, until proven otherwise. It is preferable that the witnesses who sign the bill of divorce should be the same people who witness its transmission (Rambam *Sefer Nashim, Hilkhot Geirushin* 12:15; *Shulḥan Arukh, Even HaEzer* 133:1, and in the comment of Rema, and see *Beit Shmuel* there).

NOTES

But he handed it to her in the presence of witnesses – **אֶלָּא שֶׁנְּתָנוֹ לָהּ בִּפְנֵי עֵדִים**: Rabbi Elazar maintains that witnesses who observe the transmission of a legal document constitute the main form of testimony for the transaction. Therefore, even if no witnesses have signed it, a bill of divorce can be used to enact a divorce, even *ab initio*, as long as its transmission is observed by witnesses.

And the woman can collect it even from liened property – **וְגוֹבָה מִנְּכָסִים מְשׁוּעְבָּדִים**: There are two interpretations of this phrase. According to one opinion, this line in the mishna is still discussing bills of divorce. A divorced woman is entitled to collect the value of her marriage contract. If she has a marriage contract, she must present that document in order to collect payment; if she does not, she can collect payment by presenting her bill of divorce. Rabbi Elazar is saying that she can use this unsigned bill of divorce to collect payment of her marriage contract even from liened property that has been sold, as long as the bill of divorce was transmitted to the woman in the presence of witnesses (Rabbeinu Gershom Meor HaGola).

According to the second interpretation, the mishna means to say that in the case of a promissory note that is unsigned but was transmitted in the presence of witnesses, the creditor can collect the debt even from liened property that has been sold (Rashbam).

שָׁאנֵי הָתָם דְּמִשְּׁעַת כְּתִיבָה הוּא דְּשַׁעְבֵּד נַפְשֵׁיהּ.

The Gemara answers: **There it is different, as** the husband **obligated himself** and his property immediately **from the time of** the **writing**[N] of the document, as he knew at that time that the document would be transferred in the presence of witnesses. By contrast, in the case of the mishna here, the document in the handwriting of the debtor was written without the intent of ratifying it. It was only at a later date, as an afterthought, that it was ratified, and the terms of the obligation of the debt cannot be changed at that time.

״עָרֵב הַיּוֹצֵא לְאַחַר חִיתּוּם שְׁטָרוֹת״ וכו׳. אָמַר רַב: קוֹדֶם חִיתּוּם שְׁטָרוֹת – גּוֹבֶה מִנְּכָסִים מְשׁוּעְבָּדִים, לְאַחַר חִיתּוּם שְׁטָרוֹת – גּוֹבֶה מִנְּכָסִים בְּנֵי חוֹרִין.

§ The mishna teaches: In the case of **a guarantor whose** commitment **emerged,** i.e., was written, **after the signing of** the promissory **note,**[H] the creditor can collect the debt only from unsold property of the guarantor. **Rav says:** If the guarantor's commitment is written **before the signing of the document,** the creditor can **collect** the debt from the guarantor **from liened property** that has been sold; if it is written **after the signing of the document,** the creditor can **collect** the debt only **from unsold property.**

וּמְנִין אֲמַר רַב: אֲפִילּוּ קוֹדֶם חִיתּוּם שְׁטָרוֹת – אֵינוֹ גּוֹבֶה אֶלָּא מִנְּכָסִים בְּנֵי חוֹרִין.

At other **times, Rav said: Even** if the guarantee is written **before the signing of the document,** the creditor can **collect** the debt **only from unsold property.**

קַשְׁיָא דְּרַב אַדְּרַב! לָא קַשְׁיָא: הָא דְּכָתַב בֵּיהּ ״פְּלוֹנִי עָרֵב״, הָא דְּכָתַב בֵּיהּ ״וּפְלוֹנִי עָרֵב״.

The Gemara asks: There is **a difficulty** resulting from the contradiction between one statement **of Rav to** the other statement **of Rav,** as they seem to contradict one another with regard to a guarantee that is written before the signing of the document. The Gemara answers: This is **not difficult. This** case, where Rav says the creditor can collect the debt only from unsold property, is **where it was written in** the document as follows: **So-and-so is a guarantor,** as this formulation is an independent statement, and the witnesses signing the document do not necessarily relate to that statement. And **that** case, where Rav says the creditor can collect the debt from liened property that has been sold, is **where it was written in** the document as follows: **And so-and-so is a guarantor.** The usage of the conjunctive: And, causes this clause to be an integral part of the document, so that the signatures of the witnesses relate to it as well.

וְרַבִּי יוֹחָנָן אָמַר: אֶחָד זֶה וְאֶחָד זֶה – אֵינוֹ גּוֹבֶה אֶלָּא מִנְּכָסִים בְּנֵי חוֹרִין, וְאַף עַל גַּב דְּכָתַב בֵּיהּ ״וּפְלוֹנִי עָרֵב״.

And Rabbi Yoḥanan says: In **both this** case **and that** case, the creditor can **collect** the debt **only from unsold property.** The Gemara comments: **And** according to the opinion of Rabbi Yoḥanan, this is the *halakha* **even if it is written in** the document: **And so-and-so is a guarantor.**

NOTES

As he obligated himself from the time of writing, etc. – דְּמִשְּׁעַת כְּתִיבָה הוּא דְּשַׁעְבֵּד נַפְשֵׁיהּ וכו׳: The power of a document to enable collection from liened property that has been sold is effected at the time of its writing, as that is when the publicity associated with that document is generated. Therefore, only when the debtor obligates himself at the time of the document's writing does it attain this power; it cannot be added after it is written (Rashbam).

HALAKHA

A guarantor whose commitment emerged after the signing of the note, etc. – עָרֵב הַיּוֹצֵא לְאַחַר חִיתּוּם שְׁטָרוֹת וכו׳: In a case where a loan guarantee is written before the witnesses' signatures in a promissory note, if the wording is: So-and-so is a guarantor, without the conjunctive: And, then the debt can be collected from the guarantor, but only from property presently owned by him. There are those who say that if the guarantee was undertaken with an act of acquisition in the presence of witnesses, the debt can be collected even from liened property that has been sold (*Shakh*, citing Ramah); others maintain that even in this case collection is possible only from unsold property (*Sma*). If the wording is: And so-and-so is a guarantor, with the conjunctive: And, the debt can be collected even from property that the guarantor sold. This is in accordance with the opinion of Rav and, as the Gemara concludes, Rabbi Yoḥanan as well (Rambam *Sefer Mishpatim, Hilkhot Malve VeLoveh* 26:1; *Shulḥan Arukh, Ḥoshen Mishpat* 129:7).

HALAKHA

Witnesses are signed on a greeting in a bill of divorce – עֵדִים הַחֲתוּמִין עַל שְׁאֵילַת שָׁלוֹם בְּגֵט: Preferably one should not write anything in a bill of divorce between the main text of the document and the signatures. If such text was written, for example: Send a greeting to her, the document is not valid, as it is possible that the witnesses' signatures pertain only to the greeting and not to the main text. Nevertheless, if the added text stated: And send a greeting to her, the bill of divorce is valid, as the conjunction has the effect of connecting the greeting to the text concerning the divorce. This is in accordance with the statement of Rabbi Yoḥanan, as cited by Rabbi Abbahu (Rambam *Sefer Nashim, Hilkhot Geirushin* 4:25; *Shulḥan Arukh, Even HaEzer* 130:3).

מְתִיב רָבָא: עֵדִים הַחֲתוּמִין עַל שְׁאֵילַת שָׁלוֹם בְּגֵט – פָּסוּל, חָיְישִׁינַן שֶׁמָּא עַל שְׁאֵילַת שָׁלוֹם חָתְמוּ;

Rava raises an objection from a *baraita* (*Tosefta, Gittin* 9:9): In a case where **witnesses are signed on a greeting** written **in a bill of divorce,**[H] the bill of divorce is **not valid,** as **we are concerned** that **perhaps** the witnesses **signed on the greeting** alone, i.e., they did not intend to testify to the divorce, but only to verify that the greeting was written.

וְאָמַר רַבִּי אַבָּהוּ, לְדִידִי מִיפָּרְשָׁא לֵיהּ מִינֵּיהּ דְּרַבִּי יוֹחָנָן: ״שְׁאִילוּ״ – פָּסוּל, ״וּשְׁאִילוּ״ – כָּשֵׁר!

And Rabbi Abbahu said concerning this *baraita*: **It was explained to me** personally **by Rabbi Yoḥanan** himself that it is only when the wording of the greeting begins: **Send a greeting** to so-and-so, that the bill of divorce is **not valid,** as this is an independent statement and it is possible that the signatures relate to it alone. But if the wording is: **And send a greeting** to so-and-so, the usage of the conjunctive: And, causes this clause to be an integral part of the document, and the bill of divorce is **valid.** This indicates that Rabbi Yoḥanan himself maintains that when the conjunction is used the signatures relate to the entire document.

הָכָא נַמִי דִּכְתַב ״פְּלוֹנִי עָרֵב״.

The Gemara answers: **Here too,** when did Rabbi Yoḥanan say that the creditor can collect the debt only from the guarantor's unsold property? **Where it was written: So-and-so is a guarantor.** If the conjunction is used, he can collect the debt even from liened property that has been sold.

אִי הָכִי, הַיְינוּ דְּרַב! אֵימָא: וְכֵן אָמַר רַבִּי יוֹחָנָן.

The Gemara objects: But **if so, this is** identical to the opinion **of Rav,** whereas Rabbi Yoḥanan was presented as disagreeing with Rav. The Gemara answers: That presentation was inaccurate. **Say** instead: **And so Rabbi Yoḥanan says** as Rav did.

״מַעֲשֶׂה וּבָא לִפְנֵי רַבִּי יִשְׁמָעֵאל״ וְכוּ׳. אָמַר רַבָּה בַּר בַּר חָנָה אָמַר רַבִּי יוֹחָנָן: אַף עַל פִּי שֶׁקִּילֵּס רַבִּי יִשְׁמָעֵאל אֶת בֶּן נַנָּס, הֲלָכָה כְּמוֹתוֹ.

§ The mishna relates: **An incident** occurred where such a case **came before Rabbi Yishmael,** and he said: The creditor can collect the debt from unsold property of the guarantor, but not from liened property that the guarantor has sold to others. Ben Nannas said to Rabbi Yishmael: The creditor cannot collect the debt from the guarantor at all, not from liened property that has been sold, nor from unsold property. **Rabba bar bar Ḥana says** that **Rabbi Yoḥanan says: Although Rabbi Yishmael praised Ben Nannas** after hearing his dissenting opinion (see 175b), the ***halakha*** is actually **in accordance with** Rabbi Yishmael's opinion as he stated it initially, i.e., that in the case of a guarantee that is written after the signatures, the creditor can collect the debt only from unsold property of the guarantor, but not from liened property that has been sold.

אִיבַּעְיָא לְהוּ: בְּחָנוּק מָה לִי אָמַר רַבִּי יִשְׁמָעֵאל? תָּא שְׁמַע, דְּאָמַר רַבִּי יַעֲקֹב אָמַר רַבִּי יוֹחָנָן: חָלוּק הָיָה רַבִּי יִשְׁמָעֵאל אַף בְּחָנוּק.

A dilemma was raised before the Sages: **What would Rabbi Yishmael say to me about** the case of the debtor who was being **strangled,** as depicted by ben Nannas? Perhaps he would agree in that case, since the guarantee was given under duress, that it is not valid. The Gemara suggests: **Come** and **hear, as Rabbi Yaakov says** that **Rabbi Yoḥanan says: Rabbi Yishmael disagreed** with ben Nannas **also in** the case of the debtor being **strangled.**

הֲלָכָה כְּמוֹתוֹ אוֹ אֵין הֲלָכָה כְּמוֹתוֹ? תָּא שְׁמַע, דְּכִי אֲתָא רָבִין אָמַר רַבִּי יוֹחָנָן: חָלוּק הָיָה רַבִּי יִשְׁמָעֵאל אַף בְּחָנוּק, וַהֲלָכָה כְּמוֹתוֹ אַף בְּחָנוּק.

The Gemara asks: And is the ***halakha*** **in accordance with** Rabbi Yishmael's opinion even in the case of the debtor being strangled, **or** is the ***halakha*** **not in accordance with his** opinion in that case? **Come** and **hear, as when Ravin came** he said that **Rabbi Yoḥanan says: Rabbi Yishmael disagreed** with ben Nannas **also in** the case of the debtor being **strangled, and** the ***halakha*** **is in accordance with** Rabbi Yishmael's opinion **also in** the case of the debtor being **strangled.**

אָמַר רַב יְהוּדָה אָמַר שְׁמוּאֵל: חָנוּק וְקָנוּ מִיָּדוֹ – מִשְׁתַּעְבֵּד. מִכְּלָל, דְּעָרֵב בְּעָלְמָא לָא בָּעֵי קִנְיָן. וּפְלִיגָא דְּרַב נַחְמָן, דְּאָמַר רַב נַחְמָן:

Rav Yehuda says that **Shmuel says:** If the debtor was being **strangled, and** in addition **an act of acquisition was performed with** the guarantor, the guarantor **becomes obligated** to repay the debt. The Gemara deduces: **By inference** it emerges **that a guarantor generally does not require an act of acquisition** to become obligated to pay. **And** this **disagrees with** a statement of **Rav Naḥman, as Rav Naḥman says:**

עָרֵב דְּבֵית דִּין הוּא דְּלָא בָּעֵי קִנְיָן, הָא בְּעָלְמָא בָּעֵי קִנְיָן.

It is only **a guarantor** who undertakes a loan guarantee **in** the presence of **a court who does not require an act of acquisition; this** indicates that **generally,** a guarantor **requires an act of acquisition** in order to be obligated to pay.

וְהִלְכְתָא: עָרֵב בִּשְׁעַת מַתַּן מָעוֹת לָא בָּעֵי קִנְיָן, אַחַר מַתַּן מָעוֹת – בָּעֵי קִנְיָן; עָרֵב דְּבֵית דִּין לָא בָּעֵי קִנְיָן, דִּבְהַהִיא הֲנָאָה דִּמְהֵימַן לֵיהּ – גָּמַר וּמְשַׁעְבֵּד לֵיהּ.

The Gemara concludes: **And the *halakha* is** that **a guarantor** who accepts responsibility for the loan **at the time of the giving of the money does not require an act of acquisition;** but if he accepts responsibility **after the giving of the money,**[H] he **requires an act of acquisition.** Moreover, **a guarantor** who undertakes a loan guarantee **in the presence of a court**[H] **does not require an act of acquisition, as** in return **for that gratification that** he experiences in that the court **trusts him, he resolves to obligate himself.**[N]

הדרן עלך גט פשוט
וסליקא לה מסכת בבא בתרא

HALAKHA

After the giving of the money – אַחַר מַתַּן מָעוֹת: If one lends money to another, and at a later time another party volunteers to guarantee the loan, or if someone tells the creditor when the loan becomes due: Leave the debtor alone for now, and if he does not pay by such and such a time I am a guarantor, the guarantor is not obligated to repay the debt, even if he made these statements in the presence of a court. If his guarantee was confirmed by an act of acquisition, even if it is not in court and even, in fact, if it is not seen by witnesses, he is obligated to honor his guarantee (Rambam *Sefer Mishpatim, Hilkhot Malve VeLoveh* 25:1; *Shulḥan Arukh, Ḥoshen Mishpat* 129:1, and see *Sma* and *Shakh* there).

A guarantor in court – עָרֵב דְּבֵית דִּין: If a court appoints someone to act as a guarantor of a loan, the guarantee is binding even if it was undertaken after the loan was made (*Sma*) and even if there is no accompanying act of acquisition. This situation can occur if, for instance, the court wants to enforce payment of a loan when it becomes due, and someone comes forth and tells them: Leave him for now, and I will act as guarantor. Because of the gratification the person experiences for being trusted by the court, he fully obligates himself even without an act of acquisition (Rambam *Sefer Mishpatim, Hilkhot Malve VeLoveh* 25:2; *Shulḥan Arukh, Ḥoshen Mishpat* 129:2).

NOTES

He resolves to obligate himself – גָּמַר וּמְשַׁעְבֵּד לֵיהּ: The basic principle involving all acts of acquisition instituted by the Sages is that the formalization of the agreement depends on the complete consent of the party obligating himself. If one commits, with full intent, to enter into an agreement, the act of acquisition obligates him. If sincere intent is lacking or incomplete the party is not obligated. This is the *halakha* even if he orally declares his obligation and according to some, even if he puts it in writing; if he can somehow prove that his commitment was not sincere he is not obligated. It is not a person's statement or act of acquisition per se that obligates him, but his wholehearted acceptance of the conditions of the obligation. When, in certain circumstances, the Sages determine that such sincere intent is present, they do not require an act of acquisition to formalize the obligation.

Summary of **Perek X**

Already in mishnaic times the tied document was a rarity, so that some of the Sages were not familiar with it and its *halakhot*. The preparation of such a document was intentionally rendered complicated. It had to be folded and tied several times, and the early commentaries disagree with regard to the details of these procedures. The tied document differed from an ordinary document in how the witnesses signed it, as these signatures were affixed to the reverse side of the document. In addition to these differences, the signing of the document was dated as having taken place a year after the actual signing of the document.

Most of the *halakhot* discussed in this chapter address not tied documents but ordinary ones. The Sages instituted many ordinances intended to prevent forgery and falsification of written documents, including the following:

The final line of text in a document has no legal standing and should consist of a review of the main points of the document. Also, the witnesses should sign close to the final line of text, not leaving a large enough gap for words to be added at a later time.

Effort should be made to ensure that the document is written in a uniform manner, with no words written outside the lines. Whenever an erasure or correction is required, a validation of the correction must be recorded in the body of the document. It is permitted to write a complete document on paper or parchment whose writing, including the witnesses' signatures, had been erased. Nevertheless, if the text of the document is written over an erasure while the signatures are signed on a part of the paper whose text had not been erased, the document is not valid.

If there is a contradiction between two statements in the text of a document, or if there is some ambiguity, the meaning of the document is derived from the summation at the end of the document, unless there is a disparity in the recording of the sum of the transaction in the different parts of the document, in which case the lowest sum mentioned is adopted.

A document that has become accidentally erased or smudged may have its contents reprised in a replacement document and verified by the court, based on the testimony of the original witnesses.

If a debt recorded in a promissory note is repaid in part, the creditor may keep the original promissory note and give the debtor a receipt for the amount paid. If the debt is paid in full, the creditor must return the promissory note to the debtor. If this is impossible, for example, in a case where the creditor claims that the promissory note has been lost or destroyed, a receipt is written for the debtor to prevent the creditor from demanding a repeat collection in the event the document is later found.

The party who undertakes an obligation in a legal transaction, e.g., the debtor or seller in a loan or sale, may have a document written testifying to his obligation even without consulting the other party involved in the transaction. By contrast, a creditor or a purchaser of property may not write a document without the other party's consent, as it is that other party who is undertaking the obligation. In documents concerning mutual obligations, both parties must give their consent.

The beneficiary of the transaction recorded in a document is the one who must pay the cost of writing the document, e.g., the borrower, or the purchaser or renter of property. For documents in which both sides are beneficiaries, the cost is shared.

A creditor cannot collect a debt from a guarantor without first attempting to collect the amount owed from the debtor, unless he has undertaken to become an unconditional guarantor, or unless the creditor stipulated from the outset that he maintains the right to collect from either party, according to his choice. If a guarantor takes a loan from a creditor and gives it to a debtor, the guarantor becomes solely responsible for repaying the debt to the creditor.

A guarantor is obligated to repay a debt only if the guarantee was undertaken at the time of the loan. Nevertheless, if the guarantee was accompanied by an act of acquisition, or if it was accepted in the presence of the court, it is binding even if it was undertaken at a later time.

When a creditor collects a debt from a guarantor, he can collect it only from property presently owned by him, as opposed to property sold to others after the time of the guarantee. If the guarantee was added as part and parcel of the text of the promissory note, he can collect the debt even from the guarantor's liened property that has been sold.

One who undertakes a guarantee to pay a marriage contract is not bound to honor his pledge, unless he is the father of the groom, or unless he accepted to act as an unconditional guarantor.

Several other *halakhot* were discussed in this chapter as well. A promissory note or deed of sale is automatically considered to include the right of collection from liened property that has been sold, unless it explicitly states otherwise. According to most authorities, the right to collect a debt from property owned by the debtor at the time of the loan, even if such property was subsequently sold, is by Torah law.

Image **Credits**

My Notes

My Notes

My Notes

My Notes

תלמוד בבלי

— מהדורת נאה —

בבא בתרא חלק ח

Steinsaltz
Center

ירושלים

KOREN

Please note that the number ranges that appear at the bottom of each daf of the Vilna pages indicate the corresponding pages of the Koren Talmud Bavli translation and commentary.

תלמוד בבלי

הוצאת קורֵן ירושלים

— מהדורת נאה —

מסכת בבא בתרא
דף קס. עד דף קעו:

COMMENTARY BY

Rabbi Adin Even-Israel Steinsaltz

EDITOR-IN-CHIEF

Rabbi Dr Tzvi Hersh Weinreb

EXECUTIVE EDITOR

Rabbi Joshua Schreier

•

STEINSALTZ CENTER
KOREN PUBLISHERS JERUSALEM

תורה אור

*גט פשוט — עדיו מתוכו, מקושר — עדיו מאחוריו. פשוט שכתבו עדיו מאחוריו, מקושר שכתבו עדיו מתוכו — שניהם פסולין. רבי חנינא בן גמליאל אומר: מקושר שכתבו עדיו מתוכו — כשר, מפני שיכול לעשותו פשוט. רבן שמעון בן גמליאל אומר: הכל כמנהג המדינה. גט פשוט — עדיו בשנים, ומקושר — בשלשה. פשוט שכתב בו עד אחד, ומקושר שכתב בו שני עדים — שניהם פסולין.§ **גמ'** מנהני מילי? אמר ר' חנינא, דאמר קרא: (ירמיה לב) °"שדות בכסף יקנו וכתוב בספר וחתום והעד עדים"; "שדות בכסף יקנו וכתוב בספר" — זה

(קדושין דף מט.)

גט פשוט. שטר פשוט כעין שלנו, שאינו תפור ומקושר, כדלקמן. וכל שטרות קרויין גט, כדאמרי' בעלמא (ב"ק דף לה.): וגט חוב שאין בו אחריות. ובין בגיטין ובין בשאר שטרות מיירי, כדאמרינן בגמ', כדי שלא תחלוק בין גיטין לשטרות. עדיו מתוכו. בסוף השטר, כמו שאנו נוהגין לחתום בתוכו. מקושר עדיו מאחוריו. כותב שיטה, ומניח חלק כשיעור שיטה הכתובה, וכופלה על החלק, ותופר. ואח"כ כותב שיטה, ומניח שיטה חלק, וכופלה על החלק, ותופר. וכן הרבה, כדי מקום תורף השטר. והעדים חתומין מבחוץ, כענין שפירשו אמוראי בגמרא. ובלבד שלא יהיו קשריו מרובין מעדיו, כדתנן במס' גיטין (דף פא:) דהוה ליה קרח. וטופס של שטר כתוב כולו כעין פשוט, וזהו הנקרא לפנינו "הפשוט שבמקושר". ואלו הכפילות כל כפל וכפל בפני עצמו, ונראה מבחוץ בין כפל לכפל כעין קשת הסופר כזה* וכן מוכח בגמרא שהעדים החתומין על כל קשר וקשר נקראין ונראין מבחוץ. שניהן פסולין. שלא נעשו כתיקון חכמים. ואם שט"ח הוא – אינו גובה בו מן הלקוחות, ואם גט אשה – אינה מתגרשת. שיכול. לפשוט ולעשותו פשוט, שיקרע התפירות ויפתח השטר (א) ויהיה פשוט. הכל כמנהג המדינה. בגמ' מפרש. וטעמא דמקושר מפרש בגמרא. גט פשוט עדיו שנים. מי שרוצה לעשות שטר פשוט אינו צריך להחתים בו אלא שני עדים, והרוצה לעשות מקושר צריך להחתים בו שלשה, שכך תקנו חכמים. פשוט שכתוב בו עד אחד כו'. בגמרא פריך: פשיטא. **גמ'** מנה"מ. שיש שני מיני שטרות חלוקין זה מזה בעדים ובקישור.

זה

גט פשוט עדיו מתוכו ומקושר עדיו מאחוריו. כל שטר חוב קרוי גט, כדאמר: גט חוב שאין בו אחריות, פ' "הגוזל קמא" (ב"ק דף לה.), ובפ"ק דגיטין (דף י.): כל גט שיש עליו עד כותי — פסול, חוץ מגיטי נשים ושחרורי עבדים. והאי מילתא שייך למיתני (בהאי פירקין ולא במסכת גיטין. והתם שייך למיתני) פרק "הניזקין" ולא [בסדר] נזיקין. דהכא, אגב דתנא פרק "מי שמת" בכותב שטר שכתב כל נכסיו בבריאות ובשכיב מרע — תנא הכא "גט פשוט" דאיירי בשטרות, ואגב דאיירי התם בפרק "השולח" בתיקון העולם — תנא בתריה פרק "הניזקין" דאיירי בהכי. **מקושר** עדיו מאחוריו. תימה: לרב ירמיה בר אבא, דאמר בגמרא מלמטה למעלה חתמו, ומאחורי הכתב כנגד הכתב, ליחוש דלמא כתב למעלה מעדים מאי דבעי. דסתם שטר יש בו גליון מן הצד, ומחיק ליה לשטר הראשון, ויעשנו פשוט! ואע"ג שהשטר יהיה לצד העדים שחותמין בו שחור — מ"מ אינו יכול להזדייף. דהכי משמע בכתובות (דף כא. ושם) דשחור שלהם אין יכול להזדייף, דאמר התם: האי מאן דבעי לאחויי חתימת ידיה בבי דינא — לכתוב אחספא, ואי איתא — ליחויה בשחור של קלף! אלא ודאי אינו יכול להזדייף. וא"כ היכי כשר שטר מקושר? וי"ל: דגייז ליה לגליון שבצד השטר. וא"ת: בגמרא, כי מותיב ליה לרב הונא דאמר בין קשר לקשר מאבראי: ניחוש דילמא זייף (ב) ליה וכתב מאי דבעי בפנים בסוף השטר, וסהדי של אחוריו (ג) מסהדי אכל השטר. והשתא, אמאי לא משני דגייז לקלף היתר על השטר? ומתרץ ריב"ס: דלא מצי גייז ליה, שמניחו בשביל האשרתא שרוצה לעשות בסוף. אבל מן הצדדין — מצי גייז ליה, לכך ליכא למיחש למידי. א"נ, דאימטוייט ליה לצד שחור החלק שהוא על העדים שלא יוכל לזייף אותו בתוכו. ואע"ג דאמר (לקמן דף קסג.): עדים אטיוטא חתמי — ה"מ היכא שהשטר והעדים לצד אחד, ואיכא טיוטא בין העדים לשטר. אבל הכא דסהדי חתימי מבחוץ ואיכא טיוטא(ד) בפניהם — לא אמרינן אטיוטא חתימי. וא"ת: ליחוש דכתב מאי דבעי אגליון שבין העדים עד סוף השטר, למ"ד מלמטה למעלה, ויהא השטר הבא הוא ועדיו בשיטה אחת. דהא לא מצי גייז ליה, שמניחו בשביל האשרתא! וי"ל: דמטייט ליה. אבל בלא טיוטא מצי זייף, כדפרי'. ואפי' חתימי סהדי זה תחת זה, דהשתא ליכא באותה שיטה של שטר שיזדייף כי אם עד אחד — מ"מ יכול לכתוב על אותו עד אחד שחייב לו מאה מנה, והוה ליה כתב ידו. ולכך צריך לפרש דמטייט ליה. והכי נמי לרב הונא, דאמר בין קשר לקשר, איכא למיחש דלמא ימחוק כל השטר מבפנים ויכתוב למעלה מן העדים (ה) בגליון, או מן הצד כנגד העדים, ויהיה כתב ידו בשיטה אחת עם השטר, אי לא גייז או יטייט כל מה שלמעלה מהן ושמן הצד. ה"נ איכא למיחש, בין למ"ד מלמטה למעלה בין למ"ד בין קשר לקשר, בכל השטרות פשוטים דחתימי שלשה עדים, ליחוש שימחוק כל השטר לבד העדים, ויעשה שטר מקושר כנגד אותן העדים, וכתב מאי דבעי, כיון דכשר משני לצדדין! (ו) וי"ל: דמטייט ליה מבחוץ כנגד העדים. ודוחק גדול הוא, דמשמע שכשר בלא טיוטא, מדלא מישתמיט גמרא לפרש הכי. ור' פירש: דיש לחות ההיא דכתובות (שם) דבלאו הכי מצי (ז) לפרש למימר ארישא דמגילתא, כדלקמן (דף קסז.). אלא להכי נקט חספא — דבקלף הוה טעי לכתוב במקום טוב. וגם צריך עיון אם מקושר חתום בכתב ידו מצד שני מהני, דא"כ אי הוה מחוי אשחור — דלמא עביד ליה מקושר בכתב ידו. אבל בקלפין שלנו שיכול להזדייף מצד שחור — אין ראיה לקלפין שבימיהם. **פשוט** שכתבו עדיו מאחוריו פסול. טעמא משום שמא יעשנו מקושר, ויהיה השטר מוקדם. ואפי' לא חתימי כי אם שני עדים — גזרי שנים אטו שלשה. וא"ת: והלא במקושר יש חלק בין שיטה לשיטה, וא"כ פשוט שאין בו חלק — היאך יעשנו מקושר (ח) שלא היה בו חלק? וי"ל: שהיה כתוב כסדר פשוט. והכי מוכח מר' חנינא בן גמליאל שאומר: מקושר שכתבו עדיו מתוכו — כשר, מפני שיכול לעשותו פשוט. ואם יש במקושר חלק — היאך יכול לעשות פשוט? הלא יכירו שהיה מקושר! אלא ודאי לא היה בו חלק. ותימה: למ"ד בגמרא בין קשר לקשר, (ט) סלקא דעתא מגואי, ואם אין בו חלק היאך יחתמו? וי"ל: דמ"מ בין שיטה לשיטה דחיק להו עלמא. א"נ: טעמא דפסול — כדפי' בקונטרס, משום שלא נעשה כתיקון חכמים, שנעשה פשוט ולא נחתם מתוכו. כדפסלינן ב"המגרש" (גיטין דף פז.) בכמה ענינים אפי' (י) מצד הכתב, כיון שאין נקראין העדים עם הגט. ואין לומר דהתם היינו טעמא משום שאנו חוששים שמא תוסיף על הגט מה שתרצה, לפי שאין עדים תחתיו, ולכך פוסלין אותו — הא ליכא למימר, שהרי לא משוינן שום חילוק, אלא אפי' כתוב בו "שריר וקיים", או שלא נשאר חלק מלמטה, או שחתם אחד מעדיו למטה, והשני למעלה או מן הצד — פסול, והכי נמי הכא. **מקושר** שכתבו עדיו מתוכו כשר מפני שיכול לעשותו פשוט. תימה: א"כ כל השטרות פשוטים שחתומים בהם שלשה עדים יהיו פסולים, שיעשם מקושרים ויהיו מוקדמין! ואם נאמר *כאן שנדון בפשוט — מאי קא פריך (כ) בגמ'*: לדברי ר' חנינא ב"ג אינו דומה זמנו של זה לזמנו של זה? והא בהאי מקושר אינו דין כשאר מקושרים! ואומר ר"י: דבמתני' איפליגו היכא דידוע לנו שהוא עושה הלואה שנה אחת קודם הזמן הכתוב בה, כדין מקושר, דהשתא איכא למיחש דילמא פרע ליה. והשתא פריך שפיר רבי: לר' חנינא ב"ג, כיון דהאי מקושר כתוב בו שנה אחר ההלואה — א"כ מאוחר הוא, (ל) שלא ימנה אלא מזמן הכתוב, וזימנין דזייף ביה, וכשירצה לפרוע ויאמר "אירכס לי שטרא", ויכתוב שובר "ביום פלוני פרעתי לו מנה". ואח"כ יעשה אידך שטר פשוט, ויהיו סבורין שעתה שעת הלואה! ומשני: קסבר ר' חנינא אין כותבין שובר. ומ"מ קצת קשה: אם דינו כפשוט שבא לפנינו, מאי קאמר: וכי מטא זמניה משוי ליה שטר פשוט? בלאו הכי נדון כפשוט, כדפרישית (מ) בשטר מקושר שעדיו מתוכו מגבי' בו כדין פשוט! ואומר ר"י: דאי לא משוי ליה פשוט אלא כמו שהוא, הואיל שבשובר כתוב שפרע מה שכתוב בשטר, והוא מקושר — רגלים לדבר שפרעו, ולא מגבין ביה. אבל כי משוי ליה פשוט — לא יוכלו להרגיש שהוא רמאות. וא"ת: אמאי לא הוה קשה לר' על מתני' דשטרי חוב המוקדמין פסולין והמאוחרין כשרים, דאיכא למימר כדקאמר הכא, ואמאי כשרים? וי"ל: דסבירא ליה כמאן דאמר* דמאוחרין נמי פסולין. אי נמי, כשיעשה שובר יכתוב בו "פרעתי הלואה שכתוב בו זמן פלוני", דהשתא ליכא למיחש למידי. אי נמי, (נ) שובר בלא זמן. ולכך מאוחרין כשרים. אבל הכא במקושר שעדיו מתוכו הוי *(המיוחד) ולא מסיק אדעתיה לכתוב כנגדו שובר בלא זמן. או זמן שכתוב בשטר, [שכיון] שהיה מקושר — לא מסיק אדעתיה שאינו מזמן הכתוב אלא שנה לפני הזמן. אבל מאוחרין, שבשעת כתיבת השובר ידוע שהיה מאוחר, ומסיק אדעתיה לכתוב שובר שלא יבא לידי זיוף. (ס) ונראה לי שאם יעשה שובר מקושר — תו לא אתי לידי תקלה כלל, ולא היה צריך למימר דלא כתבי שובר. **שדות** בכסף יקנו. עלה טובה קמ"ל, והכי קאמר: "וכתוב" — זה (ע) תופס, "וחתום" — זה תורף, מוכר ולוקח זמן ושדה. דתורף איקרי חתימה, כדאמרינן בגיטין (דף כא:): (פ) תלשו וחתמו ונתנו לתורף כו' (דתורף) "והעד עדים" — כמשמעו. והכי נמי אידך קרא: "ואקח את ספר המקנה" — טופס, "ואת החתום" — תורף, "ואת הגלוי" — זהו העדים, שהוא גליון של שטר. "מצות והוקים" — בפשוט נמי יש הרבה דברים שצריך ליזהר, שלא יחתמו לא מלמעלה ולא מן הצד אלא מתחתיו, ושלא ירחיקו העדים יותר משיטה אחת. וכיון דמצי למימר דאתי לפשוט, ולפרשו כמו שפירש — לית לן למימר דאתי לדרשא.

תקנו

רש"א מ"ז

נ"א כגון

[לקמן קסד.]

[לקמן קעא.]

גי' רש"א מאוחר

רבינו גרשום

גט פשוט. שטר פשוט. כגון שטרות שלנו והאי גט אפילו בשאר שטרות מיירי דכל שטרות איקרו גט כדאמרינן [כתובות נא] וגט חוב שאין בו אחריות: עדיו מתוכו. במקום הכתיבה תחת הכתיבה: מקושר. הוא עשוי כקישורין תפורות וכך היו רגילין לעשותו תחילת הקלף היו כותבין שיטה אחת זכרון עדות שהיתה בפנינו ואחר כך היו מניחין חלק כשיעור שיטה אחת והיו מקפלין שיטה ראשונה הכתובה על שיטה שניה שאינה כתובה והיו תופרין אותה שיטה הכתובה על שיטה שאינה כתובה ואח"כ כותבין בשיטה השלישית בירח פלוני בכך וכך ימים ביום פלוני ומניחין שיטה רביעית חלק וחוזרין ומקפלין שיטה הכתובה על החלק ותופרין אותו ביחד ושוב כותבין בשיטה חמישית בשנת כך וכך לבריאת עולם ומניחין שיטה ששית חלק והיו מקפלין ותופרין הכתוב על החלק וכך היו רגילין לעשות מן ו' שיטין עד שיכתוב הזמן ומאריך באותו ענין שאמרנו והיו תופרין אותן ושאר כתיבת השטר כותבין כשאר השטרות פשוטין וזה פשוט שבמקושר ומפרש בגמ' טעמא מאי הוו עבדי מקושר והיינו א) של גט מקושר שיהיו עדיו חתומין מאחר הכתיבה כדמפרש בגמ'. מפני שיכול לעשותו פשוט שיקרע התפירו' ויתפשט על הכתיבה: מנא הני מילי. דקתני מתני' דאיכא גט מקושר וצריך עדים היכן רמז מן הפסוק: וכתוב בספר.

א) נ"ל והיינו דתנן גט מקושר שהיו עדיו חתומין מאחר הכתיבה כשר וכדמפרש בגמרא וכו' ויתפשט על ידו הכתיבה:

הגהות הב"ח

(א) רשב"ם ד"ה שיכול כו' ויהיה פשוט. נ"ב עיין בתוס' דקדושין דף מט ע"א דהקשו דא"כ יהיה אויר בין השיטות וקי"ל גט קרח פסול ע"ש: (ב) תום' ד"ה מקושר עדיו וכו' דלמא זייף וכתב כצ"ל ותיבת ליה נמחק: (ג) בא"ד וסהדי של אחוריו קא מסהדי: (ד) בא"ד ואיכא טיוטא לפניהם וכו' ואפי' חתימי סהדי זה תחת זה. נ"ב פי' אליבא דמר זוטרא דנ"ל דחתמי זה תחת זה: (ה) בא"ד למעלה מן העדים או יכתוב בגליון וכו' וה"נ איכא: (ו) בא"ד דכשר משני לצדדין וצריך לומר דמטייט לי': (ז) בא"ד דבלאו הכי מצי למימר לכתוב ארישא כצ"ל ותיבת לפרש נמחק: (ח) ד"ה פשוט וכו' היאך יעשנו מקושר כיון שלא היה וכו' והכי מוכח מדאמר ר' חנינא בן גמליאל מקושר: (ט) בא"ד בין קשר לקשר קא סלקא אדעתי' מגואי: (י) בא"ד בכמה ענינים אפילו חתמו העדים מצד הכתב: (כ) ד"ה מקושר שכתבו וכו' מאי קא פריך רבי בגמ' לדברי ר' חנינא בן גמליאל הלא אינו דומה וכו' בהאי מקושר אין דינו כשאר מקושרים: (ל) בא"ד מאוחר הוא ולא ימנה אלא מזמן הכתוב בו וזימנין דזייף ביה וכשירצה לפרוע יאמר: (מ) בא"ד כדפי' דשטר מקושר: (נ) בא"ד אי נמי יכתוב שובר בלא זמן וכו' שעדיו מתוכו הוי כמאוחר ולא מסיק וכו' שכתוב בשטר דכיון שהוא מקושר לא מסיק אדעתיה שאין ההלואה בזמן הכתוב בו אלא שנה: (ס) בא"ד ונראה לי. נ"ב האי וכ"ל הוא חוזר לתרץ הקלת קשה דמאי קאמר וכי מטא זמניה משוי ליה שטר פשוט בלאו הכי נידון כפשוט ועל זה מתרץ וקאמר שאם יעשה מקושר כלומר שלא יעשהו פשוט אלא יניחהו מקושר תו לא אתי לידי תקלה כלל דודאי השובר מרע לכל השטרות המקושרין ושוב לא היה צריך למימר דלא כתבי שובר ולפי שר"י כתב בתירוצו הואיל שבשובר כתוב שפרע מה שכתוב בשטר והוא מקושר רגלים לדבר כו' על כן כתב דה"ל שיכתוב בשובר שפרע מ"ש בשטר שהוא מקושר אלא כל סתם שובר אע"פ שיש בו זמן מרע לכל השטרות המקושרין הואיל והזמן שכתוב במקושר הוא מאוחר: (ע) ד"ה שדות וכו' וכתוב זה טופס וחתום זה תורף שם מוכר וכו': (פ) בא"ד כלדאמרי' בגיטין כתבו במחובר תלשו וחתמו ונתנו לה כשר והעד עדים:

א א טוש"ע ח"מ סי' מד סעיף ע:
ב ב מיי' פכ"ז מהל' מלוה ולוה הל' ח ועיין כ"מ סמג עשין נד טוש"ע שם ס"ה:

א) לעיל כח: ע"ש וצ"ע ב) מכות ה: סנהדרין ט. ג) לקמן קסז:

תקנו רבנן מקושר כו' מספקא לן: בזמן הזה, כשכהן מגרש אשתו אם צריך לעשות מקושר, כי מתוך התקנה משמע שאין לגרש כי אם במקושר. אך לפי שאין אנו בקיאין בו בטוב — נכון יותר לעשותו פשוט, שהוא קל יותר. אי נמי: לא תקינו רבנן כי אם באותו מקום. ור"י היה אומר (ה) דתקינו רבנן מקושר — לא שיהא חובה לעשותו כן, אלא כדי שלא יפסידו נשותיהן התקינו לעשותו כן. **שלא** תחלוק בין גיטין לשטרות. שאם תפסלנה בשטרות אתי למיפסל אף בגיטין. אי נמי: אי לא עבדי שטרי חוב מקושר — אתי שיניחו (ו) לעשותו גם בגיטין. אלא מתוך שהורגלו לעשותו מקושר יעשו בגיטין. ולפירוש קמא אין להקשות משטרות שאנו פוסלין בעד כותי, וגיטין מכשירין, ולא גזרינן גיטין אטו שטרות. דהתם היינו טעמא משום דאין עדי הגט חותמין זה בלא זה, ומלכותי חתים ברישא — ש"מ חבר הוא. אבל עדי שטר חותמין זה בלא זה. **רב** ירמיה בר אבא אמר אחורי הכתב כנגד הכתב מבחוץ. אי לא אמר אלא "אחורי הכתב כנגד הכתב", ולא אמר "מבחוץ" — הוה אמינא: כנגד הכתב — היינו כלפי הכתב, ואחורי הכתב — היינו לבעלה מן הכתב, שאינו למטה כשאר חתימות. ואי [הוי] אמר "אחורי הכתב מבחוץ" — (ז) ה"א אפי' בין קשר לקשר, קמ"ל: כנגד הכתב ולא כנגד הקשר. ואי הוה אמר "מבחוץ כנגד הכתב" — הוה אמינא לגלדין. **לרב** הונא דאמר בין קשר לקשר קס"ד מגואי. ואע"ג דתנן: מקושר עדיו מאחוריו — איכא למימר דשפיר קרי אחוריו בין שיטה לשיטה, לפי (ח) (שאין) העד אחורי השיטה שתחתיו. **ואם** איתא אין זמן ואין עדים בזה מיבעי ליה. וא"ת: לר' ירמיה נמי קשה, דכיון שהיו (ט) אחוריו דרך אורך *השיטה, והיה סבור בו שהוא פשוט — היה לו לפסלו נמי משום עדים שהיו מאחוריו, דתנן: גט פשוט שכתוב עדיו מאחוריו — פסול! וכ"ת: לא ידע מתני' כלל, דהא לא ידע שיעשו שטר מקושר (י) עד שמעה לקמן, אבל קודם לכן לא. ואפי' פשוט שפסול כשעדיו מאחוריו לא היה יודע, שהרי במתני' דפסלינן ליה היינו משום שלא יעשנו מקושר ויהיה מוקדם, וכיון שלא היה יודע כלום במקושר לא היה יודע בפשוט שפסול כשעדיו מאחוריו — הא ליכא למימר, חדא, שאין סברא לומר שרבי לא היה בקי בשטר פשוט. ועוד קשה: דא"ל ר"ש בריה (כ): בין קשריו מיבלע, מנא ליה? רבי לא שנאה, ר"ש מנא ליה? ועוד, אע"פ שלא היה יודע דפסול פשוט שעדיו מאחוריו, משום דמקושר מיתני בהדי פשוט, ואיכא למימר כמו שלא היה יודע מתני' במקושר לא היה יודע גם בפשוט — מ"מ היה לו לידע מתני' דגיטין (דף פז:) דתנן התם: העדים החתומים בראש הדף מן הצד מאחוריו, בגט פשוט פסול! וי"ל: דהיה יודע רבי מתני' דפשוט ודמקושר, (ל) ולא היה יודע דבמקושר שנה מונין שתים, עד ששמעה מזונין. וכאן היה סבור שלא היו כותבין בין הקשרים שום עיקר השטר, לכך היה מתמה "אין זמן בזה"? דלא היה סבור שהיה כתוב בין הקשרים. אבל לר' ירמיה ניחא, שהיה יודע שעדיו מאחוריו. וכן יש להקשות ולתרץ לבתר דמשני מאבראי לרב הונא. אבל זה קשה: למאי פירכא (מ) הא דלעדים לא קפיד, כיון שדים להיות בין קשר לקשר? שהרי היה יודע בטיב מקושר! וי"ל, דהכי קא פריך: דאם איתא לעדים נמי היה לו להקפיד, שהם עיקר השטר, ולא היה לכותבם אלא בפשיטות השטר. ודוחק.

זה פשוט. כעין ספר. וחתום. משמע: צרור וחתום ומקושר. והעד שנים. כדאמר בעלמא (סוטה דף ב:): כל מקום שנאמר "עד" הרי כאן שנים, עד שיפרוט לך הכתוב אחד, כמו שפרט לך "לא יקום עד אחד באיש לכל עון" וגו' – מכלל דעד סתם הרי כאן שנים. מתוך שנתרבה בקשריו. שהחמיר בו הכתוב, והטריח לעשות קישורין – החמיר נמי בריבוי עדים. זה פשוט שבמקושר. (א) התופס שכתוב כעין שלנו. מצוה וחוקים. משמע שיש (ב) מיני חלוקי דינין ביניהו. עצה טובה קמ"ל. כדמפרש בריש "חזקת הבתים" (לעיל דף כט.) כדכתיב: "ונתתם בכלי חרש למען יעמדו" וגו'. בפלוגתא דר"ע ורבנן. במס' מכות, להקיש שלשה לשנים כו'. אלא מקושר מדרבנן הוא. כדמפרש טעמא לקמן. ומגרשי נשייהו. מתוך כעס. שהגט פשוט נכתב מהרה, וכשנחים מרגזם – אינם יכולים להחזיר גרושותיהן, כדכתיב: "ואשה גרושה מאישה לא יקחו" (ויקרא כא). היכן עדים. דמקושר חותמין. רב הונא אמר בין קשר לקשר. וקא (ג) סלקא דעתך השתא מבפנים. אחורי הכתב. כנגד כל הכתב מבחוץ. הכי ס"ל לרבי ירמיה בר אבא, כדמוכח לקמן, דלדידיה מחזיקין חתימת עדים כנגד כל (ד) סוף הכתב. ולדידיה אינו צריך לכתוב "שריר וקיים", שמקום חתימת העדים מקיים כל הכתב כנגדו מבפנים. ואמר רבי אין זמן בזה. בתמיה. ואם איתא. דבין קשר לקשר חתמי עדים מגואי, והרי הן מובלעין בין קשריו כמו הזמן – אמאי לא קפיד אלא אזמן? אעדים נמי הוה ליה למיבעי: אמאי אין עדים? בין קשר לקשר מאבראי. ונראין העדים בין חריצי הקשרין, כדפרישית במתני'. וניחוש דלמא זייף וכתב מאי דבעי. בסוף השטר שבמקושר, שהרי חתימי סהדי בראש השטר בין הקשרים, הואיל ואין העדים חתומים בסוף השטר. ומשני: דכתב בו. בסוף השטר "שריר וקיים" דהיינו הוכחה של סוף השטר, ואין יכול עוד להוסיף אחריו. וניחוש דלמא זייף וכתב. אחר ההוא "שריר וקיים" מאי דבעי, וכתב "שריר וקיים" אחרינא, בסוף מה שהוסיף. תרי שריר וקיים לא כתבינן. והרואה יודע שהוא זיוף. ופריך: דלמא זייף ומחיק. ומשני: האמר ר' יוחנן תלויה מקויימת כשרה. טעה הסופר והגיה ותלה תיבה או שתים בין שיטה לשיטה, ואחר כן קיימה בסוף השטר, כמו שאנו כותבין: תיבה פלונית דביני חטי שריר וקיים.
מחק

תורה אור

זה פשוט, "וחתום" — זה מקושר, "והעד" — שנים, "עדים" — שלשה, הא כיצד? שנים לפשוט, שלשה למקושר. ואיפוך אנא! מתוך שנתרבה בקשריו נתרבה בעדיו. רפרם אמר, מהכא: "ואקח את ספר המקנה את החתום המצוה והחקים ואת הגלוי"; "ואקח את ספר המקנה" — זה פשוט, "את החתום" — זה מקושר, "ואת הגלוי" — זה פשוט שבמקושר, "המצוה והחקים" — אלו דברים שבין פשוט למקושר, הא כיצד? זה עדיו שנים וזה עדיו שלשה, זה עדיו מתוכו וזה עדיו מאחוריו. ואיפוך אנא! מתוך שנתרבה בקשריו נתרבה בעדיו. רמי בר יחזקאל אמר, מהכא: "על פי שנים עדים או על פי שלשה עדים יקום דבר", אם תתקיים עדותן בשנים, למה פרט לך בשלשה? לומר לך: שנים לפשוט, שלשה למקושר. ואיפוך אנא! מתוך שנתרבה בקשריו נתרבה בעדיו. והני להכי הוא דאתו? כל חד וחד למילתיה הוא דאתא, לכדתניא: "שדות בכסף יקנו וכתוב בספר וחתום" — א)עצה טובה קא משמע לן, "ואקח את ספר המקנה" — הכי הוה מעשה, "על פי שנים עדים או על פי שלשה עדים" — ב)להקיש שלשה לשנים, בפלוגתא דרבי עקיבא ורבנן! אלא, מקושר מדרבנן, וקראי אסמכתא בעלמא. וטעמא מאי תקינו רבנן מקושר? אתרא דכהני הוו, והוו קפדי טובא ומגרשי נשייהו, ועבדי רבנן תקנתא, אדהכי והכי מיתבא דעתייהו. התינח גיטין, שטרות מאי איכא למימר? כדי שלא תחלק בין גיטין לשטרות. היכן עדים חותמין? רב הונא אמר: בין קשר לקשר, ורב ירמיה בר אבא אמר: אחורי הכתב וכנגד הכתב מבחוץ. אמר ליה רמי בר חמא לרב חסדא: לרב הונא דאמר בין קשר לקשר, קא סלקא דעתין בין קשר לקשר מגואי, והא ג)ההוא מקושר דקאתא לקמיה דרבי, ואמר רבי: אין זמן בזה? אמר ליה רבי שמעון ברבי לרבי: שמא בין קשריו מובלע? פלייה וחזייה; ואם איתא, "אין זמן בזה ואין עדים בזה" מיבעי ליה! אמר ליה: מי סברת בין קשר לקשר מגואי? לא, בין קשר לקשר מאבראי. וניחוש דלמא זייף וכתב מאי דבעי, וחתימי סהדי! דכתיב ביה "שריר וקיים". וניחוש דלמא כתב מאי דבעי, והדר כתב "שריר וקיים" אחרינא! אחד "שריר וקיים" כתבינן, תרי "שריר וקיים" לא כתבינן. וליחוש דלמא מחיק ליה ל"שריר וקיים", וכתב מאי דבעי, והדר כתב "שריר וקיים"! הא אמר ר' יוחנן: ד)תלויה מקויימת — כשרה,
מחק

וכשיעור

הגהות הב"ח

(א) רשב"ם ד"ה זה פשוט שבמקושר הטופס: (ב) ד"ה מצוה וכו' שיש שני חלוקי דינין: (ג) ד"ה רב הונא וכו' סלקא דעתיה השתא: (ד) ד"ה אחורי הכתב וכו' כנגד כל הכתב עד סוף הסטר ולדידיה אינו צריך: (ה) תום' ד"ה תקנו וכו' ור"י היה אומר דמאי דתקינו רבנן מקושר לא שיהיה חובה: (ו) ד"ה שלא וכו' שיניחו מלעשותו מקושר גם בגיטין אלא מתוך שהורגלו לעשות מקושר יעשו גם בגיטין וכו' בעד כותי וגיטין: (ז) ד"ה רב ירמיה וכו' ה"א אפי' בין קשר לקשר. נ"ב ופליג ארב הונא דאמר בין קשר לקשר דוקא אלא בכל ענין: (ח) ד"ה אחורי הכתב וכו' לפי שהעד אחורי השיטה כצ"ל ותיבת שאין נמחק: (ט) ד"ה ואם איתא וכו' דכיון שהיו העדים אחוריו לכך אורך השיטה: (י) בא"ד פירוש מזונין כדלקמן דף קסד ע"ב: (כ) בא"ד ר' שמעון בריה דרבי בין קשריו: (ל) בא"ד דפשוט ודמקושר אלא שלא היה יודע: (מ) בא"ד לבתר דמשני מאבראי לרב הונא אבל זה קשה למאי פירכא

רבינו גרשום

זהו פשוט שכתוב פשוט כספר: וחתום זה מקושר. כלומר שצרור וחתום תפור וקשור א) ביני: והעד שנים. כדכתיב לא יקום עד אחד באיש ממשמע שנאמר עד איני יודע שהוא אחד ומה ת"ל אחד ללמדך כל מקום שנאמר עד הרי כאן שנים עד שיפרוט לך הכתוב אחד ה"נ האי והעד שנים הן הואיל דלא כתב אחד: עדים שלשה. דמדקאמר והעד שנים מכלל דעדים שלשה הן: איפוך אנא. ואימא ג' לפשוט וב' למקושר. ומשני לא ס"ד דמתוך שנתרבה מן הפשוט בקשריו כדקאמרי' נתרבה נמי בעדים דליהוי משונה מן הפשוט: ורפרם אמר מהכא. דפשוט ומקושר מן התורה דכתיב ואקח את ספר המקנה וגו' ספר זה פשוט כמו ספר: חתום זה מקושר. שקשור וחתום ותפור בינו ועדיו: גלוי זה פשוט שבמקושר שאר כתיבת כל השטר הוי פשוט וגלוי מדקאמר מצוה מכלל דאיכא בהאי דליתא בהאי: רמי בר יחזקאל אמר מהכא. איכא למשמע דאיכא שני מיני גט: ע"פ שנים עדים או שלשה עדים עיין לקמן. וצריך למקושר ג' עדים ולפשוט ב'. ומקשינן לר' חנינא ולרפרם ולרמי בר יחזקאל וכי כל הני קראי דמוקמת לגט פשוט ולמקושר להכי הוא דאתא: עצה טובה קמ"ל. ירמיה הוא דאזהר להו לישראל כשתקנו שדות צריך לכם לכתוב שטרות ולהחתים עדים ויהא שמור בידכם לפי כשתלכו בגלות שמא יהרגו העדים או יוליכום בשם למקום רחוק ולא ימצאו העדים לפניך צוה להם לכתוב שטרות ולשומרן שלא יכפרו בהם המוכרין. והא נמי דאמר רפרם ואקח את ספר המקנה לאו משום דלהכי אתא אלא מעשה שהיה כך היה ולאו משום דילפינן מיניה כלום. כך אמר המורה ששמע מרבו שכך מצא כתוב שמו ב) כן דכתיב המצוה והחוקים מיכן סמכו חכמים לתיקון כל השטרות מן התורה. והאי דרמי בר יחזקאל דעל פי שנים עדים וגו' לאו להכי הוא דאתא אלא להקיש ג' עדים לשנים בפלוגתא דר' עקיבא ורבנן כל חד בראיה ליה כדתנן במס' מכות בפרקא קמא על פי שנים עדים או שלשה

וגו' אם מתקיימת העדות בשנים למה פרט לך הכתוב שלשה אלא להקיש ב' לג' מה ג' מזימין את השנים אף שנים מזימין את השלשה ור' עקיבא אמר לא בא השלישי להקל עליו אלא להחמיר וכו' אלא גט מקושר מדרבנן הוא דתקינו הכי והא דקא מפיק ליה מותחתום בספר והעד עדים קרא לאו להכי אתא אלא כדאמרן לעצה טובה אלא דסמך וראיה בעלמא אשכחו למילתייהו: ומאי טעמא תקינו רבנן גט מקושר. אתרא דכהני הוו קפדי [illegible]

[illegible]

א) אולי צ"ל תפור וקשור בינו ועדיו כצ"ל. ב) הלשון צריך תיקון [illegible]

מחק — פסול, ואע"פ שמקוים. (א)ולא אמרו מחק פסול אלא במקום "שריר וקיים", וכשיעור "שריר וקיים". ולר' ירמיה בר אבא דאמר: אחורי הכתב וכנגד הכתב מבחוץ, ליחוש דלמא כתיב מגואי מאי דבעי (א) ומחתים סהדי יתירי מאבראי, ואמר: אנא לרבות בעדים הוא דעבדי! א"ל: מי סברת עדים כסדרן חתימי? עדים ממטה למעלה חתימי. וליחוש דלמא מתרמיא ריעותיה בשיטה אחרונה, וגייז ליה לשיטה אחרונה, וגייז ליה לראובן בהדיה, ומתכשר ב"בן יעקב עד"; דתנן: א)ב"בן איש פלוני עד" — כשר! דכתיב "ראובן בן" בחד דרא, ו"יעקב עד" עלוויה. וליחוש דלמא גייז ליה ל"ראובן בן", ומתכשר ב"יעקב עד", דתנן: ב)ג"איש פלוני עד" — כשר! דלא כתיב "עד". ואיבעית אימא: לעולם דכתב "עד", דידעינן בה דהא חתימות ידא לאו

רשב"ם

מחק פסול. אף מה שהגיה עליו, אע"פ שמקויים. וכדמפרש ואזיל, שאותו המחק בסוף השטר במקום (ב) שהיה יכול לומר שהיה כתוב בו "שריר וקיים", כגון בתר ב"מנא דכשר למיקניא ביה" ומחקו, והגיה מה שרצה, ואחר כך כתב "שריר וקיים". אבל באמצע הכתב — אין לחוש, שהרי הדבר ניכר שקודם שנכתב "שריר וקיים" בזה השטר נמחק ונתקיים. וכשיעור שריר וקיים. וכל שכן אם שיעור המחק יותר מזה. ולר' ירמיה בר אבא דאמר אחורי הכתב כנגד כל הכתב מבחוץ. חותמין העדים, וממלאים מקום חתימת העדים עד סוף השטר, ולא צריך "שריר וקיים". ניחוש דלמא. יזייף וכתיב מאי דבעי מגוואי בסוף השטר, ואע"פ שאין עוד עדים כנגדו מבחוץ, ויאמר: לא הנחתי זה החלק מבחוץ אחורי זו השיטה אלא להרבות עדים גם בזו השיטה כנגדה מאחוריה, ולא נזדמן לי, כן פירש רבינו חננאל. ובספרים שלנו כתוב: ומפיש בעדים מאברהי. כלומר, נגד אותה השיטה שיוסיף מבפנים יחתום עליה עדים כנגדה מבחוץ, כדי למלאות כל השטר עדים, לקיים כל הכתוב בתוכו מצד שני כנגדו, ויאמר: כדי לרבות עדים הוא דעבדי. אע"פ שמקושר דיו בג' עדים — אני נתכוונתי לפרסם הדבר, והרביתי עדים הרבה. וכהא דתנן (גיטין דף פא:): גט קרח הכל משלימין עליו כו'. איזהו גט קרח — כל שקשריו מרובים מעדיו. אבל אם עדיו מרובים מקשריו — שפיר דמי. א"ל. רב חסדא לרמי בר חמא. אליבא דר' ירמיה בר אבא. מי סברת. עדים כסדרן (ג) כתיבי. מאחורי הכתב, שאם השטר כתוב שתי — שגם העדים חתומין שתי, ואם הכתב כתוב ערב — שגם העדים חתומין ערב, והתחילו לחתום בתחלת השטר כנגד זכרון עדות שהיתה בפנינו כו' וכולן זה תחת זה — א"כ ודאי יכול להוסיף ולזייף ולהחתים, כדקאמרת. אלא מלמטה למעלה חתימי. מתחילין לחתום מאחריו כנגד שיטה אחרונה זה (ד) תחת זה, והולכין וחותמין לארכו של שטר. ואם השטר כתוב ערב — הן חותמין שתי. וכן מפורש בגמרת ארץ ישראל: גט פשוט עדיו לרחבו, ומקושר עדיו לארכו. וכיון שמתחילין לחתום כנגד שיטה אחרונה — אין יכול להוסיף עוד ולזייף עוד מצד אחר, שאין השטר מתקיים אלא מכנגד החתימות ולמעלה. ריעותא בשיטה אחרונה. (ה) שיש כתוב שם תנאי או פרעון המזיק לבעל השטר, וגייז לה להאי שיטה אחרונה. ואף על גב דגייז ליה לראובן בהדיה, החתום כנגדה מבחוץ — הרי משתייר ביה "בן יעקב עד", ותנן דכשר בכך. בן איש פלוני עד כשר. מאחר שמכירין שזה כתב ידו של אותו בן פלוני. ומשני: דכתב ביה ראובן בן בחד דרא. בשורה אחת, ואי גייז ליה לראובן — גייז ליה נמי ל"בן" בהדיה, ולא נשאר בלתי יעקב לבדו. וקא מתכשר ביעקב עד. דאמרינן: יעקב עצמו חתם את שמו. לאו

תוספות

וכשיעור שריר וקיים. וכל שכן יותר, שימחוק שני שיטין או ג' כדי להעריס, וכתב מאי דבעי, והדר כתב "שריר וקיים". לכך פסול כל מקום שנוכל לומר: בכאן היה יכול להיות כתוב "שריר וקיים". אבל בפחות מ"שריר וקיים" — ליכא למיחש מידי.

וליחוש דלמא כתב מאי דבעי ומחתים סהדי מאבראי. אבל אי לא מחתים להו — היה פסול, שסיום העדים יש לו להיות כנגד סיום השטר. וליכא למימר דמטייט ליה מצד אחר, דשמא יעשה שם האשרתא. אנא לרבות עדים קא עבדי. ויקיים בשלשה שלמעלה, דמכל תלתא מקיימים, כדאמרי' בפרק "הזורק" (גיטין פא:). והכא לא מצי לשנויי כדלקמן: אין מקיימים אלא מעדים של מטה. דפריך לקמן: וניחוש דלמא כתב הוא ועדיו בשיטה אחת, ואמר "כדי להרבות בעדים הוא דעבדי"! ואמר: כל כי האי גוונא אין מקיימים אלא מעדים של מעלה — (ו) ה"נ לישני כאן: אין מקיימין אלא מעדים של מטה! וי"ל: דהא מתני' בשילהי "הזורק" (שם) שמע מינה מכל בי תלתא מקיימין, אבל לקמן שכתב בשיטה אחרונה — אין מקיימין.

מלמטה למעלה חתימי. וא"ת: בין לרב הונא בין לרב ירמיה, מתניתין דקתני: מאחוריו, ומפרש לה שחתומין בין קשר לקשר, ולאידך מלמטה למעלה — אמאי תקינו הכי? אלא(ז) שיהיו חתומים כולן תחת שיטה אחרונה מבחוץ, ולא יצטרך כמו כן לרב הונא לכתוב שריר וקיים! וי"ל: דכל מה שיוכלו לשנותו מפשוט היו משנים, לפי שלא יהיו הכל בקיאין לעשותו, דאדהכי מייתבא דעתיה.

וניחוש דלמא מתרמי ריעותא בשיטה אחרונה וגייז לה. וא"ת: והא אין למדין משיטה אחרונה, דהא מהדר הוא מעניינו של שטר, והיכי גייז? הא יהא פסול אם חתכה, כיון דלא מהדר! וי"ל: דבמקושר לא נהגו חזרת השטר, והיו למדין משיטה אחרונה. דבפשוט ודאי אין למדין, לפי שהעדים חתומים מבפנים, ולא דייקי, וחותמין רחוק מן הכתב שיטה, ויכול לזייף באותה שיטה אי לאו משום דאמרינן אין למדין. אבל במקושר, שעדיו מאחוריו מלמטה למעלה — מכווני שפיר לחתום כנגד שיטה אחרונה. והשתא נמי, כי למדין משיטה אחרונה(ח) — יכול להזדייף מבפנים, לפי שאין העדים חותמים כנגד אותה השיטה שזייף. וא"ת: והוא יחתום עדים כנגד הכתב שזייף מבפנים, ויקיים באידך תלתא סהדי! וי"ל: שלא היה בשיטה כי אם עד אחד חתום, ואם הוא עצמו *חתום שני פסולים, א"נ העדים שחתמו בראשונה הם טייטו בגליון שלמטה מן השטר מבחוץ, שלא יבא אדם אחריהם ויכתוב שטר באותו גליון ויהיה העד לזה שזהו כתב ידו. וא"ת: לרבי חנינא בן גמליאל מקושר שכתוב עדיו מתוכו, היאך יעשנו פשוט? הלא בפשוט איכא חזרת השטר, ובמקושר ליכא, וא"כ כשיעשנו פשוט ולא יראו חזרת השטר — יפסלוהו! וי"ל: ההיא דר' חנינא ב"ג על כרחך(ט) במקושר דמהדר, כיון שעדיו מתוכו.

וגייז ליה לשיטה אחרונה. וא"כ לר' ירמיה לא הוה כתיב ביה "שריר וקיים" במקושר, דאי הוה כתיב ביה — היכי הוה גייז ליה? הלא לא יראו "שריר וקיים" ויפסלוהו. ולרב הונא היה כתוב בו, כדמשני לעיל. אבל בפשוט, בין למר ובין למר — לא היה כתוב בפשוטים שלהם "שריר וקיים".

דכתב ראובן בן בחד דרא ויעקב עד בחד דרא עלויה. כלומר, (י) כתוב "ראובן בן" בשיטה אחרונה והיינו בחד דרא, ואחר כך "יעקב עד" לארכו של שטר. ופירש ריב"ס: אי "בן" בראש ראובן ואח"כ יעקב — הוה מצי גייז לשיטה אחרונה עד "ראו" של ראובן ועם "בן" שתחתיו, וישאר "בן יעקב". וקושיא של ריב"ס (כ) כשאפרש, שיעקב וראובן בחד דרא לארכו של שטר, ו"בן" תחת ראש ראובן. שאם לא היה כשר בהכי ב"בן" למעלה ו"יעקב עד" למטה — מאי דוחקיה לשנויי ש"בן" גדול כראובן? לימא פי' שראובן למעלה ובן יעקב למטה, דהשתא ליכא חששא למידי. ועוד: אמאי תירץ גמרא דלא כתיב ביה "עד"? לישני: כגון שכתב בו "עד", וכגון שיעקב למטה, ומעט מיעקב תחת ראובן, כדפרי'. ועוד: דהשתא לא קשיא מידי מה (ל) שהקשיתי לקמן ש"ראובן בן יעקב עד" פסול במקושר, ו"יעקב עד" גרידא כשר! אלא ודאי לא הוה מצי לתרוצי הכי, דאפילו כשראובן למעלה ו"בן יעקב" למטה, ומעט מיעקב תחת ראובן — גייז לשיטה אחרונה עם "ראו" ועם "בן" שתחתיו, ומתכשר ב"בן" של מעלה ויעקב של מטה. ולא כטועים (מ) טועים שאינו כשר בהכי — אינו, מפני תשובות חבילות מעולות שפירשנו. ואין להעלילו בלשונו, כי זדונו שוגג. אלא "בן" היה גדול ביותר, והיה מחזיק כנגד כל שם ראובן שעליו, ואחר כן יעקב, דהשתא לא מצי גייז אלא ראובן [עם בן] ביחד, ולא ישאר אלא "יעקב [עד]" והשתא ניחא הא דפריך: דלמא גייז "ראובן בן" ומתכשר ב"יעקב עד". ולא הוה מצי לשנויי ש"בן" תחת ראש ראובן ומעט מיעקב תחת ראובן, דהשתא לא מצי גייז לראובן בלא מעט מיעקב — הכי לא הוה מצי לשנויי, כדפרישית דגייז ל"ראו" ול"בן" שתחתיו, וישאר "בן" של שם ראובן (נ) ג)[וגם יעקב, ומתכשר בהכי. אלא "בן" כנגד כל ראובן. א"נ, "בן" תחת "בן" של שם ראובן] ואי גייז ל"ראו" — ישאר תרי "בן" זה תחת זה, ויעקב אחר "בן ראובן". וזה לשון ריב"א: "ראובן בן" בחד דרא ויעקב עילויה, וצריך שיכתוב "בן" תחת "בן" של שם ראובן (בן יעקב), שאם יתחיל ויכתוב כנגד תחלת ראובן למטה "בן" כנגד "ראו" — נמצא שהיה נשאר "בן" של ראובן עצמו בולט ל"בן", והוה גייז ל"ראו" של ראובן, וגם "בן" של מטה מ"ראו" עמו, ו"בן" של ראובן היה נשאר, והיה קשה כבתחלה. אבל עתה, שיכתוב ה"בן" למטה כנגד ה"בן" העליון של ראובן — ישאר "בן" אחד למטה ואחד למעלה, ויהיה ניכר הקלקול שעשה. ואפילו ימחקנו לאותו של מטה — יהא ניכר המחק, ויכירו בית דין שהוא עשה. אי נמי, צריך שיכתוב "בן" באותיות גדולות שיחזיקו כל ראובן בתחתיתו, וזהו עיקר, כי אז יהיה יותר היכרא. ואין לחוש לזה הקלקול אלא בראובן לבדו, אבל בשאר שמות לא.

ומתכשר (ס) (בבן) יעקב עד. תימה: היאך יתכשר? והלא מכירים אנו שיעקב לא חתם זה, ומה סבור לומר? דבשלמא ההיא דתנן התם (גיטין דף פז.): שני גיטין שכתוב זה בצד זה, את שהעדים נקראו עמו — כשר. ופריך בגמרא: וליתכשר האי ב"ראובן בן", והאי ב"יעקב עד", כמו שאפרשנו אחרי כן. אלא הכא היכי מתכשר? ואי בחתימת יונית שחותמים אביהן תחלה, ואיכא למימר (ע) שהאי יעקב שנשאר הוא העד, שפי' הוי ראובן בנו יעקב — זה דוחק, דא"כ ה"ל כחתימת יונית! ויש

עין משפט נר מצוה

ג א מיי' פכ"ז מהל' מלוה ולוה הל' ח סמג עשין צד טוש"ע ח"מ סי' מד סעיף ח:

ד ב ג (מיי' פ"ד מהל' גירושין הל' יב) סמג עשין נ טוש"ע אה"ע סי' קל סעיף יא:

מסורת הש"ס

א) גיטין דף פז.. ב) שם: ג) רש"א:

רבינו גרשום

ובסוף השיטה כשבא לסיימו קיימו דכתב הכי אות או תיבה פלונית דביני חיטי כשירה: מחק פסול אע"פ שמקוים. אם יש מחק באותו שטר ונכתב כלום על גבו אע"פ שמקוים לבסוף דכתב מ"ם פלוני דעל המחק פסול השטר: ולא אמרינן מחק פסול. אע"פ שמקיים: אלא במקום שריר וקיים. דאיכא למימר ודאי זייפיה בההוא שטרא: ולרב ירמיה בר אבא דאמר. לעיל: אחורי הכתב כנגד הכתב מבחוץ ליחוש דילמא כתיב מגואי. תחת בגליון: מאי דבעי. אחר שחתמו העדים מאחריו והכי שמע' האידנא [דהעדי'] התחילו לחתום מאחרי השטר כנגד כל כתיבת השטר ויכתבו כל חתימתן בשיטה אחת והתחילו לחתום מלמעלה עד למטה וכוונו כך שהאחרון סיים את חתימתו כנגד שיטה אחרונה כדי שלא יכתוב בעל שטר יותר שיטה למטה מחתימת האחרון שאם כתב שיכולין בית דין לידע שזייף. והאי רב ירמיה בר אבא וכולהו הני דלקמן לא בעי סימן של שריר וקיים אלא סיום חתימת עדים כנגד שיטה אחרונה ומש"ה מקשי וליחוש דילמא מחתים סהדי עד רביעי מבחוץ ויכתוב מבפנים כנגד חתימתו ויזייף מאי דבעי ומכוון שישים שיטה אחרונה של שטר כנגד סוף החתימה של אותו עד רביעי ואם ישאל לו בית דין למה חתמת עליו עד רביעי יאמר אנא כדי לרבות בעדים הוא דעבדי כדי שיתפרסם הדבר יותר. ומשני מי סברת דעדים כסדרן כתיבי. מלמעלה למטה בשיטה אחת דמצי לזייף. לא עדים מלמטה כנגד שיטה אחרונה מתחילין לחתום ומסיימין חתימתן כנגד שיטה העליונה. ואי אמרת אכתי ליחוש דילמא כתב מגואי לתחת מאי דבעי ויחתום עד רביעי מאבראי ליכא למיחש משום הואיל דצריך לחתום ממטה למעלה לכשר החתומין לא מצי לצמצם ולכוון שלא תהא חתימות אותותו קצרות או ארוכות האחרונות יותר מן הראשונות כדי שיגיע למקום העדים אי מזייף איכא הכירא בהכי. ואבתי אע"ג דאוקמת דעדים ממטה למעלה חתימי הא אכתי מזייף ליה דאיכא למיחש דילמא איתחמי דנכתב ריעותא בשיטה אחרונה. כגון שלא הספיק הלבלר לסיים השטר עד שפרע הלוה מקצת החוב ואותו מקצת שפרע נכתב בשיטה אחרונה שפרע לו כך וכך ומן החוב שכתוב למעלה ועכשיו גייז ליה לשיטה אחרונה שיש בה ריעותא וגייז עמה כנגדה מבחוץ ומתכשר עדיין העדות בבן יעקב עד שנשתייר מחתימת הראשון דתנן בן איש פלוני עד כשר ואתי טריף כל החוב שכתוב בו כתחילה: ומשני דכתב הכי דלא מצי לזויפי דכתיב דרא כגון ראובן ותחת ראובן כתב בן וכתב יעקב עד סמוך לראובן דאי גייז ליה לראובן לא מצי גייז ליה בלא בן ולא מתכשר החתימה ביעקב עד ולא אתי למיגז. וליחוש דכשר הוא ביעקב עד בלבד ואתי למיגז: ומשני דלא כתב בן עד והשתא ליכא למיחש דאי גייז לראובן בן לא מתכשר ביעקב לחוד: ואיבעית אימא. אפי' אי כתב יעקב עד ליכא למיחש דגייז דאמרי עדים יעקב זה כתיבת ראובן היא ולא של יעקב. [ודלמא] אמרי ב"ד שמא

הגהות הב"ח

(א) גמ' מאי דבעי (ומחתים סהדי יתירי מאברא) תא"מ ונ"ב לר"ח ל"ג ליה: (ב) רשב"ם ד"ה מחק וכו' במקום שיכול לומר כצ"ל ותיבת שהיה נמחק: (ג) ד"ה עדים כסדרן חתימי מאחורי: (ד) ד"ה אלא מלמטה למעלה וכו' כנגד שיטה אחרונה זה אחר זה. נ"ב פי' לרב חסדא אי אפשר לומר דחתימי זה תחת זה דא"כ לא קשה כל עיקר דלמא גייז ליה לראובן כו' אלא זה אחר זה קאמר ולמר זוטרא הוא דקאמר דחתמי זה תחת זה: (ה) ד"ה ריעותא בשיטה אחרונה שכתב שם תנאי או פרעון. נ"ב פי' על שטר אחר: (ו) תום' ד"ה אנא וכו' והכא נמי וכו' וי"ל דהא ממתני' דבשילהי הזורק שמע מינה דמכל בי תלתא: (ז) ד"ה מלמטה וכו' אמאי תקינו הכי אלא היה להם לתקן שיהיו חתומים כולן תחת שיטה אחרונה מבפנים ולא יצטרך כמו כן: (ח) ד"ה וניחוש וכו' כי למדין משיטה אחרונה אינו יכול לזייף מבפנים לפי שאין העדים חתומים כנגד וכו' וא"ת והלא יחתום וכו' וי"ל שלא היה בשיטה אחת כי אם עד אחד חתום ואם הוא עצמו יחתום עד שני השטר פסול אי נמי וכו' ויכתוב שטר באותו גליון ויחייב את העד לזה כתב ידו וא"ת: (ט) בא"ד דר' חנינא ב"ג על כרחך צריך לפרש במקושר דמהדר: (י) ד"ה דכתב לראובן וכו' כלומר דכתוב וכו' ופירש ריב"ס [illegible]

ספיר כמו שפרשנו: (ע) בא"ד ואיכא למימר בהאי יעקב עד שנשאר שפירוש הוי לראובן בנו של יעקב זה דוחק דא"כ הוה ליה לפרש כחתימת יוונים:

לָאו דְיַעֲקֹב הוּא. וְדִלְמָא בִּשְׁמֵיהּ דַּאֲבוּהּ חָתַם! לָא שָׁבֵיק אִינִישׁ שְׁמֵיהּ דִּידֵיהּ וְחָתֵים בִּשְׁמֵיהּ דַּאֲבוּהּ. וְדִלְמָא סִימָנָא בְּעָלְמָא הוּא דְּשַׁוְיֵהּ, דְּהָא רַב צָיֵיר א)כַּוְורָא, ר' חֲנִינָא צָיֵיר חָרוּתָא, רַב חִסְדָּא – סמ"ך, רַב הוֹשַׁעְיָא – עי"ן, ב)רָבָא בַּר רַב הוּנָא – מַכּוּתָא! לָא חֲצִיף אֱינָשׁ לְשַׁוְיֵהּ לִשְׁמֵיהּ דַּאֲבוּהּ סִימָנָא. מָר זוּטְרָא אָמַר: לָמָּה לָךְ כּוּלֵּי הַאי? כָּל מְקוּשָּׁר שֶׁאֵין עֵדָיו כָּלִין בְּשִׁיטָּה אַחַת – פָּסוּל. א"ר יִצְחָק בַּר יוֹסֵף אָמַר ר' יוֹחָנָן: אכָּל הַמְּחָקִין כּוּלָּן – צָרִיךְ שֶׁיִּכְתּוֹב "וְדֵין קִיוּמֵיהוֹן". בוְצָרִיךְ שֶׁיַּחֲזוֹר מֵעִנְיָנוֹ שֶׁל שְׁטָר בְּשִׁיטָּה אַחֲרוֹנָה. מַאי טַעְמָא?

אָמַר

לָאו דְיַעֲקֹב הוּא. אֵין בְּזֶה הַמַּלְכוּת שׁוּם אָדָם שֶׁשְּׁמוֹ יַעֲקֹב שֶׁיִּכְתּוֹב כָּךְ. וְדִלְמָא בִּשְׁמֵיהּ דַּאֲבוּהּ. יַעֲקֹב, חָתַם רְאוּבֵן, וְכֵן מִנְהָגוֹ לַחְתּוֹם לִכְבוֹד אָבִיו. וְדִלְמָא סִימָנָא שַׁוְיֵהּ. לֹא בִּשְׁבִיל שֶׁיְּהֵא שֵׁם הַחוֹתֵם כָּךְ, אֶלָּא נָהוּג הָיָה זֶה הָאִישׁ לִכְתּוֹב אוֹתִיּוֹת הַלָּלוּ לְשֵׁם סִימָן, כְּמוֹ צוּרַת חוֹתָם שֶׁבְּטַבַּעְתּוֹ, שֶׁמִּמֶּנָּה מַכִּירִים שֶׁזֶּה שֶׁל חוֹתָם זֶה. רַב צָיֵיר כַּוְורָא. צוּרַת הַדָּג הָיָה עוֹשֶׂה בִּשְׁטָרוֹת בִּמְקוֹם חֲתִימָתוֹ, וּכְבָר יָדוּעַ לָעוֹלָם שֶׁזֶּה הוּא חֲתִימָתוֹ, וּמוֹעִיל כַּחֲתִימַת שְׁמוֹ. וְהַמְפָרֵשׁ טַעַם אַמַּאי צָיֵיר כַּוְורָא וְחָרוּתָא אֵינוֹ אֶלָּא טוֹעֶה. וְשֶׁמָּא עַל שֵׁם מַעֲשֵׂיהֶם, זֶה נָהַג לֶאֱכוֹל דָּגִים, וְזֶה נָהַג בִּתְמָרִים, וְסִימָנָא בְּעָלְמָא הָיוּ עוֹשִׂים. חָרוּתָא. חֲרָיוֹת שֶׁל דֶּקֶל וַעֲנָפִים הָיָה צָר בִּמְקוֹם חֲתִימַת שְׁמוֹ. חָתִים סמ"ך. מִשְּׁמוֹ. חָתִים עי"ן. מִשְּׁמוֹ. מַכּוּתָא. תּוֹרֶן שֶׁל סְפִינָה, מסט"א בְּלַעַ"ז. מָר זוּטְרָא אָמַר לָמָּה לָךְ. כָּל הָנֵי שִׁינּוּיֵי דְּחִיקֵי לְרַבִּי יִרְמְיָה בַּר אַבָּא? הָכִי סְבִירָא לֵיהּ: שֶׁכָּל שְׁטָר מְקוּשָּׁר (א) וְעֵדִים חֲתוּמִים מִבַּחוּץ אֲחוֹרֵי הַכְּתָב לְאָרְכּוֹ, מֵרֹאשׁוֹ לְסוֹפוֹ, בֵּין מִלְמַעְלָה לְמַטָּה בֵּין מִלְּמַטָּה לְמַעְלָה, וְאֵין עֵדָיו כָּלִין בְּשִׁיטָּה אַחַת – פָּסוּל. שֶׁצָּרִיךְ שֶׁיַּתְחִילוּ לַחְתּוֹם בְּשָׁוֶה, זֶה תַּחַת זֶה, וּלְסַיֵּים בְּשָׁוֶה. הִלְכָּךְ, בֵּין שֶׁמַּתְחִילִין לַחְתּוֹם שְׁלָשְׁתָּן כְּנֶגֶד שִׁיטָּה אַחֲרוֹנָה דְּהַיְינוּ מִלְּמַטָּה לְמַעְלָה, בֵּין שֶׁמַּתְחִילִין לַחְתּוֹם כְּנֶגֶד שִׁיטָּה רִאשׁוֹנָה וּמְסַיְּימִין בְּשִׁיטָּה אַחֲרוֹנָה – אֵינוֹ יָכוֹל לֹא לְהוֹסִיף בְּסוֹף הַשְּׁטָר, שֶׁהֲרֵי אֵין חֲתִימָתָם כְּנֶגֶד הַהוּא תּוֹסֶפֶת, וְלָא לְמֵיגַז וּלְקַלֵּר רֵיעוּתָא דִּבְסוֹף הַשְּׁטָר, דְּאִי גָּיֵיז חַד מִן הָעֵדִים – גָּיֵיז כּוּלְּהוּ. כָּתַב בְּפֵירוּשׁ רַבֵּינוּ חֲנַנְאֵל: וְאע"ג דְּפָרֵיךְ ר' יִרְמְיָה כָּל מַה דְּאַקְשׁוּ עֲלֵיהּ, מַתְנִי' כְּרַב הוּנָא דַּיְיקָא, דְּקָתָנֵי: רַבִּי חֲנִינָא בֶּן גַּמְלִיאֵל אוֹמֵר מְקוּשָּׁר שֶׁכָּתְבוּ עֵדָיו מִתּוֹכוֹ – כָּשֵׁר, שֶׁיָּכוֹל לַעֲשׂוֹתוֹ פָּשׁוּט. וְאַלִּיבָּא דְּרַב יִרְמְיָה דְּאָמַר מְקוּשָּׁר עֵדָיו מִלְּמַטָּה לְמַעְלָה חוֹתְמִין – לֹא יִתָּכֵן לְהֵעָשׂוֹת הַמְּקוּשָּׁר פָּשׁוּט. וְאִי קַשְׁיָא לָךְ: אִי הָכִי, אֲפִי' לְרַב הוּנָא, אֲפִי' פָּשׁוּט שֶׁכָּתְבוּ עֵדָיו מֵאֲחוֹרָיו יְהֵא כָּשֵׁר, שֶׁיָּכוֹל לַעֲשׂוֹתוֹ מְקוּשָּׁר! הָא ל"ק, דְּהָא תְּנַן: פָּשׁוּט עֵדָיו שְׁנַיִם, וְאִם תַּעֲשֵׂהוּ מְקוּשָּׁר – הַמְּקוּשָּׁר בִּשְׁנֵי עֵדִים פָּסוּל הוּא. אֲבָל הַמְּקוּשָּׁר שֶׁעֵדָיו שְׁלֹשָׁה, אִם יֵשׁ עֵדִים בְּתוֹכוֹ, אֲפִי' אֶלֶף – כָּשֵׁר הוּא. וְעוֹד: הַמְּקוּשָּׁר אִם תַּעֲשֵׂהוּ פָּשׁוּט נִמְצָא מְאוּחָר, כִּדְלְקַמָּן, וְכָשֵׁר. וְאִם תַּעֲשֶׂה הַפָּשׁוּט מְקוּשָּׁר – יִהְיֶה מוּקְדָּם, וְהַמּוּקְדָּם פָּסוּל. הָכִי גָּרְסִינַן בְּפֵירוּשׁ רַבֵּינוּ חֲנַנְאֵל: כָּל הַמְּחָקִין כּוּלָּן צָרִיךְ שֶׁיִּכְתּוֹב קִיוּמֵיהוֹן. וְלָא גָּרַס "וְדֵין". וּפֵירוּשׁ: כָּל הַמְּחָקִין שֶׁאֵינָן בִּמְקוֹם "שָׁרִיר וְקַיָּים", דְּאָמְרִי' לְעֵיל דִּכְשֵׁרִים – צָרִיךְ לְקַיְּימָן בְּסוֹף הַשְּׁטָר לִפְנֵי "שָׁרִיר וְקַיָּים", שֶׁאִם אֵינָן מְקוּיָּימִין – אִיכָּא לְמֵימַר שֶׁמָּחַק וְזִיֵּיף וְהִגִּיהַּ כִּרְצוֹנוֹ לְאַחַר שֶׁנִּכְתַּב הַשְּׁטָר וּלְאַחַר שֶׁחָתְמוּ הָעֵדִים. וְצָרִיךְ שֶׁיַּחֲזוֹר כו'. זֶהוּ שֶׁאָנוּ כּוֹתְבִין בְּסוֹף הַשְּׁטָר "וְקָנֵינָא מִן פְּלוֹנִי בַּר פְּלוֹנִי לִפְלוֹנִי כְּכָל מַה דִּכְתַב וּמְפָרַשׁ לְעֵיל" כו', דְּהַיְינוּ שֶׁמְּפָרֵשׁ וְכוֹפֵל הָעִנְיָן הַכָּתוּב לְמַעְלָה. וְהַאי "וְצָרִיךְ שֶׁיַּחֲזוֹר" – הָכִי מְפָרְשִׁינַן לָהּ: וְצָרִיךְ שֶׁלֹּא יְהֵא כָּתוּב בְּסוֹף הַשְּׁטָר בְּשִׁיטָּה אַחֲרוֹנָה שׁוּם דְּבַר חִידּוּשׁ וְשׁוּם תְּנַאי שֶׁהַשְּׁטָר תָּלוּי בּוֹ שֶׁאֵינוֹ כָּתוּב לְמַעְלָה. לְפִי שֶׁלֹּא נִלְמַד מִשִּׁיטָּה אַחֲרוֹנָה, כִּדְמְפָרֵשׁ לְקַמָּן, וְנִמְצָא שֶׁיִּתְקַיֵּים הַשְּׁטָר הָעֶלְיוֹן בְּלֹא הַתְּנַאי, וְיִגְבֶּה בּוֹ שֶׁלֹּא כַּדִּין, אע"פ שֶׁלֹּא נִתְקַיֵּים הַתְּנַאי. אֶלָּא בִּדְבָרִים שֶׁאֵין לָנוּ צוֹרֶךְ בָּהֶן לִלְמוֹד מִמֶּנּוּ יְסַיֵּים שְׁטָרוֹ, כְּגוֹן מֵעִנְיָנוֹ שֶׁל שְׁטָר. וּמֵעַתָּה לֹא נַפְסִיד כְּלוּם אִם לֹא נִלְמַד מִשִּׁיטָּה אַחֲרוֹנָה, שֶׁהֲרֵי כְּבָר מְפוֹרָשׁ לְמַעְלָה מַה שֶּׁכָּתַב בְּשִׁיטָּה אַחֲרוֹנָה.

אָמַר

ויש לומר, דהכי פריך: וליחוש דלמא גייז ל"ראובן בן" ומתכשר ב"יעקב עד", ויהיה הלוה סבור שלא זייפו, ויהא עדיו (ב) כמו שכתבו לו, וכו'. כמה שלא יצריכנו הלוה לקיימו – לא נקיימנו, אי לא טענינן ליתמי (ג) ללקוחות ומלוה טענות זיוף — אתי שפיר, שבלא שום שכחה יוציא מהם. נחזור למשנת גיטין, דתנן התם פ' "המגרש" (דף פז.): שני גיטין (ד) שכתוב זה בצד זה, את שהעדים נקראים עמו — כשר. ופריך בגמרא: וליתכשר האי ב"ראובן" והאי ב"בן יעקב עד", דתנן: "איש פלוני עד" כשר! השתא משמע דפשיטא דקמא כשר בראובן גרידא, מדלא מייתי ראיה דכשר כמו מ"בן יעקב עד", והא אינו כשר בראובן! ועוד: לאחר שתירץ דכתב "ראובן בן" אקמא ו"יעקב עד" אבתרא, ופריך: ליתכשר האי ב"ראובן [בן]" והאי ב"יעקב עד", דתנן: "איש פלוני עד" — כשר. והשתא נמי, היכי פשיטא ליה דקמא כשר ב"ראובן בן" גרידא? (ה) ופירש רש"י ד"בראובן בן" כשר, דמשמע: אני בן של ראובן, כדרך חתימת היוונים, והוי כמו "בן איש פלוני". והאי ב"יעקב עד" — שאותו עד אחר הוא, ששמו יעקב. ופירוש זה אינו נראה, חדא — דהאי אית לן למימר ד"ראובן בן" יווני הוא, כיון שהכתב כתוב עברי? ועוד: כי נמי הוי יווני, והוה כמו "בן פלוני" — לא הוי כשר, כיון דלא כתב "עד"! ועוד פירכא קמא לא (ו) תבא שפיר. וי"ל לפרש הכי התם: מעיקרא פריך וליתכשר האי ב"ראובן" והאי ב"בן יעקב עד". כלומר, ראובן נתכוין להעיד על שני גיטין, וכתב על התחתון "ב' יעקב עד", ולהכי מתכשר, כדתנן: "בן איש פלוני עד" — כשר. וגם אהם שמו "ראובן" על הראשון, ובהכי כשר, כדתנן: את (ז) שעדים נקראים עמו — כשר, ועם הראשון נקרא ["בן] יעקב עד", ש"ראובן" קאי א"בן יעקב", ופשיטא דכשר, ולכך לא הביא ראיה להכשיר. ומשני: דכתב "ראובן בן" אקמא ו"יעקב עד" אבתרא, והשתא (ח) ידעינן דהאי "יעקב" דבתרא לא חתם ראובן, דלא חתם שמא דאבוה. ופריך: וליתכשר האי ב"ראובן בן" והאי ב"יעקב [עד]", דתנן: "איש פלוני עד כשר" כלומר, יש לנו לומר שיעקב חתם בשני "יעקב עד" ובהכי כשר, ואח"כ בא ראובן בנו והתם על ראשון "ראובן בן", וחשב שחתימת "יעקב עד" נקראת עם אותה שלו, ובהכי כשר, כדתנן: את שהעדים נקראים עמו — כשר! ומשני: דלא כתב "עד", דהשתא ודאי יעקב לא חתם על השני, דהא לא כתב "עד". א"כ דכתב "עד", ויודעים דהאי חתימת ידא לא דיעקב הוא. *דלא כתב עד. משמע: הא אם כתב "ראובן בן יעקב עד" יהיה פסול. וזה קשה, דפסלינן "פלוני בן איש פלוני עד", ומכשרינן "בן איש פלוני עד" או "איש פלוני עד". (ט) שאם חתמו מעיקרא "איש פלוני עד", שלא היה בא לידי זיוף, או "בן" למעלה ו"פלוני עד" למטה תחתיו — כמו כן יהא כשר. אדרבה, הוה לן למימר דאם חתמו מעיקרא "איש פלוני בן איש פלוני עד" יהא כשר, והכי (י) הוה לן למימר: אי גייז שיטה אחרונה עם ראובן דחתים עליו — יהא פסול, והכי הוה לן למימר! ויש לומר, דהא תנן: "בן איש פלוני עד" — כשר, "איש פלוני עד" — כשר, ולא משוי חילוק בין פשוט למקושר, ואית לן למימר דכשר הכא. (כ) אבל "פלוני בן פלוני עד" לא תנן דכשר. אע"ג ד"פלוני בן פלוני" כשר, וכל שכן כשנכתב "עד", מכל מקום כיון דלא תנן דכשר בהדיא — משוינן חילוק, דבפשוט כשר, במקושר דאתי לידי זיוף פסול. ויש שנותנין טעם, שיותר יש לנו להכשיר "איש פלוני עד" דהא איכא כמה גרים שאין להם אב, ואין יכולין לחתום שם אביהן, אלא "פלוני עד". **ודלמא** סימנא בעלמא שוויה דהא רב צייר כוורא כו'. ואם תאמר: שאני התם דאתחזק מעיקרא בדיסקי, כדאמרינן פרק "השולח" (גיטין דף לו.), אבל הכא לא! מ"מ אית לן למימר, אי חתים אינים שמיה דאבוה — שמא זה רגיל לחתום כך. **כל** מקושר שאין עדיו (ל) מאחוריו בשיטה. פי' ר"י: כשחותמין עליו מלמטה למעלה, שיהיו כולן מתחילין בשיטה אחרונה, ואין כי אם עד אחד חתום לארכו של שטר, וחתומין זה אחר זה. לפיכך, אי גייז שיטה אחרונה — יחתוך כל ראשי העדים, ולא ישאר כי אם "בן פלוני עד" וניכר הרמאות, כיון שכל העדים חתוכין. ואי מלמעלה למטה חתימי — צריך שיהיו כולם כלים בשיטה אחרונה. ולא נהירא, דמהדר לתרולי אפי' כתב "עד", וא"כ כשחותמים מלמעלה למטה וכולם כלים בשיטה אחרונה, וגייז לשיטה אחרונה — גייז בהדיה "עד" של כל החתומין! ופי' ריב"א: לעולם כסדרן חתימי. וכי תימא יזייף מגואי ויחתום מאבראי, ואמר: כדי להרבות עדים הוא דעבדי הכי — יהא פסול, דכל מקושר שאין עדיו כלים בשיטה (מ) אחרונה יהא פסול. לכך, כיון שכל העדים חתומים בשיטה אחרונה — תו לא יבא לידי זיוף, דתו לא מצי חתים מאבראי, שכולם צריכים להיות בשיטה אחת ובשיטה אחרונה. וקשיא לן מהא דאמרינן בירושלמי: מקושר לארכו של שטר חתים! ויש לפרש: כל מקושר שאין עדיו כלים בשיטה אחת פסול — כלומר שיחתום "ראובן" בשיטה אחרונה, ותחתיו "בן", ותחתיו "יעקב", ותחתיו "עד", וכן כולם. לכך, אי גייז ליה לשיטה אחרונה — יחתוך כל החתימות. **אמר** רבי יוחנן כל המחקין כולן צריך שיכתוב ודין קיומיהון. בפי' רבינו חננאל לא גרס "ודין", אלא: אי נמחק דבר אחד, ואח"כ כתב על המחק — צריך שיכתוב בסוף שטר תיבות פלוני דעל המחק. ואפי' לספרים שלנו דגרסינן "ודין" לא קשיא מידי אם אין כותבין "ודין", דלא הוי אלא שופרא דשטרא, ועוד שאנו כותבין "שריר וקיים". **וצריך** שיחזור מעניינו של שטר בשיטה אחרונה. ואם תאמר: אם בא שטר לפנינו שחתימת העדים רחוקה מן השטר שיטה אחת, ולא החזירו מעניינו של שטר בשיטה אחרונה — יהא כשר; דלמאי איכא למיחש? אי משום דאי הוה בעי (נ) מזייף באותה שיטה חלק — הא אין למדין משיטה אחרונה, ולהא ליכא

למיחש

ה א מיי' פכ"ז מהל' מלוה ולוה הל' ח סמג עשין צד טוש"ע ח"מ סי' מד סעיף ה:
ו ב מיי' שם הל' ג טוש"ע שם סעיף א:

רבינו גרשום

שמא ראובן חתם שם אביו במקום שמו וכשר הוא. ומשני לא לימרו בית דין הכי אלא לימרו הכי לא שביק איניש שמא דידיה וחתים שם אבוה וש"מ מזויף הוא. ואכתי ליחוש דאי אמרי עדים יעקב זה כתיבת ראובן היא ואמרי בית דין מה בכך דלמא שם אביו כתב לקיים חילוף חתימתו דהא רב לא הוה מחתים שמו אלא במקום שמו היה מצייר דמות דג והכל היו מכירין שזו היא חתימתו: חרותא. כמין דקל היה מצייר: רב חסדא סמ"ך. בלבד היה כותב במקום שמו: מכותא. כמין תורן של ספינה. הכא נמי איכא למימר דכתב אבוה סימן. ומשני לא חציף איניש כו': מר זוטרא אמר למה לך לשנויי כל הני. דשינויי דחיקי הוי אלא האי דקאמר ר' ירמיה בר אבא אחורי הכתב כנגד הכתב מבחוץ הכי קאמר. כל מקושר שאין עדיו [כלין] בשיטה אחת פסול. כגון ששלשתן התחילו לחתום בג' שיטות זה על גב זה והתחילו חתימתן כנגד שיטה אחרונה וחתמו ממטה למעלה וסיימו חתימתן בשיטה א) אחרונה של עדות הוי גייז לכולהו וליכא למיחש משום זיוף: כל המחקין כולם. העשוין בשטר שלא במקום שריר וקיים: צריך לכתוב. בסוף השטר: ודין קיומיהון. דכתב כך וזה מחק פלוני שבמקום פלוני שריר וקיים כדי שלא יאמר שוב נכתב ונמחק וזייף: וצריך שיחזור מעניינו של שטר. של מעלה בשיטה אחרונה:

א) נראה דל"ל וסיימו חתימתן בשיטה אחרונה ולאי גייז לשיטה אחרונה הוי גייז לכולהו וכו'.

א) גיטין דף לו. וקף ב) נ"ל רבה:

הגהות הב"ח

(א) רשב"ם ד"ה זוטרא וכו' מקושר ועדים חתומים: (ב) תוס' (בע"א) ומתכשר וכו' הלוה סבור שלא זייפו עדיו. נ"ב ותימה א"כ קא מקשי תלמודא דהא חתימה לאו די היא ונ"ל דקא מקשי למפורסם דלאו די היא תו לא חיישינן: (ג) בא"ד אי לא טענינן ליתמי וללקוחות ומלוה בטענות זיוף בלא שכחה יוציא ממנו למשנת כצ"ל ותיבות שפיר נמחק: (ד) בא"ד המגרש שני גיטין שכ' זה בצד זה את שהעדים הראשונים נקראים דתנן בן איש פלוני לפשיטא ליה דקמא וכו' כמו מבן יעקב ותימה והא אינו כשר בראובן גרידא ועוד לאחר שתירץ: (ה) בא"ד גרידא ורש"י פי' דבראובן בן כשר: (ו) בא"ד ועוד פירכא קמא לא אתי שפיר לפרש התם הכי מעיקרא: (ז) בא"ד כדתנן שהעדים נקראים עמו כשר ועם הראשון נקרא בן על שראובן קאי יעקב עד ופשיטא דכשר: (ח) בא"ד והשתא מסתמא תלינן דהאי יעקב דבתרא לא חתם ראובן דלא חתם שמיה דאבוה והכי פריך וליתכשר וכו' עם אותה שהוא: (ט) ד"ה דלא כתב וכו' פלוני עד לפי שאם חתמו מעיקרא איש פלוני עד היה: (י) בא"ד והכי הוה לן למימר דאי גייז שיטה וכו' וה"נ הוה: (כ) בא"ד דכשר הכא אבל פלוני וכו' את"ג דתנן פלוני בן פלוני כשר וכו' כיון דלא תנן בהדיא דכשר משוינן חילוק ובמקושר דאתי: (ל) ד"ה כל מקושר שאין עדיו כלים בשיטה אחת פי' רש"י כשחותמין מאחוריו מלמטה למעלה לצריך שיהיו כולן וכו' וחתומין זה תחת זה לפיכך: (מ) בא"ד דכל מקושר שאין עדיו כלים בשיטה אחת פירוש בשיטה אחרונה: (נ) ד"ה וצריך כו' דאי הוה בעי הוה מזייף כו':

אָמַר רַב עַמְרָם: אלְפִי שֶׁאֵין לְמֵדִין מִשִּׁיטָּה אַחֲרוֹנָה. אֲמַר לֵיהּ רַב נַחְמָן לְרַב עַמְרָם: מְנָא לָךְ הָא? אֲמַר לֵיהּ, דְּתַנְיָא: בהִרְחִיק אֶת הָעֵדִים שְׁנֵי שִׁיטִּין מִן הַכְּתָב — פָּסוּל, שִׁיטָּה אַחַת — כָּשֵׁר; מַאי שְׁנָא שְׁנֵי שִׁיטִּין? דִּלְמָא מְזַיֵּיף וְכָתַב, שִׁיטָּה אַחַת נַמִי מְזַיֵּיף וְכָתַב! אֶלָּא לָאו שְׁמַע מִינַּהּ: אֵין לְמֵדִין מִשִּׁיטָּה אַחֲרוֹנָה, שְׁמַע מִינַּהּ.

אִיבַּעְיָא

אָמַר רַב עַמְרָם לְפִי שֶׁאֵין לְמֵדִין מִשִּׁיטָּה אַחֲרוֹנָה. מִפְּנֵי שֶׁאֵין הָעֵדִים יְכוֹלִין לְקָרֵב חֲתִימָתָן כ"כ בְּסָמוּךְ בְּסוֹף הַשְּׁטָר, וּמַנִּיחִין רֶיוַח בֵּין הַשְּׁטָר לַחֲתִימָתָן, וְיָכוֹל אָדָם לְזַיֵּיף וּלְהוֹסִיף בֵּינְתַיִם שִׁיטָּה אַחַת. וְהִלְכָּךְ תִּקּוּן רַבָּנַן לַחֲזוֹר מֵעִנְיָנוֹ שֶׁל שְׁטָר בְּשִׁיטָּה אַחֲרוֹנָה, לְבִלְתִּי שֶׁיִּכָּתֵב בָּהּ דָּבָר הַצָּרִיךְ. (א) שֶׁהֲרֵי אִם זִיְּיפוּ וְהוֹסִיפוּ לְאַחַר זְמַן – אֵין אָנוּ מַפְסִידִין כְּלוּם אִם לֹא נִלְמַד הֵימֶנָּה, שֶׁהֲרֵי כְּבָר כָּתוּב כָּל זֶה לְמַעְלָה. וְגַם אִם זִיְּיפוּ וְיוֹסִיפוּ בְּשִׁיטַּת הַחֵלֶק שֶׁאַחַר עִנְיָנוֹ שֶׁל שְׁטָר שֶׁבְּשִׁיטָּה אַחֲרוֹנָה בֵּין הַשְּׁטָר לָעֵדִים – לֹא מַעֲלֶה וְלֹא מוֹרִיד, שֶׁהֲרֵי אֵין לְמֵדִין מִשִּׁיטָּה אַחֲרוֹנָה. וּבְשֶׁאֵין כָּתוּב בַּשְּׁטָר "שָׁרִיר וְקַיָּים" מַיְירֵי. כֵּן נִרְאֶה בְּעֵינַי טַעַם הַדָּבָר וּפֵירוּשׁוֹ, וְעִיקָּר. **הִרְחִיק אֶת הָעֵדִים שְׁנֵי שִׁיטִּין מִן הַכְּתָב פָּסוּל.** אִם אֵין כָּתוּב בּוֹ "שָׁרִיר וְקַיָּים". אֲפִי' יֵשׁ עֵדִים שֶׁלֹּא נוֹסַף בּוֹ דָּבָר זִיּוּף, מִכָּל מָקוֹם הַאי שְׁטָרָא חַסְפָּא בְּעָלְמָא הוּא, שֶׁלֹּא נַעֲשָׂה כְּתִקּוּן חֲכָמִים, וּכְמִלְוֶה עַל פֶּה דָּמְיָא. **אֶלָּא לָאו ש"מ אֵין לְמֵדִין מִשִּׁיטָּה אַחֲרוֹנָה.** הִלְכָּךְ הִרְחִיק שְׁנֵי שִׁיטִּין פָּסוּל, שֶׁיָּכוֹל לְזַיֵּיף שְׁנֵי שִׁטִּין וְנִלְמוֹד מִן הָרִאשׁוֹנָה.

אֶלָּא

למיחש, שהניחו שני שיטין חלק, והוא המלוה זייף בו שיטה אחרונה! ויש לומר דודאי (ב) כן הוא שהוא כשר. ובגיטין פרק "המביא תניגא" (דף יט:) משמע שיהא פסול, דקתני התם: האי שטרא פרסאה דחתימי עליה סהדי ישראל — גבי ביה ממשעבדי. ופריך: והא בעינן שיחזור מעניינו של שטר בשיטה אחרונה וליכא! ומשני: בדמהדר. והשתא אמאי לא משני: כשהעדים רחוקים שיטה אחת מן השטר, אי איתא דהוה כשר? ויש לומר: דעדיפא מינה משני, דאפי' לא הרחיקו כלום — כשר בדמהדר. אבל מלינו להביא ראיה דפסול מהאי דפרק קמא (ג) (דף יא.): האי שטרא פרסאה דמסריה ניהליה באפי סהדי ישראל — גבי ביה מבני חרי. ופריך רבא: והא בעינא כתב שאין יכול לזייף וליכא! בדאפילן. והא בעינא שיחזור מעניינו של שטר בשיטה אחרונה וליכא! בדמהדר. והשתא מאי פריך דבעינן חזרת השטר, למה? אי משום דלא לכתוב מאי דבעי — הא כיון דאיכא עדי מסירה מדכר דכירי, אי הוה תנאה וזייפיה — אפי' לאחר כמה ימים מדכר דכירי, כדאמר ר' יוחנן פרק שני (שם דף כג:) על (ד) מילתא דאין כותבין על נייר מחוק כו' וחכמים מכשירין. ואמר רבי יוחנן: אפילו מכאן עד עשרה ימים מכשיר ר' אליעזר, דאי הוה תנאה וזייפיה — מדכר דכיר. ואם כן, מאי קפריך הא ליכא חזרת השטר? אלמא, אע"פ שאין יכול לזייף — פסול כי ליכא חזרה. ואע"ג דר' (*אליעזר) פליג על ר' יוחנן ופוסל בר מלאלתר — מ"מ הלכה כר' יוחנן רבו. ועוד ברים "חזקת הבתים" (לעיל דף כט.) אמר אביי: "שדות בכסף יקנו" — עלה טובה קמ"ל, וזהו כסברת ר' יוחנן דהתם. והא לאו ראיה היא, דע"כ לא פריך אליביה דר' יוחנן (ה) דהא ליכא חזרת השטר, דלדידיה היכי פריך? והא בעינן כתב שאינו יכול להזדייף וליכא, דהא אמר ר' יהודה בן בתירא: אין כותבין (ו) על נייר מחוק ולא על דיפתרא, וחכמים מכשירין. ואמר ר' יוחנן: כשהכשיר ר"א — אפילו מכאן ועד עשרה ימים, דמדכר דכירי. אלא אליבא דר' אלעזר פריך, דאמר: לא הכשיר ר"א אלא לאלתר, אבל מכאן ועד עשרה ימים לא. וה"נ פריך שפיר: והא בעינן חזרת השטר וליכא, ויוכל לזייף, ולא דכירי לימים רבים. אבל לר' יוחנן — ה"נ דכשר, כיון שאין יכול לזייף מדכר דכירי. [מיהו, מלינו למימר דאף לר"י פריך], *)ולא הכשיר ר' יוחנן אפי' מכאן ועד י' ימים אלא בגיטין, דליכא רוב תנאים — הלכך מדכר דכירי. (ז) אבל בשאר שטרות מכאן ועד י' ימים לא, דרוב עניני תנאים הם בשטר, ולא דכירי לזמן מרובה. מיהו, מסתבר דפסול, גזירה אטו היכא דלא הרחיק שיטה אחת, דלא משתמיט לאפלוגי בהן, אלא בין הרחיקו (ח) ללא הרחיקו — בעינן חזרת השטר. **לפי שאין למדין כו'.** בימיהם לא היו כותבין "שריר וקיים" בפשוטין שלהם, כדאמר גבי מקושר לעיל: דכתב (ט) "שריר וקיים" — מכלל דבפשוטים לא היו כותבין "שריר וקיים". ולכך לא היו למדין משיטה אחרונה, שלא יוכל לזייף בשיטה אחת שהרחיקו העדים, והיו כותבין חזרת השטר בשיטה אחרונה, ולא שום דבר עיקר (י) שאין למדין הימנה. ואם אירע בהן מחק — היו כותבין אותו, והיו מקיימים אותו קודם שיטה אחרונה, דאחרי כן לא היו למדין כל עיקר הימנה. ויש לתמוה: א"כ, היאך הורגלנו לכתוב קיום מחקים אחר "וקנינא מיניה"(כ)? והא אין למדין משיטה אחרונה, ואין לך למדין גדול מזה. ולא היה לנו ללמוד, לפי שיכול לבא לידי זיוף כיון שהשטר כשר בלא "שריר וקיים", שפעמים לא יכתוב מתחלה "שריר וקיים", ויבא זה וימחוק מה שירצה, ויגיה, ויקיים המחק בסוף, ויכתוב "שריר וקיים"! וי"ל: כיון שהורגלנו לכתוב "שריר וקיים" — יהא פסול אם לא נכתב כן, אפילו כשאין בו מחק, והשתא לא יוכל לבא לידי זיוף. לכך אנו כותבין שפיר קיום מחקים אחר "וקנינא מיניה", ולמדין אנו (ל) היטב משיטה אחרונה, כיון שאנו כותבין "שריר וקיים". והא דכותבין "וקנינא מיניה" וכו' — לא הויא חזרת השטר, אלא לפי שעדיין עדות הקנין הוא, שבתחלה כתב: ואמר לנו "הוו עלי עדים וקנו ממני" ואחר כן ו"קנינא מיניה". והוא הדין שיכול לכתבו באמצע השטר. ולפי האי פירוש דלא צריך חזרת השטר, אם כן הא דכתבינן בגיטין "ודין (מ) דיהוי ליכי מנאי ספר תירוכין וגט פטורין" לא הויא משום חזרת השטר, דלא צריך למכתב חזרה כיון דכתבינן "שריר וקיים", ובגיטין "כדת משה וישראל" הוי במקום "שריר וקיים". ובעיא היא ב"המגרש" (גיטין דף פה: ושם) אי בעינן "ודין" או לא, ולא איפשיט. ולכך נראה שלעיקר גט אנו כותבין "ודין", ואין אנו צריכין חזרה, משום טעם שפי', ויכולים לכתוב "ודין" בשיטה אחרונה, ד"כדת משה וישראל" הוי במקום "שריר וקיים". ויש תימה: למה שינו הקדמונים לכתוב "שריר וקיים" וללמוד משיטה אחרונה, ולקיים מחקים אחר "וקנינא מיניה", כיון שחכמי הגמרא לא היו כותבין "שריר וקיים", מדקאמר: אין למדין משיטה אחרונה, ומקיימים מחקים קודם שיטה אחרונה! וי"ל: שחששו שפעמים שיטעו העדים שאינן בקיאין, וירחיקו שני שיטין. ואפילו לא יהא אדם חצוף לעשות שטר חדש בשני שיטין, כי ידאג שיכחישוהו העדים שלא חתמו על שטר זה מעולם — מכל מקום לא ידאג מלהוסיף שני שיטין, וילמדו מן העליונה, כי העדים לא יהיו זכורים שהרחיקו שני שיטין, וכיון דכתב "שריר וקיים" — למדין בטוב משיטה אחרונה. וזה שאל ר"י לר"ת על קיום מחקים שאנו כותבין בשיטה אחרונה, והשיב כמו שפירשתי, שאנו סומכין על "שריר וקיים". וקשה על האי פירוש שמשום "שריר וקיים" ו"כדת משה וישראל" שהורגלנו לכתוב לא כתבינן חזרת השטר, והלא גם הם היו כותבין "כדת משה וישראל", כדמוכח במס' ידים (פ"ד משנה ח) אמרו לדוקים: קובלים אנו עליכם פרושים, שאתם כותבין את המושל עם משה בגט. ה"ג במשניות, ולא גרסינן "את המושל עם השם", כמו שכתוב במקצת משניות, כי מה ענין השם בגט? דודאי כשגלחו בית חשמונאי היו כותבין "בשנת כך וכך ליוחנן כהן גדול לאל עליון" מקמי דאתבטילת (נ) אזכרת מן [שטריא] כדאיתא בפ"ק דר"ה (דף יח:), אבל המושל לא היו כותבין כשהיו כותבין את השם. אלא ודאי "עם משה" גרסינן. אלמא כותבין "כדת משה וישראל" בגיטין! וי"ל: שמתחלה היו כותבין "כדת משה וישראל" באמצע הגט, ואחר כך תקנוהו לכתבו בסוף הגט במקום "שריר וקיים", ולכך אין כותבין חזרת השטר. ולאחר פטירתו של ר"ת מצא ר"י בה"ג שהיה לר"ת, בתיקון הגט שעשה: (ס) כל דבר שלמדין הימנו, אם מחק או תלה — צריך לכתוב "דעל המחק" או "דביני חטי" קודם שיטה אחרונה לפני "וקנינא מיניה". אך בדברים ששנה עליהם, שכתב פעמים ושלש בתוך השטר — אז אין עיקר הגט תלוי בו — בזה הורגלו לקיים אחר שיטה אחרונה. א"כ ס"ל דאין למדין משיטה אחרונה, ו"קנינא מיניה" הוה חזרת השטר, ו"שריר וקיים" דכתבינן — על חנם הוא. וצריך ליזהר בגיטין שלא לכתוב "ודין דיהוי ליכי מנאי ספר תירוכין" בשיטה אחרונה, אלא מ"תירוכין" ואילך, שהוא כפל לשון, מאחר שאין למדין משיטה אחרונה אע"ג שאנו כותבין "שריר וקיים" בשטרות ו"כדת משה וישראל" בגיטין, שאין לכתוב דבר שהוא מעיקר הגט בשיטה אחרונה, ומבעיא לן ב"המגרש" (גיטין דף פה:) אי בעינן "ודין" או לא, ולא איפשיט. וקשיא לר"י על האי פירוש שפירש ר"ת, שאין למדין משיטה אחרונה. וקיום מחקים שהורגלו לכתוב אחר "וקנינא" היינו בדברים שאין עיקר השטר תלוי בו — א"כ יבא לידי זיוף, שימחוק בשטר דבר, (ע) ויכתוב עליהם דבר שנוי בשטר, ויקיימנו בסוף השיטה אחר "וקנינא מיניה". וכמו שאומר ר"ת מתחלה: דלמדין משיטה אחרונה — וכן נראה לר"י מדנהגו לכתוב "שריר וקיים" בשטרות, ובגיטין "כדת משה וישראל", מ"מ, נהי שאנו למדין משיטה אחרונה — הרחיק שני שיטין פסול, דלמא גייז ליה לעילאי וכתב הוא בשני שיטין, ועדיו הם בשיטה שלישית. ור"י פירש: שמא בעבור הטורח הורגלו לכתוב "שריר וקיים", דפעמים בחזרה גופה היה מחק, והיה צריך לקיימו ולחזור פעם אחרת. דנהי שאין למדין משיטה אחרונה זכות לבעל השטר — חובתו מיהא למדין, שבחובתו אין לחוש שמא יזייף. לכך היה צריך לקיים המחק של חזרה, שלא יאמר הלוה או המוכר: זכות היה לי שם ומחקתו.

איבעיא

ז א מיי' פכ"ז מהל' מלוה ולוה הל' ג סמג עשין צד טוש"ע ח"מ סי' מד סעיף א:

ח ב מיי' שם הל' ד סמג שם טוש"ע ח"מ סי' מה סעיף ו:

[נ"ל אלעזר]

רש"א *) נ"א ולאפשר דלא

רבינו גרשום

שום חידוש ממון שלא נכתב בענינו של מעלה אין למדין מאותה שיטה. דאיכא למימר אחר שנכתב ונחתם זייף הוא ולהכי כתבי בכל שטרי בשיטה אחרונה ככל מה דכתוב ומפורש לעיל דהיינו מענינו של שטר: מאי שנא שני שיטין דלמא מזייף. ומוסיף וכותב יותר ממון ומקיים ליה בשיטה אחרונה בשיטה אחת יכול לכתוב בה זיוף ומקיים בסופה אלא לאו ש"מ משו"ה שיטה אחת כשר דאי כתב ומזייף באות' [שיטה] אין למדין מכל אותה שיטה מה שאין כן בב' שיטין דילפינן מינייהו מש"ה פסול דמצי לזופי ליה:

הגהות הב"ח

רשב"ם ד"ה אמר רב ...ם וכו' לבלתי שיכתב דבר הצריך דהשתא אם יזייפו ויוסיפו לאחר אין אנו: (ב) תום' ד"ה ...ף הקודם) וצריך וכו' ...לומר דודאי בדין הוא ...א כשר אלא דבגיטין ...ק המביא תנינא משמע ...וא פסול: (ג) בא"ד ...רק קמא דגיטין האי ...רא: (ד) בא"ד ר' יוחנן ...ק שני על מתניתין דאין ...תבין לא על נייר מחוק: ... בא"ד אליביה דר' ...נן מהא דליכא חזרת ...טר: (ו) בא"ד אין ...תבין לא על נייר: ... בא"ד אבל בשאר ...רות. נ"ב עיין בתום' ...ב דגיטין בד"ה אבל ...טרות לא פירשו להדיא ...' יוחנן מודה בשטרות ...עי לאלתר: (ח) בא"ד ... הרחיקו בין לא ...חיקו: (ט) ד"ה לפי וכו' ...יל דכתב ביה שריר ...יים וכו' משיטה אחרונה ...י שלא: (י) בא"ד דבר ...קר לפי שאין למדין וכו' ...יו כותבין על אותו ...חק היו מקיימים אותם ...דם שיטה אחרונה: ...) בא"ד אחר וקנינא ...ניה קודם שריר וקיים ...א אין למדין: (ל) בא"ד ...מדין אנו בטוב משיטה ...חרונה: (מ) בא"ד ...תבינן בגיטין ודין די ...וין ליכי מנאי: (נ) בא"ד ...קמי דאתבטילת אדכרת ... שטריא כדאיתא: ...) בא"ד לר"ת בתיקון ...גט שעשה שכתב כל דבר ...ו' ששנה עליהם פעמיים ...ש בתוך השטר או אין ...יקר הגט תלוי בזה ...ורגלו כצ"ל ותיבת שכתב ...מחק: (ע) בא"ד שימחוק ...שטר דבר שעיקר השטר ...לוי בו ויכתוב עליה דבר ...שנוי וכו' כן נראה לר"י ...כו' דלפעמים בחזרה גופה:

עין משפט
נר מצוה

ט א מיי' פכ"ז מהל' מלוה ולוה הל' ד סמג עשין לד טוש"ע ח"מ סי' מה סעיף י:
י ב מיי' פ"ה מהל' עדות הלכה ו סמג עשין קט טוש"ע ח"מ סי' מה סעיף יב וסי' נא סעיף ד:
יא ג מיי' פכ"ז מהל' מלוה ולוה הל' ד סמג עשין לד טוש"ע ח"מ סי' מה סעיף יד:
יב ד מיי' פ"ה מהל' סוכה הל' כ סמג עשין מב טוש"ע א"ח סי' תרלב סעיף ב:
יג ה מיי' שם הל' יד טוש"ע שם סעיף א:

איבעיא להו שיטה ומחצה מהו. לא בעי היכא דמסיים (ג) השיטה באמצע השיטה, והניחו העדים אותו חצי שיטה הנשארת גם שיטה אחרת מהו — דפשיטא דפסול, דכתב מאי דבעי באותו חצי, ויחזור בשיטה אחרונה. אבל יש לפרש: היכא דסיים השטר בסוף השיטה, והניחו השיטה שלימה, (ד) וכתבו באמצע שיטה מהו? מי אמרינן שפסול, לפי שיזייף בשיטה שלימה ובחציה יכתוב חזרת השטר, ואין למדין מן החציה שהיא שיטה אחרונה. אבל מן השלימה למדין. או דלמא שכשר, שגם מן השיטה שלימה אין למדין שהיא אחרונה מן השטר. מיהו (ה) פשיטא דכשר, דאין למדין משיטה אחרונה היינו טעמא — שעדים לא דייקי ומרחיקין שיטה אחת. אם כן, כשמרחיקין שיטה וחותמים באמצע שיטה, כיון דליכא כי אם רוחב שיטה אחת בין העדים לשטר — אין למדין ממנה, ולכך לא יוכל לזייף, וכשר. ועוד: דומיא דהרחיק שני שיטין והרחיק שיטה אחת, דמיירי בעובי (ו) כזה [בעי] מהו? מי אמרינן לא יוכל לזייף כלום בשיטה ומחצה, או דלמא בדוחק יכתוב שני שיטין, ופסול.

איבעיא להו: שיטה ומחצה, מאי? תא שמע: הרחיק את העדים שני שיטין — (א) פסול; הא שיטה ומחצה — כשר. אימא סיפא: שיטה אחת — כשר; שיטה אחת הוא דכשר, הא שיטה ומחצה — פסול! *אלא מהא ליכא למשמע מינה. מאי הוי עלה? ת"ש, דתניא: *הרחיק את העדים שני שיטין מן הכתב — פסול, [א]פחות מכאן — כשר; *[ב]היו ארבעה וחמשה עדים חתומין על השטר, ונמצא אחד מהן קרוב או פסול — תתקיים עדות בשאר. מסייע ליה לחזקיה, דאמר חזקיה: *[ג]מלאהו בקרובים — כשר; ואל תתמה, שהרי *[ד]אויר סוכה פוסל בשלשה, [ה]סכך פסול פוסל בארבעה. איבעיא להו: שני שיטין שאמרו — הן

אלא מהא ליכא למשמע מינה. חדא דוקא, או סיפא או רישא, ותנא הא אטו הא. פחות מכאן כשר. דהיינו שיטה ומחצה. הכי גרסינן בפירוש רבינו חננאל: היו ארבעה או חמשה עדים חתומים על השטר (א) ונמצא שנים הראשונים קרובים או פסולים תתקיים עדות בשאר. מסייע ליה לחזקיה דאמר מילאהו בקרובים כשר. פירוש: אם היה בין הכתב לעדים חלק כשיעור שני שיטין, ומילא מקום החלק בקרובים — השטר ההוא כשר, ומקיימין אותו משאר העדים שבו. ולא נמצאו דברי חזקיה בפירוש בתלמוד. וי"ל: בגט קרח מדבר חזקיה, ונראין דברי חזקיה כדברי ר' עקיבא, דתנן במסכת גיטין (דף פא:): גט קרח — הכל משלימין עליו כדברי בן ננס, ר"ע אומר: אין משלימין אלא קרובים הראויים להעיד במקום אחר, כך פירש רבינו חננאל. ולי נראה לשון הראשון, שסוף הברייתא דקתני: היו עליו ארבעה או חמשה כו' — ודאי מעין תחלתה מיירי, במילוי שני שיטין הפוסלים את השטר, כדקתני רישא, ובא לומר שמילוי קרובים מכשירו. והיינו דקאמר: מסייע ליה לחזקיה, דאיירי נמי במילוי שני שיטין של חלק. דאי ברייתא בעלמא מיירי, בלא מילוי שני שיטין, ולאורויי דין עדים פסולים שיתקיים העדות בשאר — ליתנייה במסכת מכות (דף ו.) גבי ההיא פלוגתא דרבי ורבי יוסי (הגלילי) דפליגי התם בדיני ממונות אם תתקיים העדות בשאר אם לאו. וחזקיה נמי, אם בגט קרח מיירי — מה צריך סיוע מן הברייתא? מתני' דגיטין דבן ננס ור"ע יכול לסייעו. ותו, חזקיה מתני' דגיטין אתא לאשמועינן? בתמיה. ואל תתמה. מזה החלוק, כי בהיותו חלק השטר — פסול, ואם מילאו בפסולין לעדות — כשר. שהרי סוכה. בהיות בה אויר שלשה טפחים פסולה, ואם מילאו בסכך פסול, כגון בדבר המקבל טומאה — הוכשרה הסוכה, שאין סכך פסול פוסל אלא בארבעה טפחים. ורב יהודאי גאון נמי מוקי לה להא דחזקיה בהלכות עדות שלו כגון דהוה קרוב חתים ברישא, כי היכי דלא תקשי אדרב נחמן, דאמר במסכת מכות: אפילו בדיני ממונות, נמצא אחד מהן קרוב או פסול — עדותן בטילה. דהיכא דחתים קרוב ברישא — מוכחא מילתא דלכבוד עביד, ולא לעדות חתמיה. ובהא כ"ע מודו. והכי תניא בתוספתא (פ"ז דגיטין): שטר שחתמו עליו חמשה ונמצאו שלשה הראשונים קרובים או פסולים — תתקיים העדות בשאר.

[ברכות כה. וש"נ]
[תוספתא גיטין פ"ז]
[תוספתא שם]
[גיטין פז:]
[סוכה יז.]

***אלא** מהא ליכא למשמע מינה. ואי רישא דוקא — סיפא לאו דוקא, ושיטה ומחצה כשיטה אחת (ז) דקאמר כשר דמי. ואי סיפא דוקא — רישא לאו דוקא, ושיטה ומחצה כשני שיטין דפסול דמי.

***דאמר** חזקיה מלאהו בקרובים כשר. אהרחיק שני שיטין קאי. וכן מוכח ב"המגרש" (גיטין דף פז: ושם) דקאמר: ואי משום (ח) שני שיטין פסול — האמר חזקיה: מלאהו בקרובים כשר. לפירוש רבינו חננאל, שגורס בברייתא: (ט) נמצא כן הראשונים קרוב או פסול — מסייע ליה שפיר לחזקיה, דמכשיר עדים ראשונים שנמצאו קרובים. אלא לגירסת ספרים דלא גרסי ראשונים — א"כ היכי מסייע ליה? דלמא הברייתא לא מכשרת אלא כשנמצאו (י) בסוף עדים כשרים, אבל מצאו למעלה במקום שאויר פסול — אימא הקרוב נמי פסול! וי"ל: מדלא קבע ליה מקום, וקאמר סתמא: (כ) נמצא ארבעה או חמשה קרובים או פסולים כשר — שמע מינה בכל דוכתא מכשר להו. כגון הא דאמר בשילהי "הזורק" (שם דף פב.): ש"מ, אי חתים בתחלה קרוב או באמצע בין בסוף כשר, ממאי — מדלא קבע מקום. וא"ת: היכי מסייע ליה? הא בברייתא מכשיר בין קרוב בין פסול, וחזקיה לא מכשיר אלא קרוב, מדלא קאמר פסול. ומ"ט דחזקיה? וי"ל: דחזקיה סבר לה כר' עקיבא, דאמר ב"הזורק" (שם פא:): גט קרח הכל משלימין עליו, אפי' קרוב, אבל פסול — לא. אבל ברייתא סבר' כבן ננס דמכשר בגט קרח להשלים אפילו עבד, וסבר כחזקיה בחדא, בקרוב. ונראה לר"י דאין הלכה כחזקיה דסבר כר' עקיבא, אלא כבן ננס דמכשיר אפילו פסול. דאמרי' התם: כי אתו לקמיה דר' אמי, אמר: לא והשלים עליו עבד מן השוק. והשיא דר' אמי עיקר טפי, דקבע גבי פלוגתא, (ל) אבל ההיא דחזקיה לא הובאה לשם. ועוד: דסתמא דגמרא כבן ננס, דאמרי' ב"המביא תניין" (שם דף יח: ושם): אי חתים בתחלה קרוב או פסול. (מ) ומוכח התם דלכולי עלמא כשחותם בתחלה פסול, משום תנאי — כשר, אי לא אתי לאיחלופי בקיום שטרות בעלמא. ועוד: דשמא חזקיה נמי אית ליה דבן ננס, והא דאמר מלאהו בקרובים ולא קאמר בפסולים — לרווחא דמילתא קאמר, לדדברי הכל בכי האי גוונא כשר. (הג"ה. שיטה ומחלה. נראה ליישב כגון שחתומים עדים באמצע שיטה, ומספקא ליה שמא יכתוב מה שירלה בחצי (נ) השלמה. ע"כ הג"ה).

[לגיטין פז.]
[גיטין פח:]

פחות מכאן כשר. בתוספתא* מסיים כאן: וכמה יהיו העדים רחוקים מן הכתב ויהיה כשר — כדי שיהיו נקראים עמו, דברי רבי. רשב"ג אומר: מלא שיטה אחת. ר' דוסתאי ברבי ינאי אומר: מלא חתימת שני עדים. שטר שחתום עליו [ה' עדים] ונמצאו ג' הראשונים קרובים או פסולים — תתקיים העדות בשאר. ונראה לר"מ ולר"ת דמן הלד מיירי. **ואל** תתמה שהרי אויר פוסל בשלשה. וא"ת: אמאי לא מייתי ראיה מגט קרח*, שאויר פוסל וקרוב משלים? וי"ל: משום דההיא גופא תקנתא דרבנן היא, והיא גופא לריכה ראיה ממילתא דאורייתא. וא"ת: מה שייך טעם פסול אויר הגט לפסול אויר סוכה? וי"ל: (ס) ה"ק, מלאהו בקרובים כשר, ואע"ג דאויר פסול — אין לגזור מילוי קרובים אטו אויר, שהרי אויר פסול בשלשה, ופסול לא פוסל אלא בארבעה, אבל בשלשה לא פסלי ולא גזרינן אטו שלשה דאויר פסול. ועוד י"ל: דלא מייתי ראיה מגט קרח דלא גזרינן, דטעמא דאויר (ע) פסול לא הוי אלא משום דקשריו מרובין מעדיו, ולא משום שיוכל לזייף. אפי' איכא ארבעה שיטין חלקים בין עדים לעדים — כשר בטיוט בעלמא, דתו ליכא למיחש לזיוף, ולא אמר: שהדי אטיוט חתימו, כיון שאין השטר מלד שהעדים חתומין, (פ) כדאמרי' במשנה. ולכן לא גזרי קרובים אטו אויר שני שיטין, דאפילו יש בו אויר — בטיוטא בעלמא סגי. אבל הכא, דטיוטא לא מהני מידי, לפי שהעדים בלד השטר כתובים, ואי טייט ליה אמרי אטיוטא חתימי — ולכך נגזור מילוי קרובים אטו אויר, משום דבאויר אין לו תקנה. ולהכי מייתי ראיה מסוכה, שאויר פוסל בה ואין לו תקנה, ופסול כשר, ולא פסלינן ליה אטו אויר. **שהרי** אויר פוסל בשלשה. לא מיירי בסוכה גדולה (צ) שמשייר שיעור סוכה ושלש דפנות לכל לד — דאותה למה תהיה פסולה? וגם לא איירי ליושב תחת האויר — דא"כ מאי איריא שלשה? אפילו פחות נמי אמר במסכת סוכה (דף טז.) שאין ישנים תחתיו. אלא הכי פירושא: סוכה גדולה ויש לה שלשה דפנות, ויש לה אויר שלשה לכל אורך הסוכה — פסולה, שאויר שלשה מפסיק, ועתה אין נשאר בו כי אם שני דפנות לכל לד. וסכך פסול לא הוי הפסק כי אם בארבעה טפחים. אי נמי, כגון שיש לה לסוכה ארבעה דפנות, והיא סינה גדולה כל כך שישאר הכשר סוכה מכל לדי האויר. **נמצא** אחד מהם כו'. יש תימה: מהא דאמר הכא נמצא אחד מהן קרוב או פסול כשר, ולר"ע קרוב מיהא כשר, ובין בתחלה ובין בסוף בין באמצע כשר, מדלא קביע ליה מקום. ואפילו לר"ח דגרס בראשונה — לאו לאפוקי בסוף, דכ"ש הוא היכא שאין אויר פסול דכשר. והכי נמי בגט קרח לר"ע קרוב כשר. ובפ"ק דמכות (דף ה:) אמר ר"ע: אף שלשה, נמצא אחד מהן קרוב או פסול — עדותן בטלה! וי"ל: דהתם מיירי בעדים בעל פה, והיכא דלאסהודי אתו — עדותן בטלה, דשיילינן להו אי לאסהודי אתו אי למיחזי אתו, דרב נחמן פסיק התם הלכה כרבי. אבל הכא — לאו לאסהודי חתימי, אלא למילוי. והיכא שחותמין באמצע או בסוף אמרינן משום תנאי חתימי, ולאו לאסהודי קאתו. וכמו כן גבי גט קרח — לא חתימי אלא להשלים הקרח, שיהא עדים כמו הקשרים. ואע"פ דלעדות אחר על פה שיילינן אי למיחזי אתו אי לאסהודי אתו — היינו משום שלא נחקרה עדותן בב"ד. אבל בשטר — א"צ לחקור אמאי חתימי, דעדים החתומים על השטר כמי שנחקרה עדותן בב"ד דמי, כאילו נחקר שלמילוי או לתנאי חתמו. ורב יהודאי פסק על שטר שיש בו ה' עדים או יותר, ונמצא אחד מהן קרוב או פסול בתחלה

רבינו גרשום

פחות מכאן כשר. אלמא שיטה ומחצה כשר: מילאהו. אותן ב' שיטין שהרחיק העדים מן הכתב אם מילא אותן בקרובין כשר. אע"ג דאי לא הוה כתב בהו פסול להיכא דמילאהו בקרובין שהן פסולין לעדות דדמיין כמאן דליתנהו אפי' הכי כשר: ואל תתמה. על דבר זה שהרי אויר סוכה פוסל לסוכה בג' טפחים: סכך פסול. שסיככה בשפודין או בדבר המקבל טומאה פוסל בד' טפחים דאי איכא ד' טפחים מסכך פסול פסולה ואי ליכא אלא שיעור ג' טפחים מן סכך פסול כשר אע"ג דאי הוי אויר ג' טפחים היה פסול לא אמרינן סכך פסול כמאן דליתא אלא סכך פסול בג' מכשיר דבר הפסול אם היה אויר הכא נמי קרובין אע"ג דכמאן דליתנהו דמי כשר: איבעיא להו ב' שיטין שאמרו. דפסולין מי בעינן הן ואורין לאותו אויר שבין כתיבת שיטה לשיטה דכל כך ליהוו מרווחין הן ואורין או הן בלא אורין אפ"ה פסול:

הגהות הב"ח

(א) גמ' שני שיטין מן הכתב פסול הא שיטה: (ב) רשב"ם ד"ה הכי גרסינן וכו' ונמצאו שנים: (ג) תוס' ד"ה איבעיא להו וכו' היכא דמסיים השטר באמצע השיטה והניחו העדים אותה חצי: (ד) בא"ד והניחו השיטה שלימה וחתמו באמצע: (ה) בא"ד מיהו נראה דה"ה נמי פשיטא דכשר דה"ה דאין למדין משיטה: (ו) בא"ד והרחיק שיטה אחת דמיירי בעובי קו מיבעי ליה נמי בהרחיק שיטה ומחצה בעובי כזה מהו וכו' או דלמא בדוחק יכתוב: (ז) ד"ה אלא וכו' כשיטה אחת דכשר דמי כל"ל ותיבת דקאמר נמחק: (ח) ד"ה דאמר וכו' ואי משום דמופלג שני שיטין פסול: (ט) בא"ד שגורס בברייתא ונמצאו שנים הראשונים קרובים או פסולים מסייע ליה: (י) בא"ד כשנמצאו הקרובים בסוף עדים כשרים אבל נמצאו למעלה: (כ) בא"ד וקאמר סתמא היו ארבעה או חמשה ונמצאו קרובים או וכו' ש"מ אי חתים קרוב בין בתחלה בין באמצע וכו' קבע ליה מקום: (ל) בא"ד גבי פלגותא דר"ע ובן ננס אבל ההוא דחזקיה: (מ) בא"ד קרוב או פסול ואמרי לה פסול ואמרי לה כשר ומוכח התם דלכ"ע וכו' אי לא דאתי לאחלופי בקיום שטרות דעלמא: (נ) בא"ד מה שירלה בחצי השיטה עד כאן הג"ה: (ס) ד"ה ואל תתמה וכו' וי"ל דהכי קאמר וכו' ...

א) [בערוך ערך דיו א' גרס דמדיית ליה פי' דמדיית בדיו החלק כלומר עושה נקודים של דיו בין העדים לאשרתא עכ"ל]: ב) [לקמן קסו.]: (ג)[רשב"א מה"ד]: ג) [גיטין כח:]:

הֵן וַאֲוִירָן, אוֹ דִּלְמָא הֵן וְלֹא אֲוִירָן? א"ר נַחְמָן בַּר יִצְחָק: [א]מִסְתַּבְּרָא דְּהֵן וַאֲוִירָן, דְּאִי סָלְקָא דַעְתָּךְ הֵן וְלֹא אֲוִירָן, (א) שִׁיטָּה אַחַת בְּלָא אֲוִירָה לְמַאי חַזְיָא? אֶלָּא ש"מ הֵן וַאֲוִירָן, שְׁמַע מִינָּהּ. רַבִּי שַׁבְּתַי אָמַר מִשְּׁמֵיהּ דְּחִזְקִיָּה: [ב]שְׁנֵי שִׁיטִין שֶׁאָמְרוּ – בִּכְתַב יְדֵי עֵדִים וְלֹא כְּתַב יְדֵי סוֹפֵר; מ"ט? דְּכָל הַמְזַיֵּיף, לָאו לְגַבֵּי סָפְרָא אָזֵיל וּמְזַיֵּיף. וְכַמָּה? אָמַר (ב) רַב יִצְחָק בֶּן אֶלְעָזָר: כְּגוֹן "לַךְ לַךְ" זֶה עַל גַּבֵּי זֶה; אַלְמָא קָסָבַר: שְׁנֵי שִׁיטִין וְאַרְבָּעָה אֲוִירִין. רַב חִיָּיא בַּר אַמִּי מִשְּׁמֵיהּ דְּעוּלָּא אָמַר: [ג]כְּגוֹן לָמֶ"ד מִלְּמַעְלָה וְכ"ף מִלְּמַטָּה; אַלְמָא קָסָבַר: שְׁנֵי שִׁיטִין וּשְׁלֹשָׁה אֲוִירִין. רַבִּי אַבָּהוּ אָמַר: כְּגוֹן "בָּרוּךְ בֶּן לֵוִי" בְּשִׁיטָּה אַחַת; קָא סָבַר: שִׁיטָּה אַחַת וּשְׁנֵי אֲוִירִין. אָמַר רַב: לֹא שָׁנוּ אֶלָּא בֵּין עֵדִים לַכְּתָב, אֲבָל בֵּין עֵדִים לָאַשְׁרָתָא – אֲפִילּוּ טוּבָא נַמִי כָּשֵׁר. מַאי שְׁנָא בֵּין עֵדִים לַכְּתָב – דִּלְמָא מְזַיֵּיף וְכָתַב מַאי דְּבָעֵי וַחֲתִימִי סָהֲדֵי; בֵּין עֵדִים לָאַשְׁרָתָא נַמִי מְזַיֵּיף וְכָתַב מַאי דְּבָעֵי וַחֲתִימִי סָהֲדֵי! א)[ד]דִּמְטַיֵּיט לֵיהּ. א"ה, בֵּין עֵדִים לַשְּׁטָר נַמִי מְטַיֵּיט לֵיהּ! [ה]אָמְרִי: סָהֲדֵי אַטִּיּוּטָא הוּא דַּחֲתִימִי. בֵּין עֵדִים לָאַשְׁרָתָא נַמִי, אָמְרִי: בֵּי דִינָא אַטִּיּוּטָא הוּא דַּחֲתִימִי! [ו]בֵּי דִינָא אַטִּיּוּטָא לָא חָתְמִי. וְלֵיחוּשׁ דִּלְמָא גָּיֵיז לֵיהּ לְעֵילָּא, וּמָחֵיק לֵיהּ לַטִּיּוּטָא וְכָתַב מַאי דְּבָעֵי וּמַחְתִּים סָהֲדֵי, וְאָמַר רַב: שְׁטָר הַבָּא הוּא וְעֵדָיו עַל הַמְּחָק – כָּשֵׁר!

הָנִיחָא

רשב"ם

הֵן וַאֲוִירָן. שִׁיעוּר כְּתִיבַת הַשִּׁיטִין וַאֲוִיר חָלָק בֵּינְתַיִם – נִפְסָל, אֲבָל פָּחוֹת מִיכָּן – אֵינוֹ נִפְסָל. ה"ג: דְּאִי סָלְקָא דַעְתָּךְ הֵן וְלֹא אֲוִירָן לְמַאי חַזְיָא. וַהֲלֹא נִיכָּר הַזִּיּוּף, לְפִי שֶׁצָּרִיךְ לִכְתּוֹב אוֹתִיּוֹת דַּקּוֹת יוֹתֵר מִשְּׁאָר אוֹתִיּוֹת הַשְּׁטָר, כְּדֵי לָתֵת חָלָק בֵּין שִׁיטָה לְשִׁיטָה, וְאִם יִכְתּוֹב כְּתִיבָה גַּסָּה – גַּם עַתָּה נִיכָּר הַזִּיּוּף, שֶׁאֵין חָלָק בֵּינְתַיִם כִּשְׁאָר שִׁיטוֹת שֶׁבַּשְּׁטָר. שְׁנֵי שִׁיטִין שֶׁאָמְרוּ. כְּשִׁיעוּר כְּתַב יְדֵי עֵדִים, שֶׁהוּא יוֹתֵר מִכְּדֵי שִׁיעוּר יְדֵי סוֹפֵר. מַאי טַעְמָא כָּל דִּמְזַיֵּיף לָאו לְגַבֵּי סוֹפֵר אָזֵיל. אוּלַי לֹא יֹאבֶה לוֹ וְלֹא יִשְׁמַע אֵלָיו לְאוֹרוּעֵי נַפְשֵׁיהּ, אֶלָּא עוֹשֶׂה בְּצִינְעָא בְּתוֹךְ בֵּיתוֹ, וְאֵינוֹ יוֹדֵעַ לְכַוֵּין יָדוֹ בִּכְתִיבָה דַּקָּה כְּמוֹ הַסּוֹפֵר. כְּגוֹן לַךְ לַךְ זֶה עַל גַּב זֶה. לָא אָתָא לְאִיפְלוּגֵי אַדְּחִזְקִיָּה. אֶלָּא וַדַּאי בִּכְתַב יְדֵי עֵדִים מְשַׁעֲרִין כְּתִיבַת שְׁנֵי הַשִּׁיטִין חָלָק, וַעֲדַיִין צָרִיךְ אֲוִיר בֵּין שִׁיטָה לְשִׁיטָה מִלְּבַד עוֹבִי הַכְּתִיבָה, כְּדֵי שֶׁאִם יִהְיוּ שְׁנֵי "לַךְ" בִּשְׁנֵי הַשִּׁיטִין זֶה בָּעֶלְיוֹנָה וְזֶה בַּתַּחְתּוֹנָה – צָרִיךְ שֶׁלֹּא יִגַּע מֶשֶׁךְ גּוֹבַהּ הַלָּמֶ"ד שֶׁל "לַךְ" הַתַּחְתּוֹן לְהַגִּיעַ בַּךְ' שֶׁל "לַךְ" הָעֶלְיוֹן, דְּהָא זִימְנִין (ג) דְּמִינַּהְדְּדִי בַּהֲדֵי הֲדָדֵי ך' דְּשִׁיטָה עֶלְיוֹנָה וְלָמֶ"ד דְּשִׁיטָה הַתַּחְתּוֹנָה. אַלְמָא קָסָבַר שְׁנֵי שִׁיטִין וְד' אֲוִירִין. שְׁנֵי אֲוִירוֹת בֵּין שְׁנֵי הַשִּׁיטִין, מִשּׁוּם כ' דְּעֶלְיוֹנָה וְלָמֶ"ד דְּתַחְתּוֹנָה. וַאֲוִיר לְמַעְלָה מִשִּׁיטָה עֶלְיוֹנָה בִּשְׁבִיל גּוֹבַהּ לָמֶ"ד שֶׁל "לַךְ" הָעֶלְיוֹן, וַאֲוִיר לְמַטָּה מִן הַשְּׁנִיָּה בִּשְׁבִיל (ד) "לַךְ" הַתַּחְתּוֹן. וְ"לַךְ" "לַךְ" זֶה עַל גַּב זֶה – לָאו דַּוְקָא שֶׁתְּהֵא לָמֶ"ד כְּנֶגֶד לָמֶ"ד וְכ' כְּנֶגֶד כ', אֶלָּא כִּדְפְרִישִׁית, שֶׁזֶּה לְמַעְלָה בָּעֶלְיוֹנָה וְזֶה לְמַטָּה בַּתַּחְתּוֹנָה. וּשְׁלֹשָׁה אֲוִירִין. דְּבֵין שְׁנֵי הַשִּׁיטִין דַּי לָנוּ בַּאֲוִיר אֶחָד, שֶׁיָּכוֹל לְאַמֵּן אֶת יָדוֹ לְהַרְחִיק רֹאשׁ הַלָּמֶ"ד דְּתַחְתּוֹנָה מִכְּנֶגֶד רֶגֶל כ' הָעֶלְיוֹנָה. בָּרוּךְ בֶּן לֵוִי. שְׁנֵי אֲוִירִין אִיכָּא הָכָא, אֶחָד לְמַעְלָה בִּשְׁבִיל לָמֶ"ד דְּלֵוִי וְחַד לְמַטָּה בִּשְׁבִיל כ' דְּבָרוּךְ. אָמַר רַב לֹא שָׁנוּ. שְׁנֵי שִׁיטִין דְּפָסוּל, אא"כ הִרְחִיק בֵּין הָעֵדִים לַשְּׁטָר. אֲבָל אִם הוּא בֵּין הָעֵדִים לַקִּיּוּם, הַנִּקְרָא אַשְׁרָתָא עַל שֵׁם "וְאִישַּׁרְנוּהוּ וְקַיֵּימְנוּהוּ" הַכָּתוּב בּוֹ, כְּגוֹן שְׁטָר שֶׁכָּתַב בּוֹ הֶנְפֵּק דְּהַיְינוּ אַשְׁרָתָא – אֲפִילּוּ הִרְחִיק יוֹתֵר מִשְּׁנֵי שִׁיטִין כָּשֵׁר, כִּדְמַפֵּיק וְאָזֵיל – בִּמְטַשְׁטְשׁוֹ בִּדְיוֹ, וּסְתָם ב"ד אַטִּיּוּטָא לָא חָתְמִי, אֶלָּא אָעִיקָּרוֹ שֶׁל שְׁטָר. וּמְשַׁנֵּי: דִּמְטַיֵּיט לֵיהּ. כְּלוֹמַר, מְלַכְלְכוֹ בִּדְיוֹ, וְאֵין יָכוֹל לִכְתּוֹב בּוֹ שׁוּם זִיּוּף. אֲבָל אִם בָּא הֶנְפֵּק לְפָנֵינוּ וְיֵשׁ בּוֹ שְׁנֵי שִׁיטִין חָלָק בְּלֹא טִיאוּט – פָּסוּל הוּא, שֶׁלֹּא נַעֲשָׂה כְּתִיקּוּן חֲכָמִים. אַטִּיּוּטָא חָתְמִי. וְלֹא אָעִיקַּר שֶׁל שְׁטָר. כִּדְאָמְרִי' בְּגִיטִּין (דף פז.): ב) חָיְישִׁינַן שֶׁמָּא אַשְּׁאִילַת שָׁלוֹם שֶׁכָּתַב בַּשְּׁטָר חָתְמוּ, וְלֹא אָעִיקָּרוֹ שֶׁל שְׁטָר – הָכָא נַמִי כָּךְ מְעִידִין: בְּפָנֵינוּ אֲטַיֵּיט בִּדְיוֹ וְנִמְחַק, כְּדֵי שֶׁלֹּא יַחְשְׁדוּ בְּבַעַל הַשְּׁטָר. וּמְשַׁנֵּי: בֵּי דִינָא אַטִּיּוּטָא. אֵין דַּרְכָּן לַחְתּוֹם. אֲבָל עֵדִים – הַכֹּל מְלוּוִין לַחְתּוֹם, וַאֲפִי' עַמֵּי הָאָרֶץ, וְאָתֵי לְמֵיחְתַּם אַטִּיּוּטָא. וְנֵיחוּשׁ דִּלְמָא גָּיֵיז לֵיהּ. לַשְּׁטָר הָעֶלְיוֹן לְגַמְרֵי, וּמָחֵיק לֵיהּ לְטִיּוּטָא, וְכָתַב הוּא (ה) וְהַלְוָאָתוֹ וְעֵדָיו מְזוּיָּיפִין עַל הַמְּחָק. דְּאָמַר רַב שְׁטָר הַבָּא הוּא וְעֵדָיו עַל הַמְּחָק כָּשֵׁר. דְּמָה לִּי אִם חָתְמוּ עֵדִים עַל קְלָף חָלָק אוֹ עַל הַקְּלָף שָׁחוֹר, הוֹאִיל וְאָנוּ מַכִּירִין חֲתִימַת יְדֵיהֶן, וְגַם הָעֶלְיוֹן לֹא נִמְחַק אֶלָּא פַּעַם אַחַת כְּמוֹ מָקוֹם שֶׁהָעֵדִים חוֹתְמִין בּוֹ. (ו) וְגַבֵּי אַשְׁרָתָא, אע"פ שֶׁאֵין אָנוּ מַכִּירִין יְדֵי עֵדִים שֶׁלְּמַעְלָה שֶׁעַל הַמְּחָק – נִסְמָךְ עַל אַשְׁרָתָא שֶׁאַחֲרָיו שֶׁמִּתְקַיֶּימֶת עֵדוּתָן, וְהִלְכָּךְ יָכוֹל לִמְחוֹק הַטִּיּוּטָא, וּלְזַיֵּיף עֵדִים.

הָנִיחָא

תוספות

בתחלה — כשר, כדאמרינן לכוב חתמו. אבל אי חתימי בסוף — פסול. ואין נראה לר"ת, דאמר ב"המביא תניין" (גיטין דף יח: ושם): למאן דאמר שנים משום עדים וכולם משום תנאי, (ז) ולכך נמצא בסוף אחד מהם קרוב או פסול — כשר, אבל אי חתים בתחלה קרוב או פסול — אמרי לה פסול, אמרי לה כשר; מאן דאמר פסול — דאתי לאחלופי בשאר שטרות דעלמא, (ח) ולא יאמרו משום תנאי חתמו, כיון שהפסולים חתמו לכתחלה. אלמא, אפילו למאן דמכשיר בסוף — פסול לכתחלה. [וא"כ הכא] בין בתחלה בין בסוף כשר. והראשונים דגרס רבינו חננאל — לאו דוקא, אלא כל שכן הוא, אע"ג שאויר פסול. וא"ת: א"כ, אמאי כשר (ט) ולא אתי לאיחלופי בקיום שטרות דעלמא כדהתם? וי"ל: התם, מדרבנן דפסלי בתחלה משום לעדי הגט אין חותמין אלא זה בפני זה, ואי חתים בתחלה קרוב או פסול, יאמרו איך העדים העומדים שם: קרובים לשם עדות חתמו. שיכולים לחתום בתחלה אותם עדים כשרים שהיו שם וחתמו קרובים, ואתי לאכשורי קרובים. אבל בסוף — יאמרו: ב' לשם עדים, ואיך משום (י) תנאים. אבל בשאר שטרות שחותמין זה שלא בפני זה, אם נמצא פסול בתחלה — כשר, דלא אתי לאכשורי בעלמא. שידעו שלא לשם עדות חתמו, אלא כמו שמלאם החתימו, ובשעה שחתמו אלו הראשונים לא מלאו אחרים עד אחרי כן. והקשה לו ר"י: אם כן, אמאי כשרים כשנמלאו בסוף? הא אמרינן לקמן: כל כי האי גוונא אין מקיימין מעדים שלמטה — (כ) מכלל דבעלמא אין מקיימין אלא מעדים שלמטה. וא"כ, כשיראו פסולין לבסוף במקום קיום השטר — יאמרו: קרוב או פסול כשר.

וחזר בו ר"ת, ואין מכשיר כי אם בתחלה ולא בסוף, מפני שקיום השטר בסוף, כדפסיק רב יהודאי. אבל קשה מגט קרח (גיטין דף פב.) שאנו מכשירין בין בתחלה בין בסוף! וי"ל: דשאני התם דמכל תלתא מקיימין, ולא סגי בקיומא דהכא, כדמפרש התם. אבל בפשוטים, שאנו מקיימין מהשלמטה בתרי — פסול לבסוף.

שיטה אחת למאי חזיא. (ל) אי מזייף ביה וכתב ביה שני שיטין דקות — יהא ניכר שהוא מזויף, שהכך שני שיטין דקות משאר השטר. ועוד, דלא אזיל לגבי ספרא לכתוב כתיבה דקה, ואפילו אי בעי גייז ליה. ויש מפרשים: שיטה אחת בלא אוירה למאי חזיא — אין יכול לכתוב בה כלום, ואמאי אצטריך למימר הרחיק שיטה(מ) כשר? אבל לא בעי למיפרך: שני שיטין למאי חזיין. דטובא חזיין — לכתוב בו שיטה אחת, ונימא דלמדין משיטה אחרונה. דהא דאמר לעיל אין למדין — היינו למסקנא (נ) הכא דמסיק הן ואוירן, דחזו לכתוב שני שיטין דאחת, ואוירא חזיא לכתוב אחת, ולכך אין למדין. אבל מקמי דמסיק הן ואוירן — יש ללמוד אדרבה דלמדין, מדפסול הרחיק שני שיטין בלא אוירן.

כגון לך לך זה על גב זה. א"צ לפרש שרגל הכ"ף על ראש הלמ"ד, אלא אפי' לא הוי רגל הכ"ף נגד ראש למ"ד, אפ"ה הוי ד' אוירין. שאויר אחד צריך להיות בין ב' שיטין בלא רגל כ"ף וראש למ"ד, כדאמר: כגון ל' למעלה וכ"ף למטה, וקסבר ב' שיטין וג' אוירין — אלמא צריך להיות אויר בין שיטה לשיטה. ועוד אויר אחר מפני רגל כ"ף שבשיטה ראשונה, או מפני ראש למ"ד שבשיטה שניה — הוי ב' אוירין בין שיטה לשיטה. ולאו ראיה היא, דא"כ למה צריך אויר שני? באויר ראשון יכולין להיות ראש למ"ד ורגל כ"ף, כיון שאינן זה כנגד זה! אלא צריך לפרש שהן זה כנגד זה "לך" "לך", דלא יתחיל לזייף אם אין בינתים ריות, שאם יארע "לך" "לך" זה כנגד זה בזיופו, שיוכל לעשותו בריות(ס). *שיטה אחת ושני אוירין — והוי יותר משני שיטין בלא אוירן, דא"כ שיטה למאי חזיא? כדפריך לעיל. **דמטייט** ליה. פי' ר"ת: בנקודות או שורות, שניכר (ע) בחלק מעט ניכר שלא מחק מעיקרא. שאם היה מטשטשו בדיו ואין ניכר אם היה שם מחק אם לא, ואפ"ה מכשר לשטרא — א"כ יטשטש כל השטר לגמרי, וגם העדים שלמטה, ויכתוב שטר בגליון של מעלה, ויזייף עדים, והאשרתא של מטה (פ) מקיימן. ואם אין גליון למעלה ויש שיטה אחת בין העדים לכתב — יכתוב השטר ועדים באותה שיטה, והעדים הראשונים יטשטש בדיו, והאשרתא מקיימת בעדים שזייף. להכי צריך לפרש טיוט אנקודות או שורות. **שטר** הבא הוא ועדיו על המחק כשר. (צ) דהא דפסלינן בגיטין (דף כא:) שטר הבא על המחק היינו כשעדיו על הנייר. *ר' יוחנן אומר כו'. (ק) *תימה: דמשמע דאתא לפלוגי, ובמאי פליג? דהא לא פסיל אלא בלא טיוט, דאי בטיוט — אמאי פסול? וכ"ת: איכא בינייהו, דרבי יוחנן פסיל אפילו בטיוטא שני שיטין בין עדים לאשרתא, משום דימחקס ויכתוב הוא שטר ועדים על המחק, והאשרתא מקיימן, דסבירא דמקיימין מן האשרתא שבו — הא ליכא למימר, דא"כ כל שטרות שיש בהן

רבינו גרשום

שיטה אחת דאמרו. הרחיק שיטה אחת כשירה. פשיטא דכשר דלמאי חזיא הא לא מצי לזיופי דניכרת הואי הכתיבה שהיא דקה יותר מן האחרת: ב' שיטין שאמרו. פסול צריך שיהיו רחבות ככתב ידי עדים דלא בקיאי בכתיבה דצריך הרווחה טפי מסופר אומן דיודע ליישב ולצמצם כתיבתו אבל הני שיטין מקמי דליהוי פסולות צריך הרווחה טפי מאי טעמא משום דכל דמזייף לאו לגבי ספרא אזיל דמזייף ליה דסופר לא מזייף אלא הוא עצמו מזייף בצנעא בביתו ולמי שאינו מומחה בכתיבה צריך הרווחה טפי: כגון לך לך זה על גב זה. דאיכא במשך ל' מלמעלה אויר אחד ובמשך כ' מלמטה אויר אחד והכי נמי לאידך לך דהיינו ב' שיטין וד' אוירין והואיל דאיכא הרווחה כולי האי מצי מזייף ליה בכתב ידי כל אדם א) דפסול: כגון ל' מלמעלה וכ' למטה. בשני שיטין: קא סבר ב' שיטין וג' אוירין. משך ל' מלמעלה דשיטה ראשונה דהיינו אויר אחד ומשך כ' למטה משיטה שניה ב) אין תופשין אלא באויר אחד לפי שצוארו של למ"ד הוא משוך אחר כרעיה דכ' ולא מתחת רגליו: כגון ברוך בן לוי בשיטה אחת. היינו שיטה אחת וב' אוירין משך כרעיה דכ' מלמטה ול' של לוי למעלה דהשתא מצי מזייף ומשום הכי פסול: אמר רב לא שנו. אם הרחיק העדים מן הכתב ב' שיטין דפסול: אלא בין עדים לשטר. דהשתא איכא הרווחה ומצי מזייף וכיון דעדים חתימי מלמטה אתי וגבי שלא כדין: אבל אי שבק הרווחה בין חתימת העדים לאשרתא. שאם כתב למטה בגוילין אשראי קיום בית דין שטרא דקא נפק לקדמנא ואשרנוהו וקיימנוהו אפי' נמצא נמי שהניח בין עדים לאשרא שיעור ד' או ה' שיטות כשר: מאי שנא בין עדי' לשטר. שיעור ב' שיטין דפסול. דילמא מזייף וכתב. בין עדים לשטרא וגבי מכח אותו קיום בית דין של מטה דמשמע דקיימו כל מה שכתוב בשטר. ומשני [משום] הכי כשר דאותו חלק שבין העדים לאשרא דמטשטש ליה מטשטשו כולו בדיו שאין יכול לכתוב בו על גביו שום זיוף. ומקשי' בין עדים לשטר אמאי בב' שיטין פסול הא מצי מטייט ליה לאותו חלק בדיו דאינו יכול לזייף באותו מקום כלום. ומשני אי מטייט ליה בדיו בין כתב לעדים אמרי אינשי עדים אטיוטא מסהדי על מה שעל גבי חתימתן ולא על מה שכתוב בשטר ופסול השטר וכדאמר בדוכתא אחריתי אשאילת שלום חתימי כגון אם כתב בשטר פלוני אמר לנו כתבו וחתמו לפלוני שאני חייב לו מנה וכתבו בו שאני שואל בשלומו פסול השטר דאיכא למימר עדים אשאילת שלום חתימי ולאו אאותו מנה הכא נמי איכא למימר עדים לאו אשטר חתימי אלא אההוא טיוטא ופסול ומשום הכי לא מטייטינן ליה. ומקשינן בין עדים לאשרא נמי אמאי מצי לטייט הא איכא נמי למימר בי דינא אטיוטא הוא דחתימי ולא קיימו שאר השטר. ומשני הא ליכא למימר דוודאי גבי עדים דיש מהם עמי הארץ ולא דייקי חתמי אבטלה ואפי' אטיוטא אבל גבי בי דינא ליכא למימר הכי דאינהו אטיוטא שאינה כלום לא חתמי אלא אגופו של שטר קיימי וחתמו ומשום הכי מצי לשייר אפי' טובא ובלבד דמטייט ליה. ומקשי' ואכתי אמאי מצי לשיורי בין עדים לאשרא אפי' טובא אע"ג דמטייט ליה וליחוש דילמא גייז מלוה השטר עם העדים ושדי ליה ומחיק ליה לטיוטא שעל גבי אשרא וכתב מאי דבעי במקום שהיה בו הטיוטא ויכתוב כפלים ממה שהיה בשטר ומחתים איהו גופיה סהדי אחרינא על מה שכתוב בטיוטא. ואמר רב שטר הבא הוא ועדיו על המחק כשר ועוד שכתוב תחתיו אשרא שקיימו השטר וחתימת עדים וגבי ביה שלא כדין:

הניחא

עין משפט נר מצוה

יד א מיי' פכ"ז מהל' מלוה ולוה הל' ד סמג עשין לד טוש"ע ח"מ סי' מה סעיף ט:

טו ב מיי' שם טוש"ע שם ס"ח:

טז ג מיי' שם טוש"ע שם סעיף ט:

יז ד מיי' שם הל' ז וסמג שם טוש"ע שם סי' מו סעיף לב:

יח ה מיי' שם הל' י וסמג שם טוש"ע ח"מ סי' מה סעיף ו:

יט ו מיי' שם הל' ז וסמג שם טוש"ע ח"מ סי' מו סעיף לב:

הגהות הב"ח

(א) גמ' הן ולא אוירן (שיטה אחת בלא אוירה) תא"מ ונ"ב לפי' רשב"ם ל"ג ליה: (ב) שם רבי יצחק: (ג) רשב"ם ד"ה כגון לך וכו' דהא זימנין דמיהגדזין בהדי הדדי. נ"ב לשון התלמוד בפא"ע לגבי שני שורות הוושט שניקבו זה שלא כנגד זה לטרפה משום דזימנין דמהגדזין בהדי הדדי ופרש"י ז"ל מתרמי למיכווני אהדדי: (ד) ד"ה אלמא וכו' בשביל ך' של לך התחתון: (ה) ד"ה וניחוש כו' וכתב הוא הלוואתו כצ"ל: (ו) ד"ה דאמר רב וכו' ולגבי אשרתא אע"פ וכו' שמקיימת עדותן: (ז) תוס' ד"ה (בכף הקודם) נמלא כו' ואין נראה לר"ת כו' הלכך נמלא בסוף אחד מהם קרוב. נ"ב עי' מ"ש התוס' בגיטין וז"ל ואומר ר"ת דאפילו מאן דפסיל הכא לא פסיל אלא בתחלה כו' ולאחר שחזר ר"ת צריך לפרש נמי דאפי' מאן דמכשיר התם לא מכשיר אלא בתחלה אבל בסוף פסול לכ"ע וכ"כ התוס' להדיא בפ"ב דגיטין דף י"ח בד"ה אמרי לה: (ח) בא"ד שלא יאמרו משום תנאי וכו' חתמו בתחלה אלמא וכו' פסיל בתחלה: (ט) בא"ד וא"ת א"כ אמאי כשר הכא ולא אתי וכו' וי"ל התם דפסלינן בתחלה מדרבנן משום לעדי הגט: (י) בא"ד ואיך משום תנאי אבל: (כ) בא"ד מעדים שלמטה כו' מכלל: (ל) ד"ה שיטה וכו' לאי מזייף וכתב ביה וכו' שהוא מזויף כיון שהכך שני שיטין דקות יותר משאר אותיות השטר כצ"ל: [illegible]

עין משפט נר מצוה

כ א מיי' פכ"ז מהל' מלוה ולוה הל' י סמג עשין לד טוש"ע ח"מ סי' מו סעיף לג:
כא ב ג מיי' שם הל' ו טוש"ע שם סעיף לא:
כב ד מיי' שם הל' ד וסמג שם טוש"ע ח"מ סי' מה סעיף יט:
כג ה מיי' שם הל' ה טוש"ע שם סעיף יח:
כד ו מיי' שם טוש"ע שם סעיף יט:
כה ז מיי' שם הל' ט טוש"ע שם סעיף כ:

הָנִיחָא לְרַב כָּהֲנָא דְּמַתְנֵי לָהּ מִשְּׁמֵיהּ דִּשְׁמוּאֵל — שַׁפִּיר, אֶלָּא לְרַב טַבְיוֹמֵי דְּמַתְנֵי לָהּ מִשְּׁמֵיהּ דְּרַב — מַאי אִיכָּא לְמֵימַר? קָסָבַר: כָּל כִּי הַאי גַּוְונָא, [א]אֵין מְקַיְּימִין אוֹתוֹ מִן הָאַשַּׁרְתָּא שֶׁבּוֹ, אֶלָּא מִן הָעֵדִים שֶׁבּוֹ. וְרַבִּי יוֹחָנָן אָמַר: לֹא שָׁנוּ אֶלָּא בֵּין הָעֵדִים לַכְּתָב, אֲבָל בֵּין עֵדִים לָאַשַּׁרְתָּא — [ב]אֲפִילּוּ שִׁיטָּה אַחַת (א) פָּסוּל. מַאי שְׁנָא בֵּין עֵדִים לָאַשַּׁרְתָּא? [ג]דִּלְמָא גָּיֵיז לְעִילָּאֵי וְכָתַב הוּא וְעֵדָיו בְּשִׁיטָּה אַחַת, וְקָסָבַר: [ד]שְׁטָר הַבָּא הוּא וְעֵדָיו בְּשִׁיטָּה אַחַת — כָּשֵׁר; אִי הָכִי, בֵּין עֵדִים לַכְּתָב נַמִי, דִּלְמָא גָּיֵיז לֵיהּ לְעִילָּאֵי וְכָתַב מַאי דְּבָעֵי וַחֲתִימֵי סָהֲדֵי! [ה]קָא סָבַר: שְׁטָר הַבָּא הוּא בְּשִׁיטָּה אַחַת וְעֵדָיו בְּשִׁיטָּה אַחֶרֶת — פָּסוּל. וְלֵיחוּשׁ דִּלְמָא כָּתַב הוּא וְעֵדָיו בְּשִׁיטָּה אַחַת, וְאָמַר: אֲנָא לְרַבּוֹת בְּעֵדִים הוּא דַּעֲבַדִי! [ו]קָסָבַר: כָּל כִּי הַאי גַּוְונָא, אֵין מְקַיְּימִין אוֹתוֹ מִן הָעֵדִים שֶׁלְּמַטָּה אֶלָּא מִן הָעֵדִים שֶׁלְּמַעְלָה. גּוּפָא, אָמַר רַב: [ז]שְׁטָר הַבָּא הוּא וְעֵדָיו עַל הַמְּחָק — כָּשֵׁר. וְאִם

רשב"ם

הָנִיחָא לְרַב כָּהֲנָא דְּמַתְנֵי לָהּ. לְהָא דְּהוּא וְעֵדָיו עַל הַמְּחָק מִשְּׁמֵיהּ דִּשְׁמוּאֵל, אִיכָּא לְמֵימַר דִּלְרַב הָוֵי פָּסוּל, וְלֹא תִּקְשֶׁה לְרַב. אֶלָּא לְרַב טַבְיוֹמֵי כו'. וְהַךְ קַשְׁיָא בְּכָל הַשְּׁטָרוֹת שֶׁיֵּשׁ בְּהוּ הֶנְפֵּק יָכוֹל לְהַקְשׁוֹת, וַאֲפִי' הֵיכָא דְּלֵיכָּא שְׁנֵי שִׁיטִּין חָלָק בֵּין עֵדִים לִשְׁטַר אַשַּׁרְתָּא, שֶׁהֲרֵי יָכוֹל לְזַיֵּיף כָּל שְׁטָר הָעֶלְיוֹן עִם הָעֵדִים, וְלִכְתּוֹב וְלַחְתּוֹם עַל הַמְּחָק מַה שֶּׁיִּרְצֶה. וּמְשַׁנֵּינַן: קָסָבַר רַב כָּל כִּי הַאי גַּוְונָא. כְּלוֹמַר, כָּל שְׁטָר שֶׁיֵּשׁ בּוֹ הֶנְפֵּק וְהוּא וְעֵדָיו עַל הַמְּחָק — לָא סָמְכִינַן אַאַשַּׁרְתָּא, וְלֹא מִתְקַיֵּים אֶלָּא בְּהַכָּרַת יְדֵי עֵדִים הַכְּתוּבִים עַל הַמְּחָק. וְהִלְכָּךְ, הִרְחִיק שְׁנֵי שִׁיטִּין אֶת הָאַשַּׁרְתָּא מִן הָעֵדִים מִלְמַעְלָה וְטִיְּיטוֹ — כָּשֵׁר, וְסָמְכִינַן אַאַשַּׁרְתָּא, דְּהָא לָא כְּתִיבֵי הוּא וְעֵדָיו עַל הַמְּחָק דְּנֵימָא כִּי הַאי גַּוְונָא אֵין מְקַיְּימִין, וּבֵית דִּין אַטִּיּוּטָא לָא חֲתִימֵי אֶלָּא אַעִיקַּר הַשְּׁטָר. הִלְכָּךְ כָּשֵׁר הַשְּׁטָר וְהָאַשַּׁרְתָּא. וְר' יוֹחָנָן אוֹמֵר לֹא שָׁנוּ. הִרְחִיק אֶת הָעֵדִים כְּשִׁיעוּר שְׁנֵי שִׁיטִּין פָּסוּל. אֶלָּא בֵּין הָעֵדִים לַשְּׁטָר אֲבָל בֵּין הָעֵדִים לָאַשַּׁרְתָּא אֲפִי' שִׁיטָּה אַחַת פָּסוּל. וְאַע"ג דִּמְטַיֵּיט. וּמְפָרֵשׁ טַעְמָא דְּרַבִּי יוֹחָנָן, דְּקָסָבַר: שְׁטָר שֶׁכָּתוּב כּוּלּוֹ בְּשִׁיטָּה אַחַת, וְגַם הָעֵדִים חֲתוּמִין בְּאוֹתָהּ שִׁיטָּה — כָּשֵׁר. וְיָכוֹל לַחְתּוֹךְ אֶת הָעֶלְיוֹן, וְיִכְתּוֹב שְׁטָר וְעֵדִים (ב) פְּסוּלִים בְּאוֹתָהּ שִׁיטָּה, וְהָווּ נִסְמוֹךְ אָאַשַּׁרְתָּא לְקַיְּימָן. וְאִם הַשְּׁטָר כּוּלּוֹ בְּשִׁיטָּה אַחַת וְהָעֵדִים בְּשִׁיטָּה אַחֶרֶת — פָּסוּל. וְנִרְאֶה בְּעֵינַי טַעְמוֹ שֶׁל דָּבָר הוּא וְעֵדָיו בְּשִׁיטָּה אַחַת כָּשֵׁר — דְּלָא פְּלוּג רַבָּנַן בֵּין שְׁטָר גָּדוֹל לִשְׁטָר קָטָן שֶׁיְּהֵא קָטָן פָּסוּל יוֹתֵר מִן הַגָּדוֹל. אֲבָל אִם כּוּלּוֹ בְּשִׁיטָּה אַחַת, וְעֵדָיו בְּשִׁיטָּה אַחֶרֶת — פָּסוּל. וְהַיְינוּ טַעְמָא, דְּאָמְרִינַן לְעֵיל: הִרְחִיק שִׁיטָּה אַחַת חָלָק בֵּין שְׁטָר לָעֵדִים כָּשֵׁר, וְטַעְמָא כִּדְמַפְּקִינַן — אֵין לְמֵדִין מִשִּׁיטָּה אַחֲרוֹנָה. וְאִם אַתָּה אוֹמֵר כָּשֵׁר הֵיכָא דְּהַשְּׁטָר בְּשִׁיטָּה אַחַת וְעֵדָיו בְּשִׁיטָּה אַחֶרֶת — אִיכָּא לְמֵיחַשׁ דְּגָיֵיז לֵיהּ לְעִילָּאֵי, וְכָתַב בְּהַהִיא שִׁיטָּה חָלָק מַאי דְּבָעֵי, וְחָתְמֵי סָהֲדֵי. הוּא וְעֵדָיו. הַשְּׁטָר וְהָעֵדִים. וּמְשַׁנֵּי: קָסָבַר ר' יוֹחָנָן. שְׁטָר הַבָּא לְפָנֵינוּ בְּשִׁיטָּה אַחַת, וְעֵדִים בְּשִׁיטָּה אַחֶרֶת תַּחְתֶּיהָ — פָּסוּל, כִּדְפָרִישִׁית טַעְמָא — מִשּׁוּם דְּאֵין לְמֵדִין מִשִּׁיטָּה אַחֲרוֹנָה, כִּדְאָמְרִינַן לְעֵיל. (ג) וְדִלְמָא. הַיְינוּ הַךְ פִּירְכָא, דְּגָיֵיז לֵיהּ לְעִילָּאֵי וְכָתַב מַאי דְּבָעֵי וַחֲתִימֵי סָהֲדֵי. וְהָכִי פָּרֵיךְ: וְנֵיחוּשׁ וְדִלְמָא הַךְ חָלָק שֶׁהָיְתָה בֵּין שְׁטָר לָעֵדִים — זַיֵּיף בָּהּ, וְחָתַךְ אֶת הַשְּׁטָר מִלְמַעְלָה. וְדִלְמָא כְּתִיב בְּהַהִיא שִׁיטָּה חֲלָקָה שֶׁהִכְשַׁרְנוּ בֵּין הַשְּׁטָר לָעֵדִים כָּל מַאי דְּבָעֵי, וְחָתֵים נַמִי סָהֲדֵי בְּהַהִיא שִׁיטָּה, וְנִמְצָא שְׁטָר הַבָּא הוּא וְעֵדָיו בְּשִׁיטָּה אַחַת, וְכָשֵׁר. וְהָעֵדִים שֶׁלְּמַטָּה שֶׁל שִׁיטָּה הַהִיא, אוֹמֵר: הוֹסַפְתִּים עַל הָרִאשׁוֹנִים, לְפַרְסֵם אֶת הַדָּבָר יוֹתֵר. וּמְשַׁנֵּי: כָּל כִּי הַאי גַּוְונָא כו'. כְּלוֹמַר, כְּשֶׁיּוֹצִיא לְפָנֵינוּ שְׁטָר הַבָּא הוּא וְעֵדָיו בְּשִׁיטָּה אַחַת, וְיֵשׁ בּוֹ עוֹד תַּחַת אוֹתָהּ שִׁיטָּה עֵדִים אֲחֵרִים — אֵין מְקַיְּימִין אוֹתוֹ אֶלָּא מִן הָעֵדִים הַחֲתוּמִים עִמּוֹ בְּשִׁיטָּה אַחַת.

תוספות

בהן אשרתא — פסולין, שיכולין למחקו ויכתוב הוא ועדיו על המחק. אלא ודאי סבירא ליה דאין מקיימין בכי האי גוונא מאשרתא, אלא מן העדים. ויש לומר: דסבר ר' יוחנן אי מטייט ליה פסול, משום דבי דינא אטיוטא חתמי. אי נמי: איכא למימר דלא פליגי, אלא רב מיירי בטיוטא, ורבי יוחנן מיירי בלא טיוטא. (ד) א"נ, שיטה אחת בין עדים לאשרתא לרב כשר, דכל כה"ג אין מקיימין אותו מאשרתא, אלא מעדים שבו. עד כאן. **הניחא** לרב כהנא (ה) משמיה דשמואל קאמר ליה. קשה: דלדידיה מי ניחא? א"כ כל שטר מקוים ימחקנו! ויש לומר: דהא לא קשה כולי האי, דכיון שהיה כתוב מתחלה — לא יוכל למחקו שלא יהיו ניכרים האותיות. אבל מחק דטיוטא אינו ניכר, וימחקנה ויכתוב כמו שירלה. ואע"ג דבסמוך פריך: ואם תאמר חוזר ומוחק אע"פ שהיה מחוק — לפי האמת פריך, דאין חילוק בין טיוט לכתב. **שיטה** אחת נמי פסול. שיכתוב הוא ועדיו בשיטה אחת והאשרתא (ו) מקיימן. וא"ת: כי היכי דפסלינן שטר הבא הוא בשיטה אחת ועדיו בשיטה אחרת, משום שדרך עדים להרחיק חתימתן מן הכתב שיטה אחת — הכי נמי הוה לן למיפסל שטר הבא הוא ועדיו בשיטה אחת, משום שבית דין מרחיקין השיטה אחת מן העדים, ויכול לזייף באותה שיטה! ויש לומר: דסהדי לא דייקי לסמוך חתימתם, אבל ב"ד דייקי וחתמי סמוך לעדים. וכשהרחיקו שיטה אחת — פסול, שיכול לכתוב בה שטר הוא ועדיו בשיטה אחת, והאשרתא (ז) מקיימן. השתא דאתינן להכי, דפסלינן אותן שטרות שיכול לזייפינהו — א"כ לריך ליזהר באותן שטרות וכתובות שיש להן גליון, שלא יחתמו העדים זה אצל זה. שיכול לבא לידי זיוף, ולכתוב בגליון שבאורך העדים מה שירלה, והוי שטר הבא הוא ועדיו בשיטה אחת וכשר, ויחתוך כל השטר. אלא יחתמו זה תחת זה, דהשתא ליכא למיחש (ח). דאי משום שיכתוב בגליון שטר לפני העד "אני פלוני החתום חייב לפלוני מנה", והוי שטר הבא הוא והלוה בכתב ידו בשיטה אחת — משום הא לא פסלינן לשטרא, דאיהו העד הוא דאפסיד אנפשיה כשהאריך חתם במקום שיכול לזייף ולכתוב על עצמו מה שירלו. ואין לפסול השטר אלא כשיש חלק לפניהם והן חותמין זה אצל זה, שעתה יכול לעשות שטר שיש (ט) שני עדים להוליא מאחרים. אבל משום עצמו — לא, דאיהו הוא דאפסיד אנפשיה. וכן נמי אם אין גליון בשטר — לא יחתכו בסוף שיטה זה אצל זה כיון שיש חלק לפניהם, משום ההוא טעמא (י) שפירשתי, אלא זה תחת זה. אי נמי, מלינו למימר דאפי' יש גליון מרובה בראש (כ) השטר, והעדים חתומין זה אצל זה בראש שיטה של שטר — כשר, אע"פ דמלי כתיב מאי דבעי בראש גליון. דלא פסלינן שטר אלא כשיכול לזייף בחלק שהוא לורך השטר, שאינו יכול לחתכו, ואם היה חתוך היה השטר פסול, כגון שני שיטין לפני העדים, או (ל) לפני האשרתא בינו לעדים, וכגון חלק שהוא אחר השטר במקושר בסופו, שגם הוא לריך לשטר משום אשרתא. ולכך פריך לעיל: וניחוש דלמא זייף מאי דבעי כו'. אבל בחלק שאין לורך השטר, שאם היה נחתך לא היה השטר פסול, אע"ג שיכול לזייף בו מה שירלה — אין השטר פסול בכך, כגון חלק שבגליון. וגם רוב פעמים ששושבינין חותמין בכתובות זה תחת זה ומניחין חלק שני שיטין לפניהם. אלא ודאי אין בכך כלום, כיון שאין (מ) לורך השטר. (וגם קושיות שהקשו במשנה יש מהן מתורלין בתירוץ זה. עכ"ה). מיהו, אם חתמו בשטר בסוף שיטה זה אצל זה, והניחו חצי שיטה חלק לפניהם — פסול, לפי שיכולים לזייף באותו חלק. והוא לורך השטר, שאם היה נחתך — יהיה השטר פסול, דאמרינן: חלק היה *בשטר כתוב שהיו אלו העדים חתומין עליו, והוא חתכו, ועשה זה *השטר (נ) לפני העדים שיכולים להניח חלק לפניהם, כיון שאינו לורך השטר. אלא יש להן לחתום זה תחת זה. וא"ת: זה אינו לורך השטר, אותה חצי שיטה שלפני העדים, שאפי' חתוכה — אין לנו לחוש שגם היה השטר, שא"כ היה הלוה שוטה שעשה שטרו והניח חלק לפני העדים, שהמלוה היה יכול לכתוב שטר אחר כך ולחתוך זה! ויש לומר: שמא יש לנו לחוש שבאותו חתך היה שטר אחר, והניח הלוה חלק הרבה לפני העדים, לפי שחשב שאם יכתוב בו המלוה שטר אחר ויחתוך זה — יוודע זיופו (ס) ויהיה ניכר בחתוך שיש בסופו, מכל מקום לורך השטר הוא, ויש להם לעדים לחתום זה תחת זה אם חותמין בסוף שיטה ומניחין חלק לפניהם. ומ"מ, יש לומר שאין לורך השטר, שאפילו תהיה אותה חצי שיטה חלק חתוכה — יהא השטר כשר, ולא ניחוש שמא היה שם השטר שאלו העדים חתומין עליו, והמלוה כתב זה השטר — לזה אין לחוש, לפי שהלוה לא היה שוטה כל כך שהניח חלק למעלה מן העדים שיוכל המלוה לחתוך השטר הזה, וגם כל החלק שלמעלה בשוה לשטר זה, ולא ישאר חלק כי אם כנגד העדים, ויכתוב שם מאי דבעי ולא יהא ניכר זיופו. ולכך אינו [לורך] השטר, ויכולים לחתום זה אצל זה, אע"פ שמניחין חצי השיטה לפניהם שיכול לזייף בהן — בשביל כך אין לנו לפסול השטר, כיון שאינו לורך השטר, שאם היה חתוך — לא נפסל השטר בכך, שאי לחוש כלום, כדפרישית. ורבינו תם פסק כמו שפי' תחלה, שהעדים לריכין לחתום או ארישא דמגילתא אפילו זה אצל זה, או (ע) באמלע שיטה, וכ"כ שיחתמו זה תחת זה. ויש ליתן טעם בשושבינים שאין שייך באלו כלל, דהתם לא נפסל השטר בשביל השושבינים שחתומים רחוק שני שיטין, שאינם מן העדים, ואינם שייכין לשטר כלל. **גופא** אמר רב שטר הבא הוא ועדיו על המחק כשר. ואם תאמר: וניחוש שמא מעיקרא היה הוא על הנייר ועדיו על המחק (פ) *דפסול, ומחק כל השטר וכתב מאי דבעי, והוי על המחק! ויש לומר: להא ליכא למיחש, שאם מעיקרא הוה הוא על הנייר ועדיו על המחק — הוה כתוב בין סהדא לסהדא: "אנחנא סהדי

רש"ל למעלה בשטר כו' זה שטר

רש"ל דכשר

רבינו גרשום

הניחא לרב כהנא דמתני להא משמיה דשמואל. שטר הבא הוא ועדיו על המחק כשר: שפיר. דהשתא לא קשיא דרב אדרב דאמר לעיל לא שנו אלא בין עדים לשטר אבל בין עדים לאשרא אפי' טובא נמי כשר משום דמטייט ליה ולא חיישינן דלמא גייז ליה לעילאי ומחיק לטיוטא כו' משום דרב לא סבר כשמואל דאמר שטר הבא הוא ועדיו על המחק כשר אלא פסול ומשום הכי לא מחיק ליה מלוה ואפשר בתקנה דמטייט ליה ומיתוקמא מילתא דרב שפיר. אלא לרב טביומי דמתני לה משמיה דרב שטר הבא על המחק הוא ועדיו כשר השתא קשיא דרב אדרב הואיל דאמר בין עדים לאשרא אפילו טובא כשר אמאי הא אע"ג דמטייט ליה איכא למיחש דלמא גייז ליה. ומשני אפי' לרב טביומי מיתוקמא מילתא דרב שפיר דהיכא דמטייט ליה ליכא למיחש דמחיק לטיוטא דקסבר רב כל כי האי גוונא דשטר הבא הוא ועדיו על המחק א) כשר משום דאין מקיימין אותו שטר על מחק מן האשרא שבו שכתוב תחתיו אלא מן העדים שבו החתומים על המחק מקיימין אותו שאומרים לבעל השטר הבא עדים שמכירין חתימת העדים החתומים במקום מחק שהוא כתב ידן ואם לא יעידו עם מחק הוא. והואיל דאיצטריך לאייתי עדים לקיומי לא אתי למינז ואמנו להכי אפי' שייר טובא נמי לא מטייט ליה כשר דליכא למיחש דלמא מחיק ומזייף ליה: ור' יוחנן אמר לא שנו. דשביק ב) בין עדים לאשרא. אפי' שיטה ומחתים נמי עדיו באותה שיטה עצמה. וקא סבר ר' יוחנן שטר הבא הוא ועדיו בשיטה אחת כשר. ועוד שיש קיום השטר מלמטה משום הכי קאמר אפי' שיטה אחת בין עדים לאשרא פסול דלמא מזייף כי האי גוונא. אי הכי בין עדים לשטר אמאי בשיטה אחת כשר הא איכא למיחש דלמא גייז לעילאי כל כתיבת השטר וכתיב מאי דבעי בההיא שיטה כך חייב פלוני לפלוני והא חתימי סהדי בשיטה שניה שהיו חתומין ועומדין וגם קיום השטר שתחתיו. ומשני קסבר ר' יוחנן שטר הכתוב בשיטה אחת כשר (והאי) דאיכא למימר הכי מתרמי עובדא אבל להיכא דאיה בשיטה אחת ועדיו בשיטה אחרת פסול. ג) ואי אמרי' ליה אמאי חתימת העדים נמי בשיטה שניה אמר לרבות בעדים אנא עבדי כדי שיהא החוב מפורסם ואמאי כשר. קסבר ר' יוחנן כי האי גוונא אין מקיימין אותו שטר אלא מן העדים שלמעלה החתומין באותה שיטה של השטר אם יש עדים שמכירין שהיא כתיבת ידם כשר ואם לאו פסול: ואם

הגהות הב"ח

(א) גמ' אפי' שיטה אחת נמי פסול: (ב) רשב"ם ד"ה אלא בין וכו' שטר ועדיו באותה שיטה כנ"ל ותיבות פסולים נמחק: (ג) ד"ה וניחוש דלמא כו' היינו וכו' והכי פירוש וניחוש דלמא הך שיטה חלק: (ד) תוס' ד"ה (בע"א) ר' יוחנן וכו' מיירי בלא טיוטא הס"ד ואח"כ מתחיל הג"ה א"נ וכו' דכל כה"ג נמי אין מקיימי וכו' ע"כ הג"ה: (ה) ד"ה הניחא וכו' משמיה דשמואל קאמר ליה ספיר ק' וכו' אע"פ שהיה כתוב על מחוק: (ו) ד"ה שיטה וכו' והאשרתא מקיימא אותם ואח"כ: (ז) בא"ד והאשרתא מקיימת אותם השטה לאותיות. נ"ב ז"ל המרדכי כתב ר"י השטה לאותיות לאו להכי כו': (ח) בא"ד ליכא למיחש למידי דאי: (ט) בא"ד שיש בו שני עדים: (י) בא"ד ההוא טעמא גופיה שפירשתי: (כ) בא"ד גליון מרובה בראש השטר והעדים וכו': (ל) בא"ד שיטין לפני העדים או שיטה אחת לפני האשרתא וכו' אבל בחלק שאין בו לורך: (מ) בא"ד שאין לורך השטר: (נ) בא"ד ועשה זה השטר לפניהם [illegible] (ס) בא"ד [illegible] (ע) בא"ד או באמלע שיטה [illegible] (פ) ד"ה גופא וכו' ועדיו על המחק דכשר ומחק כל השטר וכתב מאי דבעי והוי הוא ועדיו על המחק וכו'.

א) נ"ל על המחק אין מקיימין אותו שטר וכו'. ב) נראה דל"ל היכא דשביק בין עדים לכתב אבל בין עדים לאשרא אפי' שיטה אחת פסול: דלמא גייז ליה לעילאי. ומחתים נמי עדים באותה שיטה וכו'. ג) נ"ל וליחוש דלמא כתב הוא ועדיו בשיטה אחת ואי אמרינן ליה וכו'.

עין משפט נר מצוה

כו א ב מיי' פכ"ז מהל' מלוה ולוה הלכה ט סמג עשין לד טוש"ע ח"מ סי' מה סעיף כ:

כז ג ד מיי' שם הל' יא טוש"ע שם סעיף כא:

כח ה ו ז מיי' שם הלכה יב טוש"ע שם סעיף כב:

כט ח שם סעיף בהג"ה:

מסורת הש"ס

א) [לעיל קלא: וש"נ]: ב) רש"ל כל כך ולהשהותו יבואו להכשיר: ג) רש"ל ונמחק בזיוף: ד) רש"ל זה: ה) רש"ל בשיטה בפני: ו) רש"ל בשביל א' וגי' כ"י ליכא למימר שיחתוך בשביל א': ז) רש"ל. ח) (רש"א רבי):

ואם תאמר: מוחק וחוזר ומוחק — [א]אינו דומה נמחק פעם אחת לנמחק שתי פעמים. וליחוש דלמא שדי דיותא אמקום עדים מעיקרא ומחיק ליה, דכי הדר מחיק ליה להאי, הוה ליה אידי ואידי נמחק שתי פעמים! אמר אביי, קסבר רב: [ב]אין העדים חותמין על המחק אלא אם כן נמחק בפניהם. מיתיבי: [ג]הוא על הנייר ועדיו על המחק — כשר; וניחוש דלמא מחיק ליה וכתיב מאי דבעי, והוי ליה הוא ועדיו על המחק! [ד]דכתבי הכי: "אנחנא סהדי חתמנא על מחקא ושטרא כתב על ניירא". דכתבי היכא? אי מלתחת — גייז ליה, אי עילאי — מחיק ליה! [ה]דכתבי בין סהדא לסהדא. אי הכי, אימא סיפא: [ו]הוא על המחק ועדיו על הנייר — פסול; אמאי פסול? הכא נמי נכתבו הכי: "אנחנא סהדי חתמנא על ניירא ושטרא על מחקא"! [השתא נמי] מאי אמרת? מוחק חוזר ומוחק — הא אמרת: אינו דומה נמחק פעם אחת לנמחק שתי פעמים! [ז]הני מילי היכא דחתימי סהדי אמחקא, היכא דלא חתימי סהדי אמחקא אלא אניירא — לא ידיע. וליתי מגילתא אחריתי ולמחוק ולידמי! לא דמי מחקא דהא מגילתא למחקא דהא מגילתא. ולקבלה לחתימות ידא דסהדי בבי דינא, ולמחוק ולידמי! אמר רב הושעיא: [ח]אינו דומה נמחק בן יומו לנמחק בן שני ימים. ולישהייה! אמר רבי ירמיה: א)חיישינן לב"ד טוען. § "רבי חנינא בן גמליאל אומר: מקושר" וכו'. § השיב רבי לדברי ר' חנינא בן גמליאל: והלא

רשב"ם

וא"ת. והלא חוזר הוא ומוחק את השטר, וזייף, וחתמי סהדי! ומשני: אין דומה חתימת העדים, שחתום על המחק שנמחק פעם אחת, לכתיבת השטר הכתוב על נמחק שתי פעמים, ויהא ניכר הזיוף. וניחוש דלמא שדי. בעל השטר דיותא בקלף במקום חתימת העדים קודם שחתמו, ומחקו, וחזר וכתב על כל הקלף, ומחקו כולו, וחתמו העדים בקלף שנמחק שתי פעמים, והשטר נכתב על המחק פעם אחת. וכי הדר מחיק ליה כדי לכתוב עליו זיוף — הוה ליה נמחק שתי פעמים כמו שנמחק מקום חתימת העדים שתי פעמים. אא"כ נמחק בפניהם. ואם יראו מקום חתימתן משונה במחיקה מן העליון — לא יחתומו. עדיו על המחק כשר. אם מכירין לחתימתן, או שהיה כתב ידם (א) במקום אחר. הוא על המחק כו' פסול. שמא מחק את השטר וזייפו. השתא נמי. חוזר עוד ומוחק ומזייף. [ומקשינן: והא אמרת אינו דומה כו'], ומשני: הני מילי היכא דחתמי סהדי על המחק, כיון שיש שני מיני מחקים בשטר אחד זה אצל זה — יכול להכיר מי נמחק יותר מחבירו. למחקא דהא מגילתא. זה עב וזה דק, ומחק של קלף עב אינו ניכר כל כך. ונקבל חתימת ידייהו בבי דינא. שלא יפסיד בעל השטר עדות של עדיו, ואחר כך נמחוק ונכתוב בההיא מגילתא גופא, ונדמייה. אית ספרים דגרסינן בהו: ונישהייה. אמר רבי ירמיה חוששין לב"ד טוענין, (ב) ולא ידעו לדקדק כל כך ב) או להשהותו להכשיר שטר פסול, הלכך פסקוהו למילתיה, ופסלו כל שטר שבעל המחק ועדיו על הנייר. ואית דלא גרסי "ונשהייה", וגרסי: רבי ירמיה אומר חיישינן לב"ד טוענין ואין נותנין לב לדמות ולמחוק. ובמקום תירוץ רב הושעיא תירץ רב ירמיה כך. השיב רבי לדברי רבי חנינא בן גמליאל. שאמר: מקושר יכול לעשותו פשוט. והלא

תוספות

סהדי חתימי על המחקא, ושטרא אניירא", כדמפרש בסמוך. ואין לחוש שמסר לו שטר פסול (ע"כ). וא"ת: שמא מחק "אנחנא סהדי" וכל השטר שלמעלה בר מן העדים, וכתב מאי דבעי? וי"ל: דלא מכשרינן הוא ועדיו על המחק אלא כשאין ריוח בין עד לעד כדי לכתוב "אנחנא סהדי". וריב"ס פירש: דאין לחוש שמא ימחוק "אנחנא סהדי", כיון דמעיקרא הוה כתב על המחק, ואם ימחקנו ה"ל נמחק ב' פעמים, והשטר שכתוב על הנייר שמחקו ה"ל נמחק פעם אחת, ויהיה ניכר הזיוף, דאינו דומה נמחק פעם אחת לנמחק שתי פעמים. ונראה לי דהיינו כשכותב על המחק, אז ניכר איזה נמחק פעם אחת ואיזה נמחק שתי פעמים. אבל הנייר מחוק גרידא, שאין כתוב עליו כלום — אותו אינו ניכר. וכן מוכח בסמוך, דפריך: וניחוש דלמא שדי ליה דיותא אמקום עדים, ומחיק ליה והדר מחיק ליה, והוה ליה אידי ואידי נמחק שתי פעמים כשימחוק אחרי כן השטר. ומאי פריך? הלא בשעה שירצו לחתום יראו (ג) מחוק פעם אחת ומקום שהמלוה מתחימם מחוק שתי פעמים! אלא ודאי אינו ניכר עד שיהא כתוב ויהא יבש. מיהו, הא לאו ראיה היא, דמצי למימר דלעדים אינו ניכר, דלא דייקי, אבל שטר הבא לפני ב"ד — ניכר, דב"ד דייקי, ולכך אי מחיק "אנחנא סהדי" — ירא̇והו ב"ד שנמחק שתי פעמים, וחתימת העדים לא נמחק כי אם פעם אחת כדינא. מיהו, קשה לרבי: דלדברי ריב"ס, תינח היכא דנכתב "אנחנא סהדי" על המחק כמו העדים, אלא היכא דנכתב "אנחנא סהדי" על הנייר — ימחקנו, וגם (ד) השטר שהוא על הנייר, ויהא שטר הבא הוא ועדיו על המחק, ואמאי כשר? וכ"ת: הוא על הנייר ועדיו על המחק לא הוי כשר אלא כשמחק בין עד לעד, במקום שיכתבו "אנחנא סהדי", אבל אי כתבו "אנחנא סהדי" על הנייר — לא. אדרבה, זה ראוי להכשיר יותר, דודאי לא עשה שום זיוף. אבל כשנמחק השטר ונמחק הריוח בין סהדא לסהדא, שיש לחוש שמא היה כתוב בו "אנחנא סהדי" (ה) ג)ומחק וזייף — אז ראוי לפסול יותר. וגם לא אשכחן חילוק בין כתוב "אנחנא סהדי" על הנייר, בין כתוב על המחק! וי"ל: דלא חיישינן שמא מחק "אנחנא סהדי", (ו) שאם כן יש ריוח בינתים בין סהדא לסהדא, ומסתמא אין כותבין (ז) ד)בזה הדיבור כנגד חתימה בפחות משני שיטין. וכמו ששני שיטין בין העדים לכתב פוסלין את השטר — כן שני שיטין בין עד לעד פוסל, דלמא יכתוב (ח) ה)ב' שיטות לפני העד. וכן משמע לקמן ששני עדים בשני שטרות מצטרפין להוציא ממון. ואין לומר שיחתום ו)בשבילו, דלענין אפוקי ממונא חשוד, דלא מהימן אלא בשבועה. והיכן יש לחוש שמא מחק "אנחנא סהדי" — היכא שהעדים חתומים זה אצל זה בחד שיטה, זה בראש השיטה וזה בסוף השיטה, ו"אנחנו סהדי" בנייר בינתים — בזה אין רגילות (ט) ד"אנחנו סהדי" על הנייר ועדים על המחק, דלמה יעשו שטות זה לכתוב "אנחנא סהדי" על הנייר, והם חתומים על המחק? יחתמו על הנייר, ודיו. וא"ת: ולמה לא תקנו (י) שטרא על הנייר ועדיו על המחק כשר בלא "אנחנא סהדי", וכשעדיו והשטר על המחק — לא יהא כשר אם לא כתבו בו "אנחנא סהדי כתיבי אמחקא ושטרא כתיבא אמחקא", דהשתא ליכא למיחש שמתחילה היה השטר על הנייר ומחקו וזייפו, שיותר היה להם לעשות תקנה כשהשטר עשוי ז)[על המחק], דאיכא למיחש ביה שנעשה זיוף, מבאותו שעדיין לא נעשה בו זיוף! וי"ל: הוא ועדיו על המחק שכיח טפי, שיש לסופר כמה טופסי שטרות שלא כוון בהן המעשה ומחקם, אבל הוא על הנייר ועדיו על המחק — לא שכיח כולי האי. ולכך תקנו "אנחנא סהדי". והשתא מיתרצא שפיר מה שהקשה ר"י על פי' ריב"ס, שיותר יש לנו להכשיר "אנחנא סהדי" כשכתוב על הנייר שלא נעשה בו שום זיוף, יותר משכתוב על המחק, דאיכא למיחש שנעשה בו זיוף. שעתה יש ליתן טעם (כ) זה שפיר, ד"אנחנא סהדי" על הנייר לא שכיח, אלא אדרבה יחתמו על הנייר ויהיה הכל על הנייר. (ל) וקשה לפי' ח)רשב"ס, שפירש בשטר הבא הוא ועדיו על המחק, שאם יש ריוח מחוק בין עד לעד פסול, דאיכא למיחש שהיה כתוב בו "אנחנא סהדי" והשטר היה כתוב על הנייר, ומחקו. א"כ, הא דקאמר: דכתבי "אנחנא" (מ) בין עד לעד — היינו כשיש נייר בין עד לעד, שאם כבר מחוק בין עד לעד למה יכתבו "אנחנא סהדי"? ירחיקו העדים זה מזה שיעור "אנחנא סהדי" ודי בכך, שאם ימחוק ויהיה הכל על המחק — יהא פסול, כדפרישית, כיון שיש ריוח בין עד לעד. וזה אינו נראה לומר שאינו מצריך "אנחנא סהדי" אלא כשיש נייר בין עד לעד, דהוה ליה לגמ' לפרש. ועוד, א"כ (נ) בשופטני עסקינן שהניחו הנייר וכתבו על המחק? ומיהו, איכא למימר שאין להקשות כשיש מחק בין עד לעד למה יכתבו "אנחנא סהדי", יניחו חלק ודיו. (ס) וזה אינו, שאם לא נצריכו לכתוב — לא יניחו בין זה לזה, ולא יחושו, כי יאמרו: למה הניחנו והרחיק חתימתי מחבירי, כיון שאינו כתוב בינתים.

וניחוש דלמא שדי דיותא אמקום עדים. פירשתי לעיל. **אי** לעילאי מחיק. לפירוש ריב"ס, שפירש כשנמחק שתי פעמים ניכר(ע) שאין כתוב עליו השתא, קשה: לישדי דיותא בין עדים לכתיבה, ולמחוק ליה, והדר לכתוב "אנחנא סהדי" וכו' דהשתא לא מצי מחיק ליה, לפי שיהא נמחק שתי פעמים ויהא ניכר. אבל לפי' רבי ניחא, שאינו ניכר, כיון שאין כתוב עליו כלום. ומיהו, עדיפא מינה משני דבלא דיותא מצי עביד בין סהדא לסהדא. **לישהייה**. מאן דלא גרים ליה (פ) סבר דכמו כן אינו דומה נמחק בן שני ימים לנמחק בן שלשה. השתא

רבינו גרשום

ואם תאמר. אמאי כשר הא מצי מלוה לחזור ולמחוק כתיבת השטר וחוזר וכותב מאי דבעי הואיל והעדים נמי חתימי על מחק. הא לא מצי למיעבד דניכר הוא דאין דומה מקום עדים שאינו נמחק אלא פעם אחת למקום השטר שנמחק ב' פעמים. לפי שנגרר הקלף ביותר ויש היכר. ואכתי אמאי כשר ליחוש דלמא שדי מלוה בתחלה נמי [קודם] דנכתב השטרא על גבי כתב מחוק זה שדי דיותא אמקום עדים להיכא דמשער דחתימי עדים ועבד הכי מעיקרא קמי דנכתב השטר ונטל אותו קלף ואשדיה דיותא א) דבמקום עדים והדר כתיב השטר על אותו שטר שלא נמחק אלא פעם אחת וחתמו העדים במקום שהיה הדיו דנמחק ב' פעמים ולפי שהשטר הוא כבר כתוב לא יכלו להבחין אם נמחק פעם אחת לנמחק ב' פעמים ואחר שחתמו העדים במקום שנמחק ב' פעמים חזר ומחק כתיבת השטר והדר וכתב מאי דבעי: והוה ליה אידי ואידי. מקום השטר ומקום העדים נמחק ב' פעמים ומזייף הכי וליכא היכרא ואמאי כשר: אמר אביי. מש"ה כשר דקסבר רב אין העדים חותמין על השטר אלא אם כן נמחק בפניהם שיראוהו קודם שיכתוב על גבי השטר וראוהו היאך נמחק דאי הדר תו ומחק במקום שהעדים חותמין הן שראוהו תחלה נמחק מכירין בין נמחק פעם אחת לנמחק ב' פעמים: מיתיבי. הוא. כתיבת השטר: על הנייר. שאינו מחוק: ועדיו על המחק כשר. ואמאי לרב דאמר שטר הוא ועדיו על המחק כשר ליחוש דלמא מחיק לנייר שכתוב בו השטר והדר וכתב מאי דבעי והוה אידי ואידי נמחק פעם אחת. ומשני משום הכי כשר דכתבי עדים הכי אנחנא סהדי כו'. אי לתתאי מן חתימת העדים גייז ליה ומחיק ליה לגוף של שטר או לעיל מן העדים מחיק ליה וליכא היכרא למלתא. ומשני דכתבו בין סהדי לסהדי דאי גייז ליה גייז לסהדי ואי ליכא עדים פסול. ואי מחיק ליה הא נמחק תרי זמני ואינו דומה נמחק פעם אחת לנמחק ב' פעמים. הוא על המחק ועדיו על הנייר פסול משום דאיכא למימר דהדר מחיק ליה ומזייף ליה. והאמרת אינו דומה נמחק כו'. והאי נמחק ב' פעמים וניכר ואמאי פסול: הני מילי היכא דכתבי סהדי אמחוקה ושטר אמחק איכא היכרא בין מחיקת מקום העדים שהוא פעם אחת ובין מחיקת מקום השטר שהוא ב' פעמים. ואכתי אמאי פסול וליתו מגילתא אחריתי ולמחוק חדא זימנא ולידמי אי דמיא ג)למחיקת הא מגילתא דהאי שטר. ומשני לא דמי מחקא דהא מגלתא למחקא דהא מגלתא לפי דקליש טפי או דעבי טפי. ואכתי אמאי פסול ליקבליה לחתימת ידיה דסהדא דחתימי בהאי שטרא דמחיק יבואו עדים ויעידו לפני בית דין יודעים אנו שזו היא כתיבת העדים החתומין ובתר דקבלו לסהדותייהו למחוק מקום חתימותייהו ולידמי אי דמי מחיקת העדים שנמחק פעם אחת למחיקת מקום השטר. וכי האי גוונא אפשר בתקנה ואמאי פסול. בן שני ימים דמחיק מחיקתו וליכא למיקם עלה דמלתא. ולשהייה לשטר ג' ימים או טפי לאחר מחיקת העדים וניחזי דהשתא אידי ואידי מכמה ימים הוא ואכתי אמאי פסול והא אפשר למבדקיה הכי. אמר ר' ירמיה להכי קא פסיק דפסול דחיישינן לבית דין טוען דכיון דחזר דכתבו עדים הכי ושטרא על מחקא סמכי עדים ולא בדקו ליה אי נמחק פעם אחת או שתי פעמים. הלכך גזרי דפסול אע"ג דאפשר בבדיקה משום בית דין טוען דלא בדקי אלא גבו לאלתר: רבי חנניה בן גמליאל אומר מקושר שכתבו עדיו מתוכו כשר מפני שיכול לעשותו פשוט. יפתח קשוריו והוי פשוט אע"פ שיש בו אויר ג' שיטות למעלה אין בכך כלום והרי

הגהות הב"ח

(א) רשב"ם ד"ה עדיו וכו' כתב ידם יוצא במקום אחר: (ב) ד"ה אית ספרים וכו' שלא ידעו לדקדק כל כך להשהותו ויבואו להכשיר וכו' ובמקום שתירץ רב הושעיא כך תירץ ר' ירמיה כך: (ג) תום' ד"ה (בדף הקודם) גופא וכו' שירצו לחתום יראו השטר מחוק פעם אחת: (ד) בא"ד ימחקנו וגם ימחוק השטר שהוא על הנייר וכו' אלא כשנמחק בין עד לעד במקום שכתבו אנחנא וכו' לאדרבה זה: (ה) בא"ד ונמחק וזייף אז ראוי לפסול יותר: (ו) בא"ד שאם כן יש ריוח בינתים. נ"ב [היינו כשהעדים חתומים זה תחת זה] ואם אין העדים חתומים זה תחת זה אלא זה אחר זה זה בראש השיטה וזה בסוף השיטה כו' התם ודאי אין לחוש שמא מחק אנחנא סהדי דלמה יעשו שטות כזה כו' והשטר כשר אע"פ שיש ריוח בינתים באותה שיטה כשיעור שיכתוב שטר לפני העד דלא יועיל שטר כשבא הוא והעד בשיטה אחת אם לא ששני עדים חתומים באותה שיטה דאפי' הוליא עליו כתיבת ידו לא מהני כשבא בשיטה אחת לפריב"ס כאשר כתוב בהגהות אשיר"י ובחתומים זה תחת זה לא היה יכול לדחות ג"כ דלמה יעשו שטות כזה כו' דהתם אם היו העדים חותמים על הנייר היו מרחיקין ב' שיטות מן השטר ודו"ק: (ז) בא"ד ומסתמא אין כותבין דבור כזה כנגד חתימה בפחות. נ"ב [כי תיבות אנחנא] סהדי וכו' ארוכה יותר מחתימת העד: (ח) בא"ד כן שני שיטין בין עד לעד פוסל דלמא יכתוב שטר אחר לפני העד וכן משמע לקמן ששני עדים בשני שטרות מצטרפין להוציא ממון אבל אין לומר שיכתוב בשבילו לענין אפוקי ממונא מחשוד דלא מהימן כצ"ל ונ"ב כלומר אבל בלא צירוף ליכא למימר דיכתוב שטר לפני העד כדי להוציא ממון בעד אחד מן החשוד על השבועה הא ליתא דהא אף כנגד החשוד אינו נאמן אלא בשבועה ומיגו דחשיד אממונא חשיד אשבועתא לא אמרינן: (ט) בא"ד בזה אין רגילות שיכתבו אנחנא סהדי: (י) בא"ד ולמה לא תקנו לשטר על הנייר: (כ) בא"ד ליתן טעם לזה שפיר: (ל) בא"ד וקשה לפי' רשב"ס. נ"ב הוא פי' שכתבו התוס' בתחלת הדבור: (מ) בא"ד אנחנא סהדי בין עד לעד: (נ) בא"ד ועוד א"כ אתו בשופטני: (ס) בא"ד יניחו חלק ודיו לזה אינו: (ע) ד"ה אי עילאי וכו' ניכר אע"פ שאין כתוב עליו: (פ) ד"ה לישהייה מאן דלא גרס ליה היינו משום דכמו כן:

א) לכאורה צ"ל וחזר ואשדי דיותא אכולה שטרא והדר כתב השטר על אותו שטר וכו'. ב) נראה דצ"ל אי דמיא מחיקה הא מגילתא למחיקה דהאי שטר.

וַהֲלֹא אֵינוֹ דּוֹמֶה זְמַנּוֹ שֶׁל זֶה לִזְמַנּוֹ שֶׁל זֶה; פָּשׁוּט, מָלַךְ שָׁנָה – מוֹנִין לוֹ שָׁנָה, שְׁתַּיִם – מוֹנִין לוֹ שְׁתַּיִם; מְקוּשָּׁר, מָלַךְ שָׁנָה – מוֹנִין לוֹ שְׁתַּיִם, שְׁתַּיִם – מוֹנִין לוֹ ג'. וְזִימְנִין דְּיָזֵיף מִינֵּיהּ זוּזֵי בִּמְקוּשָּׁר וּמִיתְרַמֵּי לֵיהּ זוּזֵי בֵּינֵי בֵּינֵי וּפָרַע לֵיהּ, וְא"ל: הַב לִי שְׁטָרַאי, וְאָמַר לֵיהּ: אִירְכַּס לִי, וְכָתַב לֵיהּ תַּבְרָא, וְכִי מָטֵי זִמְנֵיהּ מְשַׁוֵּי לֵיהּ פָּשׁוּט, וְא"ל: (א) הָנֵי הַשְׁתָּא דְּיָיפַת מִינַּאי! קָא סָבַר: אֵין כּוֹתְבִין שׁוֹבֵר. וּמִי בָּקִי רַבִּי בִּמְקוּשָּׁר? וְהָא הַהוּא מְקוּשָּׁר דַּאֲתָא לְקַמֵּיהּ דְּרַבִּי, וְאָמַר רַבִּי: שְׁטָר מְאוּחָר זֶה! וְא"ל זוּנִין לְרַבִּי: כָּךְ מִנְהָגָהּ שֶׁל אוּמָּה זוֹ, מָלַךְ שָׁנָה – מוֹנִין לוֹ שְׁתַּיִם, שְׁתַּיִם – מוֹנִין לוֹ שָׁלֹשׁ! בָּתַר דִּשְׁמַעָהּ מְזוּנִין סְבָרָהּ. הַהוּא שְׁטָרָא דַּהֲוָה כָּתַב בֵּיהּ "בִּשְׁנַת פְּלוֹנִי אַרְכָן", א"ר חֲנִינָא: יִבָּדֵק אֵימָתַי עָמַד אַרְכָן בְּאַרְכָנוּתֵיהּ. וְדִלְמָא דַּאֲרִיךְ מַלְכוּתֵיהּ! אָמַר רַב הוֹשַׁעְיָא: כָּךְ מִנְהָגָהּ שֶׁל אוּמָּה זוֹ, שָׁנָה רִאשׁוֹנָה קוֹרִין לוֹ "אַרְכָן", שְׁנִיָּה – קוֹרִין לוֹ "דִּיגוֹן". וְדִלְמָא עֲבוּרֵי עַבְרוּהוּ וַהֲדַר אוֹקְמוּהוּ! אֲמַר ר' יִרְמְיָה: הַהוּא – "אַרְכָן דִּיגוֹן" קָרְאוּ לֵיהּ. א)ת"ר: "הֲרֵינִי נָזִיר (הֵינָא")", סוֹמָכוֹס אָמַר: "הֵינָא" – אַחַת, "דִּיגוֹן" – שְׁתַּיִם, "טְרִיגוֹן" – ג', "טֶטְרִיגוֹן" – אַרְבַּע, "פֶּנְטִיגוֹן" – חָמֵשׁ. ב)תָּנוּ רַבָּנַן: אבַּיִת עָגוֹל, דִּיגוֹן, טְרִיגוֹן, פֶּנְטִיגוֹן – אֵינוֹ מְטַמֵּא בִּנְגָעִים, טֶטְרִיגוֹן – מְטַמֵּא בִּנְגָעִים. מְנָא הָנֵי מִילֵּי? דְּתָנוּ רַבָּנַן: לְמַעְלָה אוֹמֵר °"קִיר" "קִירוֹת" (ויקרא יד) – שְׁתַּיִם, לְמַטָּה אוֹמֵר "קִיר" "קִירוֹת" שְׁתַּיִם – הֲרֵי כָּאן אַרְבַּע. ג)הַהוּא מְקוּשָּׁר דַּאֲתָא לְקַמֵּיהּ דְּרַבִּי, וַאֲמַר רַבִּי: אֵין זְמַן בָּזֶה? א"ל ר' שִׁמְעוֹן ב"ר לְרַבִּי: שֶׁמָּא בֵּין קְשָׁרָיו מוּבְלָע? פַּלְיֵיהּ וַחֲזְיֵיהּ. הֲדַר חֲזָא בֵּיהּ רַבִּי בְּבִישׁוּת, א"ל: לָאו אֲנָא כְּתַבְתֵּיהּ, ר' יְהוּדָה חַיָּיטָא כְּתָבֵיהּ. א"ל: כְּלָךְ מִלָּשׁוֹן הָרַע הַזֶּה. זִימְנִין הֲוָה יָתֵיב קַמֵּיהּ וְקָא פָּסֵיק סִידְרָא בְּסֵפֶר תְּהִלִּים, אֲמַר רַבִּי: כַּמָּה מְיוּשָּׁר כְּתָב זֶה, אֲמַר לֵיהּ: לָאו אֲנָא כְּתַבְתֵּיהּ, יְהוּדָה חַיָּיטָא כְּתָבֵיהּ. א"ל: כְּלָךְ מִלָּשׁוֹן הָרַע הַזֶּה. בִּשְׁלָמָא הָתָם דאִיכָּא לָשׁוֹן הָרַע, אֶלָּא הָכָא מַאי לָשׁוֹן הָרַע אִיכָּא? מִשּׁוּם דְּרַב דִּימִי. דְּתָנֵי ד)רַב דִּימִי אֲחוּהּ דְּרַב סָפְרָא: גלְעוֹלָם אַל יְסַפֵּר אָדָם בְּטוֹבָתוֹ שֶׁל חֲבֵירוֹ, שֶׁמִּתּוֹךְ טוֹבָתוֹ בָּא לִידֵי רָעָתוֹ. אָמַר רַב עַמְרָם אָמַר רַב, שָׁלֹשׁ עֲבֵירוֹת אֵין אָדָם נִיצּוֹל מֵהֶן בְּכָל יוֹם: הִרְהוּר עֲבֵירָה, וְעִיּוּן תְּפִלָּה, וְלָשׁוֹן הָרַע. לָשׁוֹן הָרַע סָלְקָא דַּעְתָּךְ?!

אֶלָּא

וַהֲלֹא אֵין זְמַנּוֹ שֶׁל פָּשׁוּט כִּזְמַנּוֹ שֶׁל מְקוּשָּׁר. דְּאִילּוּ זְמַנּוֹ שֶׁל פָּשׁוּט, אִם נִכְתַּב בַּשָּׁנָה רִאשׁוֹנָה שֶׁעָמַד הַמֶּלֶךְ – אֵין מוֹנִין לוֹ אֶלָּא שָׁנָה, שְׁתַּיִם – מוֹנִין לוֹ שְׁתַּיִם. אֲבָל מְקוּשָּׁר, אִם מָלַךְ שָׁנָה – כּוֹתְבִין בַּשְּׁטָר שְׁתַּיִם, שְׁתַּיִם – מוֹנִין לוֹ שָׁלֹשׁ. כְּלוֹמַר, מַקְדִּימִין לוֹ שָׁנָה, שֶׁהֲרֵי מִנְהַג הָאוּמָּה כִּדְלְקַמָּן לְהַקְדִּים לַמֶּלֶךְ שָׁנָה. וְשֶׁמָּא לִכְבוֹד הַמֶּלֶךְ הָיוּ עוֹשִׂין, כְּלוֹמַר כְּבָר הֶחֱזִיק בְּמַלְכוּתוֹ שְׁתֵּי שָׁנִים. וַחֲכָמִים תִּקְּנוּ לִכְתּוֹב בִּמְקוּשָּׁר כְּמִנְהַג הָאוּמָּה, כְּדֵי לָתֵת חִילּוּקִים הַרְבֵּה וְחוּמְרוֹת בִּמְקוּשָּׁר, מִשּׁוּם תַּקָּנַת הַכֹּהֲנִים הַקַּפְּדָנִים, כִּדְאָמְרִי' לְעֵיל, כְּדֵי שֶׁלֹּא יְהֵא נוֹחַ לְגָרֵשׁ נְשׁוֹתֵיהֶן (ב). וּמַקְשִׁינַן: דִּלְמָא יָזֵיף לֵיהּ בִּמְקוּשָּׁר. דְּמוֹסִיף לֵיהּ שַׁתָּא, וּפָרְעֵיהּ בְּתוֹךְ שְׁנָתוֹ. וְא"ל: אִירְכַּס לִי שְׁטָרָא, וּכְתִיב לֵיהּ שׁוֹבָר, וּבָתַר הָכִי מְשַׁוֵּי לֵיהּ פָּשׁוּט, וְא"ל: בָּתַר דִּכְתַבִית לָךְ הַאי שׁוֹבָר הָדְרַתְּ וְיָזְפַתְּ מִינַּאי, וּשְׁטָר שֶׁלִּי מוֹכִיחַ, דִּזְמַנּוֹ בָּתַר זְמַן הַשּׁוֹבֵר. וּפָרְקִינַן: אֵין כּוֹתְבִין שׁוֹבֵר, וּלְעוֹלָם לָא פָּרַע לֵיהּ עַד דְּקָרַע (לֵיהּ) לִשְׁטָרָא. וּפְלוּגְתָּא הִיא לְקַמָּן בְּפִירְקִין בִּכְתִיבַת הַשּׁוֹבֵר. וּמִי בָּקִי רַבִּי בִּמְקוּשָּׁר. דְּקָאָמַר: זְמַנּוֹ שֶׁל זֶה לֹא כִּזְמַנּוֹ שֶׁל זֶה. וְהָא הַהוּא דַּאֲתָא לְקַמֵּיהּ דְּרַבִּי. בַּשָּׁנָה רִאשׁוֹנָה שֶׁל מֶלֶךְ, וְכָתוּב בּוֹ שְׁתַּיִם. וְאָמַר רַבִּי: מְאוּחָר הוּא זֶה. זוּנִין. שֵׁם חָכָם. כָּךְ מִנְהָגָהּ כו'. דְּרַבָּנַן תַּקּוּן בִּמְקוּשָּׁר כִּי הַהוּא מִנְהָג, לְהַפְרִיד מִלּוֹת וְחוּקִים בֵּין פָּשׁוּט לִמְקוּשָּׁר, כִּדְאָמְרַן בְּרֵישׁ פִּירְקִין. וּמְשַׁנֵּי: בָּתַר דִּשְׁמַעָהּ מְזוּנִין. אוֹתֵיב לְרַבִּי חֲנִינָא (ג). הַהוּא שְׁטָר. פָּשׁוּט. דַּהֲוָה כָּתַב בֵּיהּ בִּשְׁנַת פְּלוֹנִי אַרְכָן. לָוָה פְּלוֹנִי מִפְּלוֹנִי, וְלָא הֲוָה כָּתַב בֵּיהּ כַּמָּה שָׁנִים לְמַלְכוּתוֹ שֶׁל אוֹתוֹ מֶלֶךְ, אוֹ רִאשׁוֹנָה אוֹ שְׁנִיָּה אוֹ שְׁלִישִׁית. "אַרְכָן" זֶה מֶלֶךְ, וּבַשָּׁנָה רִאשׁוֹנָה קוֹרִין לוֹ אַרְכָן כִּדְלְקַמָּן, לְפִי שֶׁעַתָּה מְתוּקָּן הוּא, כְּמוֹ "אָרִיךְ אוֹ לָא אָרִיךְ" (סוכה דף מד:), וּכְמוֹ: "וְעַרְוַת מַלְכָּא לָא אֲרִיךְ לַנָא לְמֶחֱזֵא" (עזרא ד) – לֹא נָאֶה וְיָפֶה לָנוּ לִרְאוֹת עֶרְוָתוֹ שֶׁל מֶלֶךְ וְחֶרְפָּתוֹ. יִבְדּוֹק אֵימָתַי עָמַד אַרְכָן בְּמַלְכוּתוֹ. כִּי בַּשָּׁנָה רִאשׁוֹנָה שֶׁל מַלְכוּתוֹ נִכְתַּב שְׁטָר זֶה, וּמֵהֵיאַךְ שַׁתָּא טָרְפִי בַּעֲלֵי חוֹבוֹת לַלָּקוֹחוֹת. דַּאֲרִיךְ בְּמַלְכוּתוֹ. כְּלוֹמַר, לְאַחַר שֶׁהֶאֱרִיךְ וּמָלַךְ כַּמָּה שָׁנִים לָוָה פְּלוֹנִי זֶה מִפְּלוֹנִי. וְלֹא יִטְרְפוּ לָקוֹחוֹת אֶלָּא מִיכָּן וּלְהַבָּא! שָׁנָה רִאשׁוֹנָה קוֹרִין לוֹ אַרְכָן. מְתוּקָּן לְמַלְכוּת מֵחָדָשׁ. דִּיגוֹן. לְשׁוֹן שָׁנִים, וְקָרוֹב לִלְשׁוֹן לַעַ"ז שֶׁלָּנוּ. וְדִלְמָא עֲבוּרֵי עַבְרוּהוּ. מִמַּלְכוּתוֹ, וַהֲדַר אַמְלְכוּהוּ לְסוֹף שְׁנָתַיִם וְשָׁלֹשׁ, וּמִיקְרֵי נַמִי אַרְכָן. וְשֶׁמָּא הַשְּׁטָר נִכְתַּב כְּשֶׁמָּלַךְ בַּשְּׁנִיָּה, וְאַמַּאי יִגְבֶּה מִזְּמַן רִאשׁוֹן? אַרְכָן דִּיגוֹן קָרוּ לֵיהּ. לְפִי שֶׁהֶחֱזִירוּהוּ לְמַלְכוּתוֹ אַחַר שֶׁהֶעֱבִירוּהוּ. ת"ר הֲרֵינִי נָזִיר הֵינָא סוֹמָכוֹס אוֹמֵר הֵינָא אַחַת. כְּלוֹמַר, אִם לֹא פֵּירֵשׁ כַּמָּה נְזִירוֹת נָזַר, וְאָמַר "הֲרֵינִי נָזִיר הֵינָא" – הַיְינוּ נְזִירוּת אַחַת, לִשְׁלֹשִׁים יוֹם. וְכוּלָּם – הֵינָא דִּיגוֹן טְרִיגוֹן – כּוּלָּן לְשׁוֹן לַעַ"ז שֶׁלָּנוּ הֵם. דִּיגוֹן שְׁתַּיִם. וְיִהְיֶה נָזִיר שִׁשִּׁים יוֹם. בַּיִת עָגוֹל. הֶעָשׂוּי כְּכִבְשָׁן, שֶׁאֵין לוֹ שׁוּם פִּינַּת קֶרֶן זָוִית. דִּיגוֹן. פִּינּוֹת שְׁתַּיִם, מִצַּד אַחַת עָגוֹל וְלִדּוֹ אַחַת יֵשׁ לוֹ שְׁתֵּי פִּינּוֹת. טְרִיגוֹן. דַּעֲבִיד *כְּחוּלְיָא, וְיֵשׁ בָּהּ שָׁלֹשׁ פִּינּוֹת. פֶּנְטִיגוֹן. יֵשׁ לוֹ חָמֵשׁ פִּינּוֹת [כָּזֶה]. 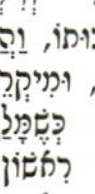 טֶטְרִיגוֹן. מְרוּבָּע. מְנָא ה"מ. דְּאֵין מְטַמֵּא בִּנְגָעִים אֶלָּא מְרוּבָּע. לְמַעְלָה. הוּא יָכוֹל לוֹמַר "וְהִנֵּה הַנֶּגַע בְּקִיר הַבַּיִת" וְכָתַב "קִירוֹת". הֲרֵי כָּאן אַרְבַּע. וְהַיְינוּ מְרוּבָּע, אֲבָל בַּיִת עָגוֹל – כּוּלּוֹ קִיר אַחַת. "וּמַרְאֵיהֶן שָׁפָל מִן הַקִּיר" לְגוּפֵיהּ אָתָא. וּבְפֵירוּשׁ רַבֵּינוּ חֲנַנְאֵל: כְּיוֹנָא בּוֹ חָמוּר, ה) אֵין לוֹ לְהַקבּ"ה בְּעוֹלָמוֹ אֶלָּא יִרְאַת הַשֵּׁם. שֶׁנֶּאֱמַר (איוב כח): "הֵן יִרְאַת ה'" שֶׁכֵּן בִּלְשׁוֹן יְוָנִי קוֹרִין לְאַחַת "הֵינָא". וְשֶׁמָּא בְּסִפְרֵיהֶם כְּתוּבָה. חֲזָא בֵּיהּ בְּבִישׁוּת. כִּסְבוּר שֶׁהוּא כְּתָבוֹ. וּבִרְצוֹנוֹ לֹא הָיוּ עוֹשִׂין מְקוּשָּׁר אֶלָּא פָּשׁוּט, לְפִי שֶׁטּוֹעִים בּוֹ. א"נ, לְפִי שֶׁהָיָה מוּבְלָע בֵּין קְשָׁרָיו יוֹתֵר מִדַּאי, שֶׁרַבִּי עַצְמוֹ טָעָה בּוֹ. יְהוּדָה חַיָּיטָא. כֵּן שְׁמוֹ. כְּלָךְ מִלָּשׁוֹן הָרַע הַזֶּה. כְּלוֹמַר, לֹא הָיָה לְךָ לְהַטִּיל אַשְׁמָה עָלָיו, הָיָה לְךָ לוֹמַר: אֵינִי כְּתַבְתִּיו. מַאי לָשׁוֹן הָרַע אִיכָּא. וַהֲלֹא בְּשִׁבְחוֹ שֶׁל ר"י חַיָּיטָא דִּיבֵּר, כְּשֶׁאָמַר יְהוּדָה חַיָּיטָא כְּתָבֵיהּ! בָּא לִידֵי רָעָתוֹ. לִידֵי גְּנוּתוֹ, מִתּוֹךְ שֶׁמְּרַבִּין בְּשִׁבְחוֹ – מַזְכִּירִין שֵׁם גְּנוּת שֶׁבּוֹ. עִיּוּן תְּפִלָּה. יֵשׁ מְפָרְשִׁין: שֶׁלְּאַחַר שֶׁהִתְפַּלֵּל דָּן בְּלִבּוֹ שֶׁיְּשַׁלֵּם לוֹ הקב"ה שְׂכָרוֹ, וְיַעֲשֶׂה הקב"ה צְרָכָיו, וְיִשְׁמַע תְּפִלָּתוֹ, לְפִי שֶׁהִתְפַּלֵּל בְּכַוָּונָה.

אָבָק

נ"ל כתובה. יעב"ץ

השתא הוא דאוזפת מינאי. פירוש: ומפסדי הלקוחות שלא כדין. אבל משום פסידא דלוה – לא איכפת לן, דאיהו הוא דאפסיד אנפשיה כשלוה בהאי שטרא, כדפרישית לעיל גבי עדים, דרית לן למיפסל לשטרא משום שיוכל לזייף על העדים עצמן, להוציא עליהם כתב ידן – דאינהו דאפסדו אנפשייהו. אי נמי, י"ל: דאין להן הפסד ללקוחות, כגון דכתב זה השטר בלא אחריות, ואפ"ה חיישינן לפסידא דלוה – שאין זה הפסד שיהא הלוה יודע ליזהר כל כך, ולא מסיק אדעתיה שיבא לידי זיוף.

בשנת פלוני. נראה לר"י דהאי "ארכן" לאו היינו מלך, אלא ממונה, שמסירים אותו משררתו לאחר שנה ואין ממונה עולמית. והיינו דפריך: דלמא עברוהו ואמלכוהו, ואע"ג דקרי ליה מלך – כן דרך לקרות שררה לשון מלוכה, כדאמר "מלך רבי יוחנן" (תענית דף כא.) "מלך רבה" (ברכות דף סד.). אבל אי "ארכן" היינו מלך – אינו דרך שיעבירוהו ממלכותו. הינא אחת. לשון יווני הוא, כדאמר (ד) (שבת דף לא:): בלשון יווני קורין לאחת "הינא". וקשה: דמאי קמ"ל? דאם אמר "הריני נזיר שתי נזירות" דהוא חייב שתי נזירות? הא פשיטא, מה לי לשון עברי ומה לי לשון יווני, מה לי לשון לעז! וי"ל: דאם אינו יודע מהו לשון דיגון טריגון, ואמר "הריני נזיר דיגון, טריגון", ואינו ו) משמע בלשון הקדש כמו דיגון (ה) שתים כו', דהאי הוי לשון לועז. והא קמ"ל דהוי כלשון חכמים, וחייב אם אמר "דיגון" שתי נזירות. וכי האי גוונא אמרינן [בנדרים] (דף י.): "הריני נזיק, נזיח, פזיח", איכא דאמרי לשון גוים הכי, וא"ד לשון חכמים [שבדו] להיות נזיר בו. עיון תפלה. הוא רע כשמהרהר בתפלתו, כדאמרינן בברכות (דף נה.): המעיין בתפלתו בא לידי כאב לב, כדאמרינן התם: אלו דברים המזכירים עונותיו של אדם: קיר נטוי, ועיון תפלה. והשתא הוי דומיא דהרהור עבירה ולשון הרע, שאינו מלוה. אבל אינו נראה, דלמה אינו ניצול בכל יום? הרבה בני אדם אינם מצפים מתי יבא תפלתם, שאינם מכוונים כל כך שיצפו (ו) תפלתם! ונראה לרבי: דעיון תפלה שהוא רע – שאינם מכוונים תפלתם, כדאמרי' (שבת קכז.) באלו דברים שאדם אוכל פירותיהם כו' – ועיון תפלה. ומזה אין אדם ניצול בכל יום, שאין שום אדם יכול לכוין בתפלתו היטב. והכי אמר בירושלמי (ברכות פ' "היה קורא" הל' י) אמר (ז) ר' מתניה: מחזקנא טיבותא לרישא דכי מטי למודים כרע מגרמיה ז).

באתרא

עין משפט
נר מצוה

ל א מיי' פי"ד מהל' טומאת צרעת הלכה ו:

לא ב מיי' פ"ז מהל' דעות הלכה ב סמג לאוין ט:

לב ג מיי' שם הלכה ד:

רבינו גרשום

והרי הוא פשוט ופשוט עדיו מתוכו. השיב ר' לר' חנניה בן גמליאל והיאך יכול לעשות ממקושר פשוט והלא אין זמנו של זה דומה לזה ואתי למטרף לקוחות שלא כדין דאילו פשוט אם מלך המלך שנה אחת כותבין בפשוט בשנה אחת למלך פלוני ואם מלך שתים מונין בו שתים ואילו בשטר מקושר אם מלך שנה אחת כשהוא עדיין בשנה ראשונה מונין שתים במקושר שכותבין בו בשנת שתים למלך פלוני לוה פלוני מפלוני כך וכך דרכן לכתוב במקושר שנה אחת יותר מחשבון שנים שמלך והשתא מצי אתי לידי תקלה דיזיף מיניה ממלוה זוזי משנה ראשונה למלך (בשטר פשוט) ועשה לו שטר מקושר וכתב בו שתים למלך פלוני ואינה אלא שנה ראשונה ומתרמי ליה זוזי ללוה ופרע לו באותה שנה ראשונה שלוה ממנו ואמר לוה למלוה החזיר שטרי שכבר פרעתיך ואמר ליה המלוה אירכס ומערים ומעכבו תחת ידו וכותב לו שפרעו וכי מטי זימניה של א) מקושר שטר שכתוב בו בשנת שתים למלך פלוני לוה פלוני מפלוני הוה מפתחו ומשוי ליה פשוט לאותו מקושר ואמר ליה הכי ב)דכתב דמהאי שטר פשוט יזפית מינאי תו השתא בשנה שניה למלך. והא גבי תרתי זימני בההוא שטרא אי אמרינן דיכול לעשותו פשוט. ומשני משום הכי אמר ר' חנינא במתני' שיכול לעשותו פשוט ולא חיישינן לכולי האי דקא סבר אין כותבין שובר אלא כשפורע לבעל חובו אינו פורע לו אא"כ מחזיר לו את שטרו וכשמחזיר לו שטרו ליכא למיחש למידי. ורבי היאך הוה מקשי הכי לדברי ר' חנינא ומי בקי רבי במקושר והא ההוא מקושר כו' ואמר רבי שטר מאוחר הוא זה משום דהוה חזי ביה יותר שנה אחרי חשבון שנות המלך שמלך. ואמר לו זונין לרבי כך מנהג אומה זו שמלך שנה מונין לו שתים ושטר מקושר הוא זה שנהגו לכתוב בו כדרך מנהג אומה זו שנה יתירא אלמא דלא בקי במקושר. ומשני בתר דשמעה מזונין הוה בקי דזמנו של מקושר אינו כזמנו של פשוט: בשנה פלוני ארכן לוה פלוני מפלוני וזה משמע ערכן כלומר בשנה שהיה ערוך ומתוקן במלכות שבשנה ראשונה שמלך קורין לו ארכן. ואמר ר' חנינא יבדק כמה שנים הן שעמד ארכן. ובאותה שנה שהיה ארכן נכתב השטר. ודלמא ארכן דאריך במלכותיה כלומר דהכי משמע שלאחר כמה שנים שהאריך במלכותו כתב השטר שלוה ממנו (ולא מחפש) ואין יכול לטרוף לקוחות שקנו מבעל חובו באותן שנים שעברו. אמר רב אושעיא לא איכא הכי אלא ארכן קורין לו בשנה ראשונה ויכול לטרוף לקוחות מאותה שנה ואילך. ודלמא עברוהו לאחר י"ח שנים או לאחר כ' שנה והדר אוקמיה וקראוהו נמי ארכן כשהחזירוהו וזה השטר נכתב בפעם שנית כשהוחזר ולא טרף כדין עד השתא. ליכא למימר הכי דא"כ ששתי פעמים המליכוהו ארכן דיגון מיקרי ליה. אלא מדלא כתב בשטרא אלא ארכן סתם אינו אלא משנה ראשונה שמלך ובדין טורף. סומכוס אומר אם אמר הריני נזיר הינא קיבל עליו נזירותו ל' יום. ואם אמר הריני נזיר דיגון קיבל עליו ב' נזירות ששים יום וכן כל כני. והאי לשון פלטין של יוני היא. בית עגול שאין לו זוית כלל. דיגון שאין לו אלא ב' זויות. טריגון ג' זויות. פנטיגון של ה' זויות. טטריגון שיש לו ד' זויות. כרוב בתים מטמא בנגעים: למעלה בפרשת נגעים כתיב ביה והיה הנגע בקירות הבית. ומצי למימר בקיר הבית מה ת"ל קירות אלא הרי כאן ב'. וכתב למטה בקירות דמצי למימר בקיר וכתב בקירות הרי ד' קירות. והכי הוי חשוב בית דמטמא בנגעים ולא בית אחר: אין זמן בזה. משום דהוה מכוסה תחת קשריו. הדר חזא ביה רבי בבישות. דקסבר שהוא כתב להאי שטר מקושר דאיכא טירחא וטעי ביה. כלומר מוטב היה לכתוב פשוט שמגולה הכל: אמר לו כלך מלשון הרע. כלומר לא היה לו לומר מי כתבו אלא היה לו לומר אני לא כתבתיו: וקא פסיק סדרא. היה גומר אחד מחמשה ספרים שבתהלים: כמה מיושר כתב זה. הרבה כתוב בדקדוק: בשלמא התם גבי שטר מקושר איכא לשון הרע. שמשליך עליו פשיעה. אבל הכא גבי ספר תהלים שאמר כו' מאי לשון הרע איכא אדרבה שבח לו שכתבו כל כך מיושר: בא לידי רעתו. כשמשבחו כל כך מפשפשין אחריו עד שאומר ממנו דבר גנאי: ועיון תפלה. שמחשב בדעתו איכון בתפלתי שיעשו לי רצונו. והיינו שדומה שמנסה לבורא ברוך שמו: לשון הרע ס"ד. וכי כל אדם

מספרי

א) נראה דצ"ל וכי מטי זימניה של שטר מקושר שכתוב בו וכו' יפתח אותו ומשוי ליה פשוט וכו'. ב) נראה דצ"ל ואמר ליה הכי שבהאי שטר פשוט יזפית מינאי וכו'.

מסורת הש"ס

א) נזיר דף ח: ע"ש [תוספתא נזיר רפ"א ע"ש]: ב) ג"ז שם ע"ש [תוספתא דנגעים פ"ו]: ג) [לעיל קס:]: ד) [ערכין טז.]: ה) [שבת לא:]: ו) רש"א משמע בלה"ק כמה: ז) [וע"ע תוס' ברכות לב: ד"ה כל ובשבת קיח: ד"ה עיון ותוס' ר"ה טז: ד"ה ועיון]:

הגהות הב"ח

(א) גמ' משוי ליה פשוט וא"ל השתא הא דיזפת מנאי: (ב) רשב"ם ד"ה והלא וכו' לגרש נשותיהן ואקשי ליה רבי ודלמא יזיף ליה כצ"ל והד"א: (ג) ד"ה ומשני וכו' לרבי חנינא כ"ג הס"ד: (ד) תוס' ד"ה הינא אחת לשון יווני הוא כדאמר בפ' הגוזלין דף ע"ו שכן בלשון יווני קורין: (ה) בא"ד כמו דיגון טריגון כו' דהאי הוי וכו' לשון נכרים הן ואיכא דאמרי לשון שבדו להן חכמים להיות בו נזיר הס"ד: (ו) ד"ה עיון וכו' שילפו לתפלתם: (ז) בא"ד בירושלמי א"ר יוחנן מחזקנא טיבותא:

אֶלָּא, אֲבַק לָשׁוֹן הָרַע. אָמַר רַב יְהוּדָה אָמַר רַב: ארוֹב בְּגָזֵל, וּמִיעוּט בַּעֲרָיוֹת, וְהַכֹּל בְּלָשׁוֹן הָרַע. בְּלָשׁוֹן הָרַע סָלְקָא דַּעְתָּךְ? אֶלָּא, באֲבַק לָשׁוֹן הָרַע.§ "רשב"ג אוֹמֵר: הַכֹּל כְּמִנְהַג הַמְּדִינָה".§ וְתַנָּא קַמָּא לֵית לֵיהּ מִנְהַג מְדִינָה?! אֲמַר א)רַב אַשִׁי: ב)בְּאַתְרָא דִּנְהִיגִי (א) פָּשׁוּט, וַא"ל: "עֲבִיד לִי פָּשׁוּט", וַאֲזַל עֲבַד לֵיהּ מְקוּשָּׁר — קְפֵידָא; נְהִיגִי מְקוּשָּׁר, וַא"ל: "עֲבִיד לִי מְקוּשָּׁר", וַאֲזַל עֲבַד לֵיהּ פָּשׁוּט — קְפֵידָא; כִּי פְּלִיגִי — בְּאַתְרָא דִּנְהִיגִי בְּפָשׁוּט וּמְקוּשָּׁר, וַא"ל: "עֲבִיד לִי פָּשׁוּט", וַאֲזַל עֲבַד לֵיהּ מְקוּשָּׁר — ג)מָר סָבַר: קְפֵידָא, וּמָר סָבַר: מַרְאֶה מָקוֹם הוּא לוֹ. ד)אָמַר אַבַּיֵי: רשב"ג וְר"ש וְר' אֶלְעָזָר, כּוּלְּהוּ ה)סְבִירָא לְהוּ: מַרְאֶה מָקוֹם הוּא לוֹ. רשב"ג — הָא דַּאֲמָרַן. ר"ש — דִּתְנַן,ו) ר"ש אוֹמֵר: אִם הִטְעָה לְשֶׁבַח — הֲרֵי זוֹ מְקוּדֶּשֶׁת. ר' אֶלְעָזָר — דִּתְנַן: ז)גהָאִשָּׁה שֶׁאָמְרָה "הִתְקַבֵּל לִי גִּיטִּי מִמָּקוֹם פְּלוֹנִי", וְקִיבְּלוֹ לָהּ מִמָּקוֹם אַחֵר — פָּסוּל, וְר' אֶלְעָזָר מַכְשִׁיר; מָר סָבַר: קְפֵידָא, וּמָר סָבַר: מַרְאֶה מָקוֹם הוּא לוֹ.§ ח)["פָּשׁוּט שֶׁכָּתוּב בּוֹ עֵד אֶחָד" כו'].§ בִּשְׁלָמָא מְקוּשָּׁר שֶׁכָּתוּב בּוֹ שְׁנֵי עֵדִים פָּסוּל — אִיצְטְרִיךְ, סָלְקָא דַּעְתָּךְ אָמִינָא: הוֹאִיל וּבְעָלְמָא כָּשֵׁר הָכָא נַמִי כָּשֵׁר, קמ"ל דְּפָסוּל. אֶלָּא פָּשׁוּט שֶׁכָּתוּב בּוֹ עֵד אֶחָד — פְּשִׁיטָא! אֲמַר אַבַּיֵי: לָא נִצְרְכָא, דַּאֲפִי' עֵד אֶחָד בִּכְתָב וְעֵד אֶחָד בַּפֶּה. אֲמֵימָר דאַכְשַׁר בְּעֵד אֶחָד בִּכְתָב וְעֵד אֶחָד עַל פֶּה. א"ל: רַב אַשִׁי לַאֲמֵימָר: וְהָא דְּאַבַּיֵי מַאי? א"ל: ט)לָא שְׁמִיעַ לִי, כְּלוֹמַר לָא סְבִירָא לִי. אֶלָּא קַשְׁיָא מַתְנִיתִין

רשב"ם

אֲבַק לָשׁוֹן הָרַע. כְּגוֹן דְּאָמְרִי "נוּרָא בֵּי פְּלָנְיָא", בַּעֲרָכִין (דף טו:). רוֹב בְּגָזֵל. רוֹב בְּנֵי אָדָם חֲשׁוּדִין עַל הַגָּזֵל, כְּעֵין גָּזֵל, שֶׁמּוֹרִין לְהֶתֵּירָא בְּמַשָּׂא וּבְמַתָּן, לְעַכֵּב אִישׁ מֵרֶיוַח הָרָאוּי לוֹ לַחֲבֵירוֹ. וְת"ק לֵית לֵיהּ מִנְהֲגָא דִּמְדִינָה. בִּתְמִיָּה, אִם רַבָּן שִׁמְעוֹן בֶּן גַּמְלִיאֵל בָּא לוֹמַר שֶׁדִּינֵי פָּשׁוּט וּמְקוּשָּׁר הַמְפוֹרָשִׁין לְתַנָּא קַמָּא, אִם יֵשׁ מְדִינָה שֶׁנָּהֲגוּ לְשַׁנּוֹת דִּינָם בְּעִנְיָן אַחֵר, הַכֹּל כְּמִנְהַג הַמְּדִינָה — וַהֲלֹא תַּנָּא קַמָּא נַמִי מוֹדֶה בְּהָא! אָמַר אַבַּיֵי בְּאַתְרָא דִּנְהִיגִי כו'. (ב) אֲתָא לְפָרֵשׁ אַבַּיֵי בְּאֵיזֶה מִנְהַג הַמְּדִינָה מָצוּ לְפְלוּגֵי תַּנָּא קַמָּא וְרַבָּן שִׁמְעוֹן. קְפֵידָא. וְאִם גֵּט אִשָּׁה — פָּסוּל לְגָרֵשׁ בּוֹ. מָר סָבַר קְפֵידָא. וְאַע"ג דְּמִנְהַג הַמְּדִינָה בֵּין בְּפָשׁוּט בֵּין בִּמְקוּשָּׁר, כֵּיוָן דְּאָמַר לֵיהּ בְּפָשׁוּט — קְפֵידָא הוּא, וְיִפָּסֵל הַמְקוּשָּׁר. וְרַבָּן שִׁמְעוֹן (ג) סָבַר: הַכֹּל כְּמִנְהַג הַמְּדִינָה, כְּלוֹמַר מַרְאֶה מָקוֹם הוּא לוֹ, שֶׁאִם טוֹרַח לוֹ לִכְתּוֹב מְקוּשָּׁר — יִכְתּוֹב פָּשׁוּט. וּמִיהוּ, אִם יִכְתּוֹב מְקוּשָּׁר — טְפֵי נִיחָא לֵיהּ, שֶׁהֲרֵי מִנְהַג הַמְּדִינָה בִּשְׁנֵיהֶם. אִם הִטְעָה לְשֶׁבַח. בְּקִדּוּשִׁין, הָאוֹמֵר "הִתְקַדְּשִׁי לִי בְּדִינָר שֶׁל כֶּסֶף" וְנִמְצָא שֶׁל זָהָב. אֲבָל בְּשֶׁבַח יוֹחֲסִין — "עַל מְנָת שֶׁאֲנִי לֵוִי" וְהוּא כֹּהֵן — לֹא אָמַר ר' שִׁמְעוֹן מְקוּדֶּשֶׁת, דְּהָא מָצְיָא הִיא לְמֵימַר: מְסָאנָא דְּרַב מִכַּרְעַי לָא בָּעֵינָא. הִטְעָה לְשֶׁבַח הַיְינוּ מַרְאֶה מָקוֹם — מִתְרַצָּה בְּשֶׁל כֶּסֶף, וְכ"ש בְּשֶׁל זָהָב. וּבְמִתְקַדֶּשֶׁת עַל יְדֵי שְׁלוּחָהּ מוֹקְמִינַן לָהּ הָתָם. פָּסוּל. שֶׁהִיא אֵינָהּ רוֹצָה לְהִתְבַּיֵּישׁ בְּמָקוֹם אַחֵר. וְר"א מַכְשִׁיר. דְּסָבַר: מַרְאֶה מָקוֹם הוּא לוֹ, לִטְרוֹחַ וְלָלֶכֶת בִּשְׁבִילָהּ עַד אוֹתוֹ מָקוֹם. וְאִם יַחְפּוֹץ לָלֶכֶת יוֹתֵר — תָּבוֹא עָלָיו בְּרָכָה. אָמַר אַבַּיֵי לָא נִצְרְכָא. לְמִיתְנֵי עֵד אֶחָד בְּפָשׁוּט פָּסוּל, אֶלָּא הֵיכָא דְּקָמְסַיֵּיעַ לֵיהּ עֵד אֶחָד בְּעַל פֶּה, וְאָתָא מַתְנִי' לְאַשְׁמוּעִינַן דְּלָא סָמְכִינַן אַשְּׁטָרָא לִטְרוֹף מִלָּקוֹחוֹת, דִּשְׁנֵי עֵדִים הַכְּתוּבִים בַּשְּׁטָר הוּא דְּמַפְּקֵי לֵיהּ לְקָלָא, וְאֵינוֹ אֶלָּא כְּמִלְוֶה עַל פֶּה, וְטָרְפָהּ מִבְּנֵי חָרֵי, כְּדִין הַמַּלְוֶה אֶת חֲבֵירוֹ בְּעֵדִים בְּלֹא שְׁטָר. וְגַם הַלֹּוֶה יָכוֹל לוֹמַר: פָּרַעְתִּי, וְלֹא יָכוֹל הַמַּלְוֶה לִטְעוֹן לַלֹּוֶה: הָיָה לְךָ לִקְרוֹעַ שְׁטָר שֶׁבְּיָדִי. מִכֵּיוָן שֶׁלֹּא נַעֲשָׂה כְּתִיקּוּן חֲכָמִים — לֹא חָשְׁשׁוּ הַלֹּוֶה, וְלֹא נִזְכַּר לְשׁוֹאֲלוֹ לַמַּלְוֶה. אֲמֵימָר אַכְשַׁר בְּעֵד אֶחָד בִּכְתָב. וּכְתַב יָדוֹ מְקוּיָּים מִמָּקוֹם אַחֵר בְּעֵדִים, וְעֵד אֶחָד נַמִי בְּעַל פֶּה מַסְהִיד עַל אוֹתָהּ מִלְוֶה. וְנִרְאֶה בְּעֵינַי דִּלְגַמְרֵי מַכְשִׁיר, אֲפִילּוּ לִטְרוֹף מִלָּקוֹחוֹת כְּאִילּוּ נֶחְתְּמוּ שְׁנֵי עֵדִים, דְּעֵד אֶחָד בַּשְּׁטָר וְעֵד אֶחָד בְּעַל פֶּה מַפְּקֵי לֵיהּ לְקָלָא. וְנִרְאִים הַדְּבָרִים כֵּן, דִּסְתָם מַכְשִׁיר — לְגַמְרֵי מַשְׁמַע. אִי הָכִי קַשְׁיָא מַתְנִיתִין. דְּפָרְכִינַן: פְּשִׁיטָא. וּמְשַׁנֵּי

תוספות

באתרא דנהיגי בפשוט וא"ל זיל עביד לי פשוט ועבד ליה מקושר. משמע: משום דא"ל "עביד לי פשוט". אבל אי א"ל סתמא "זיל עביד לי גיטא", ועביד ליה מקושר — כשר, אע"ג דבאתרא דנהיגי בפשוט. ובקדושין אמר: אע"ג דלא אמר כי אם "עביד לי גיטא", דהכי איתא בגירסא התם: באתרא דנהיגי בפשוט ועבד ליה מקושר. **אמר** אביי לא נצרכא אלא בעד אחד כו'. הכא משמע: דוקא אחד בכתב ואחד בעל פה, הא שניס בכתב כל אחד בפני עצמו — מצטרפין, ואליבא דרבי יהושע בן קרחה, וכמאן דאמר (סנהדרין דף ל:) הלואה אחר הלואה מצטרפין. א"נ, למאן דאמר לא מצטרפין, (ד) שני שטרות של עד אחד, כגון הודאה אחר הודאה, שמפרש בכל אחד ואחד "מנה דאודי לן בהאי שטרא אודי נמי קמי פלניא" — מצטרפין. דאי לא מצטרפין נמי בכי האי גוונא — לינקוט הא, וכל שכן אחד בכתב ואחד בעל פה. ומיהו יש לדחות: דעד אחד בכתב ועד אחד בעל פה לא איירי בכה"ג דהוה שייך למינקט ביה שניהם בכתב, (ה) וכגון ששניהם מעידים שראו שלוה או שמעו שהודה, דכי האי גוונא הוי שייך למינקט שניהם [בכתב] אין מצטרפין, אם אינו מצטרף שם. אלא איירי כגון שאותו שבכתב מעיד על ההלואה שראה אותה, ושבעל פה מעיד שראה שמסר (ו) השטר הזה לו, שהעד חתום בו, דבכי האי גוונא לא הוה מצי למינקט שניהם בכתב. ולהכי י)קשה נמי לאמימר, שהרי יש במסירת שטר זה שני עדי מסירה, שהעד (ז) חתום הוא כעד מסירה, דמוכיח שמסרו לו מלוה, שהוא לא היה חותם אלא בצווי של לוה. והעד שבעל פה מעיד שמסרו לוה למלוה — הלכך כשר אף על פי שלא חתם עליו אלא עד אחד, שהרי על מסירתו יש שני עדים, וקי"ל כר"א. אבל שניהם בכתב יחידין — פסולין לכ"ע, שאין על כל שטר ושטר אלא עד אחד. וסברא הוא, דלא אשכחן בשום מקום שטר בעד אחד לבד שיועיל. והכי משמע נמי מדחשיב עד אחד בכתב ועד אחד בעל פה בזה אחר זה, ואי הוי כשניהם מעידין על ראיית המלוה או על שמיעת הודאה — אמאי קרי להו זה אחר זה? והלא יכולין להיות כאחד, כגון שכתב בשטר "בפני פלוני אני החתום ובפני פלוני, לוה פלוני מפלוני מנה", ושבע"פ מעיד "בפני פלוני ובפני פלוני החתום, לוה פלוני מפלוני"! ולפי מה שפירש', דעד אחד שבעל פה היינו שמעיד על מסירת שטר שחתום בו העד — אתי שפיר הא דבעי לקמן סתמא בעד אחד בכתב ועד אחד בעל פה אי מצטרפי, דמשמע סתמא בלא פי' שלא ראו שניהם כאחד, שההלואה והמסירה לא היו כאחד, שלא היה יכול למצוא שניהם מעידין על ההלואה אלא כענין זה. שאם מעידין כל אחד על ראיית המלוה ושמיעת ההודאה — אין השטר מועיל כלל, והוי לגמרי כמאן דליתיה כיון שאין עד מעיד על מסירתו כדפרישית. ומיהו קצת קשה, כי נראה שהעד החתום חשוב כעד בשעת מסירה, שעל ידו ידוע לנו שמסר לוה למלוה. כ)ועי"ל: דהאי דלא משכחי' צירוף בעד אחד בכתב ועד אחד בעל פה לת"ק דרבי יהושע בן קרחה, היינו משום (ח) שבשניהם מעידין ראיית המלוה או שמיעת ההודאה — אין מוכיח בשטר שראו או שמעו כאחד, שראיית העד בעל פה היתה בשעת ראיה או בשעת שמיעה. אבל ראיית העד שבשטר חשבינן לה כאילו היתה בשעת מסירה, לפי שהרבה פעמים היתה בלא ראות המלוה כלל, כדתנן (לקמן דף קסז:): כותבין שטר ללוה אע"פ שאין מלוה עמו, ומוקי לה אביי (ב"מ יג.) כמאן דאמר אפילו בשטרי ל)[דלאו] אקנייתא, דעדיו בחיתומיו זכין לו. הלכך, אע"פ שאינו מוכיח (ט) השטר שלא ראה המלוה — לא חשבינן ראייתו כאחד, שאין חשוב עד בראיה זו. מאחר שאין ראייתו ידוע לנו ע"י השטר, אלא עיקר עדותו אינה אלא (י) לבדה שזה השטר מסר לוה למלוה — להכי לא חשבינן עדותו כראיית המלוה אפילו אם ראה אותו. ובירושלמי (פרק ג דכתובות) גרסינן: [זעירא בעי] עד אחד בכתב ועד בעל פה מהו [שיצטרפו? ועד אחד בכתב כלום הוא? לכך] צריכא, כשהיו שנים מצו לקיים כתב ידו של ראשון ולא מצו לקיים כתב ידו של שני. מה

עין משפט נר מצוה

לג א ב מיי' פכ"ב מהל' איסורי ביאה הל' יט:
לד ג מיי' פ"ט מהל' גירושין הל' לד סמג עשין ל טוש"ע אה"ע סי' קמא סעיף מט:
לה ד מיי' פ"ד מהל' עדות הלכה ה טוש"ע ח"מ סי' ל סעיף י:

רבינו גרשום

מספרי לה"ר הן: אבק לשון הרע. ולא ממש: רוב עונות הן בגזל. שמכזבין במשא ומתן ומשקרין: הכל כמנהג המדינה. שאם נוהגין לעשות פשוט ועשאו מקושר פסול או מקושר ועשאו פשוט פסול. מדקתני רשב"ג אומר הכל כמנהג המדינה מכלל דת"ק לית ליה מנהג המדינה. א) מדקתני פשוט שכתבו עדיו מאחריו ומקושר שכתבו עדיו מתוכו שניהן פסולין אלא כל אחד צריך להיות כתיקונו. כך ס"ל דבכל מקום צריך להלך אחר מנהגו ואם שינה פסול: אמר רב אשי. ודאי לתרוייהו סבירא להו הכל כמנהג המדינה ובאתרא דנהיגי פשוט ואמר ליה לסופר עביד למלוה פשוט כו' קפידא הוא ופסול הוא לדברי הכל והוי כמלוה על פה ואינו טורף בו לקוחות: ת"ק סבר. אע"ג דנהיגי ההוא אתרא כתרוייהו אי האי אי האי ואמר ליה עביד לי פשוט ועבד ליה מקושר מקפיד הוא שאינו רוצה שישנהו וכשישנהו פסול. ומר סבר רשב"ג כיון דנהיגי כתרוייהו מראה מקום הוא לו דהאי דקאמר ליה לעשות פשוט לאו משום דוקא קאמר ליה אלא הכי קאמר ליה עביד ליה פשוט קסבר משום דלית ליה טירחא ואם עבד ליה מקושר הכי נמי דניחא ליה הואיל והיינו נמי מנהג המדינה: אם הטעה לשבח הרי זו מקודשת. המקדש ואמר לה על מנת שאני לוי ונמצא כהן על מנת שאני עני וקבלה עליה ונמצא עשיר היינו טעות לשבח הרי מקודשת היא משום דמראה מקום הוא לה דכיון דנתרצתה להתקדש לו בכל דהו כל שכן דנתרצתה לשבח: וקבלו במקום אחר פסול. משום דלא שויא שליח לקבלה אלא בההוא מקום פלוני דקפידא הוא דבההוא אתרא לא איכפת לה אם תתזל דידעי דהיא גרושה ובדוכתא אחריתא ניחא לה להתבזות לפני בית דין. ור' אליעזר דמכשיר סבר דמראה מקום היא לו דכסבורה היא שימצאנו לבעלה באותו מקום להכי אמרה ליה במקום פלוני ואם מצאו במקום אחר הכי נמי דניחא לה: הואיל ובעלמא [...]ור. דכל גט פשוט בשני עדים כשר: הכא נמי. במקושר בשני עדים כשר קמ"ל דפסול. פשוט דבעד אחד פסול למה לי במתני' למיתני. ועד אחד על פה אפי' הכי פסול למיטרף ביה לקוחות דבמלוה על פה דמי: אמימר מכשר למיטרף

נראה לצ"ל מנהג המדינה בתמיה והא מדקתני וכו' אלמא דגם ת"ק ס"ל דבכל מקום וכו'.

מסורת הש"ס

[...]ר"ל אביי: ב) קדושין [...] ג) [לעיל טו:] [...] קדושין מח:] ה) [עי' [...] לעיל טו: ד"ה ומר [...] ו) קדושין מח:: [...]יטין סה. ח) רש"ל: [...]עירובין דף קב: וש"נ]: [...]א כשר וגי' רש"ל נמי [...] כ) רש"ל ומיהו י"ל: [...] ל) רש"א:

הגהות הב"ח

[...]גמ' דנהיגי בפשוט וכו' [...] במקושר וא"ל: [...] רשב"ם ד"ה אמר [...] וכו' אביי אתא לפרש [...]ה: (ג) ד"ה מר סבר [...] ורבן שמעון בן גמליאל [...]: (ד) תום' ד"ה אמר [...] אי נמי למ"ד לא [...]רפין מ"מ שני שטרות [...] של עד אחד: [...] בא"ד בכה"ג דהוה [...] למינקט ביה שניהם [...]ב ובשני שטרות דלא [...] כגון שניהם [...]דים שראו שלוה: [...] בא"ד שראה שמסר לו [...]ר הזה שהעד: [...] בא"ד שהעד החתום [...] כעד מסירה דמוכיח [...]סרו לו לוה למלוה שהוא [...]היה חותם: (ח) בא"ד [...] משום דכששניהם [...]דין על ראיית המלוה [...] שמיעת ההודאה אין [...]ר מוכיח שראו כצ"ל: [...] בא"ד שאינו מוכיח מן [...]ר שלא ראה המלוה לא [...]ינן ראייתו שאין חשוב [...]ל ותיבת כאחד נמחק: [...] בא"ד אינה אלא בלבד [...] השטר וכו' אפי' אם [...] אותה ובירושלמי [...]ינן עד אחד בכתב מהו [...] אחד בכתב כלום הוא [...] צריכא כצ"ל ותיבות [...]עד בעל פה נמחק:

מתניתין! הא קא משמע לן, דשנים במקושר כעד אחד בפשוט, מה התם פסולא דאורייתא, אף הכא נמי פסולא דאורייתא, תדע, דשלחו מתם חברייא לר' ירמיה: עד אחד בכתב ועד אחד על פה, מהו שיצטרפו? אליבא (א)דתנא קמא דרבי יהושע בן קרחה לא תיבעי לך, דאפילו שנים בכתב ושנים על פה לא מצטרפי, אלא כי תיבעי לך — אליבא דר' יהושע בן קרחה: שנים בכתב ושנים על פה הוא דמצטרפי, אבל עד אחד בכתב ואחד על פה לא מצטרפינן. או דלמא לא שנא? שלח להו: אני איני כדיי ששלחתם לי, אלא כך דעת תלמידכם נוטה — שיצטרפו. אמר ליה: אנן הכי מתנינן לה, דשלחו ליה חברייא לרבי ירמיה: שנים שהעידו אחד בבית דין זה ואחד בבית דין זה, מהו שיבואו בית דין אצל בית דין ויצטרפו? (ב)אליבא דתנא קמא דר' נתן לא תיבעי לך, דאפילו בחד בית דינא נמי לא מצטרפי, אלא כי תיבעי לך — אליבא דר' נתן: בחד בי דינא הוא דמצטרפי, אבל בתרי בי דינא לא מצטרפי, או דלמא לא שנא? ושלח להו: אני איני כדיי שאתם שלחתם לי, אלא כך דעת תלמידכם נוטה — שיצטרפו. מר בר חייא אמר, הכי שלחו ליה: שנים שהעידו בב"ד זה וחזרו והעידו בב"ד זה, מהו שיבוא אחד מכל ב"ד ויצטרפו? אליבא דר' נתן לא תיבעי לך, השתא עדים מצרפינן, דייני מיבעיא? אלא כי תיבעי לך — אליבא דת"ק דר' נתן: עדים הוא דלא מצרפינן, אבל דייני מצרפינן, או דלמא ל"ש? שלח להו: אני איני כדיי שאתם שלחתם לי, אלא כך דעת תלמידכם נוטה — שיצטרפו. רבינא אמר, הכי שלחו ליה: שלשה שישבו לקיים את השטר, ומת אחד מהן, צריכי למכתב: "במותב תלתא הוינא וחד ליתוהי", או לא? שלח להו: אני איני כדיי שאתם שלחתם לי, אלא כך דעת תלמידכם נוטה — שצריכין למכתב "במותב תלתא הוינא וחד ליתוהי". ועל דא עיילוהו לרבי ירמיה בבי מדרשא.§

מתני' כתוב בו "זוזין מאה דאינון סלעין עשרין" — אין לו אלא עשרין; "זוזין מאה דאינון תלתין סלעין" — אין לו אלא מנה. "כסף זוזין דאינון" ונמחק — אין פחות משתים. "כסף סלעין דאינון" ונמחק — אין פחות משתים. "דרכונות דאינון" ונמחק — אין פחות משתים. כתוב בו מלמעלה מנה ומלמטה מאתים, מלמעלה מאתים ומלמטה מנה — הכל הולך אחר התחתון. א"כ, למה כותבין את העליון? שאם (ג)תמחק אות אחת מן התחתון — ילמד מן העליון.§

גמ' תנו רבנן: (א) אמר "כסף" — אין פחות מדינר כסף; "כסף דינרין" ו"דינרין כסף" — אין פחות משני דינרין כסף; "כסף בדינרין" — אין פחות מבשני דינרין דהב, כסף. אמר מר: "כסף" — אין פחות מדינר כסף. (ד)ואימא: נסכא! אמר רבי אלעזר: דכתוב ביה "מטבע". ואימא: פריטי! אמר רב פפא: באתרא דלא סגי פריטי דכספא. תנו רבנן: "דהב" — אין פחות מדינר דהב; "דהב דינרין" ו"דינרין דהב" — אין פחות משני דינרין דהב; "דהב בדינרין" — אין פחות מבשני דינרין כסף, דהב. אמר מר: "דהב" — אין פחות מדינר דהב. (ה)אימא: נסכא! אמר רבי אלעזר: דכתב "מטבע". ואימא

תוספות

מה התם פסולא דאורייתא. למאן דאמר בפרק "המגרש" (גיטין פו.) גבי יש בו זמן ואין בו אלא עד אחד הולד כשר — בכתב ידו ועד דוקא, אבל כתב סופר ועד פסול לגמרי — אתי שפיר. אבל למ"ד נמי התם: כתב סופר ועד נמי כשר הולד, ואפי' בסופר דלא מובהק — קשה: אמאי קרי ליה הכא פסול דאורייתא? וי"ל: דההיא כאביי דהכא סבירא ליה. אי נמי, הכא מיירי שהסופר בעצמו חתם, או שכתבו קרוב או פסול.

הכא נמי פסולא דאורייתא. לאו דאורייתא ממש, דגט יתקושר מדרבנן הוי כדאמר לעיל. אלא מה שהולד ממזר מדרבנן, כי היכי דהוי ממזר בפסול פשוט — קרי ליה דאורייתא, ולאו דוקא. ורשב"ם פירש פסול דאורייתא — דלא גבי מבני חרי. ואין נראה לרבי, דאפי' (ה) כי הוי פסולא דרבנן לא היה גבי מבני חרי.

אימא נסכא. תימה לרבי: מאי קושיא? תפסת מועט תפסת! (ו) והכי הוי מצי לדחויי דנסכא פחות מדינר. מיהו, עוד קשה: דבכתובות פרק בתרא (דף קי:) אמרי': כתוב בו בבל — מגבהו ממעות שבבבל, כתוב בו כסף סתם — כל מה שירצה לוה מגבהו. פירוש: מטבע פחותה של כסף. ופריך: ואימא נסכא. ותימה: (ז) וכי נסכא פחותה מאיסר שאין בה רק[ח] [שמונה] פרוטות? ומאי שנא נסכא ממיני פרוטות? דהא "מה שירצה" קאמר התם — היינו מטבע פחות של כסף, מדפריך עלה: ואימא פריטי, ומשני: פריטי דכספא לא עבדי אינשי — מכלל דמטבע פחותה של כסף דעבדי אינשי נותן לו. והכא נמי בשמעתין משמע הכי דגריעי מאיסר, אם נפרש דמכח גריעותא מקשה "אימא נסכא", דאי לא גריע טפי מאיסר — ברישא הוי ליה לאקשויי "ואימא פריטי".

ורבינו

רשב"ם

ומשני: הא קמ"ל. מתני' דקתני פשוט שכתוב בו עד אחד פסול — שילמד מקושר ממנו, (ג) ולהכי תנייה לעד אחד, למימרא: מה עד אחד פסול דאורייתא, כדכתיב (דברים יט): "לא יקום עד אחד באיש" כו' — אף שנים שבמקושר הטילו עליו חכמים פסולא דאורייתא, ואם גט — אינה מגורשת, ואם שטר מלוה הוא — אינו טורף ממשעבדי. אבל אם יש שם עד אחד בעל פה עם עד אחד החתום בשטר — אז יהיה השטר כשר לגמרי, דמצטרפין. תדע דשלחו ליה כו'. ושלח להו דמצטרפין. דשלחו ליה חכמים לר' ירמיה לבתר דאפקוהו מבי מדרשא, כדאמר בפרק "לא יחפור" (לעיל דף כג:): אפקוה לר' ירמיה מבי מדרשא, ועל דא עיילוהו כדאמרינן במסקנא. מהו שיצטרפו. דנימא כמאן דחתימי תרווייהו, בשטרא דמי. אליבא דת"ק דר' יהושע בן קרחה כו'. פלוגתייהו בסנהדרין בפרק "זה בורר" (דף ל.) דתניא: (ג) אין עדותן מצטרפת בב"ד עד שיראו שניהם כאחד, רבי יהושע בן קרחה אומר: אפי' בזה אחר זה. אין עדותן מתקיימת עד שיעידו שניהם כאחד, רבי נתן אומר: שומעין דבריו של זה היום, וכשיבא חבירו למחר שומעין דבריו. והני שני מחלוקות, של ר"י בן קרחה ורבנן ודרבי נתן ורבנן, התם מפרש טעמא, איבעית אימא קרא ואב"א סברא. השתא. השנים החתומים בשטר ורוצין אנו לקיים עדותן בשטר שהן חתומין בו, או שנים בעל פה לענין לגבות ממון בעדותן בלא שטר — אין מצטרפין אם לא שראו שניהם כאחד את עדותן, ואע"ג דממה נפשך תרווייהו אחד מנה קא מסהדי. אליבא דר' יהושע (ד). שנים בכתב ושנים בעל פה מצטרפין, אפי' אם בזה אחר זה ראו עדותן, אבל אם עד אחד בכתב כו'. אמר ליה. רב אשי לאמימר: אנן הכי מתנינן לה כו', ולא תקשי מיניה לאביי דאמר אין מצטרפין. מהו שיבואו ב"ד. זה אצל ב"ד אחר לצרף עדותן ששמעו, וישפטו לפי העדות. אליבא דת"ק דרבי נתן. למעלה פירשתיה. וכשראו שניהם כאחד, אפס לא העידו בבית דין כאחד, בהכי פליגי רבי נתן ורבנן. ומת אחד מהן. לאחר שהעידו העדים על חתימת ידם בפני שלשה, ואין קיום השטר אלא בג', דבעינן ב"ד לקבל העדות. וחד ליתוהי. דלא מתחזי כשיקרא מאי דכתיב ברישא "במותב תלתא הוינא" ובסופו לא נחתמו אלא שנים. על דא עיילוהו. שהשיב להם כהוגן. דהא דאפקוהו ששאל שלא כהוגן: רגלו אחת חוץ לתחום ורגלו אחת בתוך התחום, ועל דא אפקוהו מבי מדרשא בפרק "לא יחפור", והשתא הוא דעיילוהו.

מתני' כתוב בו. בשטר מלוה: זוזים מאה דאינון עשרים סלעים לוה פלוני מפלוני. ואף על פי שמאה זוזי הרי הן (בכלל) כ"ה סלעים — אין למלוה אלא (מנה) כ' (ו) זוזים, דיד בעל השטר על התחתונה, והמוציא מחבירו עליו הראיה. ושמא כך פי': מאה זוזים גרועים וחסירים שאינן שוין אלא כ' סלעים. אין לו אלא מנה. מאה זוזים. שיש לפרש כך: זוזים מאה דאינון תלתין סלעים קלים, שאינן שוין אלא כ"ה סלעים, דיד בעל השטר על התחתונה. הסלע ארבעה דינרין, המנה כ"ה סלעים. ונמחק. המנין שכתוב בו אחר "דאינון". דרכונות. בלע"ז קינו"ס, והם דרכמונות שבספר עזרא (ג). ומלמטה מאתים. כשכפל דבריו בשטר. הכל הולך אחר התחתון. אלא שלא יהא כתוב בשיטה אחרונה. למה כותבין את העליון. הואיל ובסוף השטר חוזר וכופל את דבריו, שכותבין ושונין אחריות ממון זה: "כך וכך קבלתי עלי ועל ירתאי" כו'.

גמ' ת"ר כסף אין פחות מדינר כסף. "כסף לוה פלוני מפלוני". כסף דינרין או דינרין כסף אין פחות משני דינרין כסף. לוה, דהכי משמע: כסף שני דינרין לוה פלוני מפלוני. כסף בדינרין אין פחות משני דינרין זהב כסף. ד"כסף בדינרין" משמע: כסף לוה פלוני מפלוני שוה שני דינרין של זהב, וכדמפרש לקמן שכתוב "כסף בדינרי" משמע: בדינרי זהב. אבל בדינרין — היינו שני דינרין של כסף (ז) (אין פחות מכסף בשוה שני דינרין של זהב). זהב בדינרין אין פחות משוה שני דינרין של כסף. אותו זהב שלוה, וכדמפרש לקמן דדינרין משמע של כסף.

פריטי

הגהות הב"ח

(א) גמ' תנו רבנן כסף כצ"ל ותיבת אמר נמחק: (ב) רשב"ם ד"ה ומשני וכו' ולהכי תנן לעד אחד למימרא מה עד אחד פסול: (ג) ד"ה אליבא וכו' דתניא לשלש אין עדותן מצטרפת עד שיראו שניהם כאחד וכו' ואין עדותן מתקיימת עד שיעידו בב"ד עד שיעידו: (ד) ד"ה אליבא דרבי יהושע בן קרחה שנים בכתב: (ה) תוס' ד"ה הכא וכו' דאפילו אי הוי פסולא: (ו) ד"ה אימא נסכא וכו' והכא הוי מצי לדחויי: (ז) בא"ד ותימה דאי נסכא פחות אמאי לא קושיא הא דפחות ממשמונה פרוטות דהא מה שירצה קאמר התם דהיינו מטבע פחותה כצ"ל:

מסורת הש"ס

א) [לעיל דף לג. וש"נ] ב) [שם וש"ן סנהדרין ל.] ג) כ"ה גי' הרי"ף והרא"ש והגי' הנכונה שאם לא כתב אלא אות אחת. ת"ח: ד) מנחות דף קז. ע"ש כתובות דף קי: ע"ש ה) [כתובות שם מנחות שם] ו) רש"ל סלעים: ז) רש"ל מ"ז: ח) רש"ל מיני:

עין משפט נר מצוה

לו א מיי' פ"ד מהל' עדות הלכה ו סמג עשין קט טוש"ע ח"מ סי' ל סעיף יח:

לז ב מיי' שם טוש"ע שם סעיף יב:

לח ג מיי' שם פ"ו הלכה ו סמג שם טוש"ע ח"מ סי' מו סעיף כט:

לט ד מיי' פכ"ד מהל' מלוה ולוה הלכה יד סמג עשין צד טוש"ע ח"מ סי' מב סעיף ח:

מ ה טוש"ע שם סעיף ט:

מא ו מיי' פכ"ד מהל' מלוה ולוה הל' יד טוש"ע ח"מ סי' מב סעיף י:

מב ז מיי' שם טוש"ע שם סעיף ו:

מג ח ט י כ ל מ נ מיי' פכ"ד מהל' מלוה ולוה הלכה יז סמג עשין צד טוש"ע ח"מ סי' מב סעיף יג:

רבינו גרשום

למיטרף [מלקוחות]. אלא קשיא מתני'. לאמימר א"כ מאי קמ"ל מתני' פשוט שכתב בו עד אחד פסול פשיטא. ומשני הא קמ"ל דשני עדים החתומין על השטר מקושר כעד אחד דחתום בפשוט דמי: מה התם. בפשוט אי ליכא אלא עד אחד חתום איכא פסולא דאורייתא. דאפי' תפים מלוה מחמת ההוא שטרא מפקי' מיניה. אף הכא במקושר דחתימו ביה תרי סהדי בלבד הוי פסולא דאורייתא ואי תפים מפקינן מיניה דלא סגיא בלא ג' סהדי: תדע. ודאי דעד אחד בכתב ועד אחד על פה מצטרפין לעדות אחת וכשרין דשלחו ליה חבריא לר' ירמיה: אליבא דת"ק לא תיבעי לך. דאפי' שנים בכתב ושנים על פה שלא ראו זאת העדות ביחד אלא זה ראה מחלון זה שלוה פלוני מפלוני מנה והכי נמי אידך ולא היו מכירין זה את זה ודאי לא מצטרפי הואיל ולא ראו עדותן יחד: כי תיבעי לך אליבא דר' יהושע בן קרחה. דאמר בזה אחר זה מצטרפי הואיל דעל מנה אחד מסהדי ומצטרפי שנים בכתב ושנים בעל פה הכי נמי מצטרפי הואיל דמסהדי עדות אחת. אבל עד אחד בכתב ועד אחד על פה אע"ג דתרווייהו הוו לעדות אחת אהדדי לא מצטרפי הואיל דאחד בכתב ואחד על פה. או דלמא לא שנא ומצטרפי: שיצטרפו. אלמא דמצטרפי: א"ל לעולם לא מצטרפי. והאי דאמריתו דמיבעי לר' ירמיה לא הכי קא מיבעיא ליה כלל. כלומר [לא] מש"ה שלחו ליה דאנן ההיא בעיא הכי מתנינן לה. שנים שהעידו עדות אחת והעיד עד אחד עדותו בב"ד אחר ואחד העיד בב"ד אחר והלכו למדינת הים. מהו שיבא בית דין אצל בית דין ויצטרפו דכעדים דמי: אליבא דת"ק דר' נתן לא תיבעי לך דאפי' בחד בי דינא לא מצטרפי: כי תיבעי לך אליבא דר' נתן. דאמר שומעין דבריו של זה היום ולכשיבוא חבירו למחר שומעין את דבריו: שנים שהעידו בב"ד על חתימת יד שני עדים למדינת הים והשתא לא מצי הוי חד ב"ד וחזרו והעידו בב"ד אחר והלכו להן שנים מהן וחזרו העדים והעידו בב"ד והלכו להם שנים נשתייר אחד מהן מכל בית דין ובית דין מהו שיבוא אותו אחד שנשתייר מכל בית דין ובית דין דהוין ג' בתי דינין ויצטרפו לקיים השטר בעדותן. אליבא דר' נתן דאמר שומעין דבריו של זה היום וכשיבוא חבירו למחר שומעין לו. לא תיבעי לך דודאי מצטרפי. דהשתא עדים דלא בקיאי כולי האי מצטרפי. דייני דבקיאי ומובהקים לחקור ולדרוש לא כ"ש דמצטרפי. והא פלוגתא דר' נתן ור' יהושע במס' סנהדרין בפ' דיני ממונות זה בורר לו שלשה: ב"ד שישבו לקיים את השטר ומת אחד מהן. קודם שחתמו וקיום השטר צריך ג' ב"ד וצריכי למיכתב במותב תלתא הוינא כו': ועל דא עיילוהו לר' ירמיה בבי מדרשא. לכל חד וחד כדאית ליה משום דשפיר פשט [דהא] דאפקוהו (לעיל כג' לא יחפור) משום דאיבעיא ליה רגלו אחת של ניפול בתוך חמשים ורגלו אחת חוץ לחמשים מהו: כתוב בו. בשטר זוזין מאה חייב פלוני לפלוני: ונמחק אותו סכום ואינו ניכר. ודאי אין זוזי דאינון פחות משנים: דרכונות. של זהב שלועזין מוקוסי: ת"ר כתוב בשטר כסף. סתם לוה פלוני מפלוני בודאי אין פחות מדינר כסף שהוא חייב לו. ואי כתב לו כסף דינרים או דינרים כסף לוה פלוני מפלוני אין פחות משני דינרין של כסף. דינרין אין פחות משנים. אבל אם כתב כסף בדינרי חייב פלוני לפלוני משמע כסף חייב לו שהוא שוה ב' דינרין (דינרים) של זהב. אין פחות מב' דינרי של זהב מכסף חייב לו: ואימא נסכא. חתיכה של כסף קטנה חייב לו: ואימא פריטי. קטנים של כסף. דאית ביה מטבע: דלא סגיא פריטי דכספא. ומטבע שלהם אין פחותה מדינר ומשום הכי היכא דכתב כסף סתם משמע דינר: ת"ר אי כתב בשטר זהב סתם לוה פלוני מפלוני אין פחות מדינר זהב ה' פשיטים למשקל ברזל. ואי כרב זהב דינרין או דינרי זהב אין פחות משני דינרים של זהב. ואי כתב זהב בדינרין אין פחות מבשני דינרין כסף דזהב כלומר

וְאֵימָא: פְּרִיטֵי! א)פְּרִיטֵי דְּדַהֲבָא לָא עָבְדִי אִינָשֵׁי. "זָהָב בְּדִינָרִין" — אאֵין פָּחוֹת מִבִּשְׁנֵי דִּינָרִין כֶּסֶף, זָהָב. וְאֵימָא: דַּהֲבָא פְּרִיכָא בְּתְרֵי דִּינָרֵי דַּהֲבָא קָאָמַר! אָמַר אַבַּיֵי: יַד בַּעַל הַשְּׁטָר עַל הַתַּחְתּוֹנָה. ב)(רֵישָׁא דְּקָתָנֵי: "כֶּסֶף בְּדִינָרִין" — אֵין פָּחוֹת מִשְּׁנֵי דִּינָרִין זָהָב, כֶּסֶף; אַמַּאי? אֵימָא: כַּסְפָּא, נַסְכָא בִּתְרֵי דִּינָרֵי כַּסְפָּא קָאָמַר!) א"ר אַשִׁי: ברֵישָׁא — דִּכְתַב "דִּינָרֵי", סֵיפָא — דִּכְתַב "דִּינָרִין". וּמְנָא תֵּימְרָא דְּשָׁאנֵי בֵּין "דִּינָרֵי" לְ"דִינָרִין"? ג)דְּתַנְיָא: ד)גהָאִשָּׁה שֶׁהָיוּ עָלֶיהָ סְפֵק חָמֵשׁ לֵידוֹת, סְפֵק חָמֵשׁ זִיבוֹת — מְבִיאָה קָרְבָּן אֶחָד וְאוֹכֶלֶת בִּזְבָחִים, וְאֵין הַשְּׁאָר עָלֶיהָ חוֹבָה. הָיוּ עָלֶיהָ חָמֵשׁ לֵידוֹת וַדָּאוֹת, חָמֵשׁ זִיבוֹת וַדָּאוֹת — מְבִיאָה קָרְבָּן אֶחָד וְאוֹכֶלֶת בִּזְבָחִים, וְהַשְּׁאָר עָלֶיהָ חוֹבָה; מַעֲשֶׂה וְעָמְדוּ קִינִּים בִּירוּשָׁלַיִם בְּדִינָרֵי זָהָב, אָמַר רַבָּן שִׁמְעוֹן בֶּן גַּמְלִיאֵל: הַמָּעוֹן הַזֶּה! אִם אָלִין הַלַּיְלָה עַד שֶׁיְּהוּ בְּדִינָרִין; נִכְנַס לְבֵית דִּין וְלִימֵּד: הָאִשָּׁה שֶׁהָיוּ עָלֶיהָ חָמֵשׁ לֵידוֹת וַדָּאוֹת, חָמֵשׁ זִיבוֹת וַדָּאוֹת — מְבִיאָה קָרְבָּן אֶחָד וְאוֹכֶלֶת בִּזְבָחִים, וְאֵין הַשְּׁאָר עָלֶיהָ חוֹבָה. וְעָמְדוּ

פְּרִיטֵי דְּדַהֲבָא לָא עָבְדִי אִינָשֵׁי. בְּשׁוּם אַתְרָא. וְדִלְמָא בִּתְרֵי דִּינָרֵי דַּהֲבָא פְּרִיכָא קָאָמַר לֵיהּ. כְּלוֹמַר, "זָהָב בְּדִינָרִין" — תַּרְוַיְיהוּ בְּזָהָב מַיְירֵי, אֶלָּא שֶׁזֶּה מַטְבֵּעַ וְאִידָךְ הָוֵי דַּהֲבָא פְּרִיכָא, וְהָכִי קָאָמַר: דַּהֲבָא פְּרִיכָא בְּשָׁוֶה שְׁנֵי דִינָרִין זָהָב לָוָה פְּלוֹנִי מִפְּלוֹנִי. אִי הָכִי רֵישָׁא נַמִי. בֵּין דְּאִידָךְ בָּרַיְיתָא קַמַּיְיתָא דְּקָתָנֵי: "כֶּסֶף בְּדִינָרִין" אֵין פָּחוֹת מִבִּשְׁנֵי דִינָרִין דְּזָהָב כֶּסֶף — נֵימָא יַד בַּעַל הַשְּׁטָר כו', וַהֲוָה לָנוּ לְפָרֵשׁ: גְּרוּטָאוֹת כֶּסֶף בִּשְׁנֵי דִינָר כֶּסֶף. וּבֵין דְּהַךְ מַתְנִיתָא דְּקָתָנֵי: "זָהָב דִּינָרִין" וְ"דִינָרִין זָהָב" אֵין פָּחוֹת מִשְּׁנֵי דִינָרִין זָהָב — נֵימָא: אֵין פָּחוֹת מִשָּׁוֶה שְׁנֵי דִינָרִין כֶּסֶף זָהָב! רֵישָׁא דִּכְתַב דִּינָרֵי. דְּמַשְׁמַע דִּינָרֵי זָהָב, אֲבָל "דִּינָרִין" סְתָם מַשְׁמַע שֶׁל כֶּסֶף. וּמְנָא תֵּימְרָא דְּשָׁאנֵי לָן בֵּין דִּינָרֵי לְדִינָרִין. שֶׁזֶּה דִינָרִין שֶׁל כֶּסֶף וְזֶה שֶׁל זָהָב. דִּתְנַן. בְּשִׁילְהֵי פֶּרֶק קַמָּא דִּכְרֵיתוֹת: הָאִשָּׁה שֶׁיֵּשׁ עָלֶיהָ סָפֵק חָמֵשׁ לֵידוֹת — חָמֵשׁ פְּעָמִים הִפִּילָה, סָפֵק רוּחַ סָפֵק וָלָד. סָפֵק חָמֵשׁ זִיבוֹת. כְּגוֹן מְקוּלְקֶלֶת לְמִנְיָנָהּ, וְרָאֲתָה חֲמִשָּׁה חֳדָשִׁים שְׁלֹשָׁה יָמִים רְצוּפִים בְּכָל חֹדֶשׁ, סָפֵק בִּימֵי נִדָּה, סָפֵק בְּתוֹךְ אַחַד עָשָׂר יוֹם שֶׁבֵּין נִדָּה לְנִדָּה שֶׁהֵם יְמֵי זִיבָה, וְחַיֶּיבֶת בְּקָרְבָּן. מְבִיאָה קָרְבָּן אֶחָד. לִיטָּהֵר מִטּוּמְאָתָהּ: תּוֹר לְעוֹלָה וְתוֹר לְחַטָּאת. וְאֵינוֹ נֶאֱכָל, דְּחַטָּאת הָעוֹף בָּאָה עַל הַסָּפֵק וְאֵינוֹ נֶאֱכָל, כִּדְנַפְקָא לָן מִמַּתְנִי' דְּרַבִּי יוֹסֵי בְּר' חֲנִינָא בְּמַסֶּכֶת נָזִיר (דף כט.). וְאֵין הַשְּׁאָר עָלֶיהָ חוֹבָה. שֶׁבְּקוּשִׁי הִתִּירוּ לְהָבִיא חַטָּאת הָעוֹף עַל הַסָּפֵק, כְּדֵי לְטַהֲרָהּ מִסְּפֵק טוּמְאָתָהּ, מִשּׁוּם דְּהַהִיא חַטָּאת אָזְלָא לִקְבוּרָה. וְכֵיוָן דְּמִיטַּהֲרָא בְּקָרְבָּן אֶחָד, כִּדְאָמְרִינַן בְּמַסֶּכֶת כְּרֵיתוֹת — דּוּמְיָא דְּאִשָּׁה טְמֵאָה דְּמִיחַיְּיבָא חָמֵשׁ טְבִילוֹת, וּבִטְבִילָה אַחַת מִטַּהֶרֶת — תּוּ לָא מַיְיתֵי חַטָּאת מִסָּפֵק, לַהֲבִיאוֹ לְבֵית הַפְּסוּל. וְהַשְּׁאָר עָלֶיהָ חוֹבָה. וּכְגוֹן שֶׁיָּלְדָה לְאַחַר מְלֹאת. אֲבָל עַל הַלֵּידָה שֶׁבְּתוֹךְ מְלֹאת — נִפְטֶרֶת בְּקָרְבָּן אֶחָד עַל שְׁנֵיהֶם. וּמִ"זֹּאת תּוֹרַת הַיּוֹלֶדֶת" נָפְקָא לָן בְּפֶרֶק "אַרְבָּעָה מְחוּסְּרֵי כַפָּרָה" (כריתות דף ט:). הַמָּעוֹן הַזֶּה. בֵּית הַמִּקְדָּשׁ נִשְׁבַּע. עַד שֶׁיַּעַמְדוּ בְּדִינָרִין. שֶׁל כֶּסֶף. כְּלוֹמַר, שֶׁיְּהֵא בְּזוֹל. וְאֵין הַשְּׁאָר עָלֶיהָ חוֹבָה. טַעֲמָא דְּר' שִׁמְעוֹן וְר' עֲקִיבָא דְּאָמְרֵי הָתָם: תֹּאמַר עַל אַחַת וְתִפָּטֵר, מְפָרֵשׁ הָתָם בְּפֶרֶק קַמָּא. וְעָמְדוּ

ורבינו תם פירש בתשובתו דנסכא גריעא. ובין הכא ובין בכתובות (דף קי:) (א) פריך: ואימא נסכא, מכח דיד בעל השטר על התחתונה. וקשה כלפריסית. ואומר רבי: דנסכא חשיבא טובא, כיון שכתב סתם — אימור דהיינו נסכא, דמסתמא כך רלה לומר, כיון שלא פירש המטבע. ושיעור הזה לנסכא פחותה, [אפשר] שהיו יודעים כמה הוי. ולא תקשה הא דקאמר התם: פריטי דכספא לא עבדי אינשי, והכא קאמר: באתרא דלא סגי פריטי דכספא. (ב) התם הכי פריך: ואימא פרוטות של נחושת, ומשני: פריטי דכספא לא עבדי אינשי, ו"כסף" הכתוב בשטר משמע שכסף ממש הלוה לו, ולא שוה כסף. אבל הכא פריך: ואימא פריטי — פירוש: מעות ופונדיונין ואיסרין וכל שאר מטבע של כסף הפחותים מדינר קורין פריטי, ולא פריטי ממש. ומשני: דמיירי האי תנא באתרא דלא סגו פריטי דכספא, שאין הולך מטבע של כסף פחותה מדינר באותה מדינה. והך סוגיא איתא נמי במנחותה). **אי** הכי רישא נמי. פירש רבינו חננאל: רישא נמי — היינו ברייתא קמייתא: "כסף בדינרין" אין פחותין משני דינרי זהב כסף. וכן נראה לי. ואע"פ שהגמרא רלה לחלקו לשתי ברייתות, שאמר בכל אחת "תנו רבנן". אע"פ שבתוספתא שלנו ברייתא ד"זהב אין פחות מדינר זהב" שנויה תחלה קודם ההיא דכסף — נראה דההיא אינה שבתוספתא, והגמרא היה יודע שכן היא מברייתא אחת שנויה. וכעין זה נ"ל בתחלת ר"ה (דף ג:) שמחלק הגמרא ברייתא דתנו רבנן, ואע"פ שהיא אחת. (ג) והכי פריך: אימא דהבא פריכא בתרי דינרי דהבא. (ד) כיון שהזהב דינרין, ו"דינרין זהב" הן דינרי זהב — כמו כן "זהב בדינרין" יהא של זהב, כיון שבזהב משתעי שטר. כי למה י"ל שלא יהא הדינרין זהב מאחר שכתב (ה) בשטר? ועוד, כמו "כסף בדינרין" שהן דינרי זהב, א"כ סתם דינרין הן של זהב! אמר אביי: יד בעל השטר על התחתונה — לכך יש לנו לומר שהדינרין של כסף, אע"פ שיש זהב בשטר. אבל רישא דברייתא בתרייתא, (ו) אע"פ שיש בה נמי דינרין, דמשמע נמי של כסף, וסתם דינרין של כסף הן — כל כמה דלא אמר "דינרין" אין לומר שם שיהיו של כסף, ד"זהב דינרין" ו"דינרין זהב" מוכח בהדיא שהדינר של זהב. ופריך: רישא נמי, דקתני "כסף בדינרין" — יהיו של כסף! בשלמא אי לאו סיפא, הוה אמינא טעמא דרישא — [דסתם] דינרין הם של זהב עד שיפרש דינרין של כסף או זוזים, אבל כיון דאמר דדינרין הם של כסף — אפי' כשמזכיר בשטר של זהב, משום דיד בעל השטר על התחתונה! (ז) ולא גרסינן נמי "ברישא נמי נימא הכי". **אמר** רב אשי רישא דכתב דינרי. ד"דינרי" משמע בין כסף ובין זהב, ולהכי מוקמינן ההוא דסיפא בשל כסף — משום דיד בעל השטר על התחתונה, כדמשני אביי. ולא גרסינן בספרים "אלא אמר רב אשי", דלא קאתי לשנויי דאביי. ונראה לומר דאכולה ברייתא קמייתא קאמר רב אשי דכתב "דינרי" — אפי' הכי "כסף דינרי" ו"דינרי כסף" מוכיח דדינרי כסף קאמר, שאין לפרשו בענין אחר מדלא קאמר "בדינרי". דאי מודה רב אשי דברישא דקמייתא לא מיירי בדכתב "דינרי" — אמאי ו)[מפליג בין ב"ת ללא ב"ת? ליפלוג בין "דינרי" ל"דינרין"! אבל אין נראה לומר כן, כי] "כסף דינרי" ו"דינרי כסף" לא היו דינרי כסף — כי זה לא היה דיבור, ואין שום אדם כותב כן. א"נ, "דינרי כסף" ו"כסף דינרי" בלא ב"ת איכא לספוקי, ויחלוקו, אע"פ שיש לנו לומר המוציא מחבירו עליו הראיה ככל ספק ממון, שהרי יש ספק שתיקנו חלוקה, כי ההוא דרב אשי דאמר בבכורות (דף מח.): (ח) מחלה יורשין ומחלה לקוחות. ואפילו לא היו חולקים היכא דלא תפס — היכא דתפס לא מפקינן מיניה. ז)לשון ר"י. **לפי** הספרים שגורסים "עד שיהיו בדינרין" ולא גרסינן "בדינר של כסף", לא ידענא היכי פשיט מינה ד"דינרי" של זהב ו"דינרין" של כסף, דלמא האי דקאמר "דינרי (ט) של זהב" גבי זהב — מחמת הדיקות היא, אבל בלא דיקות (י) יאמר לעולם "דינרין", ולא "דינרי". וסתם "דינרי" של כסף, עד שיפרוט דינרי זהב. ולכך שנה גבי זהב "דינרי [זהב]" — שהוצרך לפרש שהן של זהב ולבא בדיקות. אבל גבי כסף לא הוצרך לפרש שהן של כסף, ושנה "דינרין" סתם, לפי שאינו דוקי! אפי' אם נפשך לומר כי כמו שיאמר "זוזי" בלא דיקות בלשון גמרא במקום "זוזים" בלשון משנה — [א"כ] בלשון גמרא אי אפשר שיהו "דינרי" של כסף, שלאותם קורא זוזי בלשון גמרא, ולהכי קים ליה ש"דינרי" הם (כ) לשון זהב — הא ליכא למימר, שאם מטעם זה רוצה להוכיח — למה הביא מתניתין דכריתות (דף ח.)? ועוד, כיון שהביא ראיה ממנה — א"כ רוצה לומר שבלשון משנה שהיא עברי היו "דינרי" של זהב! ומצאתי בתורת כהנים "עד שיהיו בדינרין של כסף". ולפי גירסת תורת כהנים מוכח שפיר, כיון ששנה "דינרי" גבי זהב ו"דינרין" גבי כסף, אע"פ שניהם דבוקים. ונראה: לספרים דגרסי' ברישא "בדינרי" לחוד — אין לריך לגרוס בסיפא "כסף", דהא לשון "בדינרי" הוא של זהב. ה"ג: **נכנס** לב"ד ולימד האשה שיש (ל) חמש לידות עליה ודאות מביאה קרבן אחד ואוכלת בזבחים ואין השאר עליה חובה. וכן כתוב בכל הספרים הכא ובכריתות בפ"ק (שם), והכי איתא בתורת כהנים. אבל יש תימה: מאי ליהוי הכא טעמא דרשב"ג דפליג לפי גירסא זו אבית שמאי ואבית הלל, דתרוייהו מודו במפלת יום פ"א שחייבת על כל לידה ולידה? ורבי יוחנן בן נורי ור"ע פ"ק דכריתות הכי אית להו, שישאר עליה חובה. אלא שר' יוחנן בן נורי אומר: תאמר על האחרונה ותהא מותרת בקדשים. פירוש: ותו ליכא למיחש שתהא סבורה ליפטר, (מ) דודאי האחרון אינו פוטר את הראשון. אבל אם לא אמרה על האחרון — איכא למיחש שתהא סבורה שהראשון פטור אפילו לידה דלאחר מלאת כמו במלאת, ואתי למפשע שלא להביא יותר. ור"ע לא חייש לפשיעה, ועל איזה שתאמר מותרת בקדשים. אבל לתרוייהו תאמר עליה חובה, כרישא דהא משנה דהכא. ועוד, היכי מייתי מעשה לסתור? אי משום דמעיקרא הוו קיימי בדינרי זהב — דהיינו מעשה לסייע, דהא משמע שזה היה טעות שהיו מחמירין, כמו שמוכיח והולך, שרשב"ג ביטל אותה חומרא! ועוד: כיון שהיתה מותרת לאכול בקדשים — למה היו עומדים בדינר זהב, כיון שיכולות לאכול בקדשים? מיהו: יש לומר משום "בל תאחר" היו דוחקות. וכספר

מסורת הש"ס: א) [במנחות קז. ליתא אמר רב פפא פריטי דדהבא ע"ז] ב) כל זה מותק רש"ל בין נ"ל אי הכי רישא נמי אמר רב אשי כו' ג) נ"ל דתנן ד) כריתות פ"א מ"ז ה) וע"ש בתוס' קז. ד"ה דלמא ו) רש"ל וגר' רש"ל ז) לשון רש"י מה"ד לשון ר"י.

עין משפט נר מצוה: מד א ב מיי' פכ"ו מהל' מלוה ולוה הלכה יז סמג עשין נד טוש"ע ח"מ סי' מב סעיף יג ע"ש בהג"ה: מה ג מיי' פ"א מהלכות מחוסרי כפרה ה"ט:

הגהות הב"ח

(א) תוס' ד"ה (בקף הקודש) אימא וכו' ובין בכתובות דפריך ואימא נסכא מכח דיד בעל השטר על התחתונה פריך וקשה כלפריסית ואומר רבי דנסכא חשיבא טובא ואפילו הכי פריך ואימא נסכא כו' כיון שכתב סתם אימור כו' כצ"ל: (ב) בא"ד התם הכי פריך ואימא פריטי ממש ומשני פריטי דכספא לא עבדי וכו' אבל הכי פריך: (ג) ד"ה אי הכי כו' נ"ב כלומר מה שקשה לפי זה כו': (ד) בא"ד בתרי דינרי דהבא קאמר כיון שזהב דינרין: (ה) בא"ד מאחר שכתב זהב בשטר ועוד: (ו) בא"ד ריישא דברייתא בתרייתא אע"פ שיש בה נמי דינרין דמשמע נמי של כסף וסתם דינרין של כסף הן כל כמה דלא אמר דינרין זהב: (ז) בא"ד דיד בעל השטר על התחתונה ולא גרסינן נמי ברישא: (ח) ד"ה אמר רב אשי כו' כצ"ל ואלו דבכורות החולקין מחלה יורשין: (ט) ד"ה לפי הספרים וכו' דינרי של זהב וכו': (י) בא"ד יאמר לעולם דינרין ולא דינרי ועוד: (כ) בא"ד שאנן כו' נ"ב פי' לשון דינרי שהוא של זהב כו': (ל) ד"ה נכנס וכו' האשה שיש עליה חמש לידות ודאות מביאה קרבן אחד ואוכלת: (מ) בא"ד ליפטר מהראשון דודאי האחרון אינו פוטר את הראשון ואפי' לידה דלאחר מלאת כמו בתוך מלאת:

רבינו גרשום

כלומר צריך ליתן לו זהב ששוה שני דינרים של כסף מזהב: אימא נסכא. חתיכה קטנה: פריטי דדהבא לא עבדי אינשי. א) ואותו מטבע של זהב הוא ומשקל דינר: זהב בדינרין כו'. אמאי יהיב שוה שני דינרים של כסף מזהב ותו לא: ואימא דהכי משמע דהבא פריכא. זהב שחוק שאינו מטבע חייב ליתן לו בשוה שני דינרים של זהב ואמאי אמר אין פחות מבשני דינרי זהב: אמר אביי. משום הכי אין גובה אלא שוה ב' דינרים של כסף מזהב דיד בעל השטר על התחתונה: אי הכי. דיד בעל השטר על התחתונה רישא דקתני כסף בדינרין אין פחות משני דינרי זהב כסף דמשמע שוה שני דינרין של זהב יתן לו מכסף אמאי. הא נמי נימא נותן כסף נסכא שאינו מטבע בשוה שני דינרין של כסף ואמאי נותן לו כסף שוה שני דינרי זהב מכסף דהיינו יד בעל השטר על העליונה: אמר רב אשי רישא משום דכתב בשטר כסף בדינרי. דמשמע דינרי של זהב ומשום הכי גובה שוה שני דינרין של זהב מכסף. וסיפא משום הכי אינו גובה אלא ב' דינרי של כסף מזהב. דכתב בשטר דינרין דמשמע דינר של כסף: ומנא תימרא. דינרי היינו זהב ודינרין הן של כסף: ספק ה' לידות. שהפילה ה' פעמים ואינה יודעת אם ולד הפילה דחייבת קרבן או אם רוח הפילה דפטורה מקרבן. והכי הוא ספק ה' זיבות שראתה ג' ימים ואינה יודעת אם בתוך י"א יום ראתה והיא זבה וצריכה קרבן או בתוך ז' ימי נדה ראתה ואינה צריכה קרבן. הואיל דמספקא לן בקרבן אחד סגיא ואוכלת בו ביום דהיינו קדשים קלים כדאמ' הביא כפרתו אוכל בקדשים ואין השאר ד' קרבנות עליה חובה להביא: אם ילדה ה' לידות ודאות או [היו עליה] ה' זיבות ודאות מביאה קרבן אחד ואוכלת בזבחים דאמרי' שם לידה אחת היא ושם זיבה אחת היא והשאר קרבנות עליה חובה להביא קרבן אחד על כל לידה ועל כל זיבה וזיבה הואיל דודאי הוא ומביאה אימתי שתרצה: מעשה שעמדו קינין בירושלים. קרבן יולדת וקרבן זבה שהן קינין תורין ובני יונה ועמדו בדינרי זהב אלמא דדינרי היינו זהב: המעון הזה. נשבע בבית המקדש: עד שיהיו בדינרים. כלומר אני אוזלם עד שיעמדו בדינר של כסף אלמא דדינרין היינו של כסף: ולמה מביאה קרבן אחד שמלמדין אותה לומר שהיא מביאה קרבן על לידה אחרונה או על זבה אחרונה ופוטרת את הראשונות דשם לידה אחת היא ושם זיבה אחת היא ואוכלת בזבחים דטהורה היא ואין השאר עליה חובה משום דאחרון פוטר את כולן ונתזלזלו קינין עד שעמדו בריבעתן היינו חצי דינר כסף ולא משום הכי קרי ריבעתן דליהוי

א) אולי נ"ל ולכן אותו מטבע של זהב בודאי הייתו משקל דינר.

וְעָמְדוּ קִינִּין בּוֹ בַּיּוֹם בְּרִבְעָתִים.§ "כָּתוּב מִלְּמַעְלָה" וכו'.§ תָּנוּ רַבָּנַן: איִלָּמֵד הַתַּחְתּוֹן מִן הָעֶלְיוֹן בְּאוֹת אַחַת, אֲבָל לֹא בִּשְׁתֵּי אוֹתִיּוֹת, כְּגוֹן: "חָנָן" מֵ"חֲנָנִי" וְ"עָנָן" מֵ"עֲנָנִי". מַאי שְׁנָא שְׁתֵּי אוֹתִיּוֹת דְּלָא? דִּלְמָא מִיתְרַמֵי שֵׁם בֶּן אַרְבַּע אוֹתִיּוֹת, וַהֲוָה לֵיהּ פַּלְגֵּיהּ דִּשְׁמָא; אִי הָכִי, אוֹת אַחַת נָמֵי — דִּלְמָא מִיתְרַמֵי שֵׁם בֶּן שְׁתֵּי אוֹתִיּוֹת, וַהֲוָה לֵיהּ פַּלְגֵּיהּ דִּשְׁמָא! אֶלָּא, שְׁתֵּי אוֹתִיּוֹת הַיְינוּ טַעְמָא — דִּלְמָא מִיתְרַמֵי שֵׁם בֶּן שָׁלֹשׁ אוֹתִיּוֹת, וַהֲוָה לֵיהּ רוּבָּא דִּשְׁמָא. אֲמַר רַב פָּפָּא: בפְּשִׁיטָא לִי, "סֵפֶל" מִלְּמַעְלָה וְ"קֶפֶל" מִלְּמַטָּה — הַכֹּל הוֹלֵךְ אַחַר הַתַּחְתּוֹן. בָּעֵי רַב פָּפָּא: "קֶפֶל" מִלְּמַעְלָה וְ"סֵפֶל" מִלְּמַטָּה, מַאי? מִי גחָיְישִׁינַן לִזְבוּב אוֹ לָא? תֵּיקוּ. הַהוּא דַּהֲוָה כְּתַב בֵּיהּ "שִׁית מְאָה וְזוּזָא", שְׁלָחָהּ רַב שֵׁרֵבְיָא קַמֵּיהּ דְּאַבַּיֵּי: שִׁית מְאָה אִיסְתֵּירֵי וְזוּזָא, אוֹ דִּלְמָא: שִׁית מְאָה פְּרִיטֵי וְזוּזָא? אֲמַר לֵיהּ: דדַּל פְּרִיטֵי, דְּלָא כָּתְבִי בִּשְׁטָרָא, דְּאַסּוּכֵי מַסְכָּן לְהוּ וּמְשַׁוֵּי

רשב"ם

ועמדו קינין. שני תורים או שני בני יונה קרויין קן. ברבעתים. ברביעית דינר. שני תורין ברובע דינר, דהיינו מ"ח פרוטות. דקל"ב פרוטות יש בדינר, בפ"ק דקדושין (דף יב.). והכי מפרש בד' מחוסרי כפרה (כריתות י:). ודכוותה אשכחן במסכת מעשר שני (פ"ב מ"ט ע"ש): ב"ש אומרים בריבעא כסף ובריבעא מעות, דהיינו ריבעא דינר. ת"ר ילמד תחתון מן העליון באות אחת. שחסר מן התחתון, כגון "חנן" מ"חנני" "ענן" מ"ענני". אבל לא בשתים. כגון "חן" מ"חנני" "ען" מ"ענני". והוה ליה רובא דשמא. דכולי האי ודאי לא ילפינן מעליון, ששתי אותיות לא חיסר הסופר, וינתן הממון למי ששמו כך כמו שכתוב בתחתון. ספל מלמעלה. "ספל אדירים" (שופטים ה) הפקיד פלוני לפלוני. קפל מלמטה. טליתות שראויין לקפל. ויש פותרין: גימטריא הוא ספל וקפל, והבל הוא. והוא הדין לכל הכלים דעלמא, אלא (א) הכי נקט משום דבעי עלה במסקנא: קפל מלמעלה וספל מלמטה כו'. מי חיישינן לזבוב. שחיסר רגלה של קו"ף ונעשית סמ"ך, ובהא נמי ילמד מעליון. תיקו. והמוציא מחבירו עליו הראיה. דכיון דמספק דינא לבי דינא — היאך יוציאו מיד המחזיק? ולא דמי לממון המוטל בספק דקיימא לן חולקין. דהתם עיקר המעשה אין ידוע לנו היאך היה, כגון שור שנגח את הפרה ונמצא עוברה בצדה (לעיל דף לג.), וכגון נפל הבית עליו ועל אמו (שם דף קנח:), הלכך פוסקין להן ב"ד את הדין שיחלוקו. אבל כל מקום שעלתה ההלכה בתיקו, הואיל ואין הדיינין יודעין לפסוק את הדין — היו שותקין, והמחזיק יחזיק במה שבידו. דאסוכי קא מסכי להו. (ב) סומכין אותן בדינרין, במקום קל"ב פרוטות כותבין דינר.
איסתרי

תוספות

ובספר רבינו תם מלאתי במשנה כריתות במילתיה דרבן שמעון בן גמליאל: והשאר עליה חובה. ומתחלה היה כתוב "ואין השאר עליה חובה", ומחק "ואין". וכן היה נראה עיקר. אבל יש תימה, שבכל הספרים (ג) הוא כתוב [ואין], בין בכריתות בין בתורת כהנים בין בכאן. עוד יש לדקדק: דלא גרסינן "ואין", דאי גרסינן ליה, כי מוקי טעמא דר"ע לפסיעה — לוקי טעמא (ד) דסבר כרשב"ג, ולא שייך פסיעה לדידיה. מיהו, יש לדחות, דמדקאמר תאמר על אחת מהן — משמע שכולן חובה עליה. (הג"ה. ובפירוש אשכנזים ראיתי כתוב: רשב"ג ורבי יוחנן בן נורי ורבי עקיבא מדמי להו לטבילתה, ופליגי אבית שמאי ואבית הלל. עד כאן). **רבעתים**. היינו רובע דינר, כדפירש בקונטרס. והכי מוכח בפרק "ארבעה מחוסרי כפרה" (כריתות דף י: ושם) דקאמר: עשירית האיפה בפרוטה מנלן? דת"ר: האומר "הרי עלי (ה) סלע" — יביא כבש, שאין לך דבר שקרב בסלע אלא כבש. ותנן: עמדו קינים בו ביום ברבעתים. ומדחס רחמנא עליה דדל להוי חד מיתסר בסלע כו', ומדרבעתיים חד מיתסר בסלע — שמע מינה דהיינו רובע דינר. ונראה דגרס "רבעתים", ולא "רבעתיים", מאחר שהוא רובע דינר כדפרישית. דאי גרסי' "רבעתיים" — א"כ צריך לפרש דהיינו שתי רבעי חלי דינר, דהיינו נמי רובע דינר — וזה לא היה שום חשבון. ועוד: דאמרינן לעיל (ו) בההוא פירקא (דף ט.): [גר] בזמן הזה צריך שיפרוש רובע לקינו, אע"ג שמביא קן שלם שתי פרידין, כדאמר התם. אלמא, כל הקן ברובע הוא. ובפרק קמא דכריתות (דף ח.) מפרש רש"י (ז) שני קינין ברבעתים, ולפי זה יוכל להיות רבעתיים. אבל אינו מיושב, דא"כ למה נקט שני קינין בשני רבעים? היה יכול לומר שלשה א)(או שני) קינין בשלש רבעים! אלא נראה דגרסינן ב)ברבעתי ופירוש קן ברובע. ובדינרי זהב נמי — קן בדינר זהב, אבל בתורת כהנים מלא רבי "רבעתיים" בשני יודין. וקשה לרבי מהא דאמרינן בפ' "הוציאו לו" (יומא דף נה: ושם ד"ה ונגרור) במתני': ר' יהודה אומר לא היה שם אלא כן אחד של זהב בלבד. ותני, רבי יהודה אומר: לא היו שופרות לקיני חובה מפני התערובות. ופריך: וניסקול ארבע זוזי ונשדי במים, והנך ליפתרו. משמע דדמי שני פרידין היינו ג)שמונה זוזי, והתם משמע חד מיתסר בסלע! ואומר רבי: דהיינו ארבע זוזי פשיטי, דהיינו איספירא, סלע מדינה, דהויא פלגא דזוזא. ד)אע"ג דאכתי הוה ליה למימר תרי זוזי, דהיינו ריבעא דזוזא — לא דק, (ח) ה) ונקיט לה שמא לפי היוקר שהיה בימיהם. ואכתי קשה לר"י: דהתם קאמר כבש חטאת דקרב בסלע, והא אמרי' בפרק בתרא דכריתות (דף כז.): מפני מה לא נתנה תורה שיעור למחוסרי כפרה — שמא יוזלו הטלאים, ואין להם תקנה לאכול בקדשים. ופריך: והא חטאת חלב דלא נתנה תורה שיעור. משמע (ט) התם דלא בעי סלע! ויש לומר: דמלוה מן המובחר להביא בסלע, דבעינן "מבחר נדריך" — מיוחד שבעדרו, ולהכי הוי דבר הגון להביא סלע בתחלה, אע"פ שכשר בפחות, כדאמרי' בפרק ו)בתרא דכריתות (שם) מדאמר רחמנא איל (י) בכסף שקלים — מכלל דכבש בן שנה בסלע. ועוד קשה לר"י: דבפרק "איזהו מקומן" (זבחים דף מח. ושם) אמר: חטאת בת דנקא, והיינו מעה, שתות דינר, והוא חד מכ"ד בסלע. ומשמע דדנקא דוקא, כגון "הראיה שתי כסף וחגיגה מעה כסף" דבחגיגה פ"ק (דף ו. ושם), ובפ"ק דבכורות (דף יא. ושם) אמרינן: "פטרוזא בת דנקא" על שה של פדיון פטר חמור, והיינו מעה! ושמא דנקא (כ) לאו דוקא. אי נמי, לכל הפחות דנקא, דהכי אמור רבנן: עין יפה — סלע, עין רעה — דנקא. ועוד יש להקשות מהא דאמר במנחות בפרק בתרא (דף קז: ושם ד"ה כבש): "הרי עלי שור" כו', כבש — יביא הוא ונסכיו בסלע. וליכא לתרוצי הא דקאמר בחטאת בת דנקא והכא סלע — שהנסכים משלימין לסלע, שהרי עשירית האיפה שיביא למנחת הכבש — בפרוטה, כדקאמר התם, והיאך ישלים מן הנסכים בשלשה ועשרים חלקים של סלע? ועוד אומר רבי: דשיבוש הוא, דחטאת אינה טעונה נסכים כדאמר בעלמא (מנחות דף ל:). אלא הכי איכא לשנויי, כדפרישית. **אם** בן למה כתוב(ל). פירש ר"י: דבשלמא אם צריך שיכתבו בשני מקומות קודם שיטה האחרונה, שאין ללמוד מן השטר עד שכתבו שתי פעמים — אתי שפיר מה שכותבין פעמים מענין הראשון של שטר, דהיינו הלואה, וענין השני שמדבר באחריות. אבל מאחר שלמדין מן התחתון לבדו — למה כותבין העליון? באחד מהן דיו! ז)**אם** בן למה כתוב העליון שאם תמחוק כו'. הא טעמא לא שייך בהא דאמר הכל הולך אחר התחתון (מ) (כדאמר). ואין למדין מן העליון כלום, ואם כתב למטה מנה — אין למדין מן העליון מאתים אם נמחק קלת מן התחתון. ועוד, דאות אחת לא שייכא כלל להני גווני. אלא מילתא באפי נפשיה היא, וקאי אהא דאמר כותבין (נ) שטר פסים המלוה פעמים, וקאמר: מה שרגילים לכפול בדברים בשטר — כגון שמות האנשים, כדאמרינן בגמ': כגון חנן מחנני, שאם תמחוק אות אחת מן התחתון — ילמוד מן העליון, שלומדין חנן מחנני, והיינו באות אחת. ובפירוש רבינו חננאל כתוב: א"כ למה כותבין את העליון — משמע כדפרישית. והא דלא קאמר: א"כ למה כותבין את (ס) התחתונה — לפי שהתחתונה עיקר. וכן פירש רבי, שלא הוצרך ליתן טעם למה כותבין התחתונה, שהרי בכל טעות שיטעה בעליון יתקן ע"י התחתון, אפי' בדבר שאין לומר שכן רלה לכתוב בעליון. ולכך כותבין התחתון, שאם יטעה — יתקן מתחתון, כי בשניהם לא יאותו שיטעה. **אבל** לא משתי אותיות. פירש רשב"ם: אלא יתן למי ששמו כך, ששתי אותיות לא חסר הסופר. ומשמע שלא היה מעמידו בנמחק האות. ואתא שפיר לספרים דגרסי במתני' "שאם לא כתב אות אחת" כו'. אבל לספרים דגרסי במתניתין "שאם תמחק" — אין לפרש כן, דהא משמע דקאי אמתניתין, דקתני: שאם תמחק אות אחת כו', ואות אחת דמתניתין נמי אין לפרש אלא כפי ברייתא זו. ואומר רבי: דבגירסא זו צריך לפרש דבנמחקו שתי אותיות מיירי, דכולי האי לא גמרינן מעליון, ולא יגבה כלל. ואע"ג דאי לאו אהדר לדיבוריה לא הוה פסלינן ליה במאי דלא כתב אלא חדא זימנא, מכל מקום (ע) נמחק ונכתב — גרע מהיכא דלא נכתב כלל. דכיון דשתי אותיות שבעליון אין ניכרות בו — שמא לא החזיר דבריו אלא לשנות השם, מאחר דחזינן ביה ריעותא בשתי אותיות. (הגה"ה. בתוספתא תניא: לעולם התחתון ילמוד מן העליון, במקושר — באות אחת ולא בשתי אותיות. ונראה לר"י: דבחזרת "וקנינא מיניה" מיירי, דמתלקינן במקושר. וצריך עיון. ע"כ הגה"ה). **דלמא** מיתרמי שם בן שלש אותיות. תימה: היכא דלא הוי רובא מיהא, אמאי לא ילמוד? (פ) ומדקאמר דלמא מיתרמי כו' — משמע דמשום הך חששא פסולין בכולהו. ותימה הוא ליגזור באחריני ולהפסידו משום הך חששא. **ספל** וקפל. פירש רבינו תם: ספל — ס' פלגי, כמו ששים אלאין דלעיל ב"מי שמת" (דף קמה.) — אלאי סלעים. קפל — ק' פלגי. ורבינו חננאל מפרש שתי לשונות: ספל — ספל ממש, כדפירש הקונטרס. קפל — כלי אחד ששמו כן. ועוד לשון אחר פירש: ספל — סאה ופלגא, קפל — קב ופלגא. **אסוכי** מסכי. לשון מנין, כמו: סך מקרי דרדקי (לעיל דף כא.), סך קירי פלסתר (ע"ז דף יא:).
ומשוי

עין משפט נר מצוה

מו א מיי' פכ"ז מהל' מלוה ולוה הלכה יד סמג עשין לג טוש"ע ח"מ סי' מב סעיף ו:
מז ב ג מיי' שם הלכה טו טוש"ע שם ס"ז:
מח ד מיי' שם טוש"ע שם סעיף טו:

רבינו גרשום

דליהוי רביעי אלא חצי קרי ריבעתן דהשתא נתזלזלו בפחות ממה שאמר ולהכי נשבע ותיקן כך שלא יתאחרו שם היולדות ושלא יתבטלו מפריה ורביה: **פים'** היה כתוב בשטר מאתים מלמעל' ומלמטה מנה או מנה מלמעלה ומאתים מלמטה הכל הולך אחר התחתון. ובלבד שלא יהא בשיטה אחרונה דאמרינן דהאי דחזר וכתבו למטה משום דלמעלה לא דק והשתא מלמטה דק. וכיון דהכל הולך אחר התחתון א"כ למה כותבין את העליון כו'. הא סיפא ע"כ מיירי בהיכא דממון שוה בין מלמעלה בין מלמטה: שאם תמחק אות אחת מן התחתון. מפרש בגמ' במאי מיירי: ת"ר האי דקתני מתני' ילמד התחתון מן העליון. באות אחת אם תמחק מן התחתון שילמד מן העליון אבל נמחקו שתי אותיות בתחתון אין למדין מן העליון. והיכי דמי ילמד תחתון מן העליון באות אחת כגון דכתב מלעיל חנני לוה כך וכך ולמטה כתב חנן דהשתא נמחק אות אחת מלמטה וילמד מלמעלה דהאי חנן היינו חנני של מעלה. והכי נמי ענן מענני אבל אי כתב למעלה חנני ולמטה חן או למעלה ענני ולמטה ען דהשתא נמחק ב' אותיות אין למדין מן העליון לתחתון דלא חדא מילתא היא: מאי שנא ב' אותיות. אם נמחקו מן התחתון דאין למדין מן העליון משום דלמא מיתרמי למעלה שם בן ד' אותיות כגון נחור והאי נח דכתב בתחתון דנמחק הוה ליה פלגא דשמא ואין למדין מן העליון: דלמא איתרמי שם בן ב' אותיות. דלוה. כגון דן נח שם וכי נמחק מהן אות השתא צריך למילף חצי השם מן העליון: אלא להיכא דנמחק ב' אותיות מן התחתון היינו טעמא דאין למדין מן העליון דלמא מיתרמי שם בן ג' אותיות כגון משה או דוד ולהיכא דנמחקו ב' אותיות מן התחתון היינו טעמא דאין למדין מן העליון משום דנמחק רובא דשמא וגזרינן ב' אותיות דהן פלגא דאין למדין אטו ב' אותיות דהוי רובא אבל היכא דנמחק אות אחת למדין מן העליון דודאי אות אחת אי נמחקת ליתא רובא דשמא: אמר רב פפא הא פשיטא לי. אי כתב מלמעלה ספל שחייב פלוני לפלוני ולמטה בשטר כתב קפל כלומר דבר מקופל וכפול כמו מקטורן שהוא מכוסה מן בגד מבחוץ או שאר בגד כפול ודאי הכל הולך אחר התחתון וגבי נמי בעל השטר קפל. אבל הא קא מיבעיא לי קפל מלמעלה וספל מלמטה מהו. מי חיישינן לזבוב ואיכא למימר בתחתון נמי קפל הוה אלא זבוב דיבק האות דרגל של ק' ועשאו ס' וגובה קפל דילמד מעליון אי לא: ההוא שטרא דהוה כרב ביה שית מאה סתם וזוזא. חייב פלוני לפלוני: אסתירי היינו סלע: וזוזא. היינו דינר: פריטי לא מצית אמרת דאסוכי מסכי להן

מסורת הש"ס

א) [כת"י או ה' קינין כב' רבעים ולמה היה לו ליקח שימכר ביחד כ' קינים כב' רבעים אלה: ב) רש"א רבעתים: ג) רש"א ד': ד) ונקט שיעור לכל קן להיות כ' פרידות אף שלא צריך אלא נגד פרידה אחת להיות חטאת ומשום חטאת שמתו בעליה ולא רש"ל: ה) כמו עוד י"ל רש"ל: ו) [נ"ל בפרק קמא דף יו"ד:] ז) שייך למתני' דלעיל קסה.:

הגהות הב"ח

(א) רשב"ם ד"ה קפל וכו' אלא נקט הכי משום: (ב) ד"ה דאסוכי קא מסכי להו סוכמין אותן: (ג) תוס' ד"ה ג כגכס וכו' שבכל הספרים היה כתוב ואין בין בכריתות: (ד) בא"ד לוקי טעמא דר"ע לפסיעה כצ"ל: (ה) ד"ה רבעתים וכו' דמ"ר האומר הרי עלי כסלע למזבח יביא כבש וכו' ומדחם רחמנא עליה דלהוי חד מיתסר בעשירות כו' ומדרבעתים: (ו) בא"ד כו' אמר גר בזמן הזה צריך שיפרש רובע לקינו: (ז) בא"ד ובפרק קמא דכריתות מפרש רש"י קינין בדינרי זהב שני קינין בשני זהובים קן לדינר זהב קינין ברבעתים ופירוש קן רביעי דינר כסף ולפי זה יוכל להיות וכו' ודהוי זה לומר שלשה בג' רבעים או ארבעה קינין בכ' רבעים אלא נראה דגרסינן קן ברבעתים ופירוש קן ברובע: (ח) בא"ד לא דק ובמה נקיט לה הכי לפי היוקר:

ומשוי להו זוזי, מאי אמרת? שית מאה איסתירי וזוזא, (א) א)(שית מאה זוזי וחד זוזא) — יד בעל השטר על התחתונה. ב)אמר אביי: ג)האי מאן דבעי למחוי חתימות ידיה בבי דינא, לא לחוי בסוף מגילתא, דלמא משכח לה אחר וכתיב דמסיק ביה זוזי, ותנן: ד)הוציא עליו כתב ידו שהוא חייב לו — גובה מנכסים בני חורין. ההוא בזבינא דאתא לקמיה דאביי, אמר ליה: ניחזי לי מר חתימות ידיה, דכי אתו רבנן מחוו לי — מעברנא להו בלא מכסא. אחוי ליה בריש מגילתא, הוה קא נגיד ביה, א"ל: ה)כבר קדמוך רבנן. אמר אביי: מתלת ועד עשר לא לכתוב בסוף שיטה, דלמא מזייף וכתב. ואי איתרמי ליה — ניהדריה לדבוריה תרין תלתא זימני, אי אפשר דלא מיתרמי ליה באמצע שיטה. ההוא דהוה כתיב ביה "תילתא בפרדיסא", אזל מחקיה ו)לגגיה דבי"ת וכרעיה, ושוייה "ופרדיסא"; אתא לקמיה דאביי, אמר ליה: מאי טעמא רויח ליה עלמא להאי וי"ו? ז)כפתיה ואודי. ההוא דהוה כתב ביה "מנת ראובן ושמעון אחי", הוה להו אחא דשמיה "אחי", אזל כתב ביה וי"ו, ושוייה "ואחי"; אתא לקמיה דאביי, אמר ליה: ח)מאי טעמא דחיק ליה עלמא להאי וי"ו כולי האי? כפתיה ואודי. ההוא שטרא דהוה חתים עליה רבא ורב אחא בר אדא, אתא לקמיה דרבא, אמר ליה: דין חתימות ידא דידי היא, מיהו קמיה דרב אחא בר אדא לא חתימי לי מעולם! כפתיה ואודי. א"ל: בשלמא דידי זייפת, אלא דרב אחא בר אדא דרתית ידיה, היכי עבדת? אמר: אנחי ידאי אמצרא, ואמרי לה: קם אזרנוקא וכתב.§ **מתני'** ט)כותבין גט לאיש אע"פ שאין אשתו עמו, י)והשובר לאשה — אע"פ שאין בעלה עמה, כ)ובלבד שיהא מכירן. ל)והבעל נותן שכר.

כותבין

רשב"ם

איסתרי. סלעים. יד בעל השטר על התחתונה. ולית ליה אלא איסתרי, דאינון כל אסתירא פלגא דזוזא, כך פירש ר"ח. ונראה לי דזוזי יקבל, דאסתירי הוו סלעים, ויש בכל אחד ארבעה דינרין. אבל אסתירא פשיטי – אינהו ודאי הוו פלגא דזוזא, דהיינו סלע מדינה, כדאמרי' בבבא קמא (דף לו:) גבי התוקע לחבירו, בעובדא דחנן בישא. **אמר אביי לא לחוי איניש חתימת ידיה כו'.** אדם שצריך לכתוב חתימת ידו על קלף ולהשליך לבית דין כדי שיכירו בית דין חתימתו, כי ההיא דאמרינן בכתובות בפרק "האשה שנתארמלה" (דף כא.), כגון ראובן ושמעון שהיו חתומין בשטר, ומת שמעון, ואין מי שיכיר חתימת שמעון אלא ראובן ואחד מן השוק. (ג) ואמרינן התם שיכתוב ראובן כתב ידו וישליכהו לבית דין, ובית דין מקיימין חתימת ידי ראובן הכתוב בשטר מכתב ידו שהשליך בב"ד, ואין צריך ראובן להעיד על כתב ידו שבשטר: "זה כתב ידי", ובאין ראובן ואחד מן השוק ומעידין על חתימת שמעון. ואמר אביי: כשיחתום ראובן להשליך לב"ד – לא יחתום בסוף הקלף, אלא בתחלתו. שלא יהא חלק מלמעלה, שמא ימלאנו אדם רע ויכתוב בחלק שלמעלה מחתימתו: "אני החתום לויתי מפלוני כך וכך ממון", ותנן: הוציא עליו כתב ידו כו', והיינו חתימת ידו, כדתנן (גיטין דף עא:): כתב סופר ועד כשר. ואמר ר' ירמיה: חתם סופר שנינו. **בזבינא.** מוכס, וישראל היה. **כי חלפי רבנן.** ותשלח כתב ידך למחול המכס, אמחול להן. **הוה נגיד.** מושך בקלף כדי שיחתום אביי מלמטה. **אמר אביי מתלת ועד י' לא לכתוב בסוף השיטה.** דמזייף וכתב לתלת "תלתין", ולארבע "ארבעין", ולחמש "חמשין", וכן עד עשר, יכתוב לעשר "עשרין". אבל אחד עשר אינו יכול לזיופי, דצריך למכתב "אחד ועשרים", וכי כתב בין אחד עשר וי"ו – נראה דחוק, ומינכר. **ואי איתרמי ליה.** ארבע או חמש בסוף שיטה. **ליהדר.** ולדכריה להאי סכומא עד דמיתרמי ליה באמצע שיטה. דאפי' אם יזייף וכתב – אין למדין אלא מן התחתון, כדקתני מתניתין. **ההוא דהוה כתב ביה תילתא בפרדיסא.** כך היה כתוב בשטר: "זבינית לפלוני בגינתא דאית לי תילתא בפרדיסא". אזל הלוקח מחקיה לגגיה דבי"ת מכאן ומכאן, ושוויה "ופרדיסא", וא"ל: מכרת לי תילתא דגינתא, וכל הפרדס כולו, והא שטרא. **ההוא שטרא דהוה כתוב ביה מנת ראובן ושמעון אחי.** דאית להו באתרא פלונית מנת חלק קרקע שיש לשני האחין. והוו להון אחא אחרינא ששמו "אחי", והוה ליה מנתא בהדייהו, ואזל הלוקח ושדא ביה וי"ו ושוייה "ואחי", וטען דמנתא דתלתא זבינית. **דרתיתא ידיה.** ידיו רותתות, ואותיות חתימתו פורחות. **אמצרא.** על חבל הנטוי משפת הנהר אל שפתו שניה, והעוברים (ג) גשר קצר נשענים בו ועוברים, והוא נע ונד כל שעה. **אזרנוקא.** סגויז"א בלע"ז, שבו דולין מים מן הבור. **קם אזרנוקא.** עלה עליה וחתם, וכל גופו נע ונד, וידיו רותתות. **מתני' כותבין גט לאיש.** כותבין וחותמין לו, והוא יגרש בו את אשתו כשירצה, אע"פ שאין אשתו עמו בשעה שנותנין לו הגט כתוב וחתום. דהא לא בעינן דעתה, שהרי היא מתגרשת בעל כרחה. **ושובר לאשה אף על פי שאין בעלה עמה.** דלדידה חוב הוא, ולבעלה הוי זכות, וזכין לאדם שלא בפניו. והיא צריכה להזהר בו שלא יבא ליד בעלה עד שתקבל כסף כתובתה. **ובלבד שיהא מכירן.** בגמ' מפרש לה. **והבעל נותן שכר.** (ד) הגט. טעמא מפרש בגמ'. ושכר השובר – דזכותו הוא, דלא תהדר ותגבה כתובתה זימנא אחריתא.

כותבין

תוספות

ומשוי (ה) ליה זוזי. תימה: זוזי נמי משוי איסתרי, דמסקי להו באיסתרי. א"כ לית לן למימר מהאי טעמא שית מאה זוזי, אלא שית מאה איסתרי, שגדולים יותר! וי"ל: דזוזי רגילים לכתוב בשטרות אע"פ שיש מטבע גדול ממנו, (ו) כדאשכחת בזוזי צורי, דקאמר בכ"מ ארבע זוזי, ולא חשבינן להם בסלעים. ופירוש רבינו חננאל, שפירש דאיסתרי יהבינן ליה, והן פחותין מזוזי, כדאמר: איסתרא פלגא דזוזא — לא נהירא, ד"מאי אמרת" אינו מתקיים בשום מקום. אלא נראה לרבי כרשב"ם, מתוך הלשון דקאמר "מאי קאמרת", דמשמע — דהא ליכא למימר, כמו: מאי אמרת לסטים מזויין כו' (קדושין דף יח.). ולספרים דגרסי: אלא מאי איכא למימר, אי שית מאה איסתרי וזוזא אי שית מאה זוזי וזוזא יד בעל השטר על התחתונה — לפי אותן ספרים יכול בטוב לפרש דאיסתרא בציר מזוזא, והוו הני זוזי זוזא צורי. מיהו, רבינו חננאל גריס: מאי אמרת שית מאה איסתרי וזוזא, יד בעל השטר על התחתונה. ור"ת היה גריס בסוכה (דף כג: ושם ד"ה כזוזא): זוזא מלעיל כאיסתרא מלתחת. ומפרש: זוז שעומד בראש ההר שהוא גדול, דומה לאיסתרא שהוא קטן לעומד למטה.

לא לכתוב בסוף שיטה. פירוש: אי כתב לשון נקבה, דכתב "תלת" ולא כתב תלתא.

אף על פי שאין אשתו עמו. וא"ת: וליחוש שמא כתב ליתן בניסן ולא נתן עד תשרי, וטרפה (ז) מלקוחות שלקחו הפירות מן הבעל עד תשרי, למאן דאמר דאף לאחר שנתן עיניו לגרשה אוכל פירות עד שעת נתינה, (ח) שלא כדין. דהכי פרכינן סוף פ"ק דבבא מציעא (דף יט.) על מלא גיטי נשים, דקאמר: בזמן שהבעל מודה יחזיר לאשה. ומשני התם, דאמרינן לה: אייתי ראיה מאימת מטא גיטא לידך. וה"מ בנפל דאיתרע הוא דמצריך הכי, אבל הכא דלא נפל — אמאי לא חיישינן להכי? ואור"י: דלא מקדים איניש פורענותא לנפשיה. הלכך, היכא דאיתיליד ריעותא דוקא חיישינן. והכי אמרינן ח)בפ"ק דגיטין (דף יח.) דלא מקדים איניש פורענותא לנפשיה, שיכתוב לה גט קודם שירצה לגרשה, וגיטין הבאים ממדינת הים — קלא אית להו.

ושובר לאשה אע"פ שאין בעלה עמה. וא"ת: וניחוש שמא כתבה ליתן בניסן ולא (ט) נתנו עד תשרי, ומזבנא לכתובתה בטובת הנאה ואזיל בעל וטריף לקוחות שלא כדין! הא פריך הכי בפ"ק דב"מ (דף כ.) על מלא שובר, ומשני: ש"מ איתא לדשמואל, דאמר: המוכר שט"ח לחבירו וחזר ומחלו — מחול, שאף מוחלת לבעל אם היתה רוצה. ואביי משני: עדיו בחיתומיו זכין לו. והא דשביק מתני' ופריך אברייתא — משום דמתני' מצי לאוקמי (י) בשטר דלית ביה הקנאה. אבל התם קתני: אין האשה מודה כו' — דמשמע שאומרת שלא נתנתו לבעל עדיין, ומה בכך אם בהקנאה מיירי. אע"ג דמצי לפרש דאומר מזוייף הוא — משמע דמיירי בכל ענין אין האשה מודה, בין שאמרה מזוייף, בין שאומרת לא נתתיו עדיין לבעל.

כותבין

רבינו גרשום

להן לפרוטות בסכום חשבון היו מצטרפין אותן ומשווי להו זוזי בשטרא ולא כתב פרוטי: יד בעל השטר על התחתונה. ולא מצבי שית מאה זוזי וזוזא: מתלת ועד עשר לא ליכתוב איניש בסוף שיטה. של שום שטר דאי כתב בסוף שיטה תלת מצי זיופי המלוה וכתב תלתין והכי נמי מארבע מצי למכתב ארבעין וכן כל החשבון עד עשר מצי לזייף אבל אי כתב אחד עשר בסוף שיטה לא מצי לזיופי ולמכתב אחד ועשרים משום דצריך למכתב ו' בין אחד ועשרים ואי מזייף להאי ו' איכא היכרא ודחיק משאר אותיות. ומשום הכי נקט מתלתא דקודם תלתא לא כתבי בשטר חשבון אלא לוה סלע כותב פלוני לוה סלע וכן לשנים כותב סלעין ולא שנים ומעוט סלעים שנים. ואי קשיא לך היכא דכתב סלע בסוף שיטה יכול לכתוב סלעין הא לא קשיא דכיון דסלעין סתם לא הוי אלא שנים משום ההוא פורתא לא מזייף אלא מתלת ולעיל דזיוף גדול הוא מזייף: ואי מתרמי ליה. בסוף שיטה חד מכל חשבון זה מתלת ועד עשר: ניהדריה לדיכוריה. בההוא שטר תרי תלת זימני כך וקיבל עליו פלוני אחריות של כך וכך סלעין ואי אפשר בחד מתלת דלא מתרמי החשבון באמצע שיטה ואי מזייף בסוף נלמוד מההוא דאמצע שיטה: ההוא שטרא דכתב ביה תלתא בפרדיסא. זבן פלוני לפלוני: אזל. הלוקח בעל השטר ומחק ב' מלמעלה ומלמטה ושויה ו' ופרדיסא דמשמע תלתא בשדה זבן ליה וכוליה פרדיסא כלומר תלתא ופרדיסא: רויח ליה עלמא להאי ו' דופרדיסא: ההוא שטר דהוה כתב ביה מנת ראובן ושמעון [אחי]. כלומר שראובן ושמעון שהן אחין מכרו לי מנת שלהן חלקן שירשו מאביהן: אזל וכתב ו' ושויה ואחי. ראובן ושמעון ואחי זבינן לי מנת שלהם: האי מאן דמחוי אחתימות ידיה בבי דינא. כדי שיכירו ב"ד אם יבוא להם היום ומחר חתימה דומה לזה שידעו שהוא חתמו ואם אינו דומה לזו שידעו שזיוף הוא: לא ליהוי בסוף מגילתא. בגליון מלמטה אלא מלמעלה דאי כתב למטה דלמא משכחת לה איניש ומזייף וכתב על גבי חתימתו דמסיק ביה זוזי כך וכך והוא חתום למטה ותנן כו': ההוא בזבינא. בעל מכס: אחוי ליה אביי חתימתו בריש מגילתא. יהיה רוצה לזייף על גבי חתימתו שיהא חייב לו: אין חתימות ידי הוא. שהיה דומה לכתיבתו: בשלמא חתימת ידי מצית לזיופי שפיר. משום דבחור אנא וכוונת כתיבתי: דרתית ידיה. מחמת שהיה זקן היו ידיו רותתות היכי מצית לכוונו: א"ל אנחי ידא אמצרא. במעבר הנהר היה נסר קטן קצר כמו גשר ומזה בשפת הנהר קבוע יתד ובעבר האחר יתד האחר וקשור חבל מזה לזה וסומכין שם ידיהן כשעוברין על גבי אותו נסר צר ומירתת מכח המים ועל אותו נסר הנחתי ידי והיתה מרתת כיד של זקן וזייפתי: זרנוקא. שקורין ציקוניא שדולין בבור דרתת ועליה הנחתי ידי: **מתני'** כותבין גט לאיש אע"פ שאין אשתו עמו. מפני שהאשה מתגרשת בעל כרחה: והשובר לאשה. אם באת אשה לב"ד ואמרה כתבו לי שובר מכתובתי שאתן לבעלי שגרשני כשיפרע לי כתובתי כותבין לה אע"פ שאין בעלה עמה: הסופר ובית דין מכירין האשה והאיש שלצורך עצמן הן מבקשין: והבעל נותן

עין משפט נר מצוה

מט א מיי' פכ"ז מהל' מלוה ולוה הל' טז ועי' בהשגות ובמ"מ סמג עשין צד טוש"ע ח"מ סי' מב סעיף טו:
נ ב טוש"ע ח"מ סי' מב סעיף ב:
נא ג מיי' פי"א מהלכות מלוה ולוה הלכה ג סמג עשין צד טוש"ע ח"מ סס סעיף ד וסי' לט סעיף ו:
נב ד ה מיי' שם פכ"ז הלכה יג סמג שם טוש"ע ח"מ סי' מב סעיף ז:
נג ו ז ח מיי' שם הלכה יב טוש"ע שם סעי' ג:
נד ט מיי' פ"ב מהלכות גירושין הל' ג ופכ"ד מהל' מלוה ולוה הל' ג סמג עשין נ וסימן נ טוש"ע אה"ע סי' קכ סעיף ג:
נה י מיי' פכ"ד מהל' מלוה ולוה הלכה ה סמג עשין צד טוש"ע אה"ע סי' קי סעיף ח:
נו כ ל מיי' שם הל' ב ועי' במ"מ ופ"ב מהל' גירושין הל' ג סמג שם טוש"ע שם וסימן קכ סעיף ג:

הגהות הב"ח

(א) גמ' שית מאה איסתרי וזוזא (שית מאה זוזי וחד זוזא) תא"מ ונ"ב ר"ח לא גרס ליה: (ב) רשב"ם ד"ה איסתרי וכו' דאמרינן וכו': (ג) ד"ה אמצרא וכו' והעוברים כו' גשר: (ד) ד"ה והבעל נותן שכר הגט: (ה) תוס' ד"ה ומשוי להו זוזי וכו' משוי להו איסתרי: (ו) בא"ד כדאשכחן בזוזי צורי: (ז) ד"ה אף וכו' וטרפה: (ח) בא"ד עד שעת נתינה שלא כדין: (ט) ד"ה ושובר וכו' ולא נתנו עד תשרי: (י) בא"ד לאוקמי בשובר דלית ביה הקנאה:

עין משפט
נר מצוה

א)אכּוֹתְבִין שְׁטָר לַלֹּוֶה ב)אע"פ שֶׁאֵין מַלְוֶה עִמּוֹ, וְאֵין כּוֹתְבִין לַמַּלְוֶה עַד שֶׁיְּהֵא לֹוֶה עִמּוֹ; בוְהַלֹּוֶה נוֹתֵן שָׂכָר. ג)גכּוֹתְבִין שְׁטָר לַמּוֹכֵר אע"פ שֶׁאֵין לוֹקֵחַ עִמּוֹ, וְאֵין כּוֹתְבִין לַלּוֹקֵחַ עַד שֶׁיְּהֵא מוֹכֵר עִמּוֹ; דוְהַלּוֹקֵחַ נוֹתֵן שָׂכָר. ד)האֵין כּוֹתְבִין שִׁטְרֵי אֵירוּסִין וְנִשּׂוּאִין אֶלָּא מִדַּעַת שְׁנֵיהֶם, ווְהֶחָתָן נוֹתֵן שָׂכָר. זאֵין כּוֹתְבִין שְׁטַר אֲרִיסוּת וְקַבְּלָנוּת אֶלָּא מִדַּעַת שְׁנֵיהֶם, חוְהַמְקַבֵּל נוֹתֵן שָׂכָר. טאֵין כּוֹתְבִין שִׁטְרֵי בֵּירוּרִין וְכָל מַעֲשֵׂה ב"ד אֶלָּא מִדַּעַת שְׁנֵיהֶם, וּשְׁנֵיהֶם נוֹתְנִין שָׂכָר; רשב"ג אוֹמֵר: ה)לִשְׁנֵיהֶם כּוֹתְבִין שְׁנַיִם, לָזֶה לְעַצְמוֹ וְלָזֶה לְעַצְמוֹ.§ **גמ'** מַאי "וּבִלְבַד שֶׁיְּהֵא מַכִּירָן"? אָמַר רַב יְהוּדָה אָמַר רַב: וּבִלְבַד שֶׁיְּהֵא מַכִּיר שֵׁם הָאִישׁ בַּגֵּט וְשֵׁם הָאִשָּׁה בַּשּׁוֹבֵר. יָתֵיב רַב סָפְרָא וְרַב אַחָא בַּר הַתָּא וְרַב הוּנָא בַּר חִינְנָא, וְיָתֵיב אַבַּיֵי גַּבַּיְיהוּ, וְיָתְבִי וְקָמִבַּעְיָא לְהוּ: שֵׁם הָאִישׁ בַּגֵּט — אִין, שֵׁם הָאִשָּׁה לָא? שֵׁם הָאִשָּׁה בַּשּׁוֹבֵר — אִין, שֵׁם הָאִישׁ לָא? וְלֵיחוּשׁ דִּלְמָא כָּתַב גִּיטָּא וְאָזֵיל וּמַמְטֵי לֵיהּ לְאִיתְּתֵיהּ דְּהֵיאַךְ, (א) וְזִמְנִין אָזְלָא כְּתָבָה אִשָּׁה שׁוֹבֵר וְיָהֲבָה לְגַבְרָא דְּלָאו דִּילָהּ! אֲמַר לְהוּ אַבַּיֵי, יהָכִי אָמַר רַב: שֵׁם הָאִישׁ בַּגֵּט, וְהוּא הַדִּין לְשֵׁם הָאִשָּׁה; כשֵׁם הָאִשָּׁה בַּשּׁוֹבֵר, וְהוּא הַדִּין לְשֵׁם הָאִישׁ. וְלֵיחוּשׁ לִשְׁנֵי יוֹסֵף בֶּן שִׁמְעוֹן הַדָּרִים בְּעִיר אַחַת, דִּלְמָא כָּתֵיב גִּיטָּא וְאָזֵיל וּמַמְטֵי לֵיהּ לְאִיתְּתֵיהּ דְּהֵיאַךְ! אֲמַר לְהוּ רַב אַחָא בַּר הוּנָא, הָכִי אָמַר רַב: לשְׁנֵי יוֹסֵף בֶּן שִׁמְעוֹן הַדָּרִים בְּעִיר אַחַת, אֵין מְגָרְשִׁין נְשׁוֹתֵיהֶן אֶלָּא זֶה בִּפְנֵי זֶה. וְלֵיחוּשׁ דִּלְמָא אָזֵיל לְמָתָא אַחֲרִיתָא וּמַחֲזִיק לֵיהּ לִשְׁמֵיהּ בְּיוֹסֵף בֶּן שִׁמְעוֹן, וְכָתֵיב גִּיטָּא וּמַמְטֵי לֵיהּ לְאִיתְּתֵיהּ דְּהֵיאַךְ! אֲמַר לְהוּ רַב הוּנָא בַּר חִינְנָא, הָכִי אָמַר רַב: מכָּל שֶׁהוּחְזַק שְׁמוֹ בָּעִיר שְׁלֹשִׁים יוֹם — אֵין חוֹשְׁשִׁין לוֹ. לָא אִיתְחַזַּק, מַאי? אֲמַר אַבַּיֵי: נדְּקָרוּ לֵיהּ וְעָנֵי. רַב זְבִיד אֲמַר: רַמָּאָה בְּרַמָּאוּתֵיהּ זָהִיר. הַהוּא תַּבְרָא דַּהֲוָה חָתִים עֲלָהּ רַב יִרְמְיָה בַּר אַבָּא, אֲתָיא לְקַמֵּיהּ הַהִיא אִיתְּתָא, אֲמַרָה לֵיהּ: לָאו אֲנָא הֲוַאי, אֲמַר: אֲנָא נַמִּי אֲמַרִי לְהוּ לָאו אִיהִי הִיא, וַאֲמַרוּ לִי: מֵיקַשׁ הוּא דְּקָשְׁיָא לָהּ וּבָגַר לָהּ קָלָא; אֲמַר אַבַּיֵי, אע"ג דַּאֲמוּר רַבָּנַן:
כֵּיוָן

כּוֹתְבִין שְׁטָר לַלֹּוֶה. לִהְיוֹת מְזוּמָּן בְּיָדוֹ לָתֵת לַמַּלְוֶה כְּשֶׁיַּלְוֶה לוֹ מָעוֹת, אע"פ שֶׁאֵין מַלְוֶה עִמּוֹ. **וְהַלֹּוֶה נוֹתֵן שָׂכָר.** בַּגְּמָרָא פָּרֵיךְ: פְּשִׁיטָא דְּהַלֹּוֶה נוֹתֵן שָׂכָר, שֶׁהֲרֵי כָּל הֲנָאָה שֶׁלּוֹ! **אֵין כּוֹתְבִין שִׁטְרֵי אֵירוּסִין.** מְפָרֵשׁ ו) בְּ"אֵלּוּ מְגַלְּחִין" (מו"ק דף יח): שְׁטָרֵי פְּסִיקְתָּא, כִּדְרַב גִּידֵּל: כַּמָּה אַתָּה נוֹתֵן לְבִנְךָ כָּךְ וָכָךְ כו'. **אֶלָּא מִדַּעַת שְׁנֵיהֶם.** אֲבִי חָתָן וַאֲבִי כַּלָּה. **וְנִשּׂוּאִין.** כְּתוּבָּה. **שִׁטְרֵי אֲרִיסוּת.** מְקַבֵּל שָׂדֶה לְמֶחֱצָה לִשְׁלִישׁ וְלִרְבִיעַ. **וְקַבְּלָנוּת.** חֲכִירוּת, כָּךְ וָכָךְ כּוֹרִין לְשָׁנָה. **שִׁטְרֵי בֵּירוּרִין.** בַּגְּמָ' מְפָרֵשׁ. **כָּל מַעֲשֵׂה בֵּית דִּין.** כְּגוֹן אַדְרַכְתָּא, דְּמוֹדְעִינַן לַלֹּוֶה וְאָזֵיל וּפָרַע בְּטֶרֶם שֶׁיִּכָּתֵב. **וּשְׁנֵיהֶם נוֹתְנִין שָׂכָר.** בְּשִׁטְרֵי בֵּירוּרִין. וּבַגְּמָ' מְפָרֵשׁ פְּלוּגְתַּיְיהוּ. **שְׁנֵיהֶם.** הָעֵדִים כּוֹתְבִין שְׁנֵי שְׁטָרוֹת, לָזֶה אֶחָד וְלָזֶה אֶחָד. **גמ' שֶׁיְּהֵא מַכִּיר שֵׁם הָאִישׁ בַּגֵּט.** הַסּוֹפֵר וְהָעֵדִים צְרִיכִין שֶׁיַּכִּירוּ שֶׁזֶּהוּ שְׁמוֹ, דְּאִיכָּא לְמֵיחַשׁ אֵין גֵּט זֶה אֶלָּא לְאִישׁ אַחֵר, וְיָבֹא לְרַמּוֹת וּלְהַגְבּוֹת כְּתוּבָּה לְשׁוּם אִשָּׁה. כִּדְתְנַן (כתובות דף פט.): הוֹצִיאָה גֵּט וְאֵין עִמָּהּ כְּתוּבָּה — גּוֹבָה כְּתוּבָּתָהּ. **וְשֵׁם הָאִשָּׁה בַּשּׁוֹבֵר.** שֶׁלֹּא תְּרַמֶּה לִיתְּנוֹ לָאִישׁ שֶׁגֵּרֵשׁ אִשְׁתּוֹ, וְתַפְסִיד כְּתוּבָּתָהּ עַל יָדָהּ. **וּמְגָרֵשׁ לָהּ.** וּמִתְכַּוֵּין לְהַתִּירָהּ לִינָּשֵׂא שֶׁלֹּא כַּדִּין. **אֶלָּא זֶה בִּפְנֵי זֶה.** דְּלֵיכָּא לְמֵיחַשׁ תּוּ מִידֵּי. **וְנֵיחוּשׁ.** דִּלְמָא נָפֵיק לוֹ לְעִיר אַחֶרֶת כו'. לַתַּנָּא דְּמַתְנִי' דְּבָעֵי (ג) מַכִּירִין, לָמָּה כּוֹתְבִין שׁוּם גֵּט לְשׁוּם אָדָם אַף עַל פִּי שֶׁאָנוּ מַכִּירִין שְׁמוֹ? וַהֲלֹא שֶׁמָּא יוֹסֵף בֶּן שִׁמְעוֹן זֶה מֵעִיר אַחֶרֶת בָּא לְכָאן, וְהָיָה שְׁמוֹ רְאוּבֵן בֶּן יַעֲקֹב, וְעַתָּה הִרְגִּיל וְהֶחֱזִיק שֶׁיִּקְרְאוּ לוֹ כָּאן רְאוּבֵן, לְפִי שֶׁרוֹצֶה לְגָרֵשׁ אֵשֶׁת רְאוּבֵן בֶּן יַעֲקֹב שֶׁבְּמָקוֹם פְּלוֹנִי. **אֵין חוֹשְׁשִׁין לוֹ.** דְּכָל כָּךְ לֹא הָיָה מַחֲלִיף שְׁמוֹ זְמַן מְרוּבֶּה, פֶּן יִוָּדַע הַדָּבָר. **בְּרַמָּאוּתֵיהּ.** יָדַע, וְיִזָּהֵר לַעֲנוֹת. הִלְכָּךְ אֵין תַּקָּנָה עַד דְּלִיתְחַזֵּק. **הַהוּא תַּבְרָא** דַּהֲוָה חָתִים עֲלָהּ רַב יִרְמְיָה בַּר **אַבָּא.** לְאַחַר זְמַן אֲתַאי הַהִיא אִיתְּתָא לְקַמֵּיהּ לִתְבּוֹעַ כְּתוּבָּה, וְאָמְרָה לוֹ: לָאו אֲנָא הֲוַאי אוֹתָהּ אִשָּׁה שֶׁאַתָּה אוֹמֵר שֶׁחָתַמְתָּ עַל שׁוֹבְרָהּ, וְשֶׁמָּא אִשָּׁה אַחֶרֶת שֶׁשְּׁמָהּ כִּשְׁמִי וְשֵׁם בַּעְלָהּ כְּשֵׁם בַּעְלִי, אֲבָל אֲנִי לֹא הִתְקַבַּלְתִּי כְּתוּבָּתִי עֲדַיִין. **אָמַר לָהּ אַף אֲנָא אֲמַרִי לְהוּ.** לְסָהֲדֵי הַחֲתוּמִים עִמִּי עַל הַשּׁוֹבֵר שֶׁאֵינָךְ אוֹתָהּ הָאִשָּׁה שֶׁחֲתַמְנוּ עַל שׁוֹבְרָהּ, וְהַדִּין עִמָּהּ. וְהֵם הֵשִׁיבוּ לִי שֶׁטָּעִיתִי בַּמֶּה שֶׁנִּשְׁתַּנָּה וְהוּחְלַף קוֹלָהּ, וְהַדִּין עִמָּהֶם, וּכְבָר הִתְקַבַּלְתְּ כְּתוּבָּתֵךְ. **מֵיקַשׁ קַשְׁיָא.** הִזְקִינָה, וּכְבָר נִשְׁתַּנָּה וְנַעֲשָׂה קוֹלָהּ עָבֶה.
כֵּיוָן

כותבין שטר ללוה. בהא נמי פריך (ג) התם: וניחוש שמא כתב ללוות כו', ומוקי לה בשטרי אקנייתא, ואביי אמר: עדיו בחיתומיו זכין לו. **וליחוש** דלמא כתביה לאתתא דלאו דיליה ומגרש לה. פירש רשב"ם: ומתכוין להתירה להנשא שלא כדין. ותימה לי: והא בפני עדים יתננו לה, והם יקראו את הגט, כדאמרינן בגיטין (דף יט:) דמיבעי לאקרויי גיטא, ויראו העדים (ד) שאין זה שם ז)האיש! ועוד: בלאו הכי ליחוש דלמא כתביה לאיתתא דלאו דיליה, כיון שאין מכירין האשה, ויכתוב הגט לאיש אחר(ה) כשמו, ויתן הגט לאיש אחר ששמו כשמו, ויתן הגט לאשת האיש ותוציא מבעלה כתובתה! וכן נ"ל דמקשה. ול"ג "ומגרש לה". **שם** האיש בגט וה"ה לשם האשה. תימה: אמאי נקט שם האיש בגט ושם האשה בשובר? וי"ל: דלא חש לפרש כולהו, אלא נקט שם אותו דמכתיב הכתב, דעלייהו קתני במתני': והוא שיהי' מכירן — שהרי הזכירן. ולהכי נקט להו רב, ומתניתין גופה לכך דברו באלו — לפי שכבר הוצרכו להזכירם. וה"ה ודאי שם האחר משום חששא אחרת.

וליחוש לשני יוסף בן שמעון הדרים בעיר אחת. ותימה: אי בהוחזקו, ואליבא דמאן? אי לר"מ דאמר דעדי חתימה כרתי — ליכא למיחש למידי, שהגט לא יהיה גט, מאחר שאין מוכיח מתוכו שהוא (ו) שלו. כדאמר ב"כל הגט" (גיטין דף כד:): כתב לגרש את הגדולה לא יגרש את הקטנה, ודייק בגמרא: הא גדולה מצי לגרש. ומוקי לה משום הכי כר"א דאמר עדי מסירה כרתי, ולא רבי מאיר. ומאי קאמר נמי שמגרשין נשותיהן זה בפני זה — אפילו הכי לא מגרש אם לא יכתבו דורות. ואי אליבא דר' אלעזר פריך — לדידיה נמי לאו גיטא הוא, שהרי צריכה להביא עדי מסירה שנתנו לה בעלה, כיון שעדי חתימה אינם מוכיחין שבעלה נתנו, וצריכה היא עדי מסירה להביאם לפנינו שבעלה מסר לה, ותבקשם ולא תמצא, ולמאי ניחוש לה? ואי בדלא הוחזקו איירי, דהשתא כרתי שפיר עדי חתימה, שאין יודעים בעיר אלא בעלה — (ז) ומאי משני: זאת אומרת שני יוסף בן שמעון הדרים בעיר אחת אין מגרשין נשותיהן אלא זה בפני זה? מה תיקון? הלא אין ידוע שיש שנים בעיר, ולעולם יגרשנה זה בשם בעלה שלא בפניו, כיון שלא הוחזקו! ואור"י: דבהוחזקו מיירי, ואליבא דר"א דקי"ל כוותיה פריך. ואף על גב דעדי מסירה כרתי, וצריכה להביא עדי מסירה, ליחוש: מאחר שכותבין לו גט בלא אשתו, אז לא יעשו הגירושין בפניהם — דלמא כתב גיטא כו'. והעדים שידעו המסירה ויכירו אותו כי שמו יוסף בן שמעון כשם הכתוב (ח) בשטר, וגם יכירו שם האשה המקבלת אותו בשם שכתוב בשטר, ולא יתנו לב לדעת אם יש עוד יוסף ב"ש אחר לבד מאותו, ואם נשותיהם שוות כמו כן, ואולי זאת אשת חברו. וכשתבא לב"ד — תביא עדי מסירה, שתאמר: אלו העדים ראו דיוסף ב"ש בעלי נתן לי הגט, והן אומרים הן, כדפרישית. ואח"כ לא יתקרוס ב"ד ודאי לומר: שמא טעיתם כך וכך, כדפרישית. ומשני, הכי אמר רב: שני יוסף בן שמעון הדרים בעיר אחת אין מגרשין נשותיהן אלא זה בפני זה. ומאחר שנתקן כך — לעולם חוקרין ב"ד ודאי אם שני יוסף היו שם, ואם היו שם שנים — אין חוששין שם כלל. וכמו שפירש רבי וליחוש לשני יוסף בן שמעון, דאיירי שהוחזקו — צריך לפרש כמו כן קושיא ראשונה, דפריך: וליחוש דלמא כתב — כשהוחזקו דוקא, דאי לא הוחזקו — לא הוה מיבעי ליה לרב למימר — וה"ה לשם (ט) האיש. ואע"ג דאביי חייש לשני יצחק בפ' "האשה" (יבמות קטו: ושם) אע"ג דלא הוחזקו — רבה לא חייש התם. ורבה נמי לא חייש היכא דלא הוחזקו, כדמוכח בפ"ק דב"מ (דף יח: ושם ד"ה נפק) (ובכל הגט). ולמאי דפרישית דמוכח ב"כל הגט" (גיטין כד: ושם ד"ה בעדי) דלר"מ אין יכולין שני יוסף בן שמעון לגרש נשותיהן עד שיכתבו דורות, כיון דעדי חתימה כרתי אין גט אלא אם כן מוכיחין עדים הכתובין בו שבעלה נתנו לה — קשה עלה דמדאוקמי פרק "המגרש" (שם דף פו: ושם) מתני' דשני גיטין ושמותיהן שוין כר"כ דוקא. ודאי: אפי' תימא ר' אלעזר. ומיהו, כר' מאיר משמע דאתיא לה שפיר. והיכי ניחא ליה לר' מאיר? הא מוכח ב"כל הגט" דלר' מאיר אין שני יוסף בן שמעון יכולין לגרש נשותיהן אלא אם כן יכתבו דורות! ויש לומר: דכי מוקי לה כר' מאיר סבר שאינם שוין לגמרי, שהרי שלשום בדורות או סימן, דעכשיו העדים החתומים מוכיחין שמיד בעלה בא הגט אם הוא בידה. ומה שקורא אותם שוין — לפי שבמקום נתינתו אין מי שיכיר הדורות. **ומחזיק** ליה לשמיה יוסף בן שמעון. תימה: מה בכך? הלא צריך שיכיר שם האשה בגט, ואשתו לא יכירו בשמה, ולא שייך למימר שיחזיק! ויש לומר: שגם אשתו באה עמו. אי נמי, מכירין את אשתו ח)[שלו על ידי פלוני ופלוני שאמרו] שהיא אשתו של זה, אבל לא שמעו איך הוא שמו, שיאמרו שפלונית היא אשת ראובן. שאם כן — יודעים שאין שמו יוסף בן שמעון.
ביון

רבינו גרשום

נותן השכר. מן הגט לסופר: אמר רב ובלבד שיהא מכיר שם האיש בגט. שכן הוא שמו בודאי שאם אין מכירין יש לחוש שמא עצמו יכנה שמו יוסף בן שמעון בשם חבירו ויוליך לאשתו של אותו ששמו כן ויתן לה הגט כדי שתגבה כתובתה מבעלה שעשה עמה קנוניא. וכן הכי נמי שם האשה בשובר צריך שיהא מכיר שם האשה בשובר שכך שמה בודאי דאם אין מכירה יש לחוש שמא תוליך זה השובר לבעלה של אשה ששמה כך ויאמר גרשתיה ופרעתיה כתובתה וזהו השובר ועשתה עמו קנוניא: וליחוש. אפי' היכי דמכיר שם האיש בגט ולא שם האשה יש לחוש דלמא שמיה כשם חבריה ושם אתתיה שכותב לה הגט יכנה אותה בשם אשת חבירו ואשתו שלו אין שמה כן כמו שכותב בגט אלא על שם אשת חבירו הוא כותב ואח"כ ממטי האי גט לאתתיה ומגרש לה על שם בעלה והיינו תקלה הואיל דאין סופר מכיר שם האשה בגט. והכי נמי שם האיש בשובר איכא למיחש כי האי גוונא הואיל דאין מכיר שם בעלה ליחוש דלמא ממטיא האי שובר לגבר אחר דשם אתתיה כשמה דהא איתתא שהיא בשובר ואתו לידי תקלה דיימר לה כבר כתובתך פרועה והרי שובר בידי הלכך צריך שיהא מכיר שם האיש והאשה. ואכתי אע"ג דמכירין שם האיש והאשה איכא למיחש לשני יוסף בן

מסורת הש"ס

הגהות הב"ח

תורה אור

א)אכֵּיוָן שֶׁהִגִּיד שׁוּב אֵינוֹ חוֹזֵר וּמַגִּיד — בצוּרְבָא מֵרַבָּנַן לָאו אוֹרְחֵיהּ לְמֵידַק. הַהוּא תַּבְרָא דַּהֲוָה חָתִים עֲלֵיהּ רַב יִרְמְיָה בַּר אַבָּא, אֲמַרָה לֵיהּ: לָאו אֲנָא הֲוַאי, אֲמַר לָהּ: ב)אִיבְרָא אַנְתְּ הֲוַת. אֲמַר אַבַּיֵי: אע"ג דְּצוּרְבָא מֵרַבָּנַן לָאו אוֹרְחֵיהּ לְמֵידַק, כֵּיוָן דְּדַק — דַּק. אֲמַר אַבַּיֵי: גהַאי צוּרְבָא מֵרַבָּנַן דְּאָזֵיל לְקִדּוּשֵׁי אִיתְּתָא, נִידְבַּר עַם הָאָרֶץ בַּהֲדֵיהּ, דִּלְמָא מְחַלְּפוּ לָהּ מִינֵּיהּ.§ "וְהַבַּעַל נוֹתֵן שָׂכָר" וכו'.§ מַאי טַעְמָא? דְּאָמַר קְרָא: °"וְכָתַב... וְנָתַן". (דברים כד) וְהָאִידָּנָא דְּלָא עָבְדִינַן הָכִי, דשַׁדְיוּהוּ רַבָּנַן אַאִשָּׁה כִּי הֵיכִי דְּלָא לְשַׁהְיֵיהּ.§ "כּוֹתְבִין שְׁטָר לַלֹּוֶה אַף עַל פִּי שֶׁאֵין מַלְוֶה עִמּוֹ" וכו'.§ ג)פְּשִׁיטָא! לָא צְרִיכָא, בְּעִיסְקָא.§ "כּוֹתְבִין שְׁטָר לַמּוֹכֵר אַף עַל פִּי שֶׁאֵין לוֹקֵחַ" וכו'.§ פְּשִׁיטָא! לָא צְרִיכָא, הבְּמוֹכֵר שָׂדֵהוּ מִפְּנֵי רָעָתָהּ.§ "אֵין כּוֹתְבִין שִׁטְרֵי אֵירוּסִין" וכו'.§ פְּשִׁיטָא! לָא צְרִיכָא, דַּאֲפִילּוּ צוּרְבָא מֵרַבָּנַן, דְּנִיחָא לֵיהּ לַחֲמוּהּ לְקָרוּבֵיהּ.§ "אֵין כּוֹתְבִין שְׁטַר אֲרִיסוּת וְקַבְּלָנוּת" וכו'.§ פְּשִׁיטָא! לָא צְרִיכָא, בְּבוּרָה.§ "אֵין כּוֹתְבִין שִׁטְרֵי בֵּירוּרִין אֶלָּא מִדַּעַת שְׁנֵיהֶם" וכו'.§ ד)מַאי שִׁטְרֵי בֵּירוּרִין? הָכָא תַּרְגִּימוּ: שִׁטְרֵי טַעֲנָתָא. רַב יִרְמְיָה בַּר אַבָּא אָמַר: וזֶה בּוֹרֵר לוֹ אֶחָד וְזֶה בּוֹרֵר לוֹ אֶחָד.§ ר"ש בֶּן גַּמְלִיאֵל אוֹמֵר: לִשְׁנֵיהֶם כּוֹתְבִין שְׁנַיִם, לָזֶה בְּעַצְמוֹ וְלָזֶה בְּעַצְמוֹ".§ ה)לֵימָא, בְּכוֹפִין עַל מִדַּת סְדוֹם קָא מִיפַּלְגִי, דְּמָר סָבַר: כּוֹפִין, וּמָר סָבַר: אֵין כּוֹפִין? לָא, דְּכוּלֵּי עָלְמָא — כּוֹפִין, וְהָכָא הַיְינוּ טַעְמָא דְּר"ש בֶּן גַּמְלִיאֵל, דְּאָמַר לֵיהּ: לָא נִיחָא לִי דְּתֶהֱוֵי זְכוּתָךְ גַּבֵּי זְכוּתִי, ו)דְּדָמֵית עֲלַאי כִּי אַרְיָא אַרְבָּא.§ **מתני'** ז)מִי שֶׁפָּרַע מִקְצָת חוֹבוֹ, וְהִשְׁלִישׁ אֶת שְׁטָרוֹ וְאָמַר לוֹ: "אִם לֹא ח)(נָתַתִּי) לְךָ מִכָּאן וְעַד יוֹם פְּלוֹנִי — תֵּן לוֹ שְׁטָרוֹ"; הִגִּיעַ זְמַן וְלֹא נָתַן — רַבִּי יוֹסֵי אוֹמֵר: יִתֵּן, רַבִּי יְהוּדָה אוֹמֵר: זלֹא יִתֵּן.§ **גמ'** בְּמַאי קָמִיפַּלְגִי? ט)ר' יוֹסֵי סָבַר: אַסְמַכְתָּא קָנְיָא, וְרַבִּי יְהוּדָה סָבַר: חאַסְמַכְתָּא לָא קָנְיָא. י)אָמַר רַב נַחְמָן אָמַר רַבָּה בַּר אֲבוּהּ אָמַר רַב: הֲלָכָה כְּרַבִּי יוֹסֵי. כִּי אֲתוּ לְקַמֵּיהּ דְּרַבִּי אַמִי, אֲמַר לְהוּ: וְכִי מֵאַחַר שֶׁרַבִּי יוֹחָנָן מְלַמְּדֵנוּ פַּעַם רִאשׁוֹנָה וּשְׁנִיָּה הֲלָכָה כְּרַבִּי יוֹסֵי, אֲנִי מָה אֶעֱשֶׂה? וְאֵין הֲלָכָה כְּרַבִּי יוֹסֵי.§ **מתני'** כ)טמִי שֶׁנִּמְחַק שְׁטַר חוֹבוֹ — ל)מַעֲמִיד עָלָיו עֵדִים, וּבָא לִפְנֵי בֵּית דִּין וְעוֹשִׂין לוֹ קִיּוּם: "אִישׁ פְּלוֹנִי בֶּן פְּלוֹנִי נִמְחַק שְׁטָרוֹ בְּיוֹם פְּלוֹנִי,

וּפְלוֹנִי

כיון שהגיד. נפקא לן במסכת שבועות (דף לג.) מ"אם לא יגיד". **צורבא מרבנן.** כגון רב ירמיה בר אבא, לאו דרכיה למידק ולהכיר בנשים כל כך. והגדה קמייתא שאמר דלאו איהי היא – לאו כלום היא, ולא מיקרי חוזר ומגיד במה שאמר לבסוף: את היא אלא שנשתנה קולך. דכיון דאמר השתא דקדקתי יפה – סמכינן עליה, ומהימנינן ליה. **אע"ג.** דאמור רבנן: צורבא מרבנן לאו אורחיה למידק, כגון רב ירמיה שטען תחלה שלא הכירה – אפי' הכי, כיון דאמר דקדקתי יפה עתה, ומכירה – סמכינן עליה, כדאמרי' גבי רב ירמיה שסמכינן על מה שאמר לבסוף, דכיון דדק דק. **נידבר.** לנהוג. **עם הארץ.** שמסתכל ומכיר בנשים. ה"ג: **מאי טעמא** דאמר קרא וכתב ונתן. **והאידנא דלא עבדינן הכי כו'.** אלא נהגו שהאשה נותנת שכר. **דלא נשהייה.** בשביל השכר, שאינו רוצה ליתן, ותתעגן. **איידי דתנא רישא כו'.** לא גרסינן, ושיבוש הוא. ויש מפרשים דאשובר קאי, ולמימרא דאיהי יהבה השכר ולא הבעל. ואיידי דתנא רישא בדידיה משום גט, שהבעל נותן שכר – תנא נמי בדידיה גבי שובר. ולאו דוקא, ואין זה שיטת גמרא למיתנייה בדידיה שיקרא משום רישא. **עיסקא.** מעות למחצית שכר. **מפני רעתה.** מום גדול שבה, או רחוקה ממנו. וס"ד יתן הוא שכר, (א) דהנאה דידיה הוא, וכדכתיב: "הקונה אל ישמח והמוכר אל יתאבל" (יחזקאל ז), וכדאמרי אינשי (בבא מציעא דף נא.): זבנת – קנית, זבין – אוביד. **אפי' צורבא מרבנן.** החתן. סד"א חמיו יתן כל השכר, שהרי משיא בתו לתלמיד חכם. **בבורה.** שצריך להובירה שנה או שנתים, ואין ריוח עתה למקבל. **הכא תרגימו.** בבבל. **שטרי טענתא.** אני סופרי הדיינין היו כותבין טענות אנשי הריב, כדי שלא יהו טוענין וחוזרין וטוענין, ועל פי אותן טענות פוסקין הדיינין את דינם. **זה בורר לו.** דיין אחד כו'. והיו כותבין בשטר: פלוני בירר לו דיין פלוני, ופלוני בירר לו את פלוני. **לימא בכופין על מדת סדום קמיפלגי.** מדת סדום, כדתנן (אבות פ"ה מ"י): האומר "שלי שלי, שלך שלך" – זו מדה בינונית, ויש אומרים זו מדת סדום. לימא ת"ק סבר: שניהם נותנין שכר, מ) ונותנין שטר אחד בין שניהם. ואם יאמר אחד מהם: לא אתן השכר, כי אני חפץ שיהא לי שטר אחד לבדי ולך שטר אחר, ויהיה "שלי שלי ושלך שלך" – כופין אותו ועושין אחד, כי מה שאמר – מדת סדום היא. ור"ש [ב"ג] סבר: אין כופין. ומשנינן: **לא דכ"ע** כופין. וטעמא דר"ש – משום דקסבר אין זו מדת סדום, שהרי חסר הוא הרבה בדבר אם יכתבו שטר אחד לשניהם, דאמר: לא ניחא לי דתיהוי זכותי בשטר אחד אצל זכותך. **דדמית עלאי כאריא ארבא.** כל שעה שתראה הכתב תבא עלי בעלילות טענותיך הכתובים בו, ואם תראה טענותיי, נבא לידי מריבה, כי איש מריבות אתה. **מתני'** **והשליש את שטרו.** המלוה והלוה מסרוהו ביד שליש, שהרי טורח היה להם לכתוב שובר, וסמכו על השליש. **גמ'** **אסמכתא.** המבטיח לחבירו דבר על מנת שיעשה דבר לעתיד, וסומך בלבו בשעת התנאי שיוכל לקיים הדבר כשיגיע זמן, וכשיגיע הזמן יאנס ולא יוכל לקיים. **לא קניא.** ואינו נתפס בתנאו, ולא יפסיד בכך. ודיני אסמכתא מפורשין בב"מ בפ' "איזהו נשך" (דף סו:) ובפ' "המקבל" (שם קד:). **כי אתו לקמיה דרבי אמי.** דייני אסמכתא. **וכי מאחר שפעם ראשונה ושניה.** כלומר, כמה פעמים לימדנו רבי יוחנן הלכה כר' יוסי, אני מה אעשה והיאך אומר לא קניא. ופסיק גמרא: ואין הלכה כר' יוסי, אף על פי שנימוקו עמו. דאסמכתא לא קניא אלא אם כן קנו מיניה בבית דין חשוב, ובדלא אנים, כדאמר במסכת נדרים (דף כז:). **מתני'** **מי שנמחק שטר חובו.** מעצמו, שנטשטש או שנפלו עליו מים. **מעמיד עליו עדים.** היודעים מאימתי נכתב ומה (ב) כתוב בו, והם עושין לו קיום בפני בית דין, וכותבין לו מה שהיה כתוב באותו השטר והזמן והמעות. **נמחק שטרו.** שהיה כתוב ביום פלוני, ופלוני ופלוני היו עדים שהיו חתומים בו – כל זה כותבין אלו המקיימין, ואחר כך חותמין את שמותם בסוף.

גמ'

כיון דדק דק. וא"ת: היכא דאמר מתחלה לאו איהי היא אמר שיכול (ג) להחזיר — כ"ש כשאומר מתחלה זאת היא, דנאמן, אע"פ שאין דרכו להסתכל בהן! תריץ: ה"ק, כיון דדק דק, ואם רוצה לחזור אינו חוזר ומגיד. (ד) **אמר** רב נחמן אמר רבה בר אבוה. גרסינן "אין הלכה" **ולא** גרסינן "הלכה" והכי משמע בפרק "ארבעה נדרים" (נדרים דף כז.): ההוא דאזיל ואתפיס זכוותיה בב"ד. אמר: אי לא אתינא עד ל' יומי — ליבטלו זכותיה. ולא אתא. אמר רב הונא: בטילן זכותיה. ופריך מרב נחמן דאמר: אין הלכה כר' יוסי דאמר אסמכתא קניא, ואמאי בטילן זכותיה? וכן הגירסא כתובה ברוב ספרים. (ה) תימה: דאמרי' ב"איזהו נשך" (ב"מ דף סו. ושם) אברייתא, אמר רב נחמן: אפי' בשעת מתן מעות לא קנה, על ההיא דהלוהו על שדהו וא"ל אם (ו) לא נתן לך כו'. איתיביה רבא כו' [אומר אני] אסמכתא קניא, ומניומי אומר אסמכתא לא קניא. ופירש רש"י: ומניומי החזירני מדברי, אבל הייתי רגיל לומר קניא, כדמשמע מתני' (ז) דפריכא ליה מינה. ומאי קאמר "מניומי החזירני"? אדרבה, רבה בר אבוה רבו החזירו! ועוד הקשה רבינו תם דרב הונא אדרב הונא; דהתם קאמר אסמכתא קניא, דבשעת מתן מעות קנה הכל, והיכי פריך *בריש נדרים (דף כז:) מהא דאמר רב נחמן אסמכתא לא קניא, והא סבירא ליה קניא! ומתרץ ר"ת: אפילו לא קניא אסמכתא בעלמא, התם ב"איזהו נשך" (שם) קניא טפי, משום דעשה לו טובה שהלוה לו, וגומר בדעתו להקנותו יותר. ועוד, דתפיס מלוה. ואין אני מבין בזה, דהא דרב נחמן (ח) עשה לו כמו כן טובה. ומיהו, מה שנתן הטעם דתפיס — אתי שפיר, דהא דרב נחמן לא תפיס אלא שליש, אלא בדרב הונא דבבא מציעא דתפיס המלוה הקרקע במשכון. ומהאי טעמא נמי אתי שפיר לרב נחמן דאמר אף לאחר מתן מעות קנה הכל, וגם שהוצרך מניומי להחזירו אע"פ שהיה יודע מילתיה דרבה בר אבוה. ועוד י"ל לרב הונא, שכל אסמכתא — שאין דעת כל אחד ואחד (ט) שתהיה האסמכתא, ואין אומרים כלל אלא להסמיך חברו על דבריו. אבל התם — אין זה להסמיכו על דבריו, אלא לגמרי הלוהו על מנת שתשקע בידו אם לא יפרעהו עד שלש שנים, ומהאי טעמא נמי אתי שפיר לרב נחמן. **מעמיד** עליו עדים. נראה שמועיל לענין זה שעושין אותו מלוה בשטר בעדות, דבשביל החתומים הבאים אחרי כן לא היה אלא מלוה ע"פ. וקיום השטר עושין ב"ד, ולא כפי' רשב"ם שהעדים עושין אותו. **ובא** לפני ב"ד. ודוקא נקט ב"ד, דאלימי לאפקועי ממונא. ולקמן נמי איירי שמביא עדים על ההיא דמי שפרע קצת חובו, בגמרא: מקרעין את השטר כו'.

ופלוני

מסורת הש"ס

א) [כתובות יח: סנהדרין מד: מכות ג.]: ב) [בחולין נט: פירש"י איברא אמת ע"ש אבל בערוך איתא אברא וכתב המוסף מלה זו מלשון ברי]: ג) [פי' פשיטא דהלוה נותן שכר]: ד) ב"מ דף כ. ע"ש: ה) לעיל [יב: וש"נ] נט.: ו) [ב"ק פה. וש"נ]: ז) נדרים כז: ב"מ קיז: ח) [צ"ל אתן וכ"א ברי"ף ורא"ש וע"ע בנדרים ובכ"מ]: ט) [נדרים כז: ב"מ מח: סו. לקמן קעג:]: י) [נדרים כז:]: כ) [עי' תוס' כתובות כ: ד"ה ורבי יוחנן וכו' ותוס' כתובות נה. ד"ה כתובו ותוס' לקמן קע: ד"ה אין הלכה]: ל) [גירסת סהמ"ש מעידין]: מ) [וכותבין]:

הגהות הב"ח

(א) רשב"ם ד"ה מפני רעתה וכו' יתן הוא שכר קמ"ל דלא דהנאה דידיה הוא: (ב) ד"ה מעמיד וכו' ומה היה כתוב בו: (ג) תוס' ד"ה כיון וכו' שיכול לחזור כ"ש: (ד) ד"ה ה"ג אמר רב נחמן אמר רבה בר אבוה אין הלכה וכו' ד' נדרים גבי ההוא דאתפיס וכו' ואמר אי לא אתינא עד תלתין יומין לבטלו כצ"ל: (ה) בא"ד ותימה דאמרינן באיזהו נשך אמר כצ"ל ותיבת אברייתא נמחק: (ו) בא"ד דהלוהו על שדהו וא"ל אם אי אתה נותן לי מכאן ועד שלש שנים ה"ה שלי ה"ה שלו איתיביה רבא כו' א"ל אני אומר אסמכתא קניא: (ז) בא"ד מתני' דפריך ליה מינה: (ח) בא"ד דהא דרב נחמן דהכא עשה לו כמו כן וכו' אלא שליש אבל בדרב הונא דבבא מציעא תפיס המלוה: (ט) בא"ד כל אחד ואחד אלא שתהיה האסמכתא:

עין משפט נר מצוה

עא א מיי' פ"ג מהל' עדות הלכה ה סמג עשין קט טוש"ע ח"מ סי' כט סעיף א:

עב ב טוש"ע אה"ע סי' קי סעיף א בהג"ה:

עג ג מיי' בהשגות הראב"ד בפכ"ח מהל' איסורי ביאה הלכה ג ובכרב אלפס יבמות פ"ד דף עו.:

עד ד מיי' פכ"ב מהל' מלוה הלכה ב ופ"ב מהל' גירושין הלכה ב סמג עשין לג ופי' נ טוש"ע אה"ע סי' קכ סעיף א:

עה ה מיי' פכ"ד מהל' מלוה ולוה הלכה ד סמג עשין צד טוש"ע ח"מ סי' רלח סעיף ב:

עו ו מיי' שם טוש"ע וסמג שם טוש"ע ח"מ סי' יג סעיף ב:

עז ז ח מיי' פי"א מהל' מכירה הל' ב סמג עשין פב טוש"ע ח"מ סי' נה סעיף א וסי' רז סעיף יב:

עח ט מיי' פכ"ג מהל' מלוה ולוה הלכה יב ועי' בהשגות ובכ"מ סמג עשין לד טוש"ע ח"מ סי' מא סעיף א וס"ב:

רבינו גרשום

בימי בחרותה ומשו"ה אין אתה מכיר אותה: ובגר לה. כמו בגרת שנתחלפה לה ימי נעוריה ונכנסת בימי בגרות: כיון שהגיד. שלא היא ואיני מכירה: [אינו חוזר ומגיד]. אפ"ה במזכירין אותו ונזכר חוזר ומגיד שצורבא מרבנן לאו אורחיה למבדק להסתכל באשה כדי שיכירה יפה ויכול לסמוך על אחרים שמכירין: כיון דדק דק. ונאמן: דלמא מחלפו לה מיניה. משום דצורבא מרבנן לאו אורחיה למידק ולא להסתכל משום צניעות אבל עם הארץ מסתכל ודייק שאינו ביישן ולא מחלפו ליה שהוא מכירה יפה: והאידנא דלא עבדינן הכי. דליתן בעל שכר משום דבעל מאחר שנכתב הגט אינו חושש אם מגיע לידה כל כך מהרה בשביל הכתובה שצריך לפרוע לה הלכך שדיוהו רבנן שכר הסופר על האשה דהיא תתן: כי היכי דלא לשהייה. שתוציא גיטה מיד הסופר כדי שלא ישהה לה פרעון כתובתה. והשובר לאשה והבעל נותן את השכר והאשה נותנת את השכר מיבעי ליה הואיל דאיהי מקבלת א) הפרעון מכתובתה. ומשני איידי דתנא רישא הבעל נותן תנא סיפא בעל נותן ולאו משום דוקא דודאי האשה נותנת שכר: אע"פ שאין מלוה עמו. משום דזכות הוא למלוה וזכין לאדם שלא בפניו: שיהא לוה עמו. משום דשטר חוב הוא לו ואין חבין לאדם אלא בפניו: והלוה נותן שכר לסופר. משום דריוח שלו הוא שהוא מקבל ונצרך הוא: פשיטא. דלוה נותן שכר דריוח שלו הוא: לא צריכא דיהיב ליה בעסקא. שנותן לו ממון שיהא חצי הריוח שלו מהו דתימא הואיל דמלוה נוטל חצי הריוח יתן שכר לסופר קמ"ל דלא אלא הלוה יתן השכירות הואיל ונהנה ממומן שלוה: אע"פ שאין הלוקח עמו. דזכות הוא לו שקונה: עד שיהא המוכר עמו. דחוב הוא לו: והלוקח נותן את השכר. בשביל שהוא זוכה שקונה: פשיטא. דלוקח נותן שכר שהוא זוכה: לא צריכא במוכר שדהו מפני רעתה. שמם שלה גדול מהו דתימא זכות הוא לו שמוכר והוא יתן השכר קמ"ל דהלוקח נותן דכל קנייה זכות הוא: פשיטא. דאין כותבין אלא מדעת שניהן עד שיתרצו שניהן: לא צריכא דאפילו צורבא מרבנן. ס"ד אמינא כותבין שלא מדעתה דכיון דצורבא מרבנן הוא תתרצה בהנהו קדושין כשיגיע לידה קמ"ל דאפי' הכי אין כותבין אלא מדעת שניהן. והחתן נותן שכר: אין כותבין שטרי אריסות. כגון שנתן פלוני לפלוני את שדהו למחצה לשליש ולרביע. או שטר קבלנות שמקבל שדהו בכך וכך כורין לשנה אלא מדעת שניהן והמקבל נותן את השכר לכותב השטר משום דאיהו משתכר: פשיטא. דמקבל נותן שכר דנהנה: לא צריכא בבורה. בשדה שהיתה בורה מזמן גדול מהו דתימא ריוח דנותן הוא שמתקן שדהו הרבה והוא יתן קמ"ל דלא: הכא. בבבל: תרגימו שטרי טענתא. שזה בורר אחד נאמן שמקבל טענותיהן וכותבן וזה בורר לו אחד שמקבל טענותיו וכותבן כדי שלא יתחלפו טענותיהן ונותנין לכל אחד טענותיו ואותן של חבירו והולכין לב"ד: רב ירמיה בר אבא אמר. היינו שטרי בירורין שכותבין שזה בירר לו דיין פלוני וזה בירר לו דיין פלוני ולהכי כותבין שאם יתחייב האחד שלא יוכל לומר אני לא קבלתי עלי פלוני להיות ב"ד: רשב"ג אומר לשניהן כותבין לזה בפני עצמו. טענותיו ולא טענותיו של חבירו והכי נמי לאידך שלא יתחלפו טענותיהם: דמר סבר. ת"ק: כופין על מדת סדום. שאם אמר האחד איני רוצה ליתן אלא מחצית שכירות הסופר לפי שיכולין כל טענותיו להיכתב בשטר אחד ויתן בעל דיני חצי השכר וחבירו יאמר איני רוצה שיכתבו טענותי עם טענותיו אלא יכתבו לו טענותיו לבד בשטר אחר ויתן הוא כל שכירות כתיבת שטרו ואני אתן כל שכירות כתיבת שטר טענותי אין שומעין לו דזה מדת סדום שלי שלי ושלך שלך אלא יכתבו לשניהן כל טענותם בשטר אחד או שטר בירור ב"ד ויתנו שניהן שכירות של שטר אחד בלבד: ורשב"ג אומר אין כופין. אלא להכי לשניהם כותבין לזה טענותיו לעצמו ולזה לעצמו וכל אחד יתן שכר שטרו: לא דכ"ע כופין והכא היינו טעמא דרשב"ג דא"ל לא ניחא לי שיהו זכיות טענותיך עם זכיות טענותי. בשטר אחד שאיני רוצה להשתתף עמך: דדמית עלי כאריא ארבא. כארי אורב: **פיס'** והשליש את שטרו. שאמר למלוה תנהו ביד שליש ביד נאמן אם לא אשלים לך הפרעון עד יום פלוני תן לו שטרו ויגבה כדמעיקרא כל חובו וילך לאיבוד מה שכבר נתתי: ב)ואם לא נתתי אסמכתא הוא שסומך בדעתו שיכול לפורעו עד הזמן ועל כן מקנה לו. ר' יוסי סבר אסמכתא קניא: שר' יוחנן למדנו. במקומות אחרים: אני מה אעשה. ואפ"ה אין הלכה כר' יוסי אלא אסמכתא לא קניא: **פיס'** מי שנמחק מקצת שטר חובו. ומתירא שמא ימחק כולו: מעמיד עליו על השטר עדים. שיקראוהו וידעו מה כתוב בו ומי הן עדיו ויביא אותן לפני ב"ד שיעידו בפניהם מה שראו בשטר. והן ב"ד עושין לו קיום. שיכתבו לו על גבי אותו שטר

פלוני

א) רבינו היה לו בכאן הגי' שהובא ברשב"ם ד"ה איידי. ב) אולי צ"ל ר"י סבר אסמכתא קניא. אם לא נתתי וכו'.

עט א ב מיי' פכ"ג מהל' מלוה ולוה הל' יג סמג עשין צד טוש"ע ח"מ סי' מא ס"א:
פ ג מיי' שם הל' יד וסמג שם טוש"ע ח"מ סי' נב סעיף א:
פא ד מיי' שם טוש"ע שם סעיף ב:
פב ה ו ז מיי' שם טוש"ע שם ס"א:
פג ח מיי' שם הל' יא סמג שם טוש"ע ח"מ סי' מא סעיף ג:
פד ט מיי' שם הל' י סמג שם טוש"ע שם בהג"ה וסי' רלט סעיף א:

"ופלוני ופלוני עדיו". § **גמ'** ת"ר: איזהו קיומו: א"במותב תלתא הוינא אנו פלוני ופלוני ופלוני, הוציא פלוני בן פלוני שטר מחוק לפנינו ביום פלוני, ופלוני ופלוני עדיו"; בואם כתוב בו "הוזקקנו לעדותי של עדים ונמצאת עדותן מכוונת" — גובה ואינו צריך להביא ראיה, ואם לאו — צריך להביא ראיה; גנקרע — פסול, נתקרע — כשר; דנמחק או נטשטש, אם רישומו ניכר — כשר. ה"ד "נקרע" ה"ד "נתקרע"? אמר רב יהודה: ה"נקרע" — קרע של בית דין, "נתקרע" — קרע שאינו של ב"ד. היכי דמי קרע של בית דין? א"ר יהודה: ומקום עדים ומקום הזמן ומקום התורף. אביי אמר: זשתי וערב. הנהו ערבאי דאתו לפומבדיתא, דהוו קא אנסי ארעתא דאינשי; אתו מרוותיהו לקמיה דאביי, א"ל: ליחזי מר שטרי' ולכתוב לן מר שטרא אחרינא עליה, דאי מיתנים חד — נקיטינן חד בידן. אמר להו: מאי אעביד לכו? דאמר א)רב ספרא: אין כותבין שני שטרות על שדה אחת, דלמא טריף והדר טריף. הוו קא טרדי ליה, אמר ליה לספריה: זיל כתוב להו הוא על המחק ועדיו על הנייר, דפסול. אמר ליה רב אחא בר מניומי לאביי: ודלמא רישומו ניכר, ותניא: נמחק או נטשטש, אם רישומו ניכר — כשר! אמר ליה: מי קאמינא שטרא מעליא? אל"ף בי"ת בעלמא קאמינא. תנו רבנן: חהרי שבא ואמר "אבד שטר חובי", אע"פ שאמרו עדים "אנו כתבנו וחתמנו ונתננו לו" — אין כותבין לו את השטר; בד"א — בשטרי הלואה, טאבל שטרי מקח וממכר — כותבין, חוץ מן האחריות שבו; רבן

גמ' הוציא. שטר מחוק לפנינו, שהיה כתוב ביום פלוני. **ופלוני ופלוני.** היו עדים שחתומים בו. ומפרש גמרא: **אם כתוב בו הוזקקנו כו'.** שעמדו אלו בית דין המקיימין וחקרו עדים החתומים בו להעיד על חתימתן, ונמצאו דבריהם מכוונין. **גובה.** מזמן ראשון הכתוב בשטר, ואין צריך ראיה אחרת. **ואם לאו** – צריך להביא ראיה אחרת על הזמן, ועל סכום המעות, ועל כל מה שהיה כתוב בשטר. **נקרע.** על ידי אדם. **נתקרע.** מעצמו. **ערבאי.** ישמעאלים. **וקאנסי לארעתא דאינשי.** ומתוך שהיו בעלי זרוע כופין בעליהן לתת גם השטרות, שלא יוכלו לערער. **ליחזי מר שטרא.** מה כתוב בו, קודם שיאנסו ממנו, וכתוב לנו אחר תחתיו. שאם יאנס אחד – ישאר לנו שני, ולזמן מרובה אם תהיה ידינו תקיפה – נערער על שדותינו, ונקח מיד הלוקחים אותם מיד הערביים. **דאמר רב ספרא.** לקמן בשמעתין. **דלמא טריף והדר טריף.** זה הלוקח שקנה שדה באחריות, וזמנין דטריף ליה מיניה בעל חוב דמוכר, ואתי איהו וטריף מלקוחות, ומחזיר להם אחד מן השטרות כדי לגבות בו מן המוכר. והדר טריף מלקוחות אחריני על ידי השטר השני, ואומר: עתה טרפו ממני, ואחזור ואטרוף מלקוחות, והרי שטר מכירתי עדיין הוא בידי. **קא טרדי ליה.** מפצירין בו. **אמר ליה לספריה זיל כתוב להו.** שטר, ומחוק אותו, ואחר כך כתוב על המחק והעדים יחתמו על הנייר, ואלו לא יתנו לב שהוא פסול, ואיפטר מהם. **אמר ליה רב אחא בר מניומי לאביי כו'.** (א) לי נראה דרב אחא בר מניומי הוה סלקא דעתיה דהכי אמר אביי לספריה, דנכתוב להו שטרא מעליא והדר נמחקיה, והדר נכתביה על המחק ונחתמו סהדי על הנייר. והכי קשיא ליה: ודלמא לא מחקי ליה שפיר, משום דבעי למיכתב עליה, והוי רושם ראשון ניכר, ואזלי ומחקי ליה להאי כתבא בתרא, ומוקי ליה אקמא, והוה ליה רושם ראשון ניכר וכשר. וראשון לא על המחק נכתב, והוה ליה כנטשטש, דאמרן לעיל: רישומו ניכר – כשר. **אמר ליה מי סברת שטרא מעליא קאמינא.** דנכתוב ונמחקיה. **אל"ף בי"ת בעלמא קאמינא.** דברים בטלים אמרתי לכתוב ולמחוק. **אבד שטר חובי.** וכתבו לי אחר תחתיו ככל הכתוב בראשון. וכגון שאין לו עדים שאבד ממנו. **כתבנו ונתננו לו.** דליכא למימר: שמא כתב ללוות ולא לוה. **בשטרי הלואה.** אפילו אם באו לכתוב חוץ מאחריות שבו – אין כותבין, דאתו למיטרף ביה מבני חרי, ושמא לא אבד הראשון, אי נמי דלמא חזר ומצאו, וטריף והדר טריף. **אבל בשטרי מקח וממכר.** אם אמרו עדים כתבנו ונתננו לו – כותבין לו אחר, חוץ מאחריות שבו. מאחר שאמת הדבר שזה הקרקע קנוי לו, והוא ירא פן ישתקע הדבר ויערערו עליו שלא כדין – כותבין לו שטר מקח בלא אחריות, כדמפרש לקמן (דף קסט:): "שטרא דנן דכתבנוהי דלא למיגבי ביה לא ממשעבדי ולא מבני חרי" כו'.
רבן

ופלוני ופלוני עדיו. החתומים בשטר, כך פירש רשב"ם. ונראה לר"י (ב) שמזכיר ב)(הוא הדין) נמי העדים שהעידו שראו אותו השטר, שאם ירצה הלוה היום או למחר לפסלן — שיוכל לפסלן. ותימה אם צריך לכתבן, (ג) שאין הגמרא מזכירן. וצריך עיון בתיקון שטרות. **אבל** בשטרי מקח וממכר כותבין חוץ מאחריות שבו. וכותבין מזמן ראשון, דאי מזמנא דהאידנא — שמא חזר ומכרה למוכר, ויוציא אח"כ שטר עליה, ויאמר: האידנא הוא(ד) דזבינתה מינך, והדר טריף שלא כדין. ורשב"ג אומר: אין כותבין אפי' בשטרי מקח וממכר. פי': דשמא אחר שקנאה החזיר שטרו למוכר, וחזר המכר. והשתא, אי לא עבדינן ליה שטרא להאי — מהימן מוכר לומר: הוא החזיר לי השטר, וחזר המכר, שהרי אין לזה שטר. אבל אם עושין לזה שטר — איך יוכל לומר שלי היא כשיוציא שטר שלו? הלא הלוקח תופס השטר שהוא שלו, ויאמר למוכר: שטר שבידך לא החזרתיו לך, אלא כשמכרת לי הקרקע כתבת לי כמה שטרות, דכותבין שטר למוכר(ה), והאחד בידך עדיין! וחכמים אומרים: מתנתו קיימת. וא"כ, גבי מקח וממכר ליכא למיחש למידי; אפי' אין שטר לזה הלוקח, שלא נכתב שום שטר — לא יוכל המוכר ליטול קרקע, שאפילו החזיר לו שטרו — אינו שלו, דהא לא חזרה מתנתו. ואפילו יש לו ראיה שנתנו לו, שכתב לו שטר שיקנה אותה, ואותיות נקנות במסירה ובשטר לכולי עלמא, או יש לו שטר מכירה במכרה לו — השתא נמי ליכא למיחש למידי, שאם כן לא יכול זה להזיקו כלום, ואפילו יש לו שטר שנכתב לו מחדש, שהרי כתוב מאותו הזמן. ותימה קצת: אם לא כתב לו שטר מכירה, אלא "קנה לך איהו וכל שעבודיה", לכה אין לחוש שמא יפסידנו הלוקח על ידי שטר (ו) שכתב לו מזמן ראשון? שאע"כ ששני השטרות יהיה כתוב בהן יום אחד — מ"מ לא יהיה מוחזק בה המוכר יותר מן הלוקח, מאחר שיהיה גם ללוקח שטר, ושמא הוא החזירו למוכר באותו יום עצמו שהקנה לו השטר מכר, שאז אין ג)(כותבין זמן ואומר שאחר כך) חזר ומכרה לו באותו היום עצמו! ואומר ר"י: דכולי האי לא חיישינן, וגם לא יהא לו פנים לומר שבו ביום החזיר לו השטר ובו ביום חזר ומכרה לו. ותימה: לרשב"ג, למאן דאמר לקמן (דף קעג.): צריך להביא ראיה, נהי דנקנות במסירה — מ"מ צריך המוכר להביא ראיה שהחזיר לו השטר, אפילו הוא בידו! ואור"י: דהכא אין צריך לכולי עלמא, דלגבילה לא חיישינן. ולפקדון נמי לא חיישינן הכא, שירא הוא להפקיד שטרי למוכר, דלמא כבש ליה ויביא עדים שהשדה היתה שלו עד עתה. תימה לר"י: שכל מוכר שדה יכול להזיק ללוקח, דכיון שכותבין שטר למוכר אע"פ שאין לוקח עמו, דזימני דכתב שני שטרות ונותן האחד ללוקח. ולאחר שלש שנים או ארבע, שיפסיד הלוקח את שטרו — יבא ויאמר: החזיר לי השטר, ויביאהו לב"ד ויגבה בלא ראיה, למאן דאמר אין צריך להביא ראיה. ואותו לא יוכל לומר לו: מתחלה כתבת, שכתבת אז הרבה שטרות, מאחר שהוא אין לו שטר, ואין יכול להוכיח שלא החזירו לו! ויש לומר: דאיכא למימר שכיון שהחזיק שלש שנים בקרקע — עומדת החזקה במקום השטר, ויכול לומר כל מה שיכול לטעון אם היה השטר בידו, כי יאמר: מה שאין לי שטרי — לא בשביל שהחזרתיו לך, אלא שלא נזהרתי לשמרו לאחר שלש שנים. ד)ותימה לרבן שמעון בן גמליאל, שמכל מקום יכול המוכר לעשות שני שטרות, כגון ראובן דכתב ב' שטרות שמכר שדה לשמעון, ויתן האחד לשמעון והאחד ללוי, ויעשה קנוניא בינו ובין לוי, ויוציא לוי אותו השטר לאחר ג' שנים שהפסיד שמעון שטרו, ויטעון כי שמעון מסרו לו ונתן לוט השדה, ולא יצטרך הוא להביא ראיה, למ"ד אין צריך להביא ראיה! וי"ל דכי האי גוונא צריך להביא. וכה"ג אמרינן לקמן (דף קעג.) דאחין הואיל ה)ושמעי להדדי — צריך להביא ראיה, ואפי' אמרי' בעלמא א"צ. ובענין אחר יש לפרש, ולא תקשה לרשב"ג (ז) ו)[ולא תצטרך] לכל זה. רשב"ג אומר אף שטרי מקח וממכר אין כותבין — כדמפרש לקמן, שיש לחוש שמא החזיר הלוקח למוכר וחזר המכר, ואם לא נכתב שטר שני ללוקח — יוציא המוכר הקרקע מיד הלוקח על ידי השטר שהחזיר לו. אבל אם נכתוב לו שטר שני ללוקח, אפילו יוציא המוכר על הלוקח השטר שהחזיר לו — לא יועיל כלום, שיאמר הלוקח: שני שטרות היו לי, ולא החזרתי לו אלא אחד. וכיון שהאחד עדיין בידו — לא חזר המכר. ז)והשתא אין להקשות: אפי' כשיש שטר ביד המוכר מה יש לו להועיל, והלא הלוקח יכול לומר לו: קודם שמכרת לי השדה כתבת שנים או שלשה שטרות, וכתבו לך כאשר חפצת, כי כותבין שטר למוכר אע"פ שאין לוקח עמו, ומה שאין שטר בידי — לפי שאבד ממני. הא לא קשה מידי, דודאי אין מועיל למוכר אלא אם כן יש עדים שזה השטר שבידו הוא אותו שנתנו ללוקח, ועתה חזר לידו. אי נמי, יבררו עדים שהחזיר לו הלוקח את השטר

רבינו גרשום

פלוני נמחק שטרו שנכתב ביום פלוני ופלוני ופלוני עדיו. שראו שם כתוב בו כך או אם הכירו השטר לפני ב"ד שיראוהו קודם שימחק כולו וראו ב"ד מה שכתוב בו וראו נמי חתימת העדים יכתבו לו איש פלוני וכו' ופלוני ופלוני עדיו שהיו חתומין בו: אנו ב"ד פלוני ופלוני שצריכין להיות שלשה: הוציא פלוני בן פלוני שטר מחוק לפנינו שנכתב ביום פלוני כלומר באותו זמן: ואם כתוב בו. באותו קיום: הוזקקנו לעדותן של עדים. שראו מה שהיה בכתב: ונמצאת עדותן מכוונת. שאמרו שהיו מכירין אף חתימת ידי העדים: גובה בעל השטר. ואין צריך להביא שום ראיה עוד: ואם לאו. שלא כתבו הוזקקנו יכול הנתבע לומר שטר מזויף מחוק הראה לעדים או לב"ד הלכך צריך עדים שיקיימו כתיבת העדים לעדות: ואם לאו. שלא נמצא מכוון שלא העידו אלא על כתיבת השטר בלבד ולא העידו שהכירו חתימת העדים צריך להביא ראיה קודם שיתבע עדים שהכירו חתימת ידי עדים שהיה על השטר שהשטר ישר הוא: נקרע. בכוונה כדמפרש לקמן: פסול. דמשמע שאחרים קרעוהו שמצאו בו דופי או פרוע היה: נתקרע. מעצמו: ומקום התורף. כתיבת הממון להכי קרי טורף שבו טורף לקוחות: הנהו ערבאי. ישמעאלים שהיו מסייעין למלך כשהיה הולך למלחמה והיו רגילין לעכב עמו במלכותו זמן גדול ושוב חוזרין למקומן ובאו עמו לפומבדיתא ונתן להם רשות לאנס קרקעות של בני אדם שבסביב העיר שיתפרנסו מהן כל ימות שהן שם: אתו מרוותיהו. בעלי הקרקע: לקמיה דאביי. ואמרו ליחזי מר שטרי' שיש לנו על אותן שדות שתופשים הערביים שהן שלנו שאנו קנאום מן בעליהן ולא הספקנו להחזיק בהן ג' שנים עד שנטלום הערביים וכשילכו להן נחזיק בשדותינו השתא לכתוב לנו מר לכל חד מיננא שטר אוחרן עלה דארעא דאי מתנים או מתביד שטרא דאית לן כדאמר התם עד תלת שנין מזדהר איניש בשטריה טפי לא מזדהר וכי מתביד נקטינן מיהא חד שטר בידן: דלמא טריף. בשטר זה לקוחות ותו לאחר זמן מפיק שטר אוחרן והדר טרפי לקוחות אחריני: הוו קא טרדי ליה. היו מפצירין עליו שיכתוב להם: כתוב להם כי האי שטרא הוא על המחק ועדיו על הנייר דפסול. לטרוף ממנו לקוחות אבל לכך יועיל להם שכל זמן שזה שטר בידם אין יכול המוכר לכפור שלא מכר: ודלמא. אע"ג דכתב על המחק ועדיו על הנייר מחק נמי לעדי קיום עד שיהא רשומו ניכר והוה ליה אידי ואידי על המחק: ותניא נמחק או נטשטש אם רשומן ניכר כשר. ואתו למיטרף נמי זימנא אחרינא: אל"ף בי"ת בעלמא קאמינא. כלומר דצי התיבות של כל השטר כותב כגון ז"ב ע"ד וכן כולו הואיל ויש בו בשטר תרי ריעותא חדא דהתיבות אינן שלמות ועוד דהוא על המחק פסול ולא מצי למטרף ביה: ת"ר וכו' ונתננו לו. שטר שאבד: אין כותבין ונותנין לו את השטר אחר. דלמא מכוב ולא נאבד ואיערומי מיערם ובעי טריף והדר טריף: במה דברים אמורים. דאין כותבין: בשטרי הלואה. כגון בעל חוב שלוה והיו קרקעותיו משועבדין למלוה ואי כתבי למלוה שטרא אחרינא טריף והדר טריף לקוחות וכל שטרי הלואה אע"פ שאין כתוב בו אחריות הרי הוא כמו שכתוב בו דכל לוה חייב באחריות החוב: אבל שטרי מקח וממכר. שמכר לו שדהו ואמר נאבד שטרא של מכירה: כותבין לו אחר חוץ מאחריות שבו. דלא כתבי בהאי שני אחריות דכיון דלית ביה אחריות לא מצי טריף ביה לקוחות ואי אמרת אם כן מה מועיל לו כיון דלא מצי למטרף ביה להכי אהני ליה דכי נקיט האי שטרא לא מצי למטען מוכר הא ארעא לא מכרתיה מעולם לך דהאי שטרא מוכיח דזבנה לו אבל לגבות לא מהני הואיל דאין בו אחריות אבל בשטר הלואה

א) ולקמן דף קסט.: ב) רש"א מ"ז:ג) ס"א כתוב בו זמן ואח"כ. רש"א: ד) נ"א ועוד תימה. רש"א: ה) ס"א דשמעי מהדדי. רש"ל: ו) גי' רש"ל: ז) נ"א ולא"ח אפי'. רש"ל:

הגהות הב"ח

(א) רשב"ם ד"ה אמר ליה וכו' לאביי כו' נראה לי דרב אחא בר מניומי הוה סלקא דעתיה דהכי וכו' והכי קא קשיא וכו' ובשר דרלאשון לא: (ב) תוס' ד"ה ופלוני וכו' שמזכירין נמי העדים וכו' הספר שנמחק שאם ירצה: (ג) בא"ד לכתבן מאחר שאין הגמרא: (ד) ד"ה אבל וכו' ויאמר האידנא הוא דהדרי' וזבינתה מינך וטריף שלא כדין כצ"ל: (ה) בא"ד דכותבין שטר למוכר ואע"פ שאין לוקח עמו והאחד בידך וכו' דלאפי' אין שטר לזה הלוקח שלא נכתב לו שום וכו' ליטול הקרקע: (ו) בא"ד שטר שנכתב לו מזמן ראשון: (ז) בא"ד ולא תקשה לרשב"ג מכל זה:

רַבָּן שִׁמְעוֹן בֶּן גַּמְלִיאֵל אוֹמֵר: אַף שִׁטְרֵי מִקָּח וּמִמְכָּר אֵין כּוֹתְבִין; וְכֵן הָיָה רַבָּן שִׁמְעוֹן בֶּן גַּמְלִיאֵל אוֹמֵר: הַנּוֹתֵן מַתָּנָה לַחֲבֵרוֹ וְהֶחֱזִיר לוֹ אֶת הַשְּׁטָר — חָזְרָה מַתְּנָתוֹ, וַחֲכָמִים אוֹמְרִים: מַתְּנָתוֹ קַיֶּימֶת. אָמַר מָר: חוּץ מֵאַחֲרָיוּת שֶׁבּוֹ. מַאי טַעֲמָא? א)א"ר סָפְרָא: אלְפִי שֶׁאֵין כּוֹתְבִין שְׁנֵי שְׁטָרוֹת עַל שָׂדֶה אַחַת, דִּלְמָא אָזֵיל בַּעַל חוֹב טָרֵיף לֵיהּ לְהַאי, וְאָזֵיל הַאי וּמַפֵּיק חַד וְטָרֵיף לָקוֹחוֹת, וְאָמַר לֵיהּ לְבַעַל חוֹב: שׁוּף לִי דְּאֵיקוּם בָּהּ וַהֲדַר תָּא טִירְפַן. וּמַפֵּיק אַחֲרִינָא וַהֲדַר אָזֵיל טָרֵיף לָקוֹחוֹת אַחֲרִינֵי. וְכֵיוָן דְּקָרְעֵנֵיהּ לִשְׁטָרָא דְּמַלְוֶה, בְּמַאי הָדַר טָרֵיף לָהּ? וְכִי תֵּימָא דְּלָא קָרְעֵנֵיהּ — וְהָא אָמַר רַב נַחְמָן: בכָּל טִירְפָּא דְּלָא כְּתִיב בֵּיהּ "קָרְעֵנֵיהּ לִשְׁטָרָא דְּמַלְוֶה" — לָאו טִירְפָּא הוּא; גוְכָל אַדְרַכְתָּא דְּלָא כְּתִיב בָּהּ "קָרְעֵנֵיהּ לְטִירְפָּא" — לָאו אַדְרַכְתָּא הוּא; דוְכָל שׁוּמָא דְּלָא כְּתִיב בֵּיהּ "קָרְעֵנֵיהּ לְאַדְרַכְתָּא" — לָאו שׁוּמָא הִיא! לָא צְרִיכָא, דְּקָאתֵי מִכֹּחַ אֲבָהֳתֵיהּ. אֲמַר לֵיהּ רַב אַחָא מִדִּפְתִּי לְרָבִינָא: וְלָמָּה לֵיהּ לְמֵימַר לֵיהּ לְבַעַל חוֹב "שׁוּף לִי בְּהַאי אַרְעָא וְאֵיקוּם בָּהּ"? תֵּיפוֹק לֵיהּ, דְּכֵיוָן דְּנָקֵיט תְּרֵי שְׁטָרֵי — טָרֵיף וַהֲדַר טָרֵיף! אִם כֵּן, נְפִישֵׁי עֲלֵיהּ בַּעֲלֵי דִּינִין. וְלִכְתּוֹב לְהַאי שְׁטָרָא מְעַלְּיָא, וְלִכְתּוֹב תַּבְרָא לַמּוֹכֵר: "כָּל שְׁטָרֵי דְּיִפְּקוּן עַל אַרְעָא דָּא פְּסוּלִין, לְבַר מִן דְּיִפּוֹק בִּזְמְנָא דָּא"! אֲמַרוּהָ רַבָּנַן קַמֵּיהּ דְּרַב פַּפָּא, וְאָמְרִי לָהּ קַמֵּיהּ דְּרַב אַשִׁי: זֹאת אוֹמֶרֶת, ב)אֵין כּוֹתְבִין שׁוֹבֵר? אֲמַר

רשב"ם

רַבָּן שִׁמְעוֹן בֶּן גַּמְלִיאֵל אוֹמֵר אֲפִילּוּ בְּשִׁטְרֵי מִקָּח וּמִמְכָּר אֵין כּוֹתְבִין. דְּס"ל אוֹתִיּוֹת נִקְנוֹת בִּמְסִירָה, כִּדִלְקַמָּן גַּבֵּי מַתָּנָה, דְּחָיְישִׁינַן דִּלְמָא לְאַחַר שֶׁכְּתָבוּ וְנָתְנוּ לוֹ שְׁטַר הַמְּכִירָה הֶחֱזִיר לוֹ לוֹקֵחַ זֶה לַמּוֹכֵר אֶת הַשְּׁטָר, וְחָזַר לוֹ מִקָּחוֹ, כִּדְאָמְרִינַן גַּבֵּי מַתָּנָה. חָזְרָה מַתְּנָתוֹ. כִּדְמְפָרֵשׁ לְקַמֵּיהּ טַעֲמָא. מַתְּנָתוֹ קַיֶּימֶת. אֶלָּא אִם כֵּן חָזַר וּמְכָרָהּ אוֹ נְתָנָהּ לוֹ בְּקִנְיָן גָּמוּר, אוֹ בִּשְׁטָר חָדָשׁ, כְּדִין לוֹקֵחַ וּמוֹכֵר. אָמַר מָר חוּץ מֵאַחֲרָיוּת שֶׁבּוֹ מַאי טַעְמָא. אֵין כּוֹתְבִין לוֹ אַחֲרָיוּת. אָמַר רַב סָפְרָא לְפִי שֶׁאֵין כּוֹתְבִין שְׁנֵי שְׁטָרוֹת עַל שָׂדֶה אַחַת. שֶׁאִם יִכְתּוֹב לוֹ שְׁטָר אַחֵר — חָיְישִׁינַן דִּלְמָא אָתֵי בַּעַל חוֹב וְטָרֵיף לֵיהּ לְהַאי שָׂדֶה, דְּאָמַר הַקּוֹנֶה אוֹתָהּ כִּי אָבַד שְׁטָרִי שֶׁהָיָה לִי עַל שָׂדֶה זוֹ וְכָתְבוּ לוֹ שְׁטָר אַחֵר עָלֶיהָ. וְכֵיוָן דְּנִטְרְפָה מִיָּדוֹ — אָזֵיל בְּהַאי שְׁטָרָא דְּכָתְבוּ לֵיהּ, וְטָרֵיף לַלָּקוֹחוֹת שֶׁקָּנוּ אַחַר שֶׁקָּנָה הוּא, וְיַעֲשֶׂה קְנוּנְיָא עִם הַבַּעַל חוֹב שֶׁטְּרָפָהּ מִמֶּנּוּ. וְאָמַר לֵיהּ שׁוּף לִי דְּאֵיקוּם בְּאַרְעָא. כְּלוֹמַר, אַל תְּעַרְעֵר עָלַי עַתָּה כְּלוּם. פֵּי': שׁוּף = בְּשׁוּפִי, כִּדְגָרְסִינַן (כתובות דף כ.): וְהוּא שֶׁאֲכָלוּם בַּעֲלֵיהֶם שָׁלֹשׁ שָׁנִים וּבְשׁוּפִי. כָּךְ אָמַר לֵיהּ: שׁוּף לִי, דְּאֵיקוּם בְּאַרְעָא אַרְבַּע אוֹ חָמֵשׁ שָׁנִים עַד דְּיִתְיַישֵּׁן הַדָּבָר, וַהֲדַר תָּא וּתְעַרְעֵר עָלַי זִימְנָא אַחֲרִיתִי. וְעָבֵיד הָכִי, וּבָתַר זְמַן מְעַרְעֵר עֲלֵיהּ וְטָרֵיף לָהּ מִינֵּיהּ, וַהֲדַר אָזַל הַקּוֹנֶה שֶׁאָמַר "אָבַד שְׁטָרִי" וְכָתְבוּ לוֹ אַחֵר, וּמַפֵּיק לֵיהּ לְהַהוּא שְׁטָרָא [קַמָּא] רש"ל דְּכָתְבוּ לֵיהּ עַל שָׂדֶה זוֹ, וְאָזֵיל וְטָרֵיף לַלָּקוֹחוֹת. וּמַקְשִׁינַן עֲלָהּ: וְכֵיוָן דְּקָרְעֵנוּהּ לִשְׁטָרָא. דְּבַעַל חוֹב, בִּזִימְנָא קַמַּיְיתָא דְּטָרֵיף — בְּמַאי קָטָרֵיף כִּי אָתֵי הַשְׁתָּא וְטָרֵיף? וְהָאָמַר רַב נַחְמָן כו'. כָּךְ הוּא הַסֵּדֶר: מַלְוֶה בָּא לְבֵ"ד וְצוֹעֵק עַל הַלֹּוֶה שֶׁיִּפְרַע לוֹ חוֹבוֹ, וּמְזַמְּנִינַן לֵיהּ לַלֹּוֶה בְּדִינָא, כִּדְאָמְרִי', וְאִי לָא אָתֵי — מְשַׁמְּתִינַן לֵיהּ, וְכוֹתְבִין שְׁטַר טִירְפָּא לַמַּלְוֶה שֶׁיֵּלֵךְ וִיפַשְׁפֵּשׁ אַחַר קַרְקְעוֹתָיו שֶׁל לֹוֶה. וְכָל מָקוֹם שֶׁיִּמְצָא מִנְּכָסָיו אוֹ מִלָּקוֹחוֹת שֶׁקָּנוּ מִמֶּנּוּ אַחֲרֵי כֵן — יַרְאֶה שְׁטָרוֹ לְבֵ"ד שֶׁל אוֹתָהּ הָעִיר, וְיִמְסְרוּ לוֹ קַרְקְעוֹתָיו לַמַּלְוֶה, וְיִכְתְּבוּ לוֹ שְׁטַר אַדְרַכְתָּא, שֶׁיְּהֵא שַׁלִּיט וְדוֹרֵךְ עַל נְכָסָיו שֶׁל זֶה לִגְבּוֹת חוֹבוֹ מֵהֶן, כִּדְמְפָרֵשׁ בְּ"הַגּוֹזֵל בַּתְרָא". וּשְׁטַר הַטִּירְפָּא יִקְרְעוּ, פֶּן יַחֲזוֹר וְיִטְרוֹף בְּבֵ"ד אַחֵר. וְיָשׁוּמוּ הַנְּכָסִים כְּדִין שׁוּמַת בֵּית דִּין כִּדְמְפָרֵשׁ בְּבֵ"ק, וּכְפִי הַשּׁוּמָא יִקָּחֵם בְּחוֹבוֹ, וְיִכְתְּבוּ לוֹ בֵּ"ד שְׁטַר שׁוּמַת הַנְּכָסִים לָדַעַת בְּכַמָּה קִבְּלָם, וּמִשּׁוּם דְּשׁוּמָא הָדְרָא לְעוֹלָם כְּשֶׁיְּהֵא לוֹ מָעוֹת לַלֹּוֶה, כִּדְאָמְרִי' [בְּבֵ"מ] (דף טז: ודף לה.). וּכְשֶׁיִּתְּנוּ לוֹ בֵּית דִּין שְׁטַר הַשּׁוּמָא — יִקְרְעוּ הָאַדְרַכְתָּא, פֶּן יַחֲזוֹר וְיִטְרוֹף בָּהּ פַּעַם שְׁנִיָּה שֶׁלֹּא כַּדִּין. וּמְשַׁנֵּי: לָא צְרִיכָא דְּאָתֵי מִכֹּחַ אֲבָהֳתֵיהּ. לְכָךְ אֵין כּוֹתְבִין שְׁנֵי שְׁטָרוֹת — דְּחָיְישִׁינַן דִּלְמָא לָאו מִכֹּחַ הַהַלְוָאָה יָבֹא וְיִטְרוֹף, אֶלָּא יָבֹא וִיעַרְעֵר כִּי זוֹ רש"ל הַשָּׂדֶה גְּזָלָהּ מֵאֲבוֹתָיו זֶה שֶׁמְּכָרָהּ לְךָ. וְהֵבִיא עֵדִים כִּי זוֹ שְׂדֵה אֲבוֹתָיו, רש"ל וְהַמּוֹכֵר שֶׁמְּכָרָהּ גְּזָלָהּ מֵאֲבוֹתָיו. וְהוֹצִיאוּהָ מִיָּדוֹ וְהֶעֱמִידוּהָ בְּיַד הַמְעַרְעֵר, רש"ל וְכָתְבוּ לַלּוֹקֵחַ שֶׁנִּטְרְפָה מִיָּדוֹ, וְכִי יֵשׁ לוֹ רְשׁוּת לִטְרוֹף הַלָּקוֹחוֹת שֶׁקָּנוּ קַרְקַע מִן הַמּוֹכֵר שֶׁמָּכַר לוֹ שָׂדֶה זוֹ הַגְּזוּלָה. וְהָלַךְ וְעָשָׂה קְנוּנְיָא הַלּוֹקֵחַ רש"ל עִם הַנִּגְזָל שֶׁלָּקַח הַשָּׂדֶה מִיָּדוֹ, וְאָמַר לֵיהּ: שׁוּף לִי, וְעָשָׂה כֵּן. וְאַחַר ד' וְה' שָׁנִים עוֹד בָּא הַנִּגְזָל וְהֵבִיא עֵדִים כִּי שָׂדֶה זוֹ גְּזָלָהּ הַמּוֹכֵר הַזֶּה וּמְכָרָהּ לָזֶה, וְטוֹרְפָהּ מִיָּדוֹ, וְחוֹזֵר הַלּוֹקֵחַ הַזֶּה בִּשְׁטָר (הַשֵּׁנִי שֶׁכָּתְבוּ לוֹ בְּעֵת שֶׁאָמַר אָבַד שְׁטָרִי) וְטוֹרֵף בּוֹ פַּעַם אַחֶרֶת. לְפִיכָךְ אָמַר רַב סָפְרָא: אֵין כּוֹתְבִין שְׁנֵי שְׁטָרוֹת עַל שָׂדֶה אַחַת. אֲמַר לֵיהּ רַב אַחָא מִדִּפְתִּי לְרָבִינָא. אַמַּאי תָּלֵינַן טַעֲמָא מִשּׁוּם דְּא"ל שׁוּף לִי וכו'? בְּלֹא טַעֲנָה זוֹ נַמִי, כֵּיוָן דְּנָקֵיט שְׁנֵי שְׁטָרוֹת בְּיוֹם אֶחָד — יָכוֹל לִטְרוֹף וְלַחֲזוֹר וְלִטְרוֹף, וּלְכָךְ אָמַר רַב סָפְרָא: אֵין כּוֹתְבִין שְׁנֵי שְׁטָרוֹת עַל שָׂדֶה אַחַת! וּמְשַׁנֵּי: א"כ נְפִישֵׁי עֲלֵיהּ מְרִיבוֹת וּמַחֲלוֹקוֹת שֶׁל בַּעֲלֵי דִּינִין בְּבַת אַחַת, וְיִתְּנוּ לֵב עַל גְּנֵיבָתוֹ. וְנִכְתּוֹב לֵיהּ שְׁטָרָא מְעַלְּיָא כו'. אַמַּתְנִיתָא פָּרֵיךְ: אַמַּאי קָתָנֵי חוּץ מֵאַחֲרָיוּת שֶׁבּוֹ — מִשּׁוּם פְּסֵידָא דְּמוֹכֵר? וַהֲלֹא יְכוֹלִין אָנוּ לַעֲשׂוֹת תַּקָּנָה, שֶׁיִּכְתּוֹב לָזֶה שֶׁאָמַר אָבַד שְׁטָרִי שְׁטָר מְעַלְּיָא, וּבְאַחֲרָיוּת, דְּאִיכָּא לְמֵימַר הַדִּין עִמּוֹ דְּוַדַּאי אָבַד שְׁטָרוֹ, וְנִכְתּוֹב לֵיהּ לְאִידָךְ לַמּוֹכֵר שׁוֹבֵר שֶׁיּוֹכִיחַ שֶׁנִּפְסַד הַשְּׁטָר הָרִאשׁוֹן שֶׁבְּיַד הַלּוֹקֵחַ, וְלֹא יָבֹא לִגְבּוֹת בּוֹ עוֹד. דְּהַשְׁתָּא לֵיכָּא לְמֵיחַשׁ דִּלְמָא טָרֵיף וַהֲדַר טָרֵיף, שֶׁהֲרֵי כְּשֶׁיּוֹצִיא הַלּוֹקֵחַ שְׁטָרוֹ הָרִאשׁוֹן שֶׁאָבַד כִּדְבָרָיו — יוֹצִיא הַמּוֹכֵר אֶת הַשּׁוֹבֵר שֶׁכָּתוּב בּוֹ "כָּל שְׁטָרֵי דְּיִפְּקוּן" כו' — כָּל שְׁטָרֵי מְכִירָה דְּיִפְּקוּן עַל אַרְעָא דָּא יְהוּ בְּטֵלִין. לְבַר מִדְּיִפְּקוּן. כְּלוֹמַר, חוּץ מִזֶּה הַשְּׁטָר שֶׁכָּתַבְתִּי לוֹ בִּזְמַן פְּלוֹנִי תַּחַת הָרִאשׁוֹן שֶׁאָמַר לִי שֶׁאָבַד מִמֶּנּוּ. זֹאת אוֹמֶרֶת כו'. מַחֲלוֹקֶת תַּנָּאִים הוּא בְּמַתְנִיתִין בְּפִירְקִין בְּשִׁטְרֵי הַלְוָאוֹת, דְּאִיכָּא לְמַאן דְּאָמַר: אֵין כּוֹתְבִין, שֶׁלֹּא יְהֵא צָרִיךְ לִשְׁמוֹר שׁוֹבְרוֹ מִן הָעַכְבָּרִים, וּמַלְוֶה שֶׁאָבַד שְׁטָרוֹ — הִפְסִיד חוֹבוֹ. וְה"ה לְשִׁטְרֵי מִקָּח, אִם אָבַד הַלּוֹקֵחַ שְׁטָרוֹ — לֹא נִכְתּוֹב לֵיהּ שְׁטָרָא מְעַלְּיָא עַל סָמַךְ הַשּׁוֹבֵר שֶׁבְּיַד הַמּוֹכֵר, שֶׁהֲרֵי לֹא יִכְתְּבוּ שׁוֹבֵר, דְּנִמְצָא מוֹכֵר צָרִיךְ לִשְׁמוֹר שׁוֹבְרוֹ מִן הָעַכְבָּרִים.

תוספות

השטר כדי שיחזור המכר. ורבנן דפליגי עליה דרבן שמעון בן גמליאל סבירא להו אין אותיות נקנות, (א) כדמפרש לקמן, וצריך לכתוב "קני לך האי שטרא וכל שעבודיה". וכיון שכותבין שמקנה לו מה שכתוב בשטר — אין לחוש אם השטר השני ביד הלוקח. שאפילו יש בידו אלף שטרי מכר קנה המוכר בחזרת השטר, כיון שכתב לו הלוקח שחזר ומקנה לו (הגה"ה. וקשה לפי פי' [*ענין בתרא זה], אמאי לא נעשה לו שטר שני שנכתב לו: "פלוני בן פלוני אמר לנו: אבד שטרי שכתבתם ושחתמתם, ועתה כתבו אחר לראיה שלא יוכל המוכר לכפור המכר בשלא אמלא עדי מסירה", וזה השטר לא יזיק כלום למוכר, שכיון שכותבין בשטר השני שמחמת שאבד הראשון כתבו השני — לא יזיק למוכר כלום. (ב) כשיוציא השטר שחזר לידו, או יביא עדים שהחזיר לו הלוקח את השטר כדי שיחזור המכר — לא יכול לומר: שני שטרות היו לי, וכל זמן שהאחד בידי לא חזר המכר. שהרי מוכיח מתוך השטר השני שלא כתב לו המוכר, אלא העדים עשאוהו אחר שהחזיר הראשון למוכר, ושיקר להם לומר שנאבד! וי"ל: דחיישינן לב"ד טועין, שכשיוציא הלוקח השטר שכתוב בו שעשאוהו העדים לפי שאמר (ג) רש"ל [שנאבד] השטר הראשון שכתבנו וחתמנו ונתננו לו — יטעו ב"ד לומר: אם לא שחקרו עדים שאבד הראשון לא כתבו לו שני. שאפילו לרבנן דאמרי לעיל בשלהי "יש נוחלין" (דף קלט:) דבי דינא בתר עדים דייקי, הכא איכא למימר דמודו, דכיון שהעדים מעידים על תחלת שטר המכר בעדות ברורה, וגם עתה באים לגמור הדבר לפי שאמר שנאבד השטר הראשון — לא היו כותבין לו אלא דבר ברור. עכ"ה). רש"א וקצת קשה לפי [ענין בתרא] זה: הא משמע ממילתיה דרשב"ג דחייש שמא חוזר המכר, אבל לאינים דעלמא — שמא נתן לו הלוקח השטר כדי לקנות השדה — לא חייש, מדקאמר: וכן היה רבן שמעון בן גמליאל אומר הנותן מתנה לחבירו כו' עד חזרה מתנתו! וי"ל: דלאינים דעלמא אם נתן לו הלוקח שטר מכר שלו כדי לקנות השדה — קנה במסירה, אע"פ שיש עדיין שטר שני בידו. ולכן לא יועיל להזיק לאינים דעלמא שטר השני, שהרי לא יכול לחזור, מאחר שמסר לו ד)שטר אחר. ודוקא למוכר לא תועיל חזרת השטר אחר, כיון שבשטר שני הנשאר ביד הלוקח כתובה חובת המוכר.

לכתוב לאידך כל שטרי דליפקון בזמנא דא כו'. וא"ת: והא מיירי שאין המוכר לפנינו, כדפרישית לעיל על מילתא דרשב"ג! וי"ל: ה)(דרשב"ג וודאי בשאינו לפנינו), אבל הכא כי פריך על הא דקאמר חוץ מאחריות שבו — [היינו] שבשום ענין אין כותבין רש"ל [אחריות], אפי' הוא לפנינו. ונראה דודאי הוה מצי לשנויי: ה"ה אם הוא לפנינו רש"ל [דכותבין. ורבותא קמ"ל, דאפי' אינו לפנינו — אפ"ה כותבין לו. אלא דעדיפא משני ליה]. **לבר** ממאן דניפוק מזמנא דא. פי': ויכתבו לו מזמן שני. אבל שטר דלעיל, דקאמר בברייתא — [היינו] דכותבין בשטר מקח וממכר, וכותבין בשטר זמן ראשון, כדפרישית לעיל.

הגהות הב"ח (א) תום' ד"ה (בכף הקודש) אבל וכו' נקנות במסירה כדמפרש לקמן: (ב) בא"ד למוכר כלום דכשיוציא: (ג) בא"ד לפי שאמר דהשטר הראשון שכתבת וחתמת ונתת לי נאבד יטעו בית דין:

פז א מיי' פכ"ג מהל' מלוה ולוה הל' י סמג עשין לד טוש"ע ח"מ סי' רלט סעיף א:

פח ב מיי' פי"ח מהל' גזלה ואבדה הל' א ופי"ט מהל' מכירה הל' ג ופי"א מהל' מלוה ולוה הל' א סמג עשין פב ולד טוש"ע ח"מ סי' לט סעיף א וסימן רכה סעיף א וסי' קיא סעיף א:

פט ג מיי' פ"א מהל' שלוחין ושותפין הל' ג ועי' בהשגות ובכ"מ סמג עשין פב טוש"ע ח"מ סי' קפב סעיף ו:

צ ד טוש"ע ח"מ סי' רמה סעיף ט:

צא ה מיי' פט"ו מהל' טוען ונטען הל' א סמג עשין לה טוש"ע ח"מ סי' קמ סעיף ד:

אֲמַר לְהוּ: בְּעָלְמָא כּוֹתְבִין שׁוֹבֵר, וְהָכָא הַיְינוּ טַעֲמָא, דִּדְלְמָא אָזֵיל בַּעַל חוֹב וְטָרֵיף מִינֵּיהּ דְּלוֹקֵחַ, וְאָזֵיל אִיהוּ וְטָרֵיף לָקוֹחוֹת, וְשׁוֹבֵר גַּבֵּי לָקוֹחוֹת לֵיכָּא. סוֹף סוֹף, לָקוֹחוֹת לָאו אַמָּרֵי דְּאַרְעָא הָדְרִי? אַדְּהָכִי וְהָכִי שָׁמֵיט וְאָכֵיל פֵּירֵי; אִי נַמִי, לְלוֹקֵחַ שֶׁלֹּא בְּאַחֲרָיוּת. אִי הָכִי, שִׁטְרֵי הַלְוָאָה נַמִי! הָתָם דְּזוּזֵי מַסֵּיק, אָמְרִי: פַּיְּיסֵיהּ בַּעַל חוֹב בְּזוּזֵי, הָכָא דְּאַרְעָא מַסֵּיק, מֵידַע יָדְעִי דְּמַאן דְּמַסֵּיק אַרְעָא — בְּזוּזֵי לָא מִפַּיֵּים. אָמַר מָר: חוּץ מִן הָאַחֲרָיוּת שֶׁבּוֹ. הֵיכִי כָּתְבִינַן? אֲמַר רַב נַחְמָן, דְּכָתְבִי הָכִי: א"שְׁטָרָא דְּנַן דְּלָא לְמִיגְבֵּי בֵּיהּ לָא מִמְּשַׁעְבְּדֵי וְלָא מִבְּנֵי חָרֵי, אֶלָּא כִּי הֵיכִי דְּתֵיקוּם אַרְעָא בִּידֵיהּ דְּלֵיקַח". אָמַר רַפְרָם, זֹאת אוֹמֶרֶת: א)באַחֲרָיוּת — טָעוּת סוֹפֵר הוּא; טַעֲמָא דְּכָתַב לֵיהּ הָכִי, הָא לָא כָּתַב לֵיהּ הָכִי — גָּבֵי. רַב אַשִׁי אָמַר: ב)אַחֲרָיוּת — לָאו טָעוּת סוֹפֵר הוּא, וּמַאי "חוּץ מֵאַחֲרָיוּת שֶׁבּוֹ"? דְּלָא כְּתִיב בֵּיהּ אַחֲרָיוּת. הַהִיא אִיתְּתָא דִּיהֲבָה לֵיהּ זוּזֵי לְהַהוּא גַּבְרָא לְמִיזְבַּן לָהּ אַרְעָא, אֲזַל זְבַן לָהּ שֶׁלֹּא בְּאַחֲרָיוּת; אַתְיָא לְקַמֵּיהּ דְּרַב נַחְמָן, אֲמַר לֵיהּ: ג)"לְתַקּוּנֵי שַׁדַּרְתִּיךְ וְלָא לְעַוּוֹתֵי", גזִיל זַבְנָה מִינֵּיהּ שֶׁלֹּא בְּאַחֲרָיוּת, וַהֲדַר זַבְנָהּ נִיהֲלָהּ בְּאַחֲרָיוּת.§ רשב"ג אוֹמֵר: הַנּוֹתֵן מַתָּנָה לַחֲבֵירוֹ וְהֶחֱזִיר לוֹ אֶת הַשְּׁטָר — חָזְרָה מַתְּנָתוֹ, וַחכ"א: דמַתְּנָתוֹ קַיֶּימֶת".§ מַאי טַעֲמָא דרשב"ג? אָמַר רַב אַסִי, נַעֲשָׂה כְּאוֹמֵר לוֹ: שָׂדֶה זוֹ נְתוּנָה לְךָ כָּל זְמַן שֶׁהַשְּׁטָר בְּיָדְךָ. מַתְקִיף לָהּ רַבָּה: אִי הָכִי, נִגְנַב אוֹ אָבַד נַמִי! אֶלָּא אָמַר רַבָּה: ד)בְּאוֹתִיּוֹת נִקְנוֹת בִּמְסִירָה קָמִיפַּלְגִי, רשב"ג סָבַר: אוֹתִיּוֹת נִקְנוֹת בִּמְסִירָה, וְרַבָּנַן סָבְרִי: אֵין אוֹתִיּוֹת נִקְנוֹת בִּמְסִירָה. ת"ר: ה)הַבָּא לִידּוֹן בִּשְׁטָר וּבַחֲזָקָה — הנִידּוֹן בִּשְׁטָר, דִּבְרֵי רַבִּי; רשב"ג אוֹמֵר: בַּחֲזָקָה. בְּמַאי קָמִיפַּלְגִי? כִּי אֲתָא רַב דִּימִי אֲמַר: בְּאוֹתִיּוֹת נִקְנוֹת בִּמְסִירָה קָא מִיפַּלְגִי,

רַבָּן

רשב"ם

אָמַר לְהוּ. רַב אַשִׁי: לְעוֹלָם אֵימָא לָךְ גַּבֵּי מַלְוֶה שֶׁאָבַד שְׁטָרוֹ – שֶׁנִּכְתּוֹב לוֹ שְׁטָרָא, אוֹ פָּרַע מִקְצַת חוֹבוֹ – דְּכוֹתְבִין שׁוֹבֵר לַלֹּוֶה, וְיִפְרַע חוֹבוֹ לַמַּלְוֶה. וְהָכָא גַּבֵּי מִקָּח וּמִמְכָּר הַיְינוּ טַעֲמָא דְּאֵין כּוֹתְבִין שׁוֹבֵר לַמּוֹכֵר כְּדֵי לִכְתּוֹב שְׁטָרָא מְעַלְיָא לַלּוֹקֵחַ – מִשּׁוּם דִּזִימְנִין דְּאָזֵיל בע"ח דְּמוֹכֵר [שֶׁהוּא לוֹקֵחַ רִאשׁוֹן שֶׁנֶּאֱבַד שְׁטָרוֹ] וְטוֹרֵף הַקַּרְקַע מִינֵּיהּ דְּלוֹקֵחַ [שֵׁנִי] וְתַבְרָא אֵינוֹ בְּיַד הַלּוֹקֵחַ אֶלָּא בְּיַד הַמּוֹכֵר, וּבְתוֹךְ כָּךְ שֶׁיֵּלֵךְ אֶל הַמּוֹכֵר וְיַרְאֶה לוֹ הַשּׁוֹבֵר – שָׁמֵיט וְאָכֵיל פֵּירֵי, כִּדְמַסֵּיק וְאָזֵיל, וְקָשֶׁה גֵּזֶל הַנֶּאֱכָל. אֲבָל גַּבֵּי שִׁטְרֵי מִלְוֶה – כּוֹתְבִין שׁוֹבֵר, דְּלֵיכָּא לְמֵימַר הָכִי, כִּדְמְפָרֵשׁ לְקַמָּן וְאָזֵיל. וּמַקְשִׁינַן: סוֹף סוֹף לָקוֹחוֹת. לָאו לְגַבֵּי מוֹכֵר אָזְלִי בִּתְמִיָּה, לִצְעוֹק עַל שָׂדֵהוּ שֶׁטָּרַף בע"ח דְּמוֹכֵר? וְיַרְאֶה לוֹ הַשּׁוֹבֵר – וְיַחֲזִיר לוֹ קַרְקָעוֹ. א"נ. זִימְנִין דְּהָוֵי לוֹקֵחַ שֶׁלֹּא בְּאַחֲרָיוּת, דְּעָבֵיד אֱינָשׁ דְּזָבֵין אַרְעָא לְיוֹמֵיהּ, וְלֹא יָחוּשׁ הַלּוֹקֵחַ לַחֲזוֹר אֵצֶל הַמּוֹכֵר – שֶׁהֲרֵי אֵין עָלָיו אַחֲרָיוּת, וְיַפְסִיד קַרְקָעוֹ שֶׁלֹּא כַּדִּין. אִי הָכִי. דְּאִיכָּא לְמֵיחַשׁ לְהָכִי, וְהִלְכָּךְ בִּשְׁטַר מִקָּח אֵין כּוֹתְבִין שׁוֹבֵר. בְּשִׁטְרֵי הַלְוָאוֹת נַמִי. אַמַּאי אָמַר דְּכוֹתְבִין שׁוֹבֵר? הָא אִיכָּא לְמֵיחַשׁ נַמִי דְּטָרֵיף הַמַּלְוֶה לָקוֹחוֹת שֶׁלָּקְחוּ מִן הַלֹּוֶה, וְתַבְרָא בִּידָא דְּלָקוֹחוֹת לֵיכָּא, אֶלָּא בְּיַד הַלֹּוֶה! וּמְשַׁנֵּי: הָתָם. גַּבֵּי הַלְוָאוֹת, כֵּיוָן דְּזוּזֵי מַסֵּיק בֵּיהּ מַלְוֶה לַלֹּוֶה – לֹא שָׁבְקֵי לֵיהּ לָקוֹחוֹת קַרְקַע שֶׁלָּהֶם לַמַּלְוֶה עַד שֶׁיֵּלְכוּ אֵצֶל הַלֹּוֶה לָדַעַת אִם פְּרָעוּהוּ זוּזֵי, מִשּׁוּם דְּמֵימַר אָמְרִי לָקוֹחוֹת: אֵימוּר פִּיּוּסֵי פַּיְּיסֵיהּ, וְלֹא אָתֵי לְמִישְׁמַט וּלְמֵיכַל פֵּירֵי. אֲבָל הָכָא, גַּבֵּי מִקָּח וּמִמְכָּר, כְּשֶׁיָּבֹא לוֹקֵחַ זֶה לִטְרוֹף קַרְקַע מִלָּקוֹחוֹת שֶׁלָּקְחוּ מִן הַמּוֹכֵר – יַנִּיחוּ לוֹ הַלָּקוֹחוֹת לִטְרוֹף, דְּאָמְרִי לָקוֹחוֹת: זֶה הַמּוֹכֵר, קַרְקַע חַיָּיב לוֹ לְלוֹקֵחַ זֶה תַּחַת שָׂדֵהוּ שֶׁאָבַד, וְכָל מַאן דְּמַסֵּיק אַרְעָא בְּחַבְרֵיהּ – לֹא מְפַיֵּיס בְּזוּזֵי עַד זְמַן מְרוּבֶּה, כְּשֶׁיִּרְאֶה שֶׁלֹּא יוּכַל לְהַעֲמִיד לוֹ שָׂדֶה. וְהִלְכָּךְ מַנִּיחִין לוֹ לִטְרוֹף עַכְשָׁיו, וּלְאַחַר זְמַן הָדַר לְגַבֵּי מָרָא דְּאַרְעָא, וּבְתוֹךְ כָּךְ שָׁמֵיט וְאָכֵיל פֵּירֵי, וְהִלְכָּךְ אֵין כּוֹתְבִין. הֵיכִי כָּתְבִינַן. הַאי שְׁטָרָא לְהָעִיד שֶׁהַשָּׂדֶה קָנוּי בְּיָדוֹ, אַף שֶׁלֹּא יִגְבֶּה לֹא מִמְּשַׁעְבְּדֵי וְלֹא מִבְּנֵי חָרֵי, דְּחָיְישִׁינַן דִּלְמָא שְׁטָרוֹ הָרִאשׁוֹן עֲדַיִין בְּיָדוֹ הוּא. דְּתֵיקוּ אַרְעָא בִּידֵיהּ. שֶׁלֹּא יוּכַל הַמּוֹכֵר לִטְעוֹן: לֹא מָכַרְתִּי לְךָ מֵעוֹלָם. אָמַר רַפְרָם זֹאת אוֹמֶרֶת. מִמִּילְּתֵיהּ דְּרַב נַחְמָן, שֶׁמַּזְקִיק לְפָרֵשׁ בְּתוֹךְ הַשְּׁטָר שֶׁאֵין בּוֹ אַחֲרָיוּת. אַחֲרָיוּת. שֶׁאֵינוֹ כָּתוּב בַּשְּׁטָר, אֶלָּא נִכְתַּב הַשְּׁטָר סְתָם – טָעוּת וְשִׁגְגַת הַסּוֹפֵר הוּא, וּכְמִי שֶׁכָּתַב בּוֹ אַחֲרָיוּת דָּמֵי. וּפְלוּגְתָּא הוּא בִּ"שְׁנַיִם אוֹחֲזִין" (ב"מ דף יד.). וְהָכִי מַסְקִינַן הָתָם (טו:) דְּטָעוּת סוֹפֵר הוּא, בֵּין בְּשִׁטְרֵי מִקָּח בֵּין בְּשִׁטְרֵי הַלְוָאָה. דְּלָא כָּתַב בֵּיהּ אַחֲרָיוּת. וְרַב נַחְמָן לֹא קָמְתָרֵץ שַׁפִּיר. זִיל זַבְנֵיהּ. מִן הַמּוֹכֵר שֶׁלֹּא בְּאַחֲרָיוּת, וּכְתוֹב הַשְּׁטָר בִּשְׁמְךָ, וְאח"כ מְכוֹר אֶת הַקַּרְקַע לָאִשָּׁה בְּאַחֲרָיוּת. מ"ט. חָזְרָה מַתְּנָתוֹ. אָמַר רַב אַסִי. קָסָבַר רַבָּן שִׁמְעוֹן בֶּן גַּמְלִיאֵל: נַעֲשָׂה כְּאוֹמֵר כו'. נִגְנַב אוֹ שֶׁאָבַד נַמִי. נֵימָא דְּאָבַד שָׂדֵהוּ, וּבָטְלָה מַתְּנָתוֹ! רַבָּן שִׁמְעוֹן בֶּן גַּמְלִיאֵל סָבַר אוֹתִיּוֹת. בֵּין דְּשִׁטְרֵי מִקָּח, בֵּין דְּמַתָּנָה — נִקְנוֹת לִמְקַבֵּל מַתָּנָה וְלַלּוֹקֵחַ בִּמְסִירַת הַשְּׁטָר. כְּלוֹמַר, אע"פ שֶׁדְּבָרִים אֵינָם נִקְנִין, כֵּיוָן דִּכְתוּבִין בַּשְּׁטָר — נִקְנִין עִם קַבָּלַת הַקְּלָף, וְכֵיוָן שֶׁהֶחֱזִיר לוֹ אֶת הַשְּׁטָר חָזְרָה מַתְּנָתוֹ. וּפְלוּגְתָּא הִיא בְּ"הַמּוֹכֵר אֶת הַסְּפִינָה" (לעיל דף עו.). וְאע"פ שֶׁפֵּירֵשׁ רַבֵּינוּ חֲנַנְאֵל דְּלֵית הִלְכְתָא כרשב"ג דְּיָחִיד וְרַבִּים הֲלָכָה כְּרַבִּים — אֲפִילּוּ הָכִי הִלְכְתָא כרשב"ג דְּאוֹתִיּוֹת נִקְנוֹת בִּמְסִירָה, וְאַף עַל פִּי שֶׁלֹּא כָּתַב לוֹ בִּשְׁטָר אַחֵר "קְנֵי לָךְ הוּא וְכָל שִׁעְבּוּדֵיהּ". דְּקַיְימָא לָן כְּרַבִּי דְּס"ל אוֹתִיּוֹת נִקְנוֹת בִּמְסִירָה בְּ"הַמּוֹכֵר אֶת הַסְּפִינָה" (שם דף עו.), דְּאָמְרִינַן הָתָם בְּמַסְקָנָא. *אָמַר רַב פַּפָּא: הִלְכְתָא אוֹתִיּוֹת נִקְנוֹת בִּמְסִירָה בְּלֹא שְׁטָר אַחֵר, וְקָאֵי רַב אַשִׁי הָתָם כְּוָותֵיהּ, דְּאָמַר: סְבָרָא הוּא כו'. וּלְקַמָּן בְּפִירְקִין (דף קעג.) נַמִי אָמְרִינַן: אוֹתִיּוֹת נִקְנוֹת בִּמְסִירָה. אַבַּיֵּי אָמַר: צָרִיךְ לְהָבִיא רְאָיָה, רָבָא אָמַר כו' — גַּם שָׁם מוּכָח דְּאַבַּיֵּי וְרָבָא סָבְרֵי דְּאוֹתִיּוֹת נִקְנוֹת בִּמְסִירָה. וְגַם שָׁם דָּחַק ר"ח וְכָתַב שֶׁאֵין הֲלָכָה כְּמוֹתוֹ אֶלָּא בִּמְסִירָה וּבִשְׁטָר, וְהֶבֶל הוּא. ת"ר הַבָּא לִידּוֹן. כְּנֶגֶד הַמְעַרְעֵר עַל שָׂדֶה שֶׁבְּיָדוֹ בִּשְׁטָר וּבַחֲזָקָה, שֶׁטּוֹעֵן: קַרְקַע זֶה קָנִיתִי מִמְּךָ, וַעֲדַיִין הַשְּׁטָר בְּיָדִי, וְגַם יֵשׁ לִי עֵדִים שֶׁאָכַלְתִּי שְׁנֵי חֲזָקָה — יִדּוֹן בִּשְׁטָר, דִּבְרֵי רַבִּי. לְקַמָּן מְפָרֵשׁ לָהּ וְאָזֵיל, וְעַל מְקוֹמָהּ אֲפָרְשֶׁנָּה לְפִי פֵּי' הָאֲמוֹרָאִים. רַבָּן שִׁמְעוֹן בֶּן גַּמְלִיאֵל אוֹמֵר בַּחֲזָקָה. לְפִי פֵּירוּשׁ הָאֲמוֹרָאִים שֶׁלְּפָנֵינוּ, יֵשׁ מֵהֶם שֶׁצָּרִיךְ לְפָרֵשׁ לר"ש דְּקָאָמַר: בַּחֲזָקָה וְלֹא בִּשְׁטָר, וְיֵשׁ שֶׁצָּרִיךְ לְפָרֵשׁ: אַף בַּחֲזָקָה, וְכָל שֶׁכֵּן בִּשְׁטָר. הִלְכָּךְ, מַה שֶּׁכָּתוּב בַּסְּפָרִים: בַּחֲזָקָה וְלֹא בִּשְׁטָר — אֵימָא אַף בַּחֲזָקָה, נִרְאֶה דְּלָא גָּרְסִינַן לֵיהּ כו'. בְּמַאי קָמִיפַּלְגִי. וּמִתּוֹךְ כָּךְ נֵדַע פֵּירוּשׁ הַבָּרַיְיתָא. רַבִּי סָבַר אוֹתִיּוֹת נִקְנוֹת בִּמְסִירָה. כִּדְקָאָמַר נַמִי רַבִּי בְּהֶדְיָא בְּפֶרֶק "הַמּוֹכֵר אֶת הַסְּפִינָה" (לעיל דף עו.) שֶׁהַמּוֹכֵר שְׁטַר חוֹב לַחֲבֵירוֹ, כֵּיוָן שֶׁמָּסַר לוֹ אֶת הַשְּׁטָר בְּיָדוֹ — קָנָה הַחוֹב, וְנִשְׁתַּעְבֵּד לוֹ לֹוֶה לָזֶה הַקּוֹנֶה כְּמוֹ שֶׁהָיָה מְשׁוּעְבָּד לַמַּלְוֶה, כָּל זְמַן שֶׁלֹּא חָזַר וּמְחָלוֹ, כִּדְאָמַר שְׁמוּאֵל *(בְּמַסֶּכֶת גִּיטִּין) (דף יג). וְה"ק: הַבָּא לִידּוֹן בִּשְׁטָר וּבַחֲזָקָה, וְטוֹעֵן רְאוּבֵן כְּנֶגֶד הַמְעַרְעֵר: שָׂדֶה זוֹ שֶׁלִּי הִיא, שֶׁהֲרֵי שִׁמְעוֹן שֶׁקְּנָאוֹ מִלֵּוִי מָסַר לוֹ שְׁטַר מְכִירָה הַכָּתוּב בִּשְׁמוֹ, וְקָנִיתִי הַשָּׂדֶה בִּמְסִירַת הַשְּׁטָר כְּאִילּוּ נִכְתַּב בִּשְׁמִי, וְגַם הֶחֱזַקְתִּי בַּשָּׂדֶה שָׁלֹשׁ שָׁנִים — נִידּוֹן בִּשְׁטָר, דִּבְרֵי רַבִּי. וְעַל יְדֵי הַשְּׁטָר שֶׁמָּסַר לוֹ הַלּוֹקֵחַ קָנוּי לוֹ הַשָּׂדֶה, דְּאוֹתִיּוֹת נִקְנוֹת בִּמְסִירָה, וְלֹא צָרִיךְ תּוּ עֵדֵי חֲזָקָה.

רַבָּן

תוספות

בעלמא כותבין שובר כו'. וא"ת: כיון דמסיק דבשטרי הלואה אימור פייסיה בעל *הבית בזוזי, וילכו הלקוחות אצל המוכר — א"כ מאי למידק מהכא דאין כותבין שובר, דאי כותבין — אם כן אמאי ו)[אין כותבין שני] שטרי הלואה, ולכתוב שובר לאידך, כדפריך הכא גבי מקח! ואומר ר"י: דבשטרי הלואה לא מצינן למכתב שובר, משום שאם כן יפסיד כל הלוואותיו שיעשה מכאן ואילך, שלא יהא זכור מן השובר, ואיכא נעילת דלת בפני לוין. אבל בשטרי מקח וממכר, אם יפסיד — יפסיד, ואין לנו להפסיד לזה משום חששא שמא יפסיד ז)[האחר לאחר זמן]. ותימה: [דסוף סוף] למ"ד כותבין שובר [מאי שנא הלואה]? ליכתיב "בר מזמנא דא ולהלן"! ושמא אנו גוזרין.

דמאן דמסיק ארעא בזוזי לא מיפיים. ותימה לר"י: אם יכול המוכר לדחותו בזוזי, למה יניחו קרקעם? אפילו היו יודעין שלא פרע לו השטר עדיין, [אלא שיכולין] לומר שיתן או קרקע או מעות, ואם אין לו — אז יחזור עליהם! וקלא רפיא אם יכול לדחותו בזוזי אם לאו. ונראה דמצי לסלוקי בזוזי. בחזקה ולא בשטר אימא אף בחזקה. פי' בקונט' דלא גרסינן ליה. ומיהו, היינו יכולין לקיימו, והוי אליבא (א) דמסקינן לקמן דמוקי לקמן פלוגתייהו בצריך לברר. ואפי' לא גרס הכא — לא היה צריך למחקו בסנהדרין (דף כג: ושם) דקאמר: והוינן, בחזקה ולא בשטר? אימא אף בחזקה, (ב) וקי"ל דבצריך לברר קא מיפלגי. דאפי' ליתיה הכא — מצינן למימר התם "הוינן בה", כדאשכחן ב"ד' אחין" (יבמות דף לא.) דקאמר גמרא על ספק קרוב כו' ואמרי': למאי הלכתא? דאי כהן אסירא ליה, ואי ערוה היא — צרתה בעיא חליצה, ואף על גב דליתיה ב"הזורק" (גיטין דף עח.) על ההיא כשנהח).

ט)ורבן שמעון בן גמליאל סבר לה כר"מ דאמר עדי חתימה כרתי. יש מקשים: דבפ"ק דגיטין (דף יא. ושם) תניא, א"ר אלעזר בר' יוסי: לא נחלקו על שטרות העולים בערכאות של גוים, דאע"פ דחותמיהם גוים — כשרים. לא נחלקו אלא כו', דרשב"ג אומר: אף הן כשרין. אלמא ס"ל עדי מסירה כרתי! ואור"י: דס"ל כר' אלעזר בגיטין ולא בשטרות, כי הנהו אמוראי ד"המגרש" בגיטין (דף פו. ושם) י)ודוחק הוא, דהא "אף אלו" קאמר — דמשמע דבשאר שטרות נמי ס"ל הכי). וצריך לומר דאליבא דרבנן דפליגי עליה קאמר להו, דאף אותם היה להם נהכשיר, כיון דסברי עדי מסירה כרתי.

אלא

רבינו גרשום

ולא מצי לוקח למטרף עוד אפי' אי כתבי ליה אחריות: אמר להו רב אשי מהא לא תפשוט דאין כותבין שובר אלא בעלמא גבי הלואה כותבין שובר והכא היינו טעמא דלא כתבי למוכר כל שטרי כו' דאי כתבי ליה להאי לוקח האי שטר שני באחריות כי טריף יתיה בעל חוב דראובן אזיל איהו וטריף לקוחות דבתריה בהאי שטר דכתב בו אחריות והדר קאמר ליה לבעל חוב שוף לי פורתא והדר טירפן ואזיל איהו וטריף לקוחות אחריני בשטרא קמא ואע"ג דכתבינן ליה למוכר שובר כל שטרי דיפקין כו' מ"מ ההוא שובר גבי לקוחות ליכא אלא גבי מוכר איתיה להכי מצי טריף ללקוחות. ומקשינן אע"ג דליתא לשובר גבי לקוחות סוף סוף כי טריף האי ללקוחות לאו לגבי מריה דארעא דזבן להו הדרי בשביל זה שטרפן ומראה להן השובר דשלא כדין טרפן: אין ודאי כיון דאיכא שובר גבי מוכר יחזיר הקרקע למריה בעל כרחו אבל איכא למיחש דאדהכי והכי דהדרי לקוחות למריה ארעא בין כך ובין כך שמיט האי פירי דההוא קרקע דטריף ואכיל להו וקשה גזל הנאכל להחזיר אי נמי דהני לקוחות שניים שטריף מינייהו שלא באחריות קנו דלא מצי הדרי למריה דארעא והוו אבדון שלא כדין הלכך לא כתבי אחריות בשטר שני דלוקח דאע"ג דכתב שובר למוכר דנפיק מיניה חורבה כדאמרן דשמיט פירי או ללוקח שלא באחריות אבל בעלמא בשטרי הלואה כותבין שובר. ומקשי' אי הכי כדאוקמת דכיון דליתיה שובר הלואה נמי אמאי כותבין שובר וניחוש נמי דאי שבקינן לשטר גבי מלוה טריף ביה לקוחות ושמיט ואכיל פירי או טריף לקוחות שלא באחריות ליכא למיחש להכי דהתם גבי מלוה דזוזי מסיק ביה בלוה אמרי הני לבעל חוב כדבעי למטרפינהו ליה זוזי חייב לך ולא קרקע שמא כבר פייסך בעל חוב שלך בזוזי וכתבת לו שובר ושטר חוב זה פסול הוא. אזלי ובדקי במילתא. אבל הכא גבי מקח וממכר דלוקח בשביל ארעא מסיק ויהיב זוזי ומאן דידעי דמוכר לא שייר לעצמו קרקע מידע ידעי נמי דמי שקונה קרקע לא מיפיים בזוזי ולא פייסו מוכר בזוזי ולא אתו למיבדק מן מוכר ואבדין קרקע שלהם שלא כדין הילכך לא כתבינן להו אחריות בהאי שטר שני רתוקי ארעא בידיה דלוקח כדי שלא יהא מוכר יכול למימר לו לא מכרתיה לך מעולם: זאת אומרת. מדכתבינן הכי שטרא דנן כו' שמעי' מיניה דאחריות טעות סופר הוא. שאם בא לפנינו שטר שאין כתוב בו אחריות אפי' הכי גבו ממשעבדי דאמרי' סופר שכח ולא כתבו כלומר מהכא דייקינן הכי טעמא דכתב ליה הכי שטרא דנן כו' הא לא כתב ליה הכי אע"ג דלית ביה אחריות גבי דאמרינן טעות סופר הוא שהיה לו לכותבו ואע"פ שלא כתב דיינינן ליה כמו שיש בו אחריות: רב אשי אמר. לעולם אחריות לא אמרינן טעות סופר הוא ומאי חוץ מאחריות שבו דלא כתב ליה אחריות ממש ולא מצי גבי ביה: זיל זבנה ניהלה. שלא באחריות. כמו שהתניתה עם המוכר. והדר זבנה ניהלה את באחריות דלתקוני שדרתיך ולא לעוותי: [illegible] ורבנן סברי אין אותיות נקנות במסירה ר"ש בן גמליאל סבר אותיות נקנות במסירה. דכיון שמסר והחזיר לו השטר חוזרה הקרקע לבעליו דשטר אפסרה דארעא הוא: הבא לידון בשטר ובחזקה. שאם אמר לו אחד לפני ב"ד מה אתה עושה בתוך שלי והוא דן עמו ואומר לו אתה מכרתה לי ויש לי שטר ועמדתי בה שני חזקה: נידון בשטר. שצריך להראות

מסורת הש"ס

א) [ב"מ יד. וש"נ:] ב) [כתובות נא. ב"ק נה.] ג) קדושין מב: ד) [לעיל עו. וש"נ:] ה) סנהדרין כג.: ו) רש"ל. ז) רש"ל. וגי' רש"ל פעם אחרת: ח) [וכו' בתוס' יבמות לא. ד"ה למאי הלכתא כגוונא דה כתבינהו: ט) וזה שייך לדף קס.] י) רש"ל. ורש"א מ"ז:

[דף עו. ושם איתא אמר אמימר]

[וע"ל לעיל קמז:]

הגהות הב"ח

(א) תוס' ד"ה בחזקה וכו' והוי אליבא דמסקינן דמוקי לקמן פלוגתייהו וכו' ואפי' לא גרסינן ליה הכא לא: (ב) בא"ד אף בחזקה כיון דקיימא לן הכא דבצריך לברר:

א) [גיטין ט: וש"נ:] ב) [שם כא. וש"נ] ג) שם ז: ד) לעיל קסז. ב"מ קף ז. עב: כתובות קף יט. [שבת שם:] ה) ב"מ ז: ו) שם ז. [ג: שבועות מה. וכתובות יח. עי' קדושין מג:] ח) רש"ל: ט) נ"א הלכה כרבי ואף רבי:

רַבָּן שִׁמְעוֹן בֶּן גַּמְלִיאֵל סָבַר: אֵין אוֹתִיּוֹת נִקְנוֹת בִּמְסִירָה, וְרַבִּי סָבַר: אוֹתִיּוֹת נִקְנוֹת בִּמְסִירָה. אֲמַר לֵיהּ אַבַּיֵי: א"כ, פְּלוּגְתָּא לְדְמָר! אֲמַר לֵיהּ: וְתִפְלוֹג. (א) אֲמַר לֵיהּ, הָכִי קָאָמֵינָא לָךְ: מַתְנִיתָא לָא מִיתַּרְצָא אֶלָּא כִּדְמִתָּרְצָא מָר, וְאִם כֵּן קַשְׁיָא דְּרַבָּן שִׁמְעוֹן בֶּן גַּמְלִיאֵל אַדְּרשב"ג! אֶלָּא אֲמַר אַבַּיֵי: הָכָא בְּמַאי עָסְקִינַן — כְּגוֹן שֶׁנִּמְצָא אֶחָד מֵהֶן קָרוֹב אוֹ פָּסוּל; וּבִפְלוּגְתָּא דְּר' מֵאִיר וְר' אֶלְעָזָר קָא מִיפַּלְגִי, רַבִּי סָבַר לָהּ כְּרַבִּי אֶלְעָזָר, דְּאָמַר: א)אעֵדֵי מְסִירָה כָּרְתֵי; וְרַבָּן שִׁמְעוֹן בֶּן גַּמְלִיאֵל סָבַר לָהּ ב)כְּרַבִּי מֵאִיר, דְּאָמַר: עֵדֵי חֲתִימָה כָּרְתֵי. וְהָא ג)אָמַר רַבִּי אַבָּא: במוֹדֶה הָיָה רַבִּי אֶלְעָזָר בִּמְזוּיָּיף מִתּוֹכוֹ שֶׁהוּא פָּסוּל! אֶלָּא אֲמַר רַבִּי אָבִינָא: הַכֹּל מוֹדִים, שֶׁאִם כָּתוּב בּוֹ: "הוּזְקַקְנוּ לְעֵדוּתָן שֶׁל עֵדִים, וְנִמְצֵאת עֵדוּתָן מְזוּיֶּיפֶת" — שֶׁהוּא פָּסוּל, כִּדְרַבִּי אַבָּא. לֹא נֶחְלְקוּ אֶלָּא בִּשְׁטָר שֶׁאֵין עָלָיו עֵדִים כְּלָל, דְּרַבִּי סָבַר לָהּ כְּר' אֶלְעָזָר, דְּאָמַר: עֵדֵי מְסִירָה כָּרְתֵי, וְרַבָּן שִׁמְעוֹן בֶּן גַּמְלִיאֵל סָבַר לָהּ כְּרַבִּי מֵאִיר, דְּאָמַר: עֵדֵי חֲתִימָה כָּרְתֵי. וְאִיבָּעֵית אֵימָא: בְּמוֹדֶה בִּשְׁטָר שֶׁכְּתָבוֹ צָרִיךְ לְקַיְּימוֹ קָא מִיפַּלְגִי, דְּרַבִּי סָבַר: ד)מוֹדֶה בִּשְׁטָר שֶׁכְּתָבוֹ — אֵין צָרִיךְ לְקַיְּימוֹ, וְרַבָּן שִׁמְעוֹן בֶּן גַּמְלִיאֵל סָבַר: צָרִיךְ לְקַיְּימוֹ. וְהָא אִיפְּכָא שָׁמְעִינַן לְהוּ! דְּתַנְיָא:ה) שְׁנַיִם אֲדוּקִין בִּשְׁטָר, מַלְוֶה אוֹמֵר: "שֶׁלִּי הוּא, וְנָפַל מִמֶּנִּי וּמְצָאתוֹ", וְלֹוֶה אוֹמֵר: "שֶׁלְּךָ הוּא, וּפְרַעְתִּיו לָךְ" — גיִתְקַיֵּים הַשְּׁטָר בְּחוֹתְמָיו, דִּבְרֵי רַבִּי. רַבָּן שִׁמְעוֹן בֶּן גַּמְלִיאֵל אוֹמֵר: יַחֲלוֹקוּ; וְהָוֵינַן בָּהּ, וְלֵית לֵיהּ לְרַבִּי הָא דִּתְנַן: ו)דשְׁנַיִם אוֹחֲזִין בְּטַלִּית, זֶה אוֹמֵר "אֲנִי מְצָאתִיהָ" וְזֶה אוֹמֵר "אֲנִי מְצָאתִיהָ" — זֶה יִשָּׁבַע שֶׁאֵין לוֹ בָּהּ פָּחוֹת מֵחֶצְיָהּ, וְזֶה יִשָּׁבַע שֶׁאֵין לוֹ בָּהּ פָּחוֹת מֵחֶצְיָהּ, וְיַחֲלוֹקוּ? וַאֲמַר רָבָא אֲמַר רַב נַחְמָן: בִּמְקוּיָּים — דְּכוּלֵּי עָלְמָא לָא פְּלִיגִי דְּיַחֲלוֹקוּ; כִּי פְּלִיגִי — בְּשֶׁאֵינוֹ מְקוּיָּם, רַבִּי סָבַר: מוֹדֶה בִּשְׁטָר שֶׁכְּתָבוֹ צָרִיךְ לְקַיְּימוֹ, הוְאִי מְקַיֵּים לֵיהּ — גָּבֵי פַּלְגָּא, וְאִי לָא — חַסְפָּא בְּעָלְמָא הוּא; וְרַבָּן שִׁמְעוֹן בֶּן גַּמְלִיאֵל סָבַר: מוֹדֶה בִּשְׁטָר שֶׁכְּתָבוֹ אֵין צָרִיךְ לְקַיְּימוֹ, וְיַחֲלוֹקוּ! אֵיפוּךְ. וְאִיבָּעֵית אֵימָא: לְעוֹלָם לָא תֵּיפוּךְ, אֶלָּא הָכָא בְּלָבָרֵר קָמִיפַּלְגִי; כִּי הָא דְּרַב יִצְחָק בַּר יוֹסֵף הֲוָה מַסֵּיק בֵּיהּ זוּזֵי בְּרַבִּי אַבָּא, אֲתָא לְקַמֵּיהּ דְּרַבִּי יִצְחָק נַפָּחָא, אֲמַר: פְּרַעְתִּיךְ בִּפְנֵי פְּלוֹנִי וּפְלוֹנִי. אֲמַר לֵיהּ רַבִּי יִצְחָק: יָבוֹאוּ פְּלוֹנִי וּפְלוֹנִי וְיָעִידוּ. אֲמַר לֵיהּ: אִי לָא אָתוּ לָא מְהֵימְנִינָא? וְהָא קַיְימָא לָן: ז)והַמַּלְוֶה אֶת חֲבֵירוֹ בְּעֵדִים — אֵינוֹ צָרִיךְ לְפָרְעוֹ בְּעֵדִים! אֲמַר לֵיהּ: אֲנָא בְּהַהִיא כִּשְׁמַעְתָּא דְּמָר סְבִירָא לִי, דְּאָמַר רַבִּי אַבָּא אָמַר רַב אַדָּא בַּר אַהֲבָה אָמַר רַב: זהָאוֹמֵר לַחֲבֵירוֹ "פְּרַעְתִּיךְ בִּפְנֵי פְּלוֹנִי וּפְלוֹנִי" — צָרִיךְ שֶׁיָּבוֹאוּ פְּלוֹנִי וּפְלוֹנִי וְיָעִידוּ. ח)[א"ל,] וְהָא אָמַר רַב גִּידֵּל אָמַר רַב: ט)הֲלָכָה כְּדִבְרֵי רַבָּן שִׁמְעוֹן בֶּן גַּמְלִיאֵל. וְאַף רַבִּי לֹא אָמַר

רשב"ם

רַבָּן שִׁמְעוֹן בֶּן גַּמְלִיאֵל סָבַר אֵין אוֹתִיּוֹת נִקְנוֹת בִּמְסִירָה. וְהִלְכָּךְ צָרִיךְ עֵדֵי חֲזָקָה; דְּכֵיוָן דְּא"ל אִידָךְ "לֵךְ חֲזַק וּקְנֵי" וְיֵשׁ לוֹ עֵדִים שֶׁהֶחֱזִיק בָּהּ — קָנָה, דְּקַרְקַע נִקְנֵית בְּכֶסֶף אוֹ בִּשְׁטַר מְכִירָה וּמַתָּנָה אוֹ בַּחֲזָקָה. וְהָכִי קָאָמַר רשב"ג: נִדּוֹן בַּחֲזָקָה וְלֹא בִּשְׁטָר. א"ל אַבַּיֵי. לְרַב דִּימִי. א"כ פְּלוּגְתָּא. דְּבָרֶיךָ, לְדְמָר — שֶׁאָמַר רַבָּה לְמַעְלָה: לְרַבָּן שִׁמְעוֹן אוֹתִיּוֹת נִקְנוֹת בִּמְסִירָה, וְאַתָּה אוֹמֵר לְרַבָּן שִׁמְעוֹן אֵין אוֹתִיּוֹת נִקְנוֹת בִּמְסִירָה. א"ל. רַב דִּימִי לְאַבַּיֵי: וְתִפְלוֹג, כְּלוֹמַר אֵינִי חוֹשֵׁשׁ. א"ל א"כ קַשְׁיָא דר"ש בֶּן גַּמְלִיאֵל כו'. דְּהָא עַל כָּרְחָךְ הוּזְקַקְנוּ לְפָרֵשׁ הַבָּרַיְיתָא דִּלְעֵיל כִּדְמָר. אֶלָּא אָמַר אַבַּיֵי. מַאי שְׁטָר דִּפְלִיגֵי בֵּיהּ רַבִּי וְרַבָּן שִׁמְעוֹן (ג) — לָאו בִּשְׁטָר הַכָּתוּב בְּשֵׁם אַחֵר וּמְסָרוֹ לָזֶה פְּלִיגִי, דְּהָא בֵּין לְרַבִּי בֵּין לְרַבָּן שִׁמְעוֹן אוֹתִיּוֹת נִקְנוֹת בִּמְסִירָה, כִּדְאָמְרִי' לְרַבִּי בְּ"הַמּוֹכֵר אֶת הַסְּפִינָה" (לעיל דף עו.), וּלְרַבָּן שִׁמְעוֹן לְעֵיל בִּשְׁמַעְתִּין כִּדְמָר. אֶלָּא בִּשְׁטַר מְכִירָה שֶׁכָּתַב בּוֹ מוֹכֵר לְלוֹקֵחַ זֶה כְּדִין קַרְקַע הַנִּקְנֵית בִּשְׁטָר, פְּלִיגֵי, וּכְגוֹן שֶׁנִּמְצָא אֶחָד מֵהָעֵדִים קָרוֹב כו'. רַבִּי סָבַר כְּרַבִּי אֶלְעָזָר. דְּאָמַר בְּגִיטִּין בְּפֶרֶק "הַמְגָרֵשׁ" (דף פו.): אֵין הָעֵדִים חוֹתְמִים עַל הַגֵּט אֶלָּא מִפְּנֵי תִּקּוּן הָעוֹלָם. דְּעֵדֵי מְסִירָה גּוֹרְמִין לִכְרִיתוּת גֵּט, וְנִמְצָא גֵּט כָּשֵׁר בִּכְתִיבָה בְּלֹא עֵדִים, אֶלָּא שֶׁיְּהֵא מוֹסְרוֹ לְאִשְׁתּוֹ לְהִתְגָּרֵשׁ בִּפְנֵי עֵדִים, דְּהָא כְּתִיב: "וְכָתַב לָהּ" — בִּכְתִיבָה לְחוּד בְּלָא חֲתִימָה מַיְירֵי. וּמִיהוּ, עֵדִים בָּעֵינַן שֶׁיִּרְאוּ שֶׁנִּתְגָּרְשָׁה. וְה"נ, כְּאִילּוּ אֵין עֵדִים בִּשְׁטָר דָּמֵי, הִלְכָּךְ נִדּוֹן בִּשְׁטָר בְּלֹא עֵדֵי חֲזָקָה, אֶלָּא שֶׁיָּבִיא עֵדִים שֶׁנִּכְתַּב וְנִמְסַר לוֹ בִּפְנֵיהֶם, שֶׁהַשָּׂדֶה נִקְנֶה לוֹ בִּשְׁטָר, אע"פ שֶׁאֵין בּוֹ עֵדִים. וְרַבָּן שִׁמְעוֹן בֶּן גַּמְלִיאֵל. אוֹמֵר: בַּחֲזָקָה הוּא קוֹנֶה, אִי א"ל "לֵךְ חֲזַק וּקְנֵי". שֶׁהַשְּׁטָר בְּלֹא עֵדִים אֵינוֹ קוֹנֶה, כְּר"מ דְּעֵדֵי חֲתִימָה עִיקָּר. דְּהַאי דִּכְתִיב "וְכָתַב" — אַחֲתִימַת עֵדִים קָפֵיד קְרָא. מוֹדֶה ר' אֶלְעָזָר כו'. דְּדַוְקָא גֵּט שֶׁאֵין בּוֹ עֵדִים כָּשֵׁר, דְּאַעֵדֵי מְסִירָה קָפֵיד רַחֲמָנָא. וּמִיהוּ, אִם חָתְמוּ שֶׁקֶר אוֹ עֵדִים פְּסוּלִים בְּתוֹךְ הַגֵּט — הֲרֵי הוּא פָּסוּל. אֶלָּא אָמַר רָבִינָא הַכֹּל מוֹדִים. רַבִּי וְרשב"ג מוֹדִים שֶׁאִם מְזוּיָּיף מִתּוֹכוֹ שֶׁהוּא פָּסוּל, כִּדְר' אַבָּא דְּמוֹדֶה ר' אֶלְעָזָר כו'. וְאִיבָּעֵית אֵימָא בְּמוֹדֶה. מְעַרְעֵר שֶׁכְּתָבוֹ לַשְּׁטָר שֶׁבְּיַד זֶה פְּלִיגֵי, וְקָאָמַר מְעַרְעֵר: לֹא *מְכַרְתִּיו לָךְ, וּמִמֶּנִּי נָפַל הַשְּׁטָר, וּמְצָאתוֹ. אֵין צָרִיךְ לְקַיְּימוֹ. דְּלָא דָּמֵי לִשְׁאָר דִּינִים שֶׁהַפֶּה שֶׁאָסַר הוּא הַפֶּה שֶׁהִתִּיר. שֶׁאֲפִילּוּ אִם הָיָה זֶה מְעַרְעֵר וְאוֹמֵר לֹא כְּתַבְתִּיו — לֹא הָיָה לָנוּ לַחְשׁוֹד אֶת זֶה הַלּוֹקֵחַ בְּכָךְ, שֶׁלֹּא נֶחְשְׁדוּ יִשְׂרָאֵל לַעֲשׂוֹת שְׁטָרוֹת מְזוּיָּיפִים. אֶלָּא שֶׁהֶחֱמִירוּ חֲכָמִים לְהִצְטָרֵךְ קִיּוּם הֵיכָא דִּמְעַרְעֲרֵי עֲלֵיהּ. הִלְכָּךְ, כִּי אָמַר כְּתַבְתִּיו — נְהֵמְנֵיהּ לְמִי שֶׁהַשְּׁטָר בְּיָדוֹ. צָרִיךְ לְקַיְּימוֹ. וְהָכִי קָאָמַר רַבָּן שִׁמְעוֹן: נִדּוֹן בַּחֲזָקָה וְלֹא בִּשְׁטָר. שֶׁהַשְּׁטָר אֵינוֹ מוֹעִיל לוֹ כָּל זְמַן שֶׁלֹּא נִתְקַיֵּים ע"י אֲחֵרִים, אע"פ שֶׁזֶּה הַמְעַרְעֵר מוֹדֶה שֶׁכְּתָבוֹ, דְּאִיהוּ אָמַר: כְּתַבְתִּי, וְקָאָמַר נַמֵּי: לֹא מְסַרְתִּיו לוֹ. וְהָא אִיפְּכָא שָׁמְעִינַן לְהוּ. בְּפֶרֶק "שְׁנַיִם אוֹחֲזִין" דְּתַנְיָא: שְׁנַיִם אֲדוּקִים בִּשְׁטָר כו'. יִתְקַיֵּים הַשְּׁטָר בְּחוֹתָמָיו דִּבְרֵי רַבִּי. וְגוֹבֶה לֵיהּ מַלְוֶה כּוּלֵּיהּ, וּכְדִמְפָרְשִׁינַן טַעֲמָא לְקַמָּן. וְהָוֵינַן בָּהּ. הָכִי קָאָמְרִינַן בְּפ' "שְׁנַיִם אוֹחֲזִין". אָמַר מָר: יִתְקַיֵּים הַשְּׁטָר בְּחוֹתָמָיו, דִּבְרֵי רַבִּי. וְגוֹבֶה לוֹ מַלְוֶה כּוּלֵּיהּ? בִּתְמִיָּה, וְלֵית לֵיהּ לְרַבִּי כו' יַחֲלוֹקוּ? וְה"נ יִגְבֶּה חֲצִי חוֹב הַכָּתוּב בַּשְּׁטָר, וְלֹא יוֹתֵר! א"ר נַחְמָן בִּמְקוּיָּים. בְּהֶנְפֵּק, כּוּלֵּי עָלְמָא לָא פְּלִיגֵי דְּפָלְגֵי בֵּין שְׁנֵיהֶם, כְּדִין מִשְׁנָתֵנוּ דִּ"שְׁנַיִם אוֹחֲזִין". אִי מְקַיֵּים לֵיהּ פָּלֵיג. כְּלוֹמַר, אָז יֵשׁ מַמָּשׁ בִּדְבָרָיו, וְיִגְבֶּה (ג) מֵהֶם חֲצִי חוֹב שֶׁבַּשְּׁטָר. וְאִידָךְ פַּלְגָּא יַפְסִיד בִּשְׁבִיל תְּפִיסַת הַלֹּוֶה שֶׁאָדוּק עִמּוֹ בַּשְּׁטָר. אֶלָּא הָכָא בְּלָבָרֵר קָא מִיפַּלְגִי. אָדָם שֶׁטּוֹעֵן לִמְעַרְעֵר: שְׁנֵי מִינֵי חֲזָקוֹת יֵשׁ לִי, אַחַת — שֶׁיֵּשׁ בְּיָדִי עֲדַיִין שְׁטַר מְכִירָה שֶׁעָשִׂיתָ לִי עַל זֶה הַשָּׂדֶה, וְעוֹד — שֶׁיֵּשׁ לִי עֵדֵי חֶזְקַת שָׁלֹשׁ שָׁנִים. וְקָאָמַר רַבִּי: נִדּוֹן בִּשְׁטָר, שֶׁצָּרִיךְ לְבָרֵר וּלְאַמֵּת אֶת דְּבָרָיו, וּלְהָבִיא אֶת הַשְּׁטָר כְּמוֹ שֶׁטָּעַן. וְעֵדֵי חֲזָקָה בְּלֹא שְׁטָר לֹא יוֹעִיל לוֹ כָּאן, מֵאַחַר שֶׁזֶּה עוֹמֵד וּמְעַרְעֵר: לֹא מָסַרְתִּי לָךְ שְׁטָר מֵעוֹלָם, וְלֹא מָכַרְתִּי לָךְ, וְשֶׁלֹּא כַּדִּין הֶחֱזַקְתָּ. וְהַלָּה טוֹעֵן: שְׁטָר יֵשׁ עֲדַיִין בְּיָדִי. וְאִילּוּ לֹא טָעַן כָּךְ — הָיָה דַּי לוֹ בְּעֵדֵי חֲזָקָה, כִּדְאָמַר בְּ"חֶזְקַת הַבָּתִּים" (לעיל כט.) דְּעַד תְּלָת שְׁנִין מִזְדַּהַר אִינִישׁ בִּשְׁטָרֵיהּ, טְפֵי לָא מִזְדַּהַר. וְרַבָּן שִׁמְעוֹן סָבַר: נִדּוֹן אַף בַּחֲזָקָה לְבַדָּהּ, כְּאִילּוּ בָּא לִידּוֹן בַּחֲזָקָה לְבַדָּהּ בְּלֹא שְׁטָר. וְכָל שֶׁכֵּן שֶׁאִם הֵבִיא שְׁטַר מְכִירָה — לָא בָּעֵי תּוּ עֵדֵי חֲזָקָה, דְּאֵין אָדָם צָרִיךְ לְבָרֵר רִיבּוּי טַעֲנוֹת שֶׁטָּעַן שֶׁאֵין צְרִיכִים לוֹ. וְכִי הֵיכִי דְּאִילּוּ טָעַן מֵעִיקָּרָא: אָבַד שְׁטָרִי, וְיֵשׁ לִי חֲזָקָה שָׁלֹשׁ שָׁנִים — דַּי לוֹ בְּכָךְ, כִּי טָעַן נַמֵּי: יֵשׁ לִי שְׁטָר עִם הַחֲזָקָה — דַּי לוֹ בַּחֲזָקָה בְּלֹא שְׁטָר. תִּבְעֵיהּ לְדִינָא. ר' חִיָּיא לְרַבִּי אַבָּא. אַטּוּ לָא מְהֵימְנִינָא. לוֹמַר "פָּרַעְתִּי" אֲפִי' בְּלֹא עֵדִים? וְהָא קיי"ל בְּפֶרֶק "שְׁבוּעַת הַדַּיָּינִין". כִּשְׁמַעְתָּךְ. דְּאָמְרַתְּ מִשְּׁמֵיהּ דְּרַב: צָרִיךְ שֶׁיָּבוֹאוּ פְּלוֹנִי וּפְלוֹנִי וְיָעִידוּ. וּמִיהוּ, אִי אָתוּ הָנֵי סָהֲדֵי וְאָמְרֵי: לֹא הָיוּ דְּבָרִים מֵעוֹלָם — הָא אָמַר רָבָא בְּפֶ' "שְׁבוּעַת הַדַּיָּינִין" (שבועות דף מא:): כָּל מִילְּתָא דְּלָא רְמִיָא עֲלֵיהּ דְּאִינִישׁ וכו'. וְהִלְכְתָא כְּרָבָא, וְנִשְׁבָּע הַלֹּוֶה שֶׁפְּרָעוֹ, וּפָטוּר. א"ל. ר' אַבָּא. וְהָאָמַר רַב גִּידֵּל אָמַר רַב הֲלָכָה כרשב"ג. שֶׁאָמַר: נִדּוֹן אַף בַּחֲזָקָה לְבַדָּהּ. דְּכֵיוָן דְּלֹא הָיָה צָרִיךְ לִטְעוֹן "שְׁטָר יֵשׁ בְּיָדִי", מֵאַחַר שֶׁאֲכָלָהּ שְׁנֵי חֲזָקָה — אֵין צָרִיךְ לְבָרֵר אֶת דְּבָרָיו, שֶׁהִרְבָּה לִטְעוֹן מַה שֶּׁאֵין צָרִיךְ. וַאֲנָא נַמֵּי, כֵּיוָן דִּבְלָא עֵדִים מְהֵימְנִינָא — אֵינִי צָרִיךְ לְבָרֵר וּלְהָבִיא עֵדִים שֶׁאָמַרְתִּי. וְאַף רַבִּי לֹא אָמַר אֶלָּא לְבָרֵר. כְּלוֹמַר, מִן הַדִּין הֲלָכָה כְּרַבָּן שִׁמְעוֹן בֶּן גַּמְלִיאֵל. שֶׁאַף רַבִּי לֹא נֶחֱלַק אֶלָּא מִשּׁוּם דִּסְבִירָא לֵיהּ דְּצָרִיךְ לְבָרֵר אֶת דְּבָרָיו אַחֲרֵי שֶׁטָּעַן "יֵשׁ לִי שְׁטָר", וְרַבִּי מוֹדֶה שֶׁאִם לֹא טָעַן — לֹא הָיָה צָרִיךְ אֶלָּא חֲזָקָה לְבַדָּהּ. וְכֵיוָן דְּלָא הָוְיָא פְּלוּגְתַּיְיהוּ אֶלָּא כְּדֵי לְבָרֵר — נִרְאִין דִּבְרֵי רַבָּן שִׁמְעוֹן בֶּן גַּמְלִיאֵל שֶׁאֵין לוֹ לְהַפְסִיד בִּשְׁבִיל שְׂפַת יֶתֶר. אָמַר

הגהות הב"ח

(א) גמ' ותפלוג (אמר ליה הכי קאמינא כו' קשיא) תא"מ ונ"ב ג"י רשב"ם א"ל קשיא כו': (ב) רשב"ם ד"ה אלא וכו' ורבן שמעון כ"נ לאו כו' לרשב"ג אותיות כו' שכתב מוכר כל"ל ותיבת בו נמחק: (ג) ד"ה אי מקיים כו' יגבה ממנו חצי חוב:

[נ"ל מסרתיו]

עין משפט נר מצוה

צב א מיי' פ"א מהל' גירושין הל' טו וט"ז הל' ב סמג עשין נ וטוש"ע ח"מ סי' נא סעיף ז וטוש"ע אה"ע סי' קל סעיף ח:

צג ב מיי' שם פ"א הל' יז וסמג שם טוש"ע ח"מ סי' נא סעיף ג וסעיף ז וטוש"ע אה"ע סי' קל סעיף יז:

צד ג מיי' פי"ד מהל' מלוה ולוה הל' יד סמג עשין צד טוש"ע ח"מ סי' סט סעיף טו:

צה ד מיי' פ"ט מהל' טוען ונטען הל' ט סמג עשין צה טוש"ע ח"מ סי' קלח סעיף א:

צו ה מיי' פי"ד מהל' מלוה ולוה הל' יד סמג עשין צד טוש"ע ח"מ סי' סט סעיף טו:

צז ו מיי' פ"ו מהל' מלוה ולוה הל' א סמג שם טוש"ע ח"מ סי' ע סעיף א:

צח ז מיי' פ"ו מהל' טוען ונטען הל' ה ועיין בהשגות ובמגיד משנה סמג עשין צה טוש"ע ח"מ סי' ע סעיף ב:

רבינו גרשום

להראות השטר ואם לא הראה השטר אלא עדי חזקה חיישינן דשמא החזיר לו השטר וחזרה מכירתו: אימא אף בחזקה. כלומר דשטר הוי עיקר ואם אין לו שטר אלא חזקה מועיל לו: רבי סבר אותיות נקנות במסירה. דכיון שמסר לו הלה את השטר קנה להכי אמר נידון בשטר דהיינו עיקר קניה: ורשב"ג סבר אין אותיות נקנות במסירה. אא"כ החזיק נמי הקרקע להכי אמר אף בחזקה: ואמר לי' אביי. לרב דימי את מוקים פלוגתייהו איפוך במאי דאוקי רבה. לרבה קרי אביי מר. א"כ פליג אדמר: אמר ליה ותפלוג. ומה בכך אנא אמינא טעמא דידי והוא אמר טעמא דידיה: אמר ליה אביי אם כן קשיא דרשב"ג אדרשב"ג. דהכא אמר איפכא כדאמר לעיל לטעמא דרב דימי: אלא אמר אביי. לא קשיא הכא אמאי אמר רשב"ג אין אותיות נקנות במסירה כגון שנמצא אחד מן העדים שבשטר קרוב או פסול. ורבי דאמר נידון בשטר סבר לה כר' אלעזר דאמר לענין גט עדי מסירה כרתי. כלומר אותן שמוסר לה הגט בפניהם היינו עיקר כריתות וה"נ קא סבר דאע"ג דעדי השטר אחד קרוב או פסול נידון בשטר בעדי מסירה שאם יש לו עדים שמסר לו את השטר שכתב לו מכירה בפניהם מועיל לו השטר: ורשב"ג סבר כר' מאיר דאמר עדי חתימה כרתי. היינו עיקר כריתות הלכך קסבר כיון דעדי חתימה דהאי שטר פסול נידון בחזקה ולא בשטר: והאמר רבא. התם במס' גיטין מודה ר' אלעזר בגט מזויף מתוכו. שאחד מן העדים קרוב או פסול פסול הגט ולא מועיל עדי מסירה. ועל מה נחלקו כגון על אותן ג' גיטין כגון כתב הגט ואין עליו עדים יש עליו עדים ואין בו זמן יש זמן ואין בו אלא עד אחד לא תינשא ואם נשאת הולד כשר דההוא לאו מזויף מתוכו וכי האי גוונא נמי בשטרי מקח במזויף מתוכו בקרוב או פסול לא פליגי. אלא בדר' אבינא פליגי דאמר ר' אבינא הכל מודים. ר' ורשב"ג שאם אמרו בית דין או כתבו הוזקקנו לעדות של עדות ונמצאת עדותן מזוייפת ונמצא אחד קרוב או פסול היינו מזויף מתוכה ואם בא לידון באותו שטר אין מועיל לו כלום עדי מסירה ועל מה נחלקו בשאין עליו עדים כלל דההוא לא הוי מזויף מתוכו רשב"ג סבר עדי חתימה כרתי וכיון דאין עליו עדים ידון בחזקה בלבד: ואיבעית אימא במודה בשטר כו' רבי סבר. כיון שמודה זה התובע בשטר שהוא כתבו לו אין צריכין לקיימו לא בחותמיו ולא להביא עדי חזקה. ורשב"ג סבר אע"פ שמודה שכתבו לו צריך לזה לקיימו להביא עדי חוקה ואם לא יכול לומר לו זה שמודה בשטר שטר אמנה הוא או שטר פסול. הלכך קאמר רבן שמעון בן גמליאל נידון בחזקה ולא בשטר: ולוה אמר שלך הוא. ברור ששלך היה שכתבתי לך ופרעתי לך והחזרת לי ונפל ממני: יתקיים השטר בחותמיו דברי רבי. כלומר יביא עדים שמכירין חתימת ידי עדים וכשר וגובה כל להכי צריך לקיימו לדברי רבי לפי שהורע כחו שנפל: רבן שמעון בן גמליאל אומר יחלוקו. הואיל דשניהן אדוקין בו האי ממון המוטל בספק ויחלוקו יפרע לו הלוה החצי בלבד: והוינן בה לרבי אמאי לא יהא דין השטר זה כדין שנים שאדוקין בטלית שלדברי הכל יחלוקו: אלא במקויים השטר כולי עלמא לא פליגי דגובה המלוה פלגא דהיינו כ"א ישבע שאין לו פחות מחציו ויחלוקו: רבי סבר אע"פ שמודה הלוה בשטר שכתבו צריך למלוה לקיימו ואי מקיים ליה גבי פלגא כדין הטלית ואי לא מקיים ליה חספא בעלמא הוא הואיל ואינו יוצא כולו מתחת ידו. ורשב"ג סבר הואיל דאדוק בחצי יחלוקו. אלמא דאיפכא שמעינן להו ולא מצית מוקמת בהכי פליגי: אלא הכא בלברר קמיפלגי. קס"ד השתא דתרווייהו סברי דחזקה עיקר והאי דקאמר נידון בשטר לא משום דצריך אלא קסבר הואיל וטען לפני בית דין דיש לו שני כחות חזקה ושטר צריך לברר טענתו שיש לו שטר להכי קאמר נידון בשטר עם החזקה. ורשב"ג סבר אין צריך לברר אלא בחזקה בלבד: מאי לברר. כי הא דרב יצחק בריה דרב יוסף הוה מסיק זוזי כו': אמר ליה. ר' אבא לר' יצחק נפחא: והא אמר רב גידל אמר רב הלכה

אָמַר אאֶלָּא לְבָרֵר! א"ל: אֲנָא נַמִּי בלְבָרֵר קָאָמִינָא.§ **מתני'** א)מִי שֶׁפָּרַע מִקְצָת חוֹבוֹ — ר' יְהוּדָה אוֹמֵר: יַחֲלִיף; רַבִּי יוֹסֵי אוֹמֵר: ב)יִכְתּוֹב שׁוֹבֵר. אָמַר רַבִּי יְהוּדָה: נִמְצָא זֶה צָרִיךְ לִהְיוֹת שׁוֹמֵר שׁוֹבְרוֹ מִן הָעַכְבָּרִים! אָמַר לוֹ רַבִּי יוֹסֵי: כָּךְ יָפֶה לוֹ, וְלֹא יֵרַע כֹּחוֹ שֶׁל זֶה.§ **גמ'** אָמַר רַב הוּנָא אָמַר רַב: אֵין הֲלָכָה לֹא כְּרַבִּי יְהוּדָה וְלֹא כְּרַבִּי יוֹסֵי, אֶלָּא גב"ד מְקָרְעִין הַשְּׁטָר וְכוֹתְבִין לוֹ שְׁטָר אַחֵר מִזְּמַן רִאשׁוֹן. אֲמַר לֵיהּ רַב נַחְמָן לְרַב הוּנָא, וְאָמְרִי לָהּ רַב יִרְמְיָה בַּר אַבָּא לְרַב הוּנָא: אִי שְׁמִיעָא לֵיהּ לְרַב הָא רס"ל [בָּרַיְיתָא,] דְּתַנְיָא: עֵדִים מְקָרְעִין אֶת הַשְּׁטָר וְכוֹתְבִין לוֹ שְׁטָר אַחֵר מִזְּמַן רִאשׁוֹן — הֲוָה הָדַר רס"א בֵּיהּ. אֲמַר לֵיהּ: שְׁמִיעַ לֵיהּ וְלָא הֲדַר בֵּיהּ, בִּשְׁלָמָא

רשב"ם

אֲמַר לֵיהּ אֲנָא נַמִּי לְבָרֵר קָאָמִינָא. כְּלוֹמַר, כְּרַבִּי סְבִירָא לִי, וְאִם לֹא בֵּירֵר
דְּבָרָיו – הִפְסִיד. וְכֵן פֵּירֵשׁ רַבֵּינוּ זְקֵנִי מ"כ בְּפֶרֶק "זֶה בּוֹרֵר" אַלִּיבָּא דְּרַבִּי,
שֶׁצָּרִיךְ לְבָרֵר, וְאִם לֹא הֵבִיא שְׁטָר – הִפְסִיד. וְיֵשׁ לָשׁוֹן אַחֵר וְאֵין בּוֹ
מַמָּשׁ. וְאע"פ שֶׁהֲלָכָה כְּרַבִּי מֵחֲבֵירוֹ – בְּהָא הִלְכְתָא כְּרַבָּן שִׁמְעוֹן, שֶׁאֵין צָרִיךְ
לְבָרֵר, כִּדְאָמַר רַב גִּידֵּל אָמַר רַב.
מתני' מִי שֶׁפָּרַע מִקְצָת חוֹבוֹ.
בְּמִלְוֶה בִּשְׁטָר מַיְירֵי, וְאִיכָּא לְמֵיחַשׁ
פֶּן יַחֲזוֹר הַמַּלְוֶה וְיִתְבַּע כָּל חוֹבוֹ.
רַבִּי יְהוּדָה אוֹמֵר יַחֲלִיף. יִקְרַע
אוֹתוֹ הַשְּׁטָר, וְיִכְתּוֹב לוֹ שְׁטָר אַחֵר לְפִי
חֶשְׁבּוֹן הַנִּשְׁאָר, מִזְּמַן רִאשׁוֹן, כִּדְמְפָרֵשׁ
בַּגְּמָרָא. יִכְתּוֹב שׁוֹבֵר. וְיִשְׁמְרֵהוּ הַלֹּוֶה.
לִשְׁמוֹר שׁוֹבְרוֹ. שֶׁאִם אָבַד שׁוֹבְרוֹ – יַחֲזוֹר
הַמַּלְוֶה וְיִגְבֶּה כָּל חוֹבוֹ. א"ל ר' יוֹסֵי כֵּן
יָפֶה לוֹ. לַמַּלְוֶה, שֶׁיִּהְיֶה הַלֹּוֶה
בְּדַאֲגַת שִׁימּוּר שׁוֹבְרוֹ. וְלֹא הַמַּלְוֶה, דְּעֶבֶד
לֹוֶה לְאִישׁ מַלְוֶה, כִּדְאָמְרִינַן בַּגְּמָרָא.
וְלֹא יֵרַע כֹּחוֹ. שֶׁל מַלְוֶה לְהַחֲלִיף שְׁטָרוֹ,
(א) כִּדְאָמַר ר' יְהוּדָה, כְּדֵי שֶׁיִּכּוֹף
לְפָרְעוֹ. **גמ'** אֵין הֲלָכָה לֹא כְּרַבִּי
יְהוּדָה. שֶׁאָמַר: יַחֲלִיף. וַאֲפִילּוּ לִכְתּוֹב
לוֹ מִזְּמַן רִאשׁוֹן עַל יְדֵי עֵדִים בְּלֹא
בֵּית דִּין. כִּדְמְפָרֵשׁ וְאָזֵיל – דְּלָא אַלִּימִי עֵדִים לִקְרוֹעַ שְׁטָר, וּלְהַחֲלִיף
וְלִגְבּוֹת מִזְּמַן רִאשׁוֹן. וְלֹא כְּר' יוֹסֵי. דְּאָמַר: כּוֹתְבִין שׁוֹבֵר, וְצָרִיךְ
לִשְׁמוֹר שׁוֹבְרוֹ מִן הָעַכְבָּרִים. וְכוֹתְבִין לוֹ שְׁטָר אַחֵר. לְפִי סְכוּם
הַמָּעוֹת שֶׁחַיָּיב לוֹ עֲדַיִין. וְרַב תַּנָּא הוּא וּפָלֵיג. אִי שְׁמִיעַ לֵיהּ לְרַב
הָא דְּתַנְיָא. לְקַמָּן בִּשְׁמַעְתִּין, בְּמִילְּתֵיהּ דְּר' יְהוּדָה בְּפוֹרֵעַ חֲצִי חוֹבוֹ,
שֶׁמְּקָרְעִין עֵדִים כּוּ' (ב). הֲוָה הֲדַר בֵּיהּ. רַב, וַהֲוָה מוֹדֶה שֶׁהֲלָכָה כְּר'
יְהוּדָה. דְּהָא רַב נַמִּי ה"ק: דְּמָה לִּי ב"ד מַה לִּי עֵדִים. שְׁמָעָהּ וְלָא הֲדַר
בֵּיהּ. דְּבָרַיְיתָא תָּנֵי: עֵדִים מְקָרְעִין, וְאִיהוּ אָמַר: ב"ד דַּוְקָא, וְלֹא עֵדִים.
בִּשְׁלָמָא

תוספות

אלא לברר. פירש רבינו תם: לברר אמיתת הדברים, ולהעמיד על האמת.
ואם ימצאו ויאמרו לא ראינו מעולם — מיחייב. אבל אם לא ימצאם
— לא אבד בכך, שאין סברא שהיה מחייבו לשלם על זה אם לא יוכל למצאן,
כי מה דין הוא זה שיפסיד בחנם אם לא יוכל לאמת דבריו שלא היה צריך
לטעון? ועוד, דהכי משמע "אנא נמי
לברר קאמינא" — ולא לחייב, שאם היה
מחייבו (ג) לברר — מה תשובה היא זו
"אנא נמי לברר"? מכל מקום היה
מחייבו! ואדרבה, מה שמזכיר לברר —
אינו כי אם קושיא על טעמו, כמו
שפירש רשב"ם ואף רבי לא אמר אלא
לברר. הלכך לא מסתבר טעמא לחייבו
משום הכי. ובשבועות פרק "שבועת
הדיינים" (דף מא:) דקאמר: אתו פלוני
ופלוני ואמרו לא היו דברים מעולם,
ואמר רבא: כל מילתא דלא רמיא עליה
דאיניש — אמר ולאו אדעתיה. תימה:
דאמר הכא צריך שיבואו פלוני ופלוני
ויעידו! וי"ל: דרבא כרשב"ג ס"ל,
כדפסיק רב (פפא). א"נ, אפי' [לרבי],
וכדפי' ר"ת, דמפרש הכא: אם לא
בירר — לא הפסיד. דיש לו לברר
כל מה שיוכל, ומ"מ אי לא משכח נהו, או אומרים להד"מ — י"ל דלא
מפסיד. אבל תימה שרשב"ם הביא על זה שצריך שיבאו פלוני ופלוני
ויעידו, משמע שרוצה להעמידה כדבי אפילו לפי' שלו. (ד) ושמא היה
רוצה לומר דגרע היכא דלא הביאם מהיכא דאייתינהו ואמרו לסד"מ,
ולא הבנתי כלל. ויש מישבים דבריו אליבא דרבן שמעון בן גמליאל,
וסובר שהלכה כוותיה. ואפי' למ"ד התם הוחזק כפרן — אתי שפיר כרבן
שמעון בן גמליאל, די"ל דלא אמר ר"ש בן גמליאל אלא דא"ל נהביא.
אין הלכה לא כר' יהודה כו'. פירש רשב"ם: דאמר עדים מקרעים
את השטר, דהכי משמע יחליף — אפילו בעדים. וכן הוא לפי
המסקנא, דשמיע ליה ברייתא ולא הדר, דאיהו מכשר בעדים ואיהו מצריך ב"ד. אבל רב נחמן לא היה סובר מילתיה דרב הכי, דא"כ — מאי הא
דקאמר לרב הונא: אי שמיע ליה כו' הוה הדר ביה ממה שהיה אומר אין הלכה כר' יהודה? מי אלימא ממתני' דמשמע נמי בעדים, ואפ"ה פליג עליה?
וא"ת: במשנה לא תני עדים בהדיא — מ"מ איהו ס"ל דעדים קאמר, ופליג עליה, דתנא הוא ופליג! ונראה לר"י: דרב נחמן סבר לה למילתיה דרב
הכי: אין הלכה כרבי יהודה דאמר יחליף וכותבין ליה מזמן שני. דס"ל דרבי יהודה מזמן שני קאמר, מדלא פירש במשנה: וכותבין לו שטר אחר מזמן
ראשון. וממאי דהדר ליה ר' יוסי: וכן יפה לו ולא יגרע כחו של זה — משמע (ה) דר' יהודה מזמן שני קאמר, דאי מזמן ראשון — מה הורעת כח
איכא? והשתא קאמר שפיר: אי הוה שמיע ליה הא דתניא: עדים מקרעין לו את השטר וכותבין לו שטר אחר מזמן ראשון — הוה הדר ממאי דמצריך
ב"ד כדי לכתוב מזמן ראשון. ולא הוה פליג אברייתא בהכי, שכל עצמו לא בא אלא לאפוקי (ו) ממה שהיה סבור שר' יהודה לא היה מכשיר מזמן ראשון
בלבד כלל אפי' בב"ד, מדלא קאמר ליה במתניתין, ובא רב לומר שאע"פ שבעדים י"ל שאין להכשיר מזמן ראשון — בב"ד מיהא ראוי להכשיר. ואי
הוה ידע דר' יהודה הוה מכשיר אפי' בעדים מזמן ראשון — לא הוה פליג עליה. ותימה: דלעיל (דף קסח.) בנמחק כותבין לו מזמן ראשון,
כן פירש רשב"ם התם: "וביום פלוני" דקאמר התם — היינו שהיה כתוב (ז) זמן ביום פלוני. והכי משמע קצת מדבעי ב"ד. ואמאי לא כותבין
הכא מזמן ראשון כי התם לרבי יהודה אליבא דרב, דהוה ס"ד דמזמן שני כותבין לר' יהודה? ומלינן למימר דרב נחמן
ס"ל דרב הוה מוקי לה ההיא דנמחק בכתיבת זמן ראשון אליבא דנפשיה, ואליבא דר' יהודה מזמן שני. דמגופה דההיא משנה לא מוכחא
לר' יהודה אי מזמן ראשון אי מזמן שני. דאפי' מזמן שני איכא למימר מזמן שני. אף על גב דמצרכי בית דין — איכא למימר שאין לעדים
לכתוב שלא מדעת לוה. ואפילו אותם עדים שעשאוהו אין רשאין לעשות אחר, שכיון שעשו שליחותן — אין חוזרין ועושין שליחותן. דומיא
דגט, שאם לוה לכתוב גט וליתן לשלוחו, שנעשה שליח להולכה וכתבו ונתנו לו, ונמחק או אבד — שאין יכולין לעשות אחר, כדמוכח בפרק
"התקבל" (גיטין דף סג:). ואע"פ שיש לתת חילוק, שבדין (ח) שבגט לא יעשו גט שני, דבעינן שיאמר לסופר "כתוב" ולעדים לחתום, ומן השני לא
אמר להם כלום. אבל הכא בלא זוי יכול להיות כשר, שאינו אלא לראיה לגלות שנשתעבדו נכסיו על ידי השטר הראשון, ואחרי שנשתעבדו
לא יפקע השעבוד. ומ"מ, אע"פ שאין דומה לגמרי לגט — נוכל לומר שאין להם לכתוב עליו שעבוד שלא מדעת. כיון שנאבד מן המלוה
אותו שכתבו ונתנו לו, על פי לוה אין רשאין לעשות אחר — כ"ש עדים אחרים, שזה השטר מזיק לו אפילו לא יכפור כלום. שאע"פ שגם אם
לא נכתב היה גובה מלקוחות שקנו אחר שנמחק הראשון כאילו היה קיים, כיון דאית ליה קלא להאי מלוה, כדמשמע ב"חזקת הבתים"
(לעיל דף מב.) אי לא משום דמאן דזיזף בצנעא יזיף — היתה מלוה על פה גובה מן הלקוחות, אף על גב דמצי לאטעוייניהו ללקוחות ולומר להן
בשעת מכר פרעתי, ושטרא ליכא לאפוקי עלייהו — מ"מ מזיק השטר השני ללוה, שאם יפרע לו ואין לו שטר — אין לו לדאוג כלום, ואם יש
שטר — זימנין דמשתמיט ולא יהיב ליה, ואמר: יהיבנא לך למחר או ליומא אוחרא, והדר גבי זימנא אחריתי. ועוד יש לומר: דרב נחמן ס"ל
דמודה רב היכא דנמחק שעושין לו בית דין שטר אחר מזמן ראשון, משום דהתם אין לחוש אם זה דומה למוקדם, כיון שבית דין
בעצמם כותבין אותו, דבית דין אלימי לאפקועי ממונא, ולא יבא לחתום בשטר מוקדם על ידי שנכשיר זה. אבל הכא — כותבין ליה עדים,
הלכך אין להם כח לחתום מזמן ראשון, שדומה למוקדם, שלא יבאו לחתום בשטרי מוקדמין. ועוד יש לומר: דגבי נמחק אין דומה כל
כך למוקדם, מאחר שזהו שטר ראשון אלא שמעתיקין אותו. אבל הכא — שטר חדש שהיו כותבין בו זמן ראשון היה דומה למוקדם.
וקצת היה משמע דבנמחק נמי (ט) זמן שני, והכי משמע לישנא קצת, דקאמר: הוציא שטר מחוק ביום פלוני. ומיהו, הוה קשה
איפכא לרב דאמר זמן ראשון, ולר' יהודה דבסמוך דאמר אפילו בעדים מזמן ראשון. ואין לומר שבנמחק אין ראוי כל כך זמן ראשון(י),
שאינו מדעת שניהם, כי כמו שפירש ר"י ורבינו שמואל נראה עיקר. תדע, דהא ב"הגוזל קמא" (ב"ק דף לח:) גבי שורף שטרות אי דאיכא סהדי כו'
— ומשמע שאז לא יפסיד כלום. ועוד תימה, דלעיל בנמחק בעי ב"ד לכ"ע, והכא קאמר ר' יהודה עדים! וזה אומר ר"י, דהכא דכתיבי מדעת
שניהם — לא בעו אלא עדים, אבל בנמחק — כותבין שלא בפני הלוה, וכיון שמזיק לו — נראה (כ) אין לעדים לעשותו שלא מדעתו.
אלא

עין משפט נר מצוה

צט א מיי' פט"ו מהל' טוען ונטען הלכה א ועיין בהשגות ובמגיד משנה סמג עשין צה טוש"ע ח"מ סימן קמ סעיף ד:
ק ב מיי' פ"ו שם הלכה ה סמג שם טוש"ע ח"מ סי' ע סעיף ב:
קא ג מיי' פכ"ג מהל' מלוה ולוה הל' טו סמג עשין צד טוש"ע ח"מ סי' נד סעיף א:

רבינו גרשום

הלכה כרשב"ג. דאמר בחזקה בלבד נידון ואין צריך לברר שיראה השטר: ואף רבי לא אמר. דנידון בשטר: אלא לברר. קאמר דמטרחינן ליה לאיתויי שטרא ואי לא מייתי לא מעכב ונאמן אף אנא נמי אע"ג דלא אתו סהדי מהימנא: אמר ליה אנא נמי לברר קאמינא לך. דיבואו פלוני ופלוני ויעידו כדי שיתבררו דבריך ובלאו הכי מהימנת. ואמר לן רבי דאמר ליה ר' יצחק נפחא אנא נמי לברר קאמינא לא כדקאמרת דרבי לא אמר דנידון בשטר אינו אלא כדי לברר ולא משום דוקא קאמר אנא סבירא לי דהאי לברר משום דוקא קאמר וצריך תרתי אף את אי לא מבררת (דצריך) לא מהימנת: **פיס'** ר"י אומר יחליף. שטרו ויכתוב שטר אחר מן המותר בלבד ויקרע שטר ראשון ויכתוב זמן שטר שני מן אותו יום שיפרע לו המקצת ואל יכתוב מזמן כתיבת שטר הראשון לפי שכיון שנקרע לא מצי טריף למפרע מן זמן ההלואה אלא מן יום כתיבת שטר שני טריף לקוחות: ור' יוסי אמר. לא יקרע שטר הראשון אלא יכתוב לו המלוה ללוה שובר ממה שפרע לו ויתן לו: אמר ר' יהודה. אם כן צריך הלוה שישמור שוברו מן העכברים שאם יאכלוהו עכברים יוציא מלוה שטרו ויגבה ממנו כל חובו כבתחלה: א"ל ר' יוסי וכן יפה לו. שיהא שומר שוברו: ואל ירע כחו של זה. ונכתב לו זמנו משעת פריע' מוטב שירע כחו של לוה משום דעבד לוה לאיש מלוה: אין הלכה כר' יהודה. דמתני' דסבירא ליה דיחליף ויכתוב מזמן שני: ולא כר' יוסי. דאמר יכתוב שיבר: אי שמיעא ליה לרב הא דתניא. דבקריעת עדים סגי הוה הדר ביה ממאי דאמר דבית דין מקרעין: אמר ליה ודאי שמיעא ליה ולא הדר. דקסבר טריף האי מלוה לקוחות בהאי חצי שטר מזמן ראשון כמו שהיה עושה כשהיה כל חובו שלם

מסורת הש"ס

א) [כתובות ע.] ב) ע"ז: וש"נ]

הגהות הב"ח

(א) רשב"ם ד"ה ולא וכו' וכדאמר ר' בברייתא כדי ש[illegible] לפרעו: (ב) ד"ה אי ש[illegible] הד"א עם ד"ה הוה נמי ה"ק שמקרעין כו' לי ב"ד: (ג) תוס' ד"ה וכו' היה מחייבו תשובה כצ"ל ותיבת [illegible] נמחק: (ד) בא"ד א[illegible] לפירוש שלו וי"ל דר[illegible] שמואל היה רוצה [illegible] (ה) ד"ה אין וכו' מ[illegible] נמי דרבי יהודה מ[illegible] (ו) בא"ד אלא לאפ[illegible] בלבד ממה שהיה ס[illegible] וכו' מזמן ראשון כלל [illegible] כצ"ל: (ז) בא"ד הזמן ב[illegible] פלוני וכו' כי התם יהודה אליבא דרב [illegible] דהוה סלקא אדעתיה [illegible] נחמן דמזמן שני כות[illegible] לר' יהודה: (ח) בא[illegible] שבדין הוא שבג[illegible] (ט) בא"ד דבנמחק [illegible] כותבין זמן שני: (י) בא[illegible] כל כך זמן ראשון [illegible] שאינו: (כ) בא"ד נר[illegible]

בשלמא בי דינא — אלימי לאפקועי ממונא, [א]אלא עדים שעשו שליחותן — חוזרין ועושין שליחותן?! ולא? והא אמר רב יהודה אמר רב: עדים כותבין אפילו עשרה שטרות על שדה אחת! רב יוסף אמר: בשטר מתנה, ורבה אמר: [ב]בשטר שאין בו אחריות. מאי ברייתא? דתניא: הרי שהיו נושין בו אלף זוז, ופרע מהן חמש מאות זוז — עדים מקרעין את השטר וכותבין לו שטר אחר מזמן ראשון, דברי רבי יהודה; רבי יוסי אומר: שטר זה יהא מונח במקומו ויכתבו שובר; ומפני שני דברים אמרו כותבין שובר: אחת — כדי שיכוף לפורעו, ואחת — כדי שיגבה מזמן ראשון. והא רבי יהודה נמי מזמן ראשון קאמר! הכי קאמר ליה ר' יוסי לרבי יהודה: אי מזמן ראשון קאמרת — פליגנא עלך בחדא, אי מזמן שני קאמרת — פליגנא עלך בתרתי. תנו רבנן: א)[ג]שטר שזמנו כתוב בשבת או בעשרה בתשרי — שטר מאוחר הוא וכשר, דברי ר' יהודה; רבי יוסי פוסל. אמר לו רבי יהודה: והלא מעשה בא לפניך בצפורי והכשרת! אמר לו: כשהכשרתי — בזה הכשרתי. והא רבי יהודה נמי בזה קאמר! אמר רבי פדת: הכל מודים, שאם הוזקקנו לעונתו של שטר, ונמצאת עונתו מכוונת בשבת או בעשרה בתשרי — ששטר מאוחר הוא וכשר,

לא

רש"י

בשלמא בי דינא. מקרעין ומחליפין אחר, וכותבין אותו מזמן ראשון לטרוף שלא כדין מזמן ראשון. דמן הדין לא הוה שטרא למיטרף אלא מיום שנכתב ואילך, אלא ב"ד אלימי ומפקעי ממונא, דהפקר בית דין הפקר, כדנפקא לן מ"אלה הנחלות" (גיטין דף לו.). **אלא עדים שעשו שליחותן.** לכתוב ולהעיד בשטר הראשון, היאך חוזרין ועושין שליחות אחרת, (א) ומי נתן להם כח זה? **ולא.** בתמיה, וכי אין עדים חוזרין ועושין? **והאמר רב יהודה אמר רב.** מי שאבד שטרו, ואמר לעדים: כתבו לי אחר — חוזרין וכותבין אפי' עשרה שטרות, אם אבדו זה אחר זה. ומשני: **רב יוסף אמר.** לעולם אין כח בידם של עדים לחזור ולכתוב שטר אחר לגבות מלקוחות. וכי קאמר רב יהודה אמר רב — ה"מ בשטר מתנה שאין בו אחריות, (ב) וכיון דהכל יודעין שנותן לו השדה — למה לא יכתבו לו שטר מתנה להיות בידו לעדות, דתיקו ארעא בידיה. **ורבה אמר.** אפי' בשטר מכירה קאמר רב יהודה דכותבין עשרה, וכגון דלית ביה אחריות. וכדאמרן לעיל (דף קסח:): חוץ מאחריות שבו. וכדאמר רב נחמן לעיל (דף קסט:): שטרא דנן דכתבנוהו לא למיגבי ביה כו'. **כדי שיכוף לפורעו.** המלוה יכוף ללוה לפורעו, שדואג פן יפסיד שוברו, וזה יוציא שטרו ותובעו כל חובו. ופרכינן: (ג) **ור' יהודה נמי מזמן ראשון קאמר.** כר' יוסי, ומה תשובה היא זו שאמר רבי יוסי כדי שיגבה מזמן ראשון? **הכי קאמר ליה רבי יוסי כו'.** דרבי יהודה לא פירש דבריו כל כך, אלא יחליף סתמא קאמר ליה לר' יוסי, כדתנן במתניתין. **בחדא פליגנא.** דכותבין שובר כדי שיכוף לפורעו. **בתרתי פליגנא עלך.** (ד) כי כותבין שובר, וגובין מזמן ראשון. **ת"ר שטר שכתב בו זמנו בשבת או בעשרה בתשרי.** כגון במקומות שמונין לחדשי החמה וכתב בשטר "בט"ו לירח פלוני", וכשאנו נזקקין לכוין מתי אירע יום ט"ו של אותו חדש — נמצא עונתו ביום שבת, או ביום עשירי לתשרי, דהיינו יוה"כ. והכל יודעין שלא נכתב לא בשבת ולא ביוה"כ, ונמצא שלא נכתב באותו יום המוכיח בשטר, אלא או מוקדם הוא ופסול, או מאוחר וכשר. **שטר מאוחר הוא וכשר דברי ר' יהודה.** דס"ל לרבי יהודה: כל שטר מאוחר כשר, ואפילו אותו שאין להוכיח מתוכו של שטר אם מאוחר הוא ואם לאו. וכ"ש זה, שזמנו ביום השבת וביום הכפורים, שהזמן מוכיח שהוא מאוחר. ואפי' רבי יוסי מודה ביה, דלא נפיק מיניה חורבא מהאי, כדמפרש ואזיל. והא ליכא למימר שמא מוקדם הוא ופסול, כמו שפירש רבינו חננאל — הלא תרחה דרמינן עלה דמתניתין (סנהדרין דף לב.), דתנן: אחד דיני ממונות ואחד דיני נפשות בדרישה וחקירה, שנאמר (ויקרא כד): "משפט אחד יהיה לכם", הא דתניא בתוספתא בתחלת מסכת מכות: שטר שכתוב בו זמנו באחד בניסן בשמיטה, ובאו עדים ואמרו: "היאך אתם מעידין על שטר זה שנמסרה לכם עדות זו במקום הזה, והלא באותו היום עמנו הייתם במקום פלוני" — שטר ועדיו כשרין, חיישינן שמא איחרוהו וכתבוהו. ושקלו וטרו ר' חנינא ורבינא לאוקמי תרוייהו מתני' ומתניתא ולא דמו חדא מנייהו, וקי"ל דלא מותבי' תיובתא אלא ממשנה או ברייתא שהיא הלכה. ותו, הא בהדיא אמרי': קיום שטרות מדרבנן הוא, דאי מדאורייתא — לא בעינן, דקי"ל כריש לקיש, דאמר (כתובות דף יח:): עדים החתומים על השטר נעשה כמי שנחקרה עדותן בבית דין, ורבנן הוא דאצרכינהו קיום. ש"מ שבעל הבא לפסול את השטר עליו הראיה, הלכך מעמידין שטר זה בחזקת מאוחר, והטוען כי מוקדם הוא כדי לפסלו — עליו הראיה. **ור' יוסי פוסל.** שטר מאוחר דעלמא, שאין בתוכו הוכחה כלל, כדמפרש לקמיה. **והלא מעשה בא לפניך בצפורי.** בשטר מאוחר, והכשרת. **א"ל כשהכשרתי בזה.** שכתוב זמנו בשבת וביוה"כ הכשרתי, שמתוכו מוכיח שלא נכתב בזמנו, שהרי אין ישראל כותבין שטרות בשבת וביום הכפורים, והכל ידינו שהוא מאוחר, ולא נפיק מיניה חורבא כדלקמן. אבל במאוחר בעלמא, שזמנו כתוב ביום ראוי לכתיבה, ולא יוודע אם מאוחר הוא אם לאו — בההוא פליגנא עלך, ופסילנא. וטעמא לקמן. **אמר ר' פדת הכל מודים.** ר' יהודה ור' יוסי, בכל שטרות מאוחרין בענין זה, שכשאנו נזקקין למנות למתי מגיע עונתו של שטר, ונמצאת עונת הזמן הכתוב בו מכוון ביום השבת או בעשרה בתשרי — שטר מאוחר הוא זה, וכשר לדברי הכל. דדמי כמי שכתוב בתוכו "שטרא דנן דכתבנוהו לאו בזמניה כתבנוהו אלא אנן סהדי איחרנוהו וכתבנוהו", שהרי הכל יודעים שלא נכתב בשבת וביום הכפורים, ויכירו שהוא מאוחר, ולא אתי לידי חורבא כדמפרש לקמן. (ה) וה"ק ר' פדת: הכל מודים בההוא שטר דקתני כדאתא שטר שכתוב זמנו בשבת כו' דכשר, והיינו דקאמר ליה ר' יוסי: בזה הכשרתי.

לא

תוספות

אלא עדים שעשו שליחותן כו'. תימה קצת על הלשון, דמשמע (ו) שעשו שליחותן כבר גורם שלא יעשו. כי ההיא ד"התקבל" (גיטין דף סג:) דכתבי "תפוותא" ושמה היה "נפוותא", וקאמר: עשו עדים שליחותן ולא יכתבו עוד — התם ניחא, אבל הכא אין ליישב כלל, דכ"ש אם לא עשו שליחותן מעולם דהויא לה מלוה על פה, שאין יכולין לכתוב מזמן ראשון — דא"כ ה"ל מוקדם גמור! ועוד, דהתם בגיטין מה שאין יכולין לעשות שליחותן — זהו משום ששליחותן פסקה משעה שעשו את הראשון, ואם יעשו אחר — אין זה שליחותו של הבעל, שלא צוה לכתבו. אבל אם מלוה לכתוב שני — יכולין לעשות. והכא, אע"פ שלוה מלוה להם לכתוב לעשות שטר ראשון — לא יעשו, דאל"כ מאי דוחקיה דמלוה לקרוע שטר הראשון אם אין הלוה כופהו לכך? ואם כן רוצה הלוה בכך. דאין לומר כי הלוה אינו רוצה אלא מזמן שני — כי מה טענה היה לו בזה? וע"כ צריך כאן לפרש כן: וכי עדים אע"פ שעשו שליחותן וכבר חלה שעבוד על ידן, יכולין לעשות בשביל כך שטר אחר כיוצא בראשון מאחר שדומה למוקדם? ואפי' אם מלוה להם הלוה — אין זו סברא, שאם כן יאמרו כל שטר מוקדם כשר, ואתי למיחתם בשטר מוקדם. אבל במה שיכתבו לו ב"ד מזמן ראשון — לא יבא לחתום בשטר מוקדם, כי ידעו שהוא פסול, ובזה יתלו הכשרו, שב"ד אלימי לאפקועי ממונא. והלשון מגומגם ביותר.

כותבין אפילו עשרה שטרות. ואם תאמר: למאי דס"ד דבאחריות מיירי, תקשי הא דאמר לעיל (דף קסח:): אבל בשטרי מקח וממכר כותבין חוץ מאחריות שבו! וי"ל: דלעיל הכי פירושו, דהוא אמר אבד שטר חובי, וחיישינן דלמא טריף והדר טריף. אבל הכא איירי בשידוע לנו שנאבד, או ראינוהו שנשרף.

מזמן ראשון. ר' יהודה לא פירש לר' יוסי מזמן ראשון, אבל ברייתא היא שנויה במילתיה דרבי יהודה לפי האמת.

שאם הוזקקנו (ז) לעדותו של שטר. הא לישנא משמע שאין כתוב להדיא כך, אלא [ב]ג' בניסן [ג]והוא חל ביום חמישי, ועתה נמצאת ג' בניסן מכוונת בשבת. וכן ביום שני בשבת שניה של תשרי, [ד]והוא חל בשבת — נמצאת עונתו מכוונת ביום הכפורים. ותימה: נימא דטעה בקביעא דירחא, ויהיה כשר לרבי יוסי, ואמאי פסול? ולר' יהודה נמי, ניחא טפי למימר הכי ממה שנאמר שנכתב [ה] (לחוכא) בעלמא. בשלמא ליום הכפורים — לא קשיא מידי, כיון שמזכיר באיזה יום לשבוע שאותו יום היה ידוע שהיה יום הכפורים — שבזה לא היה טועה, אלא משבת קשה! ואומר ר"י: דמיירי אחר רובו של חדש, כדאמר ב"היו בודקין" (סנהדרין דף מא:) דאי אפשר דלא שמע.

מתקיף

עין משפט נר מצוה

קב א מיי' פכ"ג מהל' מלוה ולוה הל' יב סמג עשין צד טוש"ע ח"מ סי' נג סעיף א:

קג ב טוש"ע ח"מ סי' רלט סעיף א בהג"ה:

קד ג מיי' פכ"ג מהל' מלוה ולוה הלכה ד סמג עשין צד טוש"ע ח"מ סי' מג סעיף יד:

רבינו גרשום

שלם דבית דין יש להם כח לעשות כן: אלא עדים שעשו שליחותן. בפעם ראשונה שחתמו כשהיה כל החוב שלם כשטורף מאותו זמן מי יש להן כח לחזור ולעשות שליחות אחרת לקרוע ולכתוב שטר שני ולחתום בו שיטרוף מזמנו של ראשון והא נפרע לו החצי והאי שטרא אחרינא הוא: ומקשי' ולא. ואין כח לעדים לחזור ולעשות שליחות אחרת: והאמר רב יהודה כותבין העדים אם רצו אפי' עשרה שטרות על שדה אחת. היינו כמה שליחות: ומשני רב יוסף אמר בשטר מתנה. יכול לעשות אפי' עשר' שטרות לפי שבשטר מתנה אם יוציא בע"ח ממנו המתנה (אינן) יכולין העדי' לכתוב אפי' י' שטרות שלא באחריות דכיון שאין בהם אחריות לא מצי טריף בהו לקוחות. אבל בשטרי הלואה שיוכלו לטרוף בהן אין כח לעדים לחזור ולעשות שליחות אחרת לקרוע ולכתוב אלא בית דין אלו ולא עדים: מאי ברייתא. דאמר רב נחמן ואי שמיעא ליה לרב. זו היא עיקר הברייתא דתניא הרי שהיו נושין כו'. ומפני ב' דברים אמרו כותבין שובר. שניהן תקנת המלוה אחד כדי שיכוף ללוה לפורעו שמפחד שמא יאבד שוברו ונמצא זה מוציא שטרו וגוב' חובו משלם. ואחר ששטרו קיים ויכול לטרוף הלקוחות מזמן ראשון אע"פ שיפרע לו מקצת חובו: ומקשי' והא ר' יהודה נמי מזמן ראשון אמר. אם כן במאי קא פליג ר' יוסי עליה: הכי קאמר ליה ר' יוסי לר' יהודה אי מזמן ראשון קאמרת. כדאמינא אנא: פליגנא עלך בחדא. דאמינא דכותבין שובר ואת אמרת דליחלף: ואי מזמן שני קאמרת. כדאוקימנא לטעמא במתני': פליגנא עלך בתרתי. דסבירא לי דגובה מזמן ראשון וכותבין שובר: שזמנו כתוב בשב' או בי' בתשרי. שהוא יום הכפורים לוה פלוני מפלוני והוא הדין נמי בשאר מועדים בידוע ודאי שההלואה לא היתה באותו היום אלא להכי כתבו כך להודיע שזמן השטר מאוחר הוא כשר: ור' יוסי פוסל. דמחזי כשיקרא: והלא מעשה בא לפניך. בשטר שכתב בו והכשרת אמר לו כשהכשרתי בזה הכשרתי. שנכתב זמנו בשבת ור' יוסי הוה פוסלו: הכל מודים. בין ר' יהודה בין ר' יוסי שאם כתב שכתבו העדים הוזקקנו לידע עונתו של שטר ונמצא כו' דידוע ששטר מאוחר הוא וכשר. לפי שהואיל שבכונה דקדקו העדים וכתבו כן בידוע כדי ללמדנו ששטר מאוחר הוא ובההוא אמר בזה הכשרתי:

מסורת הש"ס

...תוספתא למכות פ"א ... ב) לפי האמת נ"ל ...ניסן. רש"ל: ג) פי' ר"ח ... ד) פי' ר"ח תשרי: ... ה) [נ"ל לחוכה]:

הגהות הב"ח

...רשב"ם ד"ה אלא וכו' ...נתן: (ב) ד"ה ומשני ...דכיון להכל: (ג) ד"ה ...ינן והא רבי יהודה: ... ד"ה בתרתי פליגנא ... דכותבין כצ"ל ותיבת ...מחק: (ה) ד"ה אמר ... פדת וכו' כדמפרש ...ן הס"ד ואח"כ מתחיל ...ה והכי קאמר: ...תוס' ד"ה אלא וכו' ...מע דלפי שעשו וכו' ... יעשו עוד כי ההיא: ... ד"ה שאם הוזקקנו ...תו של שטר וכו' אחר ... נ"ב ולפי זה נ"ל ...ה כתוב בשטר י"ז בניסן:

עין משפט
נר מצוה

קה א ב מיי' פכ"ג מהל' מלוה ולוה הלכה טז סמג עשין צד טוש"ע ח"מ סי' נב סעיף ב:
קו ג מיי' שם הל' א וסמג שם טוש"ע ח"מ סי' מג סעיף ז:
קז ד מיי' שם הל' ב טוש"ע שם סעיף יג:
קח ה מיי' שם הל' ז טוש"ע שם סעי' יב:
קט ו מיי' שם הלכה ז טוש"ע שם סעי' כד:

לא נחלקו אלא בשטר מאוחר בעלמא, דרבי יהודה לטעמיה, דאמר: א)אין כותבין שובר, ולא נפיק מיניה חורבא; ורבי יוסי לטעמיה, דאמר: כותבין שובר, ונפיק מיניה חורבא. אמר רב הונא בריה דרב יהושע: אפילו למ"ד כותבין שובר, הני מילי אפלגא, אבל אכוליה לא. ולא היא, (א) א אפי' אכוליה כתבינן; ב כי הא דרב יצחק בר יוסף הוה מסיק ביה זוזי ברבי אבא, אתא לקמיה דרבי חנינא בר פפי, אמר ליה: הב לי זוזיי. אמר ליה: הב לי שטראי ושקול זוזך. אמר ליה: שטרך אירכס לי, אכתוב לך תברא. אמר ליה, הא רב ושמואל דאמרי תרווייהו: אין כותבין שובר! אמר: ב)מאן יהיב לן מעפריה דרב ושמואל רמינן בעיינין, הא רבי יוחנן והא ריש לקיש דאמרי תרווייהו: כותבין שובר. וכן כי אתא רבין אמר ר' אילעא: כותבין שובר. ומסתברא ג)דכותבין שובר, דאי סלקא דעתא אין כותבין שובר, אבד שטרו של זה – יאכל הלה וחדי? מתקיף לה אביי: ואלא מאי, כותבין שובר? אבד שוברו של זה – יאכל הלה וחדי? א"ל רבא: ד)אין, "עבד לוה לאיש מלוה". ה)תנן התם: ג שטרי חוב המוקדמין – פסולין, ו והמאוחרין – כשרין. א"ר המנונא: לא שנו אלא שטרי הלואה, אבל שטרי מקח וממכר – ה אפילו מאוחרין נמי פסולין; מ"ט? זימנין דמזבין ליה ארעא בניסן וכתיב ליה (ב) בתשרי, ומתרמי ליה זוזי ביני ביני וזבין ליה מיניה. וכי מטי תשרי מפיק ליה ואמר ליה: הדר זבנתה מינך. אי הכי, שטרי הלואה נמי, זמנין דיזיף בניסן וכתיב ליה שטרא בתשרי, ומתרמי ליה זוזי ביני ביני ופרע ליה, ואמר ליה: הב לי שטראי, וא"ל: אירכס לי, וכתיב ליה תברא. וכי מטי זמניה מפיק ליה וא"ל: (ג) הני השתא הוא דיזפת מינאי! קסבר: אין כותבין שובר. אמר ליה רב ייסר לרב כהנא, ואמרי לה רב ירמיה מדיפתי לרב כהנא: (ד) והאידנא ו)דכתבינן שטרי מאוחרי וכתבינן תברא, (אמאי קעבדינן הכי? א"ל:) בתר דאמר להו ר' אבא לספריה: כי כתביתו שטר מאוחרי, כתבו הכי: "שטרא דנן לא בזמניה כתבניה, אלא אחרנוהו וכתבנוהו". א"ל רב אשי לרב כהנא: (ה) והאידנא דלא קא עבדינן הכי! בתר דאמר ליה רב ספרא לספריה: כי כתביתו הני תברי, אי ידעיתו זימנא דשטרא – כתבו, אי לא – כתבו סתמא, ו דכל אימת דנפיק לרעיה. אמר ליה רבינא לרב אשי, ואמרי לה רב אשי לרב כהנא: והא

לא נחלקו אלא בשטר מאוחר בעלמא. שמגיע עונתו ביום חול, ולא יוודע אם מאוחר אם לאו. ונפיק מיניה חורבא. אליבא דר' יוסי, כדמפרש ואזיל. ויש מפרשים: א"ר פדת הכל מודים שאם הוזקקנו כו' – שכך כתוב בתוך השטר, "הוזקקנו לעונתו של שטר ונמלאת" כו', וכל זה דכתב בשטר – לדעת כן נכתב, שידינו שאין ישראל כותבין בשבת, וידעו שהוא מאוחר. לא נחלקו אלא בשטר מאוחר בעלמא, שכתוב בו זמנו בשבת או בעשרה בתשרי, ולא חזר וכתב בו "הוזקקנו לעונתו של שטר" כו'. וכל זה הבל ולינות הוא; חדא – דהכי הוה ליה למימר: אמר ר' פדת הכל מודים שאם כתב בו הוזקקנו כו'. ועוד: כיון דכתב זמנו בשבת, למה לי למכתב "הוזקקנו" כו'? הא מאליה אנו יודעין שלא נכתב ביום השבת וביום הכפורים, ומאוחר הוא. כדפי' לעיל. דרבי יהודה. דמכשיר – לטעמיה, דאמר: אין כותבין שובר, הלכך לא חייש. בין מאוחר לכשנכתב בזמנו, לעולם אינו פורע עד שיקח השטר ויקרענו, וכיון שנקרע השטר – לא חייש למידי. ור' יוסי. דפוסל המאוחר. לטעמיה דאמר כותבין שובר. היכא דפרע מקצת חובו. וה"ה היכא דפרע כל חובו וטוען מלוה אירכס שטרי, כדמפרש לקמן – כותבין שובר ונותנין ללוה, להודיע שפרע כל חובו. והלכך האי שטר מאוחר פסול הוא כו'. (ו) ואמר ליה אירכס לי. וה"ה בלא אירכס, היכא דפרע חצי חובו וכתבו שובר ללוה – יכול המלוה להוציא אחרי כן שטר חובו שכתוב זמנו אחר זמן השובר, ויאמר: ממון אחר הוא זה שלוית ממני אחרי כן. ויגבה כל חובו משלם, שהרי אין ידוע שהוא מאוחר. אבל שטר שכתוב זמנו בשבת ועשרה בתשרי – לא מצי למימר השתא הוא דיזפת מינאי. אמר רב הונא בריה דרב יהושע כו'. מלתא באפי נפשיה היא. הני מילי פלגא – פן יחזור המלוה ויתבע כל חובו, אבל אכוליה חוביה – לא, דמלוה אפסיד אנפשיה שלא נזהר לשמור את שטרו. ומסתברא דכותבין שובר. אכוליה חוב, היכא דאירכס שטרא. יאכל הלה וחדי. בתמיה: ישמח באכילת ממון אחרים חנם? עבד לוה לאיש מלוה. מוטב שיהא טורח ודאגת שמירת שטר מוטל על הלוה יותר מן המלוה. תנן התם. בסדר זרעים, בפרק אחרון דמסכת שביעית. המוקדמים פסולין. שכתבוהו באחד באייר, ובתוך השטר הקדימו וכתבו בו באחד בניסן – פסולין, דאתי למיטרף לקוחות שלא כדין. ואפי' מזמן שני לא גובה, כדאמרינן ב"איזהו נשך" (ב"מ דף עב.): ר' יוחנן אמר אפי' תימא רבנן, גזירה שמא יגבה מזמן ראשון. אבל מוקדמין בענין זה שנכתב בו באחד בניסן, ובאחד בניסן כתבוהו, ולא לוה עד תשרי, דאתא למיטרף לקוחות שלא כדין דמניסן ועד תשרי – בזה נחלקו בפרק "שנים אוחזין", רב אשי מוקי לה בשטרי הקנאה, ואביי אמר: עדיו בחתומיו זכין לו, ומיום כתיבת השטר שיעבד נפשיה, והלכך כשר. והמאוחרים כשרין. שכתבוהו באחד בניסן, וכתבו בתוך השטר באחד באייר. וכ"ש אם לוה בניסן ולא נכתב עד אייר, דכשר, שהרי מחל לו שעבוד של חדש שעבר. אמר רב המנונא לא שנו. דמאוחרים כשרים, אלא בשטרי הלואה, כדאמרן לעיל: ר' יהודה לטעמיה דאמר אין כותבין שובר, ולא נפיק מיניה חורבא. ורב המנונא ס"ל אין כותבין שובר, כדמתרץ לקמן, הלכך ליכא למיחש למידי. אבל בשטרי מקח וממכר אפי' מאוחרים פסולים. דזמנין דמזבן ראובן שדהו לשמעון בניסן על מנת שאם יגיע לדמים יחזירנה לו, וכשכתב שטר מקנה כתב בו "ראובן מכר שדה לשמעון בתשרי". וחזר ראובן ולקח שדהו משמעון בתמוז, וכששאל שטר מקנה, אמר ליה שמעון: אירכס לי. ואפילו למ"ד אין כותבין שובר – הכא מודה, דמה יפסיד שמעון אם לא יפדה ראובן שדהו? הלכך אפילו אם יכתוב לו שמעון לראובן שובר שפדה שדהו בתמוז – יחזור שמעון ויוציא שטרו הכתוב בתשרי, ויאמר: אחר שפדית חזרתי ולקחתיה ממך, והא שטרא. א"ה שטרי הלואה נמי כו'. כדאמרן לעיל אליבא דר' יוסי, דפסיל שטר מאוחר משום הך חורבא. קסבר רב המנונא אין כותבין שובר. הלכך מאוחרין כשרין כדאמרן אליבא דר' יהודה. (ז) האידנא כתבינן שטרי מאוחרין וכתבינן תברא. ולא חיישינן לחורבא דנפיק מיניה לר' יוסי לעיל. אמר ליה בתר דאמר להו ר' אבא לספריה כו'. ליכא למיחש מידי. דכיון דכתוב בתוך השטר שכתוב בו זמנו בשבת ועשרה בתשרי, דאכשרנא לעיל בין לר' יהודה בין לר' יוסי. דכיון דידעינן ביה בשטר שהוא מאוחר – לא אתי לידי חורבא, ושוברו מוכיח עליו שהוא פרוע, והאי דקדים ליה שובר היינו משום דשטר מאוחר כתבוה, כמו שכתבו בתוכו "אנן סהדי איחרנוהו", ואפי' ר' יוסי בזה מכשר. א"ל רב אשי לרב כהנא (ח) האידנא לא עבדינן הכי. אלא כתבינן שטר מאוחר וכתבינן תברא, ולא כתבינן בתוך השטר "איחרנוהו וכתבנוהו", ואפ"ה לא חיישינן לחורבא דר' יוסי. אדכרתון זמנא דשטרא כתובו. בתוך השובר: "פלוני פרע לפלוני חוב פלוני כך וכך של אותו השטר שכתוב בו זמן פלוני". ואז לא יוכל לרמות, שאפי' כתב את השטר מאוחר – הרי השובר מוכיח עליו דהוא פרוע. ואי לא. אדכרתון זמן הכתוב בשטר – כתבו השובר סתמא. שלא יהא כתוב שום זמן בשובר, אלא סכום המעות שהיו כתובין בשטר כותבין בשובר, דכי היכי דכל אימת דנפק השטר שכתוב בו סכום ממון כזה – לורעיה השובר, לא שנא אם השטר קודם לשובר לא שנא מאוחר הימנו, דהא תברא סתמא כתוב. ומעתה צריך המלוה ליזהר שלא ילוה עוד ללוה הזה כסכום ממון הכתוב בשובר, דהא תברא מרע ליה, ואם הלוהו כסכום ממון ההוא – הוא ניהו דאפסיד אנפשיה.
והאידנא

מתקיף לה אביי. (ט) נראה לר"י דקבלה מרבא. וכן הא דאמרי' בסוטה (דף ז: ושם ד"ה אתר) על משנה שוברת כתובתה ויולאת, ש"מ: כותבין שובר? אמר אביי: תני מקרעת – נראה דדיחויא הוא, דמהכא ליכא למשמע מינה, דהא בשמעתא דהטוען אחר מעשה ב"ד פרק "שנים אוחזין" (ב"מ דף יז: ושם ד"ה הוליאה) משמע דס"ל דכותבין שובר.

בתר דאמר ליה רב ספרא לספריה כי כתביתו האי תברא כו'. שמא היו *שוכחין לכתוב "האי שטרא" כו', ע"כ כתבו זה אי

רבינו גרשום

לא נחלקו אלא בשטר מאוחר דעלמא. דאין כתוב בו כן: ר' יהודה לטעמי' דאמר אין כותבין שובר. אלא מחליף השטר או מחזירו כשנפרע כולו כיון דאין כותבין שובר אע"ג דמאוחר הוא השטר לא נפיק מיניה חורבה. משום דמחזיר השטר עצמו ללוה בשעת פרעון: ורבי יוסי לטעמיה דאמר כותבין שובר. ולא מחזיר השטר עצמו הלכך האי שטר מאוחר פסול הוא משום דנפיק חורבה דפרע ליה זוזי ביני ביני בטבת: והני מילי אפלגא. דשלא פרע לו אלא פלגא מחצית הממון כותבין שובר ומניחין השטר שלם ביד המלוה מאי טעמא כדאמרינן לעיל מפני שני דברים אמרו כותבין שובר אחד כדי כו': אבל אכוליה. אי פרע ליה כל השטר לא כתיב שובר אלא מחזיר לו השטר עצמו: ואתא לקמיה דר' חנינא בר פפי. לדינא: אמר ליה. ר' אבא שהיה לוה: הא רב ושמואל דאמרי תרוייהו אין כותבין שובר. ואם לא תחזיר לי שטר עצמו לא אתן הפרעון: אמר ליה ר' חנינא בר פפי לר' אבא הא דמייתית ראיה מרב ושמואל כל כך היו חביבין עלינו דמאן יהיב לן מעפרייהו ומלין עיינין מינייהו מרוב חביבות. ברם הא ר' יוחנן וריש לקיש דאמרי כותבין ומצינו למיסמך עלייהו וזיל פרע ליה. דאי ס"ד אין כותבין שובר. אלא אם אינו מחזיר לו את השטר לא יפרע (אלא) אם כן אבד שטרו של זה שאינו יכול להחזירו לו. יאכל הלה. הלוה ממונו של מלוה וחדי: מתקיף לה אביי. ואם כותבין שובר ואבד שוברו יוציא הלה את שטרו ויחזיר ויגבה ממנו לפי שנאבד שוברו ויאכל ממונו [של] לוה פעם שניה וחדי: א"ל רבא אין. ודאי כותבין שובר שאם נאבד השטר שיפרע שאע"ג דאיכא למיחש דלא נאבד (ומעידין) אפ"ה כותבין משום דעבד לוה לאיש מלוה דבין כך ובין כך צריך לפרוע לו: ומתרמי לי' זוזי ביני ביני. בתמוז וזבין ליה מיניה. כלומר פריק לארעיה מיניה. לענין הלואה קסבר אין כותבין שובר אלא צריך להחזיר לו השטר עצמו ושוב שהחזירו אין יכול להוציאו אבל בשטרי מקח וממכר אין נוהג שובר דלא מצי למימר ליה אי לא כתבת לי שובר לא פרקנא לארעאי דלוקח מה איכפת לו אם לא יפדנה: והא האידנא. גבי שטר הלואה כתבינן מאוחרין וכתבינן תברא ולא חיישינן לדלמא מפיק לשטר והדר טריף: אמר ליה. היינו בתר דתיקן ר' אבא הא תקנתא דאמר לספרא כי כתביתו שטרא מאוחר כתבי הכ וכו' דכיון דכתיב ביה דלא בזמנא איכתב אלא מאוחר הוה להכי לא מצי גבי ביה זימנא אחריתי דאמרינן שמא זמנו נכתב אחר הפרעון הלכך כותבין שובר דליכא למיחש מידי: אי ידעיתו זמניה דההיא שטרא כתבו בתברא שטר פלוני זמנו בכך וכך נפרע ואי לא ידעיתו זמן השטר כתבו לתברא בלא זמן סתם דכל אימת דמפיק הא שטרא בתר הכי והאי מפיק ליה לתברא מרע לשטרא דכיון דאין בו זמן י"ל אחר זמן של שטר זה פרע לך והא

מסורת הש"ס

א) [שבת עט.]: ב) [ע חולין סח:] ועי' ערוך עפר א': ג) [כתובות וש"נ]: ד) [עי' תוס' כה טז: ד"ה כותבין]: ה) יז. עב. סנהדרין לב. ב. א. שביעית פ"י מ"ה קנז: : ו) רש"א דלא ע הכי ומ"ז:

הגהות הב"ח

(א) גמ' ולא היא אפילו: (ב) שם א בניסן וכתב ליה ש בתשרי: (ג) שם השתא הוא דיזפת ותיבת הני נמחק: (ד) ר' ירמיה מדיפתי כהנא והא האידנא דלא עבדינן הכי דכתבינן ש מאוחרי וכתבינן ת אמר ליה בתר דאמר ר' אבא כצ"ל: (ה) שם אשי לרב כהנא האידנא דלא קא עב הכי אמר ליה בתר דא להו רב ספרא לספ כי כתיבתו הני ת אי אדכרתון זי (ו) רשב"ם ד"ה לטע

והא האידנא דלא קעבדינן הכי! אמר ליה: רבנן תקוני תקיני, מאן דעביד – עביד, מאן דלא עביד – איהו הוא דאפסיד אנפשיה. אמר להו *רבא בר רב שילא להנהו כתבי שטרא אקנייאתא: כי כתביתו שטרי אקנייאתא, אאי ידעיתו יומא דקניתו ביה – כתבו, ואי לא – כתבו יומא דקיימיתו ביה, כי היכי דלא מתחזי כשקרא. א)אמר להו רב לספריה, וכן אמר להו רב הונא לספריה: בכי קיימיתו בשילי – כתבו בשילי, ואע"ג דמסירן לכו מילי בהיני; כי קיימיתו בהיני – כתבו בהיני, ואף על גב דמסירן לכו מילי בשילי. *אמר רבא: גהאי מאן דנקיט שטרא בר מאה זוזי, ואמר: שוויה ניהלי תרי בני חמשין – לא משוינן להו. מאי טעמא? עבדו רבנן מילתא דניחא ליה למלוה וניחא ליה ללוה; ניחא ליה למלוה – כדי שיכוף לפורעו, וניחא ללוה – כי היכי דניפגם שטריה. ואמר רבא: דהאי מאן דנקיט תרי שטרי בני חמשין, ואמר: שוינהו ניהלי חד בר מאה – לא משוינן ליה, עבוד רבנן מילתא דניחא ליה למלוה וניחא ליה ללוה; ניחא ליה למלוה – כי היכי דלא ניפגום שטריה, וניחא ליה ללוה – כדי שלא יכוף לפורעו. אמר רב אשי: ההאי מאן דנקיט שטרא בר מאה זוזי, ואמר: שוונהי ניהלי חד בר חמשין – לא משוינא ליה. מ"ט? אמרינן: האי מיפרע פרעיה, ואמר ליה: הב לי שטראי, ואמר ליה: אירכס לי, וכתיב ליה תברא, ומפיק ליה האי ואמר ליה: האי אחרינא הוא.§ **מתני'** ב)ושני אחין, אחד עני ואחד עשיר, והניח להן אביהן מרחץ ובית הבד; עשאן לשכר – השכר לאמצע. עשאן לעצמו – הרי העשיר אומר לעני: קח לך עבדים וירחצו במרחץ, קח לך זיתים ובא ועשה בבית הבד. זשנים שהיו בעיר אחת, שם אחד יוסף בן שמעון ושם אחר יוסף בן שמעון – אין יכולין להוציא שטר חוב זה על זה, ג)ולא אחר יכול להוציא עליהן שטר חוב. ד)חנמצא לאחד בין שטרותיו: "שטרו של יוסף בן שמעון פרוע" – שטרות שניהן פרועין. כיצד יעשו? ישלשו, ואם היו משולשין – יכתבו סימן, ואם היו מסומנין – ה)יכתבו כהן.§ **גמ'** ההוא שטרא דנפק (א) לבי דינא דרב הונא, דהוה כתיב ביה "אני פלוני בר פלוני לויתי מנה ממך",

אמר

רשב"ם

(ג) והאידנא לא עבדינן הכי. אלא כתבינן שטר מאוחר סתמא, דלא כתיב "איחרנוהו וכתבנוהו" וכתבינן תברא עלייהו" בשעת פרעון, וכתבינן זמן בשובר ולא כתבינן ליה סתמא, ולחורבא דרבי יוסי לא חיישינן. להנך דכתבי אקנייאתא. כותבי שטר מתנה שאין כתוב בהן אחריות, ולא אתי למיטרף מלקוחות. אי נמי, שטר מכירה שכתב בהן אחריות, שדינו לטרוף לקוחות משעת מכירה. דעדים מפקי ליה לקלא בלא שטר, כדאמרינן ב"חזקת הבתים" (לעיל דף מא:), אמר רב: המוכר שדהו בעדי' – גובה מנכסים משועבדים, וכדמפרש התם טעמא: מלוה אזוזי קא רמית כו'. הלכך, אי ידעיתון ההוא יומא דאקניתון ביה מן הנותן מתנה או מוכר מכירה – כתבו עכשיו אותו היום שנתנה המתנה והמכירה, דליכא למיחש שמא אחרי כן נתנה לאחר שלא כדין. (פסק) ודוקא שטרי אקנייתא, אבל שטרי הלואה שיש בו אחריות – לא יכתוב אלא יום שעומד בו עכשיו, דא"כ הוה ליה מוקדם ופסול, דאתי למיטרף לקוחות מזמן הכתוב בשטר שלא כדין. דלעולם אין לקוחות משועבדים לשום אדם כל זמן שלא נכתב שטר, עד שיקחו מן הלוה קרקעות אחר שנכתב השטר המשעבד נכסיו. הלכך, אי כתבי יומא שנעשית ההלואה בשטר זה – פסול הוא, דאתי למיטרף לקוחות שלקחו בין ההלואה לכתיבת השטר, והם לא נשתעבדו עד לאחר כתיבת השטר. דעדים החתומים על השטר אינהו מפקי ליה לקלא, כדאמרי' לענין הלואה ב"חזקת הבתים", ולקוחות שלקחו אחרי כן – אינהו הוא דאפסידו אנפשייהו. אבל מקמי כתיבת השטר – שפיר זבון. ואפילו נכתב ביום ונחתם בלילה חשבינן ליה מוקדם ופסול, דהא לא אשתעבוד לקוחות אלא מיום חתימה ואילך, ואיהו אתי למיטרף מיום כתיבתו שלא כדין. והכי תנן ב"המביא גט" (גיטין דף יז.): נכתב ביום ונחתם בלילה – פסול, ורבי שמעון מכשיר. שהיה ר' שמעון אומר: כל הגיטין שנכתבו ביום ונחתמו בלילה – פסולין, חוץ מגיטי נשים. והתם מפרש טעמא לענין גיטי נשים. מיהו, לענין שאר שטרות לכ"ע פסולין.(ג) פסק. אמס, רבינו חננאל פירש: דהא דרבה בר שילא שמעינן מינה דשטרא דכתיב בההוא יומא דקנו מיניה, ובתר כמה יומי אסהידו עליה הנהו סהדי קמאי – שפיר דמי, מדקאמר: אי ידעיתו יומא דאקניתו – כתבו ההוא יומא. ואף על גב דחתמי עליה האידנא – שפיר דמי, דלא אשכחן דבעו חתימת ההוא יומא אלא גט אשה בלבד, דתנן בגט: נכתב ביום ונחתם בלילה – פסול, וכן הלכה הוא. כך פר"ת. אך לא יתכן, אלא כמו שפירשתי, וכדפי' מתניתין דגיטין. כי יתביתו בשילי. ואתם כותבין שם אותה העיר בשטרי מכירה או שטרי הלואה או שטרי מתנה או זכרון עדות – כתבו בתוך השטר מקום שאתם יושבים שם בשעת כתיבה. כלומר: במקום פלוני כתבנו הך מה שראינו במקום פלוני. בהיני. מקום. האי מאן דנקיט. מלוה דנקיט שטר מלוה בר מאה זוזי, ואמר להם: כתבו לי תרי בני חמשים, שכשיפרע לי הלוה חמשים זוזי אקרע שטרא של חמשים, ולא יהיה צריך לכתוב שובר – לא כתבינן שלא מדעת הלוה. מ"ט עבוד רבנן מילתא. שתקנו שלא ישנה שטרו מכמות שהיה, דניחא ליה כו'. כי היכי דליכוף ולפרעיה. כשיפרענו לוה למלוה חצי חובו – יכופנו מלוה לפרוע לו השאר, כי ידאג הלוה פן יפסיד שוברו ויתבעהו מלוה כל חובו. כי היכי דליפגום שטרו. כשיפרע חמשים זוז הרי נמצא שטר שביד מלוה פגום, ותנן (כתובות דף פז.): הפוגמת כתובתה לא תפרע אלא בשבועה. וה"ה לכל השטרות, כדאמרי' במסכת שבועות: וכי מה בין זה לפוגם שטרו כו', בפ' "שבועת הדיינין" (דף מא.). כי היכי דלא ליפגום שטרו. אך כשיפרענו חמשים זוז יחזיר לו שטר של חמשים, ונשאר בידו שטר של חמשים שני שלם. אמר רב אשי האי מאן דנקט שטר. מלוה בר מאה זוזי, ואמר להו לספרי: כתובו חד בר חמשים מההוא זמן ראשון, שהרי פרע לי המותר וקרעו שטר זה – לא כתבינן ליה שטר אחרינא, לא מזמן ראשון, וכל שכן מזמן זה של יום כתיבה ואילך. שמא שטר פרוע הוא זה ויש לו שובר ללוה עליו, ויוציא המלוה עליו שטר של חמשים, ויאמר: חוב אחר הוא זה, שהלויתי לך פעם אחרת. **מתני'** הרי עשיר אומר לעני כו'. ואפי' למאן דאמר בפרק קמא (לעיל דף יג.) דאית דינא דגוד או אגוד – שאני הכא, ד"גוד" איכא, "אגוד" ליכא. והכי מתרץ לה התם. קח לך עבדים. דבהיא חזקה שהניחו אביו יהיה לעולם, ולא יניחו לו להרבות ולהביא בני אדם במרחץ, אלא מבני ביתו. אינן יכולין להוציא שטר חוב זה על זה. שיכול הלה לטעון: שטר זה שבידך אני החזרתיו לך כשהחזרת לי ממון שלוית בו ממני. ולא אחר יכול להוציא. על אחד מהם, דכל חד מצי מדחי ליה אצל חבירו, אא"כ יש עדים בדבר שמעידין: זה לוה מזה. אבל מן השטר אין יכולין להביא ראיה. נמצא לאחד בין שטרותיו כו'. בגמ' פריך עלה מרישא, ומפרש לה שפיר. כיצד יעשו. אם רוצים ללוות זה מזה, או מאיש אחר, או לקנות קרקע. ישלשו. אבי אביו, ויכתוב: יוסף בן שמעון בן יעקב, וזה יכתוב: יוסף בן שמעון בן נפתלי. משולשים. ששמותיהן ושמות אביהן ושמות אבי אביהן שוין. יכתבו סימן. יוסף בן שמעון שהוא גוץ, או לבן, או גיחור, לוה מיוסף בן שמעון שהוא ארוך או שחור. ואם היו (ד) סימניהן. שוין. יכתבו כהן. אם אחד מהן כהן, יכתבו: יוסף כהן לוה מיוסף ישראל. **גמ'** ההוא שטרא דנפק (ה) לבי דינא דרב הונא. והיה מוחזק בו אדם אחד שהיה טוען: פלוני בן פלוני הכתוב בזה השטר כתבו וחתמו ומסרו לי, לפי שהלויתיו כך וכך ממון. וכדתנן מתניתין בפירקין (דף קעה:): הוציא עליו כתב ידו שהוא חייב לו – גובה מנכסים בני חורין. ואת שמי לא הוצרך לכתוב, שהרי מסרו לי, וכתב לי "ממך" – כלומר ממי שמוחזק בשטר.

אמר

תוספות

אי ידעיתו יומא דאקניתו ביה כתובו. בשטרי אקנייתא דוקא, אבל בהלואות לא איירי, כך פירש רשב"ס. ואומר ר"י: דלא שנא במכר לא שנא במתנה איירי, דאפילו בשטרי מקח וממכר משכחת לה, כגון דכתבי מדעת [ז]עדים דללקוחות — ליכא הכא פסידא כלל, דיש קול למקח וממכר, וליכא למיחש למידי. **כתבו** בשילי. היני ושילי קרובות זו לזו, להכי נקט להו. שאפילו בשתי עיירות קרובות זו לזו כתבו על שם העיר שתעמדו בה בשעת כתיבה. וגם היו רגילין תדיר להיות בהיני ושילי, והכי אמרינן בגילה (דף כה: ע"ש): הוי מכתפי (ו) לה בשבתא דריגלא משילי להיני ומהיני לשילי. **עבידו** ליה תרי שטרי כו'. מאי טעמא כו'. תימה: אמאי לא קאמר דפרוע הוא, כדאמר רב אשי בסמוך? ואומר ר"י: דהכא איירי אפי' ידעינן שאינו פרוע.

מינך

עין משפט נר מצוה

קי א מיי' פכ"ג מהל' מלוה ולוה הלכה ו סמג עשין צד טוש"ע ח"מ סי' מג סעיף יט:

קיא ב מיי' פ"א מהל' גירושין הל' כח ופכ"ג מהל' מלוה ולוה הלכה ו סמג עשין נ וסמג עשין צד טוש"ע ח"מ סי' מג סעי' כ וטוש"ע אה"ע סי' קכז סעיף ו:

קיב ג ד ה מיי' פכ"ג מהל' מלוה ולוה הל' יז יח סמג עשין צד טוש"ע ח"מ סי' מג:

קיג ו מיי' פ"ו מהל' שכנים הל' כ סמג עשין פב טוש"ע ח"מ סי' קעג סעיף ו:

קיד ז מיי' פכ"ד מהל' מלוה ולוה הלכה ח סמג עשין צד טוש"ע ח"מ סי' מט סעיף ז:

קטו ח מיי' שם טוש"ע שם סעי' ט:

רבינו גרשום

והא האידנא. דעבדינן שטר מאוחר וכתבי תברא ולא כתבי בסתמא אלא כתבי בהו זמן ולא חיישינן: אמר ליה רבנן תקוני תקיני. כנגד הרמאי ולכתוב שובר בסתם מאן דעבד הכי עביד. אין יכול המלוה לחזור ולגבות ממנו כלום ומאן דלא עביד הכי שוברו בסתם אם המלוה רמאי הוא יכול לחזור ולגבות דאיהו דאפסיד אנפשיה דאיבעי ליה למכתב שוברו בסתם כדתקינו רבנן: כי קיימיתו בשילי. שם מקום ואתם רוצים לכתוב באיזה מקום נכתב השטר כתבו שנכתב בשילי: ואע"ג דמסירן לכו מילי בהיני. כלומר אע"ג דבהיני היתה ההלואה ושם מסרו לכם המעשה שתהיו עדים בדבר ואם לא הספקתם לכתוב שם השטר כתבו שנכתב בשילי ולא בהיני דלא מיחזו כשיקרא וכן כי קיימיתו בהיני כו': שטרי אקנייתא. שום שטר שיש בו קנין: ואי לא. דלא בעיתו למכתב מיומא דקיימיתו ותרצו לכוון באומדן דעתא את הקנין ולא ידעיתו בברור אימת הוה ותכתבו בתר אומר מיחזו כשקרא: ניחא ליה למלוה וניחא ליה ללוה. דלא ליהוי אלא חד שטרא ניחא ליה ללוה דליפגום שטרא דמלוה דכיון דלית ליה אלא חד שטר ופרע ממנו חציו נמצא השטר פגום דאין יכול המלוה ליפרע ממנו עוד אלא בשבועה כדתנן הפוגם את שטרו לא נפרע אלא בשבועה: וניחא ליה למלוה. שיהא לו שטר אחד גדול שאם פרע לו הלוה חציו וזה כותב לו שובר על חציו וכיון דיש ביד המלוה עדיין שטרו שלם יכוף הלוה את עצמו וימהר לפרוע לו הכל שמתירא שמא יאבד שוברו ויוציא הלה את שטרו ויאמר שלא פרע לו עדיין כלום: ניחא ליה למלוה דלא ליפגום שטריה. שאם פרע האחד השני לא יפרע ממנו כלום ולא יפגום וגובה ממנו בלא שבועה: וניחא ליה ללוה. הואיל שאין החוב שלו כולו בשטר אחד אם פרע לו האחד מחזיר לו אותו שנפרע כולו ואין בידו אלא שטר אחד שלא נפרע ממנו כלום ואין יכול לכופו ולהפחידו שיתבע ממנו יותר ממה שחייב לו שהרי החזיר לו השטר הפרוע ולא נשאר בידו אלא אותו שעדיין לא פרע ממנו כלום: ואמר שויה ניהליה חד בר חמשין. שמוחל החצי: לא משוינן. מאי טעמא דאמר האי לוה פרעיה כוליה ואמר ליה הב לי שטרי שפרעתיך ואמר אירכס כו' ואמר ליה הא אחרינא הוא ועדים כדי שלא יכירוהו: **פיס'** עשאן אביהן האי מרחץ ובית הבד לשכר. כדי להשכירן ליטול מהן שכר רחיצה ושכר דריכה יכול העני לכופו לעשיר שישכיר אותם ויחלקו השכר לאמצע: עשאן אביהן לעצמו. ולא להשכירן לאחרים יכול העשיר לכופו לעני שלא להשכירן אלא אומר לו לעני קח לך. כלומר כדרך שאבינו היה עושה לעצמו ולא היה משכיר: אני פלוני בן פלוני לויתי ממך סתם. ולא היה כתוב שמו של מלוה:

אמר

מסורת הש"ס

ג) גיטין פ. יבמות קטז. ב) לעיל יג.: [גיטין כד:] ג) ב"מ כ: ה) [עי' תוספות תוכות כד: ד"ה אמנה:] ד) רש"א ר"ע מדעת עדיהם:

נ"א רבה

רש"א כי היכי דלא מתחזי כשקרא וכן הוא גי' הרי"ף והרא"ש

הגהות הב"ח

(א) גמ' דנפק בבי דינא דרב הונא: (ב) רשב"ם ד"ה והא האידנא לא עבדינן וכו' דלא כתיב בהו אוחרנוהו: (ג) ד"ה להנך וכו' פסק ודוקא שטרי אקנייתא וכו' לכ"ע פסולין ע"כ פסק אמס רבינו חננאל: (ד) ד"ה ואם היו מסומנין סימניהן שוין: (ה) ד"ה ההוא וכו' בבי דינא: (ו) תוס' ד"ה כתבו וכו' מכתפי ליה בשבתא:

קטז א מיי' פ"א מהל' גירושין הלכה כו סמג עשין נ טוש"ע אה"ע סי' קכו סעיף ז:
קיז ב מיי' פכ"ד מהל' מלוה ולוה הל' ט סמג עשין צד טוש"ע ח"מ סי' נ וסי' סח סעיף י:
קיח ג מיי' שם וסמג שם טוש"ע ח"מ סי' מט סעיף ז:

אָמַר רַב הוּנָא: "מִמְּךָ" — אֲפִילּוּ מֵרֵישׁ גָּלוּתָא, וַאֲפִילּוּ מִשָּׁבוּר מַלְכָּא. א)אֲמַר לֵיהּ רַב חִסְדָּא לְרַבָּה: פּוּק עַיֵּין בָּהּ, דִּלְאוּרְתָּא בָּעֵי לָהּ רַב הוּנָא מִינָּךְ. נְפַק דַּק וְאַשְׁכַּח, דְּתַנְיָא: גֵּט שֶׁיֵּשׁ עָלָיו עֵדִים וְאֵין בּוֹ זְמַן, אַבָּא שָׁאוּל אוֹמֵר: אאִם כָּתוּב בּוֹ "גֵּרַשְׁתִּיהָ הַיּוֹם" — כָּשֵׁר. אַלְמָא: "הַיּוֹם" — הַהוּא יוֹמָא דְּנָפֵיק בֵּיהּ מַשְׁמַע, בהָכָא נַמִי "מִמְּךָ" — מֵהַהוּא גַּבְרָא דְּנָפֵיק מִתּוּתֵי יְדֵיהּ מַשְׁמַע. אֲמַר לֵיהּ אַבַּיֵי: וְדִלְמָא אַבָּא שָׁאוּל כְּרַבִּי ב)אֱלִיעֶזֶר סְבִירָא לֵיהּ, ג)דְּאָמַר: עֵדֵי מְסִירָה כָּרְתֵי, אֲבָל הָכָא לֵיחוּשׁ לִנְפִילָה! אֲמַר לֵיהּ: לִנְפִילָה לָא חָיְישִׁינַן. וּמְנָא תֵּימְרָא דְּלָא חָיְישִׁינַן לִנְפִילָה? דִּתְנַן: שְׁנַיִם שֶׁהָיוּ בְּעִיר אַחַת, שֵׁם אֶחָד יוֹסֵף בֶּן שִׁמְעוֹן וְשֵׁם אַחֵר יוֹסֵף בֶּן שִׁמְעוֹן — אֵינָן יְכוֹלִין לְהוֹצִיא שְׁטַר חוֹב זֶה עַל זֶה, וְלֹא אַחֵר יָכוֹל לְהוֹצִיא עֲלֵיהֶן שְׁטַר חוֹב; גהָא הֵם עַל אֲחֵרִים — יְכוֹלִין, וְאַמַּאי? לֵיחוּשׁ לִנְפִילָה! אֶלָּא לָאו שְׁמַע מִינַּהּ: לִנְפִילָה לָא חָיְישִׁינַן. וְאַבַּיֵי? לִנְפִילָה דְּחַד לָא חָיְישִׁינַן, לִנְפִילָה דְּרַבִּים חָיְישִׁינַן.

וְאֶלָּא

רשב"ם

אָמַר רַב הוּנָא. "מִמְּךָ" מַשְׁמַע אֲפִילּוּ מֵרֵישׁ גָּלוּתָא. כְּלוֹמַר, שֶׁמָּא רֵישׁ גָּלוּתָא אוֹ אָדָם אַחֵר הִלְוָהוּ, וְנָפַל מִמֶּנּוּ וּמְצָאתוֹ. וְאֵין לְפָרֵשׁ שֶׁבָּא רַב הוּנָא לוֹמַר שֶׁיִּגְבֶּה שְׁטָרוֹ זֶה הַמּוּחְזָק, דְּמַשְׁמַע: כָּל מִי שֶׁמּוּחְזָק בִּשְׁטָר, וַאֲפִילּוּ רֵישׁ גָּלוּתָא מוּחְזָק בּוֹ, שֶׁאֵין רָגִיל לְהַלְווֹת, יִגְבֶּה לוֹ בּוֹ – דְּא"כ הֲוָה לֵיהּ לְמֵימַר (א) כִּדְלְקַמָּן: "מִמְּךָ" — הַהוּא [גַּבְרָא] דְּנָפֵיק מִתּוּתֵי יְדֵיהּ מַשְׁמַע. וְאֵין בּוֹ זְמַן. וְהוּא אֶחָד מִשְּׁלֹשָׁה גִּיטִּין פְּסוּלִין, וְאִם נִיסֵּת הַוָּלָד כָּשֵׁר, בְּפֶ' "הַמְגָרֵשׁ" (גיטין דף פו.). אֲנִי הַיּוֹם גֵּירַשְׁתִּיךְ כָּשֵׁר. קס"ד הַשְׁתָּא, כֵּיוָן דְּעֵדִים קָא חָזוּ לֵיהּ בִּידֵיהּ וְכָתוּב בּוֹ "הַיּוֹם" — הֲרֵי כָּתַב בּוֹ זְמַן. הַהוּא יוֹמָא דְּנָפֵיק. בְּבֵ"ד לְהִתְגָּרֵשׁ הָאִשָּׁה מַשְׁמַע, וְחָשְׁבִינַן לֵיהּ כִּזְמַן גָּמוּר. ה"נ מַשְׁמַע מִמְּךָ כו'. דְּהָא חָזוּ לֵיהּ ב"ד בְּיָדוֹ, וּכְמִי שֶׁנִּכְתַּב שֵׁם הַמַּלְוֶה בִּשְׁטָר דָּמֵי. דִּלְמָא אַבָּא שָׁאוּל. לָא חָיֵישׁ לְשׁוּם זְמַן בְּגִיטִּין בְּדִיעֲבַד, וּכְדְר' אֱלְעָזָר ס"ל, דִּתְנַן בְּפֶ' "הַמְגָרֵשׁ" (שם): שְׁלֹשָׁה גִּיטִּין פְּסוּלִין, וְאִם נִיסֵּת הַוָּלָד כָּשֵׁר: כָּתַב בִּכְתַב יָדוֹ וְאֵין עָלָיו עֵדִים, יֵשׁ עָלָיו עֵדִים וְאֵין בּוֹ זְמַן, יֵשׁ בּוֹ זְמַן וְאֵין בּוֹ אֶלָּא עֵד אֶחָד — הֲרֵי אֵלּוּ שְׁלֹשָׁה גִּיטִּין פְּסוּלִין, וְאִם נִיסֵּת הַוָּלָד כָּשֵׁר. ר"א אוֹמֵר: אע"פ שֶׁאֵין עָלָיו עֵדִים, אֶלָּא שֶׁנְּתָנוֹ לָהּ בִּפְנֵי עֵדִים — כָּשֵׁר, וְגוֹבָה מִנְּכָסִים מְשׁוּעְבָּדִים, שֶׁאֵין הָעֵדִים חוֹתְמִין עַל הַגֵּט אֶלָּא מִפְּנֵי תִּיקּוּן הָעוֹלָם. וְכִי הֵיכִי דְּרַבִּי אֱלְעָזָר מַכְשִׁיר לֵיהּ בְּלֹא עֵדִים מִשּׁוּם טַעֲמָא דְּעֵדֵי מְסִירָה כָּרְתֵי – ה"נ מַכְשִׁיר לֵיהּ בְּלֹא זְמַן מִשּׁוּם הַאי טַעֲמָא גּוּפֵיהּ. כִּדְקָתָנֵי יֵשׁ עָלָיו עֵדִים וְאֵין בּוֹ זְמַן בְּהַאי מִשְׁנָה דִּשְׁלֹשָׁה גִּיטִּין פְּסוּלִין, וַעֲלַהּ קָאֵי ר' אֱלְעָזָר וְאָמַר: אע"פ שֶׁאֵין עָלָיו עֵדִים בְּהַאי שְׁטָר שֶׁאֵין בּוֹ זְמַן – כָּשֵׁר, שֶׁאֵין הָעֵדִים חוֹתְמִין עַל הַגֵּט אֶלָּא מִפְּנֵי תִּיקּוּן הָעוֹלָם. וְה"נ אֵין כּוֹתְבִין בּוֹ זְמַן אֶלָּא מִפְּנֵי תִּיקּוּן הָעוֹלָם דְּבַת אֲחוֹתוֹ וּפֵירוֹת, כִּדְמְפָרֵשׁ בְּפֶ' ("כָּל הַגֵּט") ["הַמֵּבִיא תִּנְיָינָא"] (שם דף יז.), וְכֵיוָן שֶׁנְּתָנוֹ לָהּ בִּפְנֵי עֵדִים — הֵם יָעִידוּ עַל הַזְּמַן וְעַל הַגֵּט. וְהַאי דְּמַצְרִיךְ אַבָּא שָׁאוּל לִכְתּוֹב בּוֹ "אֲנִי הַיּוֹם גֵּירַשְׁתִּיךְ" – לָאו מִשּׁוּם זְמַן, דְּהָא אֵין זֶה זְמַן, וְלִזְמַן לָא חָיֵישׁ כְּר' אֱלְעָזָר. אֶלָּא דְּבָעֵי אַבָּא שָׁאוּל יָדַיִם מוֹכִיחוֹת דְּמִשָּׁעָה שֶׁקִּבְּלָה הַגֵּט נִתְגָּרְשָׁה מִיָּד. שֶׁאִם לֹא נִכְתַּב "מֵהַיּוֹם" בְּגֵט זֶה שֶׁאֵין בּוֹ זְמַן – מִנַּיִן לָנוּ שֶׁיְּהֵא גֵּט? שֶׁמָּא אֵין בְּדַעְתּוֹ לְגָרְשָׁהּ מִיָּד בְּגֵט זֶה עַד סוֹף שָׁנָה אוֹ שְׁנָתַיִם לְאַחַר קַבָּלָתָהּ! הִלְכָּךְ בָּעֵי אַבָּא שָׁאוּל שֶׁיִּכְתְּבוּ "הַיּוֹם" אֲחֵרֵי שֶׁאֵין זְמַנּוֹ כָּתוּב בּוֹ שֶׁיּוֹכִיחַ עָלָיו, כְּר' יוֹסֵי דְּאָמַר (לעיל דף קלו.) זְמַנּוֹ שֶׁל שְׁטָר מוֹכִיחַ עָלָיו. וְהַאי דְּאָמַר אַבָּא שָׁאוּל – הַיְינוּ דְּכָתְבִינַן בְּגֵט "מִן יוֹמָא דְּנַן וּלְעָלַם". אֲבָל הָכָא לֵיחוּשׁ לִנְפִילָה. וְכִדְרַב הוּנָא, דְּאָמַר: "מִמְּךָ" – אֲפִילּוּ מֵרֵישׁ גָּלוּתָא, וְשֶׁמָּא מֵאַחֵר נָפַל וּמְצָאוֹ זֶה. הָא הֵן עַל אֲחֵרִים מוֹצִיאִין. אֶחָד מֵהֶן שֶׁיֵּשׁ לוֹ שְׁטָר עַל אַחֵר שֶׁיִּגְבֶּה מִמֶּנּוּ, וְלֹא יָכוֹל זֶה לִטְעוֹן "מֵחֲבֵירְךָ נָפַל וּמְצָאתוֹ". נִמְצֵינוּ לְמֵדִין שֶׁמִּי שֶׁמּוּחְזָק בִּשְׁטָר – יָכוֹל לִגְבּוֹת מִלְוֶה מֵאִישׁ אַחֵר הַכָּתוּב בְּתוֹכוֹ, וְאע"פ שֶׁהַשְּׁטָר אֵין מוֹכִיחַ מִי הַמַּלְוֶה. וְה"ה "לָוִיתִי מִמְּךָ". וְאַבַּיֵי לִנְפִילָה דְּחַד לָא חָיְישִׁינַן. כְּגוֹן שְׁטָר שֶׁבְּיַד יוֹסֵף בֶּן שִׁמְעוֹן שֶׁיֵּשׁ לוֹ עַל אֶחָד מִן הַשּׁוּק, דְּהַיְינוּ נְפִילָה דְּחַד וּמְצִיאָה דְּחַד – הֵיכִי אִיתְרְמִי מִילְּתָא דְּמִיּוֹסֵף בֶּן שִׁמְעוֹן נָפַל וְיוֹסֵף בֶּן שִׁמְעוֹן מְצָאוֹ? הִלְכָּךְ לָא חָיְישִׁינַן. אֲבָל גַּבֵּי "לָוִיתִי מִמְּךָ מָנֶה" דְּהַיְינוּ נְפִילָה דְּרַבִּים, שֶׁיֵּשׁ לָחוּשׁ מֵאִישׁ אַחֵר בָּעוֹלָם נָפַל וְאִישׁ אַחֵר בָּעוֹלָם מְצָאוֹ, כְּגוֹן זֶה שֶׁמּוּחְזָק בּוֹ – הָתָם וַדַּאי חָיְישִׁינַן וְלֹא יִגְבֶּה בּוֹ. (הג"ה. חָיְישִׁי' לִנְפִילָה דְּיָחִיד וְאַשְׁכְּחוּ רַבִּים, ע"כ). עִיקַּר הַלָּשׁוֹן כֵּן הוּא: לִנְפִילָה דְּרַבִּים חָיְישִׁינַן. כְּלוֹמַר, שֶׁמְּצָאוֹ שׁוּם אָדָם בָּעוֹלָם. אֲבָל לְשֶׁמְּצָאוֹ יָחִיד יוֹסֵף בֶּן שִׁמְעוֹן – לָא חָיְישִׁינַן. וְרַבֵּינוּ חֲנַנְאֵל פֵּירֵשׁ: וְאַבַּיֵי לִנְפִילָה דְּחַד וְאַשְׁכְּחֵיהּ הַאי דִּשְׁמֵיהּ כִּשְׁמֵיהּ דְּהַאי – לָא חָיְישִׁינַן, שֶׁאִילּוּ מִן הָאַחֵ' נָפַל הָיָה צוֹעֵק וּמְבַקֵּשׁ, וְכֵיוָן שֶׁלֹּא צָעַק נִתְבָּרֵר כִּי לָזֶה שֶׁמְּצָאוֹ הוּא. אֲבָל לִנְפִילָה דְּרַבִּים, דְּלָא יָדְעִינַן מִי הוּא – חָיְישִׁינַן.

וְאֶלָּא

תוספות

מינך אפי' מריש גלותא. לשון שאלה הוא. וכן ההיא דאמר רב הונא: חיישינן לשני סוררי ב"כל הגט" (גיטין דף כז.) וב"שנים אוחזין" (ב"מ דף יח: ושם). ד)[וה"פ]: אפי' מריש גלותא שאין רגיל להלוות, נאמר אפילו באותו דגבי אי תפיס ביה? ה)אבל רשב"ם אין תופס בו עיקר. ואין נראה לר"י מה שמפרש: אפילו מריש גלותא — שאנו חוששין שמא אדם אחר הלוהו ונפל ממנו ומצאו (ב) לזה. מה לי לתלות בריש גלותא אותו אדם אחר? ולישנא נמי לא משמע כלל הכי. ומה שהקשה למה שפי', דהוה ליה למימר: ההוא [גברא] דנפק מתותי ידיה משמע — נראה דלא קשה כלל, דלרב הונא הוה מספקא ליה, ודרך שאלה היה אומר: אם נתחייב אותו כלל, דמשמע אפילו מריש גלותא אף על פי שאינו רגיל להלוות (ג) לו כלל?! אלא ש"מ "מינך" לא חשיב משמעות והבל הוא, ומשום אדם לא יגבוהו, ו)[או לא].

עדי מסירה כרתי. והא ז)דכתוב ביה "היום" — לא משום דצריך זמן, אלא שאם מתנה בעל פה שום תנאי, אם ימות מחולי זה או כשימות — שתהא אז מגורשת מעכשיו, וכדפסיק לעיל (דף קלו.) כרבי יוסי, דאמר: זמנו של שטר מוכיח עליו, והוי כאומר "מהיום". אבל היכא דלא מתנה שום דבר — לא צריך כלל "מהיום". והא דפירש רשב"ם דבעי למיכתב "מהיום" משום דבעי אבא שאול ידים מוכיחות — אין נראה לר"י, דהא אמרי' (גיטין דף יז.): זמן לא תקנו אלא משום פירות או משום בת אחותו, ור' אלעזר לא [הוה] בעי זמן ח)[כלל], דס"ל עדי מסירה כרתי, כמו שסובר רשב"ם עצמו. וגם זהו תימה להוסיף טעם חדש לאבא שאול, דבעי "היום" משום הוכחה. אבל הכא ליחוש לנפילה. תימה: מאי שייכא הכא פירכא דר"א בהלואה? הוה מצי למימר: נהי (ד) נמי דמשמע מההוא גברא כו' — מ"מ ליחוש לנפילה. ואפילו הוה סובר כר"מ הוה מצי למיפרך הכי! ואומר ר"י דהכי פירושה: אלמא "מהיום" — מההוא יומא דנפק ביה משמע, ה"נ "ממך" — מההוא גברא דנפק מתותי ידיה משמע, שרוצה לומר לכל אדם שימלא בידו, כי משמעות חשוב הוא ולא הבל ושילנות. וכן משמע שיגבה כל מי שימלא, וכן דעת הכתיבה היתה. ושטרי אקנייתא אתי שפיר, שמשעבד עכשו מה שלא לוה עדיין, מש"ה שעבד לו אפילו לא ילוה לעולם, כדאמרי' ב"שנים אוחזין" (ב"מ דף טו:): מלא שטרי הקנאה בשוק — יחזירם לבעלים. מאי אמרת? שמא כתב ללוות ולא לוה — הא שעבד ליה נפשיה. הלכך לא שייך למיחש לנפילה הכא. ואפילו בלא אקנייתא הוה מצי לאוקומי לפי' ר"ת ד"הנושא" (כתובות דף קב. ד"ה אליבא) דמפרש התם שיכול אדם להשתעבד לחבירו אפילו לא לוה ממנו, כגון שיכתוב (ה) השטר: אני חייב לך מנה, ויכתבנו ויתננו לו לשם כך. ופריך: דלמא אבא שאול כר' אלעזר ס"ל, ולא בעי זמן כו', ו"היום" משמע: יומא ט)דנפק מבעל הבית, ולא דנפק מב"ד. ולא הוצרך "מהיום" אלא אם התנה "אם מתי" כדפרישית לעיל. אבל הכא — ליחוש לנפילה, ד"ממך" נמי לא משמע אלא (ו) שנתנו לו, כי היכי ד"מהיום" משמע סתם משמעותו משעת הגירושין, ולתפוס על בת אחותו לא יוכל — דהא עדי מסירה צריך. וה"נ משמע הכא — אותו שנתנו לו דוקא, ולא למוצאו — א"כ איכא למיחש לנפילה! ומשני: לנפילה לא חיישינן. ותחלת שאלה דרב הונא נראה לר"י לפרש כן: "ממך" — אפילו מריש גלותא, אע"פ שאין רגיל להלוות כלל תם אפילו אנו ידעינן בבירור שלא הלוהו, וגם אין רגילות להקנות לו וליתן לו שטר הקנאה כלל — אפ"ה מקנה לו, מטעמא דפרישית. או לא, דשמא אין לנו לתלות אלא באותו שנתנו לו — הלכך חיישינן לנפילה, דלא קני אם לא מסרו לו. ועוד יש לפרש: אבל הכא ליחוש לנפילה. כלומר, לא מיבעיא דלא משמע (ז) ההוא גברא כו', והבל הוא, ואפי' הוה משמע — ליחוש לנפילה! ומשני: לנפילה לא חיישינן. וקושיא ראשונה לא חשש לתרץ, משום דכר' אלעזר לא מתוקמא, דהא מצריך "מהיום". וטעמא שפירשתי למעלה הוא דחוק, ולא סבירא ליה לרבה ההוא דיחויא. וכן מצינו בשאר מקומות בגמ' שאין חושש לתרץ קושיא ראשונה כלל. לנפילה דחד. פירוש: (ח) שאין לתלות שנפל אלא מאחד לבד, כי היכי דמתרמי שמזה נפל. לנפילה דרבים — פירוש: דיש לחוש מכל בני אדם שבעולם שנפל מזה או מזה, יש לתלות בנפילה. י)ואלא הא דתניא כו'. לנפילה דחד חיישינן, ומתני' בבאין בהרשאה, וברייתא במוציאין זה בלא זה.

והכא

רבינו גרשום

אמר רב הונא. אין אדם יכול לגבות בזה השטר כלום שכשמוציאו זה המלוה אע"פ שהוא כתב ידו של לוה אמר הלוה מה אתה מבקש ממני והלא כתבו ממך סתם משמע אפי' מריש גלותא או משאר כל אדם היאך אתה יכול לגבות ממני: פוק עיין ביה. שתמצא ראיה שדומה למעשה: דלאורתא בעי לה רב הונא ממך. שתאמר לו ראיה שדומה למעשה זה: ואין בו זמן כו' אבא שאול אומר אם כתוב בו. אפי' זמן כזה שגירשתיה היום אע"ג דאין יודע איזה יום קאמר כשר הגט אלמא באיזה יום שיבוא הגט לבית דין יש לומר היום משמע ההוא יומא דקא נפיק ביה משמע שבאותו יום גירשה וכשר. הכי נמי ממך משמע מההוא גברא דנפיק שטרא מתותי ידיה משמע דנאמן ולא מצי למימר ממך אפי' משבור מלכא: אמר ליה אביי לרבה דלמא אבא שאול. דאמר דכשר הגט משום ההוא טעמא קאמר דגירשתיה היום סתם כשר דאע"ג דלא ידעי' באיזה יום נכתב הגט אלא שידע באיזה יום מסרו לה כשר דס"ל כר' אלעזר דאמר עדי מסירה כרתי: אבל הכא. דכתב ממך ניחוש לנפילה דיכול לומר לו אין אתה המלוה שמא מן המלוה אחר נפל השטר ומצאת אותו: אמר ליה רבה לעולם ראיה שלי [ראיה] ודקא פרכ' ליחוש לנפיל'. לנפילה לא חיישינן: מנא תימרא דלא חיישינן לנפילה דתנן. במתניתין שנים שהיו בעיר אחת [ששמותיהן שוות] שניהן אין יכולין להוציא שטר חוב זה על זה שזה יכול לומר לזה אתה חייב לי וממני נפל השטר ואתה מצאתו וזה יכול לומר לזה אתה חייב לי וממני נפל השטר ואתה מצאתו או יכול לומר לו פרעת לי והחזרתי לך השטר: ולא אחר יכול להוציא שטר חוב על אחד מהן. שיכול כל אחד לומר לו איני חייב לך אלא חבירי. נמצא למלוה שטר אחד בין שטרותיו ששטרו של יוסף בן שמעון פרוע אע"ג שיש לו שטר אחר על יוסף בן שמעון שאינו פרוע שטרות שניהן פרועין שכל אחד יכול למימר לו שטר שלי הפרוע: כיצד יעשה אם אחד [רוצה ללוות] מחבירו: ישלשו. יכתוב כל אחד שמו ושם אביו ושם זקנו שמא שמות זקנים אינם שוין ובכן יחקר הדבר: ואם הוו משולשין יכתוב לו סימן המשפחה ואם היה סימנם שוה יכתוב כהן אם אחד מהן כהן יכתוב פלוני כהן. ואם יש באחד מהן סימן אחד או ארוך או גוץ או שחור יכתוב אותו סימן. קתני מיהת מתני' ולא אחר יכול להוציא שטר חוב על אחד מהן הא אחד מהן על אחרים יכול להוציא ואמאי ליחוש לנפילה. ולימא ליה לוה לא ממך לויתי אלא מחבירך ונפל ממנו ומצאת אותו וכן נמי נימא לאידך אלא ש"מ מדהן על אחרים יכולין להוציא ולא מצי ליה למימר מחבירך נפל ש"מ דלנפילה לא חיישינן: ואביי משיב לנפילה דחד. כגון מלוה אחד ששמו יוסף בן שמעון לא חיישינן. דמזהיר זהיר ביה והכא ליכא ספיקא אלא דחד גברא בלבד של חבירו ששמו כשמו. אבל לנפילה דרבים היכא דכתב לויתי ממך איכא לספוקי דרבים דלכל חד מעלמא משמע ממך הלכך חייש לנפילה במאי

מסורת הש"ס

א) [ב"מ יח: ב: גיטין ...] ב) [נ"ל אלעזר]: ג) [... ע: וש"נ]: ד) רש"ל ... רש"א אפי' והוא לדבור ... ה) רש"א אבל פי' ... שתופס כו' אין ... ו) רש"ל: ז) רש"א ... היום: ח) רש"א: ט) ... דנפק מידו ולא דנפק ... י) [בתי' הג"ה. אלא ... דתניא כו' א"כ לנפילה חיישינן ומתניתין בהרשאה ומבר דמוליאין זה על זה ע"כ] ועיין רש"א:

הגהות הב"ח

(א) רשב"ם ד"ה אמר הונא וכו' כדלקמיה ... (ב) תום' ד"ה מינך ונפל ממנו ומצאו זה ד... לו לתלות בריש גלו... (ג) בא"ד להלוות כלל ... ותיבת לו נמחק: (ד) ... אבל וכו' נהי דממך מ... מההוא גברא: (ה) בא"ד שיכתוב בשטר אני ח... (ו) בא"ד לא משמע ... אותו שנתנו לו: (ז) בא"ד דלא משמע מהה... (ח) ד"ה לנפילה ... פירוש כשאין לתלות ... אלא מאחד בלבד לתלות בנפילה כי ... מתרמי שמזה נפל ה... ואח"כ מ"ה לנפילה ... דמכל בני אדם:

וְאֶלָּא הָא דְּתַנְיָא: כְּשֵׁם שֶׁאֵין מוֹצִיאִין שְׁטַר חוֹב זֶה עַל זֶה — כָּךְ אֵין מוֹצִיאִין עַל אֲחֵרִים, בְּמַאי קָמִיפַּלְגִי? בְּאוֹתִיּוֹת נִקְנוֹת בִּמְסִירָה קָמִיפַּלְגִי, תַּנָּא דִידָן סָבַר: א)אוֹתִיּוֹת נִקְנוֹת בִּמְסִירָה, וְתַנָּא בָּרָא סָבַר: אֵין אוֹתִיּוֹת נִקְנוֹת בִּמְסִירָה. וְאִי בָּעֵית אֵימָא: דְּכוּלֵּי עָלְמָא — אוֹתִיּוֹת נִקְנוֹת בִּמְסִירָה, וְהָכָא בְּצָרִיךְ לְהָבִיא רְאָיָה קָא מִיפַּלְגִי; תַּנָּא דִידָן סָבַר: אֵין צָרִיךְ לְהָבִיא רְאָיָה, וְתַנָּא בָּרָא סָבַר: ב)צָרִיךְ לְהָבִיא רְאָיָה. דְּאִיתְּמַר: אוֹתִיּוֹת נִקְנוֹת בִּמְסִירָה — אַבַּיֵי אָמַר: צָרִיךְ לְהָבִיא רְאָיָה, וְרָבָא אָמַר: אאֵינוֹ צָרִיךְ לְהָבִיא רְאָיָה. אָמַר אַבַּיֵי: מְנָא אָמִינָא לָהּ? דְּתַנְיָא: באֶחָד מִן הָאַחִין שֶׁהַשְּׁטָר חוֹב יוֹצֵא מִתַּחַת יָדוֹ — עָלָיו לְהָבִיא רְאָיָה; מַאי לָאו הוּא הַדִּין לְאַחֲרִינֵי? וְרָבָא אָמַר: שָׁאנֵי אַחִין, דְּשָׁמְטוּ מֵהֲדָדֵי. אִיכָּא דְּאָמְרִי, אָמַר רָבָא: מְנָא אָמִינָא לָהּ? דְּתַנְיָא: אֶחָד מִן הָאַחִין שֶׁהַשְּׁטָר חוֹב יוֹצֵא מִתַּחַת יָדוֹ — עָלָיו לְהָבִיא רְאָיָה; אַחִין הוּא דְּשָׁמְטוּ מֵהֲדָדֵי, אֲבָל אַחֲרִינֵי לָא. וְאַבַּיֵי? אַחִין אִיצְטְרִיכָא לֵיהּ, סַלְקָא דַּעְתָּךְ אָמִינָא: כֵּיוָן דְּשָׁמְטוּ מֵהֲדָדֵי — אֵימָא מִיזְדְּהַר זְהִירֵי, וְלָא צְרִיכֵי לְהָבִיא רְאָיָה, קמ"ל. וְאֶלָּא הָא דְּתַנְיָא: כְּשֵׁם שֶׁמּוֹצִיאִין הֵן שְׁטַר חוֹב עַל אֲחֵרִים — כָּךְ מוֹצִיאִין זֶה עַל זֶה, בְּמַאי קָמִיפַּלְגִי? בְּכוֹתְבִין שְׁטָר לַלֹּוֶה וְאע"פ שֶׁאֵין מַלְוֶה עִמּוֹ, קָמִיפַּלְגִי; תַּנָּא דִידָן סָבַר: ג)כּוֹתְבִין שְׁטָר לַלֹּוֶה וְאַף עַל פִּי שֶׁאֵין מַלְוֶה עִמּוֹ. זִמְנִין דְּאָזֵיל לְגַבֵּי סָפְרָא וְסָהֲדֵי, וְאָמַר לְהוּ: "כִּתְבוּ לִי שְׁטָרָא, דְּבָעֵינַן לְמֵיזַף מִיּוֹסֵף בֶּן שִׁמְעוֹן חַבְרִי", וּבָתַר דְּכָתְבִי וְחָתְמִי לֵיהּ, נְקִיטָא לֵיהּ וְאָמַר לֵיהּ: "הַב לִי מְאָה דִּיזָפְתְּ מִינַּאי"; תַּנָּא בָּרָא סָבַר: אֵין כּוֹתְבִין שְׁטָר לַלֹּוֶה עַד שֶׁיְּהֵא מַלְוֶה עִמּוֹ.§ "נִמְצָא לְאֶחָד בֵּין שְׁטָרוֹתָיו: 'שְׁטָרוֹ שֶׁל יוֹסֵף בֶּן שִׁמְעוֹן פָּרוּעַ' — שְׁטָרוֹת שְׁנֵיהֶם פְּרוּעִין" וכו'.§ טַעְמָא דְּנִמְצָא, הָא לֹא נִמְצָא — מָצֵי מַפֵּיק; וְהָאֲנַן "וְלֹא אַחֵר יָכוֹל לְהוֹצִיא עֲלֵיהֶן שְׁטַר חוֹב" תְּנַן! אָמַר רַבִּי יִרְמְיָה: בִּמְשׁוּלָּשִׁין. וְנֶחֱזֵי תַּבְרָא בִּשְׁמָא דְּמַאן דִּכְתִיב! אָמַר רַב הוֹשַׁעְיָא: גבִּמְשׁוּלָּשִׁין בַּשְּׁטָר וְאֵין מְשׁוּלָּשִׁין בַּשּׁוֹבֵר. אַבַּיֵי אָמַר, הָכִי קָאָמַר: (א) דנִמְצָא לַלֹּוֶה בֵּין שְׁטָרוֹתָיו "שְׁטָרוֹ שֶׁל יוֹסֵף בֶּן שִׁמְעוֹן עָלַי פָּרוּעַ" — שְׁטָרוֹת שְׁנֵיהֶם פְּרוּעִין.§ "כֵּיצַד יַעֲשׂוּ? יְשַׁלְּשׁוּ" כו'.§ תָּנָא: האִם הָיוּ שְׁנֵיהֶם כֹּהֲנִים — יִכְתְּבוּ דּוֹרוֹת.§ **מתני'** והָאוֹמֵר לִבְנוֹ "שְׁטָר בֵּין שְׁטָרוֹתַי פָּרוּעַ וְאֵינִי יוֹדֵעַ אֵי זֶהוּ" — שְׁטָרוֹת כּוּלָּן פְּרוּעִין; נִמְצָא לְאֶחָד שָׁם שְׁנַיִם — הַגָּדוֹל פָּרוּעַ, וְהַקָּטָן אֵינוֹ פָּרוּעַ.§ **גמ'** אָמַר רָבָא: ז"שְׁטָר לְךָ בְּיָדִי פָּרוּעַ" — הַגָּדוֹל פָּרוּעַ, וְהַקָּטָן אֵינוֹ פָּרוּעַ; "חוֹב לְךָ בְּיָדִי פָּרוּעַ" — שְׁטָרוֹת כּוּלָּן פְּרוּעִין. אֲמַר לֵיהּ רָבִינָא ד)לְרָבָא: אֶלָּא מֵעַתָּה, "שָׂדִי מְכוּרָה לָךְ" — שָׂדֶה גְּדוֹלָה מְכוּרָה לוֹ, "שָׂדֶה שֶׁיֵּשׁ לִי מְכוּרָה לָךְ" — כָּל שְׂדוֹתָיו מְכוּרִין לוֹ? הָתָם חיַד בַּעַל הַשְּׁטָר עַל הַתַּחְתּוֹנָה.§ **מתני'** ה)טהַמַּלְוֶה אֶת חֲבֵירוֹ עַל יְדֵי עָרֵב — לֹא יִפָּרַע מִן הֶעָרֵב, וְאִם

ואלא הא דתניא כו'. לכ"ע פריך, דהא אפילו אביי מודה דלנפילה דחד לא חיישינן — וא"כ אמאי תניא בברייתא שאין יכולין להוציא על אחרים? במאי קא מיפלגי. כיון דלאו בחיישינן לנפילה פליגי. תנא דידן סבר. לנפילה דחד לא חיישינן. מאי איכא למימר? דלמא איהו יהיב ליה — אותיות נקנות במסירה, ועל כרחו יפרע לו למי שהשטר בידו. ותנא ברא סבר אין אותיות נקנות במסירה. ומתוך כך ידחה הלוה לזה, ויאמר: פקדון הוא אצלך, ולזה יאמר: אין השטר בידך. ומיהו, אם כתבו הרשאה זה לזה — על כרחו ישלם לו. ואב"א דכ"ע אותיות נקנות במסירה. בלא שטר מכירה [אחר], כדפסקי' הלכתא בפ' "המוכר את הספינה" (לעיל עז.) כרבי, וכדאמר רב אשי: אותיות מילי נינהו, ומילי במילי לא נקנו, היכא שמסרו לו ונתנו. אך ראיה ועדים צריך שמסרו לו לזה בפניהם, דלא נימא פקדון הוא אצלו או השמיטו ממנו. ובהכי פליגי מתני' ותנא ברא, בפלוגתא דאביי ורבא. ורבא אמר אין צריך. אלא העמידהו בחזקת המוחזק בו. אחד מן האחין ששטר חוב יוצא מתחת ידו. או בשם אביהם או בשם מלוה אחר, וטוען: אחיי נתנוהו לי, והם אומרים: אתה חטפתו. מיזהר זהירי. ולא יכול להשמיט מיד אחיו, כי נזהר איש מאחיו. וסד"א: אין צריך המוחזק בו להביא ראיה, קמ"ל. אלא הא דתניא כו'. ג' מחלוקות בדבר. זימנין דאזיל לגבי ספרא כו'. כסבור הוא לרמות בו חבירו ולגבות ממנו בשטר זה, והוא אינו יודע מה ששנינו שאין יכול להוציא על חבירו ששמו כשמו. אא"כ מלוה עמו. ומסתמא שניהם היו במעמד מקום שנכתב, וכיון דאינהו ידעי ואין מקפידים זה על זה — לא חיישינן תו לשום רמאות, כיון דלנפילה לא חיישינן. נמצא לאחד. מלוה: "שטרו של יוסף בן שמעון שחייב לי ממון פרוע" — שטרות שניהם פרועים. ואע"ג דאמרן בשילהי "שנים אוחזין" (ב"מ כ:) סימפון היוצא מתחת ידי מלוה אינו אלא כמשחק ופסול — הא אוקימנא להך משנה התם, כגון שנמצא השטר בין שטרותיו (ב) קרועין, הלכך השובר כשר. במשולשין. פירוש: בשטר שלשה דורות "יוסף בן יעקב בן יצחק", ובאידך כתב "יוסף בן יעקב בן דוד". ובשובר כתב סתם "יוסף בן יעקב", כדמתרץ לקמן. הלכך איתרע כחם, והם בחזקת פרועים, שכל אחד טוען: שלי פרוע, והמלוה אינו יכול להכחישו, הואיל ונמצאו השטרות בין השטרות קרועים. אביי אמר. מתני' כשנמצאו בבית לוה מיירי, והכי קתני: נמצא ללוה אחד בין שטרותיו שובר שהשטר שהיה נושה בו יוסף בן שמעון פרוע הוא, והיו שני יוסף בן שמעון נושים בו. ואילמלא זה השובר היו שניהם נפרעין ממנו שטרותם, כדאוקמינן שהם יכולין להוציא שט"ח על אחרים. ועכשיו בזה השובר הורע חזקתם, דקיי"ל: יד בעל השטר על התחתונה, וכשיוציא כל אחד מהם שטרו — אומר לו: הנה השובר עליו. ומיהו, נראה בעיני שאם שניהם באים בהרשאה זה מזה על הלוה — יכולין לגבות אחד מן השטרות ממ"נ מן הלוה, שהרי מודה הוא בע"כ בשני השטרות, אלא שפרע אחד מהן. ומיהו, אי טעין לוה ואומר: לשניכם פרעתי, והשובר נכתב סתם על שניהם — נראה בעיני דטענה מעלייתא היא. אבל היכא דמודה בב' הלוואות, אלא שפרע אחת, נהי נמי דהורע כח המלוין לגבות כל אחד חובו, אבל יעשו שטר ביניהם ויגבו בין שניהם מן הלוה שטר אחד, ע"י שיכתבו הרשאה זה לזה. עלי. שאני חייב לו. תנא אם היו שניהם. משולשים וכהנים. יכתבו דורות. מרובעים: יוסף בן יעקב בן יצחק בן אברהם, יוסף בן יעקב בן יצחק בן דוד. דכולי האי לא יהיו שמות אבותיהן שוין. **מתני'** האומר לבנו. מלוה בשעת מיתתו. ואיני יודע איזהו. והלוה האמינני, ולא החזרתי שטרו, ואיני רוצה ליענש. שטרות כולן פרועין. חוץ מאותן שיאמרו: עדיין לא פרענו. נמצא. ללוה אחד שם בבית המת שני שטרות, שלוה ממנו שני הלוואות — הקטן אינו פרוע, דשטר בין שטרותיו קאמר, דמשמע אחד ולא שנים. **גמ'** חוב לך בידי. משמע: מה שאתה חייב לי, ואפי' כתוב החוב בהלוואות דקות, בשטרות הרבה. א"ל רבינא לרב אשי אלא מעתה שדי מכורה לך. שדהו הגדולה מכורה לו. שדה שיש לי מכורה לך. מי נימא כל שדותיו מכורין לו קאמר? כמו "שדה אדום" קנפיינ"א (כתיב) וכמו "ובהמה רבה" (יונה ד). ומשני: התם יד בעל השטר על התחתונה. דהמוציא מחבירו עליו הראיה, דהיינו לוקח. ומילתיה דרבא דלעיל נמי משום האי טעמא דיד בעל השטר על התחתונה, דהיינו מלוה. הלכך "חוב לך בידי פרוע" — כל השטרות שיש לו עליו פרועין. **מתני'** לא יפרע מן הערב. תחלה, עד שיתבע את הלוה לדין ויחייבוהו ב"ד. ואם אין לו מה לשלם — אז יפרע מן הערב. הכי מפרשינן לה בגמרא במסקנא.

ואם

והכא בצריך להביא ראיה קא מיפלגי. ופלוגתא דמתני' וברייתא ליתא בפלוגתא דאביי ורבא, דמצריך ראיה — מודה דלא חיישינן לנפילה ופקדון היכא דשמיה כשמיה, כדקאמר בפרק (בתרא) [ט"ו] דיבמות (דף קטו. וסס) דקאמר אביי: לנפילה לא חיישינן. אי לפקדון, כיון דשמיה כשמיה — לא מפקיד גביה. אבל הך ברייתא — (ג) חיישי' לנפילה או לפקדון דיוסף בן שמעון, דאפילו בשני יוסף בן שמעון מצרכי ראיה. ורבא אמר א"צ להביא ראיה, ולעיל בפרק "המוכר את הספינה" (דף עז. ד"ה אמר) פירשתי.

אביי אמר הכי קאמר נמצא כו'. והא דמוקי לה ב"שנים אוחזין" (ב"מ ד' כ:) כגון שנמצא השטר בין שטרותיו פרועין — לאו היינו אליבא דאביי, דאיהו מוקי לה בשובר היוצא מתחת יד הלוה כשאר שוברין. אלא אליבא דר' ירמיה אתיא.

שטרו של יוסף בן שמעון עלי פרוע שטרות שניהם פרועין. אע"ג (ד) דבשטר אחד שיש לו עליהם אין יכול להוציא עליהם, משום דחיישינן בכל אחד שמא חבירו של כל אחד כתבו, (ה) אע"פ [דחד] ודאי לוה — [הכא לא אמרינן] חיישינן שמא חבירו של כל אחד ואחד כתבו והחתימו, אע"ג דודאי אחד פרע. וטעמא — משום דמספיקא לא מפקינן ממונא.

שניהם כהנים. ה"ה שניהם ישראלים, אלא משום דתני' לעיל: היה "אחד מהן כהן" — תני כהנים.

חסורי

רבינו גרשום

במאי פליגי. מתני' וברייתא: באותיות נקנות במסירה פליגי מר סבר. תנא דמתני' דדייקינן ממתני' הא הן על אחרים יכולין להוציא משום דקסבר אותיות נקנות במסירה שאם טוען הלוה איני חייב לך אלא לחבירך יכול לומר לו נהי כדאמרת דלחברי אתה חייב ולא לי הרי השטר בידי וקניתיו ממנו וחבירי נתנו לי במסירה ואותיות נקנות במסירה ונפל ממנו לא מצית אמרת דהא אמרן לנפילה דחד לא חיישינן הלכך יכולין להוציא על אחרים: ומר סבר אין אותיות נקנות במסירה. ויכול לומר לו לחבירך אני חייב ולא לך והוא לא יכול לקנות לך החוב במסירת השטר דאין אותיות נקנות במסירה ולא בעל חוב דידי את ולחבירו נמי מצי אמר לאו בעל דברים דידי את ואין בידך השטר: והכא בצריך להביא ראי'. עדי מסירה דתנא דברייתא סבר צריך להביא ראיה עדי מסירה ואם אין לו עדי מסירה אינו יכול להוציא שטר על אחרים: עליו להביא ראיה. עדי מסירה שאביו מסרו לו ונתנו לו לבדו: מאי לאו הוא הדין לאחריני. לשני יוסף בן שמעון שמוציא האחד שטר על אחרים שצריך להביא ראיה עדי מסירה שחבירו נתנו לו בפניהם: ורבא אמר לך. לאו הוא הדין לאחריני אלא שאני אחד מן האחין אמאי צריך להביא ראיה דאחין משמטי אהדדי. יד כל אחד גונב מאחיו דמורה היתרא לעצמו לפי שיורש הוא להכי צריך להביא ראיה אבל בעלמא אותיות נקנות במסירה ואין צריך להביא ראיה: ואביי. אמר לך לכולי עלמא צריך להביא ראיה ומאי שנא דנקט ברייתא אחד מן האחין דאחין אצטריכא ליה. סד"א כיון דאחין משמטי אהדדי אימא מיזהר זהיר ומעיין כל אחד שלא ישמוט אחיו כלום מירושת אביו קודם חלוקה והואיל דזהירי אימא היכא דיוצא שטר חוב מתחת ידי אחד לא יהא צריך להביא ראיה דהוא אביו נתנו לו שאם היה מחזיק בו לאחר מיתת אביו היו מרגישין וסד"א דאין צריך ראיה קמ"ל דצריך וכל שכן אחריני דלא זהירי דצריך להביא ראיה: ותנא ברא סבר אין כותבין שטר ללוה עד שיהא מלוה עמו. הלכך כיון דבפניו נכתב מהימן אידך כל אימת דמפיק ליה להכי מוציא שטר זה על זה: טעמא דנמצא. בין שטרותיו דשטר יוסף בן שמעון פרוע דמשום הכי לא מצי מפיק הא לא מצא מפיק: (משום) במשולשין. שכתוב יוסף בן שמעון בן לוי דניכר איזה יוסף חייב לו: ומקשי' אי הכי כיון דמיירי במשולשין אם כן אמאי קתני נמצא לאחד בין שטרותיו כו' שטרות שניהן פרועין ואמאי שניהן פרועין וכיון דמשולשין ששם זקנם אינם שוה וניחזי תברא שכתב יוסף בן שמעון בן לוי בשמא דמאן יוסף כתב. כיון דניכרין בשם זקנם ואידך דלא כתב תברא על שמיה ליפרע משטריה: אמר רב אושעיא במשולשין בשטר להכי מצי מפיק. ואין משולשין בשובר להכי שניהן פרועין דלא ידעי תברא דמאן כתב: אביי אמר כו'. לעיל מהדר אמאי לעיל טעמא דנמצא הא לא נמצא מצי מפיק והא אנן תנן כו'. וקא מתרץ אביי דוקיא דמתניתין באידך גיסא דלא קשיא מידי והכי קאמר נמצא לאחד בין שטרותיו שטר של יוסף בן שמעון שיש לו עלי פרוע הוא ואית לאידך יוסף שטרא נמי עלי' השטרות שניהן פרועין והשתא דייק טעמא דנמצא משום הכי לא מצי מפיק הא לא נמצא מצי מפיק יוסף בן שמעון מיניה היינו כדדייקי' ברישא הא הן על אחרים יכולין להוציא אבל אחרים אין יכולין להוציא עליהן והשתא ליכא למפרך והאנן תנן ולא אחר כו': יכתבו דורות. ירבעו או יחמשו עד שלא יהו שוין: פים' נמצא לאחד. לוה: שם שנים. שטרות כיון דהוא אמר לבנו שטר א' פרוע ולא שנים מכלל דזה לוה שיש לו שם שני שטרות האחד אינו פרוע ואפי' הכי אמרינן שטר גדול הוא דפרוע והקטן אינו פרוע משום דיד בעל השטר על התחתונה: שטר לך בידי פרוע. ויש לו ב' שטרות עליו אמרינן הגדול פרוע ולא הקטן ויד בעל השטר על התחתונה: ואם אמר חוב לך בידי פרוע. כלומר חוב הוית חייב לי ופרעת כיון דאמר חוב סתם ויש לו כמה שטרות עליו כולן פרועין: אמר ליה רבינא לרבא. לרישא מקשי למאי דאמר הגדול פרוע. אלא מעתה שדה אחת שלי מכורה לך והיה לו ב' שדות גדולה וקטנה הכי נמי דאמרינן שדה גדולה מכר לו ואם אמר לו כל שדה שיש לי מכורה לך משמע דמודה כל שדותיו מכורין לו (לא כי היכי) דאמר בשטר יד בעל השטר על התחתונה ומתרץ רבא לא סלקא דעתך דשדה גדולה מכר ולא קטנה ואמרי' קטנה מכורה ולא גדולה: לא יפרע כדמפרש

עין משפט נר מצוה

קיט א מיי' פ"ד מהל' מלוה ולוה הל' ז ופ"ו מהל' מכירה הל' יא ועי' בהשגות ובכס"מ סמג עשין צד טוש"ע ח"מ סי' סו סעיף יח:

קכ ב מיי' פ"ט מהל' נחלות הלכה ז סמג עשין צו טוש"ע ח"מ סי' סב וסו"ע בהג"ה:

קכא ג מיי' שם טוש"ע ח"מ סי' מט סעיף ט:

קכב ד ה מיי' פכ"ד מהל' מלוה ולוה הל' א סמג עשין צד טוש"ע ח"מ סי' מט סעיף ז:

קכג ו מיי' פי"ג מהל' יב סמג עשין צד טוש"ע ח"מ סי' מט סעיף כג:

קכד ז מיי' שם טוש"ע שם סעיף כג:

קכה ח מיי' פכ"ה מהל' מכירה הלכה יט סמג עשין צד טוש"ע ח"מ סימן ריד סעיף יב:

קכו ט מיי' פכ"ה מהל' מלוה ולוה הלכה ב סמג עשין צד טוש"ע ח"מ סי' קכט סעיף ח:

רס"ל ועי' רש"א

מסורת הש"ס

א) [לעיל עו. וש"נ], ב) [עי' תוס' יבמות קטו. ד"ה תמאה], ג) [לעיל קסו:], ד) לפי גי' רשב"ם צ"ל לרב אשי, ה) כתובות דף מח.

הגהות הב"ח

(א) גמ' אביי אמר הכי קאמר בין על אחרים מוציאין נמצא ללוה: (ב) רשב"ם ד"ה נמצא וכו' קרועין: (ג) תום' ד"ה והכא וכו' אבל הך ברייתא ס"ל דחיישינן לנפילה: (ד) ד"ה שטרו וכו' אע"ג דבשטר שיש לו עליהם כל"ל ותיבת אחד נמחק: (ה) בא"ד חבירו של כל אחד כתבו אע"ג דחד ודאי לוה הכא בשובר לא אמרינן שמא חבירו כל"ל:

תורה אור

א)ואם אמר לו "על מנת שאפרע ממי שארצה" — יפרע מן הערב; רשב"ג אומר: אם יש נכסים ללוה — בין כך ובין כך לא יפרע מן הערב. וכן היה א)רבן שמעון בן גמליאל אומר: ב)הערב לאשה בכתובתה, והיה בעלה מגרשה — ידירנה הנאה, שמא יעשו קנוניא על נכסים של זה ויחזיר את אשתו.§ **גמ'** מאי טעמא? רבה ורב יוסף דאמרי תרוייהו: גברא אשלימת לי, גברא אשלימי לך. מתקיף לה רב נחמן: האי דינא דפרסאי! אדרבה, בתר ערבא אזלי! אלא, בי דינא דפרסאי, דלא יהבי טעמא למילתייהו. אלא אמר רב נחמן: מאי לא יפרע מן הערב — ב)לא יתבע ערב תחלה. תניא נמי הכי: ג)המלוה את חבירו על ידי ערב — לא יתבע ערב תחלה, ואם אמר "על מנת שאפרע ממי שארצה" — יתבע ערב תחלה. א"ר הונא: מנין לערב דמשתעבד? דכתיב: °"אנכי אערבנו מידי תבקשנו". (בראשית מג) מתקיף לה רב חסדא: הא קבלנות היא, דכתיב: ג)°"תנה אותו על ידי ואני אשיבנו"! (שם מב) אלא ד)אמר רבי יצחק, מהכא: °"לקח בגדו כי ערב זר ובעד נכריה חבלהו"; (משלי כ) ואומר: °"בני אם ערבת לרעך תקעת לזר כפיך, נוקשת באמרי פיך נלכדת באמרי פיך, עשה זאת אפוא בני והנצל כי באת בכף רעך לך התרפס ורהב רעיך", (שם ו) ה)אם ממון יש לו בידך — התר לו פיסת יד, ואם לאו — הרבה עליו ריעים. אמר אמימר: ערב דמשתעבד — מחלוקת ר' יהודה ור' יוסי; (א) לרבי יוסי דאמר: ו)אסמכתא קניא — ערב משתעבד, לר' יהודה דאמר: אסמכתא לא קניא — ערב לא משתעבד. אמר ליה רב אשי לאמימר: ז)הא מעשים בכל יום, דאסמכתא לא קניא, וערב משתעבד! אלא אמר רב אשי: בההוא הנאה דקא מהימן ליה — ד)גמר ומשתעבד נפשיה.§ "ואם אמר על מנת שאפרע ממי שארצה" כו'.§ אמר רבה בר בר חנה אמר רבי יוחנן: ה)לא שנו אלא שאין נכסים ללוה, אבל יש נכסים ללוה — לא יפרע מן הערב. והא מדקתני סיפא, רבן שמעון בן גמליאל אומר: אם יש נכסים ללוה — (ב) לא יפרע מן הערב, מכלל דתנא קמא סבר: לא שנא הכי ולא שנא הכי! חסורי מחסרא והכי קתני: המלוה את חבירו על ידי ערב — לא יפרע מן הערב, ואם אמר "על מנת שאפרע ממי שארצה" — יפרע מן הערב; במה דברים אמורים — בשאין נכסים ללוה, אבל יש נכסים ללוה — לא יפרע מן הערב; ו)וקבלן, אף על פי שיש נכסים ללוה — יפרע מן הקבלן; רבן

ואם אמר לו על מנת כו'. בגמרא אמרינן: חסורי מיחסרא והכי קתני כו', ומפרש לה. **בין כך ובין כך לא יפרע מן הערב.** תחלה. **הערב לאשה בכתובתה.** ואין לבעל נכסים, והיה בעלה מגרשה, וצריך הערב לפרעה כתובתה מכיסו. **ידירנה.** הבעל הנאה על דעת רבים, נדר שאין לו הפרה, שלא יוכל להחזירה. דחיישינן שמא דעתו להחזיר את אשתו ולאכול כתובתה לאחר שנתקבלה כתובתה מן הערב, וקנוניא בעלמא הוא דעבדי בעל ואשתו על נכסיו של ערב. **גמ' מאי טעמא.** לא יפרע מן הערב? דקסלקא דעתך השתא לא יפרע כלל קאמר מתני'. דלא מהני ערבות אלא להכי, שאם מת לוה או ברח — אז יפרע מן הערב. אף אם הלוה בפניו בשעה שתובע מלוה את חובו, כיון שהעמידו ערב ללוה בפניו — פטור. **גברא אשלמת לי.** הפקדת הלוה, על מנת שאם ימות או יברח שאפרע ממוני, והרי אני מחזירו לך ותתבענו בדין — ואני פטור. **מתקיף לה רב נחמן האי דינא.** דמתניתין, שלא יפרע הערב כלום — דינא דפרסאי הוא. וקס"ד השתא דהכי קאמר: שמנהג פרסיים לדון כן, דאמר ליה גברא אשלמת לך. **בתר ערבא אזלי.** אף כשיש נכסים ללוה. **דלא יהבי טעמא למילתייהו.** שגם זה דבר שאינו הגון הוא, לומר שלא יפרע מן הערב כלל א"כ מאי אהני ערבות? אלא ודאי להכי נכנס בערבות, שאם אין נכסים ללוה — שישלם לו ערב תחתיו את הממון. **לא יתבע ערב תחלה.** דלא נעשה ערב אלא על מנת אם ימות הלוה, או ימאן לבא לדין, או שיתחייבוהו בית דין ולא יהיה לו מה לפרוע — אז יפרע מן הערב. **ואם אמר לו על מנת כו'** יתבע מן הערב תחלה. וכגון שאין נכסים ללוה. דהכי מפרשי' לה מתני' לקמן. **מנין לערב שמשתעבד.** באמירה בעלמא, בלא קנין. **קבלנות.** לקמן מפרש: "תן לו ואני קבלן". ובאמירה בעלמא הוי קבלן, והכי מוכח לקמן בשמעתין. אבל אם נשא ונתן ביד — אמרינן לקמן דאין למלוה על הלוה כלום. **תנה אותו על ידי.** כלומר, כאילו (ג) מקבלו בידי אחזירנו לך. **לקח בגדו.** למלוה קאמר קרא: קח בגדו של ערב, כי ערב בשביל איש זר — דהיינו אמירה בעלמא, דלא כתיב הכא קבלנות. **בני אם ערבת לרעך.** ממון, או נוקשת באמרי פיך — שחרפתו וגדפתו — עשה זאת אפוא בני והנצל משני דברים הללו: על כי באת בכף רעך, דהיינו ממון שיש לו עליך — לך התרפס, התר לו פיסת ידך ותן לו מעותיו. ורהב רעך, על שחרפתו — הרבה עליו ריעים, ובקש מחילה. **רבי יהודה סבר אסמכתא לא קניא.** והיינו אסמכתא: אם לא יפרע לך — אני אשלם לך. וכל "דאי" הוי אסמכתא — סומך ובוטח בלבו שהלוה יפרענו, ואילו היה יודע שלא יפרע הלוה — לא היה נכנס בערבות. **דאסמכתא לא קניא.** דפסיקנא הלכה כרבי יהודה. **גמר** (ד) **ומשתעבד.** בלב שלם, ושליחותא דערב קא עביד מלוה, כאילו הוא עצמו הלוה. **לא שנו.** אפי' דאמר על מנת כו'. **אע"פ שיש נכסים ללוה יפרע מן הקבלן.** אם ירצה המלוה. רבן

חסורי מחסרא והכי קתני. פירש ר"ת בכתב ידו: חסורי מחסרא והכי קתני המלוה את חבירו על ידי ערב לא יפרע מן הערב. הכי פירושו, והכי הלכתא: לא יתבע מן הערב תחלה, אע"פ שאין לו נכסים (ה) ללוה, דהיינו קרקעות. אלא יתבע מן הלוה תחלה, ואם הוא רחוק — ימתין לו, או ילך לשם לתבעו ולכופו. דלא מחפינן לנכסי דערב, (ו) דלמא אי איתיה הכא ללוה הוה יהיב ליה מטלטלי למלוה. ואם אמר "על מנת שאפרע ממי שארצה תחלה" כו' — ולא יצטרך להמתין ולחזור אחר הלוה. דמשום דלמא פרע ליה מטלטלין לא מטרחינן ליה למלוה, כיון דאתני. וכגון שאין נכסים ללוה, דהיינו קרקעות, כדמסיק ואזיל: בד"א כו', אבל יש נכסים ללוה, דהיינו קרקעות — יתבע הלוה תחלה ויכופנו, ולא נטריח את הערב, כיון דאיגלאי מילתא שיכול להפרע מן הלוה. אבל כשאין נכסים ללוה, ואתני "ממי שארצה אפרע" — מספיקא לא מטרחינן לחזור ולהמתין ללוה, אלא יפרע מן הערב כדפרישית. **וקבלן, אף על פי שיש נכסים כו'.** ושמש מדות בערבות: א' — המלוה על ידי ערב ולא אתני "ממי שארצה אפרע" — תובע הלוה תחלה בב"ד, בין שיש לו ובין שאין לו נכסים ללוה. ואם לא יוכל לכופו ללוה, ולא ציית דינא — נכנס לבית של ערב. ב' — אם התנה "ממי שארצה אפרע" ואין לו נכסים ללוה, דהיינו קרקעות — נפרע מן הערב תחלה. פי': אם ירצה לדון עם הערב תחלה, ואם ירצה — יתבע מן הלוה תחלה. כדאמרינן: אם אמר "ממי שארצה אפרע" — יפרע מן הערב, ש"מ דברצון המלוה תליא מילתא. ג' — ואם יש לו נכסים ללוה, אפילו אתני — נפרע מן הלוה תחלה. ד' — וקבלן, דהיינו "תן לו ואני נותן לך", בין יש לו נכסים ללוה בין אין לו — נפרע מן הערב תחלה. ה' — נושא ונותן ביד — יפרע מן הערב ולא מן הלוה, שאין למלוה על הלוה כלום. ואם לא מצא שום (ז) להפרע מן הערב — חוזר על הלוה מדר' נתן, דקיימא לן כוותיה דאפילו בבעל חוב דעלמא. וכולהו ערבין בעי קנין, בר מקבלן וערב בשעת מתן מעות. וקבלן דהיינו "תן לו ואני אתן לך". אי נמי — שאינו מזכיר לשון הלואה ח)אלא לשון פרעון, דקאמר ט)"יט" דונראי" ולא קאמר י)"ייט" דיבראי", דהלכתא כרבא. ולא לימא "ואני קבלן". וקונין בכליו של קונה, וכגון דנקיט ביה שלש על שלש, דבציר מהכי לא מהני אם אינו כלי. ואין חילוק בין עור לשק, כדאמרינן ב"שנים אוחזין" (ב"מ דף ז.): כיון דנקט ביה שלש על שלש, לשון רבינו תם. ואם היה כתוב בשטר שנעשה פלוני בן פלוני קבלן — אומר ר"י דהוי קבלן. דאע"ג דלא כתב בו "תן לו ואני נותן לך" שלא פירש היאך אמר, מכל מקום קבלן קאמר דהוי. מקמי

רבינו גרשום

כדמפרש בגמ' לא יתבע ע"י בתחלה: ואם אמר. בשעת הלואה: על מנת שאפרע ממי שארצה. וקיבל עליו הערב: יפרע מן הערב. וכיוצא בו אמר רשב"ג הערב לאשה בכתובתה בשביל בעלה והיה בעלה מגרשה. ואין לבעל נכסים לפרוע כתובתה ידירנה הנייה. שלא יחזירנה לעולם ויפרע לה הערב כתובתה שאם אינו מדירה איכא למימר קנוניא עשו ביניהן על נכסיו של זה הערב ושוב כשיפרע לו הערב כתובתה יחזיר לו זה את אשתו ויאכל נכסיו של ערב: מאי טעמא. לא אפקת מן הערב: דאמר לו ערב גברא אשלימת לי. כלומר לוה הפקדת בידי שאהיה ערב שלא יברח וגברא אשלימי לך אותו אדם עצמו אני אחזירו לך ושוב איני נזקק לך: האי דינא דפרסאי הוא. דדיינו בגיותא שאין יורדין לעיקר הדין אלא פוטרין לאלתר הנתבע כמו שנראה להם לפי שעה: אדרבה פרסאי בתר ערבא אזיל א) דבר תימה הוא היאך יכול ערב לסלק עצמו ולומר לו גברא אשלמת לי וכו' והלא יכול לומר לו המלוה אי לא את לא הוה נפקי זוזאי מתחת ידאי. ואלא מאי לא יפרע מן הערב תחלה אלא ללוה יתבע תחילה ואם אין (יפרע) נכסים ללוה יפרע מן הערב: תניא נמי הכי. כדאוקימנא דהאי לא יפרע לא יתבע הוא: לקח בגדו כי ערב זר. אלמא דמשתעבדי ב) ולמה קרא נמי דכתיב ערבת לזר כפיך וגו' לך התרפס ורהב רעיך או תפרע לו או הרבה עליו רעים לפייסו שיתן לך זמן עד שתפרע לו על יד על יד: ולר' יוסי דאמר אסמכתא קניא ערב משתעבד. דערבות נמי אי הוו כמו אסמכתא שהוא דאי כלומר דאי לא פרע לך לוה פרעי לך אנא וגמר ומשעבד נפשיה בלב שלם: לא שנו. דהיכא דאמר על מנת שאפרע ממי שארצה שיפרע מן הערב אלא בשאין נכסים ללוה: מכלל דתנא קמא סבר לא שנא יש לו לא שנא אין לו. יגבה מן הערב וקשיא לר' יוחנן: ואמר לך חסורי מחסרא והכי קתני כו'. והא דקא דייקת מכי דתנא קמא סבר לא שנא הכי ולא שנא הכי דיפרע מן הערב בקבלן קאמר. דקבלן אע"פ שיש נכסים ללוה הפרעון מן הקבלן: ורשב"ג סבר אחד זה ואחד זה אחד ערב ואחד קבלן ביש נכסים ללוה לא יפרע מה
חוץ

א) נראה דחסר כאן וצריך לציין על הגמ' אלא בי דינא דפרסאי דלא יהבי טעמא למילתייהו. דבר תימה הוא וכו'. ב) אולי צ"ל ולמה מהך קרא נמי וכו'.

עין משפט נר מצוה

קכז א מיי' פכ"ה מהל' מלוה ולוה הל' ד סמג עשין לד טוש"ע ח"מ סי' קכט סעיף יד:

קכח ב מיי' פי"ז מהל' אישות הלכה ט ועיין בהשגות ובמגיד משנה סמג עשין מח טור וש"ע אה"ע סימן קב סעיף ז:

קכט ג מיי' פכ"ה מהל' מלוה ולוה הל' ג סמג עשין לד טוש"ע ח"מ סי' קכט סעיף ח:

קל ד מיי' שם הל' ב טוש"ע שם סעיף ב:

קלא ה ו מיי' שם הל' ד ועיין בהשגות ובמגיד משנה טוש"ע שם סעיף יד עיין בטור:

מסורת הש"ס

א) [ערכין כג.: ב] קנט.: ג) [וכן מילתא אותו וגו' כאוכן הוא אבל יהודה אמר אערבנו. ומהרש"א נדחק לייחב הפלוגתא לאמנם לע טסחא של פרסת מקך סי' ל"ח ג א"ל רב חסדא יהודה גופיה לוה דכתיב שלחה הנער אלא א"ר חסדא מ בני אם ערבת לרעך] ד) ב"מ קטו: ה) [פז. ב"מ קטו:] ו) קסח. וש"נ: ז) וב"וכו' ולא לשון: ט) פי' אני ליתן לך: י) פי' אני לפרוע לך:

הגהות הב"ח

(א) גמ' לר' יוסי ד אסמכתא. נ"ב ע"ל קסח ע"א: (ב) שם נכסים ללוה בין כך כך לא יפרע מן ה מכלל דת"ק: (ג) רש ד"ה תנה אותו כו' כו קבלתיו בידי: (ד) גמר ומשעבד נפשיה שלם: (ה) תום' ד"ה ח וכו' אע"פ שאין לו נכס ידועים ללוה: (ו) ב לנכסי הערב דלדלמא הוה איתיה ללוה הכה יהיב וכו' שהרלה א אינו לריך להמתין ולח (ז) בא"ד לא מלא סוס להפרע וכו' ש"כ הכה דעלמא וכו' בכעל ערבין בעו קנין ולא היינו תן לו וכו' אב אינו מזכיר:

רַבָּן שִׁמְעוֹן בֶּן גַּמְלִיאֵל אוֹמֵר אִם יֵשׁ נְכָסִים לַלֹּוֶה — אֶחָד זֶה וְאֶחָד זֶה לֹא יִפָּרַע מֵהֶן. א)אָמַר רַבָּה בַּר חָנָה אָמַר ר' יוֹחָנָן: כָּל מָקוֹם שֶׁשָּׁנָה רשב"ג בְּמִשְׁנָתֵנוּ — הֲלָכָה כְּמוֹתוֹ, חוּץ מֵעָרֵב, וְצִידוֹן, וּרְאָיָה אַחֲרוֹנָה. אָמַר רַב הוּנָא: "הַלְוֵהוּ וַאֲנִי עָרֵב", "הַלְוֵהוּ וַאֲנִי פּוֹרֵעַ", "הַלְוֵהוּ וַאֲנִי חַיָּיב", "הַלְוֵהוּ וַאֲנִי ב)(נוֹתֵן") — כּוּלָּן לְשׁוֹן עַרְבוּת הֵן; "תֵּן לוֹ וַאֲנִי קַבְּלָן", "תֵּן לוֹ וַאֲנִי פּוֹרֵעַ", "תֵּן לוֹ וַאֲנִי חַיָּיב", "תֵּן לוֹ וַאֲנִי ב)(נוֹתֵן") — כּוּלָּן לְשׁוֹן קַבְּלָנוּת הֵן. אִיבַּעְיָא לְהוּ: "הַלְוֵהוּ וַאֲנִי קַבְּלָן", "תֵּן לוֹ וַאֲנִי עָרֵב", מַאי? אָמַר ר' יִצְחָק: לְשׁוֹן עַרְבוּת — עַרְבוּת, לְשׁוֹן קַבְּלָנוּת — קַבְּלָנוּת. רַב חִסְדָּא אָמַר: כּוּלָּן לְשׁוֹן קַבְּלָנוּת הֵן, בַּר מֵ"הַלְוֵהוּ וַאֲנִי עָרֵב". רָבָא אָמַר: אכּוּלָּן לְשׁוֹן עַרְבוּת הֵן, בַּר מִ"תֵּן לוֹ וַאֲנִי נוֹתֵן". א"ל מָר בַּר אַמֵימָר לְרַב אַשִׁי, הָכִי אָמַר אַבָּא: "תֵּן לוֹ וַאֲנִי נוֹתֵן" — אֵין לַמַּלְוֶה עַל הַלֹּוֶה כְּלוּם. בוְלָא הִיא, לָא מִיפְּטַר לֹוֶה מִינֵּיהּ דְּמַלְוֶה געַד שֶׁיִּשָּׂא וְיִתֵּן בַּיָּד. הַהוּא דַּיָּינָא רס"ל דְּאַחְתֵּיהּ לַמַּלְוֶה לְנִכְסֵי [דְּלֹוֶה] מִקַּמֵּי דְּלִתְבְּעֵיהּ לַלֹּוֶה, סַלְּקֵיהּ רַב חָנִין בְּרֵיהּ דְּרַב יֵיבָא. אֲמַר רָבָא: מַאן חַכִּים לְמֶעְבַּד כִּי הָא מִילְּתָא, אִי לָאו רַב חָנִין בְּרֵיהּ דְּרַב יֵיבָא! קָסָבַר: ג)נִכְסֵיהּ דְּבַר אִינִישׁ אִינּוּן מְעָרְבִין יָתֵיהּ; וּתְנַן: ד)הַמַּלְוֶה אֶת חֲבֵירוֹ ע"י עָרֵב — לֹא יִפָּרַע מִן הֶעָרֵב; וְקי"ל: לֹא יִתְבַּע עָרֵב תְּחִלָּה. ההַהוּא עָרְבָא דְּיָתְמֵי דִּפְרָעֵיהּ לַמַּלְוֶה מִקַּמֵּי דְּלוֹדְעִינְהוּ לְיָתְמֵי, א"ר פַּפָּא: ה)פְּרִיעַת בע"ח מִצְוָה, וְיַתְמֵי לָאו בְּנֵי מֵיעֲבַד מִצְוָה נִינְהוּ; וְרַב הוּנָא בְּרֵיהּ דְּרַב יְהוֹשֻׁעַ אֲמַר: ה אֵימַר צְרָרֵי אַתְפְּסֵיהּ.

מַאי

רשב"ם

רַבָּן שִׁמְעוֹן בֶּן גַּמְלִיאֵל אוֹמֵר אִם יֵשׁ נְכָסִים לַלֹּוֶה. אֶחָד עָרֵב וְאֶחָד קַבְּלָן — לֹא יִפָּרַע אֶלָּא מִן הַלֹּוֶה. בְּמִשְׁנָתֵנוּ. וְלֹא בַּבָּרַיְיתָא. חוּץ מֵעָרֵב. מִשְׁנָה זוֹ. אֶלָּא יִפָּרַע מִן הַקַּבְּלָן וְאַע"פ שֶׁיֵּשׁ נְכָסִים לַלֹּוֶה, כְּרַבָּנַן. וְצִידָן. בְּ"מִי שֶׁאֲחָזוֹ" בְּמַסֶּכֶת גִּיטִּין. וּרְאָיָה אַחֲרוֹנָה. בְּסַנְהֶדְרִין, בְּפֶרֶק "זֶה בּוֹרֵר", שְׁנֵי מִשְׁנָיוֹת שֶׁל רְאָיָה (א) זוֹ: כָּל זְמַן שֶׁמֵּבִיא רְאָיָה כו' — בָּרִאשׁוֹנָה הֲלָכָה כְּמוֹתוֹ, בָּאַחֲרוֹנָה אֵין הֲלָכָה כְּמוֹתוֹ. כּוּלָּן לְשׁוֹן עַרְבוּת הֵן. דְּהָא לְשׁוֹן הַלְוָאָה קָאָמַר: הַלְוֵהוּ, הוּא יִהְיֶה לֹוֶה וַאֲנִי פּוֹרֵעַ אִם לֹא יִפְרַע לְךָ. תֵּן לוֹ. מְסוֹר הַמָּמוֹן בְּיָדוֹ וַאֲנִי אֶפְרָעֲנּוּ לְךָ. אֵין כָּאן לְשׁוֹן הַלְוָאָה, אֶלָּא שְׁלִיחוּתֵיהּ דְּהַאי דְּקָאָמַר "תֵּן לוֹ" עָבֵיד מַלְוֶה. לְשׁוֹן עַרְבוּת עַרְבוּת. לָא שְׁנָא קָאָמַר "הַלְוֵהוּ", וְל"ש קָאָמַר "תֵּן לוֹ". וְרַב חִסְדָּא אָמַר כּוּלָּן לְשׁוֹן קַבְּלָנוּת הֵן. וַאֲפִי' "תֵּן לוֹ וַאֲנִי עָרֵב", אֲפִי' "הַלְוֵהוּ וַאֲנִי פּוֹרֵעַ", "הַלְוֵהוּ וַאֲנִי חַיָּיב", "הַלְוֵהוּ וַאֲנִי נוֹתֵן לְךָ". בַּר מֵהַלְוֵהוּ וַאֲנִי עָרֵב. דְּכֵיוָן דִּנְקַט לְשׁוֹן הַלְוָאָה וּלְשׁוֹן עַרְבוּת — אָז מוֹצִיא מִכְּלַל קַבְּלָנוּת. וְרָבָא אָמַר כּוּלָּן לְשׁוֹן עַרְבוּת הֵן. אֲפִילּוּ "הַלְוֵהוּ וַאֲנִי קַבְּלָן", "תֵּן לוֹ וַאֲנִי פּוֹרֵעַ", "תֵּן לוֹ וַאֲנִי חַיָּיב" — דְּמַשְׁמַע: אֲנִי אֶפְרַע בִּשְׁבִילוֹ אִם לֹא יִפְרַע הוּא. בַּר מִתֵּן לוֹ וַאֲנִי נוֹתֵן לְךָ. וְכ"ש "תֵּן לוֹ וַאֲנִי קַבְּלָן". וְקַיְימָא לָן כְּרָבָא דְּהוּא בַּתְרָא. וְדַוְקָא "תֵּן לוֹ וַאֲנִי נוֹתֵן", דִּשְׁנֵיהֶם לְשׁוֹן מַתָּנָה (ג) — מַשְׁמַע קַבְּלָנוּת, שֶׁבְּאוֹתוֹ לָשׁוֹן שֶׁצִּיוָּהוּ לִמְסוֹר לָזֶה קִבֵּל עָלָיו לְפָרְעוֹ, דְּמַשְׁמַע כְּאִילּוּ קִבֵּל הוּא עַצְמוֹ מִיַּד הַמַּלְוֶה. בְּעַרְבוּת — לֹא יִפְרַע מִן הֶעָרֵב תְּחִלָּה אֶלָּא מִן הַלֹּוֶה. וּבְקַבְּלָנוּת — מֵאֵיזֶה שֶׁיִּרְצֶה יִפְרַע, כְּרַבָּנַן דְּמַתְנִיתִין. אֲבָל אִם נָשָׂא וְנָתַן בַּיָּד — אֵין לַמַּלְוֶה עַל הַלֹּוֶה כְּלוּם. אִינּוּן עָרְבִין בֵּיהּ. כִּדְכְתִיב (משלי כב): "אִם אֵין לְךָ לְשַׁלֵּם לָמָּה יִקַּח מִשְׁכָּבְךָ מִתַּחְתֶּיךָ", וּכְתִיב (דברים כד): "יוֹצִיא אֵלֶיךָ הָעֲבוֹט הַחוּצָה". וְקַיְימָא לָן לֹא יִתְבַּע מִן הֶעָרֵב תְּחִלָּה. אֵין נָכוֹן לְהַטְרִיחַ אֶת הֶעָרֵב חִנָּם, דִּלְמָא מְפַיֵּי לֵיהּ לֹוֶה. וְהוּא הַדִּין לְנִכְסֵי דְּאִינָשׁ — לָמָּה נְזַלְזֵל בִּנְכָסָיו לְהוֹרִיד בָּהֶן אֶת הַמַּלְוֶה חִנָּם, שֶׁמָּא יְסַלְּקֶנּוּ לֹוֶה בְּמָעוֹת וְלֹא יִצְטָרֵךְ לֵירֵד בִּנְכָסָיו. הַהוּא עָרְבָא דְּיַתְמֵי. אֲבִיהֶם לָוָה בְּחַיָּיו, וְזֶה נַעֲשָׂה עָרֵב לַמַּלְוֶה בִּשְׁבִילוֹ. וּלְאַחַר מוֹתוֹ פָּרַע הֶעָרֵב תְּחִלָּה, מִקַּמֵּי דְּנִתְבְּעִינְהוּ לְיַתְמֵי. כְּלוֹמַר, מִשֶּׁלּוֹ פָּרַע וְלֹא מִשֶּׁל יְתוֹמִים, שֶׁלֹּא הִסְפִּיק לְתָבְעָם, וְעַתָּה חוֹזֵר עֲלֵיהֶם וְתוֹבְעָם. פְּרִיעַת בע"ח מִצְוָה. הֶעָרֵב עַתָּה נַעֲשָׂה בע"ח, וּמִלְוָה עַל פֶּה הוּא, וּמִצְוָה לְפָרְעוֹ. וְאִם יְתוֹמִים פְּחוּתִים מי"ג (ג) — דְּלָאו בְּנֵי מֵיעֲבַד מִצְוָה נִינְהוּ, וְכִי גָּדְלֵי — לִישְׁתָּעֵי דִּינָא בַּהֲדַיְיהוּ, כִּדְאָמַר בְּ"חֶזְקַת הַבָּתִּים" [נ"א דרבא] (לעיל לג.) גַּבֵּי עוּבְדָּא *דְּרַבָּה בַּר שַׁרְשׁוֹם. רַב הוּנָא בְּרֵיהּ דְּרַב יְהוֹשֻׁעַ אָמַר. לְעוֹלָם יַתְמֵי בְּנֵי מֵיעֲבַד מִלְוָה נִינְהוּ, כִּדְאָמַר בַּעֲרָכִין בְּפֶרֶק "שׁוּם הַיְתוֹמִים" (דף כב.): יַתְמֵי דְּאָכְלִי דְּלָאו דִּידְהוּ — לֵיזְלוּ בָּתַר שִׁיבְקַיְיהוּ. אֶלָּא הַיְינוּ טַעֲמָא דְּלָא גּוֹבֶה עָרֵב מִיַּתְמֵי עַד דְּגָדְלֵי, וְיֵדְעוּ לִטְעוֹן וְלַחֲזוֹר אַחַר דִּינָם — דְּאִיכָּא לְמֵימַר: אֵימוֹר צְרָרֵי אַתְפְּסֵיהּ אֲבִיהֶם לַמַּלְוֶה בְּחַיָּיו, לִפְטוֹר אֶת הֶעָרֵב. [נ"ל כל] וְהִלְכָּךְ, *עַל מִלְוָה עַל פֶּה אִיכָּא לְמֵיחַשׁ דִּלְמָא פְּרָעֵיהּ אֲבוּהוֹן בְּחַיָּיו. וְאַע"ג דְּקיי"ל לְקַמָּן בְּפִירְקִין: מִלְוָה עַל פֶּה גּוֹבֶה מִן הַיּוֹרְשִׁין — הָנֵי מִילֵּי כְּגוֹן דְּשַׁמְתּוּהוּ וּמִית בְּשַׁמְתֵּיהּ, אִי נַמִּי כְּשֶׁחַיָּיב מוֹדֶה. וּפָסְקִינַן לְקַמָּן הִלְכְתָא כְּרַב הוּנָא בְּרֵיהּ דְּרַב יְהוֹשֻׁעַ דְּאָמַר דְּלָא חָיְישִׁינַן לְמֵימַר יַתְמֵי לָאו בְּנֵי מֵיעֲבַד מִלְוָה נִינְהוּ, אֶלָּא בְּכָל חוֹב שֶׁאָנוּ יוֹדְעִין שֶׁלֹּא פָּרְעוּ אֲבִיהֶן בְּחַיָּיו, אוֹ שֶׁאֵין אָנוּ יוֹדְעִין אֶלָּא שֶׁאָמַר אֲבִיהֶן "תְּנוּ" — נוֹתְנִין כִּדְפָסְקִינַן בַּעֲרָכִין, וְאֵין מַמְתִּינִין עַד דְּגָדְלֵי, כִּדְשַׁלְחוּ מִתָּם דְּהִלְכְתָא כְּרַב הוּנָא בְּרֵיהּ דְּרַב יְהוֹשֻׁעַ. וְרָבָא נַמִּי, דְּפָסַק בַּעֲרָכִין (שם:) הִלְכְתָא דְּאֵין נִזְקָקִין לְנִכְסֵי יְתוֹמִים אֶלָּא אִם כֵּן רִבִּית אוֹכֶלֶת בָּהֶן, וְאִם אָמַר "תְּנוּ" נוֹתְנִין — נִרְאֶה בְּעֵינַי דְּלָא פָּלִיג אַדְּרַב הוּנָא, (ד) כֵּיוָן דְּחַיָּיב מוֹדֶה כְּמַאן דְּאָמַר "תְּנוּ" דָּמֵי. וּמָר אָמַר חֲדָא וּמָר אָמַר חֲדָא וְלָא פְּלִיגֵי, רַב הוּנָא אַיְירֵי בְּחַיָּיב מוֹדֶה אַף עַל גַּב דְּלָא אָמַר "תְּנוּ", וְרָבָא אַיְירֵי בְּאוֹמֵר "תְּנוּ" אַף עַל גַּב דְּאֵין חַיָּיב מוֹדֶה. וְכָל הָנֵי גְּבִיָּיתָן מִמְּקַרְקְעֵי דְּיַתְמֵי. וְנִרְאֶה בְּעֵינַי דִּבַזְּמַן הַזֶּה דְּלֵיכָּא מְקַרְקְעֵי כָּל כָּךְ, אַע"ג דְּקיי"ל מִטַּלְטְלֵי דְּיַתְמֵי לָא מִשְׁתַּעְבְּדֵי לְבע"ח — בַּזְּמַן הַזֶּה דִּינָם לִגְבּוֹת מִמִּטַּלְטְלֵי דְּשָׁבַק לְהוֹן אֲבוּהוֹן, כְּמוֹ שֶׁתִּקְּנוּ הַגְּאוֹנִים בִּכְתוּבַּת אִשָּׁה, דְּפָסְקִינַן הִלְכְתָא מִמְּקַרְקְעֵי וְלָא מִמִּטַּלְטְלֵי, וַאֲפִילּוּ הָכִי נָהֲגוּ לִגְבּוֹת מִמִּטַּלְטְלֵי. וּמֵבִיא אֲנִי רְאָיָה מֵהַהוּא דִּכְתוּבּוֹת (דף סז.) דְּאַרְנְקֵי דִּמְחוֹזָא, דְּאִשָּׁה גּוֹבָה כְּתוּבָּתָהּ מֵהֶם מִשּׁוּם דְּאַסְמְכַתַּיְיהוּ עֲלַיְיהוּ, וְהוּא הַדִּין לְבַעַל חוֹב דְּגָבֵי מִטַּלְטְלֵי דְּיַתְמֵי הֵיכָא דְּיָדוּעַ לָנוּ שֶׁאֲבִיהֶן הָיָה חַיָּיב לָזֶה. וְכֵן הֲלָכָה לְמַעֲשֶׂה, דְּהָא אָמְרִינַן לְקַמָּן: מִלְוֶה עַל פֶּה גּוֹבֶה מִן הַיְּתוֹמִים כְּדֵי שֶׁלֹּא תִּנְעוֹל דֶּלֶת בִּפְנֵי לֹוִין, וְאִי מִמִּטַּלְטְלֵי דְּשָׁבַק לְהוֹן אֲבוּהוֹן לֹא גּוֹבֶה — אֵין לְךָ נְעִילַת דֶּלֶת גָּדוֹל מִזֶּה, דְּהָא לָא שְׁכִיחֵי לָן מְקַרְקְעֵי.

מַאי

תוספות

מקמי דלודעינהו ליתמי כו'. מיהר לפרוע ולא הודיעם אם ירצו לפרוע לו כלום. שאם היה מודיעם — שמא היו פורעין. מיהו, אם לא היו רוצים לפרוע — נפרע מן הערב, דהיינו אין לו נכסים ללוה. דודאי אם אין לו נכסים ו)(שאין) יכול הערב לדחותו עד אחר שישכיר עצמו ויקנה נכסים, מה לי אם ידחה אותו עד שיגדלו היתומים, מה לי אם ידחה אותו עד שישכיר עצמו. *ואם כתב בו התקבלתי. שכתב בעל חוב כן — גובה. בשלמא לרב הונא משכחת לה בשחייב מודה, דליכא למיחש לצררי. אלא לרב פפא היכי משכחת לה? וא"ת: אי בשחייב מודה, אפי' לא כתב "התקבלתי"! ויש לדחות: דכי לא כתב "התקבלתי" — להכי לא גבי מיתומים, דחיישי' שמא לא גבה המלוה ממנו. ומשני: שאני התם, דלהכי כתב ליה "התקבלתי" — דליהוי כחיה אלים, וליהוי כמלוה בשטר. וכן גרס רבינו חננאל: משכחת לה בשחייב מודה, ומפרש כדפרישית, דאלים משום דהוי (ה) בשטרא. וקשיא לן: דבערכין פ' "שום היתומים" (דף כב: ושם) מוכח דאיירי רב הונא ורב פפא במלוה בשטר. דפריך התם: שום היתומים ל' יום, בשלמא לרב הונא — מוקי לה בשחייב מודה, אלא לרב פפא במאי מוקי לה? אמר לך רב פפא: איבעית אימא בכתובת אשה, משום חינא. אבל בבעל חוב בשטר — לא מצי מוקי לה. אלא איירי ודאי אפילו בשטר. ועוד קשיא: כיון דמוקי מילתיה במלוה על פה — א"כ אפילו בני מיעבד מלוה נינהו נמי אין לגבות מהן, דטוענין ליורש שפרע, שהאב היה נאמן לומר "פרעתי", ואפילו גדולים נינהו פטורין מהאי טעמא! ועוד: מאי משני דלהכי כתב ליה "התקבלתי", דהוי כמלוה בשטר? מה יש לו לכתיבת המלוה להועיל לערב לגבות מיתמי, מאחר שהלוה לא כתב כלום! והיה נראה לפרש: דאם כתב בו "התקבלתי" גובה — היינו: אם כתב בשטר "התקבלתי מן הערב", שכך כתב הלוה גם לערב בתוך השטר, ליפות כחו, לדוחקו ולפטרו לשלם חובו למלוה אף אם לא יתבענו המלוה עדיין — גובה. בשלמא לרב הונא בריה דרב יהושע — ניחא, דאיהו חייש לצררי, והכא ליכא למיחש לצררי, דכיון שכתב גם לערב "התקבלתי" ועשאו כמלוה לתבעו מעצמו — אין רגיל להתפיס צררי למלוה. אבל ברישא אינו גובה, משום דחייש לצררי, דלמא אתפסיה למלוה, ואע"פ שיש ערב. וזה אין לחוש בכתב לו "התקבלתי" — דלמא אתפסיה צררי לערב — שאין רגילות להתפיס ליה צררי, כדאמרינן לקמן דבגוי ליכא למיחש לצררי — אלמא אין מתפיס לערב, דאם כן ניחוש שמא התפיס לערב. ואפילו למאן דפריך: אדרבה כו' (ו) אי לאו דאתפיס צררי לערב לא הוה מקבל לערב, כדפי' בקונטרס — הכא מיהא לא מתפיס לא למלוה ולא לערב. אלא לרב פפא קשיא: הא לאו בני מיעבד מלוה נינהו! שאני התם דלהכי כתב לו "התקבלתי" — שיהא לו כח לגבות מן היתומים,

ושעבד

רבינו גרשום

חוץ מערב. הא דקאמר במתני' דבין כך ובין כך לא יפרע מן הערב: צידן. במס' גיטין מעשה בצידן באחד שאמר לאשתו הרי זה גיטך על מנת שתביא אצטליתי ואבד אצטליתו אינו גט: רשב"ג אמר נותן דמיה והרי הוא [גט] ולית הלכתא כוותיה: וראיה אחרונה. במס' סנהדרין אמר רשב"ג מה יעשה זה שלא היה יודע שיש לו עדים ומצא עדים ולא היה יודע שיש לו ראיה והביא לו ראיה כו': כולן לשון ערבות הן. כיון שאמר לו בלשון הלואה: כולן לשון קבלנות הן. כיון שאמר לו בלשון נתינה דנתינה היינו קבלנות כדאמרי' לעיל תנה אותו על ידי דהיינו קבלנות: איבעיא להו הלוהו ואני קבלן. וכן כי אמר ליה תן לו ואני ערב מאי מי אזלינן בתר תן לו דהיינו קבלנות או בתר ואני ערב דהיינו ערבות: אמר רב יצחק. תפוס לשון אחרון להיכא דאמר ליה לבסוף ואני ערב היינו לשון ערבות ולהיכא דאמר לבסוף ואני קבלן היינו לשון קבלנות אע"ג דאמר מעיקרא הלויהו: בר מתן לו. דהיינו תנה אותו על ידי ואני אשיבנו אליך היינו קבלנות גמורה: ולא היא לא מפטר לוה מיניה דמלוה עד שישא מיד המלוה ליתן ללוה דהשתא לא קיבל הלוה מיד מלוה כלום להכי אין לו עליו כלום אלא הקבלן אפי' יש נכסים ללוה: מאן היה לסלוקיה ההוא דיינא אלא רב חנן בר אבא. דקסבר נכסוהי דברנש אינון ערבין ליה ולא היה לו ליפרע מן הנכסים דהיינו הערב עד שיתבע מן הלוה תחלה דשמא אילו תובע הוה היה פורעו ממקום אחר: ההוא ערבא דיתמי. שהיה א' ערב של אביהן במלוה שעל פה ומת האב והיה הערב ליתומין פורע החוב למלוה מנכסיו של עצמו מקמי דלודעינהו ליתמי והיה רוצה הערב לגבות מן היתומין מה שפרע למלוה: רב פפא אמר פריעת בעל חוב. למלוה במלוה שבעל פה ואין בה קנין לא חיוב הוא לפורעו כיון דאין לו שטר ולא עדות וקנין אלא מצוה היא שיפרע לו הודאת מלוה על פה ואילו היה הלוה קיים היה רוצה לקיים מצוה זו היו בית דין חובטין אותו עד שיאמר רוצה אני ויפרע והשתא שמת ובניו יתומין קטנים הן יתמי לאו בני מיעבד מצוה נינהו עד דגדלי והלכך לית עלייהו לפרוע לא למלוה לערב כלום ולא פריעי ליה להאי ערב כלום אבל אי היה בשטר היו מחובין לפרוע: ורב הונא בריה דרב יהושע. אמר להכי לא פרעי יתמי כלום לערב דאימור אביהן קמי דמת שמא אתפסיה צררי למלוה כשיעור חובו

עין משפט נר מצוה

קלב א מיי' פכ"ה מהל' מלוה ולוה הל' ה ועי' בהשגות ובמ"מ סמג עשין צד טוש"ע ח"מ סי' קכט סעיף יז:

קלג ב ג מיי' שם פכ"ו הל' ג סמג שם טוש"ע ח"מ שם סעיף יט:

שייך לע"ב

קלד ד ה מיי' שם הל' ו ועיין בהשגות ובמ"מ סמג שם טוש"ע ח"מ סי' קל סעיף ז:

הגהות הב"ח

מַאי בֵּינַיְיהוּ? אִיכָּא בֵּינַיְיהוּ אכְּשֶׁחַיָּיב מוֹדֶה. אִי נַמִי, בדְּשַׁמְּתוּהוּ וּמֵת בְּשַׁמְתֵּיהּ. א)שָׁלְחוּ מִתָּם: שַׁמְּתוּהוּ וּמֵת בְּשַׁמְתֵּיהּ — גהִלְכְתָא כְּרַב הוּנָא בְּרֵיהּ דְּרַב יְהוֹשֻׁעַ. מֵיתִיבֵי: דעָרֵב שֶׁהָיָה שְׁטַר חוֹב יוֹצֵא מִתַּחַת יָדוֹ — אֵינוֹ גּוֹבֶה, הוְאִם כָּתוּב בּוֹ "הִתְקַבַּלְתִּי מִמְּךָ" — גּוֹבֶה; בִּשְׁלָמָא לְרַב הוּנָא בְּרֵיהּ דְּרַב יְהוֹשֻׁעַ מַשְׁכַּחַת לָהּ — כְּשֶׁחַיָּיב מוֹדֶה, אֶלָּא לְרַב פַּפָּא קַשְׁיָא! שָׁאנֵי הָתָם, (א) לְהָכִי טָרַח וּכָתַב לֵיהּ "הִתְקַבַּלְתִּי". והַהוּא עָרְבָא דְּגוֹי דְּפָרְעֵיהּ לְגוֹי מִקַּמֵּי דְּלִתְבְּעִינְהוּ לְיַתְמֵי. א"ל רַב מָרְדְּכַי לְרַב אַשִׁי, הָכִי אָמַר אֲבִימִי מֵהַגְרוֹנְיָא מִשְּׁמֵיהּ דְּרָבָא: אֲפִילּוּ לְמ"ד חָיְישִׁינַן לִצְרָרֵי — ה"מ יִשְׂרָאֵל, אֲבָל גּוֹי, כֵּיוָן דְּבָתַר עָרְבָא אָזֵיל — לָא חָיְישִׁינַן לִצְרָרֵי. א"ל: אַדְּרַבָּה: אֲפִילּוּ לְמ"ד לָא חָיְישִׁינַן לִצְרָרֵי — הָנֵי מִילֵּי יִשְׂרָאֵל, זאֲבָל גּוֹיִם, כֵּיוָן דְּדִינַיְיהוּ בָּתַר עָרְבָא אָזְלִי, אִי לָאו דְּאַתְפְּסֵיהּ צְרָרֵי מֵעִיקָּרָא — לָא הֲוָה מְקַבֵּל לֵיהּ.§ "וְכֵן הָיָה רשב"ג אוֹמֵר: הֶעָרֵב לָאִשָּׁה בִּכְתוּבָּתָהּ" [וכו'].§ ב)מֹשֶׁה בַּר עַצְרִי עָרְבָא דִּכְתוּבָּתָהּ דְּכַלָּתֵיהּ הֲוָה, רַב הוּנָא בְּרֵיהּ צוּרְבָא מִדְּרַבָּנַן הֲוָה וּדְחִיקָא לֵיהּ מִילְּתָא, אָמַר אַבַּיֵי: לֵיכָּא דְּנֵיזִיל דְּנַסְבֵּיהּ עֵצָה לְרַב הוּנָא, דְּנִגָרְשָׁהּ לִדְבֵיתְהוּ, וְתֵיזִיל וְתִגְבֵּי כְּתוּבָּה מֵאֲבוּהּ, וַהֲדַר נַהְדְּרָהּ? א"ל רָבָא: וְהָא יַדִּירֶנָּה הֲנָאָה תְּנַן! א"ל אַבַּיֵי: אַטּוּ כָּל דִּמְגָרֵשׁ — בְּבֵי דִינָא מְגָרֵשׁ? לְסוֹף אִיגַּלַּאי מִילְּתָא דְּכֹהֵן הוּא. אֲמַר אַבַּיֵי, הַיְינוּ ג)דְּאָמְרִי אֱינָשֵׁי: בָּתַר עַנְיָא אָזְלָא עֲנִיּוּתָא. וּמִי אֲמַר אַבַּיֵי הָכִי? וְהָא ד)אָמַר אַבַּיֵי: חאֵיזֶהוּ רָשָׁע עָרוּם? זֶה הַמַּשִּׂיא עֵצָה לִמְכּוֹר בִּנְכָסִי' כְּרשב"ג! טבְּנוֹ שָׁאנֵי, וְצוּרְבָא מֵרַבָּנַן שָׁאנֵי. וְהָא עָרֵב הוּא, [וְקַיְימָא לָן:] עָרֵב דִּכְתוּבָּה ילָא מִשְׁתַּעְבֵּד! כקַבְּלָן הֲוָה. הָנִיחָא לְמ"ד: קַבְּלָן דִּכְתוּבָּה אע"ג דְּלֵית לֵיהּ נִכְסֵי לְבַעַל מִשְׁתַּעְבֵּד — שַׁפִּיר, אֶלָּא לְמַאן דְּאָמַר: אִי אִית לֵיהּ מִשְׁתַּעְבֵּד, אִי לֵית לֵיהּ לָא מִשְׁתַּעְבֵּד — מַאי אִיכָּא לְמֵימַר? אִיבָּעֵית אֵימָא: מֶיהֱוֵי הֲוָה לֵיהּ וְאִישְׁתַּדּוּף. וְאִיבָּעֵית אֵימָא: לאַבָּא לְגַבֵּי בְּרֵיהּ שַׁעְבּוּדֵי מְשַׁעְבֵּד נַפְשֵׁיהּ. דְּאִיתְּמַר: ה)עָרֵב דִּכְתוּבָּה — דִּבְרֵי הַכֹּל לָא מִשְׁתַּעְבֵּד, קַבְּלָן דְּבַעַל חוֹב — דִּבְרֵי הַכֹּל מִשְׁתַּעְבֵּד, קַבְּלָן דִּכְתוּבָּה וְעָרֵב דְּבַעַל חוֹב — פְּלִיגִי, מָר סָבַר: אִי אִית לֵיהּ נִכְסֵי לַלֹּוֶה — מִשְׁתַּעְבֵּד, אִי לֵית לֵיהּ — לָא מִשְׁתַּעְבֵּד; וּמָר סָבַר: בֵּין אִית לֵיהּ וּבֵין לֵית לֵיהּ — מִשְׁתַּעְבֵּד. ו)וְהִלְכְתָא: (ב) מעָרֵב, בֵּין אִית לֵיהּ וּבֵין לֵית לֵיהּ — מִשְׁתַּעְבֵּד, נבַּר מֵעָרֵב דִּכְתוּבָּה, דְּאע"ג דְּאִית לֵיהּ לַבַּעַל — לָא מִשְׁתַּעְבֵּד; מַאי טַעְמָא? מִצְוָה הוּא דַּעֲבַד וְלָאו מִידֵּי חַסְרָהּ. ז)אָמַר רַב הוּנָא: סשְׁכִיב מְרַע שֶׁהִקְדִּישׁ כָּל נְכָסָיו, וְאָמַר "מָנֶה לִפְלוֹנִי בְּיָדִי" — נֶאֱמָן, חֲזָקָה אֵין אָדָם עוֹשֶׂה קְנוּנְיָא עַל הֶקְדֵּשׁ. מַתְקִיף לָהּ רַב נַחְמָן: וְכִי אָדָם עוֹשֶׂה קְנוּנְיָא עַל בָּנָיו? דְּרַב וּשְׁמוּאֵל דְּאָמְרִי תַּרְוַיְיהוּ: עשְׁכִיב מְרַע שֶׁאָמַר "מָנֶה לִפְלוֹנִי בְּיָדִי", אָמַר "תְּנוּ" — נוֹתְנִין, לֹא אָמַר "תְּנוּ" — אֵין נוֹתְנִין; אַלְמָא חאָדָם עָשׂוּי שֶׁלֹּא לְהַשְׂבִּיעַ אֶת בָּנָיו, הָכָא

מַאי בֵּינַיְיהוּ. כֵּיוָן דְּבֵין לְמָר וּבֵין לְמָר אֵין הֶעָרֵב גּוֹבֶה עַכְשָׁיו מִיַּתְמֵי. כְּשֶׁחַיָּיב מוֹדֶה. בִּשְׁעַת מִיתָתוֹ, דְּלֵיכָּא לְמֵיחַשׁ לִצְרָרֵי. לְרַב הוּנָא גָּבֵי מִיַּתְמֵי, לְרַב פַּפָּא לָא גָּבֵי עַד דְּגָדְלֵי. דְּשַׁמְּתוּהוּ וּמֵית בְּשַׁמְתֵּיהּ. שֶׁלֹּא רָצָה לִפְרוֹעַ בְּחַיָּיו. שְׁלַחוּ מִתָּם. הֵיכָא דְּשַׁמְּתוּהוּ וּמֵית בְּשַׁמְתֵּיהּ — הַדָּבָר יָדוּעַ שֶׁלֹּא פְּרָעוֹ, וּכְמִי שֶׁחַיָּיב מוֹדֶה דָּמֵי. הִלְכְתָא כְּרַב הוּנָא בְּרֵיהּ דְּרַב יְהוֹשֻׁעַ. דְּגָבֵי מִיַּתְמֵי, וְלָא אָמְרִינַן יַתְמֵי לָאו בְּנֵי מֵיעֲבַד מִצְוָה נִינְהוּ. "הִלְכְתָא" גָּרְסִי' וְלָא גָּרְסִי' "וְהִלְכְתָא". הַיּוֹצֵא מִתַּחַת יְדֵי עָרֵב. וְתוֹבֵעַ אֶת הַיְּתוֹמִים, וְאָמַר: פָּרַעְתִּי חוֹב שֶׁל אֲבִיכֶם, וְהַשְּׁטָר מוֹכִיחַ, שֶׁהֲרֵי הֶחֱזִירוֹ לִי הַמַּלְוֶה. אֵינוֹ גּוֹבֶה. עַד דְּגָדְלֵי יַתְמֵי וּמִשְׁתַּפְּעֵי דִּינָא בַּהֲדַיְיהוּ. וְאָז יִשָּׁבַע וְיִפָּרַע מֵהֶם, כְּדִין הַבָּא לִיפָּרַע מִנִּכְסֵי יְתוֹמִים. וְאִם כָּתַב בּוֹ. הַמַּלְוֶה: "הִתְקַבַּלְתִּי מִמְּךָ" מִן הֶעָרֵב. דִּלְהָכִי כָּתַב לֵיהּ הִתְקַבַּלְתִּי. דְּהָוֵי עָרֵב מוּחְזָק בִּשְׁטָר שֶׁיֵּשׁ לוֹ עֲלֵיהֶם, וְלָא חֲשִׁיבָא מִלְוֶה עַל פֶּה. וּבְמִלְוֶה בִּשְׁטָר מוֹדֶה רַב פַּפָּא דְּגָבִינַן מִיַּתְמֵי, דְּלָא אָמְרִינַן הָכָא מִלְוֶה אֶלָּא חוֹב, וּמוּטֶּלֶת עֲלֵיהֶם לִפְרוֹעַ בְּעַל כָּרְחָם. אֲפִילּוּ לְמ"ד חָיְישִׁינַן לִצְרָרֵי. ה"מ בְּמַלְוֶה שֶׁהוּא יִשְׂרָאֵל, שֶׁדִּינוֹ שֶׁל לֹוֶה לִפְרוֹעַ לַמַּלְוֶה, שֶׁהֲרֵי הַמַּלְוֶה לֹא יִתְבָּעֶנּוּ לֶעָרֵב תְּחִלָּה. אֲבָל. הֵיכָא דְּהָוֵי הַמַּלְוֶה גּוֹי — אֵין הַלֹּוֶה מַתְפִּיסוֹ לְגוֹי צְרָרֵי, דְּהָא יָדַע יִשְׂרָאֵל דְּגוֹי הָדַר בֵּיהּ וְגוֹבֶה זִמְנָא אַחֲרִיתִי מִן הֶעָרֵב. מֵעִיקָּרָא. כְּשֶׁנַּעֲשָׂה הַיְּהוּדִי עָרֵב לַגּוֹי, אִי לָאו צְרָרֵי אַתְפְּסֵיהּ לֶעָרֵב — לָא הֲוָה מְקַבֵּל לֵיהּ לִיכָּנֵס בַּעֲרֵבוּת, שֶׁהֲרֵי זֶה יוֹדֵעַ בְּוַדַּאי שֶׁהַגּוֹי יַחֲזוֹר עָלָיו וְלֹא עַל הַלֹּוֶה. וְהִלְכָּךְ לָא גָּבִינַן מִיַּתְמֵי עַד דְּגָדְלֵי. עַצְרִי. כֹּהֵן הֲוָה, וְאִי מְגָרֵשׁ — תּוּ לָא מָצֵי מְהַדַּר לָהּ. וְהָאָמַר אַבַּיֵי. בְּפֶ' "יֵשׁ נוֹחֲלִין". אֵיזֶהוּ רָשָׁע עָרוּם. (ג) הַמִּתְעַבֵּר עַל רִיב לֹא לוֹ, וּמְבַטֵּל מַחֲשֶׁבֶת הַנּוֹתֵן שֶׁאָמַר "נְכָסַי לְךָ וְאַחֲרֶיךָ לִפְלוֹנִי", וּבִרְצוֹנוֹ לֹא הָיָה רִאשׁוֹן מוֹכֵר לַאֲחֵרִים לְהַפְסִיד "אַחֲרֶיךָ". עָרוּם — דְּמִכָּל מָקוֹם מַצְלִיחַ הוּא, וּמַה שֶּׁעָשָׂה עָשׂוּי, שֶׁהַנּוֹתֵן לֹא מִיחָה בִּשְׁעַת הַמַּתָּנָה. כְּרשב"ג דְּאָמַר: אִם קָדַם רִאשׁוֹן וּמָכַר — מַה שֶּׁעָשָׂה עָשׂוּי. כִּי אֵין לַאֲחֲרֶיךָ אֶלָּא מַה שֶּׁיְּשַׁיֵּיר רִאשׁוֹן, וַהֲרֵי לֹא שִׁיֵּיר לוֹ כְּלוּם. (ד) וְהָא קַיְימָא לָן. לְקַמָּן בִּשְׁמַעְתִּין. מַאי אִיכָּא לְמֵימַר. דְּהָא לָא הָווּ לֵיהּ נִכְסֵי לְרַב הוּנָא, וְלֹא נִשְׁתַּעְבֵּד אָבִיו. אִי בָּעֵית אֵימָא (ה) הָווּ. לְרַב הוּנָא בְּשָׁעָה שֶׁנַּעֲשָׂה אָבִיו עָרֵב, וְגָמַר וּמַקְנֶה, מִתּוֹךְ שֶׁהָיָה סָבוּר שֶׁלֹּא יַפְסִיד. דִּבְרֵי הַכֹּל לָא מִשְׁתַּעְבֵּד. כִּדְמְפָרֵשׁ טַעְמָא לְקַמָּן: מִצְוָה הוּא דַּעֲבַד וְלָאו מִידֵּי חַסְרָהּ. כִּי לֵית לֵיהּ נִכְסֵי לָא מִשְׁתַּעְבֵּד. דְּלֹא גָּמַר בְּלִבּוֹ לְשַׁעְבֵּד נַפְשֵׁיהּ, וְאֵינוֹ אֶלָּא פְּטוּמֵי מִילֵּי, שֶׁיִּרְאֶה לְהַפְסִיד. וְאִיכָּא לְמֵימַר אֲמוֹרָאֵי פְּלִיגִי בְּהָא מִילְּתָא, וּשְׁמַעְתַּיְיהוּ לָא אִיתְפָּרְשׁוּ בַּגְּמָ'. בְּכוּלְּהוּ מִשְׁתַּעְבֵּד. אע"ג דְּלֵית לֵיהּ נְכָסֵי. מִצְוָה הוּא דַּעֲבַד. הַמְשַׁדֵּךְ בְּזִוּוּגָן אֵין דַּעְתּוֹ לִפְרוֹעַ הָעֲרֵבוּת, אֲבָל מִתְכַּוֵּין לְזִוּוּגָן, שֶׁע"י עֲרֵבוּת זוֹ מִתְרַצִּין. וְלֹא מִידֵּי חַסְרָהּ לָאִשָּׁה, דְּהָא טַב לְמֵיתַב טַן דּוּ, וּלְטוֹבָתָהּ נִתְכַּוֵּין. מַתְקִיף לָהּ רַב נַחְמָן וְכִי אָדָם עוֹשֶׂה קְנוּנְיָא עַל בָּנָיו. לְהַנְחִיל לַאֲחֵרִים וּלְהַפְסִיד אֶת בָּנָיו? וְאַפ"ה אָמְרֵי רַב וּשְׁמוּאֵל: אִם לֹא אָמַר "תְּנוּ" — אֵין נוֹתְנִין לְאוֹתוֹ פְּלוֹנִי, אע"ג דְּהוֹדָה שֶׁיֵּשׁ לוֹ מָנֶה מִשֶּׁל פְּלוֹנִי בְּיָדוֹ. אֶלָּא מַאי אִית לָךְ לְמֵימַר, הַאי אֵין נוֹתְנִין לוֹ — דְּאָדָם עָשׂוּי שֶׁלֹּא לְהַשְׂבִּיעַ כו', נִתְכַּוֵּין שֶׁלֹּא יַחֲזִיקוּהוּ כְּעָשִׁיר, לֹא הוּא וְלֹא בָּנָיו. הָכָא

ושעבד נכסיו לזה, ויש לו כח לזה. מיהו, קשה לר"י מן התוספתא, דקתני: ואם כתב בו בע"ח. ולשון "בו" משמע כפירוש ר"ח. ויש לפרש קצת לפירוש ר"י, כי הלוה מכל מקום כתב לו כך, אבל הבעל חוב לוה לכתוב לו כדי שיהא הערב קבלן גמור. והא דאמר מלוה על היתומין לפרוע חובת אביהן — פירש ר"י: דהיינו במלוה על פה, ובמקום שלא נשארו קרקעות מאביהן כי אם מטלטלין, ולא כייפינן ליתמי עבור כן אפי' היו גדולים, כדמוכח פרק "מי שהיה נשוי" (כתובות דף צא:) גבי קטינא (ו) דאביי, דמדקטריף בעל חוב — אלמא גדולים היו. והא דפסקינן לקמן מלוה על פה גובה מן היורשים — היינו במקרקעי, דומיא דאינו גובה מן הלקוחות. **אטו** כל דמגרש כו'. שמא יפרע בלא ב"ד, ובלא הדרה. **בר** מערב דכתובה. דאף על גב דאית ליה — לא משתעבד. ומילתיה דרשב"ג מיירי באבא לגבי ברא, דמשעבד נפשיה (הג"ה. ותימה למורי: אמאי לא פריך ממתניתין). **שכיב** מרע שאמר מנה לפלוני בידי כו'. קשה לר"י: הא דבעי פ' "מי שמת" (לעיל דף קמח:): שכיב מרע שהקדיש כל נכסיו מהו? תפשוט מהכא דאם עמד אינו חוזר. דאי חוזר — חוזר (נמי) [כמו] במתנתו, וא"כ פשיטא דנאמן, ומאי קנוניא שייך? והלא היה יכול לחזור בו מיד! ונראה לר"י: דמיירי בשכיב מרע שהקדיש כשהיה בריא את נכסיו, ואמר השתא נמי מנה לפלוני בידי — נאמן. והאי דנקט שכיב מרע — משום דדוקא השתא מהימן, כדאמרינן בפרק "שום היתומים" (ערכין דף כג.) ובפ' "שבועת הדיינים" (שבועות דף מב:) דאין אדם חוטא ולא לו. אבל בבריא — ודאי חיישינן. **אדם** עשוי שלא להשביע את בניו. והיינו בשלא תבעוהו ואמר מעצמו. אבל תבעוהו והודה — חייב, כדאמר לקמן בשמעתין, דטעמא דלהשביע את בניו לא שייך התם. ו"משטה אני בך" נמי לא טענינן, (ז) אף על גב דבריא אי לא טעין טענינן ליה, דאין אדם משטה בשעת מיתה, כדאמרינן בסמוך. והא דאדם עשוי כו', אמר רבי דמשמע: אפי' לא טעין טענינן ליה, דאמר ב"זה בורר" (סנהדרין דף כט: ושם): ההוא דקרו ליה "קב רשו", אמר: מאן מסיק בי אלא פלניא ופלניא. תבעוהו לדינא קמיה דרב נחמן. אמר: אדם עשוי כו'. משמע דרב נחמן הוה טעין ליה הכי. ורב

רבינו גרשום

חובו ולא היה חייב כלום למלוה: מאי בינייהו. בין רב פפא ורב הונא מכדי בין למר ובין למר לא פרעי יתמי לערב: איכא בינייהו כשחייב מודה. שאביהן הודה בשעת מיתתו שעדיין לא פרע למלוה כלום למאן דאמר אימור צררי אתפסיה הכא לא אתפסי' ופרעי יתמי לערב מאי דפרע למלוה ולמאן דאמר יתמי לאו בני מיעבד מצוה נינהו אע"ג דהודה בשעת מית' דחייב למלוה (ולמאן דאמר) לא יפרעו להערב דיתמי לאו בני מיעבד מצוה נינהו ולא פרעי ליה לערב כלום: א"נ איכא בינייהו. דתבעיה מלוה ללוה קמי בית דין ושמתוהו דליפרע ליה ומת בשמתיה ולא פרע ליה למאן דאמר צררי אתפסיה הכא כיון דמת בשמתא לאו מידי אתפסוה ומחייבי יתמי למיפרע לערב מה שפרע למלוה ולמאן דאמר פריעת בעל חוב מצוה יתמי לאו בני מיעבד מצוה נינהו ולא פרעי ליה מידי: שלחו מתם היכא דשמתוהו ומית בשמתיה. אפ"ה הלכ' כרב הונא בריה דרב יהושע דחיישינן דלמא צררי אתפסיה ולא הספיק לתבוע להפר שמתא עד שמת הוא [אבל] אי ודאי בריר לן דלא אתפסי' צררי מחייבי יתמי לשלמי לערב אע"ג דמלוה על פה היה: מיתיבי ערב שהיה שטר חוב של מלוה יוצא מתחת ידו ואמר שפרע למלוה והחזיר לו השטר ותובע מן היתומין שישלמו מה שפרע למלוה אינו גובה מהן כלום דחיישינן שמא לא פרע למלוה אלא נפל השטר מן המלוה ומצא הערב ואע"ג דהאי חוב בשטר הוא הואיל וזה שטר על שם המלוה נכתב ולא על שם הערב להכי אינו גובה הערב דלגבי ערב מלוה על פה הוא דאין לו שטר על היתומין שחייבין לו: ואם כתב בו. בשטר כתיבת המלוה שכתב לערב התקבלתי ממך חובי. גובה מן היתומים דהשתא ליכא למיחש לנפילה וכיון דכתב ביה התקבלתי דמי כמאן דאית ליה שטר על היתומין: בשלמא לרב הונא בריה דרב יהושע. דחייש לצררי וכל היכא דודאי פשיטא לן דלא אתפסיה צררי מחייבי יתמי לשלומי הכא נמי כיון דהכא מלוה בשטר הוא איכא למימר לא הוה מתפיס ליה צררי אלא אם כן מהדר ליה שטרא וכיון דלא אהדר ליה שטרא פשיטא דלא אתפסיה לצררי ומשום הכי גובה ערב בשכתב לו התקבלתי דדמי כמאן דאית ליה שטרא על יתמי: אלא לרב פפא. דאמר יתמי לאו בני מיעבד מצוה נינהו במלוה על פה סוף סוף אע"ג דמלוה הוה ליה שטרא מעליא הא התקבלתי דאית ליה לערב עלי' יתמי לאו שטר גמור הוא והוה לענין ערב כמלוה על פה ואמאי גבי מיתמי: אמר לך רב פפא. להכי טרח וכתב ליה התקבלתי דליהוי לה׳ האי התקבלתי כמאן דאית ליה לערב שטר גמור על יתמי ומש"ה גובה מינייהו. ההוא ערבא דגוי שהיה ערב לגוי בשביל שהלוה לראובן ומת ראובן ופרעיה ערב לגוי: הני מילי למלוה ישראל. איכא למיחש דלמא אתפסיה לוה צררי קודם מיתתו משום דמלוה תובע ללוה: אדרבה. הכא איכא למיחש דדילמא לערב גופיה אתפסיה צררי דכיון דידע האי ערב דגוי בתר דידיה אזיל ולא בתר לוה לא הוה מקבל למהוי ליה ערב אי לאו דאתפסיה צררי לערב הלכך לא גבי הערב כלום מיתמי: אמר ליה אביי אטו כל דמגרש בבי דינא רבא מגרש. אפי' לפני בית דין הדיוט יכול לגרש דלא ידעי [דמצרכה] לידור הנאה ולא אדרי ליה: איגלאי מילתא דכהן הוה. רב הונא ולית ליה תקנה לגרשה דאי מגרש לה לא מצי לאהדורה: והיכי הוה אביי משיא עצה. למיעבד קנוניא והא אמר אביי כו': שאני הכא. דבנו היה רב הונא וליכא העברת ירושה כדאמר׳ (לעיל דף קל:) אם אמר על מי שראוי ליורשו דבריו קיימים. ועוד משום צורבא מרבנן ודחקא ליה מלתא שאני מאינש דעלמא: ואכתי מאי עצה הואי. והא ערב דכתובה לא משתעבד למיפרע כדאמר לקמן דמצוה עבד דזווגן (מאי) [ולאו מידי] חסרה: קבלן הוה. דמשתעבד: אלא למאן דאמר אי לית ליה לא משתעבד מאי איכא למימר. הא רב הונא לא הוה ליה נכסי כשנעשה אביו ערב בשבילו: אבא לגבי בריה. כשנעשה קבלן בשבילו משעבד נפשיה אע"ג דלית ליה לבן מפני חיבת הבן: מר סבר. איכא למאן דאמר אי אית ליה נכסי כו׳: מצוה עבד. כלומר דלא גמיר ושעבד נפשיה אלא האי דנעשה לו ערב משום מצוה נתכוון כדי שיזדווגו שניהם ולא מידי חסרה שלא נתנה לו כלום על ידו: נאמן. ונותנין מנה לפלוני: לא אמר תנו אין נותנין. אע"ג דאיכא למימר אין אדם עושה קנוניא על בנו דניחא ליה לבנו יותר מבאחר ואי לאו דהוה חייב לאחר מנה לא הוה אמר ואפי' [הכי] אם לא אמר תנו אין נותנין. ודאיכא למימר כי לא אמר תנו האי דאמר הכא מנה לאחר בידי להכי קאמר

עין משפט נר מצוה

קלה א ב ג מיי' פכ"ו מהל' מלוה ולוה הל' ו סמג עשין צד טוש"ע ח"מ סי' קל סעיף ו:
קלו ד ה מיי' שם הל' ז טוש"ע שם סעי' ז:
קלז ו ז מיי' שם הל' ו טוש"ע שם סעי' ז:
קלח ח ט י כ ל מיי' שם פכ"ה הלכה ו ופי"ז מהל' אישות הל' ט ועי' בהשגות ובמ"מ סמג שם וסי' מח טוש"ע אה"ע סי' קב סעיף ו ז:
קלט מ מיי' פכ"ה מהל' מלוה הלכה ב סמג עשין צד טוש"ע ח"מ סי' קכט סעיף ב:
קמ נ מיי' שם הל' ו ועי' בהשגות ובמ"מ ופי"ז מהל' אישות הל' ט ועי' בהג"ל סמג שם טוש"ע אה"ע סימן קב סעיף ו ז:
קמא ס מיי' פ"ז מהל' ערכין הל' יט ועי' בהשגות ובכ"מ סמג עשין קלא טוש"ע ח"מ סי' רנה סעיף ג:
קמב ע מיי' פ"י מהל' זכיה הל' ג סמג עשין פב טוש"ע שם סעיף ב:

מסורת הש"ס

א) [ערכין כג. ובפירש"י ע"ש]: ב) שם כג.: ג) שם ב"ק לב. [חולין קה:]: ד) לעיל קלז. כתובות לה: סוטה כא: ערכין כג:: ה) גיטין מט: [ערכין כג:]: ו) רש"ל והלכת' אכולהו משתעבד בר: ז) שבועות מב: [ערכין כג.]: ח) [סנהדרין כט:]:

הגהות הב"ח

(א) גמ' להכי טרח: (ב) שם והלכתא בכולהו משתעבד בר מערב דכתובה כצ"ל ותיבות ערב בין אית ליה ובין לית ליה נמחק: (ג) רשב"ם ד"ה איזהו רשע ערום רשע המתעבר: (ד) ד"ה וקיימא לן כצ"ל ותיבת והא נמחק: (ה) ד"ה איבעית אימא מיהוי הוה לרב הונא: (ו) תום' ד"ה (בע"א) ואם וכו' גבי קטינא דארעא דקטריף בעל חוב: (ז) ד"ה אדם וכו' לא טענינן ליה אע"ג:

הכא נמי, אדם עשוי שלא להשביע את עצמו! כי קאמר רב הונא התם — דנקיט שטרא. מכלל דרב ושמואל — דלא נקיט שטרא; אמר "תנו" — נותנין?! מלוה על פה הוה, א) ורב ושמואל דאמרי תרוייהו: מלוה על פה — אינו גובה לא מן היורשין ולא מן הלקוחות! אלא אמר רב נחמן: אידי ואידי דנקיט שטרא, ולא קשיא: א הא דמקויים, הא דלא מקויים; אמר "תנו" — קיימיה לשטריה, לא אמר "תנו" — לא קיימיה לשטריה. אמר רבה: שכיב מרע שאמר "מנה לפלוני בידי", ואמרו יתומין "פרענו" — נאמנין; "תנו מנה לפלוני", ואמרו יתומין "פרענו" — אין נאמנין. כלפי לייא? איפכא מסתברא! אמר "תנו מנה", ב כיון דפסקה אבוהון למילתא — איכא למימר דפרעיה. ג "מנה לפלוני בידי" — כיון דלא פסק אבוהון למילתא — ב) איכא למימר דלא פרעיה! אלא אי איתמר הכי איתמר: ד שכיב מרע שאמר "מנה לפלוני בידי", ואמרו יתומין: חזר ואמר לנו אבא "פרעתי" — נאמנין, מ"ט? אדכורי מידכר; ה "תנו מנה לפלוני", ואמרו יתומין: חזר ואמר אבא "פרעתי" — אין נאמנין, דאם איתא דפרעיה, לא הוה אמר "תנו". בעי רבא: שכיב מרע שהודה, מהו? צריך לומר "אתם עדי", או אין צריך לומר "אתם עדי"? (א) ג) צריך שיאמר "כתובו", או אין צריך לומר "כתובו"? אדם משטה בשעת מיתה, או אין אדם משטה בשעת מיתה? בתר דבעיא הדר פשטה: ד) ו אין אדם משטה בשעת מיתה, ה) ז ודברי שכ"מ ככתובין וכמסורין דמו. § **מתני'** ו) ח המלוה את חבירו בשטר — גובה מנכסים משועבדים, ט על ידי עדים — (ג) גובין מנכסים בני חורין.

הוציא

רש"י

הכא נמי. גבי הקדש, איכא למימר לכך נתכוין, ואמאי קאמר רב הונא נאמן, ונותנין לו המנה? **כי קאמר רב הונא דנקיט שטרא.** ההוא מלוה, וזה הודה לו. ופרכינן: מכלל דרב ושמואל מיירי בדלא נקיט. והלכך אין נותנין לו כי לא אמר "תנו". אי הכי, כי אמר "תנו" אמאי נותנין? מלוה על פה היא כו', ואי ז) (לאו) משום טעמא דמלוה לקיים דברי המת — לא היה להם ליתן בשביל דברי אביהם עד לאחר מותו. **אלא אמר רב נחמן.** בין זה שאמר שכ"מ "מנה לפלוני בידי" והוא בא ליפרע מן ההקדש, ובין זה הבא ליפרע מבניו — כולהו שטרי נקיטי דמסקי ביה בהאי שכיב מרע מנה, ולא קשיא. **הא.** דהקדש — במקויים, דאיכא הנפק. **אמר תנו** קיימיה לשטריה. ולא צריך מלוה לקיומיה. **לא אמר תנו.** חיישינן דלמא משום שלא להשביע את בניו אמר הכי, ולא גבי עד דמקיימי לשטריה. **דכיון דפסקה אבוהון.** שגמר דבריו וצוה לפרוע. **מ"ט.** ח) (ג) [דלא?] דלמא אידכורי מידכר, והלכך לא רצה לומר עדיין "תנו". **שכיב מרע שהודה.** בעל חובו טוען לו: מנה לי בידך, ואמר לו: הן. דכה"ג אמרינן בסנהדרין בפ' "זה בורר" (ד' כט:) דצריך שיאמר "אתם עדי", ואי לא — מצי א"ל משטה אני בך. **צריך שיאמר כתובו.** דאמרי' ב"חזקת הבתים" (לעיל מ.): הודאה בפני שנים — צריך שיאמר "כתובו". **ודברי** שכ"מ ככתובין וכמסורין. וא"צ לומר "כתובו". **מתני' המלוה את חברו** בשטר. אפי' אין כתוב בו אחריות, הא פסקינן הלכתא ב"שנים אוחזין" (ב"מ טו:) דאחריות טעות סופר הוא, וכמי שכתוב בו אחריות דמי. **משועבדים.** מכורין.

הוציא

תוספות

ורב ושמואל דאמרי תרוייהו מלוה וכו'. וא"ת: והא דברי שכיב מרע ככתובין וכמסורין דמו; (ד) מאחר דאם כתבו ונתנו היו נותנים — השתא אמאי אין נותנים כמחלק כל נכסיו? וי"ל: לא דמי, דהיכא דנותן מטעם מתנה — בודאי תקנו שיהיו ככתובין וכמסורין, שמא תטרף דעתו עליו. אבל מלוה להן ליתן מכח מלוה ולא מטעם אחר — אין לו אלא מכח מלוה כאשר בתחלה, והלכך אין נותנין. **הא** דמקויים. וא"ת: (ה) הא דנקט שטרא מקויים — צריכין למימר דנאמן? ועוד: מה אנו צריכין לנאמנות? ממילא גבי ע"י שטר שבידו! ועוד: למה לי הקדש? ועוד: מאי איריא שכ"מ, דאין אדם חוטא ולא לו, כדמפרש בפ' "שום היתומים" (ערכין דף כג. ושם)? אפי' בריא נמי! וי"ל: דכולהו איצטריך לגבות בלא שבועה. דאי לא הוה אלא שטרא — הוה בעי שבועה, כדתנן (כתובות דף פז.): הבא ליפרע מנכסים משועבדים לא יפרע אלא בשבועה, ואפילו הקדש. אי לא (ו) שכ"מ, ואי לא נאמנותו — הוה [בעי] שבועה, דמה לי משתעבד לגבוה מה לי משתעבד להדיוט. והכי מפרש בהדיא בפ' "שבועת הדיינים" (שבועות דף מג:) על הא דקתני (ברייתא): אבל נשבעים לקטן ולהקדש ליפרע מנכסי הקדש. (ופריך) תנינא: (כו') מנכסים משועבדים כו'! סד"א הנ"מ הדיוט, אבל הקדש לא חיישינן לקנוניא — קמ"ל. ופריך: והא א"ר הונא שכ"מ כו'! ומשני: דוקא שכ"מ, דאין אדם חוטא ולא לו. ומכאן נראה לרבי הא דמבעיא לן פ' "הניזקין" (גיטין דף נ:) גבי אין נפרעין מנכסים משועבדין במקום שיש נכסים בני חורין אפילו הן זיבורית, במתנה מאי? בההיא דמנכסים משועבדים לא יפרע אלא בשבועה הוי ודאי, ה"ה מתנה דנשבעין כשבאין ליפרע ממנו. דפשיטא ליה נמי הכא, דמה לי משתעבדי לגבוה מה לי משתעבדי להדיוט. אלמא, להדיוט בכה"ג בעי שבועה. **הא** דלא מקויים. וא"ת: כי היכי דאי לא מקויים ט)[אמרינן] שהוא מזוייף, והאב אמר שלא להשביע את בניו — בהא נמי לימא (ז) שלא להשביע את בניו, ופרוע הוא. ומדברי האב אין ראיה! ואין לומר דא"כ היו נותנים על ידי שבועה אם היה מקויים, שא"כ אלא לישבע שלא נפרע, וזה יכול הוא לעשות, ולא שייך לומר "אין נותנים". אבל בלא מקויים, דבעי קיום י)[קודם שיפרע] — שייך לומר "אין נותנים". דהא גבי הקדש אמרו נאמן במקויים, ולא טענינן ליה פרוע ויצטרך שבועה, אלא נאמן בלא שבועה, כדמוכח ההיא דשבועות (דף מג:) שהבאתי לעיל! אלא נראה לרבי: דהיכא דנקט ההוא מלוה שטרא (ח) ומקיים — אין הלוה רגיל לעולם לומר שלא להשביע שחייב לו מנה כמו שכתב בשטר, היכא דפרעיה, שלא יהא סבורים העולם שלא פרעו. **אלא** אי איתמר כו'. לא בעי למימר: "אלא איפכא איתמר", דידע גמרא שאמר על "מנה לפלוני בידי" דנאמנים. **חזר** ואמר לנו **אבא פרעתי נאמנים דלמא אדכורי** מדכר. היינו "פרעתי קודם לכן", כ)[כדקאמר: דלמא] אדכורי מדכר — [היינו] באותה שעה, כדמוכח בסמוך, [דקאמר]: אי איתא דפרעיה כו'. והכא נאמנים — משום שהוא (ט) היה נאמן לומר פרעתי קודם לכן, מגו דנאמן לומר פרעתי אחרי כן. כדתנן: מנה לי בידך! א"ל: הן. למחר א"ל: תנהו לי. נתתיו לך — פטור, אלא דמשביעין אותו שבועת היסת מדרבנן. ואף הם יכולים לומר פרענו אחרי כן. והא דאמר אין נאמנים כיון דלא פסקה למילתיה — היינו דטפי מסתבר לומר שם אין נאמנין, מ"תנו מנה לפלוני". ואומר רבי: הא דאמר סוף פ"ק דגיטין (דף יד.): הנהו גנאי דעבוד עסקא בהדי הדדי כו', לסוף לא פש גביה ולא מידי, ומסיק דהאי דאקני למריה ארעא זוזי דפשו גביה — קנין בטעות הוא, וחוזר. ומפרש ר"ת ורבינו חננאל: שהיו הן מודים שטעו תחלה בחשבון, שאם לא כן — לא היה נאמן, שא"כ אין לך קנין מועיל (י) לעולם, שיאמר "טעיתי", וגם יאמר היאך טעה — הא לאו הוכחה היא, דודאי הוא יכול להיות נאמן בכמה מקומות מגו דהוה מצי למימר "פרעתי אחרי כן", כדאשכחן הכא. אלא נראה דלא מיבעיא שנאמן לומר שטעה כשאמר "מנה לפלוני בידי", אלא הוא נאמן לומר פרעתי כבר — מגו דמצי למימר פרעתי אחרי כן. ומ"מ יכול הוא להיות דהתם צריך שיהו מודים שטעה אחרי כן, משום דקנין חשוב כ"תנו" דהכא, דאי פרעיה — לא הוה אמר "תנו", ומה לי לשקר במקום עדים הוא. ה"נ התם, אי איתא דטעה דלא פש גביה מידי — לא הוה מקני. וי"מ דדוקא בשכ"מ שייך למימר אדכורי מדכר, שאין דעתו מיושבת עליו, אבל בריא — לא.

ודברי שכ"מ ככתובין וכמסורין דמו כו'. האי "ככתובין" לא הוי ככתובין דלעיל פ' "מי שמת" (דף קנא.). דהתם קאמר שהם ככתובים וכמסורין כבר, דלא בעי קנין. אבל הכא לא בעי למימר דדוקא ככתובין וכמסורין, אלא אלימו טובא כדברים הכתובים, הלכך הוי כאילו אמר "כתבו". והרבה יפוי כח עשו חכמים בשכיב מרע בלא ההוא דלעיל דלא בעי קנין, כי ההיא דאמר בפרק קמא דגיטין (דף יד:) ד"הולך" כ"זכי" בשכיב מרע, אפילו לא הוי בבריא כזכי.

המלוה את חבירו בשטר כו'. [על ידי] עדים גובה מנכסים בני חורין. הכא תנן בהדיא דמלוה על פה לא גבי ממשועבדים ל)[מדרבנן]. והא דפרש"י פרק "הניזקין" (גיטין דף נא. ושם) דמזון האשה והבנות גובין מנכסים בני חורין לפי שאין קלוטים, אבל היו קלוטים היו גובין אע"פ שאין כתובים, משום דהוה כמלוה ע"פ — ליתא, ואגב ריהטא לא עיין בה. אלא טעמא דאכילת פירות למזון האשה והבנות דגבי אם היו קלוטים, אפילו אין כתובים — משם דקלא אית להו. מ)והקשה ה"ר יעקב מקורביי"ל: אם כן היאך נשבעין במודה מקצת הטענה? והא אין נשבעין על כפירת שעבוד קרקעות! ואומר רבי: כגון שמחל שעבודו. א"נ, בדליכא עדים. דהא דשעבודא דאורייתא — היינו על פי עדים, אבל על פי עצמו — לא. ובפרק קמא דבבא מציעא (דף ד: ושם) הארכתי יותר מבכאן.

גבו

עין משפט נר מצוה

קמג א מיי' פ"ז מהל' ערכין הל' יט סמג עשין קלא טוש"ע ח"מ סי' רנה סעיף ג:

קמד ב ג מיי' פ"י מהל' זכיה ומתנה הל' י ועי' בהשגות ובמ"מ סמג עשין פב טוש"ע ח"מ סי' רנה סעיף ד:

קמה ד ה מיי' שם הל' ח ט טוש"ע שם סעיף ה:

קמו ו מיי' שם פ"ח הלכה ד סמג שם טוש"ע ח"מ סימן פא סעיף ב:

קמז ז מיי' שם הל' ב סמג שם טוש"ע ח"מ סי' רנ סעיף א:

קמח ח מיי' פי"א מהל' מלוה ולוה הל' ד סמג עשין צד טוש"ע ח"מ סי' לט סעיף א וסי' קיא סעיף א:

קמט ט מיי' שם וסמג שם טוש"ע ח"מ סי' לט סעי' א:

רבינו גרשום

קאמר (באדם) שלא להשביע את בניו שלא יאמרו בני אדם כמה ממון מניח להם ונותנין בו עין: הכא נמי. בשכיב מרע שהקדיש נכסיו ואמר מנה לפלוני בידי כיון דלא אמר תנו לו איכא למימר אינו חייב לו ואלא להכי קאמר הכי דאדם עשוי שלא להשביע את עצמו שאם יקום מחליו שלא יאמרו עליו בני אדם מזל גדול של עושר יש לפלוני שקיבץ ממון כל כך ואמאי אמר רב הונא נאמן: כי קאמר. דנאמן כגון דנקיט האי בעל המנה שטר חוב על אותו שכיב מרע [שאמר] שיש לו מנה בידי. מכלל דרב ושמואל אע"ג דלא נקיט בעל המנה שטר: לא קשי' התם גבי הקדש נקיט בעל המנה א) שטר ולא מקוים הלכך אי אמר תנו מנה לפלוני קיימי' שכיב מרע לשטריה בהאי דהודה דישר הוא ונותנין לו: דפסקה למילתי' דאמר תנו איכא למימר דפרעוה וקיימוה צואת אביהן: מאי טעמא. נאמן כיון דלא אמר תנו משום דלא אדכר בדיוקא דחייב ובתר הכי אידכר דפרע ליה: ב) וצריך למימר שכיב מרע שמודה ליה לעדים אתם עדי או כתבו לו [כמו] בבריא איצטריך לומר כן ואי לא אמר כן (כבריא) יכול לומר משטה אני בך ה"נ אם לא אמר שכיב מרע אתם עדי מצי יתמי למימר משטה היה בו משחק היה בשעת מיתה ואי לא מצי למימר:

א) נ"ל ולא קשיא התם גבי הקדש נקיט בעל המנה שטר מקויים אבל רב ושמואל מיירי בדנקיט שטרא ולא מקויים וכו':
ב) נ"ל צריך שכ"מ שהודה למימר לעדים אתם עדי וכו':

הגהות הב"ח

עין משפט נר מצוה

קנ א מיי׳ פי״א מהל׳ מלוה ולוה הלכה ג ופכ״ב הל׳ א סמג עשין צד טוש״ע ח״מ סימן סט סעיף א וכמור סי׳ לט:

קנא ב מיי׳ פכ״א מהל׳ מלוה ולוה הל׳ א ועי׳ בכ״מ סמג שם טוש״ע ח״מ סימן קכט סעיף ז:

קנב ג מיי׳ פכ״א מהל׳ מלוה ולוה הל׳ א סמג שם טוש״ע ח״מ סימן קיא סעיף א:

קנג ד מיי׳ פי״א שם הלכה ד סמג שם:

קנד ו מיי׳ שם פי״ט הל׳ ה סמג שם:

קנה ז ח מיי׳ שם ופי״ב מהל׳ נזקי ממון הל׳ כב סמג עשין סו טוש״ע ח״מ סי׳ תי סעיף לח:

א) א הוֹצִיא עָלָיו כְּתַב יָדוֹ שֶׁהוּא חַיָּיב לוֹ — גּוֹבֶה מִנְּכָסִים בְּנֵי חוֹרִין. ב) ב עָרֵב הַיּוֹצֵא לְאַחַר חִיתּוּם שְׁטָרוֹת — גּוֹבֶה מִנְּכָסִים בְּנֵי חוֹרִין. מַעֲשֶׂה וּבָא לִפְנֵי ר׳ יִשְׁמָעֵאל, וְאָמַר: גּוֹבֶה מִנְּכָסִים בְּנֵי חוֹרִין. אָמַר לוֹ בֶּן נַנָּס: אֵינוֹ גּוֹבֶה לֹא מִנְּכָסִים מְשׁוּעְבָּדִים וְלֹא מִנְּכָסִים בְּנֵי חוֹרִין. אָמַר לוֹ: לָמָּה? אָמַר לוֹ: הֲרֵי ג הַחוֹנֵק אֶת אֶחָד בַּשּׁוּק, וּמְצָאוֹ חֲבֵירוֹ וְאָמַר לוֹ "הַנַּח לוֹ [וַאֲנִי אֶתֵּן לְךָ]" — פָּטוּר, שֶׁלֹּא עַל אֱמוּנָתוֹ הִלְוָהוּ; אֶלָּא אֵיזֶה הוּא עָרֵב שֶׁהוּא חַיָּיב? "הַלְוֵהוּ וַאֲנִי נוֹתֵן לְךָ" — חַיָּיב, שֶׁכֵּן עַל אֱמוּנָתוֹ הִלְוָהוּ. ג) וְאָמַר רַבִּי יִשְׁמָעֵאל: הָרוֹצֶה שֶׁיַּחְכִּים — יַעֲסוֹק בְּדִינֵי מָמוֹנוֹת, שֶׁאֵין לְךָ מִקְצוֹעַ בַּתּוֹרָה (א) יוֹתֵר מֵהֶן, וְהֵן כְּמַעְיָין הַנּוֹבֵעַ, ד הָרוֹצֶה שֶׁיַּעֲסוֹק בְּדִינֵי מָמוֹנוֹת — יְשַׁמֵּשׁ אֶת שִׁמְעוֹן בֶּן נַנָּס.§ **גמ׳** אָמַר עוּלָּא: ד דְּבַר תּוֹרָה, אֶחָד מִלְוֶה בִּשְׁטָר וְאֶחָד מִלְוֶה ע"פ — גּוֹבֶה מִנְּכָסִים מְשׁוּעְבָּדִים, מַאי טַעְמָא? ה שִׁעְבּוּדָא דְּאוֹרַיְיתָא, וְאֶלָּא מָה טַעַם אָמְרוּ: מִלְוֶה עַל פֶּה אֵינוֹ גּוֹבֶה אֶלָּא מִנְּכָסִין בְּנֵי חוֹרִין? מִשּׁוּם פְּסֵידָא דְּלָקוֹחוֹת. אִי הָכִי, מִלְוֶה בִּשְׁטָר נַמִי! הָתָם אִינְהוּ נִינְהוּ דְּאַפְסִידוּ אַנַּפְשַׁיְיהוּ. וְרַבָּה אָמַר: דְּבַר תּוֹרָה, אֶחָד מִלְוֶה בִּשְׁטָר וְאֶחָד מִלְוֶה עַל פֶּה — אֵינוֹ גּוֹבֶה אֶלָּא מִנְּכָסִים בְּנֵי חוֹרִין, מ"ט? שִׁעְבּוּדָא לָאו דְּאוֹרַיְיתָא, וּמָה טַעַם אָמְרוּ: מִלְוֶה בִּשְׁטָר גּוֹבֶה מִנְּכָסִים מְשׁוּעְבָּדִים? כְּדֵי שֶׁלֹּא תִּנְעוֹל דֶּלֶת בִּפְנֵי לוִֹין. אִי הָכִי, מִלְוֶה עַל פֶּה נַמִי! הָתָם לֵית לֵיהּ קָלָא. וּמִי אָמַר רַבָּה הָכִי? וְהָא ו) אָמַר רַבָּה: גָּבוּ קַרְקַע — יֵשׁ לוֹ, גָּבוּ מָעוֹת — אֵין לוֹ! (ב) וְכִי תֵימָא: אֵיפוֹךְ דְּרַבָּה לְעוּלָּא וּדְעוּלָּא לְרַבָּה, וְהָא ה) אָמַר עוּלָּא: ו דְּבַר תּוֹרָה, בַּעַל חוֹב דִּינֵיהּ בְּזִבּוּרִית! (אֶלָּא) רַבָּה טַעֲמָא דִּבְנֵי מַעֲרָבָא קָאָמַר, וְלֵיהּ לָא סְבִירָא לֵיהּ. רַב וּשְׁמוּאֵל דְּאָמְרִי תַּרְוַיְיהוּ: ו) מִלְוֶה עַל פֶּה — אֵינוֹ גּוֹבֶה לֹא מִן הַיּוֹרְשִׁין וְלֹא מִן הַלָּקוֹחוֹת, מ"ט? שִׁעְבּוּדָא לָאו דְּאוֹרַיְיתָא. ז) ר׳ יוֹחָנָן וְר׳ שִׁמְעוֹן בֶּן לָקִישׁ דְּאָמְרִי תַּרְוַיְיהוּ: מִלְוֶה עַל פֶּה — גּוֹבֶה בֵּין מִן הַיּוֹרְשִׁין וּבֵין מִן הַלָּקוֹחוֹת, מ"ט? שִׁעְבּוּדָא דְּאוֹרַיְיתָא. מֵיתִיבֵי: ח) ז הַחוֹפֵר בּוֹר בִּרְשׁוּת הָרַבִּים, וְנָפַל עָלָיו שׁוֹר וַהֲרָגוֹ — פָּטוּר; וְלֹא עוֹד, אֶלָּא ח שֶׁאִם מֵת הַשּׁוֹר — יוֹרְשֵׁי בַּעַל הַבּוֹר חַיָּיבִים לְשַׁלֵּם דְּמֵי שׁוֹר לִבְעָלָיו! אָמַר ר׳ אֶלְעָא אָמַר רַב: בְּשֶׁעָמַד בַּדִּין. וְהָא הֲרָגוֹ קָתָנֵי! ט) אָמַר רַב אַדָּא בַּר אַהֲבָה: שֶׁעֲשָׂאוֹ טְרֵפָה. וְהָא אר"נ תָּנֵי י) תַּנָּא: מֵת וּקְבָרוֹ! הָתָם, דְּיָתְבִי דַּיָּינֵי אַפּוּמָּא דְּבֵירָא וְחַיְּיבוּהוּ. אָמַר

רשב"ם

הוֹצִיא עָלָיו. מַלְוֶה. כְּתַב יָדוֹ. שֶׁל לֹוֶה, שֶׁהוּא חַיָּיב לוֹ מָמוֹן, וְאֵין כָּאן עֵדוּת אַחֶרֶת. גּוֹבֶה מִנְּכָסִים בְּנֵי חוֹרִין. דְּלֹא גּוֹבֶה מִמְּשׁוּעְבָּדִים אֶלָּא מִלְוֶה הַכָּתוּב בִּשְׁטָר שֶׁיֵּשׁ בּוֹ עֵדִים. דְּכֵיוָן דְּאִיכָּא תַּרְתֵּי, שְׁטָר וְעֵדִים — מַפְּקֵי לֵיהּ לְקָלָא, וְלָקוֹחוֹת הוּא דְּאַפְסִידוּ אַנַּפְשַׁיְיהוּ, שֶׁלֹּא חָקְרוּ בַּדָּבָר, וְיַנִּיחוּ בְּנֵי חָרֵי לַמּוֹכֵר לִגְבּוֹת מֵהֶם. עָרֵב הַיּוֹצֵא כו׳. שֶׁכָּתַב בְּתוֹךְ הַשְּׁטָר אַחַר חֲתִימַת הָעֵדִים: "אֲנִי פְּלוֹנִי בֶּן פְּלוֹנִי עָרֵב". גּוֹבֶה מִנְּכָסִים בְּנֵי חוֹרִין. מִן הֶעָרֵב בְּעַרְבוּת שֶׁבְּעַל פֶּה, דְּמִלְוֶה ע"פ הִיא, כֵּיוָן דְּלָא חֲתִימֵי עֵדִים עַל הָעַרְבוּת. וְה"ה לְעָרֵב בְּלֹא שְׁטָר אַחַר מַתַּן מָעוֹת. אָמַר לֵיהּ בֶּן נַנָּס אֵינוֹ גּוֹבֶה. דְּכָל עָרֵב שֶׁלְּאַחַר מַתַּן מָעוֹת לָא הָוֵי עָרֵב, שֶׁלֹּא עַל אֱמוּנָתוֹ וְהַבְטָחָתוֹ שֶׁל עָרֵב זֶה הִלְוָהוּ. **גמ׳** שִׁעְבּוּדָא דְּאוֹרַיְיתָא. "יוֹצִיא אֵלֶיךָ הָעֲבוֹט" (דברים כד) — וְה"ה לְמִקַּרְקְעֵי. לָאו דְּאוֹרַיְיתָא. וּקְרָא בְּמַשְׁכְּנוֹ שֶׁלֹּא בִּשְׁעַת הַלְוָאָתוֹ, בְּב"מ (דף קיד:). (ג) מִשּׁוּם פְּסֵידָא דְּלָקוֹחוֹת. שֶׁלֹּא יוּכְלוּ לְהִזָּהֵר בְּדָבָר שֶׁאֵין יָדוּעַ לָעוֹלָם. וּמִי אָמַר רַבָּה. שִׁעְבּוּדָא לָאו דְּאוֹרַיְיתָא? וְהָא אָמְרִינַן בְּפֶ׳ "יֵשׁ נוֹחֲלִין" (לעיל דף קכד:): שָׁלְחוּ מִתָּם: בְּכוֹר נוֹטֵל פִּי שְׁנַיִם בַּמִּלְוֶה. וְאָמַר רַבָּה עֲלָהּ: גָּבוּ קַרְקַע בְּחוֹבַת אֲבִיהֶם — יֵשׁ לוֹ, דִּכְמַאן דְּמִשְׁתַּעְבֵּד בְּחַיֵּי אֲבוּהוֹן דָּמֵי, וְקָרֵינָא בֵּיהּ "בְּכֹל אֲשֶׁר יִמָּצֵא לוֹ" — אַלְמָא שִׁעְבּוּדָא דְּאוֹרַיְיתָא! כ) אֵיפוּךְ גָּבוּ קַרְקַע אֵין לוֹ גָּבוּ מָעוֹת יֵשׁ לוֹ. דְּמָעוֹת הִלְוָהוּ וּמָעוֹת מְשַׁלֵּם, וְדָמֵי טְפֵי לַ"אֲשֶׁר יִמָּצֵא לוֹ". בע"ח דִּינֵיהּ בְּזִיבּוּרִית. וְנָפְקָא לֵיהּ בְּפ"ק דְּב"ק (דף ח.) מֵ"וְהָאִישׁ אֲשֶׁר אַתָּה נוֹשֶׁה בוֹ יוֹצִיא" וגו׳ מָה דַּרְכּוֹ שֶׁל אָדָם לְהוֹצִיא — פְּחוּת שֶׁבַּכֵּלִים. אַלְמָא שִׁעְבּוּדָא דְּזִיבּוּרִית דְּאוֹרַיְיתָא. וּמְשַׁנֵּי: לְטַעֲמַיְיהוּ דִּבְנֵי מַעֲרָבָא קָאָמַר. דְּאָמַר הָתָם: נוֹטֵל פִּי שְׁנַיִם בַּמִּלְוֶה בְּמִקַּרְקְעֵי אָמוּר וְלֹא בְּמָעוֹת. וּמִיהוּ, לְדִידֵיהּ סְבִירָא לֵיהּ דִּבְכוֹר אֵינוֹ נוֹטֵל פִּי שְׁנַיִם, וְלָא שְׁנָא גָּבוּ קַרְקַע וְלָא שְׁנָא גָּבוּ מָעוֹת, דְּשִׁעְבּוּדָא לָאו דְּאוֹרַיְיתָא. יוֹרְשֵׁי בַּעַל הַבּוֹר חַיָּיבִין לְשַׁלֵּם. אַלְמָא מִלְוֶה ע"פ גּוֹבֶה מִן הַיּוֹרְשִׁים, וְקַשְׁיָא לְרַב וּשְׁמוּאֵל. כְּשֶׁעָמַד בַּדִּין. דְּמַעֲשֵׂה ב"ד כְּמִלְוֶה בִּשְׁטָר דָּמֵי. שֶׁעֲשָׂאוֹ. הַשּׁוֹר טְרֵיפָה, וְעָמַד בַּדִּין קוֹדֶם שֶׁיָּצְתָה נִשְׁמָתוֹ. וּקְבָרוֹ. הַשּׁוֹר דְּחָפוֹ וּקְבָרוֹ בְּתוֹךְ קַרְקָעִית הַבּוֹר. אַפּוּמָּא דְּבֵירָא. לִפְנֵי מוֹתוֹ. אָמַר

תוספות

גבו קרקע יש לו גבו מעות אין לו. אע״ג דמיניה (ד) איירי, מ״כ מעות אין לו, דלאו הני מעות שבק אבוהון, אע״ג דהיינו מיניה. קרקע אמאי יש לו? ל) אלא ודאי עיקר שעבוד הוא על קרקע. אלמא, שעבוד קרקע לקוחות דאורייתא. **דבר** תורה ב״ח דינו בזבורית. תימה: היכי מוכח מהכא דשעבודא דאורייתא? דלמא היינו מיניה, דמיניה פשיטא דגבי בין קרקע ובין סובין. ושמא עולא אמרה על הא דפ׳ "הניזקין" (גיטין דף מח:) דאין נפרעין מנכסים משועבדי׳ במקום שיש בני חורין ואפי׳ הן זיבורית, דמשום פסידא דלקוחות אוקמוה אדאורייתא. ומדקאמר "אוקמוה אדאוריית׳" — משמע דהתם נמי דאוריית׳ הוא. מיהו, לא אשכחן דקאמר איהו בהדיא הכי. אבל הגמרא קאמר התם ב"הניזקין" (שם נ.): כדעולא, דאמר עולא כו׳ ומשום פסידא דלקוחות כו׳. ואפילו (ה) אומר בהדיא הכי — לא הוה דוקא, דשפיר משמע אוקמוה אדאורייתא דמיניה הוא. ונראה, שמא מדקאמר בזבורית — משמע קרקע זבורית, מדלא הזכיר סובין. ואין נראה לפרש דהאי דמ״ד לאו דאורייתא — היינו אפי׳ מיניה. דהא פשיטא שחייב לשלם, ואם אין לו מעות — פשיטא דאינו פטור בכך, אלא יתן לו סובין או קרקע, (או) ימכר ויתן לו מעות. אלא בשעבוד לקוחות איירי, שמשועבדים. אע״פ דכתב ליה אחריות בהדיא — לאו דאורייתא הוי האי קנין, דמדאוריית׳ לא יוכל לשעבד בחובו את נכסיו מן הלקוחות, אע״פ שיכול למכרן. ומה שפי׳ רשב״ם גבי שעבוד דאוריית׳ הוי האי קנין — דכתיב "יוציא אליך את העבוט". וגבי לאו דאורייתא, פי׳: והא דכתיב "יוציא אליך העבוט" — במשכנו שלא בשעת הלואתו בב״מ (דף קיד:) (לא) — משמע דבשעבוד דמיניה פליגי. ולא ידע רבי מאי קאמר. וגם לא הבנתי מה שאומר למ״ד לאו דאורייתא, דקרא במשכנו (ו) בשלא בשעת הלואתו. כ״ש דהוי דאורייתא, דבשלא בשעת הלואתו — הוא גבייה מחוב! **אינו** גובה לא מן היורשים. תימה: כיון דמלוה בשטר גובה מן היורשים, אע״ג דשעבוד לאו דאורייתא — שלא בשטר נמי מ״ט לא גבי? מה לי היכא דאית ליה קלא מה לי היכא דלית ליה קלא? וי״ל: (ז) מי שמלוה בעדים אינו חושש לקלא. ולגבייה דלקוחות לא תקנו חכמים לגבות מן היורשין. **לא** מן היורשין. וקשה לר״י: דב"ארבעה אבות" (ב״ק דף יא: ושם) גבי הלכה גובין מן העבדים, אמר ר״א: אפילו מיתמי? לא, מיניה. מיניה, אפילו מגלימא דעל כתפיה! ומשני: שעשאו אפותיקי ומכרו. משמע: אבל מיתמי לא גבי. ותימה: דפסקינן לקמן דמלוה ע״פ גובה מן היורשין ולא מן הלקוחות, אלמא גובה טפי מן היורשין ממן הלקוחות. והתם גבי טפי מלקוחות! ותירץ רבי: דודאי מלקוחות גבי טפי מדגבי מיורשים, אע״ג דעדיפי לקוחות הכא, כדאשכחן גבי מוכר שדהו בעדים גובה מנכסים משועבדים, דקאמר לעיל ב"חזקת הבתים" (דף מא: מב.): אפסודי אפסדי אנפשייהו, ואע״ג דאינו גובה מן היורשין. וטעמא — משום שעשו חולפא לקנות דבר שיש עליו קול שהיה משועבד, והאי טעמא לא שייך ביורשין. ומהאי טעמא גבי נמי מלקוחות התם ולא מן היורשין. מיהו, אין נראה לרבי, שמוכר שדהו בעדים גובה מן היורשין כמו מן הלקוחות, מאחר דאית להו קלא, כמו שמלוה בשטר גובה מן היורשין לרב ושמואל אע״פ שמלוה ע״פ אינו גובה, הואיל ואית להו קלא, ומטעם תקנה, כמו שתקנו במלוה דגבי משום נעילת דלת. והכי נמי אשכחן בסנהדרין (דף לב.): ומה טעם אמרו דיני ממונות לא בעינן דרישה וחקירה — שלא תנעול דלת בפני לוין. ואפילו בכל דיני ממונות שבעולם אנו דנים בלא דרישה וחקירה משום תקנת השוק, בין בדיני ירושה בין בדיני מקח. ה״נ, טעמא משום דנעילת דלת — לאו דוקא, והוא הדין במקח וממכר כדפרישית. וכן בעמד בדין דבסמוך, ומשום קלא גובה מן היורשים ומן הלקוחות שלא תפתח דלת הלווים. ובההיא ד"ארבעה אבות" (ב״ק דף יא:) נראה דבעי למימר כדפרישית התם, אלא כגון שעשאו אפותיקי. ועמד בדין דבסמוך, מספקא לרבי אי משום קלא אי משום תפיס למוחזק, דכל מעשה ב״ד אין משמיטין, ואי הוה מעשה ב״ד — הוה טעמא דעמד בדין משום דהוי כמוחזק בכך, ואי לא איירי אלא בכתובה — הוי טעמא דעמד בדין משום דאית ליה קלא. והלכך גבי מן יורשין משום פתיחת דלת בפני הגזלנין, וכ״ש [מן] הלקוחות. וזה נראה עיקר, דעמד בדין משום קלא הוא ולא משום דתפיס, דאונס ומפתה גופייהו בעמדה בדין נעשה כמלוה ומשמיטין, לברייתא דתניא כוותיה דשמואל ב"המביא תניין" (גיטין דף יח.).

דיתבי דיינא אפומא. ותימה: אמאי תני ר״נ וקברו? מאחר דפרשינן לה הכי, וסבירא ליה אינו גובה מן הלקוחות! ואומר רבי: דאיכא למימר דקמ״ל שאע״פ שקרי״ב זה החופר למיתה מיד, שהשור היה ממיתו והכהו — מועיל דין שדנים שם, ולא אמרינן גברא קטילא דייני.

גובה

רבינו גרשום

שעבודא. שמשועבדין לו נכסים של לוה למלוה מדאורייתא הוא דכתיב עבד לוה לאיש מלוה: אי הכי מלוה בשטר נמי. לא נטרוף ממשעבדי משום פסידא דלקוחות: התם אינהו. לקוחות אפסדי אנפשייהו דכיון דידעי דהוי חייב ממון למלוה בשטר דשטר קלא אית ליה לא הוה לי׳ למזבן מיני׳: שעבודא לאו דאורייתא. וקרא אסמכתא בעלמא הוא: לית ליה קלא למלוה על פה ולא ידעי לקוחות דלוה מיניה ולא גבי מינייהו: ומי אמר רבה הכי. דשעבודא לאו דאורייתא: והאמר רבה. בפרק יש נוחלין גבו יתומים מבעל חוב קרקע בחובת אביהן יש לבכור פי שנים בה דכיון דמשעבדי לאבוהון דמי כממון שלו ונוטל בה בכור פי שנים. מדקאמר שקיל בכור פי שנים בה אלמא שעבוד׳ דאוריית׳: וכי תימא איפוך. והאמר עולא דבר תורה בע״ח בזיבורית אלמא דקסבר עולא דשעבוד׳ דאוריית׳ ולא מצית אפכית ליה: אלא לעולם קסבר רבה דשעבודא לאו דאוריית׳ והא דקאמר רבה גבו קרקע יש לו לטעמא דבני מערבא קאמר. דשלחו מתם בכור נוטל פי שנים במלוה וקאמר רבה מסתבר טעמייהו בקרקע וליה לא ס״ל דשקיל בה פי שנים דקסבר שעבודא לאו דאורייתא: ונפל עליו שור. בתוך הבור: והרגו. לחופר: פטור. בעל השור לפי שהוא עצמו גרם לו תקלה שחפר ברה״ר: ולא עוד אלא שאם מת השור. והחופר יורשי בעל הבור חייבין לשלם דמי שור לבעלים והא הכא האי חוב דיורשי בעל בור משלמים אינו בשטר אלא בעל פה אלמא דמלוה על פה גובה מן היורשין וקשיא לרב ושמואל. ומתרץ ר׳ אילעא בשעמד בדין ונתחייב החופר קודם שמת וכל פסק דין מב״ד דמי כמלוה בשטר להכי יורשי בעל הבור משלמין דמלוה בשטר גובה מן היורשין: והא הרגו. השור קתני אלמא דלא עמד בדין ואפ״ה משלמין יורשין אע״ג דהוה מלוה על פה: ומתרץ רב אדא לא הרגו לאלתר אלא עשאו טריפה. דאינו יכול לחיות וחייבוהו בית דין קודם שמת והוי כמלוה בשטר: והא תני תנא והרגו ומת בבור וקברוהו ואפ״ה יורשין חייבין לשלם אע״ג דלא עמד בדין. ומתרץ לעולם חייבוהו ב״ד קודם שמת והיה כמלוה בשטר

מסורת הש"ס

א) לעיל קמז. כתובות פח. ב) גיטין כח. כתובות קב ג) ברכות סג: ד) ב״ק ט: לעיל קכה: ה) ב״ק יא: גיטין נ. ו) [לעיל מב. קב קדושין יג: ב״ק קד: ערכין ז: ז.] קדושין שם ח) [ערכין ז. כל הענין ט) [גיטין מג.: י) ובערכין ז. אי׳ תנא: כ) [עי׳ רש״י שהיה לרשב״ם גירס אחרת: ל) רש״ל לו כ״ז: דלמא לאו הני קרקע שבק אבוהון וגם לאו מיניה הוי שהרי מעות הלוהו אלא ודאי כו׳:

הגהות הב"ח

(א) במשנה מקצוע בתורה גדול מהן: (ב) גמ׳ גבו מעות אין לו ורב נחמן אמר גבו מעות יש לו איפוך לרבה ודרב נחמן לרבה והא שמעתתא לא אזלא הכי כדאמרינן לעיל לידיך קשיא כו׳ וכי תימא איפוך כל״ל: (ג) רשב״ם ד״ה משום קודם ד״ה לאו: (ד) תוס׳ ד״ה גבו כו׳ אע״ג דמיניה הוא מכל מקום מעות אין לו דלאו הני מעות שבק אבוהון ופריך קרקע אמאי יש לו אע״ג דהיינו נמי מיניה כיון דלאו הני קרקע שבק אבוהון שהרי מעות הלוהו אלא ודאי עיקר שעבוד כל״ל: (ה) בא״ד ואפי׳ אמר בהדיא הכי לא הוה דוקא דבמיניה הוא מדקאמר בזיבורית כל״ל: (ו) בא״ד דקרא במשכנו בשלא בשעת הלואתו כו׳: (ז) ד״ה אינו כו׳ וי״ל כיון דמי שמלוה:

א) קדושין יג: בכורות מח: ב) גיטין פו.: ג) שם פז. ד) גיטין פו: ה) [ועי' תוס' מנחות נח: ד"ה אליבא לדאמר] ו) [ועי' תוס' קדושין יג: ד"ה אמר רב פפא] ז) [ועי' רש"י ד"ה] ח) [ועי' תוס' גיטין ג: ד"ה וגובה]

א)אמר רב פפא, א הלכתא: מלוה על פה — גובה מן היורשין ב ואינו גובה מן הלקוחות; גובה מן היורשין — כדי שלא תנעול דלת בפני לוין, ואינו גובה מן הלקוחות — דלית ליה קלא. § "הוציא עליו כתב ידו שהוא חייב לו — גובה מנכסים בני חורין" וכו'. § בעא מיניה רבה בר נתן מר' יוחנן: הוחזק כתב ידו בבית דין, מאי? אמר ליה: ג אף על פי שהוחזק כתב ידו בבית דין — אינו גובה אלא מנכסים בני חורין. מתיב רמי בר חמא: ב)שלשה גיטין פסולין, ואם נישאת — הולד כשר, ואלו הן: ד כתב בכתב ידו ואין עליו עדים, ה יש עליו עדים ואין בו זמן, יש בו זמן ואין בו אלא עד אחד — הרי אלו שלשה גיטין פסולין, ואם נישאת — הולד כשר; רבי אלעזר אומר: ו אף על פי שאין עליו עדים, אלא שנתנו לה בפני עדים — כשר, וגובה מנכסים משועבדים! שאני התם (א) דמשעת כתיבה הוא דשעבד נפשיה. § "ערב היוצא לאחר חיתום שטרות" וכו'. § אמר רב: קודם חיתום שטרות — גובה מנכסים משועבדים, לאחר חיתום שטרות — גובה מנכסים בני חורין. זמנין אמר רב: אפילו קודם חיתום שטרות — אינו גובה אלא מנכסים בני חורין. קשיא דרב אדרב! לא קשיא: ז הא דכתב ביה "פלוני ערב", הא דכתב ביה "ופלוני ערב". ור' יוחנן אמר: אחד זה ואחד זה — אינו גובה אלא מנכסים בני חורין, ואף על גב דכתב ביה "ופלוני ערב". מתיב רבא: ג)ח עדים החתומין על שאילת שלום בגט — פסול, חיישינן שמא על שאילת שלום חתמו; ואמר רבי אבהו, לדידי מיפרשא ליה מיניה דרבי יוחנן: ט "שאילו" — פסול, "ושאילו" — כשר! הכא נמי דכתב "פלוני ערב". אי הכי, היינו דרב! אימא: וכן אמר רבי יוחנן. § "מעשה ובא לפני רבי ישמעאל" וכו'. § אמר רבה בר בר חנה אמר רבי יוחנן: אף על פי שקילס רבי ישמעאל את בן ננס, הלכה כמותו. איבעיא להו: בחנוק מה לי אמר רבי ישמעאל? תא שמע, דאמר ר' יעקב אמר רבי יוחנן: חלוק היה רבי ישמעאל אף בחנוק. הלכה כמותו או אין הלכה כמותו? תא שמע, דכי אתא רבין אמר רבי יוחנן: חלוק היה רבי ישמעאל אף בחנוק, והלכה כמותו אף בחנוק. אמר רב יהודה אמר שמואל: י חנוק וקנו מידו — משתעבד. מכלל, דערב בעלמא לא בעי קנין. ופליגא דרב נחמן, דאמר רב נחמן:

ערב

אמר רב פפא הלכתא כו'. לעיל פירשתי גביית מלוה מן היתומים, וגם בפרק "שום היתומים" בערכין (דף כג:) אמר רבא: הלכתא, אין נזקקין לנכסי יתומים כו'. **בעא** מיניה רבה בר נתן מרבי יוחנן הוחזק כתב ידו בבית דין מהו. לאחר זמן, שמסר לו הלוה למלוה כתב ידו שהוא חייב לו ממון, ובא בב"ד והודה בפניהם שהוא כתב ידו, וכתבו לו ב"ד הנפק, הוא הנקרא אשרתא וקיום השטר. **מאי.** מי אמרינן: הרי הוא מעשה כשטר שיש בו עדים, ויגבה ממשעבדי. דאחריות טעות סופר הוא, דכל שטר מלוה ומכירה שחותמים בו עדים — גובין ממשעבדי כאילו כתוב בהן אחריות. או דלמא קיום שטר אינו מועיל לשום שטר אלא להחזיקו בב"ד לכמות שהיה מקודם לכן, שאילו ימותו עדים או לוה — לא יוכל לטעון שטר זה מזויף הוא, דב"ד קיימוהו, ויגבה בו המלוה, וגם זה לא יגבה אלא מבני חורין. ולהכי אהני ב"ד — שלא יוכל לוה לומר "אין זה כתב ידי". **פסולין.** לינשא בו. **ואין עליו עדים.** אלא שנמסר לה בפני עדים, דעדי מסירה כרתי ליה בדיעבד. **הרי אלו כו'.** בגיטין מפרש "הרי אלו" דרישא ו"הרי אלו" דסיפא למעוטי מאי, והתם מפרשא כולה. **כשר.** לכתחלה, דסבירא ליה עדי מסירה כרתי. **וגובה מנכסים משועבדים.** כלומר, ואם שטר מלוה הוא אותו השטר הכתוב בכתב ידו ואין בו עדים, אלא שמסרו בפני עדים — גובה מנכסים משועבדים. והכי מפרש התם ר' יוחנן אליבא דר' אלעזר בפ' ["המביא תניינא"] (גיטין כב:) שאפי' בשאר שטרות גובה מנכסים משועבדים בעדי מסירה בלבד. אלמא, הוציא עליו כתב ידו שהוא חייב לו, ומסרו בפני עדים — גובה ממשעבדי, וכל שכן הוחזק בבית דין! ה"ג: **שאני התם דבשעת כתיבה הוא דשעבד נפשיה.** כשנכתב השטר — נכתב כדי למסרו בפני עדים, שיהו עדי מסירה במקום עדי חתימה. הלכך, כיון דלר' אלעזר עדי מסירה כרתי — כאילו נחתמו בתוך השטר דמי. אבל אנו מיבעיא לן בהוציא כתב ידו בעלמא ששמו של לוה חתום בו, שזה מסר לו במקום הודאה, שלא יוכל לחזור ולכפור בו ולומר "פרעתי" כל זמן שחתימתו ביד מלוה, (ג) שלא נעשה השטר בלשון של שטר שעדים חתומים בו, ואחר זמן החזיקו בב"ד, וכשהלוהו — כמלוה על פה הויא, ותו לא מלו ב"ד בקיומן לעשותו שטר שיש בו אחריות נכסים, שהרי לא לדעת כן נכתב מתחלה. כן נראה בעיני שמועה זו, וכן עיקר. ואית דגרסי: משעת הכתובה. ולא ירדו לשיטת השמועה. **פלוני ערב.** הפסיק הענין, ודלמא לא אסהדי עדים אלא אשטרא דלעיל לחוד. **ופלוני ערב.** וי"ו מוסיף על ענין ראשון, ועל השטר ועל הערבות חתימי סהדי. **ושאילו** כשר. שעל הכל העידו עדים. **הלכה כמותו.** כר' ישמעאל, דגובה מנכסים בני חורין. **חנוק מה לי אמר רבי ישמעאל.** דלמא משום צערא דחבריה שנחנק נמי גמר ומקנה. או דלמא מתכוין הוא להצילו מחניקה, ומלוה הוא דקא עביד, ולאו מידי חסריה, ולא הוי ערב.

ערב

גובה מן היורשים כדי שלא תנעול דלת בפני לוין. הכא מוקי הך מילתא אליבא דכולי עלמא, בין למאן דאמר דאורייתא בין למאן דאמר לאו דאורייתא. ובפרק קמא דקדושין (דף יג: ושם) אמרינן: גובה מן היורשים — שעבודא דאורייתא. ואינו גובה [מן הלקוחות כו']. ויש לפרש דרב פפא לא אמר אלא: מלוה על פה גובה מן היורשים ואינו גובה מן הלקוחות, וגמרא מפרש לה הכא למאן דאמר שעבודא לאו דאורייתא, והתם למאן דאמר שעבודא דאורייתא. והוי כמו "איכא דאמרי" מילתא דהכא ודהתם. וכעין זה מצינו ב"המקבל" (ב"מ דף קיב. ושם) דבעו מיניה מרב ששת: קבלן עובר "בבל תלין" או לא, אומן קונה בשבח כלי או לא, ד)וב"הגוזל קמא" (ב"ק דף צט.) משמע שלא שאלו ממנו אם אומן קונה בשבח כלי או לא. ובשם ה"ר אליהו מ"כ מפרש דהא דפסיק רב פפא התם דשעבודא דאורייתא — היינו לענין קרבן, כגון האשה שמתה יביאו היורשים עולתה, דאיירי התם לעיל במשנה. וכן משמע התם מתוך פירוש רבינו חננאל, וכן עיקר ה).

משעת כתיבה שעבד נפשיה. ו)כדפירש בקונטרס. ולא גרסינן "משעת כתובה", דהוי משמע דעדי חתימה כרתי בכתובה לרבי אלעזר. וזה אינו, דהא אפילו אין בכתובה עצמה אלא עדי מסירה — כשר, כדאמרינן דאמר ר"א בין בגיטין בין בשטרות, וקיימא לן כוותיה בין בגיטין בין בשטרות מההיא ד"זה בורר" (סנהדרין דף כח: ושם). ז)(הג"ה) [הכא] נמי דכתב ביה "אני פלוני ערב". ותימה: דאם כן ליהוי כ"שאילו"! ותירץ מורי ר': דשאני שאילו, שדומה שסותר הגט. ולעיל (דף קסב:) נמי אמרינן: מילאהו בקרובין — כשר.

והלכה כמותו אף בחנוק. קשה לר"י על ההיא ד"הנושא" (כתובות דף קא: ושם קב. ד"ה אליבא) דאמר ר' יוחנן באומר לחבירו "חייב אני לך מנה" בשטר, דאלימא מילתא דשטרא וכמאן דאמר להו "אתם עדי" דמי, ומוקי נפשיה כר' ישמעאל, *דלא פליג עליה ר' ישמעאל אלא משום דסבר דערב לאחר מתן מעות משתעבד, כדאמר דהלכה כמותו אף בחנוק. ורבי יוחנן גופיה [אפשר דס"ל] כשאמר לו בשוק "הנח לו ואתן לך" — פטור, דליכא אלימות' דשטר כלל, ומנלן דסבר אלימא מילתא דשטרא? ונראה לרבי: דחנוק נמי, דהכא בשטר טעמא דאלימא מילתא דשטרא *גמר ומשעבד נפשיה. ופי' בקונטרס דלא גרסינן בתר הכי: הנך כולהו בעו קנין. וכן נראה, כי כבר פירש דין כולם. ובפירוש רבינו חננאל הוא משמע לפרשו כך: בין בחנוק בין בלא חנוק, בין בשטר ובין בבעל פה, בעי קנין. ויש ספרים שאין כתוב בהן כלל, ונחת לזה מזה.

הדרן עלך גט פשוט וסליקא לה מסכת בבא בתרא

קנו א מיי' פי"א מהל' מלוה ולוה הל' ד' סמג עשין לד טוש"ע ח"מ סי' קז סעיף א:
קנז ב מיי' שם וסמג שם טוש"ע ח"מ סי' לט סעיף א ומי' קיא סעיף א:
קנח ג מיי' שם הלכה ג וסמג שם טוש"ע ח"מ סי' קו סעיף א:
קנט ד מיי' פ"א מהל' גירושין הלכה יד ועי' בהשגות וכמ"מ סמג עשין נ טוש"ע אה"ע סי' קל סעיף כ:
קס ה מיי' שם הלכה כה ועי' בהשגות ובכ"מ וסמג שם טוש"ע אה"ע סי' קל סעיף ה:
קסא ו מיי' שם טוש"ע אה"ע סי' קלג סעיף א:
קסב ז מיי' פכ"ה מהל' מלוה ולוה הל' ח סמג עשין לד טוש"ע ח"מ סי' קכט סעיף ז:
קסג ח ט מיי' פ"ד מהל' גירושין הלכה כה סמג עשין נ טוש"ע אה"ע סי' קל סעיף ג:
קסד י מיי' פכ"ה מהל' מלוה ולוה הל' א סמג עשין לד טוש"ע ח"מ סי' קכט סעיף א:

הגהות הב"ח

(א) גמרא שאני התם דמשעת: (ב) רשב"ם ד"ה גרסינן וכו' ביד מלוה ולא נעשה:

רבינו גרשום

בשטר ולהכי משלמין יורשין: הוחזק כתב ידו בב"ד. שהעידו לפני ב"ד שזו כתיבת יד לוה מאי. מי אמרינן כיון דהוחזק בבית דין דמי כמלוה בשטר וגובה מנכסים משועבדים או דלמא כיון דלא חתימי עליו עדים הוה כמלוה על פה וגובה מבני חורין: אמר ליה אף על פי שהוחזק כו'. הואיל דלא חתימי עליו עדים: ר' אלעזר אומר אע"פ שאין עליו עדים. אלא הואיל שכתב בכתב ידו ונתנו לה בפני עדים כשר וגובה כתובתה מנכסים משועבדים. אלמא אף על גב (בלא חתימת) [דלא חתימי] עדים עליה גבי ממשעבדי וקשי' לר' יוחנן. ואי קשי' לך היכי מצית מקשי גברא מגברא מר' אלעזר לר' יוחנן. תריץ הכי א) ברייתא' היא ומברייתא מצי מקשי. ואמר לך ר' יוחנן הא לא קשיא לי דהתם אמאי גבי ממשעבדי דאיכא כתובתה בידה דאיכא שטרא מעליא דמשעת כתובה שעבד נפשי' אבל הכא דלא שטר מעליא הוא דאין עליו עדים במאי מצי גבי ממשעבדי: ערב היוצא לאחר חיתום שטרות. שכתב מתחת חתימת העדים ופלוני ערב גובה המלוה מאותו ערב מנכסים בני חורין לפי שהואיל שנכתב לאחר חתימת העדים כמלוה על פה דמי שיש לו על הערב: ג) מעשה בא לפני ר' ישמעאל בערב היוצא אחר חיתום שטרות: שלא על אמונתו הלוהו. פירש ר' שלא על אמונתו של ערב הלוהו לפי שלא היה בשעת מתן מעות והכא איכא למימר כיון דנכתב הערב לאחר החיתום איכא למימר לא הלוה בשעת מתן מעות ולא על אמונתו הלוהו דלא אמר בשעת מתן מעות על מנת שאפרע ממי שארצה להכי אינו גובה אפי' מבני חורין: ישמש את שמעון בן ננס. שבקי הוא הרבה בדיני ממונות: הא דכתב ביה בשטר קודם [ופלוני ערב] ואח"כ חתמו העדים משמע זו מוסיף על ענין ראשון דכי היכי דחתמי על מה שכתוב בשטר חתמו נמי על מאי דכתב ביה ופלוני ערב. אבל אי כתב קודם חתימת העדים פלוני ערב משמע דהיינו מילתא אחריתא ועדים לא חתמו ג) אלא אפי' לרב והוי שטר גופיה על פה וערב במלוה על פה לא טרף מלוה מערב אלא מבני חורין אעיקר שטרא ולא אפלוני ערב הלכך אינו גובה אלא מנכסים בני חורין: לדידי מיפרשא לי מיניה דר' יוחנן. היכא דמי קתני ברייתא דפסול אי כתב בגט בסוף כדת משה וישראל שאילו בשלום פלוני ושוב חתמו עדים איכא למימר על שאילת שלום חתמו שאלו עדים שזה שואל בשלום פלוני אבל אעיקר הגט אין מעידין ואי כתבו בסופו ושאילו בשלום פלו' ושוב חתמו כשר דמשמע דאשאילת שלום ועל כל מאי דכתב בגט חתמו וגובה כתובה מנכסים משועבדים ואמאי קאמר ר' יוחנן אחד זה ואחד זה אין גובה אלא מנכסים בני חורין ואע"ג דכתב ביה ופלוני ערב. ומשני לא התם נמי בההוא קאמר ר' יוחנן דגובה מבני חורין היכא דכתב ביה פלוני ערב אבל אי כתב ביה ופלוני ערב גובה מנכסים משועבדים ומקשי' היינו דרב דרב הכי נמי אמר. ומתרץ אימא וכן אמר ר' יוחנן כרב: אע"פ שקילס ר' ישמעאל את בן ננס. דאמר ישמש את בן ננס: הלכה כמותו. כר' ישמעאל דגובה מנכסים בני חורין: חלוק היה ר' ישמעאל. על בן ננס אף בחונק דגובה מן הערב מנכסים בני חורין: חנוק וקנו מידו. אחד שהיה חונק חבירו בשביל חובו ומצאו חבירו ואמר ליה הנח לו ואני אתן לך וקנו מן זה הערב שיפרע בשבילו משתעבד. מכלל דערב דעלמא משתעבד בלא קנין:

והלכתא

א) לכאורה צ"ל מתניתין היא. ועי' גיטין פז ע"ב. ב) מכאן עד ד"ה הא לא כתב ביה שייך למתני'. ג) נ"ל לא חתמו אלא אעיקר שטרא ולא אפלוני ערב והוי כערב ע"פ וערב וכו' אלא מבני חורין:

קסה א מיי׳ פכ״ה מהל׳ מלוה ולוה ה״ב סמג עשין לד טוש״ע ח״מ סי׳ קכט סעיף ב:
קסו ב מיי׳ שם הל׳ א טוש״ע שם ס״א:
קסז ג מיי׳ שם הל׳ ב טוש״ע שם ס״ב:

עָרֵב דְּבֵית דִּין הוּא דְּלָא בָּעֵי קִנְיָן, הָא בְּעָלְמָא בָּעֵי קִנְיָן. וְהִלְכְתָא: עָרֵב א בִּשְׁעַת מַתַּן מָעוֹת לָא בָּעֵי קִנְיָן, ב אַחַר מַתַּן מָעוֹת – בָּעֵי קִנְיָן; ג עָרֵב דְּבֵית דִּין לָא בָּעֵי קִנְיָן, דִּבְהַהִיא הֲנָאָה דִּמְהֵימַן לֵיהּ – גָּמַר וּמְשַׁעְבֵּד לֵיהּ.§

עָרֵב דְּבֵית דִּין לָא בָּעֵי קִנְיָן. דִּבְהַהִיא הֲנָאָה דְּקָא מְהֵימְנִי לֵיהּ ב״ד גָּמַר וּמְשַׁעְבֵּד נַפְשֵׁיהּ. הָכִי גָּרְסִינַן: וְהִלְכְתָא עָרֵב בִּשְׁעַת מַתַּן מָעוֹת לָא בָּעֵי קִנְיָן. וְאִם כָּתַב בְּתוֹךְ הַשְּׁטָר לְאַחַר חִיתּוּם שְׁטָרוֹת – גּוֹבֶה מִנְּכָסִים מְשׁוּעְבָּדִים. שֶׁלֹּא בִּשְׁעַת מַתַּן מָעוֹת בָּעֵי קִנְיָן. וַאֲפִי׳ חָתוּם בְּתוֹךְ הַשְּׁטָר. וְאִי חָתוּם לְאַחַר חִיתּוּם – בָּעֵי קִנְיָן, וְגוֹבֶה מִבְּנֵי חוֹרִין. וְלָא גָּרְסִינַן: הָנָךְ כּוּלְּהוּ בָּעֵי קִנְיָן.

והלכתא ערב מתן מעות לא בע ומשתעבד דמצי ליה אי לאו א נפיק זוזי מתחר דלאחר מתן מעור חנוק בעי קנין. דב״ד לפני ביר דהיינו נמי לאחר

מערת לא בעי קנין. כך אמר המורה משום רבו א) דהנך כולהו בעי קנין לא מתרצתא היא משום דאין עוד ערב אלא הני די

א) נראה דל״ל כך אמר המורה משום רבו דמאן דגרס כאן והנך כולהו בעו קנין לא מתרלתא היא וכו׳:

הדרן עלך גט פשוט וסליקא לה מסכת בבא בתרא

The following paragraph is recited three times:

הַדְרָן עֲלָךְ מַסֶּכֶת בָּבָא בָּתְרָא וְהַדְרָךְ עֲלָן, דַּעְתָּן עֲלָךְ מַסֶּכֶת בָּבָא בָּתְרָא וְדַעְתָּךְ עֲלָן, לָא נִתְנְשֵׁי מִנָּךְ מַסֶּכֶת בָּבָא בָּתְרָא וְלָא תִתְנְשֵׁי מִנַּן, לָא בְּעָלְמָא הָדֵין וְלָא בְּעָלְמָא דְאָתֵי.

יְהִי רָצוֹן מִלְּפָנֶיךָ יהוה אֱלֹהֵינוּ וֵאלֹהֵי אֲבוֹתֵינוּ, שֶׁתְּהֵא תּוֹרָתְךָ אֻמָּנוּתֵנוּ בָּעוֹלָם הַזֶּה, וּתְהֵא עִמָּנוּ לָעוֹלָם הַבָּא. חֲנִינָא בַּר פַּפָּא, רָמֵי בַּר פַּפָּא, נַחְמָן בַּר פַּפָּא, אֲחַאי בַּר פַּפָּא, אַבָּא מָרִי בַּר פַּפָּא, רַפְרָם בַּר פַּפָּא, רָכִישׁ בַּר פַּפָּא, סוּרְחָב בַּר פַּפָּא, אַדָּא בַּר פַּפָּא, דָּרוּ בַּר פַּפָּא.

הַעֲרֶב נָא יהוה אֱלֹהֵינוּ אֶת דִּבְרֵי תוֹרָתְךָ בְּפִינוּ וּבְפִי עַמְּךָ בֵּית יִשְׂרָאֵל, וְנִהְיֶה אֲנַחְנוּ וְצֶאֱצָאֵינוּ (וְצֶאֱצָאֵי צֶאֱצָאֵינוּ) וְצֶאֱצָאֵי עַמְּךָ בֵּית יִשְׂרָאֵל, כֻּלָּנוּ יוֹדְעֵי
תהלים קיט שְׁמֶךָ וְלוֹמְדֵי תוֹרָתְךָ לִשְׁמָהּ. מֵאֹיְבַי תְּחַכְּמֵנִי מִצְוֹתֶךָ כִּי לְעוֹלָם הִיא־לִי: יְהִי־לִבִּי תָמִים בְּחֻקֶּיךָ לְמַעַן לֹא אֵבוֹשׁ: לְעוֹלָם לֹא־אֶשְׁכַּח פִּקּוּדֶיךָ כִּי־בָם חִיִּיתָנִי: בָּרוּךְ אַתָּה יהוה לַמְּדֵנִי חֻקֶּיךָ: אָמֵן אָמֵן אָמֵן סֶלָה וָעֶד.

מוֹדִים אֲנַחְנוּ לְפָנֶיךָ יהוה אֱלֹהֵינוּ וֵאלֹהֵי אֲבוֹתֵינוּ שֶׁשַּׂמְתָּ חֶלְקֵנוּ מִיּוֹשְׁבֵי בֵּית הַמִּדְרָשׁ, וְלֹא שַׂמְתָּ חֶלְקֵנוּ מִיּוֹשְׁבֵי קְרָנוֹת. שֶׁאָנוּ מַשְׁכִּימִים וְהֵם מַשְׁכִּימִים, אָנוּ מַשְׁכִּימִים לְדִבְרֵי תוֹרָה, וְהֵם מַשְׁכִּימִים לִדְבָרִים בְּטֵלִים. אָנוּ עֲמֵלִים וְהֵם עֲמֵלִים, אָנוּ עֲמֵלִים וּמְקַבְּלִים שָׂכָר, וְהֵם עֲמֵלִים וְאֵינָם מְקַבְּלִים שָׂכָר. אָנוּ רָצִים וְהֵם רָצִים, אָנוּ רָצִים לְחַיֵּי הָעוֹלָם הַבָּא, וְהֵם רָצִים לִבְאֵר
תהלים נה שַׁחַת, שֶׁנֶּאֱמַר: וְאַתָּה אֱלֹהִים תּוֹרִדֵם לִבְאֵר שַׁחַת אַנְשֵׁי דָמִים וּמִרְמָה לֹא־יֶחֱצוּ יְמֵיהֶם וַאֲנִי אֶבְטַח־בָּךְ:

יְהִי רָצוֹן מִלְּפָנֶיךָ יהוה אֱלֹהַי, כְּשֵׁם שֶׁעֲזַרְתַּנִי לְסַיֵּם מַסֶּכֶת בָּבָא בָּתְרָא כֵּן תְּעַזְרֵנִי לְהַתְחִיל מַסֶּכְתּוֹת וּסְפָרִים אֲחֵרִים וּלְסַיְּמָם, לִלְמֹד וּלְלַמֵּד לִשְׁמֹר וְלַעֲשׂוֹת וּלְקַיֵּם אֶת כָּל דִּבְרֵי תַלְמוּד תּוֹרָתְךָ בְּאַהֲבָה, וּזְכוּת כָּל הַתַּנָּאִים וְאָמוֹרָאִים וְתַלְמִידֵי חֲכָמִים יַעֲמֹד לִי וּלְזַרְעִי שֶׁלֹּא תָמוּשׁ הַתּוֹרָה מִפִּי וּמִפִּי זַרְעִי וְזֶרַע זַרְעִי
משלי ו עַד עוֹלָם, וְיִתְקַיֵּם בִּי: בְּהִתְהַלֶּכְךָ תַּנְחֶה אֹתָךְ בְּשָׁכְבְּךָ
משלי ט תִּשְׁמֹר עָלֶיךָ וַהֲקִיצוֹתָ הִיא תְשִׂיחֶךָ: כִּי־בִי יִרְבּוּ יָמֶיךָ
משלי ג וְיוֹסִיפוּ לְּךָ שְׁנוֹת חַיִּים: אֹרֶךְ יָמִים בִּימִינָהּ בִּשְׂמֹאולָהּ
תהלים כט עֹשֶׁר וְכָבוֹד: יהוה עֹז לְעַמּוֹ יִתֵּן יהוה יְבָרֵךְ אֶת־עַמּוֹ בַשָּׁלוֹם:

The following paragraph is recited three times:

הַדְרָן We shall return to you, tractate *Bava Batra,* and your glory is upon us. Our thoughts are upon you, tractate *Bava Batra,* and your thoughts are upon us. We will not be forgotten from you, tractate *Bava Batra,* and you will not be forgotten from us; neither in this world nor in the World-to-Come.

יְהִי רָצוֹן May it be Your will, Lord our God and God of our ancestors, that Your Torah will be our avocation in this world and will accompany us to the World-to-Come. Ḥanina bar Pappa, Ramei bar Pappa, Naḥman bar Pappa, Aḥai bar Pappa, Abba Mari bar Pappa, Rafram bar Pappa, Rakhish bar Pappa, Surḥav bar Pappa, Adda bar Pappa, Daru bar Pappa.

הַעֲרֶב נָא Please, Lord our God, make the words of Your Torah sweet in our mouths and in the mouths of Your people, the house of Israel, so that we, our descendants (and their descendants), and the descendants of Your people, the house of Israel, may all know Your name and
study Your Torah for its own sake. Your commandments Psalms 119
make me wiser than my enemies, for they are ever with me. Let my heart be undivided in Your statutes, in order that I may not be put to shame. I will never forget Your precepts, for with them You have quickened me. Blessed are You, O Lord; teach me Your statutes. Amen, Amen, Amen, Selah, Forever.

מוֹדִים We give thanks before You, Lord Our God and God of our ancestors, that You have placed our lot among those who sit in the study hall and that you have not given us our portion among those who sit idly on street corners. We rise early and they rise early. We rise early to pursue matters of Torah and they rise early to pursue frivolous matters. We toil and they toil. We toil and receive a reward and they toil and do not receive a reward. We run and they run. We run to the life of the World-to-Come and they run to the pit of destruction,
as it is stated: But You, God, will bring them down into Psalms 55
the pit of destruction; men of blood and deceit shall not live out half their days; but as for me, I will trust in You.

יְהִי רָצוֹן May it be Your will, Lord my God, just as you have assisted me in completing tractate *Bava Batra* so assist me to begin other tractates and books and conclude them to learn and to teach, to observe and to perform, and to fulfill all the teachings of Your Torah with love. And may the merit of all the *tanna'im* and *amora'im* and Torah scholars stand for me and my descendants so that the Torah will not move from my mouth and from the mouths of my descendants and the descendants of my
descendants forever. And may the verse: When you Proverbs 6
walk, it shall lead you, when you lie down, it shall watch over you; and when you awaken, it shall talk with you
be fulfilled in me. For in the Torah your days shall be Proverbs 9
multiplied, and the years of your life shall be increased.
Length of days is in her right hand; in her left hand are Proverbs 3
riches and honor. May the Lord give strength to His Psalms 29
people; the Lord will bless His people with peace.

The following קדיש requires the presence of a מנין.

יִתְגַּדַּל וְיִתְקַדַּשׁ שְׁמֵהּ רַבָּא
בְּעָלְמָא דְּהוּא עָתִיד לְאִתְחַדָּתָא
וּלְאַחֲיָאָה מֵתַיָּא, וּלְאַסָּקָא יָתְהוֹן לְחַיֵּי עָלְמָא
וּלְמִבְנֵא קַרְתָּא דִירוּשְׁלֵם, וּלְשַׁכְלָלָא הֵיכְלֵהּ בְּגַוַּהּ
וּלְמֶעְקַר פָּלְחָנָא נֻכְרָאָה מֵאַרְעָא
וְלַאֲתָבָא פָּלְחָנָא דִשְׁמַיָּא לְאַתְרֵהּ
וְיַמְלִיךְ קֻדְשָׁא בְּרִיךְ הוּא בְּמַלְכוּתֵהּ וִיקָרֵהּ
(נוסח ספרד: וְיַצְמַח פּוּרְקָנֵהּ וִיקָרֵב מְשִׁיחֵהּ)
בְּחַיֵּיכוֹן וּבְיוֹמֵיכוֹן וּבְחַיֵּי דְכָל בֵּית יִשְׂרָאֵל
בַּעֲגָלָא וּבִזְמַן קָרִיב, וְאִמְרוּ אָמֵן.

יְהֵא שְׁמֵהּ רַבָּא מְבָרַךְ לְעָלַם וּלְעָלְמֵי עָלְמַיָּא.

יִתְבָּרַךְ וְיִשְׁתַּבַּח וְיִתְפָּאַר וְיִתְרוֹמַם וְיִתְנַשֵּׂא
וְיִתְהַדָּר וְיִתְעַלֶּה וְיִתְהַלָּל
שְׁמֵהּ דְּקֻדְשָׁא בְּרִיךְ הוּא
לְעֵלָּא מִן כָּל בִּרְכָתָא
/בעשרת ימי תשובה: לְעֵלָּא לְעֵלָּא מִכָּל בִּרְכָתָא/
וְשִׁירָתָא, תֻּשְׁבְּחָתָא וְנֶחֱמָתָא, דַּאֲמִירָן בְּעָלְמָא
וְאִמְרוּ אָמֵן. (קהל: אָמֵן)

עַל יִשְׂרָאֵל וְעַל רַבָּנָן
וְעַל תַּלְמִידֵיהוֹן וְעַל כָּל תַּלְמִידֵי תַלְמִידֵיהוֹן
וְעַל כָּל מָאן דְּעָסְקִין בְּאוֹרַיְתָא
דִּי בְּאַתְרָא (בארץ ישראל: קַדִּישָׁא) הָדֵין, וְדִי בְּכָל אֲתַר וַאֲתַר
יְהֵא לְהוֹן וּלְכוֹן שְׁלָמָא רַבָּא
חִנָּא וְחִסְדָּא, וְרַחֲמֵי, וְחַיֵּי אֲרִיכֵי, וּמְזוֹנֵי רְוִיחֵי
וּפֻרְקָנָא מִן קֳדָם אֲבוּהוֹן דִּי בִשְׁמַיָּא
וְאִמְרוּ אָמֵן.

יְהֵא שְׁלָמָא רַבָּא מִן שְׁמַיָּא
וְחַיִּים (טוֹבִים) עָלֵינוּ וְעַל כָּל יִשְׂרָאֵל
וְאִמְרוּ אָמֵן.

Bow, take three steps back, as if taking leave of the Divine Presence, then bow, first left, then right, then center, while saying:

עֹשֶׂה שָׁלוֹם/ בעשרת ימי תשובה: הַשָּׁלוֹם/ בִּמְרוֹמָיו
הוּא יַעֲשֶׂה בְרַחֲמָיו שָׁלוֹם, עָלֵינוּ וְעַל כָּל יִשְׂרָאֵל
וְאִמְרוּ אָמֵן.

The following Kaddish requires the presence of a minyan.

Magnified and sanctified may His great name be,
in the world that will in future be renewed,
reviving the dead and raising them up to eternal life.
He will rebuild the city of Jerusalem
and in it re-establish His Temple.
He will remove alien worship from the earth
and restore to its place the worship of Heaven.
Then the Holy One, blessed be He,
will reign in His sovereignty and splendor.
May it be in your lifetime and in your days,
(*Nusaḥ Sepharad:* make His salvation flourish,
and hasten His messiah,)
and in the lifetime of all the House of Israel,
swiftly and soon – and say: Amen.

May His great name be blessed for ever and all time.

Blessed and praised,
glorified and exalted,
raised and honored,
uplifted and lauded
be the name of the Holy One,
blessed be He,
beyond any blessing,
song, praise and consolation uttered in the world –
and say: Amen.

To Israel, to the teachers,
their disciples and their disciples' disciples,
and to all who engage in the study of Torah,
in this (*in Israel add:* holy) place or elsewhere,
may there come to them and you great peace,
grace, kindness and compassion,
long life, ample sustenance and deliverance,
from their Father in Heaven –
and say: Amen.

May there be great peace from heaven,
and (good) life for us and all Israel –
and say: Amen.

Bow, take three steps back, as if taking leave of the Divine Presence, then bow, first left, then right, then center, while saying:

May He who makes peace in His high places,
in His compassion make peace for us and all Israel –
and say: Amen.